PSYCHOLOGY
Its Principles and Applications

PSYCHOLOGY
Its Principles and Applications

Sixth Edition

T. L. Engle

Louis Snellgrove

HARCOURT BRACE JOVANOVICH, INC.
New York Chicago San Francisco Atlanta Dallas

About the Authors

T. L. Engle is widely known for his contributions to high school psychology courses. Dr. Engle has taught psychology and other subjects in high schools for fourteen years and has instructed secondary school teachers in education courses. A Professor Emeritus of Psychology, he recently retired from Indiana University at Fort Wayne.

Dr. Engle has written numerous articles for professional journals in the fields of high school psychology, social psychology, and mental retardation. He has served as chairman of several APA committees and has read papers at APA meetings on the subject of teaching psychology at the secondary school level.

Louis Snellgrove is a professor of psychology at Lambuth College (Jackson, Tennessee). He has taught at the high school level and has been a full-time counselor to high school students. For five years Dr. Snellgrove systematically collected and disseminated more than 175 projects and activities for the teaching of psychology to over 1500 high schools.

In addition to publishing articles on psychology, Dr. Snellgrove is the author of *Psychological Experiments and Demonstrations*. He has been active as a member of APA and a participant of many APA activities related to the high school.

ACKNOWLEDGMENT: For permission to reprint copyrighted material, grateful acknowledgment is made to the American Psychological Association for the excerpts on pages 206 and 209 from the *American Psychologist*, vol. 24, no. 11, November 1969, pages 1039–1041, copyright © 1969 by the American Psychological Association and excerpts on page 466 from "Human Nature and the Peace: A Statement by Psychologists," the *Third Yearbook of the Society for the Psychological Study of Social Issues*, copyright 1945 by the American Psychological Association.

Copyright © 1974, 1969, 1964, 1957, copyright 1950, 1945 by Harcourt Brace Jovanovich, Inc. All rights reserved. No part of this publication may be reproduced or transmitted in any form or by any means, electronic or mechanical, including photocopy, recording, or any information storage and retrieval system, without permission in writing from the publisher.

Printed in the United States of America.

ISBN 0-15-374830-3

Contents

UNIT 1 WHAT IS PSYCHOLOGY   1

Chapter 1 Studying Psychology   2
Some Questions for Which you May Be Seeking Answers
What Psychology Is
The Place of Psychology Among the Sciences
What Psychology Is Not
Are Psychologists Hypnotists?
Can Psychologists Read People's Minds?
Methods of Psychological Study

UNIT 2 LEARNING   28

Chapter 2 Principles of Learning   30
What Is Learning?
Trial-and-Error Learning
Classical Conditioning
Terms Related to Classical Conditioning
Operant Conditioning
Terms Related to Operant Conditioning
Operant Conditioning and Punishment
Operant Conditioning and Programmed Learning
Learning
Learning by Insight
Controversial Areas of Learning

Chapter 3 How to Learn Efficiently   57
Transfer
Other Factors in Learning Efficiency
   1. *Motivation*
   2. *Meaningfulness*
   3. *Knowledge of Results*
   4. *Massed vs. Distributed Practice*
   5. *Whole Learning vs. Part Learning*
   6. *Mnemonic Devices*
   7. *Overlearning*
   8. *Latent Learning*
   9. *Serial Learning*
The Progress of Learning
Remembering
Forgetting

v

Chapter 4 The Process of Thinking   87
    Basic Elements of Thinking
    Concepts
    Uncritical Thinking
    Creative Thinking
    Imagining
    Reasoning
    Computer vs. Human Thinking
    Applying Principles of Learning to Taking Examinations

UNIT 3   UNDERSTANDING HUMAN BEHAVIOR   114

Chapter 5 Understanding Personality   116
    The Development of Personality
    Some Theories of Personality
    Scientific Techniques for Measuring Personality
        1. *Ratings*
        2. *Inventories*
        3. *Interviewing*
        4. *Behavior Sampling*
        5. *Projective Techniques*

Chapter 6 How Behavior Develops   140
    Development
    Physical Development
    Motor Development
    Language Development
    Emotional Development
    Social Development
    How Personality Develops
    Mental Development

Chapter 7 Measuring Intellectual Ability   163
    The Meaning of Intelligence
    Individual Tests of Intelligence
    Group Tests of Intelligence
    The Intelligence Quotient (IQ)
    Practical Applications of Intelligence Tests
    Mental Retardation
    Superior Intelligence
    Criticisms of Tests

UNIT 4 PATTERNS OF BEHAVIOR 190

Chapter 8 **Heredity and Environment** 192
Inherited Characteristics
Some Studies of Heredity
Heredity and Maturation
Influences of the Environment Before Birth
Influences of the Environment After Birth
Interaction of Heredity and Environment

Chapter 9 **Biological Influences on Behavior** 214
The Nervous Systems
Reaction Time
The Brain
Convulsive Disorders
Glands
Emotional Behavior
Instincts, or Species-Specific Behavior
The Effect of Sleep on Behavior

Chapter 10 **Getting to Know Your Environment** 239
Attention
Sensation and Perception
Vision
Hearing
Other Sense Fields
Sensory Deprivation

UNIT 5 EMOTIONAL AND BEHAVIORAL ADJUSTMENTS 266

Chapter 11 **Facing Frustration and Conflict** 268
Frustration and Conflict
Desirable Ways of Responding to Frustration and Conflict
Adjustment Mechanisms
Cognitive Dissonance

Chapter 12 **Some Emotional Problems of Adolescents** 292
Inferiority
Daydreaming
Thrills and Thrill-Seeking
Family Conflicts
Dating and Romantic Love
Assuming the Roles of Men and Women

vii

Chapter 13 **Behavior Disorders and Their Treatment**   316
   Behavior Disorders in Our Society
   Neurotic Behavior
   Psychosis
   Functional Psychoses
   Organic Psychoses
   Personality Disorders
   Treatment of Behavior Disorders

UNIT 6   SMALL GROUPS   344

Chapter 14 **The Family Group**   346
   The Family
   Marriage
   Love Between Children and Parents
   Children
   The Development of Conscience in Children
   The Problem of Lying
   The Problem of Cheating
   The Problem of Discipline
   The Problem of Fear
   Television Watching

Chapter 15 **The Peer Group**   371
   The Generation Gap
   Peer-Group Influence
   Friendship
   Popularity
   Leadership in Peer Groups

Chapter 16 **Behavior in Small Groups**   393
   The Composition of Small Groups
   The Size and Efficiency of Small Groups
   Belonging to Small Groups
   Some Characteristics of Small Groups
   How Roles Vary in Different Groups
   Communication Within a Group
   The Classroom as a Small Group
   Famous Studies of Behavior in Small Groups

UNIT 7 PSYCHOLOGY AND SOCIETY   426

Chapter 17 Some Social Relationships   428
Would You Help a Person in Distress?
Social Facilitation
Social Competition
The Effects of Competition
Social Cooperation

Chapter 18 Psychology and Problems of Society   454
Social Attitudes
Propaganda
Crime and Delinquency
War
Drugs
Pollution
Overpopulation
The Role of Psychology in Solving Social Problems

Chapter 19 The World of Work   482
Choosing Your Vocation
Scientific Studies of Work
Thinking Work
Psychology As a Vocation
Looking Ahead

GLOSSARY   509
INDEX   525
ILLUSTRATION CREDITS   535

SPECIAL TEXT FEATURES

UNIT 1 FEATURE: Extrasensory Perception   26
UNIT 2 FEATURE: How Much Should We Control our Environment?   112
UNIT 3 FEATURE: What Is Intelligence?   188
UNIT 4 FEATURE: The Work of Dr. Anastasi   264
UNIT 5 FEATURE: Dr. Clark and Social Behavior Disorders   342
UNIT 6 FEATURE: Love and Aggression   424
UNIT 7 FEATURE: Studying and Predicting Behavior   506

unit 1

WHAT IS PSYCHOLOGY?

chapter 1 Studying psychology

chapter 1
Studying Psychology

You are beginning a study of the subject of psychology. Why did you decide to study psychology? How will this study fit into your general educational background? In what ways will your study of psychology be of value to you in the years following high school?

Of course, the interests and needs of students differ greatly from one student to another, but probably every student is seeking answers to some basic life questions. Perhaps you have some personal problems for which you are seeking solutions. Perhaps you feel baffled by some of the social problems you face now and know you will have to face in later life. Maybe you are curious about certain aspects of man and his environment and want to know more about them.

Some Questions for Which You May Be Seeking Answers

This section includes some questions that are of interest to and are asked by many high school students. No doubt you can add even more questions of your own.

Personal questions. Am I very different from other people my age? Am I afraid of more things than most people? How can I get along better with the members of my family? How should I treat my grandparents, who are getting old and difficult? Am I handicapped by being an only child in my family, or the oldest, or the youngest, or an intermediate? What can I do about being anxious or nervous? How will I know if I am in love and ready for marriage? How can I know what vocation or profession to enter? If I become very interested in psychology, how can I become a psychologist? Is smoking really harmful? What about

What Psychology Is

Different books may give slightly varying definitions of psychology. The following, however, is a generally acceptable definition: PSYCHOLOGY is the science that studies the behavior of organisms. Three words in this definition—science, behavior, and organisms—require further examination.

Science. Like other sciences, psychology is a systematic study. The work of any science is based on factual investigation, experiments, and other systematic means of collecting information, or data. It is not based on prejudiced opinion or unsupported judgment. The goal of all sciences is a better understanding of man and all the forces, conditions, and influences that make up his environment.

Scientists collect data by research, that is, by systematic, careful, firsthand observation of facts or events. These observable facts or events are known as phenomena. Research usually involves description by measurement, reported in mathematical terms. But science does not stop when a set of facts has been described. The next step is to try to relate and explain what is described, to construct theories. A THEORY is simply a general principle, based on considerable data, proposed as an explanation for what is observed. It is a statement of relations among facts, supported by a comprehensive study of facts. Through research, scientists may be able to offer a well-grounded explanation of what has happened in the past and thus make it possible to predict what will happen in similar situations in the future. Long's study of yellow fever, for example, led scientists to the theory that mosquitoes caused the disease and to the prediction that control of mosquitoes would cut down the disease.

It must be stressed that no science has all the facts on or all the answers to the problems it investigates. Science gives the best answers it can on the basis of the evidence it has. As investigation goes on, new facts are collected, and theories may have to be changed. Observations made with the help of man-made satellites led to revisions in our knowledge of the shape and dimensions of the earth. The most reliable reference sources and maps must be revised as scientists establish new facts.

Behavior. We have defined psychology as the science that studies behavior. In the sciences words that are familiar often have a different and specific definition, and "behavior" is such a word. In psychology BEHAVIOR refers to those activities of a human being or other organism that can be observed directly or by means of special instruments or techniques. Such activities as walking, running, and speaking are forms of behavior, but no more so than less easily observed forms. As an example, a person charged with a crime may appear calm, revealing no easily detectable behavior that suggests fear or guilt. With instruments, however, a psychologist may be able to measure such behavior because of telltale changes in the person's blood pressure, breathing, and pulse rate. Psychologists have techniques for studying and measuring many other kinds of behavior, such as learning, remembering, and reasoning.

Organisms. Psychologists use the word ORGANISM to refer to any living animal. Although psychologists are primarily interested in human beings, they often make studies of chimpanzees, rats, pigeons, and other animals.

The mind in psychology. Perhaps you are surprised that there is no mention of the mind in our definition of psychology. At one time, it is true, psychology was described as the study of the mind. You may have heard or read discussions of the mind-body problem—the problem of the relation of mind, or that which is mental, to body, or that which is physical. This problem is based on the assumption that it is possible and profitable to consider mental behavior as separate from physical behavior.

Modern psychologists are not much concerned with a mind vs. body problem. They do not regard mind and body as separate entities. Behavior that is called mental—for example, thinking—is a part of the functioning of the entire organism. Nevertheless, such words as mind and mental are so common in our language that we cannot get away from them. It would take a very stilted teacher to announce to his class, "Bear in your organism that there will be an examination next Friday" rather than "Bear in mind that there will be an examination next Friday." Psychologists and physicians find it convenient to speak of mental health, even though they do not assume that there is a mind whose health can be completely separated from the health of the whole person.

The word "mind" is an example of a HEURISTIC CONCEPT, or a concept that is useful in understanding and explaining something but that has no physical counterpart or way of proving if the concept is true or false. Although the term "mind" is used occasionally in such fields as psychoanalysis, it should be used cautiously, and is best left out of a definition of psychology.

The Place of Psychology Among the Sciences

To understand the nature of psychology, it is helpful to consider how this science is related to other sciences. All sciences share certain methods and aims. They all grew out of philosophy. The ancient philosophers strove to understand the nature of man and the universe, and modern scientists (as well as philosophers) are still working toward this goal. In modern times so much knowledge has accumulated that scientists have found it necessary to concentrate on specialized areas. Thus, there are many sciences. Psychology draws upon the accumulated knowledge of several of these sciences and is drawn upon by them.

Since it would take volumes to trace all the relationships of psychology with other sciences, we will consider only a few representative and important relations.

How is psychology related to chemistry and biology? Although it might seem that the research chemist in his laboratory is far from the field of psychology, there is a close relationship between behavior and body chemistry. Some forms of behavior disorders that were formerly spoken of as sicknesses of the mind can now be explained in terms of body chemistry. We are learning much through psychopharmacology—the study of the effects of drugs and poisons on psychological functions. Today pharmaceutical houses are devoting much research effort to problems of the nervous system, developing such aids as the ataractic (tranquilizing) drugs.

Biology is another science that contributes to psychology. The relation of biology to psychology will be evident throughout this book—as, for example, in the study of emotions, which requires a knowledge of the activity of the glands and parts of the brain.

How is psychology related to anthropology and sociology? The sciences of anthropology and sociology are closely allied to psychology. Cultural (or social) anthropology studies the culture—the way of life—of man. Although once focused on the behavior of nonliterate peoples, anthropology is becoming more and more concerned with the behavior of so-called civilized as well as so-called primitive peoples. Through his studies of widely divergent cultures, the anthropologist assists the psychologist in understanding the influences of environment on the behavior of individuals.

Like cultural anthropology, sociology studies the behavior of human groups. Sociology is especially concerned with group life and social organization, chiefly in literate societies such as our own. Sociologists study such areas as growth and shifts of population, urban and rural living, voting trends, delinquency, and crime.

Data from all these studies contribute to understanding the behavior of the individual. In some areas—as in the study of families and other small groups—sociology is very close to the branch of psychology called social psychology. The distinction is that the psychologist focuses primarily on the individual, while the sociologist focuses primarily on the group.

To sum up the discussion of the place of psychology among the sciences, we may paraphrase a section from a report on the place of psychology in education: Psychologists (this report states) seek to provide a basic science of human thinking, learning, skills, motives, conduct, and so on, that will serve all the sciences of man—such as anthropology, sociology, political science, and law—in much the same way that biology now serves the agricultural and medical sciences.

What is the difference between psychology and psychiatry? Psychiatrists are physicians who specialize in the prevention, diagnosis, and treatment of both mild and severe "mental" disorders. They hold the M.D. degree from some university school of medicine. They are licensed, as are all physicians, to prescribe drugs, perform surgery, and use other medically accepted techniques.

Psychologists, with rare exceptions, do not hold an M.D. degree. They are not licensed to prescribe drugs, perform surgery, or use treatments that by law are restricted to medical men. Psychologists usually have a Ph.D. degree in psychology. However, some of them hold an Ed.D. (Doctor of Education) degree from a university school of education. A few hold a Psy.D. (Doctor of Psychology) degree from the graduate school of some university, although not many universities currently offer this degree. Some psychological work is done by individuals with M.A. (Master of Arts) or M.S. (Master of Science) degrees. In many states psychologists are licensed to practice PSYCHOTHERAPY, or the treatment of personality and behavior disorders by psychological methods.

The fields of psychology and psychiatry often overlap, and psychologists and psychiatrists frequently cooperate with one another, such as working together in clinics.

What is the difference between psychology and psychoanalysis? Many people confuse the science of psychology with PSYCHOANALYSIS, a method of treatment for mental disorders and a body of psychological theory. Psychoanalysis was developed under the leadership of Sigmund Freud (1856–1939), a Viennese physician. His work has been carried on and expanded by many students and followers.

Although we avoid incorporating the word "mind" in our definition of psychology, psychoanalysts are very likely to use the term. In fact, in his early writings Freud had much to say about the unconscious part of the mind, a part containing all the information, desires, wishes, and concepts that a person cannot recall to consciousness under ordinary circumstances, but that nevertheless greatly influence his life.

Freud, and others of his time, placed a great deal of emphasis on early childhood experiences as a means of understanding the individual personality. More recently, psychoanalysts have stressed the role of the later environment and social interaction in influencing personality developments. Psychoanalysis has been very helpful in showing that emotional disturbances are frequently the result of a conflict between bodily needs and desires and the demands of social customs and rules.

Because psychoanalysis is based mainly on clinical rather than on laboratory procedures, especially in the earlier writings, many experimental psychologists do not look upon it with a great deal of favor. However, CLINICAL PSYCHOLOGISTS—psychologists concerned with the diagnosis and treatment of personal and social maladjustment—often find the theories and techniques of psychoanalysis of practical use in their work.

What Psychology Is Not

We have been using the term "psychologist" so far to refer to a scientist with professional standards and proper training in a recognized college or university. Unfortunately, like the members of every profession, psychologists have the problem of combating charlatans and quacks, persons who call themselves psychologists but are not qualified to use that title.

Pseudo-scientists. Some people work around the fringes of psychology, appealing to individuals who want advice about personal problems. Phrenologists, astrologers, numerologists, and others of their kind promise quick diagnosis, advice, and therapy. Having examined the bumps on your head, the phrenologist will claim that he is able to tell you all about yourself. The astrologer, who studies

Going to a fortune-teller for advice on personal matters is an unscientific approach to solving individual problems, even if much of the information you are told may seem to be accurate and the experience may be an interesting one.

the positions of the stars, and the numerologist, who looks at the letters in your name, also make the same claims. Their "treatment" may consist of nothing more than telling you to think "I am a success" or "I live gloriously." As any student of science knows, behavior is too complex to be understood in such simple terms. The mere fact that these individuals tell a troubled person exactly what to do is an indication that they are not professionally trained. A trained psychologist helps troubled persons develop insight into their own problems and work out their own solutions.

Many of these people pass themselves off under titles that, to the uninformed, may sound impressive. Although such titles as "Certified Grapho-Analytical Psychologist," "Doctor of Chiro-Deo-Therapy," or "Doctor of Metaphysics" may sound like academic degrees, they were probably bought from one of the more than 200 so-called schools or even colleges that are nothing but diploma- or degree-mills. In one of these schools it is possible to get four "doctor's" degrees in twenty months at a mail-order cost of $250. An accredited Ph.D. normally requires a minimum of seven years of study beyond high school.

Anyone seeking to consult a psychologist should not hesitate to ask about the psychologist's qualifications. The well-trained and ethical psychologist will be glad to give this information. The quack will try to bluff and avoid giving direct answers. Or he may claim to have training, but the education he reports may be worthless.

Phrenologists, astrologers, and quacks who use mail-order degrees are sometimes called "pseudo-scientists." They use some of the terms and even a few of the procedures of science, but their work is not scientific. Genuine scientists and pseudo-scientists occasionally are involved in common or overlapping fields. Hypnosis and telepathy ("mind reading") are two examples. Showing how psychologists work in these "mysterious" areas will help clarify the nature of scientific psychology.

Are Psychologists Hypnotists?

The best answer to this question is that some psychologists sometimes use hypnosis. It is one of the many accepted techniques of psychotherapy, although some psychologists question its basic value. They feel that hypnosis may be used to treat symptoms of personality and behavior disorders without treating the basic difficulties of individuals. Occasionally experimental psychologists make use of hypnosis as a control in experiments.

Even though it is not a major field of interest to most psychologists, some brief discussion of hypnosis is in order, since many students are curious about this topic. However, no one, including students, should play around with hypnosis.

What is hypnosis? Sometimes placed in the realm of mystery or magic, HYPNOSIS is an artificially induced state, at times resembling sleep, although the biological processes in a hypnotized person are not exactly the same as those of a person in normal sleep. Furthermore, the person who has been hypnotized is usually very much open to suggestion, while the person in normal sleep is usually open to very little, if any, suggestion. Although the hypnotized person may appear to be asleep, he understands what is said to him and is able to carry out simple directions. The hypnotized person may be so much open to suggestion that he seems to have lost his ability to make judgments. He may believe almost anything that is told him and do almost anything requested of him. There are limits, however, to what he can be made to do.

How is hypnosis produced? There is no certain formula or mysterious technique to follow in producing a state of hypnosis. Some psychologists induce a state of hypnosis in one way, some in another.

One instrument used in inducing hypnosis is an automatic variable strobe light. It consists of a light that flashes at a specific rate per second, while the subject stares fixedly at it. The flashing light is thought to block the *alpha wave*, one of the electrical waves sent out by the brain. The alpha wave seems to be associated with sleep. When the individual goes to sleep under ordinary circumstances, the alpha wave disappears. The blocking of the wave when the subject is awake tends to make him more relaxed and sleepy and therefore more susceptible to being hypnotized. The presence of the flashing lights also gives the subject something on which he can concentrate.

Other methods for producing hypnosis include the use of droning sounds and specific objects, such as a pencil, to which the subject directs his attention. Still other methods involve no mechanical aid of any kind. They rely on the spoken word, attempting to get the subject to concentrate on a specific thought.

Whatever the particular techniques used, the fundamental procedure involves narrowing the subject's attention so that he is aware only of what the psychologist is saying to him. As the subject's attention is narrowed, he becomes less and less critical toward accepting the suggestions made to him. The suggestions can also be placed on a phonograph record or a tape recording, so that the hypnotist is not even present during the process of producing a hypnotic state.

Who may be hypnotized? Some believe that only a person with a "weak will" can be hypnotized. As a matter of fact, most normal persons can be hypnotized if they are willing, will allow sufficient time, and will cooperate in the process. The subject must be able to concentrate on what is said and done by the person who is about to hypnotize him. Very young children usually cannot concentrate for a period long enough to enable them to be hypnotized, and they are not sufficiently familiar with the language to understand all the suggestions made to them. The same may be said of mentally retarded individuals and persons suffering from some forms of mental illness.

Perhaps you have wondered if you can be hypnotized without your knowledge. You may have read stories in which a hypnotist slipped behind his intended victim and hypnotized him before he ever knew what was happening. But by now you are aware that the person being hypnotized must concentrate on what the hypnotist is saying and doing. If the subject does not know that the hypnotist is around, he cannot give the necessary cooperation and concentration. Therefore, it would be extremely difficult for anyone to hypnotize you without your knowledge and consent.

Still another notion is that a victim may be hypnotized and then left, never to awaken to normal life. Actually, the person who has hypnotized another merely has to suggest to the other that he awaken, and he will do so. In case the victim is not told to awaken, he will eventually do so anyway, just as he would awaken from normal sleep.

As to the relationship between personality traits and hypnosis, there have been no significant consistent findings that any one pattern of personality traits is more susceptible to hypnosis than any other. How easily a specific individual can be hypnotized depends on his desire, or fear, whether conscious or unconscious, to be put into a state of hypnosis and his ability to concentrate on what the psychologist or hypnotist is saying and doing.

One way of hypnotizing a person is to have the subject focus all his attention on a pencil held directly in front of him, while the psychologist utters soothing words and makes suggestions.

How do hypnotized persons behave? Perhaps you have never seen a demonstration of hypnosis. The following is a description of some characteristic behavior.

After the person is put into a state of hypnosis, he can accept the suggestion that he will feel no pain when a pin is jabbed into his hand. A pin that is then stuck into his hand will not cause him to flinch or show any sign of pain. Or the psychologist can tell the person that he is going to be stuck with a pin and that it will hurt. If the psychologist then touches the person with his finger, the person will jump and show all the signs of having experienced pain. The subject is unable to tell the difference between this suggested pain and real physical pain.

At the present time we do not understand nor can we adequately explain why this phenomenon takes place. Some experimental data reveal that nerve impulses do travel from the point of stimulation, such as the finger, to the brain and that the brain somehow denies the presence of the pain impulse to it. But we do not know how the person feels pain when there is no specific or known stimulation.

A hypnotized person can often recall facts from far back in his experience. He may be able to recall the name of the person who sat in front of him in the first grade in school, although in a normal state he may not be able to recall the name of the student who sat in front of him in class yesterday. A subject can, in some cases, give the license number of an automobile he owned or drove five or six years earlier, although in a normal waking state he may not even know the license number of his present car. However, a person who is hypnotized does not have any mysterious possession of facts he has never known or facts he has known only superficially. A psychologist demonstrating hypnotism once asked a woman whom he had hypnotized, "What was the license number on your car five years ago?"

She seemed disturbed and did not answer for a minute. Finally she said, "I didn't have a car five years ago."

It is possible to suggest to a hypnotized person that he is to perform a particular act after he has been awakened. This procedure is called POSTHYPNOTIC SUGGESTION. The following classroom demonstration was an example of this procedure. A psychologist hypnotized a student and suggested to him that he would perform a certain action after being awakened. The student was told that when the psychologist looked at his watch, he was to jump up and yell very loudly, "Let's go!" When the subject was awakened, he remembered nothing of what had happened during his hypnotic state. Classwork was resumed. After some time the psychologist casually glanced at his watch. Instantly the student jumped to his feet and shouted, "Let's go!" Then he sat down in great confusion and embarrassment, unable to imagine why he had done such a thing.

In this instance the suggested act was performed a short time after the subject was awakened from the hypnotic state. Other cases have been reported in which posthypnotic suggestions were carried out months after the original suggestions were given.

Hypnosis can be divided into different degrees or states, such as light and deep. Contrary to popular belief, the person being hypnotized into a light state of hypnosis is aware of what is going on around him. Those who have been hypnotized in this way report that it is very much like going to sleep. Perhaps you can remember that period of time, often called the "twilight zone" of sleep, in which you are on the verge of going to sleep or waking up. You are aware of what is going on around you and you find it difficult to either fall into a deep sleep or wake up completely.

Some practical uses of hypnosis. The medical profession has used hypnosis to eliminate or reduce the pain of terminal cancer, severe burns, and childbirth. There is evidence that hypnotic methods may be as effective as morphine and other opiates in minimizing pain with some patients. With other patients, though, hypnosis reduces suffering and discomfort but does not eliminate pain entirely.

In some surgical cases hypnosis has been used sucessfully instead of a chemical anesthetic. Appendectomies have been performed with no anesthetic other than hypnosis. Instead of giving an anesthetic, some dentists have suggested to hypnotized patients that

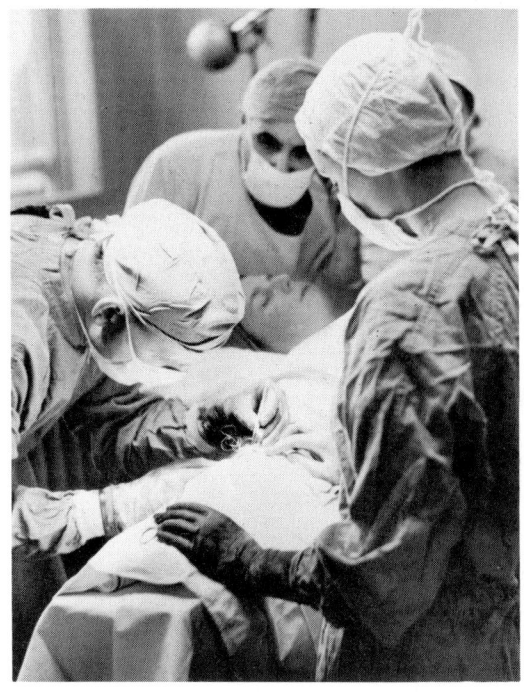

Hypnosis was used as an anesthetic on this patient undergoing minor arm surgery. The patient, a nurse anesthetist at the hospital, was able to return to work that same day.

they would feel no pain when their teeth were extracted—and the patients reported no pain.

Hypnosis may also be used in connection with psychotherapy. Many persons have unreasonable fears that interfere with their lives. Such a fear may well have had its beginning in a single incident of early childhood. A person may be unable to recall the incident that originally produced this particular fear. Nevertheless, the incident continues to influence his behavior and to make his life unhappy. Under hypnosis he may recall the event. Once the incident is identified, it can be dealt with. A course of explanation and suggestion will help the person overcome his fear. Some psychotherapists have used hypnosis to control behavior, such as smoking, through posthypnotic suggestion. Others have resorted to hypnosis to get cooperation from otherwise resistant persons, such as an individual who refuses to cooperate in taking a test that will help the psychotherapist study his basic personality.

Lost articles have been found through the use of hypnosis. In a normal waking state a person may be unable to recall where he left an article, but under hypnosis he may easily remember where he put it.

Because of the many uses of hypnosis and because it helps to give insight into behavior, psychologists have shown increasing interest in research in this area. The American Psychological Association recognizes the work of those psychologists who have diplomas granted by the American Board of Examiners in Psychological Hypnosis.

The beginning student of psychology, however, is not prepared to carry out scientific experiments involving hypnosis. The use of hypnosis should be left to professional persons. Some states even have legal restrictions concerning the use of hypnosis.

Can Psychologists Read People's Minds?

Probably you are ready to assume that if psychologists do not talk much about minds, they are not likely to talk much about reading other people's minds. Actually, there are some well qualified psychologists who are very much interested in the problem of "mind reading," or telepathy. They study telepathy and other related subjects that fall under the category of parapsychology.

Parapsychology. The prefix *para-* means "at the side of," so parapsychology is concerned with material of a psychological nature that is apart from the main body of psychological knowledge and interest. Perhaps someday material that is now classified as parapsychology will be generally accepted as psychology.

Specifically, parapsychology is the study of the two major subfields of extrasensory perception (ESP) and psychokinesis (PK). EXTRASENSORY PERCEPTION investigates experiences where it is said that knowledge is acquired independently of the known senses. Extrasensory literally means "outside the senses" or "apart from the senses." (Some psychologists prefer to use the term "neosensory perception." The prefix *neo-* means "new." They think of the phenomena referred to as extrasensory as phenomena involving a new sense or a new combination of known senses.) Extrasensory perception consists of three main areas: (1) TELEPATHY, or the transfer of thought from one person to another without the use of the senses, (2) CLAIRVOYANCE, or the extrasensory perception of objects rather than the thoughts of another person, and (3) PRECOGNITION, or the perception of future events by ESP. For further information on ESP, see pages 26–27.

The other major subdivision of parapsychology, PSYCHOKINESIS, or PK, is the study of experiences in which the thought of an individual is said to influence the performance of some physical object or event.

The various areas of parapsychology do not include such items as occultism, spiritualism, or mediums, which are, respectively, studies of the supernatural (such as ghosts), the supposed control of the supernatural, and those who believe they can communicate with the dead.

Telepathy. One of the areas of parapsychology that many laymen find interesting is telepathy, spoken of popularly as "mind reading." TELEPATHY has been defined as the "communication of thought from 'mind' to 'mind' by other than the usual means of sensory stimulation." Sensory stimulation means the stimulation of a sense organ, such as the eye. Usually we communicate our thoughts by either vocal sounds (auditory stimuli) or written words (visual stimuli). Theoretically, we can communicate thoughts to others by means of any of the senses. In telepathy thoughts are conveyed without using any of the senses.

How is telepathy explained? We need not assume that there are supernatural or mysterious explanations for telepathy, or "mind reading," since telepathy can be studied in the laboratory. To date, there is no conclusive scientific evidence either for or against telepathy. But experiments have shown that what is often supposed to be extrasensory communication of thought is really sensory communication.

In one experiment ten books were placed in a row. The experimenter chose one of these books by secretly casting lots. Then he stood somewhat behind the subject and acted as a "mental" guide. He concentrated his thinking upon the book he had chosen by casting lots. This procedure was repeated many times. By pure mathematical chance the subject could have selected the correct book in 10 percent of the total number of tries. Yet in this experiment he selected the correct book in 25 percent of the total number of tries. Was the subject reading the experimenter's mind, or was he getting slight sensory cues? Blinders were put on the subject so that he could not see the experimenter out of the corners of his eyes. Also, the subject's ears were plugged so that he could not hear any slight sounds made unintentionally by the experimenter. Under these conditions, which prevented sensory cues, his score for correct selection dropped to the pure mathematical chance of one out of ten.

Coincidence is often mistaken for telepathy. There are stories about friends, living hundreds of miles apart, who have not seen or written to each other for years, suddenly writing to each other on the same date. Is this long-distance "mind reading"? There is no reason to assume that thought waves have been sent out and received. Possibly both had just watched a television program or read a newspaper article that reminded each of the other. Or perhaps years before, on a date that they had both made note of then, the two friends had had an interesting experience together. Although they may not be aware of it, the date in itself serves as the stimulus for each to think about, and then write to, the other.

The simultaneous letter writing could also be due to chance alone. Out of the tens of thousands who actually write letters, it is likely that two people will write letters to each other at the same time by chance.

The writing of the two letters on the same date is so unusual that it is news. Each friend

In this experiment on telepathy, the young man on the left tries to state the number and suit of the three cards that he cannot see, but whose identity the subject on the right tries to communicate to him by telepathy.

tells his acquaintances about the incident. People remember this case and ignore the other thousands of letters that were written on different dates. They also ignore the thousands and thousands of friends who are separated, think of each other often, yet never write.

The judgment of psychologists regarding telepathy. Telepathy is an unsolved problem of science. At one time a sampling of members of the American Psychological Association were asked to indicate whether or not they believed extrasensory perception to be an established fact. Only about 5 percent of these psychologists expressed the belief that extrasensory perception was an established fact. Twenty-five to 35 percent regarded extrasensory perception as a likely possibility. The majority, however, merely regarded the investigation of such problems as a "legitimate scientific undertaking." In other words, most psychologists were open-minded to the possibility that telepathy might prove to be a fact, but very few of them believed that enough accurate data were available to come to a conclusion now.

Although in the nineteenth century there was some research in the field of what today we would call extrasensory perception, we usually think of the early 1930's as the beginning of the modern scientific attempt to study the various phenomena of ESP. Some research suggests that those who believe in ESP have more success with it than those who reject the idea. Studies also suggest a fade-out in ESP— that is, early trials are more successful than later ones.

Most of the studies of extrasensory perception have been made by individuals who were not psychologists. Although much scattered work is being done, probably fewer than fifty trained psychologists are investigating ESP. There is a need for well-trained men and women to carry on research using the best of modern methods. Only after much research can the concept of telepathy and other kinds of extrasensory perception be understood in scientific terms.

Methods of Psychological Study

We have defined psychology as the science that studies the behavior of organisms. But how does the psychologist go about studying behavior scientifically? What methods might he use to study telepathy, for instance? Actually, the psychologist uses the same general methods of study as do scientists in all fields. Some of these methods and techniques that are especially suited to studying the behavior of organisms are described below.

Natural observation. Before the development of psychology as a science, men observed and recorded examples of behavior. Even today psychologists use natural observation as a check on laboratory and other scientific work. We can learn something about maternal behavior by observing mother monkeys with their young in South America. We can learn about how individuals adjust to social situations by observing them and their companions at informal social gatherings. We can find out about an individual's attitudes by listening to his conversation.

Natural observation quite often includes the use of tape recorders, motion pictures, and other permanent ways of recording data. Although natural observation gives a record of activities, it has the serious disadvantage of providing little or no information about why or how behavior occurs. Nevertheless, it does allow us to study organisms in their natural environment rather than in the artificial environment created by directed or laboratory observation.

Directed observation. Directed observation (sometimes called experimental or laboratory observation) is a refinement of the uncontrolled observing of behavior that we all do. Psychologists, however, make observations under controlled conditions and according to a planned schedule. For example, they may plan to observe how children react to specific toys. All details, even though they seem trivial, are noted immediately either in shorthand or by a camera or some other recording device.

One example of directed observation is the use of the one-way mirror, as shown below. A psychologist can observe through the mirror the behavior of a child engaged in play therapy, yet the child cannot see the psychologist.

The case-study method. Psychologists, social workers, and psychiatrists often use the case-study method as they attempt to help children and adults with problems of adjustment. These trained persons strive to get impartial and objective descriptions of the background forces that have probably influenced an individual's development. The case record includes information concerning family background, home life, neighborhood activities, school experience, health, and so on. This method is based on the idea that the more we know about an individual, the better we will be able to understand and help him.

The case-study method is valuable and even indispensable in some psychological work. Nevertheless, it has certain limitations. For instance, information often has to be obtained from parents, teachers, and other associates of the individual under study. These informants may unintentionally give partial and biased reports rather than the impartial and objective reports that psychologists need.

Interviews. In psychology, sociology, and other fields, interviews are widely used to obtain data. Your physician may have included an interview as part of his diagnostic technique when you went to see him. Your teacher and guidance counselor may have interviewed you. Certainly you have been interviewed if you have ever applied for a job. Public-opinion researchers interview a sample of the population to gauge attitudes toward soaps, toothpastes, or other commercial products or to forecast voting trends. Psychologists use interviews for such purposes as compiling a case record on an individual or studying prejudices in groups.

The value of data from an interview depends on how well the interviewer has been trained for his job. For instance, a good interviewer is careful to establish rapport—that is, an unconstrained and cooperative relationship with the interviewee. He knows in advance what questions he is going to ask and the general order in which he will ask them. Nevertheless, he keeps the interview flexible enough so that both parties can bring out topics not on the list of questions. The skilled interviewer can enrich the record by noting little hesitancies, tenseness, or topics the interviewee seems to try to avoid.

The entire interview may be tape-recorded so that the interviewer can play it back to himself for further consideration. He may call in other trained interviewers to hear and evaluate the entire recorded interview.

The interview method is widely used, but it is subject to serious limitations. One is the difficulty of eliminating the personal prejudices of the interviewer. Another is the difficulty of expressing the results of an interview in exact terms. A person may be recorded as "favorable" toward a group. But how favorable—100 percent? 50 percent? This sort of doubt rules out the precise measurement that is essential to all scientific work. Despite these shortcomings, however, interviews conducted by well-trained persons using modern techniques may yield scientifically valuable data.

The questionnaire method. The questionnaire method was developed in the latter part of the nineteenth and early part of the twentieth century to provide greater accuracy in studying human behavior. This method consists of giving a list of questions on some subject to a selected group of individuals. Occasionally, the questions are asked directly in an interview. The questions do not constitute a test with right or wrong answers. Rather, they are designed to gather facts about the individual or to elicit his opinions. The answers to the questions can be treated statistically.

There are dangers in the use of the questionnaire method. An individual answering a questionnaire may give inaccurate replies. If he is asked very personal questions, the respondent may deliberately falsify his responses. Moreover, an investigator does not receive replies from 100 percent of those to whom he sends his questionnaire. Frequently, less than 50 percent reply and those who do reply may not be a representative sample of the group under study. In spite of these limitations, however, a thoughtfully formulated questionnaire sent to carefully selected groups may give valuable information about general trends in behavior.

Tests and similar methods of measurement. As you study psychology, you will find frequent references to tests and other such methods of measurement. Psychologists have devoted much time to developing tests of intellectual ability. They have also designed aptitude tests, which help predict what an individual is likely to be able to accomplish when and if he receives training in a given field. They have developed measuring devices that give clues to an individual's basic vocational interests. Psychologists have techniques for measuring attitudes toward social problems. They have developed techniques that enable one individual to rate other individuals on specified characteristics. In addition, psychologists have a number of techniques for measuring personality. During your school years you have taken many achievement tests designed to measure the extent to which you have mastered subject matter. If the tests were standardized ones, probably psychologists were involved in constructing them.

Tests and similar methods of measurement are valuable in psychology. They give more objective data than interviews and questionnaires. They give results that can be expressed in statistical terms, and often an individual's score can be compared with scores for large groups. Nevertheless, tests must be used with care. Some people think a psychologist can give them a few tests and then tell them exactly what college to attend, what job to take, and which person to marry. There is no such magic in tests. Results must be interpreted by experts. Even with the best interpretations, test results do not give full and final answers to individual problems. Test results must always be used as a means to an end, never as an end in themselves, or the results are useless. They are only one aspect in studying the behavior of an organism.

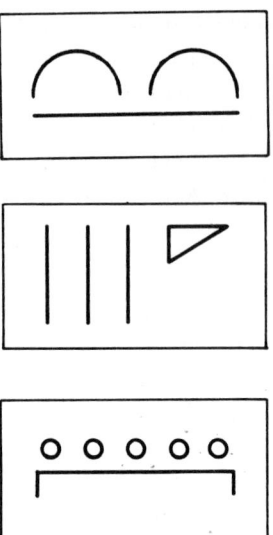

Psychologists have also developed creativity tests. For example, fifth-grade children are shown items similar to these three and are asked to imagine what these patterns might be. Most children give routine answers—such as two igloos, for the first item—but a few give original, creative responses.

The experimental method. You may think of experiments as activities carried out in laboratories containing dials, meters, rows and rows of bottles, glass tubing, and so on. Some experiments require such elaborate equipment, but many worthwhile experiments can be carried out in the classroom with the aid of simple apparatus. Method rather than apparatus determines the value of the work, although the accuracy of the equipment influences the accuracy of the ultimate results. The experimental method permits better control of conditions and provides for more accurate measurement than do other methods of study.

An experiment usually begins with the statement of a HYPOTHESIS, a tentative assumption or proposition that is to be tested. One of the oldest ways of stating a hypothesis is the "if-then" method. For example, the following might be a hypothesis: *"If* students eat no lunch, *then* they will do less well in their afternoon classes than they would otherwise."

In an experiment there must be at least two VARIABLES, or conditions that can change in amount or quality. There is always an INDEPENDENT VARIABLE, the factor that produces the effects being examined in the experiment. This variable is manipulated and controlled by the experimenter in some systematic and predetermined manner. The independent variable is also usually the stimulus acting upon the organism in the experiment. A STIMULUS is any object, event, or situation that causes a response by the organism.

Related to the independent variable is the DEPENDENT VARIABLE, the changed condition that is considered to be a consequence of, or to depend on, the independent variable. The dependent variable in an experiment is generally the *response* of the organism, which is caused by the action of the stimulus. An illustration will clarify the use of variables in experiments.

What procedures are used in an experiment? Suppose a psychologist wanted to conduct an experiment on the effect of a limited amount of sleep on students' examination grades. He might put forth the hypothesis, "If the sleep of students is limited the night before an exam, then their exam grades will be lower than they would be otherwise." For him to know that lower grades were not caused by factors other than insufficient sleep—for example, by differences in age, sex, amount of study, or intellectual ability—he must control or eliminate the possibly influential variables other than insufficient sleep that might cause exam grades to be lower. One way of doing this is to match two groups of students carefully. For every student in one group there would be a student of the same age, sex, socioeconomic background, and intellectual ability in the other group. Members of both groups would spend the same specified amount of time studying for the exam.

The psychologist might then instruct one group of students to get at least eight hours of sleep the night before the exam. To the other group he might give instructions to get only four hours of sleep prior to the exam. The experiment would thus investigate the effect of a particular condition (a limited amount of sleep the night before an exam). Psychologists call the group in which the condition under study is present (in this case, the group that gets little sleep) the EXPERIMENTAL GROUP. The group in which the condition is not present is called the CONTROL GROUP.

Since the amount of sleep is the factor being manipulated and is the stimulus acting upon the students, amount of sleep is the independent variable in the experiment. Examination grades are the dependent variable, since lower exam grades are, according to the hypothesis, a consequence of insufficient sleep and a response to the stimulus.

"I'm suffering a real identity crisis...I keep getting assigned to the control group."

After giving the experimental and control groups identical examinations, the psychologist would study the grades and compare the performance of the two groups. If the students in the experimental group earned lower grades than those in the control group, the psychologist's hypothesis would be supported.

The experimental method is basic to modern psychology. Much of the information presented in this textbook is based on evidence produced by experiments.

Why do psychologists use animals in experiments? Though interested chiefly in human behavior, psychologists do much experimental work with animals. They may use rats, pigeons, chimpanzees, or almost any other animal as subjects for experimental work. (In psychology a SUBJECT is the organism, human or animal, participating in an experiment, whose responses constitute the dependent variable in the experiment.) The physical structure, and to some degree the social behavior, of many animals resembles that of man, so that work with animals leads the way toward scientific studies of human beings.

Animal behavior can be controlled to an extent that is not possible with human beings. A rat, for example, can be raised from birth in a cage, where a record can be kept of everything that happens to it. The rat can then be used in a learning experiment with the certainty that it has had no opportunity to learn except under the conditions of the experiment. Human beings, on the other hand, have many experiences that cannot be controlled or even recorded by an experimenter but that may influence experimental data.

Another advantage of using animals as subjects is that many animals have relatively short life spans and reproduce at rapid rates. Thus a psychologist can study the behavior of several generations within a relatively short period of time. A third advantage is that experiments involving brain or other surgery or involving the use of certain drugs can be performed with animals but not with man.

Although the psychologist studies animals to get clues to human behavior, he is careful to avoid ANTHROPOMORPHISM, or the attributing of human characteristics to other beings besides man. For example, we see a dog "begging" for a bone. When he barks, we may say that he "speaks" for the bone. When he buries the bone, we may be tempted to say that he thinks to himself, "I am not hungry now, so I will bury it in this hole to keep the puppy next door from running off with it." Thinking in terms of words that make complete sentences is a human characteristic, and there is no evidence that lower animals think in this way. We may be tempted to attribute language to the lower animal partly because we have been brought up on fairy stories suggesting that animals and even inanimate objects can talk. Although we can learn much about human behavior by observing the behavior of lower animals, it is inaccurate to attribute human characteristics to them.

20 WHAT IS PSYCHOLOGY?

One word of caution: Do not attempt experiments that involve injury or discomfort to an animal. Such work should be done only under restricted conditions by a trained scientist, who can take the responsibility for judging that his project is for the eventual benefit of mankind. The American Psychological Association (APA), a national professional organization for psychologists, has a Code of Ethics for the handling of animals under experimental conditions. This Code covers the living conditions of experimental animals and the ways in which such animals can and cannot be treated before, during, and after experiments.

How are experimental data reported? If you want to learn how psychologists bring together, summarize, and evaluate experimental evidence, consult the *Psychological Bulletin,* a journal published by the American Psychological Association which summarizes research in specialized areas, or some other periodical containing articles by psychologists. Some articles may be difficult to understand in detail because of the technical language, but they will add to your appreciation of the scientific method in psychology.

Rather than include all the mathematical terminology and statistical details that psychologists sometimes use in designing, recording, and reporting their work, this textbook will often summarize experiments. When research is cited and one case is given to illustrate a point, students sometimes wonder, "What of it? One experiment with a small group of children or a litter of rats doesn't prove anything." That is true, but the experiment may illustrate basic principles and provide useful research. There is not enough space in any one book to cite all the evidence supporting a principle.

If you do some supplemental reading in current journals, you may find reports of experimental data or theories that are not in agreement with what is said in the textbook. In this case, the first step is to examine the source of the report. Sometimes the press describes as a "revolutionary discovery" what is really a hypothesis that has yet to be tested. If the report is from a truly scientific source, then fresh data and new ideas have emerged since this textbook went to press. The rapid progress of modern science is one factor that keeps the field of psychology exciting and challenging.

THE PHYSIOLOGY OF MEDITATION

Is the meditative state that is achieved by yogis and other Far Eastern mystics accompanied by distinct physiological changes? A study of volunteer subjects in the U.S. indicates that it is

How capable is the human organism of adjusting to psychologically disturbing changes in the environment? Our technological age is probably testing this capacity more severely than it was ever tested in the past. The impact of the rap... ...unprecedented in... ...the...

...of her subjects actually was able to stop his heart. In 1957 two American physiologists, M. A. Wenger of the University of California at Los Angeles and B. K. Bagchi of the University of Michigan Medical School, conducted a more extensive investi... ...collaboration with ...dia Insti... ...h...

practitioner; confined in a sealed metal box, the meditating yogi markedly reduced his oxygen consumption and carbon dioxide elimination.

These tests strongly indicated that meditation produced the effects through ...l of an "involuntary" ...nism ...ly, presumably... ...ic ...T...

When you see a headline about some scientific matter in a magazine or newspaper, do you automatically believe it? or do you first examine the source of the article?

Terms to Know

As you study psychology, you will learn many new terms as well as some new meanings for terms already in your vocabulary. Such terms will be listed at the close of each chapter. Checking your knowledge of the specific meanings of these terms will help serve as a review and as preparation for examinations.

anthropomorphism	heuristic concept	psychiatry
behavior	hypnosis	psychoanalysis
case-study method	hypothesis	psychokinesis
clairvoyance	independent variable	psychology
clinical psychologist	interview	psychotherapy
control group	"mind"	questionnaire method
dependent variable	natural observation	stimulus
directed observation	organism	subject (in an experiment)
experimental group	parapsychology	telepathy
experimental method	posthypnotic suggestion	theory
extrasensory perception	precognition	variable
	pseudo-scientist	

Topics to Think About

The questions below are not examination questions for which there are right or wrong answers. They are designed to stimulate your thinking about problems that interest psychologists. If the questions are discussed in class, members may disagree. If psychologists were consulted, they might disagree. Disagreement, followed by careful thinking, theories, and research, is how progress is made in any field of learning.

1. Are there more social problems today, and are they more intense than in previous generations?

2. Many young people disagree with the thinking of older persons on personal and social problems. Why?

3. Have you ever had any experiences that seem to suggest telepathy? If so, what evidence was there that telepathy took place? Is there any possible explanation for what happened?

4. Would you permit anyone to try to hypnotize you? Why or why not?

5. Psychologists use animals in their experiments quite often. Do the results obtained from animals apply also to human beings? How is it possible to show that such results are applicable to human behavior?

6. Do you think that psychology is as "true" a science as biology, chemistry, or physics?

22 WHAT IS PSYCHOLOGY?

7. One writer has stated that if an experiment explains the behavior of 80 percent of a group, the use of the data is limited unless it also explains the behavior of the other 20 percent. Do you agree or disagree? Why?

8. Do you think that psychologists or sociologists do the most good for society? Give your reasons.

Suggestions for Activities

Remembering and even understanding what is said in each chapter of a textbook is not enough. The more personal experiences you can have with psychology, the broader your view and the better your understanding of the subject.

At the close of each chapter there will be suggestions for activities. You may wish to conduct surveys or to make and use apparatus. Probably there will not be time for all of you to carry out each suggestion. Perhaps committees can be designated to conduct certain activities and report back to the class for discussion. If it is inconvenient to carry out some of these activities in your school or community, you may wish to suggest other similar ones.

1. Ask several persons who have not studied psychology to complete some or all of the following sentences, and then compare their sentences. Keep all these materials and restudy them toward the end of the course. (1) Psychology is useful to people because... (2) Psychology is popular with many people because... (3) To me, common sense and psychology... (4) Some things psychologists tell us are... (5) In terms of ability to judge people, psychologists... (6) Psychologists ought to... (7) Psychologists know less about behavior than... (8) Psychology teaches you how to... (9) By studying psychology a person can... (10) Psychologists can predict behavior by... (11) Many psychologists are... (12) As scientists, psychologists are...

2. Look for "Psychologists" in the classified section of your telephone directory or in the directory of the nearest large city. If there are psychologists or psychological services listed, what can you learn about their qualifications?

3. Try to find out whether or not your state has any regulations restricting the use of the title "Psychologist" (most states do). If there are regulations, what qualifications do they require for psychologists? If there are no restrictions, are psychologists in your state doing anything to bring about a licensing law?

4. Ask several friends who have not studied psychology to define "mind." Record their responses, bring them to class, and compare these definitions with the discussion of "mind" in the text.

5. If you have ever seen a demonstration of hypnosis, report on it. Was it done for entertaining purposes? What methods were used to produce hypnosis? Was the hypnotized person asked to say or do anything that might have been embarrassing? What training in psychology did the hypnotist have?

6. Many amateur entertainers mystify their audiences by giving demonstrations of "mind reading." Perhaps you can arrange such a demonstration in class. Will the entertainer admit that he is using one kind of trick or another, even though he may not be willing to tell his secret method of operation? Can you figure out how he achieves the effects of telepathy?

7. Check your school or public library to see if it has any psychological journals. The American Psychological Association publishes many journals, including the *American Psychologist, Journal of Applied Psychology, Journal of Educational Psychology,* and *Journal of Experimental Psychology.* These are, however, only a few of the journals published by the APA. There are more than sixty different journals published by qualified organizations which contain articles relating to psychology. In addition to professional journals, there are also magazines such as *Psychology Today, Human Behavior, People Watching,* and *Trans-Action* that contain interesting and informative articles on psychology.

 ## Suggestions for Further Reading

In addition to your study of this textbook, class discussions, lectures by your teacher, activities of various kinds, and experiments, you will wish to broaden your knowledge of psychology still further through supplemental reading. At the close of each chapter there will be "Suggestions for Further Reading."

Some of the books suggested are introductory college textbooks. Such books present much the same material as is given in your textbook, but treat it in more detail. Other of the suggested readings are taken from lists recommended for high school students. Some of the suggestions offered below are books of readings, containing selections on appropriate topics of interest. A few of the books do not fit the traditional lists of readings, but present material of a psychological nature written by persons who are not professional psychologists.

Do not consider these "Suggestions for Further Reading" as complete reference lists. Only limited space is available at the close of each chapter. New books and booklets are being published all the time. Your teacher or librarian might assist you in finding recent material. There is always new and interesting material to read in the field of psychology.

Annual Editions: Readings in '72 Psychology, Guilford, Conn.: The Dushkin
　　Publishing Group. A collection of eighty-five articles from periodicals such as
　　Time and the *American Scientist* on a wide range of psychological topics. This
　　paperback is reissued each year.
Dethier, V. F., *To Know a Fly,* Holden-Day, 1962. The author makes learning seem
　　like fun and research sound exciting.
Doherty, Michael, and Kenneth M. Shemberg, *Asking Questions About Psychology:
　　An Introduction to What Psychologists Do,* Scott, Foresman, 1970. A paperback
　　in which the authors try to answer some of the questions of students who
　　are taking an introductory course in psychology. Part I of this book is on
　　"Asking Questions," Part II on "Some Answers," and Part III on conclusions,
Hilgard, E. R., R. C. Atkinson, and Rita Atkinson, *Introduction to Psychology,* 5th
　　including principles of research.

ed., Harcourt Brace Jovanovich, 1971. This is a widely used college textbook. Chapter 1: "Psychology as a Behavioral Science"; pages 156–59, on ESP; and pages 172–78, on hypnosis as an altered state of awareness.

Johnson, Cecil E. (ed.), *Contemporary Readings in Behavior,* McGraw-Hill, 1970. This paperback contains eighteen selected readings on animal behavior—for example, on ants, wolves, bears, seals, and apes. There are short biographical sketches of the scientists whose works are included.

Kagan, J., M. M. Haith, and Catherine Caldwell, *Psychology: Adapted Readings,* Harcourt Brace Jovanovich, 1971. The editors of this book of readings have selected materials that are of basic psychological interest and have modified them enough so that the beginning student of psychology can read them with sustained interest. The readings cover fourteen major psychological topics. Each topic is introduced by a headnote that discusses the reading. See Selection 1, "On Attention," by William James; and Selection 2, "Psychology as the Behaviorist Views It," by John B. Watson.

Kagan, J., and E. Havemann, *Psychology: An Introduction,* 2nd ed., Harcourt Brace Jovanovich, 1972. One of the authors of this book is a psychologist, the other a professional writer. It has considerable value for supplemental reading by high school students. See Chapter 1, which contains an introduction to the field of psychology, including material on the history of psychology and scientific methodology, as well as applications of psychology to society today.

Lindgren, H. C., and D. Byrne, *Psychology: An Introduction to a Behavioral Science,* 3rd ed., John Wiley, 1971. Although a college textbook, this one has been recommended for reading by high school students. See Chapter 1, "Psychology as a Science and a Profession," and page 139 on ESP.

Lorenz, K., *King Solomon's Ring,* Thomas Y. Crowell, 1952 (paperback, Apollo). This book tells of experiences and experiments with animals. It is written in an interesting style and contains many amusing incidents.

McCollom, I. V., "Psychological Thrillers: Psychology Books Students Read When Given Freedom of Choice." *American Psychologist,* vol. 26 (1971), pages 921–29. An annotated list of fifteen books on psychology that students find particularly enjoyable.

McConnell, R. A., "ESP and Credibility in Science," *American Psychologist,* vol. 24 (1969), pages 531–38. Contains information about ESP experiments as well as references to literature on ESP.

Readings in Psychology Today, CRM Books, 1969. A collection of articles on many phases of psychology that have appeared in the magazine *Psychology Today.*

Rhine, J. B., and J. G. Pratt, *Parapsychology,* rev. ed., Charles C. Thomas, 1967. See Chapter 1, "A Field of Science," which describes the field of parapsychology, and Chapter 2, "Objective Research Methods," which contains an elementary discussion of research methods.

Ruch, Floyd L., and Philip C. Zimbardo, *Psychology and Life,* 8th ed., Scott, Foresman, 1971. See Chapter 1, "Unraveling the Mystery of Man's Behavior," and Chapter 2, "Psychology As a System of Scientific Inquiry."

Wertheimer, M., M. Bjorkman, I. Lundberg, and D. Magnusson, *Psychology: A Brief Introduction,* Scott, Foresman, 1971. Although this book can be used in colleges and junior colleges, it was written for high schools and for general reading. It is an adaptation of a Swedish text, translated and adapted for American usage. See Chapter 1, "Psychology Is Based on Controlled Observation and Experiment," which will expand your knowledge of what psychology is and how it operates.

EXTRASENSORY PERCEPTION

Do you believe in extrasensory perception (ESP)? Why, or why not? How would you go about conducting experimental research on ESP?

Extrasensory perception is a controversial subject in psychology. There is a considerable amount of evidence for ESP. However, a great deal of it is not the result of controlled experimentation in a laboratory. Most of the scientific studies of ESP have been done by individuals who were not psychologists.

One set of experiments on extrasensory perception was performed by the author Upton Sinclair in the 1920's, after he discovered that his wife seemed to have this unusual ability. Sinclair, or another person, would draw a picture and then have Mrs. Sinclair attempt to draw a picture like it, without looking at the original picture. Sometimes Mrs. Sinclair would hold the original picture in her hand while concentrating. Other times the original picture would be drawn many miles away. Of the 290 trials that were held, Upton Sinclair rated 23 percent as hits—very close reproductions of the original pictures—53 percent as partial hits, and 24 percent as failures. Below you can see one of the partial hits. The original drawing of the American flag is on the left and Mrs. Sinclair's matching drawing is on the right.

Research on extrasensory perception has also been conducted by a few psychologists under controlled experimental conditions. The psychologist whose name has stood out in the field of ESP for many years is Dr. Joseph B. Rhine. In his early research at Duke University, Dr. Rhine used a special deck of ESP cards. The deck consisted of twenty-five cards, five each of the following five suits: a star, a circle, a square, a plus sign, and wavy lines. An experimenter with the cards was stationed in one building on the campus while a subject remained in another building. Each had synchronized watches. Starting at a preestablished time, once each minute the experimenter would remove the top card from the deck and lay it face down, without looking at it. Thirty seconds later the subject would record his "impression" of the card. There was no means of communication between the experimenter and the subject except possible extrasensory perception. After each deck of cards was completed, the experimenter recorded the order of the cards. Later, Dr. Rhine compared this record to the record of the subject's responses. A score of 5 correct out of 25 could be expected by pure chance. In 1850 trials, the average score was 7.53 out of 25. Certain subjects made fairly consistent scores well above chance. Occasionally, more than twenty of the twenty-five cards were named correctly.

Since then Dr. Rhine and others have conducted far more complex experiments with ESP. Some of the experimenters have backgrounds in statistics, physics, biology, and physiology. One physicist, Dr. R. A. McConnell, left engineering electronics after reading a magazine article about Rhine's experiments, which inspired him to study scientific reports on ESP and interview many of the participants. Dr. McConnell, now a research professor of biophysics at the University of Pittsburgh, has conducted numerous laboratory experiments on parapsychology and has written many articles on the existence of ESP.

Most psychologists, however, do not agree with him that ESP is real. Some skeptical psychologists will be convinced only when there is an experimental procedure that produces ESP consistently on demand. At this point scientists have not been able to guarantee that extrasensory perception will take place under controlled conditions every time that it is attempted. Therefore many psychologists have suspended judgment on whether ESP is real or imaginary until more substantial evidence is presented.

What is your position in this controversy? What sort of evidence would you require to be convinced of the reality of ESP? If you are interested, you might read more about the subject. Perhaps the evidence you require already exists.

unit 2

LEARNING

chapter 2　Principles of learning

chapter 3　How to learn efficiently

chapter 4　The process of thinking

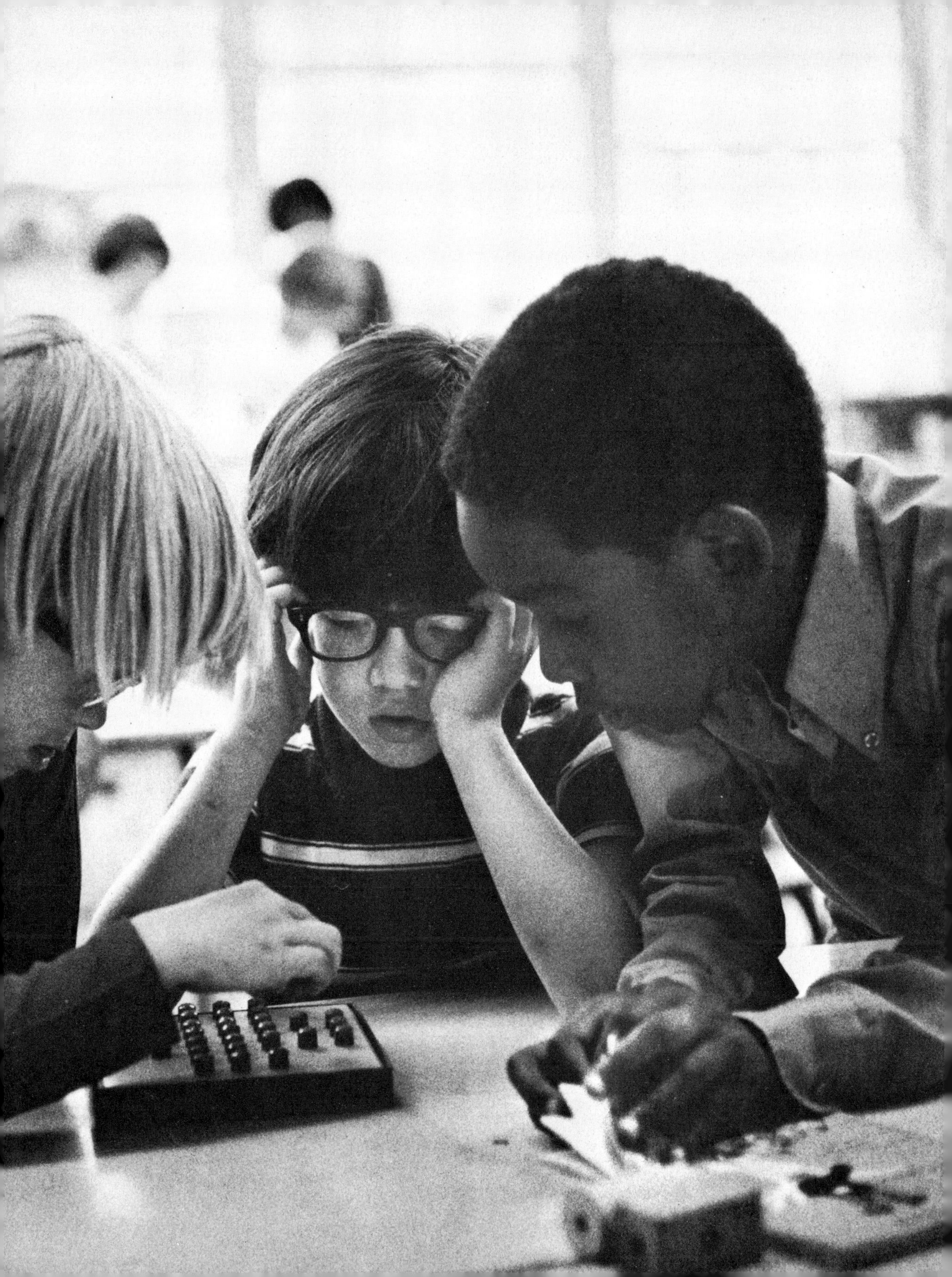

chapter 2

Principles of Learning

PSYCHOLOGY DEALS with human behavior. The most studied area of human behavior is the topic of learning. Learning takes place within an organism from birth (and possibly even before birth) to death. It is so important that without learning, man, and many other organisms, would die. If you suddenly forgot everything you had ever learned, and there was no one around to help you, how long do you think you could survive? A day? Two days?

Knowledge of some of the principles of learning will help you work more efficiently not only in school but in other areas as well. There are no short-cut methods of learning that will instantly make your life easier. However if you apply them properly, the principles of learning will help you perform better in school and in your other daily activities.

What Is Learning?

You have been learning all your life, and you will continue to learn for the rest of your life. Learning is not restricted to what you do in school. It is true that some of your most constructive learning takes place in school—through books, laboratory work, shop work, and other activities. You also learn, however, in a less formal way from friends, movies, television, newspapers, and jobs. Before you started school, you were learning in your home and at play with other children.

LEARNING refers to relatively permanent changes in behavior that occur as a result of practice or other past experience. Characteristically, learning involves acquiring the ability to do something that you have not done before, or at least the ability to use previously acquired reactions in new and different combinations. Some learning involves acquiring and using facts; some, acquiring and using skills.

Not all behavior has to be learned. Some behavior—like blinking your eyes when a puff of air strikes them—occurs automatically. Such automatic behavior, which does not require previous experience or practice, is called a REFLEX.

Still other unlearned behavior is mainly the result of physical growth and development. For example, as a baby grows and develops, he is able to crawl. We say, "The baby has learned to crawl," but what we really mean is that the child's nerves and muscles have developed to a point where crawling becomes possible. In early adolescence a boy's voice changes, a result of the growth of his vocal cords. Such changes are due to physical growth and development rather than to learning.

In this chapter we will use the term "learning" to refer to changes in behavior that are not reflexive and are not primarily the result of physical growth.

Trial-and-Error Learning

Early in the twentieth century a great deal of experimental work placed animals and human beings in situations where they tried, over and over, to learn some desired bit of behavior. In these experiments the subjects seemed to blunder onto the solution to the problem by trial and error. To provide an incentive for the subjects' efforts, the experimenter gave food or some other reward for a correct response. For an incorrect response he often provided punishment, such as a low-voltage electric shock.

Puzzle boxes. Some of the early work on learning used puzzle boxes for experimental purposes. The boxes were so constructed that an animal placed in the box could turn a knob or push a latch that would allow him to escape. He was then rewarded with food. Typically, the animal had many trials and made errors the first time he was put into the box, but eventually he happened to turn the knob. On subsequent trials the animal made fewer and fewer useless movements, or errors, until finally he could turn the knob immediately on being placed in the box.

Mazes. Mazes were also used in much of the early experimental work on learning. A maze is simply a device having a series of pathways, some of which are blind alleys but one of which is the correct path to the goal. The animal or person is presented with the task of taking a path through the maze without entering any blind alleys. Many responses can be tried, but only one is correct.

Some mazes are large enough to permit people to walk about in them, while other smaller mazes are not much bigger than a book. The subjects are blindfolded and asked to find their way with a finger or stylus through a small maze consisting of grooved paths or raised ridges. When mazes of the same design are used with humans and with laboratory animals, the results do not differ greatly. People seem to make about the same number of trials and errors as the animals. In fact, there have been some experiments reported in which rats had scores somewhat superior to those made by human beings.

Although research using mazes is not so common today as it was earlier in the century, students can still discover much about the learning process by performing simple experiments with mazes. Modern mazes are usually of the T or Y type; that is, the learner starts along a straight path but comes to a point where he must turn either left or right. Turning left, for example, may lead to no reward or even to punishment of some kind (often an electric shock); turning right may lead to a reward of some kind (often food, in the case of animal subjects). Even earthworms can learn this type of maze.

Multiple-T mazes are usually used with higher animals and human beings. In experiments with such mazes every turn in the wrong direction at each junction point is counted as an error. Today we generally use elimination of errors as a measure of learning rather than the counting of time spent, since otherwise the learner can speed up his movements without actually improving his learning.

Sometimes scientists use a double-alternation temporal maze. In such a maze the animal or person must learn to turn to the left some of the time and to the right some of the time, in a definite pattern determined by the experimenter. Monkeys are able to learn such intricate sequences as rrllrrllrrllrrll (two turns to the right, two to the left, and so on). Human beings over four years of age can learn the solution to a double-alternation maze. Rats ordinarily cannot solve such a problem.

Today psychologists have other methods for studying learning. They speak in terms of conditioning rather than of the older trial-and-error learning. Many people use the term "conditioning" as if it were a synonym for learning. To the psychologist, however, conditioning has a specific technical meaning as one aspect of learning.

Classical Conditioning

CLASSICAL CONDITIONING refers to a learning situation in which a response is evoked by a certain stimulus (which did not previously evoke it) as a result of combining this stimulus for a number of trials with a stimulus that normally did elicit the response. Although this definition may seem a bit difficult to understand, a few examples of classical conditioning will make it clear.

Pavlov's famous experiment. Have you ever felt your mouth water at the sight or smell or even the thought of a tasty bit of food? Ivan Pavlov (1849–1936), a Russian scientist, observed this "mouth watering" when he fed the dogs in his laboratory. He decided to follow up his observation by studying the

This maze of hedges at Hampton Court, England, requires the use of trial-and-error learning. Because the hedges are above eye-level, people inside the maze cannot see the whole problem and must use trial-and-error learning to get out.

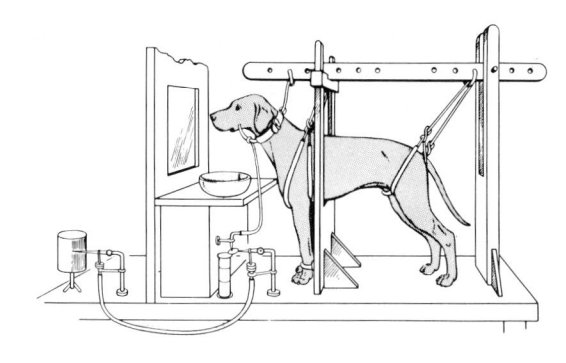

The apparatus used by Pavlov in his experiments in classical conditioning. Food could be placed in the bowl by remote control. The dog's salivation was recorded automatically.

phenomenon of salivation under controlled experimental conditions. Pavlov designed an apparatus that held the dog in a desired position. A tube attached to the dog's cheek near one of the salivary glands drained off the saliva and permitted accurate measurement of the flow. The apparatus was in a soundproof room. There was a one-way-vision screen between the experimenter and the dog, which permitted the experimenter to see the dog, although the dog could not see the experimenter.

Powdered meat was placed in the mouth of the hungry dog and, as usual, saliva flowed. The flow of saliva became known as the UNCONDITIONED RESPONSE (UCR)—the response that occurs normally, with no learning necessary. The meat Pavlov called the UNCONDITIONED STIMULUS (UCS) because it was the normal, unlearned agent for causing salivation. Next, the experimenter sounded a bell just before he delivered meat to the dog. Several more times he sounded the bell and presented the meat immediately after. Then, when he sounded the bell without presenting the meat, he found that the dog's saliva flowed. The dog had been conditioned to salivate at the sound of the bell. The sound of the bell had become a CONDITIONED STIMULUS (CS) and the salivation at the sound had become a CONDITIONED RESPONSE (CR). A new association had been formed.

Other conditioning experiments. It is easy to demonstrate classical conditioning. Picture a subject seated with one arm resting on a table. Electrodes are attached so that he can receive a safe but noticeable shock through his hand and finger. When he gets a shock, he normally jerks his finger without having to learn to do so.

At the beginning of the experiment the subject hears a bell rung. He does not jerk his finger, because he has no reason to give such a response. Next, the bell is rung and a shock is given almost at the same time. This bell-followed-by-shock routine is repeated a number of times, to which the subject always responds by a finger jerk. Then, although the subject does not know what is going to happen, he hears the bell ring but does not receive the accompanying shock. Again, he jerks his finger. Conditioning has taken place.

In summary, remember that the UCS (unconditioned stimulus) is a stimulus that normally evokes a UCR (unconditioned response); that is, the UCR is an unlearned response to the UCS. The CS (conditioned

A diagram of classical conditioning

UCS (Electric shock) — Unlearned → UCR (finger withdrawal)

CS (Bell) — Learned ⇢ CR (finger withdrawal)

PRINCIPLES OF LEARNING

stimulus) is a stimulus that is associated with the UCS and eventually evokes a CR (conditioned response), which is similar to but not identical with the UCR. The CR is usually weaker in strength than the UCR. The diagram on page 33 will help you understand the procedures. The dotted line indicates that the connection between the CS and the CR is learned.

Some practical applications of classical conditioning. Classical conditioning has been used for practical purposes outside the laboratory. In one case a baby girl showed none of the usual reactions to sound. The parents, afraid that she was deaf, asked a psychologist to determine whether or not the baby could hear. When a bell was rung, the baby made no observable responses. The sole of her foot was then scratched with a pin. She drew up her leg and cried. Then the bell was rung and the baby's foot was scratched at practically the same time. After a considerable number of such pairings, the psychologist rang the bell without scratching the sole of the baby's foot. She drew up her leg and cried. A conditioned response had been formed. The anxious parents knew that their baby could hear, although for some unknown reason she had not been giving the usual responses to sound stimulation.

An interesting, common, and highly practical application of the principle of classical conditioning is the electrically charged wire fence for enclosing livestock. A fence with a few strands of charged wire, insulated at all points of contact with the fence posts, will serve as well as the much more expensive "hog-tight, bull-strong, and horse-high" fence. Animals that touch the charged wire receive a harmless but disagreeable shock. In some cases, even one experience of shock will condition an animal against trying to pass under,

A single strand that is electrically charged makes an effective and inexpensive fence. Contact with the electric charge quickly conditions horses to stay in the pasture.

through, or over the fence. The expense of the conditioning will be slight, for current is used only during those instants when animals touch the fence. Soon all the animals in an enclosure become so well conditioned that they cannot be induced to go near the wire.

Counter-conditioning. Another practical application is the use of a procedure known as counter-conditioning to eliminate undesirable behavior, such as alcoholism. COUNTER-CONDITIONING consists of conditioning the stimulus to a different response, usually for the purpose of getting rid of certain learned, unacceptable behavior. The individual may be given a drug (emetine for alcoholics) that produces nausea when the individual tastes alcohol. Later, when he desires alcohol, he associates the feeling of nausea with alcohol and avoids drinking. Counter-conditioning is also used to reduce fear and anxiety.

There is some criticism of the procedures involved in counter-conditioning, when used alone, because they treat the symptoms of the undesirable behavior rather than the underlying causes. When used in conjunction with appropriate treatment of underlying causes, this method has more success, especially when the substituted desirable behavior is rewarded. In one experiment overweight subjects were divided into an experimental group and a control group, and were asked to list the foods they most desired, such as pies, cakes, candies, and doughnuts. The subjects were then to handle each food, one at a time, think about each, and, finally, smell it. Immediately after smelling the food each subject placed a gas mask over his face and a noxious odor was blown into the mask. All subjects in the experimental group lost weight during conditioning and nearly one year later still had an average weight loss of more than nine pounds, while subjects in the control group gained an average of one pound. In addition to conditioning the subjects to avoid certain foods, the study involved establishing an experimenter-subject personal relationship, in which the experimenter talked at length with the subjects about weight reduction, listened to their problems, insisted that they lose weight, and praised them as their weight decreased. The successful results with the experimental group were attributed to using the counter-conditioning procedures in conjunction with establishing a personal relationship and rewarding the desirable behavior of losing weight.

Terms Related to Classical Conditioning

Psychologists use a number of technical terms in discussing classical conditioning. Five terms will be defined here: extinction, spontaneous recovery, reinforcement, generalization, and discrimination.

Extinction and spontaneous recovery. When a conditioned stimulus (CS) is presented without the unconditioned stimulus (UCS), the conditioned response (CR) will gradually diminish and eventually cease. This process is called EXTINCTION. To illustrate extinction, we can refer to the bell-and-shock experiment previously described. If the bell (CS) is sounded a number of times without the shock (UCS) being given, the subject will cease to give the finger jerk (CR) when the bell is sounded. The conditioned response will have been extinguished. To consider another example, in the case of the electrified fence, what may happen if the farmer turns off the current? The conditioned response (avoiding the fence) may last for a while, but if animals touch the fence accidentally and are not shocked, the conditioned response will be weakened or will no longer occur. The fence will have lost its value because extinction has taken place.

Some conditioned responses are difficult to extinguish. A CR of fear, for instance, may persist even though the original object or situation (the UCS) may not have been present for years. In one study it was found that fifteen years after their last war experience sailors still responded physiologically more than the average person to a rapidly sounding gong, a signal used in the navy to announce battle stations.

After extinction has apparently occurred, however, if there is a rest period and then the conditioned stimulus is given, the conditioned response will probably reappear. The reappearance of the conditioned response without reinforcement is known as SPONTANEOUS RECOVERY. Both extinction and spontaneous recovery can be illustrated in graphic form (see below). At point A in the conditioning, the conditioned stimulus (CS) is presented without the unconditioned stimulus (UCS). The strength of the conditioned response (CR) may actually continue to increase for a few trials, but as the CS is continually presented without the UCS, the strength of the CR will begin to decrease. This would be the beginning of the extinction period. Then, at point B, after a period of time and without any intervening reinforcement, the CS is presented to the subject. When this occurs, the CR will again appear in the subject's behavior as spontaneous recovery. For example, a rat conditioned to press a lever for food will, after a rest period, begin pushing the lever again, even though he receives no food. One way of measuring remembering is to compare the number of trials necessary for the organism to regain the original strength of the CR after extinction has taken place.

Reinforcement. In classical conditioning the procedure of presenting the unconditioned stimulus immediately following the conditioned stimulus is called REINFORCEMENT. As the examples cited in the preceding pages have shown, the unconditioned stimulus (shock, for example) strengthens the tendency for the response (in this case, the finger jerk) to be made and thereby increases its probability of occurrence.

Reinforcement may be PARTIAL or INTERMITTENT. Once a conditioned response has been established, it will continue to be elicited when there is only occasional reinforcement with the unconditioned stimulus. The student who no longer jerks his finger because the bell has been sounded a number of times without the accompanying shock will begin jerking his finger again as soon as the bell and shock are paired one or more times.

In one well-known experiment two groups of subjects were conditioned to blink their eyes when a light went on. One group had a puff of air (UCS) directed toward their eyes every time a light (CS) was turned on. Another group of subjects had the puff of air directed toward their eyes only half of the time the light was turned on. The group receiving reinforcement only half the time became conditioned almost as well as the group receiving reinforcement every time. Next, the responses of both groups were extinguished by presenting the light without the puff of air. The group that was reinforced only half the time persisted longer in eye blinking after no puff of air was given than did the group receiving 100-percent reinforcement, indicating that intermittent reinforcement may result in greater persistence in behavior than does 100-percent reinforcement.

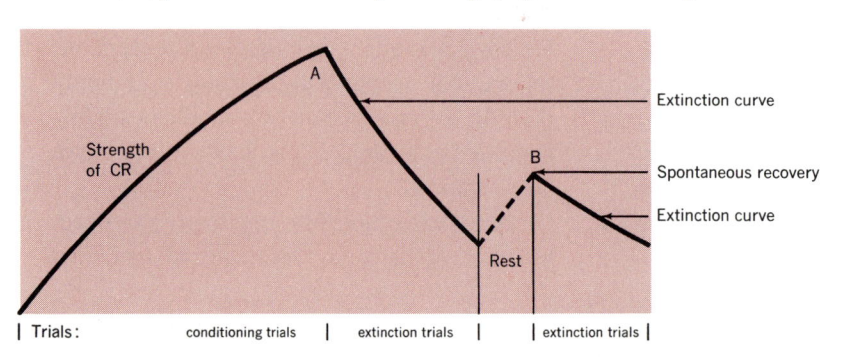

A diagram of extinction and spontaneous recovery

These two pictures illustrate one instance of generalization. On the left, a little girl is patting and making friends with a large furry dog. Above, the girl generalizes her response to large furry animals and wants to pat the tiger.

Generalization. It might seem that learning in everyday life situations would require a tremendous number of different conditioning experiences. In a way this is true, but allowance must be made for generalization. When a conditioned response has been established to a certain stimulus, other similar stimuli will also bring about that response. That is, there will be GENERALIZATION.

An example of generalization can be found in the experiment on weight reduction mentioned earlier (on p. 35). One subject was conditioned (by breathing in noxious odors through a gas mask immediately after smelling a food) to avoid several foods containing grease. She was not specifically conditioned to avoid french fries. Yet when she smelled french fries, which contain grease, she nearly became ill.

We know from experience that we perspire, "break out in a cold sweat," under severe emotional strain. This perspiration can be measured. In one experiment individuals were given an electric shock severe enough to be unpleasant and even fear-producing.

When they perspired, their skin response was measured. The electric shock (UCS) was then paired with a tone of a certain pitch (CS). Conditioning took place, and the subjects perspired to that particular tone even when the shock was not given. Next, the particular tone was replaced by tones slightly higher and slightly lower, yet the conditioned response of perspiration continued. Generalization had occurred.

Then tones farther from the original tone were introduced. Although the skin response of perspiration was evoked by these tones, the reactions were less marked than those for the original tone. This experiment suggested a general rule that the greater the similarity between stimuli, the greater the generalization between them.

Some of the fears of children may be understood in terms of stimulus generalization. For example, a child may be beaten by a bully at school, which causes the child pain and produces vasoconstriction (blood vessel constriction). The sight of the bully, or even hearing his name, may then become

PRINCIPLES OF LEARNING **37**

a conditioned stimulus that evokes vasoconstriction—the child turns pale. Later on, generalization may take place and he may turn pale when he sees someone who resembles the bully of earlier days. It is possible that a number of fears of older children and adults can be explained in terms of generalization.

Discrimination. We have noted that there is a tendency to respond to all stimuli of a similar kind in the same way. Related to, but also in contrast to, generalization is discrimination. DISCRIMINATION refers to a tendency to respond to a particular stimulus in one way and to respond to similar stimuli in another way. Discrimination is established by reinforcing the desired response but withholding reinforcement for the generalized responses and thereby extinguishing them.

We can condition a dog to salivate at the sound of a tone of a certain pitch. Now if we present a tone somewhat different from the original tone, the dog will salivate to it. This is an example of generalization. If, however, we present food (reinforcement) whenever the first tone is sounded but do not present food when the second tone is sounded, the dog will soon salivate to the first tone only. There will be discrimination.

A child learns to respond by saying "Daddy" at the sight of his father, but for a while there is likely to be amusing generalization as he applies the term to any man he sees. However, the response "Daddy" is reinforced by some expression of pleasure on the part of the parents only when the child applies it to his father. It is not reinforced for other men. Soon there is discrimination, and the term "Daddy" is applied only to the father.

Perhaps you have already observed the fact that extinction, spontaneous recovery, generalization, discrimination, and the original acquisition of a response are all accomplished by furnishing or by withholding reinforcement for the response. The point at which reinforcement occurs in the conditioning process is one of the major differences between classical and operant conditioning.

Operant Conditioning

Of more relevance to formal learning than classical conditioning is operant conditioning. The word "operant" is used because the subject "operates" on the environment to bring about a result. In everyday learning we are more likely to encounter cases of operant conditioning than classical conditioning. OPERANT CONDITIONING may be defined as the strengthening of a stimulus-response association by following the response with a reinforcing stimulus. The stimulus is reinforcing if it strengthens the response that precedes it, thus increasing the probability of the response occurring.

What are some differences between classical and operant conditioning? An illustration will help to make clear the distinction between classical and operant conditioning. In a laboratory a dog has two electrodes attached to one of its feet. Whenever the current is turned on, the dog receives a shock (UCS) and so lifts its foot (UCR). If a bell is sounded (CS) each time the dog is shocked, it will soon be conditioned to lift its foot (CR) when the bell is sounded, even though it is not shocked. This is a case of classical conditioning.

A contemporary psychologist, Professor B. F. Skinner, has done a great deal of work on operant conditioning. For animal experi-

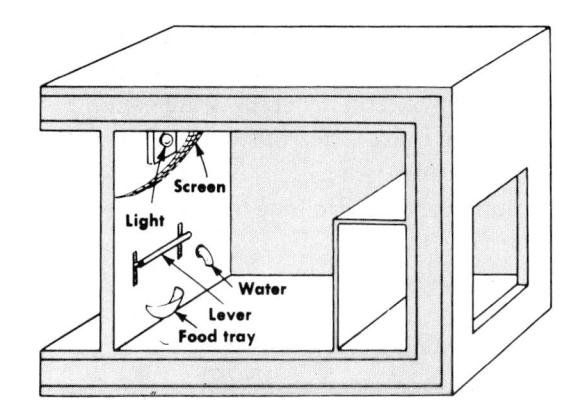

This apparatus was designed by B. F. Skinner for animal experiments in operant conditioning. When a rat presses the bar, food appears.

ments he developed a box (above), one side of which contained a protruding bar with a food cup below. When a hungry rat was placed in the box, the rat began to explore it. In the course of its wandering, it usually pushed the bar by accident. The apparatus was designed so that whenever the bar was pressed, a pellet of food fell into the cup. After a few such experiences of pressing the bar and receiving food, the hungry rat was conditioned to press the bar in order to get food. It operated on the environment to bring about a desired result. This is operant conditioning. (See feature on pp. 112–13.)

In past years it was thought that classical conditioning procedures were concerned with involuntary responses, such as salivating, involving the autonomic nervous system, and operant procedures with voluntary responses, such as pressing a bar, involving the central nervous system. However, in recent years this difference has been challenged by experiments showing that animals can be operantly conditioned to change heartbeat, blood pressure, intestinal contractions, temperature, and salivation, which are under the control of the autonomic nervous system. For example, in one study a baseline of normal heart rate was established for a group of rats. One group was rewarded for an increase in heart rate and another group was rewarded when they showed a decrease. It was possible to teach a rat to slow its heart rate from 350 to 250 beats per minute within a short period of time. Several rats even slowed their heart rate down so far that they died (although this was not the intention of the researchers). Other rats learned to increase their heart rate.

Many of the same principles that apply to classical conditioning also apply to operant conditioning, but there are important differences. One difference is that in operant conditioning the subject takes a larger role in the procedure. The rat in the Skinner-box experiment is an operator, not just a salivator or foot raiser. Another difference is that in classical conditioning the unconditioned stimulus, such as an electric shock, is specifically known, but in operant conditioning the unconditioned stimulus must be inferred. For example, in operant conditioning when a rat presses a lever to obtain food, the unconditioned stimulus may be inferred to be hunger. Further examples of the operant principle follow. They will illustrate other important differences between operant conditioning and classical conditioning.

Some operant conditioning experiments with animals. In one experiment a pigeon was taught to make complete turns in a clockwise direction. Making complete clockwise turns is not part of a pigeon's unlearned behavior. When first placed in the Skinner conditioning box, the pigeon merely wandered about, but in a relatively short time he learned that he could obtain food in the food tray (this box had no lever). Then the psychologist began training him. Of course, the pigeon had no way of knowing that he was supposed to turn clockwise, but in the course of his random movements he chanced to turn a few degrees in a clockwise direction. Immediately the psychologist reinforced this behavior with some grain.

The pigeon continued to make random movements, but each time he turned a bit more in a clockwise direction, the movement was reinforced. The pigeon received grain for a quarter turn, for between a quarter and a half turn, and so on, to a complete clockwise turn. Obviously, movements in a counterclockwise direction were never reinforced. Soon the pigeon was regularly making clockwise turns to get food.

This procedure, in which the experimenter rewards the organism each time it makes an overt response that approximates (resembles) the ultimate desired response, is called SUCCESSIVE APPROXIMATIONS. On successive trials each response must be more like the desired response for reinforcement to occur. When the desired response occurs, reinforcement follows only that response.

The experiment with the pigeon illustrates an important distinction between operant and classical conditioning. During classical conditioning the order of events is stimulus-reinforcement-response (with the UCS as the reinforcement). To insure that the response occurs, reinforcement is given before each response. During operant conditioning, however, the order is stimulus-response-reinforcement. Reinforcement follows the response, and it follows only a correct response.

Animals can be taught to do a wide variety of activities—elephants can be taught to sit on stools, for instance—through operant conditioning procedures. Many of the tricks that animals perform in circuses are learned through operant conditioning.

Can operant conditioning be used for animal training? Using their knowledge of operant conditioning, modern psychologists have been able to train animals efficiently and successfully. They simply reinforce those responses that meet their requirements and extinguish all others by withholding reinforcement. For example, two psychologists trained a hen to play a five-note tune on a small piano. They provided reinforcement in the form of grain for desired responses as they occurred in correct order, and presented no grain for undesired behavior.

Owners of pets quite often use operant-conditioning procedures to train their animals. And professional animal trainers employ more elaborate and precise methods of conditioning than pet owners. A professional dog trainer, for example, usually has a specific training area in which the dog's behavior is strictly controlled. Most professional dog trainers use verbal commands as reward and punishment for correct and incorrect responses. Army trainers emphasize verbal praise as the reinforcement, occasionally associating verbal praise with food. To train a dog to sit down, for instance, the trainer gives the command "Sit." If the dog does not make the appropriate response within a short period of time, the trainer gently forces the dog into a sitting position, waits until the dog relaxes, and then gently praises the dog, using such terms as "Good dog." To train dogs as retrievers, professional trainers also use specific methods and verbal reinforcement. The trainer may fasten to the ground all but the object he wants the dog to retrieve. As training progresses, the tied-down objects will eventually be left alone and only the desired object will be retrieved. Each time the dog runs after and brings back the appropriate article, the animal is rewarded with verbal praise.

In one interesting experiment operant conditioning was used to teach pigeons to select visually all rejects among drug capsules, such as a capsule that had a double cap or a rough edge. The pigeons viewed the capsules from behind a glass window and rejected capsules by pecking on the glass. They were reinforced only when they correctly selected a reject, which had been mixed in a random order with acceptable capsules and placed on an endless conveyor belt during the training period. The pigeons were able to differentiate between acceptable and unacceptable capsules on a 99-percent correct basis within one week of daily training. Because of some of the problems involved, such as the huge number of pigeons needed to inspect the more than 20 million capsules manufactured in one day, pigeons were never put to work on an actual inspection line. But animals can be trained to perform these and many other tasks through operant conditioning.

Is operant conditioning used with human beings? Operant conditioning is no more limited to animals than is classical conditioning. Reinforcing desired responses is a standard procedure in teaching, for instance. In one experiment the subjects were asked to make up sentences using words printed on cards. Each card contained a verb and six pronouns —*he, I, she, they, we,* and *you.* Each sentence had to contain one of the pronouns and the verb. The experimenter provided reinforcement by saying "Good" whenever a sentence containing the pronouns *I* or *we* was given. The production of sentences containing the other pronouns was not reinforced. In the course of eighty trials there was a steady increase in the number of sentences containing *I* and *we,* whereas with a control group of subjects, to whom no reinforcement was given, there was no increase.

In another experiment a psychologist and his subject carried on an informal conversation. Whenever the subject used a sentence beginning with "I think," "I believe," or a similar expression, the psychologist reinforced it by saying "You're right" or by otherwise expressing agreement. No reinforcement was given for other sentences. The record showed a steady increase in the number of sentences beginning with "I think" and similar expressions. Chairpersons of committees and leaders of discussion groups often use this technique to encourage discussion.

Terms Related to Operant Conditioning

Some of the terms that are used in classical conditioning are also used in operant conditioning; for example, extinction, spontaneous recovery, reinforcement, generalization, and discrimination. In this section we will see how these words are used in operant conditioning.

Extinction and spontaneous recovery. In classical conditioning extinction takes place if the conditioned stimulus is repeated without repeating the unconditioned stimulus. Similarly, a learned response in operant conditioning can be extinguished by withholding reinforcement. A pigeon that has been conditioned to make clockwise turns ceases to do so if he no longer gets food whenever he makes such a turn. As in classical conditioning spontaneous recovery will occur—the extinguished response of clockwise turns will reappear spontaneously when, after a period of time, the pigeon is again placed in the cage or experimental situation.

We have already considered the experiment in which subjects were conditioned to express their opinions by reinforcing all statements which began with "I think," "I believe," and so on. In a later part of the experiment no reinforcement was given following such statements. That is, the experimenter simply said nothing when such sentences were used. There was a marked drop in the number of sentences beginning with "I think" and the like. The chairperson of a committee or the leader of a discussion group might use this technique to squelch some members of the group who were taking too much of the group's time for their personal opinions. Spontaneous recovery can be seen in these cases, too, when the group meets once more and some of the same individuals again begin talking too much.

Reinforcement. In classical conditioning reinforcement often comes in the form of an unpleasant sensation, such as a mild electrical shock. You may already have recognized, however, that in operant conditioning a response is typically reinforced with a reward, such as food. The reinforcement is *positive* if presenting it strengthens a response, as in the case of giving the pigeon food. The reinforcement is *negative* if removing it strengthens a response, as in the turning off of a somewhat unpleasant electrical stimulation. In either case the reinforcement amounts to a reward.

One aspect of reinforcement to consider is the delay in time between performance of the correct response and reinforcement of that response. The principle of the GOAL GRADIENT states that the shorter the delay in receiving a reward after a correct response, the more likely it is for an organism to learn that response. Even a delay of fifteen seconds will have an effect on the learning of a response. This would mean, for instance, that students performing educational procedures correctly should receive more immediate and frequent rewards than is usually the case, especially at early grade levels. As the individual becomes

"WHAT REALLY GRIPES ME IS THAT I CAME **THAT** CLOSE TO BEING PUT IN THE GROUP ACROSS THE HALL!"

older, he is better equipped to profit from delayed rewards. One study indicated that black teen-age students from a low socioeconomic status group were less likely to choose a delayed, but larger, reward than were white teen-agers from a low socioeconomic group. According to the experimenters in this study, perhaps the difference is that blacks saw less relationship between their present behavior and their future behavior than did the white students. Possibly the black students had received fewer immediate and frequent rewards for appropriate responses in their earlier years.

Aside from the importance of the time between the response and the reinforcement in operant conditioning, there is the question of how frequently a correct response is reinforced. Reinforcement may be given each time that a correct response occurs, which generally results in fast acquisition of a learned response. However, in real-life situations we are not usually rewarded after every correct response, yet we persist in certain behavior for years.

Partial or intermittent reinforcement. Animals and men continue to perform many acts even when there is only partial or intermittent reinforcement. The gambler continues to put his money in the slot-machine or to play the roulette wheel, even though such behavior is reinforced by winning only a small part of the time.

It is possible that intermittent reinforcement may account for superstitions. On one play the gambler snaps his fingers just after he has rolled the dice, and the number he wants happens to appear. Although undesired numbers appear following subsequent finger snappings, once in a while his finger-snapping behavior happens to be reinforced. Consequently, he goes through the ritual each time he throws the dice. He acts as though snapping his fingers after the dice have left his hand in some way causes the dice to stop in a desired position.

A pigeon can be conditioned to peck at an illuminated disk to get food. After this behavior has been conditioned, it is not necessary to give the pigeon food every time it pecks at the disk to have it continue pecking. In one experiment a pigeon was rewarded with food only twelve times an hour (about every five minutes), although it pecked at the disk about 6,000 times an hour. Some pigeons have been kept pecking at an illuminated disk several thousand times with only one reinforcement of food. There is experimental evidence that other animals, and man, too, will perform faster and over longer periods of no reinforcement when the initial response has been established under partial reinforcement.

Knowledge of intermittent reinforcement can assist a person in breaking some habits and developing others. Habits are tendencies toward a particular kind of behavior that have become relatively fixed by repeated performance. Take, for instance, the habit of smoking. This particular bit of behavior has usually been reinforced so many times that extinction may be difficult. Suppose that a person wishes to stop smoking but decides to start out by limiting his smoking to once a day or even once a week. Knowledge of the effects of intermittent reinforcement suggests that even occasional smoking will keep the undesired habit in force. On the other hand, intermittent reinforcement can be used to keep desired behavior in force.

Intermittent reinforcement can be given on several types of schedules. The two basic types are ratio and interval. In RATIO SCHEDULES the reinforcement depends on the number of responses between reinforcements. A *fixed-ratio* (FR) schedule means that the organism is reinforced for a fixed number of responses, such as for every fifth correct response. A *variable-ratio* (VR) schedule means that the number of responses between reinforcements varies, so that a pigeon might be reinforced after its first response, then after its third, then its fifth, its sixteenth, and so on.

In INTERVAL SCHEDULES reinforcement is determined by the time between responses. A *fixed-interval* (FI) schedule means that the response of the organism is reinforced after a fixed time period. In this schedule the organism might receive reinforcement every two minutes, assuming that within the two-minute period a correct response has been made. If the organism has not made a correct response at the end of the two-minute period, reinforcement is withheld until a correct response is made. Reinforcement is given again after the next two-minute period. In a *variable-interval* (VI) schedule the time between reinforcements varies throughout the conditioning procedures.

It is possible to design conditioning procedures so that you can use different schedules, but the total amount of reinforcement will be equal. For example, you could use an FR schedule on the basis of every fifth correct response (twenty reinforcements for 100 correct responses), and construct another procedure so that the organism is rewarded on a random basis (VR schedule) twenty times for 100 correct responses. When reinforcement is withdrawn, learned behavior will usually persist longer when learned under a variable schedule than when learned under a fixed one.

Another factor that influences the persistence of learned behavior is the number of rewards received by the organism—even when the total amount of the reward is kept constant. For example, chickens will continue learned behavior longer if they are reinforced forty times with forty half grains of corn, than if you give them a whole grain of corn twenty times. A young boy whom you want to mow the lawn three times will probably mow more readily for several small payments than he would for one lump sum payment after the first mowing.

Secondary reinforcement. Instead of being a direct reward, reinforcement can have a secondary stage. A SECONDARY REINFORCEMENT is a stimulus that has been associated with something that does satisfy needs to the extent that it can act as a reward by itself. Money is a good example of a secondary reinforcer. To maintain his family a man must provide food, clothing, and shelter for them. However, when he works, he does not earn these items directly. Instead he earns money which he can then use to buy these necessities.

The following experiment provides another example of secondary reinforcement. As a result of operant conditioning, chimpanzees were required to do certain work, such as moving a lever, to get poker chips. They formed an association between work and poker chips (which had already been linked with raisins). In one test three of the four chimpanzees worked as hard for poker chips as they did for raisins. The poker chips had a secondary reinforcement value, though in themselves they had no direct value to the chimpanzees. The poker chips had acquired a value similar to that of money for humans.

After these animals had learned to work for "money," the experimenters gave the chimpanzees poker chips before beginning the sessions during which the animals could secure more chips by working at the machines. The amount of work done was reduced noticeably. One animal ordinarily worked for about twenty chips at a single work session. When, however, the experimenter gave him thirty chips before he began the work session, he would work for only about three chips. Perhaps these effects of a "handout" involve a principle that also applies to human behavior.

This chimpanzee has been conditioned to work for poker chips, a secondary reinforcement, which he can insert into the "Chimp-o-mat" to obtain food, a primary reinforcement.

Generalization and discrimination. In our discussion of classical conditioning we spoke of generalization and discrimination. Both procedures are also common in operant conditioning. In the experiment just mentioned, after the chimpanzees learned that a poker chip of one color was good for a raisin, they would work for poker chips of another color. This was generalization. If, however, a chip of a certain color was regularly reinforced with food and a chip of another color was not reinforced with food, discrimination developed. They learned not to work for chips that could not be used to obtain food.

One scientist has designed procedures in which no errors are made in teaching an organism to discriminate. He first taught pigeons to discriminate between red and green circles, in which they did make mistakes. After they had learned to distinguish between the two colors, vertical lines were superimposed on the red circle and horizontal lines on the green circle. The pigeons were reinforced when they selected the correct color, which they had already learned. The colors in the circles were gradually faded away, leaving only the vertical and horizontal lines. The pigeons were able to discriminate between the lines without making any mistakes. Such learning with no errors tends to be stable over a long period of time. Similar techniques have been used to teach mentally retarded people discriminations that were previously thought to be impossible.

Operant Conditioning and Punishment

As we have said, operant conditioning involves reward for desired behavior rather than punishment for unwanted behavior. Even in the case of the dog conditioned to lift its paw to avoid a shock, the animal is rewarded—its reward is not being shocked. In classical conditioning, on the other hand, it is shocked whenever the bell sounds.

Is reward more effective than punishment? Punishment for doing what is considered undesirable is our traditional method for training children and adults as well as animals. We may punish the dog that does not obey a command. Parents punish a small child because he refuses to take his medicine. Society punishes adults with fines if they drive too fast. Operant conditioning suggests the possibility that it might be better to reinforce desired behavior rather than to punish undesired behavior. We might pat or feed our dog for obeying the command, give a child a little treat whenever he takes his medicine without a fuss, or give citations for careful driving.

As we have seen, hungry rats can be conditioned to press bars if that behavior is reinforced with food. We can test the strength of this learning by seeing how long it takes to extinguish the behavior when no food is given. If, during extinction, we slap the rat for pressing the bar, will it cease pressing the bar more quickly than a rat that is not slapped? There is evidence that the bar-pressing response of the slapped rat is not extinguished with any fewer responses than is the bar pressing of the rat that is not punished. By analogy, we might question the effectiveness of some systems of punishment used with many criminals.

Punishment effectively stops undesirable behavior, but the behavior may reappear if punishment ceases. Also, punishment results in behavior that is less predictable than behavior that comes from rewarding desirable responses, because although punishment tells the individual what not to do, it often does not indicate what he should do. Nevertheless, threat of punishment is an important factor in our lives. The person who feels his skin begin to scorch from the sun seeks the shade to avoid becoming sunburned, and the driver of a speeding car slows down when he sees a policeman because of the threat of punishment. Furthermore, mild punishment is useful to a child if it helps him learn essential caution, say, about fire, hot water, and traffic. The experimental evidence does suggest, however, that punishment extinguishes behavior only sometimes, while reward usually reinforces behavior. In many cases we might do better to use reward for desired behavior rather than punishment for undesired behavior.

Operant Conditioning and Programmed Learning

Now that we have finished a quick survey of operant conditioning and terms related to it, let us look at an interesting and important use to which operant conditioning has been put—programmed learning.

What is programmed learning? Programmed learning uses the operant conditioning techniques of presenting an organism with stimuli, to which the organism responds and receives reinforcement for a correct response. In programmed learning subject matter is presented to the learner in a series of small steps, technically called *frames*. Each of the frames presents the learner with material that requires him to make an active response, either by answering a question or completing a statement. The learner finds out immediately whether or not he has given a correct response. If his response is correct, it is immediately reinforced by the knowledge that he is right.

The steps, or frames, of programmed materials are so arranged that the student is not likely to make many errors. If he does make an error, he discovers it immediately and so does not go on in the wrong direction. He spends his time learning what he should learn rather than unlearning what he stumbled onto by error.

The student using programmed materials is in much the same kind of learning situation as the student who has a private tutor sitting beside him. Both situations present materials when the subject is ready for them, help the learner to respond correctly by giving hints, promptings, and suggestions, and both provide immediate knowledge of results.

There are two basic ways to arrange programmed material: according to a linear program or according to a branching program. In the *linear* program the individual moves step by step in a line through the material

This programmed material is presented on a computerized outlet station (a screen or typewriter). It instructs students step by step on a particular topic and provides a "branch" of supplementary material to help those students who answer incorrectly.

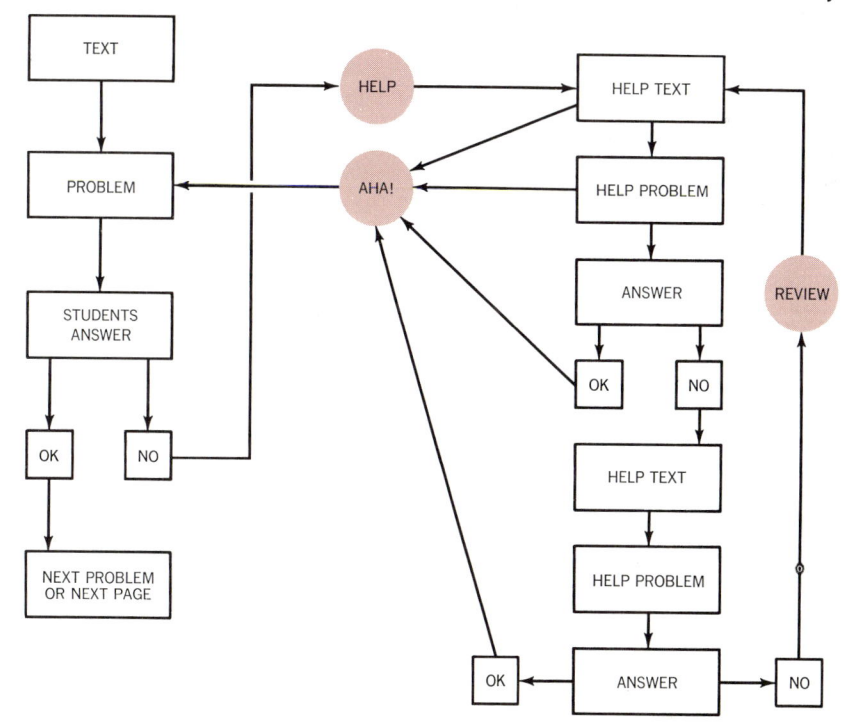

regardless of whether his answers are right or wrong. In the *branching* type of program the student is given an alternative sequence depending on his answer. If he responds correctly, he is presented with the next question, and if he does exceptionally well, he may be given an opportunity to skip some material. On the other hand, if he makes an error, he will be branched off into some supplementary material on the subject that he answered incorrectly. For example, if a child learning to read has trouble with the word "church" in a sentence, he may be shown a picture of a church. If he still cannot read the word, he will receive another branch of instructional material to help him learn it.

Teaching machines. Teaching machines are educational devices designed to present programmed material to the learner. A teaching machine can be elaborate, involving a computer and other complex pieces of equipment, or it can be simple, with hand operation taking the place of electronic devices. In the hand-operated machines a question is asked or an incomplete sentence is presented in a window at the left of the machine, and the student writes his answer beside it. By means of a lever, he can then move his answer to a position under a transparent cover. At the same time the correct answer is moved into view. If his answer agrees with the correct answer, he can go on to new material. If the teaching machine is a computer, it sends out instructions on a screen or through earphones at an individual student station. The student responds on a special typewriter or writes on the screen with a special pen. His response is evaluated by the computer and determines which item in the lesson sequence he will receive next.

Some people are wary of the idea of teaching machines. They regard them as a recent fad, although psychologists have been working to develop such machines since 1926. The skeptics insist that a personal teacher-student relationship is necessary for any and all kinds of learning to take place. Some seem to fear that teaching machines will take over completely. However, there is no reason to believe that teaching machines will replace good teachers. Rather, the use of teaching machines can free teachers from time-consuming routine work, thereby giving them more time for valuable personal teacher-student relationships.

There is a great deal of evidence that teaching machines can do a good job in education from kindergarten to college and beyond. To take just one example, a group of adults, using a teaching machine, were able to learn as much German vocabulary in 48 hours of instruction as college students ordinarily learn in an entire semester.

Programmed books. In programmed books there are a number of frames on each page. The correct response to each frame may appear next to or below the frame on the same page. In using a programmed book, the student indicates what he believes to be the correct response to a frame, looks next to or below the frame (where the answer has been under a cover, such as a strip of cardboard), or turns to the next page, and immediately learns if his response is correct. Perhaps you are asking, "What prevents the student from looking at the answer before he writes his response, and merely copying the correct response in the blank?" The answer is that there is nothing to prevent the student from uncovering the answers and cheating himself in this way. A programmed book is designed to encourage the student in his learning by breaking the process into simple steps and reinforcing the correct response at each step. The book, however, cannot force the student to learn. If he looks ahead for answers, he is failing to make use of an aid to efficient learning.

Some advantages of programmed materials. Although they cannot replace classroom teachers, under some circumstances programmed books and teaching machines may be able to teach more efficiently. They permit the learner to progress at his own speed, neither holding back the rapid learner nor forcing the slow learner to advance more rapidly than is reasonable for him.

In working with individuals who are physically handicapped so that they move awkwardly and respond very slowly, the teacher, in spite of himself, may become impatient or otherwise discourage the learner. Programmed books and teaching machines cannot become impatient, no matter how slowly the learner responds.

In industry each new employee has to learn many facts. The military services also have a great deal of technical material that must be taught to new men in a time-saving and efficient manner. Programmed books and teaching machines are part of the answer to efficient learning of much new material.

Learning by Insight

Early in this chapter we saw how a learner may find the solution to his problem by blundering on it through trial and error. Then we went on to classical conditioning, in which an individual learns a specific response by having it paired several times with a specific stimulus. In operant conditioning the individual learns to respond in a particular way because that response is reinforced after he makes it. Now we turn to yet another way that an individual learns a particular response—through insight.

What is insight? Often the word "insight" is used to refer to an almost mysterious understanding of the inner nature of things, an understanding that comes without previous experience or thinking. But psychologists cannot accept such a meaning for the word. To the psychologist, INSIGHT is the relatively sudden perception of relationships that results in the prompt solution of a problem. It is not a blind, chance hitting upon a solution to a problem. Although insight is often a relatively sudden perception that follows a period of little or no apparent progress, it is based on previous experience. Actually, the perception may appear somewhat gradually in the sense that an individual may see a number of minor relationships before he has the final insight into the problem.

Animal experiments that illustrate insight. One psychologist placed fruit beyond a chimpanzee's reach outside its cage. Within the cage there were two bamboo sticks, neither of which was long enough to reach the fruit. The chimpanzee nevertheless tried first one stick and then the other. It even pushed one stick with the other toward the fruit, but of course could not rake in the fruit. The chimpanzee then seemed to give up in its attempt to solve the problem.

Later, while playing with the sticks, the chimpanzee happened to hold one in such a way that it came into a straight line with the other. The chimpanzee pushed the thinner stick into a hole in the end of the thicker

In this experiment of learning by insight, a chimpanzee is faced with the problem of obtaining a bunch of bananas that is out of reach (upper left). Then it has insight (lower left). It piles up the crates beneath the fruit, climbs onto the top crate, and grabs the bananas, which are now within its reach (upper right).

stick. Now there was a new relationship or pattern. Instead of two short sticks that could not be used to reach the fruit, there was one long stick. The chimpanzee jumped up, ran to the side of the cage, and used this long stick to rake in the fruit. This successful bit of behavior was reinforced by the reward of eating the fruit. Thus, we could say that the chimpanzee would be conditioned to repeat its efforts. The basic learning in this case, however, depended on the animal solving its own problem, after a considerable time, by insight. Trying solutions that did not work may have helped the chimpanzee find the satisfactory answer, since it had made various attempts to use the sticks before arriving at the sudden solution.

Some examples of human insight. Soon after the publication of the above research, another psychologist carried out similar experiments with children of preschool age. In one case a toy was placed outside a child's playpen, where the child could not reach it with his hands. Some children spent a great deal of time trying vainly to reach the toy with their hands even though there was a stick in plain sight in the pen. Other children seemed to spend a while "sizing up" the situation. Then they would pick up the stick and rake in the toy.

Have you ever had insight into some problem, say a problem in a mathematics course? Perhaps you worked long and hard on the problem, using methods you had learned previously. There were many trials that were not reinforced by the satisfaction of a solution. Then, perhaps rather suddenly, you saw a relationship that you had not seen before and the whole problem became clear. Maybe you said, "Aha, I see it! How simple! How could I have missed seeing the solution in the first place?" The answer is that you had not reached the point of insight into the problem. Sometimes insight is called the "Aha" experience.

What causes the learner to have insight? Even in what seem to be sudden perceptions, the subject has had some previous experience with the tools involved in the problem. The chimpanzee and the children had had previous experiences with sticks. The student has had much previous experience with mathematical processes and principles. Also, the subjects have had the experience of making several incorrect attempts and have therefore already ruled out some possibilities.

This brings up an important difference between insightful learning and many cases of conditioning. When a situation is worked out through insight, the learner is often aware of steps in his thinking. In conditioning, on the other hand, the learner is hardly likely to recall that he said to himself, "I see a light. The light is associated with a shock. I will jerk my finger."

Human subjects can be asked about their thinking experiences, but with animals we have to depend on observable behavior. By using special instruments and techniques we can record and observe animal behavior that might not be noticed otherwise. In one experiment rats were required to learn to choose from a row of four doors the one door that would give access to food. One door was white, one medium gray, one light gray, and one black. The food was always behind the white door. During the trials the experimenter was able to count the number of times that each rat looked back and forth from one door to another. He spoke of such looking back and forth as "vicarious trial and error." A casual observer might have said that the rat learned suddenly to go to the white door without any trial-and-error experience. The experiment suggests, however, that looking at the gray and black doors was a substitute for trying them.

Insight, then, is not something that comes "out of the blue." For example, a student would be unsuccessful if he came to an examination unprepared, expecting to solve the problems by insight. To have insight, he needs preparatory experience with the material covered in the course.

Controversial Areas of Learning

We have examined some, but not all, theories of learning. You may wonder why we did not discuss all of the topics under a single learning theory. The reason is that no one learning theory today can explain all of the different kinds of learning that occur. Although there is agreement on many points, there are some aspects of learning on which psychologists disagree. In these last few paragraphs we will mention some of the areas of learning that are in controversy.

Psychologists generally agree that reinforcement facilitates learning, but they disagree on whether reinforcement is absolutely necessary for learning to take place. Some psychologists believe that learning occurs only when reinforced, but admit that the specific reinforcer is difficult to identify in some experiments. They believe that a response associated with the reduction of a need (such as the need for food) is learned to the extent that when the same need or drive (the hunger drive) arises again, there will be a tendency for that same, or a very similar, response to occur. But such persons have a difficult time explaining why rats, given prior access to water, will learn a maze when they receive a saccharine solution of water as a reward, since the saccharine has no nutritional value and therefore cannot reduce a need or drive, and the rats have no need for water.

There is also disagreement as to whether learning occurs gradually or suddenly. Insight, as we have seen, stresses the suddenness of learning, whereas conditioning theories explain learning as a gradual process. Conditioning theories assume that what is learned is a connection between a stimulus and a response, and as successive trials occur this connection becomes stronger and stronger.

Another area of controversy exists among cognitive theorists and conditioning psychologists. Cognitive theorists accept the same experimental data as stimulus-response theorists, but offer a different interpretation of the data. For example, cognitive theorists explain an organism learning a maze or puzzle box in terms of brain processes, or expectancies. They say that the organism responds because it has learned to expect that a particular stimulus will be followed by another —it is learning "what leads to what." Stimulus-response theorists, on the other hand, emphasize a chained sequence of responses. However, there is agreement that cognitive theory explains higher forms of learning, such as problem-solving and reasoning, better than stimulus-response theory. A stimulus-response approach to learning is very useful for memorizing dates, names, and facts, and facts are the cornerstones of higher learning. For example, you must be able to distinguish between the letters of the alphabet before you can learn to read. The cognitive approach to learning is most helpful for having students organize and understand what they learn.

In summary, there is no single theory of learning today that will adequately explain all aspects of different learning situations. Some psychologists are still concerned with basic principles of learning, and are trying to develop models that will explain a larger amount of the data related to learning. Other psychologists have shifted away from emphasis on learning theory to studies of memory with its storage and retrieval problems. Still other psychologists are concerned primarily with the practical application of our present knowledge of learning to human behavior. One such program involves behavior modification, which is the attempt to change undesirable behavior to more acceptable behavior through the use of learning techniques. As psychologists continue to study and provide more factual data on the subject of learning, we should come to better understand the overall processes and uses involved.

Terms to Know

branching program	goal gradient	reflex
classical conditioning	insight	reinforcement
conditioned response (CR)	intermittent (or partial) reinforcement	secondary reinforcement
		spontaneous recovery
conditioned stimulus (CS)		successive approximations
	interval schedule	teaching machine
counter-conditioning	learning	unconditional response (UCR)
discrimination	linear program	
extinction	maze	unconditioned stimulus (UCS)
fixed-interval (FI) schedule	negative reinforcement	
	operant conditioning	variable-interval (VI) schedule
fixed-ratio (FR) schedule	positive reinforcement	
frame	programmed book	variable-ratio (VR) schedule
generalization	programmed learning	ratio schedule

Topics to Think About

1. Assume that you have the necessary qualifications and are employed as a teacher of learning theory at a university. Which theory would you adopt to explain how organisms learn? Why would you choose this particular theory and not some other?

2. Soldiers preparing for possible combat duty are sometimes required to crawl across a field with live bullets whizzing over them. What principle of learning is being used? Are you in favor of, or do you oppose, this method of learning? Why?

3. Do you think social scientists should use principles of operant conditioning to try to shape the behavior of large masses of our population? If so, who should decide what behavior is most desirable—what is best for society now and in the future? How could such behavior shaping be done?

4. In one experiment, when the chimpanzees were given "money" *before* the work session, they did less work (see page 45). Do you think the various forms of charity and government aid will result in individuals not really trying to earn a living? Why or why not?

5. How would you like to attend a school where all of the teaching is done by teaching machines? What would you like about it and what would you dislike?

6. What do you think is the most efficient method of learning? Try to plan a school curriculum that utilizes this method of learning.

Suggestions for Activities

1. Cut out of cardboard or paper two crosses similar to the ones shown below. The crosses are to be of equal size. Cut each along the dotted line. Fit the four pieces together to form a square. Note how you go about the solution. Do you learn how to solve the puzzle by trial and error, by insight, or by a combination of both? Do you talk to yourself as you work? Give the puzzle to a friend. Does he or she suddenly see the relationship and say, "Oh, I see"?

(In case you are unable to solve the problem, the solution is given on page 56. Do not look at it until you have done your best.)

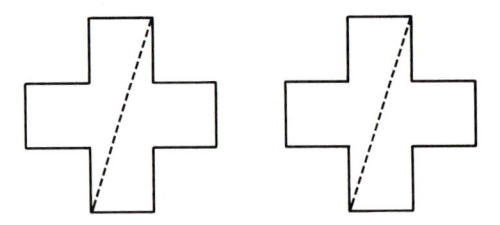

2. Make a multiple-T maze (perhaps like the one shown below) by tacking or gluing strips of wood on a 12-inch-square sheet of plywood. The strips can be ¼ inch wide by ¼ inch high. Blindfold a subject, place his finger at the starting point, and tell him to find his way to the goal end of the maze. Count the number of times he turns in the incorrect direction whenever he must choose between left and right at the cross of a T. Repeat the runs through the maze as many times as possible in the time available or until the subject makes no errors for several runs.

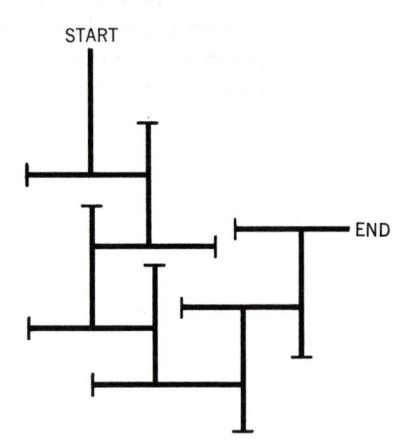

The experiment can be varied by making a maze in which the subject must turn to the left at the first choice, to the right at the second, to the left at the third, and so on. You could have some other pattern such as llrrllrrll. Does the subject "catch on" to the pattern? With some subjects you might reinforce desired behavior by saying "good" as soon as they start in the correct direction. Does this immediate reinforcement result in more efficient learning?

54 LEARNING

3. Another type of finger maze can be constructed by gluing straight pieces of a wire coat hanger onto a piece of wood. They can be glued in a Y- or a T-maze pattern. Round each end of the wire off before joining them together, so that the person will not scratch his or her finger or have a clue to the correct turn in the maze. When you construct such a maze, do not give away the sequence of turns to anyone. Have several blindfolded individuals begin at the "start" point and proceed to the "end" as quickly as possible. Keep count of the number of correct and incorrect responses per trial and the number of seconds it takes the person to go from the beginning of the maze to the end. To have learned the maze, each person must go through at least two consecutive trials without error. Have as many persons learn the maze as time permits, making certain that each remaining subject does not see the maze before his turn.

Make a graph and include the mean (average) number of errors per trial and the mean number of correct responses. Also include the mean time per trial for all subjects. In graphing the data, place trials on the horizontal or bottom axis (abscissa) and the frequency of errors, correct responses, and time on the vertical axis (ordinate). What shape does the curve have? Where did the fastest and slowest learning take place?

4. Try this simple conditioning experiment with one or more children. Place one of your hands flat on a table and have the child do the same. Instruct him to raise his hand every time you raise your hand. After a few such trials, begin using your hand to tap on the table with a pencil about a second before you lift your hand. After a number of such trials, does the child begin to raise his hand following the pencil tap but before you lift your hand? Tap the pencil without raising your hand. Does the child lift his hand? Continue to tap the pencil without raising your hand. Does the child cease raising his hand?

5. If you have a pet that has some behavior you dislike, try to eliminate the behavior by using the principles of operant conditioning. Remember not to cause the animal any physical pain. Perhaps you might scold your pet when it has the undesirable behavior, and reward it when it behaves the way you would like. Keep an accurate record of your activities and the responses of your pet, and write a report on procedures and outcomes.

6. Does your school make use of any teaching machines or programmed books? If you are able to locate any, use such devices or books as a basis for a class discussion of operant conditioning. Is the learner likely to make errors? What happens if he does? How is reinforcement given? Do you find that the effectiveness of teaching machines decreases as you continue to use them? In your opinion, do programmed books promote more, or less, efficient learning than traditional textbooks?

7. Teachers quite often use verbal statements or other actions as reinforcers. The reinforcement may be either positive or negative. For example, one teacher might remark, "That's a good paper." Another might say, "Do not come to class late again without a very good excuse." Over a period of several days, make a list of statements and actions made by teachers that would illustrate principles of reinforcement or learning. (Do not include the names of the teachers on any such list.) See if you can also note what effect the teacher's reinforcement has on the behavior of the other person or persons involved.

Suggestions for Further Reading

Daniel, Robert S. (ed.), *Contemporary Readings in General Psychology,* 2nd ed., Houghton Mifflin. See pages 95–98, "How to Teach Animals," an article by B. F. Skinner telling how to apply principles of conditioning to the training of pets.

Hediger, H., *The Psychology and Behavior of Animals in Zoos and Circuses,* Dover Publications. This paperback is a translation of a book originally written in German by a Swiss zoologist.

Hilgard, E. R., R. C. Atkinson, and Rita Atkinson, *Introduction to Psychology,* 5th ed., Harcourt Brace Jovanovich. See Chapter 8, "Learning and Conditioning."

Kagan, J., M. M. Haith, and Catherine Caldwell (eds.), *Psychology: Adapted Readings,* Harcourt Brace Jovanovich. See Selection 3, "The Salivary Reflex in Dogs," by Ivan Pavlov; and Selection 4, "Pigeons in a Pelican," by B. F. Skinner.

Kagan, J., and E. Havemann, *Psychology: An Introduction,* 2nd ed., Harcourt Brace Jovanovich. See Chapter 2 on learning, which includes sections on shaping human behavior and the possible role of operant conditioning in therapy.

Matthews, W. H., *Mazes and Labyrinths: Their History and Development,* Dover Publications. An illustrated account (paperback) of labyrinths and mazes from ancient to modern times.

Neill, A. S., *Summerhill,* Hart. This paperback describes a radical approach to teaching and child-rearing in a school.

Ruch, Floyd L., and Philip G. Zimbardo, *Psychology and Life,* 8th ed., Scott, Foresman. See Chapter 5, "Learning About Events and Consequences."

Skinner, B. F., "Baby in a Box," *Ladies' Home Journal,* vol. 62, (October 1945), pages 30–31. An article about how Skinner made use of his operant-conditioning box in raising his daughter.

Skinner, B. F., *Beyond Freedom and Dignity,* Knopf. A book that describes the advantages of using operant conditioning procedures to control large masses of people for the benefit of society.

Skinner, B. F., "Teaching Machines," *Scientific American,* vol. 205 (1961), pages 91–102. An interesting and very informative discussion by the man who devised the first series of successful teaching machines. He describes in detail the usefulness of teaching machines and the roles that they can play in teaching individuals a variety of subjects.

Skinner, B. F., *Walden Two,* Macmillan. Skinner describes a utopian community, which incorporates some of his operant conditioning concepts.

"Skinner's Utopia: Panacea, or Path to Hell?" *Time* (September 20, 1971), pages 47–53. Some biographical and descriptive material on Skinner and his contributions.

Wertheimer, M., et al., *Psychology: A Brief Introduction,* Scott, Foresman. See pages 78–98, 108–09, on unlearned behavior, habits, classical and operant (instrumental) conditioning, programmed instruction, and insight.

Answer to puzzle on page 54

chapter 3
How to Learn Efficiently

Now that you are familiar with some of the principles and theories of learning, you may be interested in the application of these principles. The following chapter applies the principles of learning to various life situations. Most of the topics in this chapter can be applied directly to your schoolwork and to your role as a student. In operant conditioning, for instance, learning involves active work on the part of the subject. And it is particularly true in school that learning is something you do, not something that is done to you or for you.

As you read this chapter, you might watch for answers to the question "How can I make my learning most efficient?" Even the most conscientious student can give only a part of the hours in each day to study. Therefore, the time available should be used to all possible advantage. The topics in this chapter can help you increase the efficiency of your learning.

Transfer

Will a person's study of French help him learn Spanish? Will learning to reason in geometry help an individual develop the kind of reasoning required to argue a law case? That is, will learning in one field transfer to other fields? Many teachers used to believe that transfer of training was a key to education. They spoke of a "mind" consisting of a number of faculties, such as reasoning and memory. They thought that hard drill in certain subjects would develop and discipline these faculties. Thus, if a student mastered French or Russian, he would increase his general ability in languages. Today, however, psychologists do not believe that there are faculties that can be developed by exercise, as muscles might be. Experiments have shown that studying French does not seem to cause any general improvement in using languages. French does help, however, with words in other languages that have the same origin as those in French. That is, transfer of training is not the key to all learning problems, but it is an important factor in learning. Transfer takes place from one specific experience to another—from the experience of learning French vocabulary to learning Spanish vocabulary, for example.

We can define TRANSFER as the effect of previous learning on later learning or later performance. Improvement in a given bit of learning as a result of earlier learning is called *positive transfer*. When earlier learning interferes with the learning of new material, it is known as *negative transfer*.

Why is positive transfer important? We can see the importance of positive transfer if we review the topic of generalization. For instance, chimpanzees that have learned to work for a poker chip of one color will work for chips of other colors. To use an obvious example from human learning, a child who has learned to write with a pencil on paper can also write with chalk on a chalkboard. Generalization of this kind saves much time in learning.

Schools do not maintain that the way to learn Spanish is to study French and hope for positive transfer. The way to learn Spanish is to study that language. For practical reasons, however, schools try to foster transfer whenever it can be useful. For example, since the technical school can seldom afford the expensive equipment found in industry, it makes use of less expensive equipment to teach principles, and trusts that there will be positive transfer. Since the medical student cannot begin practicing surgery with living persons, he works with animals and cadavers, later transferring this experience to living human patients. The person learning to drive an

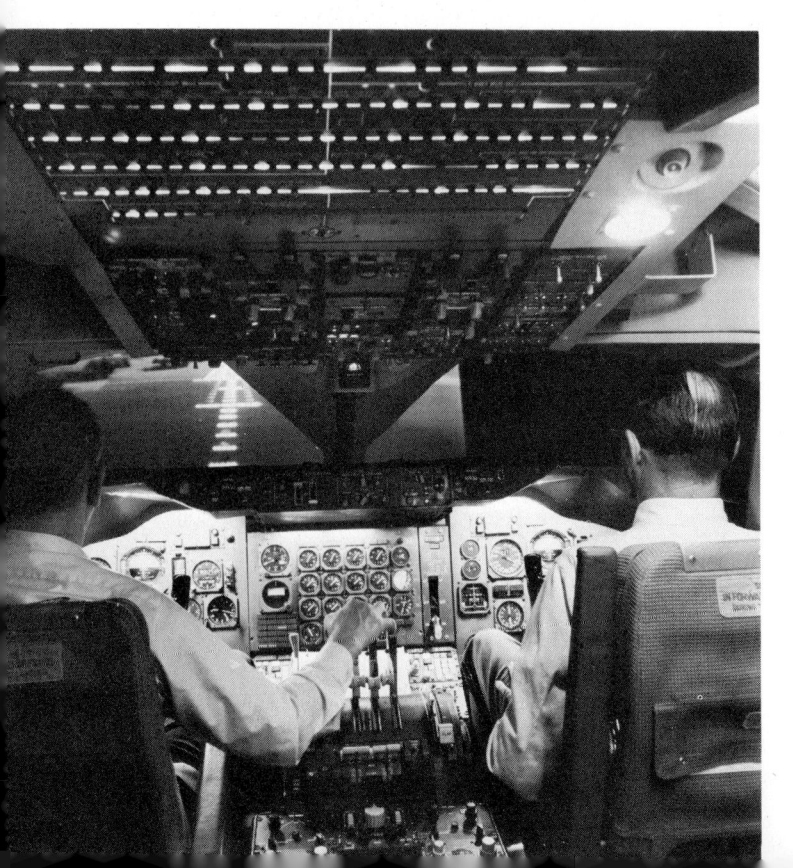

Many commercial pilots learn to fly on the ground by using a flight simulator, as shown here. There is positive transfer —pilots apply what they learned in the simulator to flying in the air in a real plane.

automobile cannot be permitted to go out on the highway in heavy traffic for his first experience. In some driver-training courses he is seated in a carlike apparatus and shown a moving picture taken from a car in actual highway operation. In the safety of his simulated car, he learns something about how to drive under conditions in which he can evaluate his own correct and incorrect performances. Later this training transfers to actual automobile operation. In this same way, your study of the psychology of learning will transfer to all of your courses and make you a more efficient student.

Experimental studies of transfer. Over the years many experimental studies have produced a great deal of evidence that learning in one situation will transfer to other situations, although the amount of transfer is often not as extensive as was once assumed. We will consider two of these studies.

Every experienced typist knows that there is some, although possibly slight, difficulty in changing from one kind of typewriter to another—for example, in changing from an electric to a manual typewriter. That is, there is some negative transfer. On the other hand, there is a great deal of positive transfer, for a person does not have to learn the entire skill of typing each time he changes typewriters.

Radiomen in the navy are required to have, among other skills, some proficiency in typing. One experiment involved two groups of men matched for age, years of educational background, general ability, and radio code aptitude. Members of the control group began training on manual typewriters while members of the experimental group began training on electric typewriters. After three weeks of basic typing instruction, the experimental group was changed to manual typewriters. Both groups were tested at frequent intervals.

The experimental group showed a marked drop in performance on the first test after changing to manual typewriters. On the whole, though, there was considerable positive transfer because the experimental group had learned key placement on the electric typewriter and therefore knew the key placement on the manual typewriter. There was some negative transfer, however, since the "feel" of the two kinds of typewriters is different. For example, the person who has learned to type on an electric machine strikes the keys with less force and reaches a shorter distance from key to key than he would in typing on a manual machine.

Evidence suggests that knowledge of facts and principles can transfer to practical problems. One psychologist was interested in measuring the extent to which training in facts and principles of human behavior would transfer to the practical problems of diagnosing difficulties and assisting individuals having such difficulties. College students taking courses concerned with adolescent behavior, educational psychology, and mental hygiene were tested not only with the usual subject-matter tests but also with case-study tests in which they could apply what they knew. The data indicated that although knowledge of facts and principles about adolescent behavior was positively related to ability to diagnose specific cases and apply appropriate remedial procedures, the relationship was not great. Perhaps the courses should have been taught with more emphasis on transfer.

How are stimulus-response relationships involved in transfer? Many instances of transfer can be understood in terms of associations between stimuli and responses. The highest positive transfer results when the stimuli and responses of two tasks are identical. Thus, to learn to type on an electric typewriter, an individual does better to practice on an electric typewriter than to practice on a manual one. Although not so highly positive, transfer is also positive when the individual is learning to make old responses to new stimuli. For example, a psychologist asked a group of subjects to learn paired lists of nonsense syllables. If you care to try a similar experiment, make a list such as *gak-bic, suf-lar,* and so forth. Later, ask your subjects to learn lists such as *sen-bic, zyz-lar,* and so on. You will note that the stimulus syllable *gak* is first followed by the response syllable *bic.* Later a new stimulus syllable *sen* is followed by the old response *bic.* In other words, you will be asking your subjects to learn old responses to new stimuli. The psychologist found that if his subjects had had a considerable amount of practice on the original list, there was positive transfer—they learned the second list more easily for having learned the first list.

As a rule, however, learning to make new responses to old stimuli results in negative transfer. Continuing your experiment, you could have a group of subjects learn paired lists of nonsense syllables (*gak-bic, suf-lar,* and so on) thoroughly. Then ask your subjects to learn such lists as *gak-zam, suf-reg.* You will note that the stimulus syllable *gak* is first followed by the response syllable *bic.* Later the same stimulus syllable *gak* is followed by a new response syllable, *zam.* In other words, you will be asking your subjects to learn new responses to old stimuli. The psychologist who carried out a carefully controlled similar experiment found that there was negative transfer. That is, his subjects learned the second list with more difficulty because they had learned the first list.

If you have already studied Spanish and plan to study French, you may experience some negative transfer. When asked to give the French equivalent (response) for a certain English word (stimulus), you may find yourself giving the Spanish word rather than the French word. For "dog" you may say "perro" instead of "chien." You will have been asked to learn a new response to an old stimulus, with a resulting negative transfer.

Another way to express the relationship of stimuli and responses to positive and negative transfer is by using symbols. If we allow S_1 to represent the original stimulus, R_1 the original response, S_2 a different stimulus, and R_2 a different response, we can diagram the relationship. Then, S_1-R_1 becomes the original stimulus-response situation; S_1-R_2 is a situation involving the original stimulus but a different response to the same stimulus; and S_2-R_1 is a stimulus different from the original but where the same response is given.

For example, a red light (S_1) previously evoked a braking action (R_1), but in an experimental situation the subject must now put the brakes on (R_1) to a green light (S_2). In such a situation as S_2-R_1 there will be some positive transfer, for when new stimuli are used, positive transfer will result in most cases if the response remains the same, as the diagram below indicates. If, however, the individual had to make a new response (pressing the accelerator-R_2) to the old stimulus (red light-S_1), there would probably be negative transfer. Generally, when stimuli are the same, as responses to the stimuli become more different, negative transfer will increase. The situation could be diagrammed as follows:

$$S_1\text{-}R_1$$
positive transfer
$$S_2\text{-}R_1$$

$$S_1\text{-}R_1$$
negative transfer
$$S_1\text{-}R_2$$

How can the amount of transfer be increased?
Many experiments, as well as everyday observations, show that transfer can and does occur, but those who teach and those who learn must not assume that there is automatic spread of training and experience from one field to another. They must strive to secure such transfer.

Modern educators recognize the need for coordinated training in both theory and practice. Laboratory courses and projects of various kinds are designed to promote transfer from theories to everyday life situations.

At the university level, medical students are required to have, in addition to their classwork, actual practical experience with persons who are ill. Dental students are required to apply their knowledge to persons needing dental care. Individuals who plan to become teachers not only study psychology and other subjects to learn how to teach but also have actual experience in teaching, under supervision.

A broad background of learning is conducive to transfer. The more we know, the easier it is to learn related material. A good background in mathematics makes learning a science easier because there are so many elements in common. College students often find that after the first few courses in a subject field, later courses in that field are somewhat easier because of transfer.

A student's attitude toward transfer is very important. Although some transfer will take place without an active effort on your part, it is much more likely to occur if you strive for it. The influence of attitudes toward transfer has been demonstrated with college students. Three groups of students were each divided into two equivalent sections. One section in each of the three groups was told that their previous training would help them in a new task about to be assigned. That is, it was suggested to them that their previous training would transfer. The other sections were given no such suggestion. On the new task, the three sections with favorable attitudes toward transfer made superior records compared with the three sections in which no one had suggested that there would be transfer. One way to use learning time efficiently is to look for similarities in various courses and for applications outside of school—to apply principles learned in one situation to other situations.

In the future, positive transfer will probably become more important in the educational process. With the constant increase in the contents of various courses such as biology, chemistry, physics, and psychology, it will become more and more difficult for any one teacher to try to teach all the information

A child who can ride a tricycle can transfer her knowledge of how to use the pedals and handlebars when she begins to ride a two-wheel bike.

in any one course. Therefore, what an individual learns in one course will have to transfer and relate to other courses to a greater extent than happens today. For example, emphasis on the scientific method as one way of discovering information and facts would transfer to many different courses.

Other Factors in Learning Efficiency

Striving for transfer is only one of many ways to make efficient use of the time available for learning. Psychologists have studied many other ways. We will consider some of them here, along with the experimental evidence and practical applications.

1. Motivation

The section on transfer stressed that striving for transfer is important. This idea suggests the importance of wanting to learn, of being motivated. In psychology, MOTIVATION refers to the regulation of behavior to satisfy the needs of an individual. It is concerned with the goals toward which one is working. Motivation is a basic concept in psychology. Here, however, we will limit our discussion to satisfying needs and working toward goals through efficient studying.

Although a certain amount of incidental learning may take place without our intending to learn, the intent is essential to efficient studying. The student who is motivated takes an active interest in his work and therefore is much more likely to succeed than a student with a passive attitude. Sometimes students become indifferent to certain courses because they have studied some of the same subject matter in other courses or have learned it outside the school so that the work is too easy for them. Sometimes they become indifferent because they do not understand the material being presented to them. Sometimes the subject matter does not seem interesting and students become bored. Whenever a student finds his work too easy, too difficult, or boring, he is likely to become passive rather than active in his studying. In such a case, the student must remember that he can become more active. Textbooks usually offer suggestions for further reading. Teachers are glad to suggest additional reading or other activities that will be more difficult or easier or clearer, depending on the student's needs.

Many times students feel virtuous when they put a book aside and say, "There, I have read my lesson for tomorrow!" But such reading may have been passive, a mere "soaking up" process. Have you ever read a page and then realized that you had only a vague idea of what it said? Experimental evidence has shown the value of reviewing and reciting to yourself as you read. In reading or any other kind of study, take an active role in what you are learning.

The most immediate kind of motivation in day-to-day schoolwork comes from being given immediate knowledge of results when you make responses in class. For example, if you answer a teacher's question correctly, knowing immediately that you are correct not only reinforces that correct response but also helps maintain your satisfaction with and interest in the learning. Immediate knowledge of results is very important for motivation as well as for reinforcement.

Effective motivation for learning comes when a student sees his studying as a means to achieve his goal—a professional career, for example. Short-range motivating devices are also useful. In addition to checking on progress, tests and examinations play a role in motivating learning. Many teachers give weekly or biweekly tests. They believe that such frequent testing provides continuous motivation and, at the same time, serves to diagnose difficulties and to suggest remedial steps. Frequent testing has many advantages, but there can also be drawbacks. The student must guard against a tendency to feel, "Well, that's over!" after each test. He may fail to fit each part on which he has been tested into the total structure of the course.

Examination results are usually turned into grades, and striving for passing grades or honor grades motivates many students. Report cards or other notices to parents may also spur the learner on. A certificate or diploma may become a goal in itself.

Unfortunately, many students are more motivated to learn about school subjects because they fear failure or punishment or want a superficial reward than because of a desire to learn for the sake of learning. Research has shown that a subject will learn materials more readily if he knows in advance that he will be punished if he fails to recall them. Similarly, he will pay closer attention to and rehearse more often those items that have a higher reward value than those with a lower payoff value. However, you can greatly aid your learning and retention, and also enjoy learning more, if you study school subjects for the sake of knowing something about them.

Does competition motivate learning? In our culture competition generally provides motivation. Athletic events, sales contests in business, team rivalry in fund drives for charity, and student rivalry for high grades and honors are all examples of competition providing motivation.

Psychologists have studied competition in learning situations. In one experiment 814 children served as subjects. They were striving to develop proficiency in adding. For the control part of the experiment, the children were first told that they were to work simply for practice. The mean (average) number of examples they worked per minute was 41.4. In another part of the experiment cooperative effort was encouraged. The children were told that their individual scores would count toward their class average and that there would be a prize for the best class. The mean score was 43.9. In still another part of the experiment the children were told that they were being tested to see who could add fastest in the school, second fastest, and so on. There were individual prizes for those with the best scores. The mean score was 46.6. Certainly this experiment suggests the motivational value of competition for children in our culture. It should be added that a follow-up study found that cooperation could be effective under some conditions, such as when boys were competing against girls.

Competition is a mixed blessing. We tend to overlook the effects of competition on those who do not win. Students have spent many bitter hours in disappointment because they did not quite make the grades they strove for or were not elected to some honor group. The student who barely makes the coveted honor may have been no better a student than the one who did not quite make it. Every teacher must use a cut-off point in deciding between A's and B's, between B's and C's, and between which grades earn honors and which do not.

Remember that an individual can always compete with his own previous record—and win. In the long run, such competition may well be worth more to the individual than competition against a fellow student and may result in happier interpersonal relationships. The student who can set realistic goals for himself and can succeed in achieving them is likely to remain highly motivated.

Competition can be an important factor in motivating people to learn. In basketball, for instance, the competition to excel as a player and to defeat the other team can motivate boys to improve their skill at throwing baskets, dribbling, or playing defense.

2. Meaningfulness

Experimental evidence as well as everyday experience leads us to believe that meaningful material is much easier to learn than nonsense syllables. The psychologist may ask his subjects to learn nonsense syllables for experimental purposes, but in school studies and everyday experiences we are more likely to work with material that is meaningful and therefore relatively easy to learn. Even though the value of meaningfulness in learning is rather obvious, it is worthwhile to sum up a few suggestions concerning its importance in your studies.

The greater the variety of experiences a student may have, the easier future learning will be. That is, the more basic information a student has, the more meaning he will find in each new chapter or book or course. When the basic principles and rules in a subject field are understood, new material in that field will be relatively easy to learn. The student who neglects the early lessons in a mathematics course is almost sure to run into great difficulty later on. Mathematical formulas can be little more than nonsense material if basic principles are not understood. The student who neglects fundamental rules of grammar is not likely to finish his study of a foreign language with flying colors.

Material for which the "why" is understood is relatively easy to learn. Many experiments and other illustrations are included in this book so that you will understand why psychologists are able to state conclusions and make recommendations.

Material for which there is an immediate application, or for which some application seems likely in the future, is easier to understand and learn than material that is "purely theoretical." Sometimes students despair of certain courses because they don't see any use for the material they are asked to learn. Often teachers can help them see applications for what seems to be general or theoretical material.

3. Knowledge of Results

Although at times persons and animals seem to learn in spite of unfavorable learning conditions, they learn more efficiently under favorable conditions. One favorable condition is to have knowledge of the results of the learning effort. Sometimes knowledge of results is called PSYCHOLOGICAL FEEDBACK.

The following experiment illustrates the effects of psychological feedback in a learning situation. The subjects were blindfolded, allowed to feel a 4-inch piece of wood with their hands as often as they wished, and were asked to draw a line equal to the length of the piece of wood. Responses were considered accurate if they were within .2 inches of the correct length. Two groups had 200 practice trials to determine whether or not they were equal in ability at the outset. Then for seven days one group was told whether their estimate of the length was accurate or not—they were given knowledge of results (although they were not told the direction of their error, if any). The other group practiced for nine days, but were not told the results of their responses—they received no feedback. After seven days the feedback group was changed to a nonfeedback procedure for an additional seven days.

The results of the experiment are shown in the graph on this page. Although the number of subjects was small, the results do show distinct differences. The feedback group made consistent progress in percent of correct responses, whereas the nonfeedback group made no consistent progress. Even after the feedback group was changed to a nonfeedback situation, they performed better than the original nonfeedback group.

The principle of psychological feedback also functions in our daily lives in social situations. For example, we constantly monitor how other persons react toward us. We consider the feedback and, as a result, may change our own behavior toward them.

There are many applications of feedback that affect you as a student. For instance, you can make use of the principle that knowledge of the results aids learning when you take an examination. Unfortunately, many students do not bother to check over examinations after handing them in to see which questions they fail to answer correctly. Their interest seems to be in their grade rather than in improved learning. For best results, you should obtain knowledge of correct and incorrect

The results of an experiment showing the effects of knowledge of results on learning. The group who received psychological feedback performed better than the nonfeedback group.

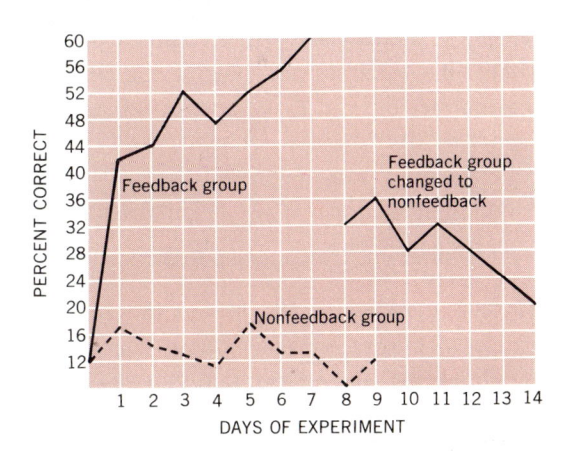

answers as soon as possible after the completion of an examination. Some teachers make it a practice to have a key available for students to study as soon as examination papers are turned in. Pages in the textbook or other sources of information are indicated on the key so that the students can check their answers.

One experiment, conducted over an entire semester, used freshman students in a college chemistry course. Some students checked the answers to short tests as soon as they handed in their papers. Other students did not have knowledge of results until the next meeting of the class. The students who had immediate knowledge of their results on short tests—immediate feedback—made significantly higher grades on the final examination than the students who had to wait to learn the results of their tests.

Objective tests do not give the student an opportunity to express himself in a well-organized fashion, but they can be used very effectively to provide immediate knowledge of results. One testing device requires the student to punch holes in a special answer sheet. A red dot appears whenever the correct answer is punched, thus providing immediate knowledge of results. One psychologist developed an answer sheet in which, when the student marked his choice of answers, the mark turned blue if the answer was correct but red if the answer was incorrect.

4. Massed vs. Distributed Practice

MASSED PRACTICE refers to the running together of practice sessions during which material is being learned. DISTRIBUTED PRACTICE refers to a type of practice in which the sessions are separated by rest periods.

Which type of practice is more efficient? At one time the answer to this question was simply that distributed practice results in more efficient learning than massed practice. Modern research has indicated, however, that there is no such simple answer. The question is complicated by such factors as the following: in massed practice, fatigue may reduce efficiency; in distributed practice, forgetting is likely to occur between sessions; in massed practice, the student may become bored; but, on the other hand, he may become bored if a learning task stretches over too long a period of time because practice is spaced. Probably the best answer is that the relative efficiency of massed and distributed practice depends on the type of learning task involved.

Much experimental work has been done on practice in learning motor skills. These experiments have often been performed using mazes, tracking (the subject must keep a stylus in contact with a moving target), or mirror tracing. In general, the research literature suggests that in learning a motor skill, performance is superior under conditions of distributed practice, particularly during the early stages of learning.

In a classic experiment carried out early in this century, a psychologist assigned his subjects the task of transcribing words into numbers according to a code. There were four groups, each of which practiced a total of 120 minutes. Group I practiced 10 minutes twice a day for six days, Group II practiced 20 minutes a day for six days, Group III practiced 40 minutes every other day, and Group IV practiced 2 hours at one sitting. The resulting data, shown on the graph on page 67, certainly suggest that distributed practice is more effective for this simple task than is massed practice.

For more complex learning, however, results are different, as the following experiment shows. Subjects were required to learn to make a nonsense-syllable response to certain symbols. The subjects were divided into six groups. Three groups learned under conditions of massed practice, in which there were only eight seconds between trials. The other three groups learned under conditions of distributed practice—two minutes between trials. Three tasks differing in complexity were assigned to each group. One task consisted of a simple association. A symbol was presented alone, but after two seconds a nonsense syllable was presented with it. Later the subject was required to indicate the correct nonsense syllable when only the stimulus symbol was presented. The second task was similar except that each stimulus symbol was combined with two response terms, only one of which was correct. The third task was similar, but there were three choices.

The relative effectiveness of variously distributed practice periods

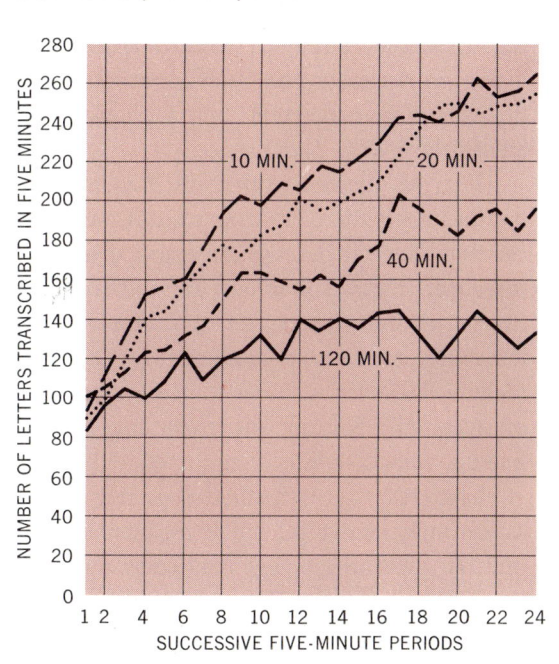

Mean Number of Trials Required to Learn Certain Nonsense Material Under Conditions of Massed and Distributed Practice

	NUMBER OF CHOICES		
	ONE	TWO	THREE
Massed practice	26.85	37.45	40.70
Distributed practice	21.05	34.00	39.40

The table shown above indicates the mean number of trials required for the subjects to be able to give one recitation without errors. For both the massed and distributed practice groups, the number of trials required increased as the complexity of the problem increased. Also, the difference between massed and distributed practice groups decreased as the task became more complex. There is further evidence that in complex learning, where the seeing of relationships is important, massed learning may be superior to distributed learning.

Some practical suggestions about massed and distributed practice. In general, research literature indicates that in learning which is largely a matter of skill, as is typing, some form of distributed practice is best. This is especially true during the early periods of practice, although at later stages more massed practice may be desirable. In the learning of serial material—material which requires that certain responses be made in a prescribed order, as in a poem—the evidence seems to suggest the superiority of distributed practice. In nonserial learning, where responses are independent of each other, as in a vocabulary list, the superiority of distributed practice is less pronounced than in serial learning. As learning becomes more and more complex, and as the individual seeks to learn ideas and principles, the advantage of distributed over massed practice becomes less. In fact, experimental evidence seems to indicate that the best procedure is massed practice at first, followed by distributed practice.

Perhaps you hoped to find a simple formula that would enable you to set up an efficient study schedule. Learning is too complex for any simple, invariable rules. Nevertheless, the suggestions just given can be helpful to you. Future research may give us further suggestions.

5. Whole Learning vs. Part Learning

Requiring students to memorize a great deal of material verbatim is less common than it was many years ago, but some such requirements still exist. The music student must memorize long passages of music to play in a concert. The student of dramatics must memorize his speeches and possibly the speeches of his fellow actors. The student in literature courses may be required to memorize selected passages. Usually foreign language vocabulary must be memorized.

A student striving to be efficient in his work may raise the question "Should I try to learn this material as a whole or should I break it up into parts and learn it part by part?" There was a time when psychologists felt that experimental evidence indicated very clearly that it was more efficient to learn an entire selection as a whole rather than to break it down into parts and finally combine the parts into a whole. But more recent evidence suggests that there are too many variables involved to permit any sweeping general rule in favor of the whole method. Whether or not the whole method is superior to the part method seems to be related to the general intellectual ability of the learner. For example, we have evidence that the whole method is more efficient for children of superior intellectual ability than for children of normal ability. Also, the more a learner uses the whole method, the more effective it becomes for him. In cases in which the learner is using distributed practice, the whole method seems to be superior to the part method.

Some practical suggestions about whole and part learning. Some students work more efficiently when using the whole method than when using the part method, but there are some students who work more efficiently if they use the part method. You will need to determine for yourself which method is better for you, and you cannot depend on your general impression. You will have to test out both methods with a variety of courses. Keep track of the time spent, and try to check your learning by seeing how much you remember and what grades you get.

Most students find that they can learn meaningful passages more efficiently by the whole method than by the part method. On the other hand, disconnected material, such as a foreign language vocabulary, probably can be learned as efficiently, and perhaps more efficiently, by the part method.

For the student who needs frequent encouragement, there is often an advantage in the part method because his learning is reinforced at frequent intervals. He can feel that he is "getting someplace." Therefore, he is less likely to become discouraged. The part method, however, imposes the additional task of eventually putting the parts together to make a whole.

Using the whole method does not necessarily imply studying a whole assignment as a unit. A given assignment may consist of two or more logical units. When the student learns one of these logical parts, he is learning a psychological whole, even though it is not the complete assignment.

For greatest learning efficiency, the whole and part methods may be combined. In many learning situations it is probably best to begin with the whole method, while feeling free to concentrate at any time on a particularly difficult or important part. By using the part method with the difficult sections, the learner need not spend time going over material he already knows well. At the end of his study session he should round out his learning with a brief return to the whole method to review and to check on his learning.

6. Mnemonic Devices

In an attempt to be efficient in his learning, a student may sometimes turn to MNEMONIC (ni-'män-ik) DEVICES such as catchwords, jingles, and formulas to help him recall particular facts. No doubt you know the little jingle beginning, "Thirty days hath September, April, June, and November." The jingle helps you remember the facts. Similarly, the rhyming of *two* and *blue* may help you remember that Columbus discovered America in 1492:

> In fourteen hundred ninety-two
> Columbus sailed the ocean blue.

Actors and actresses often combine the part and the whole method of learning in preparing for a play. They may read their lines and memorize certain passages for one scene in the play. Yet they also may read through their part as a whole, and rehearse the entire play as a unit.

HOW TO LEARN EFFICIENTLY

Then there is the story of the schoolboy who put down 1493 on his examination paper because

> In fourteen hundred ninety-three
> Columbus sailed the deep blue sea.

The possibility of making such mistakes is always present when we depend on mnemonic devices. Nevertheless, mnemonic devices can be of some value in learning simple facts and organizing the information to be remembered. For example, "Roy G. Biv" can help you remember the order in which the colors appear in the spectrum (red, orange, yellow, green, blue, indigo, and violet).

However, there is always the danger of spending too much time on developing and using mnemonic devices and not enough time on understanding what is being learned. Anyone who attempts to depend heavily on mnemonic devices will eventually become bogged down in the devices themselves. The efficient student will place more emphasis on understanding and applying information than on using mnemonic devices.

7. Overlearning

Suppose you have to memorize a poem or a speech or a vocabulary list. You study until you can close your book and recite the material without a mistake. Why study more? There is experimental evidence that materials learned to the level of a single perfect recitation are forgotten more rapidly than materials that are studied more thoroughly, or OVER-LEARNED. The student who studies only to the point of being able to recite the material perfectly one time will probably find that he can no longer repeat it perfectly when the day comes for examination.

In a classic experiment on overlearning, adults were asked to learn lists consisting of twelve nouns of one syllable each. Some of the lists were repeated over and over until the subject had learned them well enough to repeat them once without error. As soon as he met this criterion, he studied these particular lists no further. For other lists, the subject went on with his repetitions to the extent of 50-percent overlearning. For example, if four repetitions had been required to meet the criterion of one errorless repetition, the subject went on to a total of six repetitions. For still other lists, the subject went on to the extent of 100-percent overlearning—if four repetitions had been required to meet the criterion, the subject went on to a total of eight repetitions. Learning was measured at intervals for twenty-eight days by testing how much of the lists the subjects could remember.

The results of this experiment are shown on page 71. From this graph you will note that overlearning results in a material increase in what is remembered, especially over longer periods of time. Note also, however, that a law of diminishing returns seems to be operating. There is less difference in the amount remembered between 50-percent overlearning and 100-percent overlearning than there is between no overlearning and 50-percent overlearning. The results of overlearning carried to 200 percent bear out the generalization about diminishing returns. For the student who must budget his time, some overlearning is clearly indicated. But even the student with unlimited time available must be aware of the fact of diminishing returns. He might improve his grades somewhat by poring over the same material hour after hour, but he is paying a high price for an increasingly smaller return.

The above experiment should not be taken as evidence of how much overlearning you should do in your schoolwork. If you

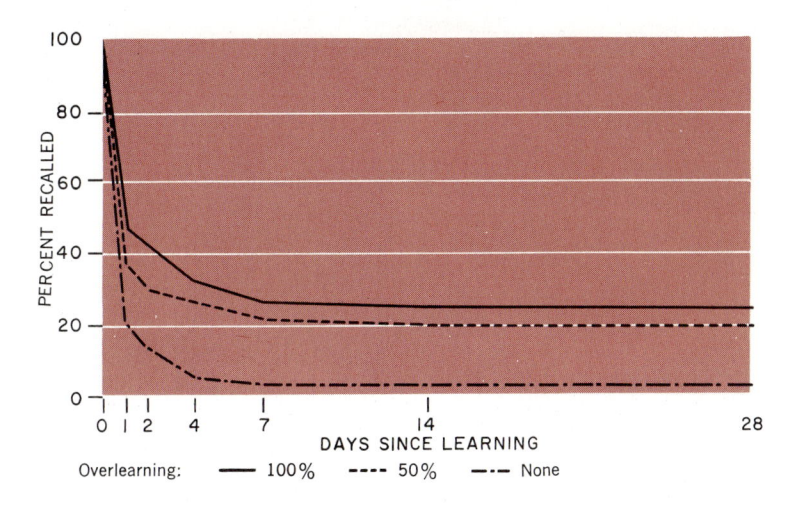

Retention following no overlearning and two degrees of overlearning

thoroughly understand the material you are studying, and if it is material that involves understanding relationships rather than material that requires rote learning, you may need very little time for overlearning.

8. Latent Learning

Learning that takes place in the absence of reinforcement but is utilized only when reinforcement is given is known as LATENT LEARNING. There is some experimental evidence that such learning occurs—that animals, for instance, learn even though they are not rewarded. Three groups of rats were tested in maze running. One of the groups was permitted to wander through a maze but was never rewarded with food. (Some psychologists feel that the handling the rats received from the experimenters served as reward, even though they may have received no food.) Another group was always fed on completing the run of the maze. A third group was permitted to wander about in the maze for ten days but was not rewarded until the eleventh day. When presented with food reinforcement, this third group quickly took the short path through the maze, equaling or even excelling the maze-running ability of the group that had been reinforced from the first.

In our everyday activities we have many experiences in which we do not seem to learn but later find that some learning has taken place. We may feel that we have learned practically nothing on certain days or in certain classes. Yet there may have been latent learning. It is encouraging to think that this learning may be there at some later time when it is needed.

9. Serial Learning

When an organism learns a series of responses in some particular order, it is called SERIAL LEARNING. For example, an experimenter presents the material to be learned on a memory drum (a drumlike device which, as it revolves, exposes briefly through a small opening each item to be learned). After the subject has seen the list one time, he tries to state in advance the next item that will appear in the opening. Each item becomes a

A memory drum, such as the one shown above, is very useful for studying serial learning. The first item to be memorized appears in the opening. Then the circular drum revolves one notch and exposes the next item in the series.

cue or stimulus for the appearance of the next item. By keeping score of the errors made by the subject, the experimenter can plot his learning curve.

Does the position of an item in a series have an effect on learning that item? Although we do not know why it occurs, the items or words appearing first and last in the series are learned more easily than the items appearing in the middle of the list. Some psychologists believe that the first and last items are learned more easily because they occupy special positions in the series. They mark the beginning and the end of the series, and therefore stand out more than the other items. It is true that the serial effect becomes less when the subject does not know where the list begins and ends.

Learning to live in today's society is not unlike serial learning, in that we must learn certain responses before we can proceed to new responses. Even our educational system has required courses. For example, you must first learn certain responses in mathematics before you can progress to more difficult math courses. In fact, even within courses you must learn sequential responses as you progress through the course. Each response becomes a cue or stimulus for the appearance of the next response in the series.

The Progress of Learning

Thus far we have discussed a number of the problems and techniques involved in learning. Now we will consider the entire process of learning a set of facts or a skill. How fast should that process be? Should we expect to improve at a steady rate until we achieve mastery?

Graphs of learning can show us how learning progresses. We encountered graphs that show the progress of learning when we studied feedback in trials, estimating the length of a piece of wood, and when we examined massed vs. distributed practice. To keep track of the progress of learning, experimenters plot their data on graphs.

As you perhaps noticed on the learning graphs mentioned above, the amount of learning is usually shown on the vertical axis, and the amount and kind of practice is shown on the horizontal axis. The dependent variable is indicated on the vertical axis and the independent variable on the horizontal axis. Take a look at the learning graph on page 65 showing the effects of knowledge of results in making accurate responses. The dependent variable, the amount of learning (percent of correct responses), is plotted on the vertical axis, or ordinate. The independent variable (the number of days of the experiment—controlled by the experimenter) is plotted on the horizontal axis, or abscissa.

There is some reason to believe that if we are able to measure the process of learning a skill or set of facts from the very beginning to at least a fair degree of mastery, the graph of our data would show an S-shaped (sigmoid) curve, as indicated in the figure on this page. Learning progress is generally very slow at first, then speeds up, and finally slows down. Suppose we were to measure the complete process of how an individual learns his native language. The newborn infant exercises his vocal cords. Soon he hears sounds. He is learning, although very slowly, to speak the language he hears. There are great individual differences, but generally the first word is uttered somewhere between eight and twenty months of age. The child continues to make meaningful sounds. By the age of four he may have a vocabulary of more than 1500 words. During his school years, his vocabulary continues to grow at a fairly steady rate. Then there is a slowing down in the acquisition of vocabulary, although he adds new words and drops some old words throughout his life.

Graphs of learning data for an individual are characteristically irregular. One day he may not have as good a record as on a previous day. Perhaps the learning process itself is irregular, or perhaps the irregularity is a result of inability to measure all that is really taking place as a person learns.

Some experiments on learning result in curves that show increasing returns. Such learning curves are said to show POSITIVE ACCELERATION. They resemble the first part of the S-shaped curve. Some experiments on learning result in curves that show UNIFORM ACCELERATION, or the same amount of improvement for equal units of practice. They resemble the middle of the S-shaped curve. Still other experiments result in curves that show decreasing returns, or NEGATIVE ACCELERATION. They resemble the last part of the S-shaped curve. Most learning curves are of the last-mentioned shape, probably because measurement does not begin until after much of the total learning has been completed. Also, the learner may be reaching his limit. For example, a typist may be reaching the point beyond which his fingers will not move more rapidly. (Most of us, however, cease to improve long before we reach this limit.)

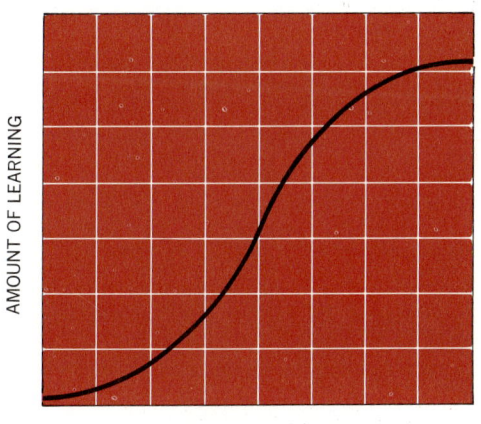

AMOUNT OF LEARNING

AMOUNT OF PRACTICE

HOW TO LEARN EFFICIENTLY

Sometimes students become discouraged because they slow up in a given learning process. The discouragement may not be warranted. They may be nearing the end of the total learning process, or at least they may have reached a fair degree of mastery. On the other hand, the slowing up may be just a temporary phenomenon.

Plateaus. Occasionally, but not frequently, one or more plateaus may be found in a learning graph. A PLATEAU is a period of little or no apparent progress in learning. It is preceded by measurable learning and is followed by measurable learning. A plateau is more likely to be found in data that are based on learning a complex skill than on data that are based on learning a simple skill.

At one time, psychologists conducted a study of workers learning a particular industrial job. Part of the data obtained from this study is shown in the graph on this page. Note that the rapid initial learning was followed by a plateau (marked off by two broken vertical lines). Note, too, that there was further rise in skill following the plateau.

If you ever learned to type, do you think data on your progress might have shown a plateau? Individuals who learn to ski often feel that they go through a period that would appear on a graph as a plateau. Did you have a plateau while learning to play a musical instrument? If you are a radio "ham," you may have had a plateau in your learning of the code.

Why does a plateau occur? A number of possible explanations have been offered for the plateau that is found in some learning graphs. It has been said that a plateau is likely to occur when the learner becomes bored. The beginning student of typing is quite enthusiastic; he is on his way to a good job, and his motivation is high. In time, however, the novelty wears off, he becomes discouraged, he loses interest, and his progress levels off. It may be, of course, that the plateau is a cause of boredom rather than a consequence of it. At any rate, a short period of no practice may be helpful. During this rest period, detrimental habits may be extinguished. The learner may return to the original practice material with renewed enthusiasm. A graph of his learning will show that he then leaves the plateau.

A plateau may occur when the learner has to discover a more efficient work method. For example, some individuals learn to type by the hunt-and-peck system. They may achieve considerable speed with this system, but they do not become excellent and efficient typists. If they decide to become good typists, they must change to the touch system. A plateau may occur as the change is made, but as they acquire skill in the touch system, they leave the plateau. Lessons from a skilled

The progress and the plateau made by workers in learning an industrial job.

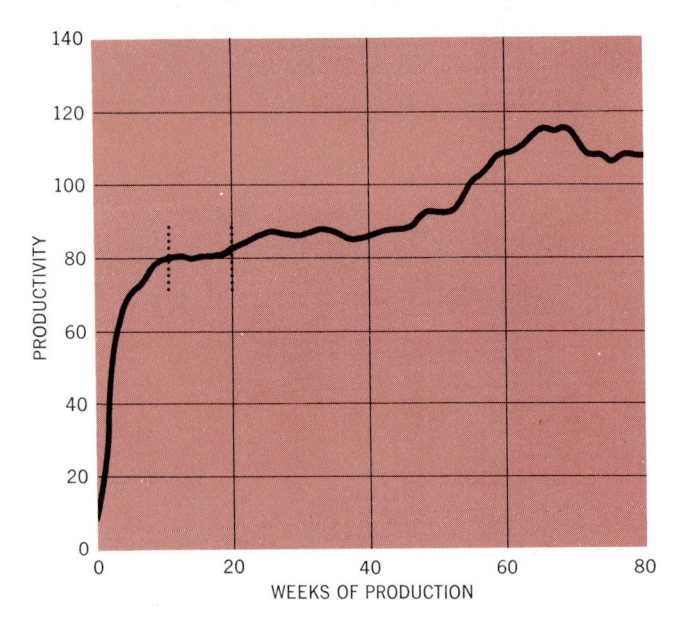

teacher may help an individual to leave a plateau. If, for example, your progress in learning to play a musical instrument has leveled off, a music teacher might help by instructing you to change the position of your hands or of the mouthpiece on your lips.

A plateau may appear because the learner has not understood earlier material. Sometimes a course has to move so rapidly from one topic to another that the learner does not master each step as it is presented. He will leave the plateau when he assimilates this earlier material.

A plateau may occur because the learner becomes tense. He feels that he is "dumb" because he isn't making progress. Knowing that a plateau is only a temporary thing and that further progress will come should relieve tension and help the learner rise above the plateau.

It is encouraging to realize that the plateau may not represent an actual lack of improvement. Although the learning curve does level off temporarily, it may be that if we could measure the learning process more accurately and in more detail, we would find that progress is steady. The apparent plateau might be eliminated.

Remembering

Inherent in the discussion of learning has been the idea of remembering. We learn with the thought that at some time later we will be able to recall what we have learned. In this section we will consider some of the experimental work that has been done on retention—on what is retained or remembered. To be studied scientifically, retention must be measured. Psychologists have performed experiments using many different methods of measuring memory. We will consider three basic methods here.

The method of relearning. The method of relearning, sometimes called the "method of savings," can be illustrated by a classic experiment of the German psychologist Hermann Ebbinghaus. To avoid the effects of previous learning, he introduced the use of nonsense syllables in his experiments on learning. Serving as his own subject, he memorized lists of nonsense syllables, carefully recording the amount of time required to learn each list to the point of making two errorless recitations. Following various intervals, he relearned the lists, again keeping a record of the time required. The difference between the time required for the original learning and the time required for relearning was a measure of retention. The table on this page summarizes his data in terms of percent of material retained when measured by this method.

Are these data disturbing? Are you asking yourself, "Why bother to learn? I'll forget most of what I learn in a month anyway"? Note, however, that this experiment employed nonsense syllables. There is greater retention for meaningful material.

Another well-known experiment indicates that material once learned can be relearned with less effort than material not learned

Retention of Lists of Nonsense Syllables, as Measured by Ebbinghaus

INTERVAL BETWEEN LEARNING AND RELEARNING	PERCENT RETAINED
None (immediate recall)	100
20 minutes	58
1 hour	44
9 hours	36
24 hours	34
2 days	28
6 days	25
31 days	21

previously, even though the original learning occurred early in life and a long interval elapsed between learning and relearning. A psychologist read selected passages of Greek to his child when the child was between fifteen and thirty-six months of age. Each day for three months passages were read to the child. At the end of each three months, new passages were selected and read. When the child was eight and one-half years of age, and again when he was fourteen years of age, he was required to memorize these same passages. In addition, at these ages he was required to memorize new Greek passages of equal length and apparently of equal difficulty. At eight and one-half years, 317 repetitions were required to memorize the passages that had been heard in early childhood, but 435 repetitions were required to memorize the new passages. In other words, 27 percent fewer repetitions were required for the passages heard in infancy. It is true that by the age of fourteen years the saving was reduced to 8 percent, but the remarkable fact is that there was retention for what was obviously nonsense material to the young child.

Sometimes students become pleasantly aware of the fact that they have actually retained learned material that they believed had been completely forgotten. Perhaps you have studied a foreign language in high school. Later in college or while traveling you may need to read, write, or speak this language. At first it may seem that you have completely forgotten your high school language training. Yet it takes much less time to relearn vocabulary than to learn a comparable amount of vocabulary in a language that you have never studied.

The method of recall. In this method of studying retention the individual is asked to reproduce certain material that he has learned in the past. For example, the subject may be asked to learn a list of nonsense syllables or words. Later his retention is measured by giving him the first syllable or word and asking him to respond with the remainder of the list. By dividing the number of items he can reproduce by the number of items originally learned, we obtain a retention score expressed as a percentage.

A more refined method of measuring recall involves anticipation. Again a list of nonsense syllables or words is learned. Later the syllables or words are exposed one at a time through the aperture of a memory drum at intervals of a few seconds, in the same order as in the list that the subject has learned. During this interval between exposures the subject tries to anticipate what the next syllable or word will be.

As students you have a great deal of experience with the recall method of measuring retention of learned material. In a French class, for example, you may be asked to conjugate the verb *faire*. Following this minimal stimulus, you try to recall the various forms of the verb. Essay examination questions are typically used to measure retention by the method of recall. Perhaps you have often felt that you really know much more than you were able to recall during an examination.

The method of recognition. Following an examination, you have probably talked over the questions and answers with some of your classmates. Perhaps there was one question for which you could recall practically no material. The friend mentions the answer he gave and you recognize immediately that his answer represents what you had learned but could not recall.

Objective examination questions are typically used to measure retention by the method of recognition. For example, an objective test may contain a question such as the following:

> The strengthening of a stimulus-response association by following the response with a reinforcing stimulus which strengthens the response that precedes it is a definition of what kind of conditioning? (A) Classical. (B) Pavlovian. (C) Operant. (D) Respondent.

Isn't it easier to recognize the correct response to this question than it would be to recall the response to the question, "How can we define operant conditioning?"

Objective examinations can cover many more points than essay examinations. The student has a better chance to indicate just how much of the material he has retained. If he has forgotten two or three points on an essay examination, and if these two or three points happen to be stressed, his score is not an accurate measure of his total retention for the material in the course. Yet it is also true that objective examinations do not give the student an opportunity to organize and express his thinking in the form in which he will do most of his reporting throughout life. A good examination program combines essay and objective questions—it uses both the method of recall and the method of recognition.

Does an extensive vocabulary help retention? Language assists us in remembering specific material. This was demonstrated in an experiment involving the naming of colors. The psychologists performing the experiment pointed out that humans are able to distinguish about 7,500,000 different "colors." However, the English language has less than 4,000 names for colors, and only about 8 of these occur very commonly (red, orange, yellow, green, blue, purple, pink, brown).

The subjects for the experiment were college students, all of whom spoke English as their native language and none of whom was color-blind. First, each subject looked at selected groups of 4 colors. Then the subject was shown a card containing 120 colors and was asked to identify the 4 he had just seen. Data indicated that those colors that were easiest to recognize were those most easily named. The subjects remembered (recognized) most quickly those colors with familiar names.

The same experiment was carried out with Zuñi Indians. In the language of the Zuñi Indians, there is but a single name for the colors we denote as orange and yellow. Although English-speaking subjects never confused orange and yellow in the recognition test, Zuñi subjects frequently did so. That is, both the laboratory study and the field study indicated an agreement between vocabulary and ability to remember (recognize) a color.

The practical suggestion that can be made on the basis of this experiment is that students should learn the vocabulary of each field they study. To aid you in retaining psychological terms, this book lists vocabulary at the end of each chapter.

Are general or exact words easier to remember? Sometimes, in a sincere effort to do good work, students attempt to memorize verbatim the material in their textbooks. Later, they are greatly disturbed to find that they cannot recall material studied in this way. Psychologists have found that longtime retention is greater for ideas and concepts that have been mastered than for statements that have been memorized verbatim.

In one scientific study students were required to recognize the correctness or incorrectness of statements on the basis of a passage they had read previously. Some of the statements they were asked to recognize were

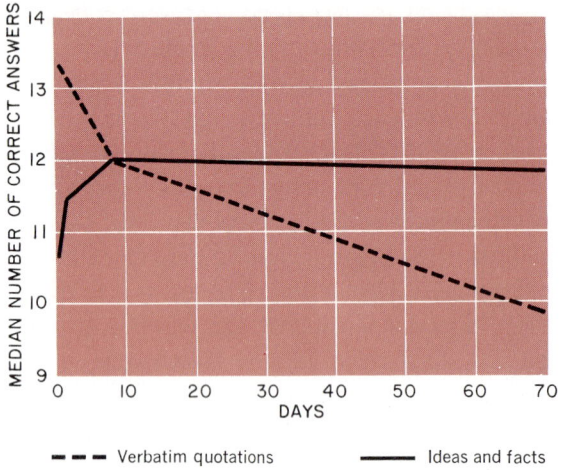

The retention of general ideas compared with the retention of exact words

--- Verbatim quotations   ⎯⎯ Ideas and facts

worded exactly as they had been in the passage. Others were worded differently, although expressing the same general idea as the original passage. Retention was measured at various intervals over a period of seventy days. The results are shown above.

In this experiment there was actually a rise in retention of essential ideas and facts for a number of days following the reading of the passage. This rise occurred even though retention of essential ideas was at first somewhat lower than verbatim retention. Some loss followed the initial rise in retention of essential ideas, but this loss was slight compared with the loss for verbatim retention.

Apply the results of this experiment to your own studying. Do you merely try to memorize what the book says, or do you try to understand the fundamental meaning of what you read?

Can you remember what is heard during sleep? It has been estimated that in a normal lifetime a person spends approximately twenty-two years sleeping. If some of this time can be salvaged for learning purposes, total learning—and free time for recreation—can be increased. Some research reports seem to show that people can remember what they hear while sleeping. For example, two psychologists attempted to teach the words of three songs, each one eight to twenty-seven lines in length, to a lightly sleeping woman by playing each song to her five times a night for three successive nights. She did not know the songs before the experiment began, but following the sleep training she was able to write the lyrics for two of the songs without error and for the other song with only minor errors.

It has been shown that subjects can discriminate auditory signals during a light stage of sleep. Furthermore, spoken names are incorporated into dreams when presented at a time when the subject is dreaming. One recent study included a tape-recorded training session in which the subjects were told that they would hear paired Russian-English words while they slept. None of the subjects had any prior knowledge of Russian and the probability of a subject correctly guessing the paired words was zero. The average recall after five nights of sleep was 13 percent. It was 17 percent during light sleep early in the night in the last two nights of the experiment. When the subjects heard the training tape during light sleep late at night, their scores ranged from 12 to 30 percent retention. Another feature of this study was that retention while asleep seemed to improve with training.

However, the individual who spends his time learning while awake will still learn more than the one who spends an equal amount of time trying to learn when asleep. At any rate, the student certainly should not depend on having his textbooks read to him while he sleeps!

Forgetting

There are a number of theories that attempt to explain why we forget, although none of them seem to answer adequately all of the problems involved. We shall examine six of these basic theories: (1) elapse of time, (2) inattention, (3) retroactive inhibition, (4) proactive inhibition, (5) motivated forgetting, and (6) distortion of the memory trace.

1. *Elapse of time.* One of the oldest theories of forgetting is based on the belief that when we learn, a *memory trace* is laid down in the nervous system, and especially in the brain. Learning causes a physical change in the brain and nervous system that disappears with the passage of time. The fading of the memory trace after a lapse of time is sometimes called "organic decay." To date there is little evidence to support this belief. One argument against this theory is that some apparently "lost" event is later remembered. Particularly in old age, individuals can often remember events that happened when they were much younger. For example, there is a record of one man who, at the age of ninety, suddenly recalled a poem of eight lines which he had learned at the age of fifteen. He could not remember having reheard the poem during the interval of seventy-five years.

2. *Inattention.* Another explanation for some forgetting is a lack of attentiveness when we are supposed to be learning. For example, when we are introduced to someone, unless we are paying close attention it is sometimes very difficult, if not impossible, to recall the person's name after a few seconds.

3. *Retroactive inhibition.* The theory that new learning may interfere with old learning is called RETROACTIVE INHIBITION. For example, in one experiment subjects were required to learn a list of nonsense syllables (List A) and then learn a different list of nonsense syllables (List B), after which they were required to recall List A. The control group, who learned only the nonsense syllables on List A, was able to recall more of List A than the experimental group. The control group did not have any new learning to interfere with their memory of List A.

Another example of retroactive inhibition is one experimental study in which subjects were asked to memorize lists of adjectives. Following this learning, other learning activities were introduced, which consisted of the following lists: (1) adjectives that were synonyms of the original list, (2) adjectives that were antonyms of the original list, (3) adjectives that were unrelated in meaning to the original adjectives, (4) nonsense syllables, and (5) three-place numbers. After the original learning, the subjects were divided into five groups. Each of the five groups learned a different one of these five lists, while one group of subjects rested after the original learning and made no attempt to learn another list of any kind. The percentages of recall following the rest and following various learning activities are indicated in the table below. The interval of time between original

Retention of Original Learning Following Rest or Other Learning

INTERVAL ACTIVITY	PERCENT RETAINED
Rest (no further learning)	45
Learning:	
Digits	37
Nonsense syllables	26
Unrelated adjectives	22
Antonyms	18
Synonyms	12

learning and recall was ten minutes. Certainly the data in this table suggest that retroactive inhibition is greatest when the original learning is followed by the learning of very similar material. Also, note the effect on recall of rest following the original learning.

4. *Proactive inhibition.* Proactive inhibition is similar to retroactive inhibiton, except that the sequence of the interference of learning material is reversed. That is, PROACTIVE INHIBITION is the interference of earlier learning with newer learning. In one experiment subjects first learned List A, next List B, and then were asked to recall List B. A control group showed that the prior learning of List A did interfere with the recall of List B. Actually, evidence has shown that experience with learning lists does improve the learning of new lists, but it also shows that past experience in learning such lists interferes with the recall of lists or information of a similar nature. Such interference is considerably less, though, when the material learned is meaningful. Also, through overlearning the individual becomes much less susceptible to interference.

5. *Motivated forgetting.* An important aspect of forgetting not previously stated is the individual's motives. One instance in which an individual is motivated to forget is REPRESSION, an unconscious process by which we make memories inaccessible to recall, presumably because we become uncomfortable when we do recall them. Such memories are not lost because of an organic decay or time lapse, since under hypnosis these memories can be recalled. In one experiment subjects were hypnotized and told that upon waking they would not be able to remember certain critical words suggested to them while under hypnosis. When the subjects awoke, hints were given to them but they could not remember the critical words. The cues for the critical words were not consciously recognized by the subjects in their wakened state. To prove that these words were not permanently forgotten, the subjects had also been given a post-hypnotic suggestion that when they were given permission to remember the words, they would be able to do so. When the subjects received verbal permission to remember, they did recall all of the repressed words.

Another factor related to motivation and memory is a phenomenon called the ZEIGARNIK (Zi-'gär-nik) EFFECT. As the story goes, a Russian psychologist, Zeigarnik, and her students were astounded by the memory of a waiter who could remember long, detailed orders without writing them down. But once the waiter had completed the order, he was unable to remember what he had brought. The result was a classic experiment which concluded that uncompleted tasks are remembered better than completed ones. Further experiments have refined this conclusion, and we now have evidence that the Zeigarnik effect of remembering uncompleted tasks better than completed ones applies only to nonstressful situations. In stressful situations, an individual may be more motivated to forget uncompleted tasks.

6. *Distortion of the memory trace.* In recent years there has been considerable progress in experiments analyzing memory on a biochemical basis. Although this theory is much too complex to present in detail, the following is a general explanation. In an experiment with flatworms that had learned the conditioned response of contraction to a light, a substance containing RNA (ribonucleic acid) was taken from their bodies and injected into untrained flatworms. The untrained but injected flatworms were subjected to the same classical conditioning procedures as the original flatworms and learned the response much faster than a control group, which were injected with RNA from untrained flatworms. A similar experiment was performed on rats with the same results. It is thought that the RNA molecules contain a biochemical substance related to the specific learning task of the animals.

In another experiment goldfish learned an avoidance response to a light signal, after which the response was extinguished. Extracts of RNA from these goldfish were injected into other goldfish that had learned the same avoidance response. A control group of goldfish was also used. Goldfish injected with an RNA extract from the original group extinguished their avoidance responses much faster than the non-RNA-injected control group. Thus, it seems as if RNA may be associated not only with learning tasks but also with learning to extinguish responses.

Some interesting studies of memory traces have been conducted with the sea hare, a small mollusk about seven inches in length. The sea hare was trained for several days by exposing it to twelve hours of light and twelve hours of darkness. Then one nerve cell was removed and electrodes attached to it for recording electrical activity. At the beginning of each twenty-four hour cycle, when the twelve hours of light had occurred in the training period, the electrical activity in the individual nerve cell rose, indicating that the nerve cell not only had learned in the original situation, but also had remembered.

Some researchers have found that RNA produces favorable changes in memory for humans. Also, injected RNA seems to have better results than RNA taken orally. Attempts have been made to develop chemicals that will cause the human body to manufacture larger amounts of cerebral RNA.

Forgetting takes place when there is some interruption or distortion of the biochemical memory processes. Evidence has shown that there are chemicals that can destroy the transfer of learning effects related to RNA. Also, electroconvulsive shock (ECS) is known to influence the length of time an act is remembered. ECS involves the administering of an electric current that produces immediate temporary unconsciousness in the organism. Different rats that had learned a task were given ECS at various intervals after learning the task. It was found that there was a relationship between retention of the learning and how soon ECS was given after the learning. The shorter the time interval between the learning and the ECS, the less the rats retained, as measured by relearning. Perhaps the ECS destroyed the memory trace before it became part of the long-term memory. In terms of RNA, there may have been biochemical disruption of the RNA molecule that contained the data involved in learning the task.

What are long-term memory and short-term memory? One theory hypothesizes that there are actually two kinds of memory, one for short-term memory (STM) and another for long-term memory (LTM). Every bit of information we receive, according to this theory, is stored for a very short period of time in STM, where it may or may not be coded and eventually stored in LTM. (*Coding* refers to the process of transforming one type of energy into another.) While the information is in STM, it can be recalled perfectly. Because of its limited capacity and the flow of new information arriving constantly from the senses, STM can store information only briefly. If information is successfully coded, it can be kept in LTM, which is like a large storage room. The question then is, "Why is it difficult to recall some information from LTM?" One possible answer is that some information never reaches LTM. Another conceivable explanation is that there is no sufficient stimulus present for the individual to

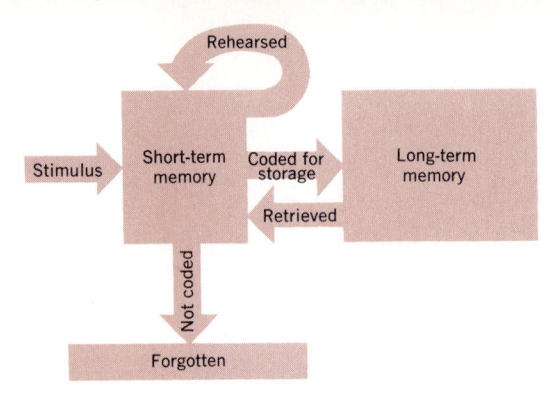

A theory involving two storage mechanisms

locate the information properly once it is stored in LTM. It is one thing to store information away and still another to find it at a later time, especially when it can be filed under many different headings.

No single belief or theory can answer all questions related to forgetting, just as no single learning theory can currently account for all the processes involved in learning. At present we must use a number of different approaches to explain forgetting. But all the approaches agree that forgetting is an active process, not a passive one.

How does sleep affect retention? Experiments have shown that learning followed by rest is retained better than learning followed by an activity. We usually seem to rest most completely when we sleep. Therefore, is retention of learning followed by sleep markedly greater than retention of learning followed by waking activity? To answer this question, six subjects were tested twenty-four, forty-eight, seventy-two, and ninety-six hours after the original learning. There was consistently greater retention of learning in sessions followed by sleep. Other experiments indicate that details of organized material are remembered better if the learning is followed by sleep rather than by waking activity but that essential items are retained about as well after remaining awake as after sleeping.

Would it be best to have periods of relaxation after each class period? In practical school situations, such a plan is not possible. Experimental evidence and the experience of teachers suggest, however, that after a student learns one set of materials he should then, if possible, learn a very different kind of material. You may wish to make use of this practical suggestion for planning your study schedule. In fact, by applying the different principles of learning and forgetting you have just studied, you can improve your learning and retention considerably.

Terms to Know

coding
distributed practice
forgetting
latent learning
long-term memory (LTM)
massed practice
memory trace
mnemonic device
motivated forgetting
motivation

negative acceleration
negative transfer
overlearning
part learning
plateau
positive acceleration
positive transfer
proactive inhibition
psychological feedback
recall

recognition
repression
retention
retroactive inhibition
serial learning
short-term memory (STM)
transfer
uniform acceleration
whole learning
Zeigarnik effect

Topics to Think About

1. Suppose you decide to learn to read and speak the Chinese language and know someone who can instruct you. How much transfer do you think there would be from English to Chinese? Suppose you decide to learn the Russian language. Would there be more or less transfer from English to Russian than from English to Chinese?

2. Assuming that you are attending a school where marks are given, how would you like to attend a school where no marks are given? Would you have more or less motivation to learn than you have in a school where marks are given and even emphasized?

3. For most efficient school learning, how often do you think examinations should be given—or should they be given at all?

4. Which kind of examination questions do you prefer: (1) short answers of a word or few words in which you are asked to *recall* what you have learned, or (2) multiple-choice or matching questions in which you are asked to *recognize* what you have learned? Can you give an explanation for your preference in terms of the process of learning and forgetting?

5. Suppose you develop a desire to learn to play an instrument such as the piano. Do you think that it would be better to learn by "ear" or by learning to read the music? Why?

6. Do you think that girls are more highly motivated toward academic achievement than boys, or the other way round? Why do you think this is the case?

7. Since people are motivated and able to learn, why do teachers have such a difficult time getting students to learn their particular course material?

Suggestions for Activities

1. The following experiment will demonstrate the effects of active vs. passive attitudes in learning. The teacher or some member of the class should select two passages of poetry by the same author that seem to be of equal difficulty. One passage should be marked A and the other B. The passages should be eight lines in length. In some random way, divide the class into two groups. Members of Group I should read and reread the A passage as often as possible in a fixed period of time, say three minutes. The members of this group should be instructed to make no effort to recall the material as they read. Group II should read and reread the A passage as often as possible in a fixed period of time equal to half the time allowed Group I, say one and a half minutes. The members of Group II should then spend the other half of the time in actively reciting the passage to themselves. In this recitation time, they should read two lines at a time, close their eyes and try to recite these lines, then go on to the next two lines, and so on. Immediately following the period of reading or reading-study, have members of both groups write as much of the poem as they can remember. The score for each individual is the number of words that he can recall correctly.

In a second part of the experiment, use the B passage and reverse the procedure. Group II should spend the entire time reading and rereading the material without making any attempts at recall. Group I should divide reading and reciting as Group II did in the first part of the experiment. Data can be secured in the same way as for the first part. Do the combined data suggest any tentative conclusions? Can you improve the experiment by using four groups of subjects?

2. Ask your parents, other relatives, and friends what mnemonic devices they use now or have used in the past. Make a collection of these devices. Then put together a class scrapbook on the basis of the material brought in by various students. How many of the mnemonic devices represent efficient learning procedure? How many are more trouble than they are worth?

3. Make a weekly work-study-play schedule for yourself and follow the schedule for several weeks. Does such a schedule result in more efficient study? Does it result in more time for recreation?

4. Write a ten-word sentence on an index card. Next take ten different words and write them in a random order on another card. Then select someone who is not taking and has not had this course and for ten seconds show him the card with the ten randomly written words. Afterward, ask him to write down as many words as he can remember. Next present the card with words in sentence form for ten seconds and ask him to write down these words. On which list did he remember more words? Ask him to explain why.

5. Take fifty small index cards and number them from 1 to 50. Divide a tabletop in half by placing a small board or a piece of string down the middle so that there is a right side and a left side. Next shuffle the cards thoroughly. Hand the cards to someone and instruct the person to place all even-numbered cards on the right side of the table and all odd-numbered cards on the left side, as fast as he can without making any mistakes. If he places a card on the wrong side, he must replace it on the correct side. Time him to see how fast he can correctly place all cards on the table. Repeat this same procedure for at least ten trials, timing each trial, or until there is no further decrease in time for three consecutive trials. Then have the person reverse the order of placing the cards on the table; even-numbered cards on the left side and odd-numbered cards on the right. What happens to the time it took to place the cards? For Trial 3, have him put the even-numbered cards on the left side and the odd-numbered cards on the right side, using the same number of trials as were used for the reverse procedures at the beginning. Did he learn fastest in the Trial 3 procedures? How do you explain your results?

6. Try to recite some rather long bit of poetry that you learned in elementary school or earlier. Probably you have forgotten much of it. Undertake to relearn the poetry, noting to what extent you are able to say, "It came back to me." Then try to memorize an equally long piece of poetry that is new to you. After one week, try to recite both passages. Which passage took the most time to memorize, the one that you were relearning, or the one that you were learning for the first time?

7. Write the small letters a, b, d, e, h, k, p, s, y, and z at the top of a piece of paper. Ask several subjects to begin printing each letter upside down at a signal from you. Record the time it takes a subject to complete a trial, and repeat for ten trials. Then count the number of errors made by each subject on each trial, subtracting five seconds for each error per trial. (An error would be the printing of a letter right side up.) Combine the data for several subjects and construct a graph. A class discussion of this activity might include such questions as: Why combine data for several subjects? What effect, if any, did the correction of five seconds for each error have upon the shape of the curve?

8. Make a list of twelve nonsense syllables. Type each nonsense syllable in approximately the same location on a separate index card, using lowercase letters. Tell a subject that you will show him the cards one at a time for five seconds each, and that he is to try to remember each syllable in order. After the subject has seen the syllables once, he is to use the first syllable as a stimulus to say the second syllable, the second syllable to recall the third one, and so on, using the last syllable as a stimulus to recall the first one. After each trial, give the subject a thirty-second rest. A third person should keep a record of any errors (syllables called incorrectly or in the wrong order). Continue until the subject correctly recalls the list two consecutive times.

Then construct a graph, using the number of errors made for each syllable. Where do most errors occur? Which are the most frequently remembered syllables? What principles does this illustrate? It may be necessary to combine data for several subjects to obtain meaningful results.

9. Type a list of twelve nonsense syllables on separate index cards, but type every other syllable in capital letters and the rest in lowercase letters. Repeat the procedures in Activity 8 above. Are there differences between how subjects learned the syllables in capital and lowercase letters?

10. At the end of each chapter in this book is a list of words to be added to your vocabulary. Secure a card index or possibly an indexed blank book. Record words from preceding lists that you believe you might have difficulty using in your own writing about or discussion of psychology. Record the meaning of each word. Add to this list as you continue with your study of psychology. Frequent study of this index list and review of it near the close of the course will be excellent preparation for a final exam as well as for long-time retention.

Suggestions for Further Reading

Hilgard, E. R., R. C. Atkinson, and Rita Atkinson, *Introduction to Psychology,* 5th ed., Harcourt Brace Jovanovich. See Chapter 9, "Memory," and Chapter 10, "Optimizing Learning."

Kagan, J., M. M. Haith, and Catherine Caldwell (eds.), *Psychology: Adapted Readings,* Harcourt Brace Jovanovich. See Selection 5, "On Remembering"; Selection 7, "Memorizing, Recoding, and Perceptual Organization"; and Selection 8, "Mechanization in Problem Solving: A Case of Rigid Behavior."

Kagan, J., and E. Havemann, *Psychology: An Introduction,* 2nd ed., Harcourt Brace Jovanovich. Chapter 3 discusses such topics as three kinds of memory: short- and long-term memory, coding, and retrieval. Chapter 4 is devoted to learning efficiency, including school learning.

Meenes, Max, *Studying and Learning,* Random House. This is a paperback written specifically for high school students and contains many useful suggestions about better study habits and principles of learning that can be used to promote learning.

Psychology Today: An Introduction, CRM Books. See Chapter 18, "Human Information Processing"; and Chapter 19, "Human Learning and Memory."

Ruch, Floyd L., and Philip G. Zimbardo, *Psychology and Life,* 8th ed., Scott, Foresman. See Chapter 6, "Human Learning and Memory."

Wertheimer, M., et al., *Psychology: A Brief Introduction,* Scott, Foresman. See pages 62–64, 98–108, 109–12, 219–20, on curiosity, learning and practice, forgetting, probability and learning, transfer, and training and education.

chapter 4
The Process of Thinking

MOST LEARNING requires remembering and using past experience. The ability to recall a tune, name, or formula, or to recognize and define a foreign word implies that certain processes are going on within the learner. Through some activity within the human organism, principles learned in mathematics can be transferred to computing batting averages or analyzing the school budget. You can use words and numbers to work on problems "in your head," and you can talk about them or write them down. This kind of activity involves thinking.

Just what is thinking? For many centuries philosophers and scientists have been concerned with understanding thought. In modern times psychologists, too, have been trying to define and explain thinking. Today, although definitions of thinking differ, they usually share certain basic elements.

Basic Elements of Thinking

To an observer it might appear that an individual arrives suddenly at the solution to a problem without any previous behavior. But the solution to a problem may not be as sudden as it seems. An individual may sit and think about his problem. He may say to himself, "If I try method A, I'll run into difficulty W; if I try method B, I'll run into difficulty X. Will I run into difficulty if I use method C? Ah—that is the method that will solve the problem." In other words, the individual had engaged in previous behavior—thinking.

Many other forms of behavior, such as strenuous muscular activity, are much easier to observe and measure than thinking is. We can easily measure how much work a man does when he lifts a weight, or how hard a rat pulls on a harness as it approaches a food tray. We speak of such easily observed and measured activity as EXPLICIT BEHAVIOR.

Other behavior, such as thinking, is not easily and directly observable, but can often be inferred from explicit behavior. If we watch a child solve a puzzle, we can observe his movements, and from them we infer that he is thinking. Or we can use very delicate instruments to detect the tiny, inaudible muscular movements of the speech apparatus during thinking. Such behavior that is not easily and directly observable by another person without the aid of special, sensitive measuring instruments is called IMPLICIT BEHAVIOR.

Thinking implies more than mere perception by the individual—more than simply becoming aware of objects, qualities, or relations by means of the sense organs. It also implies more than the mere manipulation of objects. Thinking implies the manipulation of symbols. We may define THINKING, then, as implicit activity by which an organism becomes aware of and manipulates past experience through the use of symbols.

Symbols. Suppose that while attending a basketball game you notice several students wearing red and white ribbons. Since you know that red and white are the colors of West Side High School, you think, "They attend West Side High School." The red and white ribbon is a symbol representing that school—its teams, student body, teachers, and building. A SYMBOL, then, is anything that becomes a representative substitute for something else. Flags, pins, colors, and badges frequently serve as symbols for organizations of people. Gestures, diagrams, pictures, and numbers may serve as symbols in our thinking.

Letters and the words they form are symbols. On a white page you see the black marks **MAN,** and these marks convey a

The shapes of international traffic signs, as well as the drawings themselves, are symbols. What do these shapes and drawings represent? (Answers are on page 111.)

meaning to you. These marks, arranged as they are, have become a symbol for a specific class of organism. On another white page you see a black mark, 人. This mark probably has no meaning for you unless you are familiar with Chinese symbols, or ideographs. To a person familiar with Chinese ideographs, 人 suggests or represents man —it is a representative substitute for man. The ideograph 山 is a representative substitute for a mountain to those who read Chinese. To those of us who do not, the printed word or symbol "mountain" has more meaning.

We recognize the symbols **"MAN"** and "mountain" rather than 人 and 山 because our past experience has taught us printed words rather than ideographs. Therefore, using past experience is another element in thinking. If we see that a bolt needs tightening, we think of the word or symbol "wrench." Our past experience tells us that we need to make use of the object for which the word "wrench" is the symbol. In other words, thinking about what we are to do involves manipulating our past experience to work out a solution to a current problem.

Language. The development of language and the development of thinking are closely related. Vocabulary has been described as the stock-in-trade of the thinker. This statement is clear to anyone who has had the pleasure of observing children develop their language ability. Sometimes we are amused by what seems to be the child's incorrect use of words, but we are usually amazed at how fast a normal child's vocabulary increases. As a rule, the vocabulary development of retarded children is much slower than that of normal children. Every teacher of retarded children is acutely aware of the limitations in language, and so in thinking, of such children. On the other hand, the vocabulary development of very superior children is much more rapid than that of normal children, and teachers are often amazed at the superior child's ability to think more clearly than most children of his age.

A child's use of words, as well as the number of words in his vocabulary, changes as he grows older and develops thinking ability. Early in his development the child uses a single word instead of a sentence. "Drink" may mean "I want a drink." The single-word sentence is characteristic of the child of eighteen months, but by the age of three years the average sentence contains three or four words. By the age of five years the child may be using sentences of at least four or five words, and by the time he is in the third grade his sentences have increased to an average length of about ten words. When he is completing high school, his sentences are almost twice as long as in the third grade.

Concepts

Concepts are important in thinking. A CONCEPT is the meaning that an individual attaches to the qualities or characteristics that are common to otherwise diverse objects, situations, or events. In forming a concept, an individual thinks of similarities and groupings, and associates them with a word or other symbol that he can use thereafter to describe other similar objects, situations, or events.

In what way are an apple and a banana alike? If asked this question, small children are likely to insist that an apple and a banana are not alike, that one is round and the other is long. Of course, an apple and a banana are both part of the concept of fruit. Furthermore, the concept of fruit can be applied to other objects: oranges, pears, pineapples, grapes, apricots, avocados, lemons, figs. As an individual advances in this thinking and areas of knowledge, his concepts become more specific. To the botanist all seed-bearing plants produce fruits. Although a tomato is commonly called a vegetable, the botanist's concept of fruit would cause him to classify the tomato as a fruit.

Adults often develop concepts by looking up a definition in a dictionary. The text of this book, the glossary, and your teacher provide you with definitions to guide you in your formation of psychological concepts.

Can animals form concepts? There is evidence that animals can develop concepts. In one experiment rats were required to develop a concept of triangularity. They were shown cards bearing triangles, rectangles, circles, and other geometric figures. Whenever a rat jumped at a card bearing a triangle, it was rewarded. Whenever it jumped at a card bearing any other geometric figure, it was

Concept formation develops with age. Here a four-year-old child notes that two squat jars contain the same number of beans (top). Yet when the beans from one jar are poured into a narrow, high container (above), he thinks that the high container has more beans (below).

punished. Eventually, the rats learned to jump only at the cards containing the original triangle or at cards showing other kinds of triangles. In some way these rats had developed a concept of triangularity.

How do children form concepts? It is fascinating to watch a child as his processes of thinking develop, as he forms concepts. A pioneer in this interesting field of study has been a Swiss psychologist, Jean Piaget (jȯn pē-ä-'jā). The following is a brief summary of the basic stages of concept development found by Piaget and his followers. Note that the age range for each stage is wide and subject to individual variation.

From birth to about two years of age the child's thinking may be described as sensorimotor—that is, through his senses he learns that his activities are related to objects in his environment. In early infancy his activity is largely reflexive. He does not always differentiate between himself and his environment. Suppose we take a rattle with which a five-month-old infant is playing and, while he is watching, we place the rattle under a blanket. The infant is likely to act as if the rattle no longer exists. He may cry over the loss. Three months later, though, if we do the same thing, he will probably lift the blanket to look for the lost toy. He will be relating his activity to objects in his environment.

By about two years of age the child has a limited vocabulary and he begins to use thought and imagination to solve his problems. From two to four years of age his behavior shows increasing signs of symbolic activity, especially in the use of words. Perhaps the child says "kitty." This word refers to a specific cat, probably the family cat. However, this one word may mean such different ideas as "Where is the cat?" or "Give me the cat!" Objects begin to become symbols, to stand for other objects. For example, a two-year-old's wood toy blocks may stand for bricks in the toy building he constructs.

From about age four to about age seven the child is able to think in terms of classes of objects and events. He has some ability to handle number concepts. His thinking is often based on the most prominent features of what he observes. Suppose he is shown a wide glass half full of water. Then, while he is watching, the water is poured into a slender cylinder. He is likely to say that there is more water in the cylinder than in the glass. If several pennies are placed in a row on the table in front of him and then another row of pennies is laid close to the first, consisting of the same number and spacing, the child will probably say that there are the same number of pennies in both rows. However, if the pennies in the second row are placed so that there is more space between each penny and consequently the entire row is longer than the first row, the child is likely to say that there are more pennies in the second, or longer, row.

By about seven to eleven years of age the child is able to think about and group several concrete concepts and relate them to problems he is trying to solve. Now he can understand that the amount of water poured from the wide glass to the slender cylinder is the same. Furthermore, he can understand that if conditions are reversed and water is poured from the slender cylinder to the wide glass, the amount of water is also the same.

From about ages eleven to fifteen years the individual reaches the final stages of concept formation. He is able to think in abstract terms. He can set up a hypothesis and test it to determine whether or not it is correct. He can imagine various possibilities in a problem he is trying to solve.

How do you form concepts? One psychologist, working with human subjects, presented them with material similar to the figure on this page. He asked them to identify the characteristics that distinguished *dax* from non-*dax*, and then to define the nonsense syllable *dax*. What does *dax* mean? Did you note that all the figures at the left are similar in certain respects? Are all the figures at the right similar in some ways to those at the left but at the same time different in at least one important respect? The psychologist who reported this experiment found that many subjects could correctly identify figures that are

Look closely at these figures. What do you think DAX are? (Answer is on page 92.)

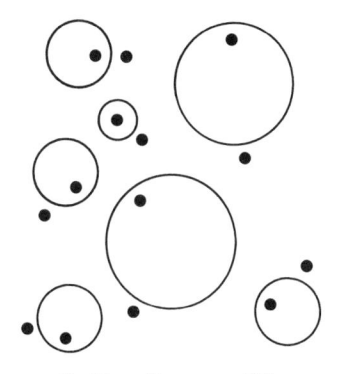

All of these figures are DAX .

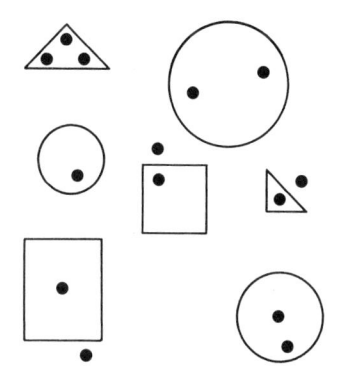

None of these figures are DAX .

dax, even though they could not express the principle in words. Did you verbalize your concept? Did you spend most of your time looking at the figures on the left or looking at the figures on the right? It was found that the subjects in the reported experiment learned much more from studying the positive examples at the left than from studying the negative examples at the right. (*Dax* are circles having one dot inside and one outside.)

This experiment may have given the impression that the development of concepts is a quick and simple experience. On the contrary, we develop and even change many of our concepts over days, months, and years. In the formation of concepts it is important to have wide and varied experiences. Sometimes high school and college students become too narrow in their training, taking only subjects that seem to have immediate, practical value and avoiding subjects that will give them experiences in a wide variety of situations. In the course of a lifetime we must learn thousands of concepts, which should include broad as well as specialized concepts.

Can animals learn to express concepts through speech? As we have seen, animals can develop concepts. Also, animals do have a limited number of vocal signals by which they communicate with one another and, to some extent, with man. But can they be taught to convey their thoughts to man through speech? To answer this question we will consider four experiments in communication with chimpanzees.

In the first study a professor of psychology and his wife raised a baby chimpanzee with their own baby son for a period of nine months. The chimpanzee, named Gua, learned to understand about ninety-five words, but did not learn to talk.

In another case a man and his wife, both psychologists, took an infant chimpanzee called Viki into their home and attempted to teach her to speak. They patiently tried shaping Viki's lips so that she would express certain sounds under specific conditions. After three years of loving care and training, Viki could repeat only three sounds with recognizability and meaning. The words were: Mama—to refer to the woman psychologist, Papa—referring to the man psychologist, and cup—for the cup from which she was fed.

Perhaps the very limited speech success with Viki and no speech success with Gua was due to the structure of a chimpanzee's vocal apparatus. Maybe chimpanzees simply cannot make the sounds of human speech with any degree of ease.

Therefore, a third study involved teaching a female chimpanzee, Washoe, the American sign language. (This is the sign language used by deaf persons in the United States and Canada.) Between the ages of one and four years, Washoe lived in a house trailer, where she heard no spoken words. When in the trailer, her trainers always communicated with each other by means of the sign language. They trained Washoe by putting her hands in the proper position for a sign and then guiding her movements in the desired direction. For example, she was taught to make a beckoning motion with her hands. This meant "come" or "give me." She used this beckoning motion for both human beings and animals, and even for objects out of her reach. At the end of the three-year period, Washoe could use about eighty-five signs correctly.

A still more recent experiment has attempted to teach a chimpanzee, Sarah, to communicate with human beings by using metal-backed plastic pieces to represent specific words. First, Sarah was taught to associate a specific plastic piece with a particular

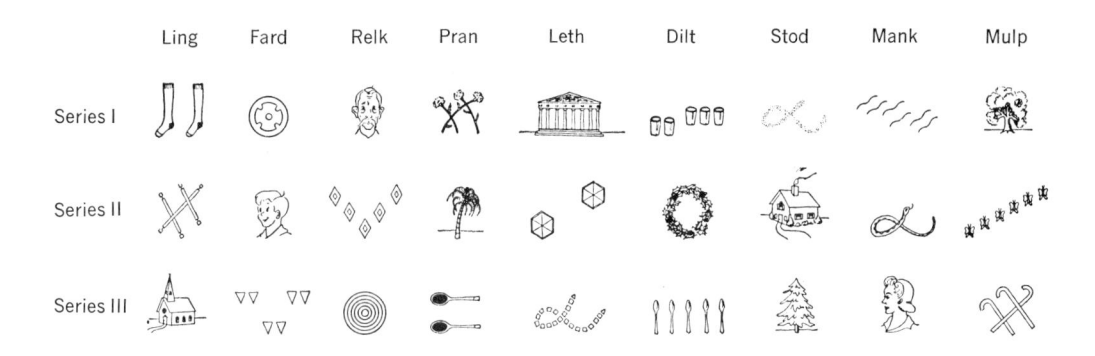

	Ling	Fard	Relk	Pran	Leth	Dilt	Stod	Mank	Mulp
Series I									
Series II									
Series III									

Try this experiment in concept formation. Each nonsense syllable represents a concept illustrated by the drawing in Series I that appears below it. Look at each drawing in Series I and find the matching concept in Series II and in Series III. What concept does each syllable represent? (Answers on page 94.)

piece of fruit. This was a simple process of conditioning. She was given the fruit only when she placed the correct metal-backed plastic piece on a magnetic board. She learned the symbol associated with each of nine different fruits. Also, she learned to associate certain other pieces of plastic with each of her four trainers.

Next, Sarah was taught to associate two "words," that is, two pieces of plastic representing two specific concepts. She learned, for example, that if she placed the symbol for Mary, one of her trainers, and the symbol for apple on the board at the same time, Mary would give her the desired apple. Sarah did not receive an apple if she used a plastic piece designating any of the other three trainers when Mary was present.

To test further whether or not Sarah understood the meaning of the symbols, the trainers taught her to associate four specific pieces of plastic with four colors: red, green, blue, and yellow. Also, she was taught the plastic symbol for "on." The trainer then put the symbols for "green on red" on the board and gave Sarah a green card and a red card. She learned to put the green card on the red card, and soon Sarah worked at 80- to 90-percent accuracy most of the time. In all, the trainers taught her over 120 different "words."

One day Sarah even gave her trainer a "test." She arranged some incomplete statements on one side of the board and a list of possible completions on the other side, much like a matching test question. Sarah then pointed to each combination of statement and completion in turn, and seemed to want the trainer to signal at each correct answer. The trainer admitted that it took her some time to figure out what Sarah wanted *her* to learn!

The results of these experiments suggest that chimpanzees, and presumably other animals, cannot really be taught to talk with human beings—at least not without a great deal of work for very limited success. But evidence seems to be building up that chimpanzees can think in terms of symbols and can communicate with human beings by using symbols other than words.

THE PROCESS OF THINKING

Uncritical Thinking

Man is very proud of his ability to think, and justifiably so when he compares himself with lower animals. Yet when he compares some of his thought processes with mature thinking, man is far less proud. The concepts developed in childhood are selfish, for the child tends to think of himself as the center of the world. As we grow more mature, we learn to respect the importance of other individuals and of social institutions. Unfortunately, our thinking often continues to be limited, such as when we feel sure that we go to the best school, that the political party to which we belong is the only one that can govern wisely, or that our family is better than other families in the neighborhood. Sometimes we swing the other way and say, probably without meaning it, that our school is the worst in the world, that our political party is totally corrupt, and so on.

We are capable of thinking about schools, political parties, and families critically. Although we could analyze them and find both good and bad features, all too often we do not bother to think critically. It is frequently easier to accept incomplete information than to examine an issue more thoroughly. Our friends may be prejudiced, too. As long as we associate only with people who have prejudices similar to our own, we are likely to retain our uncritical thinking. As we look at the following examples of uncritical thinking in our society, consider what the risks of such thinking might be.

"All-or-nothing" thinking. Popular fiction, films, television, and other mass media may frequently encourage us to go all out one way or the other in our thinking. The child watching the thrilling television program is apt to think that there are just two kinds of people in the world: the "good guys" and the "bad guys." He may not realize that goodness-badness is a continuum—that bad guys have some good characteristics and that good guys have some bad characteristics.

As the individual matures, he becomes interested in romantic stories, films, and television programs. He comes to believe that he must be either completely in love or not in love at all. This belief seems to be easier than thinking about friendships in general and evaluating romance in the framework of general social relationships.

One use of "all-or-nothing" thinking in the early days of television was to put all the heroes in westerns—the "good guys," such as the Lone Ranger (above)—on white horses.

The syllables on page 93 represent concepts of concrete objects, spatial forms, and numerical quantities: Ling—*2;* Fard—*circularity;* Relk—*face;* Pran—*one line crossing two lines;* Leth—*building;* Dilt—*5;* Stod—*a looped form;* Mank—*6;* Mulp—*tree.*

94 LEARNING

Many individuals tend to think that they have either good jobs or bad jobs. This "all-or-nothing" thinking is easier than evaluating their jobs according to what various jobs offer and what sort of job they can reasonably hope to get.

Confusing coincidence with cause. Sometimes events seem to go together, as when there is a spell of cold, wet weather and a large number of people have head colds. We often jump to the conclusion that the cold weather caused the colds. However this is not a scientific conclusion unless we have screened out all other causes. We would also need to know how many people actually had colds before and after the bad weather. To assume that because B is found with A, A caused B is uncritical thinking. Both A and B might be related to or caused by C. For example, statistics indicate that church weddings are less likely to be followed by divorce than are weddings not performed in churches. Uncritical thinking might suggest that our divorce problem would be lessened by urging, or even requiring, all couples to be married in churches. The basic factor, of course, is that persons who have fairly stable home backgrounds and religious beliefs tend to marry in a church. Stable home backgrounds and religious beliefs are factors that often contribute to stable marriages.

Delusions. Perhaps the most extreme examples of uncritical thinking are found in the delusions of mentally ill persons. A DELUSION is a false belief that persists in spite of evidence to the contrary. The ill person may insist that he is a great general who is being held prisoner in a concentration camp. It can be pointed out to him that he has no military record and that the hospital in which he finds himself has practically none of the characteristics of a concentration camp, but he continues to think of himself as a great general being persecuted by the enemy. He is incapable of critical thinking.

To cite a much less extreme case, students sometimes insist that they are brilliant but that all the teachers "have it in for them." It can be pointed out to them that they have done poorly on objective, standardized tests in which no teacher judgments were involved. It can be pointed out that teachers have asked them to come in for personal help. Nevertheless, they continue with their uncritical thinking.

Creative Thinking

Sometimes schools are criticized for not producing students who can do truly creative thinking. Our schools are said to turn out technicians but not creative thinkers. Actually, it has been estimated that of all the individuals who have lived in historical times, only about two in a million have become truly distinguished for their creative thinking. Yet, although we cannot all achieve great artistic and scientific creativity, most of us are capable of some creative thinking. Schoolwork often calls for creativity.

In creative thinking the individual strives to discover new solutions to problems, to see new relationships, or to find new modes of artistic expression. He tries to discover new and better ways of achieving goals. His thinking brings into existence something that is new for society, or at least for himself. For contrast, consider "do-it-yourself" kits. We buy the parts, we follow the directions, and behold—we have made a radio, we have constructed a useful piece of furniture, or we have cooked an edible meal. Perhaps we buy a numbered canvas and set of correspondingly numbered bottles of paint, and we paint a picture. Such activities may be fun, they serve as recreation, and they may produce useful results. But they do not give us the opportunity to do creative thinking. Similarly, in laboratory or shop courses it is possible to follow directions and get by—or to try to do more and thus to learn more.

What is artistic creativity? The true artist does more than copy nature. He creates. Like the scientist, he recombines or reorganizes ideas according to some specific pattern in an attempt to achieve some goal or to solve some problem. Can such a process be measured? One psychologist developed a test in which the subject was required to recombine familiar ideas according to certain patterns. In one part of the test the subject was told to recombine given lists of words into as many meaningful, grammatical sentences as possible. For example, how many sentences can you make using the following ten words: *men, sky, is, fight, that, the, slow, bright, of, far?* In another part of the test the subject was asked to make as many pieces of furniture or house furnishings as possible out of ten blocks. The complete test was administered to professional artists, college art majors, and college students not majoring in art. The mean scores of both the professional artists and art majors were significantly higher than the mean scores of the college students not majoring in art. They displayed more creativity as measured by the test.

The steps in creative thinking. In various courses you may be assigned to write term papers. In laboratory or shop courses you may be asked to design new apparatus or tools. Later, you may have a job that requires you to devote some of your time to creative thinking. For example, you may be asked to prepare constructive reports and to preside at meetings in which plans and policies are discussed. Many individuals have found that the following four steps are helpful to all creative thinking.

1. *Preparation.* Preparation in creative thinking may be a very long process, possibly requiring weeks, months, or years. Although Einstein wrote his famous creative treatise on relativity in a few weeks, he had spent seven years in preparation for the writing. Such extended study is not possible in all creative work, but preparation does mean enough time for a "soaking-up" process. The individual reads widely, he may attend lectures, he talks with others interested in his problem, he strives to have personal experience in the field about which he is thinking. He often finds it useful to keep a card index of notes and lists of references. Undoubtedly he will follow some blind leads, since he will have such a mass of material that he can easily become confused. Such confusion should not be discouraging, however, for it seems to be a normal part of the process of creative thinking.

2. *Incubation.* After collecting many facts and opinions during the stage of preparation, creative thinkers usually find it helpful to put their work aside for a while and do something else, such as engaging in some recreational activity. They have their equipment at hand and they have at least a rough map of the road they are to follow. But before setting out on their journey, they consciously take time to permit their thinking to incubate.

The period of incubation is not a matter of resting because the individual is tired, discouraged, or bored. It is a definite step in the process of creative thinking. During this period of incubation, although the individual does not work on his problem, he may find himself thinking about it at odd times.

Albert Einstein often went through several steps in creative thinking before arriving at theories that revolutionized physics. Einstein's development of his "general" theory of relativity came as a flash of insight or inspiration only after many years of reflection.

An application to schoolwork should be noted here. All too often students leave the writing of term papers and other creative work until it is nearly time to hand the assignment in. They procrastinate. They do not complete the preparation stage early enough to allow for a period of incubation. The absence of this important step often causes their reports to be little more than jumbles of facts and opinions, representing only the preparation stage of the creative process.

3. *Inspiration.* There is nothing magical about inspiration as the term is used here. It is simply a rather sudden solution of a problem already studied. The thinker may not be able to trace the steps by which he has reached his solution, but his inspiration has followed preparation and incubation. There is a dropping out of irrelevant material, a seeing of new relationships. Often the new ideas come very rapidly and, although it is still difficult, thinking becomes enjoyable as the goal is neared.

The student who puts off all preparation of a report until the last minute may hope to have a sudden inspiration and be able to write a brilliant report, but he is doomed to disappointment. He is neglecting the first two essential steps in creative thinking. Unfortunately, some school assignments are of such a nature that the student merely collects facts in a routine manner without ever being required to see new relationships, without ever having the pleasant experience of inspiration.

4. *Verification and revision.* All too often the student is satisfied to stop with the step of inspiration—if he gets that far in his attempt at creative thinking. More work is needed, however. In scientific thinking, for example, the inspiration may have been incorrect or only partly correct. Objective data are necessary to confirm the correctness of the inspiration. The scientist will have to go to his laboratory and verify his hypothesis or theory by experimentation. He will have to add to his observations. He may need to read further about the thinking of others along similar lines, and then revise his thinking a number of times. A painter or author also needs to check and recheck his work to be sure that he has achieved the artistic effect he wanted. He is very likely to make at least minor changes as a result of this verification process.

The four distinct steps that seem to be necessary for creative thinking are difficult steps. The thinker who follows them can, however, look for the reward of knowing that he is out of the rut, that he has achieved something truly worthwhile.

Does "brainstorming" help creative thinking? BRAINSTORMING is a method of thinking in which an individual attempts to solve problems by listing all the possible solutions that occur to him, without attempting to evaluate them until some later time. In one experiment two groups of college students, matched on the basis of grades, age, and sex, acted as subjects. The following brainstorming instructions were given to the first group: "You are to list all the ideas that come to your mind, without judging them in any way. Forget about the quality of the ideas entirely. We will count only quantity on this task. Express any idea that comes to your mind. As you go along, you may combine or modify any of the ideas that you have already listed in order to produce additional ideas. Remember that quantity and freedom of expression without evaluation are the key points."

To the second group the instructions were: "You are to list all the good ideas you can think up. Your score will be the total number of good ideas. Don't put down any idea unless you feel it is a good one."

The results indicated that significantly more ideas of good quality were produced under brainstorming instructions than under nonbrainstorming instructions. Why? The men performing the experiment suggested that in the customary course of our thinking, we tend to inhibit ideas because we are afraid of criticism by others or even by ourselves. Brainstorming seems to reduce this fear and thereby encourages more ideas, including better ideas. Creative thinkers may make many false starts in the process of developing their ideas, but they successfully get out of the rut of everyday thinking.

Are we more likely to do superior creative thinking in groups or alone? A psychologist performed an experiment that enabled him to compare group performance and individual performance in a task involving creative thinking. His ninety-nine subjects included college students who were majoring in psychology or preparing to teach in elementary schools. The task assigned was to produce eight interesting and novel sentences for children just learning to read. Some subjects worked alone first and then in a group of three persons, others worked in a group first and then alone. All of them spent eighteen minutes working under each condition. As an added control, some subjects worked individually in both periods.

The subjects working in groups were told that they were to hand in only one report of sentences for their group. It was suggested that they might wish to use the technique of brainstorming. As an incentive, the subjects working in groups were told that they would receive $5.00 per person for the best group report, and $2.50 per person for the next best report. Subjects working alone were told that the individual turning in the best set of sentences would receive $10.00, and the individual with the next best set would receive $5.00.

The results showed that the groups performed at a level below that of the most creative individual in that group, but above that of the least creative individual in that group. The psychologist performing this experiment concluded that for maximum creative productivity it may be best to have individuals work alone.

Some characteristics of a creative person. From past experimental data psychologists know that some individuals are more creative than others. Because creative persons contribute a great deal to society, it is worth investigation to determine whether creative individuals have any behavior characteristics in common.

One way of determining characteristics of creative persons is to select a group of such persons and study them at length and in detail. Several different studies have shown that creative individuals are more flexible and more willing to analyze their own impulses than most people, have a good sense of humor, are independent in both thought and action, and prefer the complex to the ordinary. Such individuals also tend to devote less than the average amount of time to social behavior, perhaps because of the amount of time and energy that goes into their work. The important question, however, is whether they became creative and then developed the tendency to devote energy to work or whether they became creative as a result of strong dedication to and concentration on their work. Although we do not know the answer today, longitudinal studies examining creativity in young children and continuing to study them as they grow into adults may eventually discover the best conditions for promoting creativity.

Perhaps you are wondering why intelligence has not been listed as a major aspect of creativity. Although there is a positive relationship between the two, there is not much relationship over the entire range of intelligence. For individuals with high IQ's the relationship between creativity and intelligence is very small. It seems that motivation and personality are more important variables than intelligence in influencing creativity among individuals with high IQ's. Nevertheless, a basic level of superior intelligence seems to be necessary for creativity. There is very limited creativity in a school for retarded individuals.

Even though creative individuals do tend to have the characteristics described, you should be extremely hesitant about categorizing individuals one way or another. Simply because a person possesses the aspects described does not automatically make him creative, nor does a lack of such characteristics guarantee that he is not creative.

Imagining

Psychologists used to spend a great deal of time discussing whether thinking involved having images of one kind or another. They determined that most, if not all, individuals do have some imagery. A popular phrase used to describe imagery is "seeing with the mind's eye." Can you picture how the breakfast table looked this morning? Can you recall the sound of a very close friend's voice? Such images occur in normal thinking.

Eidetic images. Particularly vivid images are called eidetic (ī-'det-ik) images. An EIDETIC IMAGE is an image that is so vivid that it almost seems to the individual as if he is having a sensory experience, although he knows that he is not. The person with eidetic imagery is popularly said to have a "photographic mind." Some examples will clarify the term "eidetic imagery."

Studies of eidetic imagery are often conducted by showing a picture to subjects for a short length of time, such as thirty seconds or less. Then the picture is removed and the subject is asked to report on the details. The picture may contain an unusual word or a word in a foreign language. The subject with clear eidetic imagery will be able to spell the word both forward and backward. Why? He can "see it."

To test your eidetic imagery, observe this picture for 20 seconds, then close the book and see how accurately you can reproduce it.

One psychologist tells of a law student suspected of cheating on an examination. One of the questions on the examination asked for a detailed account of a law case given in the textbook. The student's answer to this question was a word-for-word reproduction of the case given in the textbook. The professor assumed that the student had had his textbook open during the examination, but the student denied the charge. He said that just before the examination he had looked over the case and then on the examination had been able to recall such a clear image of the page that he could reproduce it on the examination paper. Since the members of the faculty committee investigating the case were skeptical, they decided to test the student. He was given a page of unfamiliar material and permitted to study it for five minutes. At the end of that time the material was taken away and he was asked to reproduce it. He did so—writing some four hundred words without a single error. Even punctuation was exactly the same.

Eidetic imagery is most common in the visual field, but may occur in others. For example, a music teacher who was also a minor composer made it a rule not to use printed music material in his teaching. He simply wrote off on ruled paper the music he thought the student needed for practice. Once, while writing out music for a student, the teacher hesitated a minute or so and then went ahead with his writing. The student asked "Why did you stop, and what let you continue with your writing?" The reply was "I had forgotten just how that part went, but as soon as I heard the orchestra play it, I could write it for you."

How valuable is eidetic imagery? Eidetic imagery might be useful for examinations, but having such imagery is not necessarily a mark of superior intellectual ability. In fact, there is some evidence that persons who regularly engage in the highest and most abstract kind of thinking are not likely to use visual imagery. As you have grown older and have turned to more and more abstract thinking, you probably have less vivid imagery than you had as a child. Eidetic imagery is more common in children than in adults.

Psychologists believe that most individuals have at least some experiences involving images and that such images may be helpful in certain kinds of thinking. However, psychologists today tend to feel that images play a minor rather than a major role in thinking.

Imagination. The word "imagination" implies having images. But today psychologists do not stress this meaning of the word. To the psychologist IMAGINATION is the reproduction and reorganization of past experiences into a present ideational experience. We may imagine what we are going to do next week, next month, or a year from now, but the imagined future experiences are based on our past experiences. Television programs suggest what it will be like for man to live on some other planet. In these programs the conditions found on the other planet and the organisms living there are somewhat different from those on earth, but the influence of earthly experiences is clearly discernible. An eyewitness account of another planet may well indicate conditions beyond our wildest imagination.

Related to imagination is AUTISTIC THINKING, in which the individual remakes his world into a place that is more like the world in which he wishes to live than is his real world. In some cases the word FANTASY is used to describe imaginative and usually pleasant thinking in which the individual finds relief from his frustrations by living in a visionary world of his own. Daydreams are yet another form of imaginative thinking.

Reasoning

One main area of thinking is reasoning. In REASONING, a present problem is solved on the basis of general principles derived from at least two previous experiences. The new solution is not a mere reproduction of earlier solutions. It represents the adapting of earlier solutions to fit the present problem.

Although man is considered to have more ability to reason than lower animals, some psychologists have experimental evidence that animals can solve problems involving very simple reasoning. Other psychologists, however, are not sure that such thinking should be called reasoning. Therefore, we shall concentrate on experimental evidence based on human subjects.

How well do children reason? A psychologist carried out an experiment to determine to what extent a child could reason out how to reach a desired toy. The figure on page 102 is a simple version of the apparatus he used. A child could walk through the various pathways. Entrance to any pathway was from a booth partitioned off by curtains. For a first experience the child was permitted to explore the apparatus. Then he was removed through the exit to pathway Y. Next he was taken around the outside of the apparatus to the booth permitting entrance to pathway W. There he encountered a toy windmill that would play a tune, much to the delight of the child. This was his second experience.

The child was then taken to the booth permitting entrance to pathway X and told to find the windmill. Note that he could not go directly to the windmill without combining his first and second experiences—knowledge of the apparatus and knowledge of where the windmill was. It was found that with increasing age came greater ability to do this

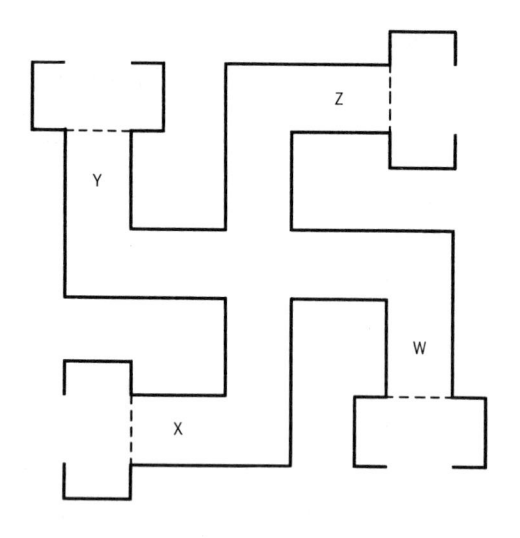

Apparatus to test children's reasoning ability

simple kind of reasoning. In some of his experiments the psychologist found that the percentage of children who could combine such isolated experiences increased from about 20 percent at four years of age to 71 percent at six years of age. By eight years, 100 percent of the children could do this kind of reasoning.

How well do college students reason? In another experiment conducted by the psychologist just mentioned, 384 college students in elementary psychology classes were used as subjects. The psychologist was interested in learning whether instruction in how to reason would improve the solution of problems involving reasoning—that is, would there be transfer?

The students were given three kinds of problems to solve, of which only one will be described here. A string was fastened to the ceiling and was of such length that the end came to the top of a stationary table in the room. Another string, six feet in length, was fastened to the wall six feet above the floor. The problem was to tie the two strings together. Conditions were so arranged that when the subject held one of the strings, he could not reach the other. Several solutions were demonstrated, one of them being to tie one of the strings to a chair halfway between the two positions. However, the students were not permitted to use this answer or any version of it in their solutions. Available in the room were such materials as washers, pliers, bolts, and chalk. How would you have solved the problem?

The students were divided into two groups. The control group went to work on the problem without any suggestions on how to reason. The experimental group was given a lecture on reasoning. On the string problem there was very little difference in percentages of correct solutions by the two groups. (The desired solution was to convert one of the strings into a pendulum by means of a weight available in the room.) For the experiment as a whole, however, the mean percent of correct solutions by the control group was 39.7, for the experimental group 49.2. The instruction in how to reason seemed to have made a difference.

In the above experiment it was assumed that the two groups were equal in general ability, an assumption that might or might not have been correct. In a refinement of the experiment, 169 students were given problems in different orders, which permitted the same students to serve in both control and experimental groups. The data of this experiment revealed that the lecture on reasoning about doubled the successes.

You might like to try one of the problems in that part of the experiment. On page 103 are three rows of three dots each. Your problem is to pass through each of the dots with four straight lines without lifting your pencil from

• • •

• • •

• • •

the paper and without retracing any line. (Copy the dots and do the exercise on a piece of paper. The solution is on p. 111.)

Inductive and deductive reasoning. Reasoning is often described in terms of two types—inductive reasoning and deductive reasoning. To understand these two types of reasoning, we can use a hypothetical experiment on the relation between insufficient sleep and low exam grades. INDUCTIVE REASONING moves from specific cases to general principles. The thinker discovers common characteristics in otherwise separate and unique events. For example, suppose that before formulating his hypothesis, the psychologist noticed that students who were tired when they came to an exam seemed to score low grades on it, even though they were prepared. He might then reason inductively from the specific cases of low-scoring students being tired to the general principle that insufficient sleep caused the students to make low scores.

On the other hand, the psychologist may have arrived at his hypothesis by DEDUCTIVE REASONING, in which the thinking moves from general principles to specific cases or consequences. The psychologist may have begun with the general principle that people who are tired are less efficient than are those who are not tired. He then may have deduced that in the specific cases where students are tired they will not perform well on exams, even when prepared for them.

In our daily problem solving we seldom reason a problem through by using only the inductive or only the deductive method. We change from one form to the other and back again many times as we think through our problems.

Computer vs. Human Thinking

Can machines think? A can opener is a machine, but few people would suggest that a can opener can think. An ordinary typewriter is a machine that can be used in thinking and communication, but we wouldn't say that a typewriter can think for itself. Don't depend on a typewriter to write term papers for you. On the other hand, modern high-speed computers are machines that can assist man in his thinking so much that we may be tempted to say they can think. Popularly, but not scientifically, such machines are sometimes referred to as "electronic brains."

Computers can solve many complex problems. However, computers are not organisms. On page 88 we defined thinking as an activity of organisms. We have seen that animals can think. Unlike computers, animals have a body structure, including a nervous system much like man's. It has been said that at present even our largest computers are not nearly as complex as the brain of a chicken.

What do computers do? There are two basic kinds of computers. One kind counts by means of digits or exact numbers and is called a *digital computer*. An example of a very simple digital computer is the abacus. It dates back to the days of the Greeks and Romans and is still found in Oriental countries. It is used in some American schools to teach children about numbers. Other examples include the adding machine and the cash register. Modern digital computers can solve extremely difficult problems at a very high speed.

A second kind is the *analogue computer,* which is basically a measuring device. Your watch is an analogue computer measuring the passage of time. A thermometer is an analogue computer that measures temperature by the height of a liquid in a tube. The analogue computers that scientists use are much more complex than these examples and rely on the computer programs that scientists design to measure and solve particular problems.

Persons in the computer field now speak of a third kind of computer that combines digital and analogue operations.

How do human thinking and computer "thinking" compare? You may remember from Chapter 3 that psychological feedback, or knowledge of results, is important in learning. In the computer field FEEDBACK, or the process of a given bit of activity modifying subsequent activity, is essential to computer "thinking." Both man and electronic computers use feedback to help solve problems.

Suppose you think, "This room in which I am working has become too warm." You turn a regulator on your furnace. As the temperature in the room drops, you begin to feel uncomfortably cool, so you regulate the furnace again but in the opposite direction. You have had feedback, which you have used to

This shows the insides of a computer, the complex wiring and connections that make the capabilities of a computer so extensive. The inside of a human brain is even more complex, containing numerous nerve cells, making contacts constantly, and enabling human beings to think.

help solve the problem of regulating the room temperature.

Now suppose you have a thermostat on the wall. You set it for what you have decided is a desirable temperature. If the temperature rises above this point, the thermostat has feedback indicating that the room is warmer than the desired temperature. It operates to turn down the furnace. As soon as the temperature in the room falls below the desired degree, the thermostat has feedback and turns up the furnace. The thermostat performs the same operations that you performed when you turned the furnace regulator up or down. Would you say the thermostat was "thinking"?

In industry, formerly, complex machines were operated by the thinking and skills of highly trained mechanics. Today electronic computers can feed various messages into such machines so that the machines turn out the desired products.

One great advantage that an electronic computer has over man is that it never "forgets" what has been fed into it and is still properly stored in it. Also, a computer can combine its "thoughts" in new and complex ways at a very rapid rate. An expert chess player can feed the intricacies of chess combinations into a computer. Afterward, when the expert and the computer play a game of chess, the computer is likely to win.

Simple and complex machines can aid man in his thinking, and may be able to do "thoughtlike" tasks in a very short time as compared to the time required for man to perform the same tasks. Electronic computers seem to be giving us a better idea of how man thinks, and even how his central nervous system operates, than we had before the development of such machines. On the other hand, it takes man with his very complex nervous system to build and feed programs into and then analyze data obtained from high-speed electronic computers.

The scientific study of the regulation and control of information, whether found in machines, individual persons, or social groups, is called CYBERNETICS. Some cyberneticists have even suggested that man is basically an information transmitter, and that man's intellectual ability rests on the amount of information that is fed into him. Would you agree?

Applying Principles of Learning to Taking Examinations

By this time in your school career you are quite familiar with taking examinations. They are part of the learning process. Undoubtedly you have had to answer both essay questions and objective examinations in the past, and probably will again in the future. Below are a few suggestions to aid you in taking both types of examinations.

Essay questions. Essay-type examinations give you an opportunity to recall and write down in an organized fashion what you have learned.

1. Be sure to do what is asked. Some examination questions ask the student to explain, summarize, compare, critically evaluate, trace, define, or prove some point. Follow the instructions. If told to define, do not merely illustrate. If told to compare, do not merely explain one part.

2. Read all questions first, before beginning to answer any. Otherwise you may waste time bringing out a point in one answer that should be brought out in another. As you read over the questions, jot down any points that you want to include in any given answer, since under the pressure of the examination you may not think of the point again until after you have handed in your paper.

3. *Outline* an answer, at least in your thinking, before beginning to write it. Otherwise you are likely to ramble, breaking one of the rules of good English composition.

4. *Use technical terms*—provided you know their meanings. They express ideas more clearly than nontechnical terms.

5. *Leave space at the end of each answer.* You should reread your examination paper before handing it in. When you do so, a point may occur to you that you wish to include. Put it in the space left for such an emergency rather than in the margin or between lines.

6. *Apply the rules of grammar,* spelling, and punctuation to any subject field in which you are writing.

Objective examinations. Objective questions may seem easier than essay questions because they require recognition rather than pure recall. Studies have shown, however, that there is usually a great similarity between grades on essay and objective examinations.

1. *Mark answers clearly.* Follow directions. A statement marked "True" that you meant to be "False" can only be considered incorrect. On examinations scored by stencils or by machine, answers not clearly indicated according to the directions are counted as omitted. If you wish to change an answer, be sure that you erase the old answer thoroughly.

2. *Check lightly any answers that you are uncertain of.* Later you can go back and either verify or change your answers. Questions answered in the meantime may have helped to clear up these previously doubtful answers.

3. *Be careful in answering true-false or yes-no questions.* There are various ways of scoring answers to such questions. Sometimes the student is simply scored on the number of correct answers. Sometimes his score is the number of correct minus the number of incorrect responses. (This method of scoring is designed to discourage guessing.) Try to find out how true-false and yes-no answers are to be scored, and govern your answering of doubtful questions accordingly.

4. *Watch for sweeping generalizations.* In true-false questions, especially in the social sciences, statements containing such terms as "always," "never," "invariably," "without question," "everyone," and "no one" are likely to be false.

Sweeping statements are usually false because there are so many points that are still uncertain. On the other hand, questions containing such terms as "there is some evidence that," "some authorities say that," "generally," "frequently," and "sometimes" are likely to be true. Watching for such terms may help you in answering doubtful questions. Nevertheless, a guide such as this is no substitute for accurate and thorough knowledge.

5. *Read the directions carefully when answering multiple-choice questions.* You may be instructed to choose just one of the several answers given. Or you may be directed to select the two or possibly more best answers. In either case, be sure to note the directions. To give more answers than the instructions indicate will mean that the answers will be counted as incorrect, even though they may include the correct answers.

When you take an objective test, such as a test with multiple-choice questions (shown here), it is usually better to first answer all the questions that you are sure of, and then to go back and fill in those answers you need to ponder.

A multiple-choice question may seem hopeless at first glance. If, however, you begin by checking off any answers that are clearly incorrect, you will limit the choices. You will run a much better chance of giving the correct answer than if you try to choose from all the answers given.

6. *Be systematic when answering matching questions.* In answering matching questions you should work down one column looking for matches in the other column. Random looking around in hopes of finding matches is an inefficient use of time and is confusing. It is better to mark those matches that you are certain of and to fill in lightly those that you have some doubts about. Eventually you may be able to make all matches correctly, even though at first the question seemed very difficult.

7. *Change answers if you are sure you made a mistake.* Frequently the question is asked, "Should you change answers, or is the first impression more likely to be correct?" If the first answer has been just a guess, the

THE PROCESS OF THINKING **107**

first impression will probably have a slight advantage. But you should not hesitate to change answers if you believe you have made an error. One psychologist studied 28,000 answers on true-false and multiple-choice questions. He found that the majority of students raised their scores by changing answers that they believed to be incorrect. Only one-fourth of them lowered their scores by making such changes. Do not change answers just to be changing them, hoping that luck will be on your side. But do not hesitate to make changes if you have reason to do so.

8. *Budget your time.* In answering objective questions remember that all answers will probably have the same value in the total score. There is some virtue in working out the answer to a difficult question. In an examination, however, it is foolish to spend so much time on one question that you do not get to twenty-five or thirty others that you could have answered readily and correctly. Also, save a little time to go back over the questions and clear up doubtful points or complete uncertain answers.

We have already stressed the importance of psychological feedback—knowledge of results. Check over your errors on examinations and learn why certain answers were incorrect or insufficient. Otherwise you may never clear up incorrect impressions.

Terms to Know

all-or-nothing thinking
autistic thinking
"brainstorming"
concept
creative thinking
cybernetics

deductive reasoning
delusion
eidetic image
explicit behavior
fantasy
feedback
imagination

implicit behavior
inductive reasoning
reasoning
symbol
thinking
uncritical thinking

Topics to Think About

1. If you were a teacher, how would you go about getting students to think, instead of just memorizing facts? What kinds of thinking would you emphasize the most?

2. Can individuals really think in more than one language? What evidence do you have for your answer?

3. To what extent do politicians make their appeals through truly critical thinking?

4. Can computers take over the thinking that man has been doing for centuries? What would be the advantages and disadvantages?

5. Which are better measuring devices, objective or essay exam questions? Why?

6. How can you teach individuals to be creative? What conditions would promote creativity? inhibit creativity? Consider conditions within a home, classroom, job, country, and the world in general.

7. Do you consider the works of Pablo Picasso to be creative art? Why?

Suggestions for Activities

1. The following activity (suggested by Dr. Paul J. Woods in APA's *Periodically*, April 30, 1971) will give you an idea of the kind of "thinking" that a computer does. Arrange your desks or chairs in rows. The first student in each row is to compose a sentence and then select one word from the sentence that becomes his or her word. The student will then write on a card the one word that *follows* his or her word in the sentence, and pass the card to the next student in the row. The second student will then compose a sentence using the word he received and pass on to the third student in the row the word in his sentence *following* the word he received from the first student. Continue the process to the end of the row.

Record on the chalkboard the word received by some designated student—for example, it might be the fifth student in each row. Then for each row the teacher will write on the board a "sentence" constructed of the words each student received, in the sequence that the words were passed. Do any meaningful sentences begin to emerge?

The activity can be varied by having each student pass on the two words following the word he received. You may even wish to try passing on three words. Do you find that the more words that are passed on, the greater is the coherence of the sentences?

2. Some members of the class might present a short play in pantomime. Is such symbolization as efficient as word symbols in conveying ideas?

3. Arrange to listen in on various children's conversations for short periods of time, say five minutes. Record everything that is said. If available, a tape recorder will make the job easier. How many different words did each child use? Did older children use more words than younger children? Were there any examples of questionable or incorrect usages of words? Report your findings to the class.

4. You may wish to arrange to take the *Watson-Glaser Critical Thinking Appraisal* (published by Harcourt Brace Jovanovich). It measures five aspects of the ability to think critically: to draw sound inferences from a statement of facts; to recognize assumptions implied by a statement; to reason logically by deduction; to reason logically by interpretation; to discriminate between strong and weak arguments. The test can be completed in a fifty-minute class period.

5. Read a newspaper editorial and analyze it—perhaps an editorial concerned with some political problem. On the whole, is the editorial sound? Are there any evidences of uncritical thinking?

6. Bring to class examples of newspaper or magazine advertising for household cleansers, toothpastes, cola drinks, alcoholic beverages, and aspirins. Note such advertising on radio and television. Are the statements in the advertising justified on the basis of scientifically determined facts? Do advertisers sometimes use language to induce uncritical thinking on the part of the public?

7. Present the following to someone who is not taking this course:

All A is B.
All C is B.
Therefore, some C is A.

Ask the person if, according to the statements, the conclusion is true. To show that it is not true on the basis of the premises alone, show the person the following diagram.

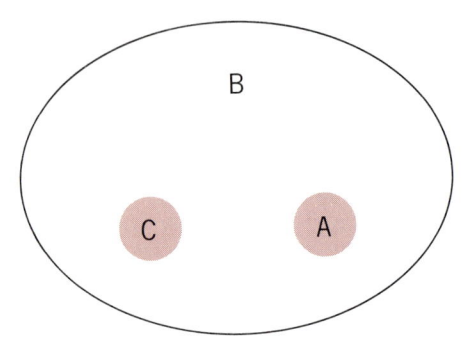

From the diagram it can been that B is only something that A and C share in common with each other. The conclusion stated above is, therefore, incorrect.

8. Have one student demonstrate inductive reasoning in geometry. Have another student demonstrate deductive reasoning in geometry. Can you give examples of such reasoning in literature? What sort of reasoning is demonstrated in Poe's tale *The Gold-Bug?*

9. Make a study of Jean Piaget's theories describing the stages of concept development that children go through. Then read A. A. Milne's *Winnie-the-Pooh,* a famous children's story, and see how many aspects of Piaget's levels of concept development are illustrated by the behavior of the characters in the story.

Suggestions for Further Reading

Brown, A. E., and H. A. Jeffcott, Jr., *Absolutely Mad Inventions,* Dover Publications. A humorous paperback originally published in 1932, based on records of inventions from the United States Patent Office. You may wonder about the creative thinking involved in some of the inventions.

Hilgard, E. R., R. C. Atkinson, and Rita Atkinson, *Introduction to Psychology,* 5th ed., Harcourt Brace Jovanovich, See Chapter 11, "Language and Thought."

Kagan, J., M. M. Haith, and Catherine Caldwell (eds.), *Psychology: Adapted Readings,* Harcourt Brace Jovanovich. See Selection 12, "Teaching Sign Language to a Chimpanzee"; Selection 13, "How Shall a Thing Be Called?"; and Selection 14, "Toward a Theory of Creativity."

Kagan, J., and E. Havemann, *Psychology: An Introduction,* 2nd ed., Harcourt Brace Jovanovich. See Chapter 5, which takes up such topics as the importance of language, concepts, thinking, and problem solving.

Psychology Today: An Introduction, CRM Books. See Chapter 20, "Problem Solving."

Ruch, Floyd L., and Philip G. Zimbardo, *Psychology and Life,* 8th ed., Scott, Foresman. See Chapter 8, "To Think, To Reason, To Create."

Wertheimer, M., et al., *Psychology: A Brief Introduction,* Scott, Foresman. See pages 66–67, 112–13, on conflicts in thinking and concept formation.

Answer to symbols on page 88. Shapes: triangular traffic signs are for danger; circular signs for driving instruction; rectangular for information. Drawings: ∾ sign indicates curves; line through horn means horn blowing is prohibited; P signifies authorized parking; walking figure means pedestrian crossing.

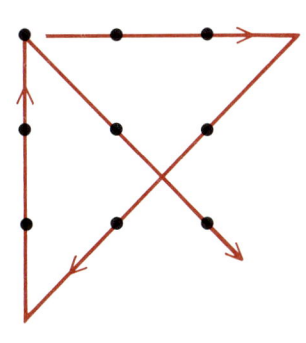

Answer to problem on page 103. If you are unable to solve this problem, was it because you thought only in terms of keeping all your lines within the area bordered by the dots? The instructions did not make this a requirement.

HOW MUCH SHOULD WE CONTROL OUR ENVIRONMENT?

When you have children, would you be willing to raise them in a "Skinner box" (like the one shown on page 39)? This "box," invented by Dr. B. F. Skinner, a professor of psychology at Harvard University and one of the leading psychologists in the world today, is not the same as the apparatus he used for his laboratory work with rats and pigeons. Dr. Skinner referred to this "box" as an "air crib." He raised his daughter, Deborah, in it for about two and a half years. The air crib was glassed in so Deborah could see all that was going on in the room, just as she would in a more conventional playpen. Since the temperature was automatically controlled, the baby could be naked in the crib and thus avoid the usual movement restrictions of clothing and blankets. Furthermore, she was not subject to diaper rash. The air in the crib was filtered so that she was not exposed to germs.

Despite the many advantages of the air crib, the public did not accept it. Many people were horrified that anyone, especially a psychologist, would raise his own baby in such a mechanical contraption. All kinds of dire predictions were made about the effects of the "box" on the child. The critics overlooked the fact that Deborah was frequently taken from the air crib so that she could be cuddled and played with. She knew parental love, just as other babies do who are raised in more conventional cribs, and certainly more than babies raised under conditions in which there is very little love. Now as an adult, Deborah says she considers that she had a happy babyhood.

Although the public has not adopted it, the air crib is still active in the Skinner family. Deborah's sister, Julie, is using a modern version with her daughter, Justine—Dr. Skinner's granddaughter. This "box" is enclosed with clear plexiglass. The air temperature is thermostatically controlled so that Justine sleeps in only a diaper and undershirt. Justine spends as much or as little time in the "box" as she would in an ordinary crib.

The air crib is only one of Skinner's many accomplishments. It is but one of Skinner's applications of his principles of operant conditioning to human use. Another example that has stirred public controversy is his best-selling book *Beyond Freedom and Dignity,* in which Dr. Skinner discusses the need for making use of the psychological principles of operant conditioning and positive reinforcement to shape human behavior in our society. Skinner claims that since our environment determines our behavior, we should control the environment of everyone in our society to produce the behavior needed for survival.

Do you agree with Dr. Skinner that environmental conditioning determines our behavior? Can you think of ways in which you use, or could use, operant conditioning to improve your life and help solve the problems of our society?

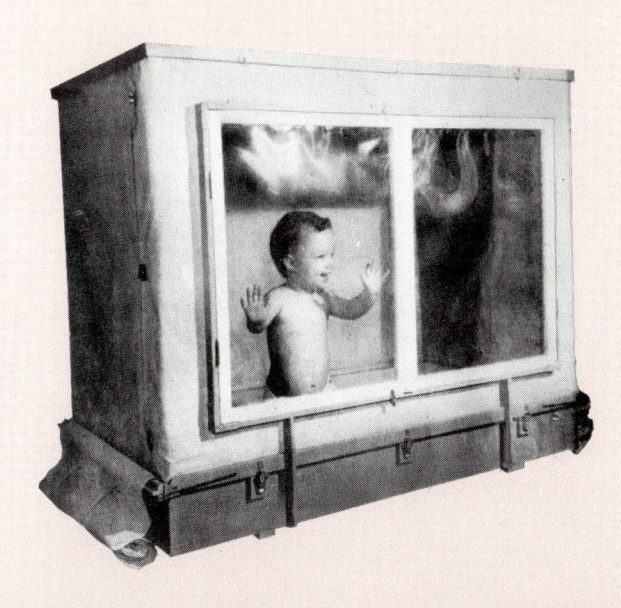

unit 3

UNDERSTANDING HUMAN BEHAVIOR

chapter 5   Understanding personality

chapter 6   How behavior develops

chapter 7   Measuring intellectual ability

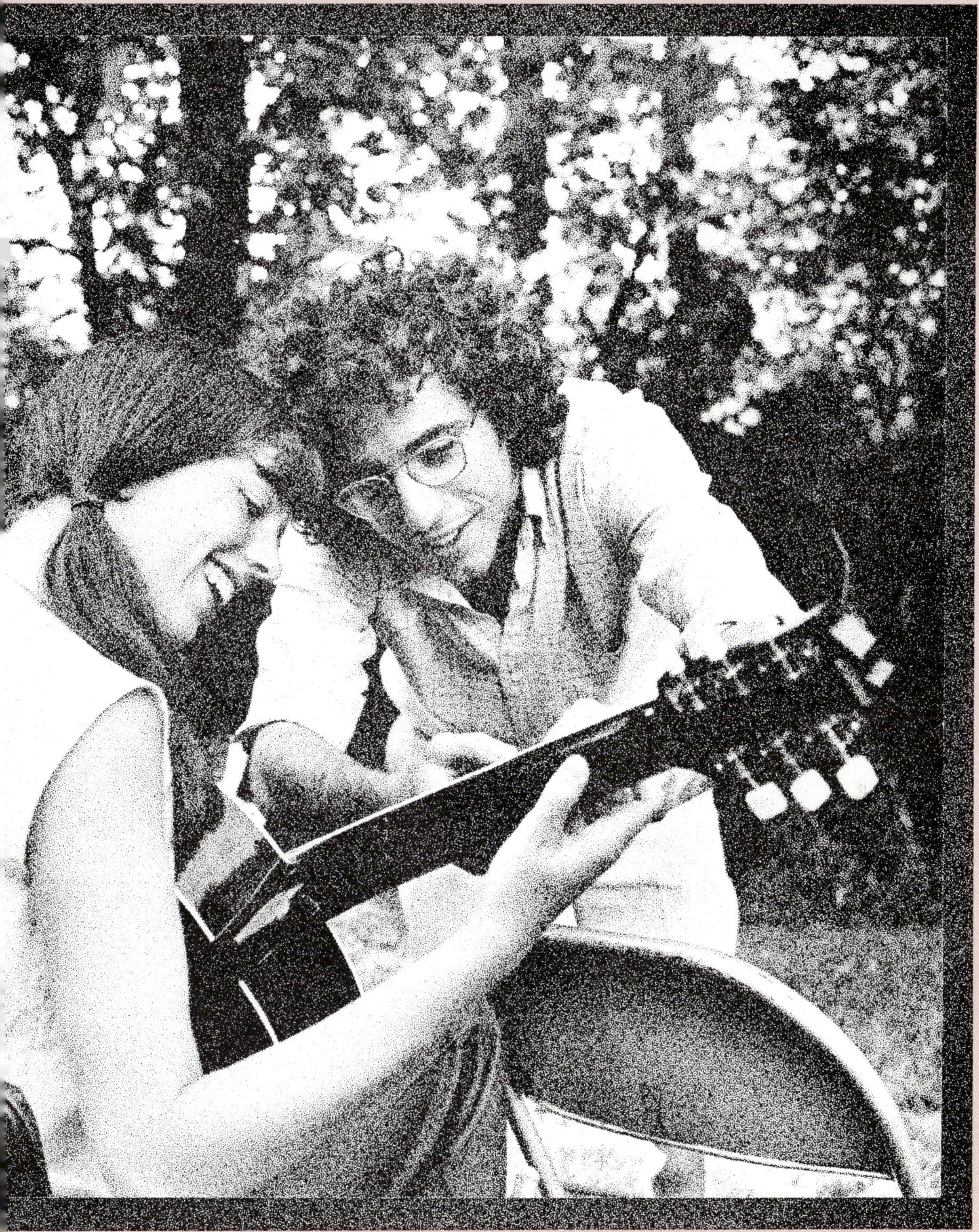

chapter 5
Understanding Personality

MANY WORDS in our language are used vaguely in everyday speech. Yet to psychologists these terms have definite, scientific meanings. The word "personality" is an example. What is the popular use of this term, and how does it differ from the scientific meaning?

The popular concept of personality. In the popular view personality is a wonderful quality we all want to have. The ambition of many Americans is to possess a "winning" or "charming" or "dynamic" personality. Unfortunately, not everyone—so goes the mistaken popular view—has this almost magical advantage.

Advertising has helped formulate the concept of personality that many people hold. Magazines, television, and newspapers run some advertisements in the form of romantic picture stories. Scene 1—A pretty girl is sitting at home, crying. She has no boyfriends, no social life, no date for the big dance. Scene 2—A friend drops a hint, or the girl overhears two friends talking in the next room. Scene 3—The girl is brushing her teeth with "Dento" toothpaste, washing her hair with "Sudso" shampoo, eating "Atomic" vitamin pills, or covering her face with "Madame X's Skin Revitalizer." Scene 4—The girl, greatly cheered up and wearing a new outfit, is surrounded by handsome young men. They always look like movie stars, and they want nothing so much as to dance with the girl. Now she is popular because her skin is clear, her hair is shiny, she has a sparkling smile and boundless energy. In short, she has "personality." Advertising asks us to believe that we can buy personality—in a large, economy-size bottle from the corner drugstore.

The psychological definition of personality. Actually, "personality" is difficult to define, and psychologists vary somewhat in their definitions. It may be said, however, that PERSONALITY is the sum total of an individual's reactions to his environment as determined by his perceptions and his reactions to his perceptions. Personality is, therefore, the unique or individual pattern of a person's life. It is the fundamental organization of an individual's characteristic attitudes toward others, his habits of thought and ways of expression, his interests and ambitions, his plan of life, and his attitude toward life in general. It is an error to think of personality as one quality that some persons have and others lack. Everyone has a pattern of life and reacts to his environment, and therefore everyone has a personality.

Perhaps you have noted that we have not used the word "character" in connection with personality. It is a popular word referring to the general moral and ethical outlook and the social conduct of an individual. Psychologists are concerned about such aspects of life, but they include them under the general term "personality."

The Development of Personality

How does personality develop? How do our patterns of behavior build up? There are no simple answers to these questions. Personality is very complex, and many factors, such as intellectual ability, biological foundations of heredity, and certain anatomical and physiological factors, influence its development. Since we discuss these factors in other chapters, here we will mention briefly some additional factors in the development of personality.

The early years of life are very important to the development of personality. Even during the first few weeks of life, infants differ in their

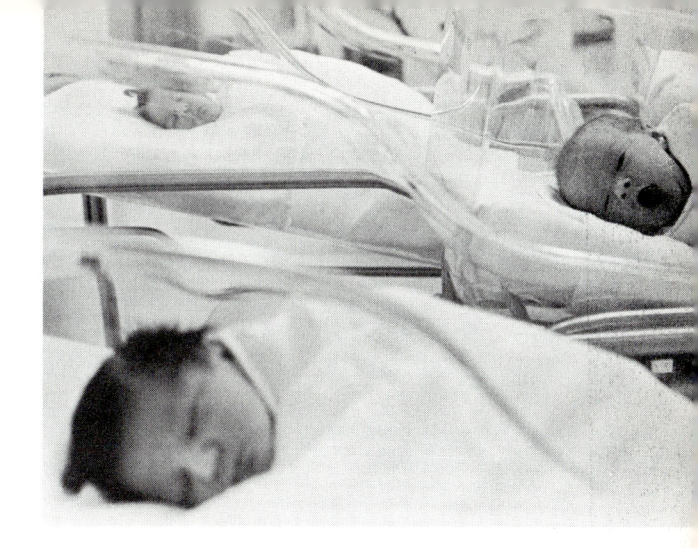

Immediately after birth children begin to show differences in behavior. These infants already have developed individual reactions—some sleep more than others; some are more active.

behavior (although such differences are primarily biologically determined). For example, some will cry, others will not cry; some infants are active, others are more passive. Distinctive patterns of adjusting to the environment are seen by the fourth month of life or slightly later. During the first half of the first year of life, behavior starts to become individualized as the infant reacts to food, clothing, light, dark, and so on. The child begins to show that complex pattern called "personality." There is evidence that personality patterns established in the early years of a child's life usually persist into adult years, although the way in which these personality patterns are expressed may change, and experiences in later life, such as contacts in business, organizations, and clubs, can greatly modify them.

How does the home affect personality? In America the home plays a major role in the development of personality because basic foundations of personality are laid down early in life, and most of the child's early life is spent in the home. Different home environments produce different personalities. Some parents constantly tell their children what they must not do, rather than showing them what they should do. Such repressive treatment by parents may have undesirable effects, causing the child to be defiant or to withdraw from contacts with other people or to live in a world of daydreams. Some parents make nearly all the decisions for their children, while others give children an opportunity to make decisions for themselves. What clothes the child wears each day or whether he eats oatmeal or cornflakes for breakfast is not important. But it is very important for the child to develop habits of making decisions. Such habits are basic to the development of a personality marked by independence.

Affection in the home has a strong bearing on the personality development of children. By affection in the home we mean the degree to which children feel free to confide their problems to their parents, the degree to which parents are interested in and recognize the work and play of the children, and the degree to which there is mutual sharing of work and play in the family. In one psychological study a group of ten-year-old children were asked to rate the degree of affection in their family relations. It was found that children who had indicated that there was a great deal of genuine affection in their family relations tended to be responsible and honest in their social relationships, whereas children from homes with little family affection were more likely to be irresponsible and dishonest.

How does the order of his birth in the family affect a child's personality? Psychological studies of the personalities of children in various ORDINAL POSITIONS (that is, the order in which the children were born) have failed to indicate that birth order establishes a biological effect on the kind of personality that a child develops. A child's ordinal position in a family does, however, alter the circumstances under which he is reared. For example, the first-born child is an only child for some period of time, while the second-born child is reared from birth with another sibling. Such differing circumstances do contribute to differing personality patterns. One study has indicated that the older child in a two-child family tends to be serious, shy, and oriented toward adults, while the younger child tends to be cheerful, easy-going, and less studious than his older sibling.

Other studies have consistently shown a relationship between birth order in a family and certain other variables. For example, eminent individuals are more likely to have been first-born, or the eldest, children. Also, an overproportionate number of first-born children are likely to go to college, and an even larger percentage will go on to graduate school. Both male and female first-born have been found to be more socially conforming than later-born children; and first-born females, when fearful, desire the company of others more strongly than do later-born females.

How does his society influence an individual's personality? At first, a child learns something of his society through his home life. Then, as he grows older, he has more and more social contacts outside the home. His personality development is shaped by his contacts in the schoolroom, on the playground, in a church, synagogue or temple, and in play activities with children in the neighborhood. Through his home and social contacts he gradually learns what is expected of him as a member of the society in which he lives. The social group in which the child is reared will help him learn ways of behaving that are accepted by his society. To understand an individual's behavior we must also understand the society in which the child is reared.

Perhaps we can get a good idea of how much a society influences personality by looking at some ways in which societies, or large groups of people who share common traits, customs, or ways of behaving, may differ from one another.

In some societies of the world, such as the Balinese, orthodox Hindu, and Hopi Indians, we do not find the striving for financial success that is characteristic of many people in the United States. In some societies an individual's lifework is determined by the occupational group into which he is born— if he is born a farmer's son, he will be a farmer. Societies may differ from one another in a multitude of ways, such as the amount of emphasis they place on individual achievement, the worth and rights of the individual, education, marriage, standards of individual achievement, and money or material wealth. The types of achievement stressed and the amount of emphasis that a particular society puts on them help determine the personalities of the members.

There are also differences among social groups within a society. The standards of these social groups can influence personality development. The personalities of members of different social groups often reflect the differences in standards and values set by their groups.

In summary, remember that personality is determined by the home in which the person is reared, as well as the social group with which he associates and the society in which he is raised. If you had been reared in a different society and a different geographical setting, you might have a quite different personality.

Some Theories of Personality

Over the years, as psychologists have sought to learn about personality, they have introduced a number of theories to explain its nature. Before examining these, however, we will briefly look at how some people develop their own informal personality theories.

Informal personality theories. There are many groups of people who react to an individual by sizing him up on the basis of subtle clues and then fitting him into a specific classification. These classification systems are used to get other people to do something. However, they are not recognized as formal, scientific personality theories.

Informal theories are based on empirical evidence—the knowledge of personality has been learned from observations and experiences. Individuals obtain information about a given person and then attempt, on the basis of this information, to come to certain conclusions about that person. For example, a fortune-teller, by looking at a wedding band on a young woman's finger, might consider that she has problems with her husband, finances, or children—common problem areas of a young married woman. The fortune-teller may begin by stating that the young woman has problems—as all people do. By watching for specific clues, such as a frown, the eyelids opening wider, a smile, or tears, and using such clues to guide what to say, the fortune-teller can arrive at certain conclusions about the person.

Police interrogators may look for clues to obtain information about the personality of a subject, which they use in deciding how to handle the person. For example, from clues they may decide that a youthful first offender would be susceptible to hearing how much his

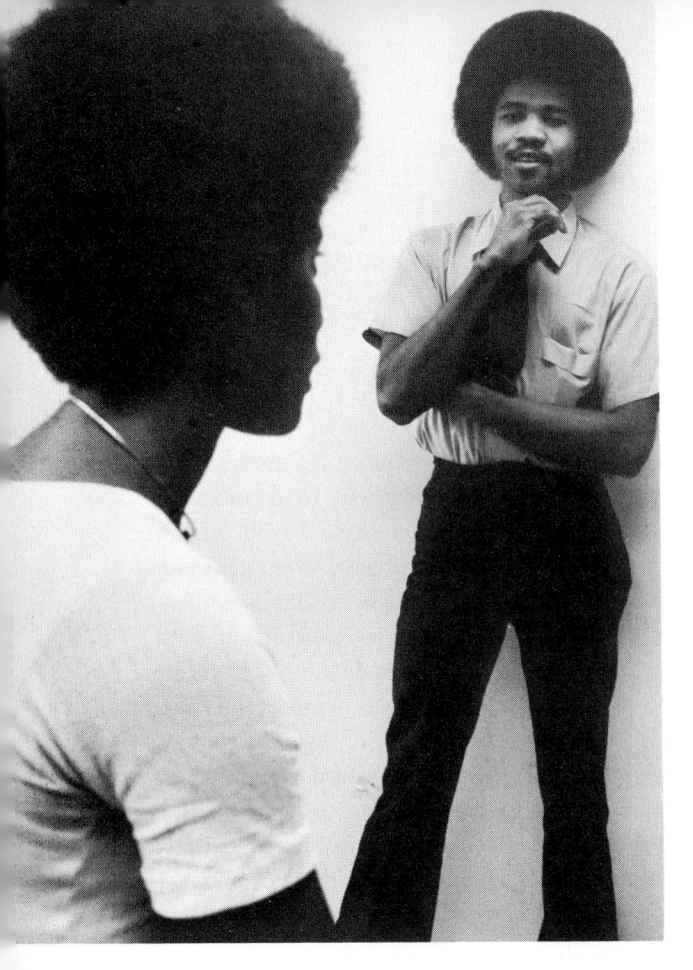

Do you have ways of judging people you first meet—ways of deciding what sort of personality they have and how to approach them?

family will be hurt by his actions, a timid person may be approached by friendliness, and a disinterested person may be flattered to give him a feeling of importance.

Other groups of individuals, such as doctors, lawyers, politicians, salesmen, and teachers, whose primary job depends on getting someone else to do something, also use these same techniques. They usually try several different approaches with people, discarding those techniques that do not seem to work and retaining those that succeed.

These are all ways in which different persons use their own informal personality theories to describe and handle others. We will now consider some theories advanced by psychologists.

The trait theory of personality. A TRAIT is a more or less permanent pattern of behavior. Traits are categories of an individual's personality that can be observed, described, and measured. Therefore, we can use traits to indicate similarities and differences between people.

One study has shown that the English language includes approximately 18,000 terms, mostly adjectives, which describe what might be called traits of personality. There is much overlapping in meaning among these terms.

One trait theory, based on statistical analysis, speaks of PRIMARY TRAITS—traits that are characteristic of most individuals in a society. There are about a dozen of these primary personality traits. Each trait is usually expressed as a pair of words of opposite meaning. The trait is described in terms of two extremes, and individuals are scored on a scale somewhere in between the two extremes, depending on the degree to which they have the particular trait. Examples of some primary personality traits are: (1) easygoing, genial, friendly *vs.* inflexible, hostile, suspicious; (2) intelligent, independent, thoughtful *vs.* foolish, frivolous, slipshod; (3) emotionally stable, realistic, patient *vs.* evasive, emotionally changeable, unrealistic; and (4) dominant, self-assertive, headstrong *vs.* submissive, self-effacing, sensitive.

The introvert-extrovert theory. An early theory of personality that persists today, at least in popular thinking and generally without the sanction of psychologists, is one originated by the Swiss psychiatrist Carl Jung (yủng). He classified persons as introverts or extroverts. By INTROVERTS, he meant those people who respond primarily to internally oriented stimuli, such as their own ideas and inner thoughts. By EXTROVERTS he meant those people who respond primarily to external stimuli, such as ideas from others and social situations.

Psychologists have made up lists of activities, interests, and attitudes that reflect introversion and extroversion. Among the traits considered characteristic of introversion are being hurt easily, daydreaming frequently, blushing often, keeping in the background on social occasions, suffering from stage fright, showing reluctance about making friends (especially with the opposite sex), worrying over possible misfortune, being unable to make decisions, being critical of others, showing excessive concern over gossip, taking meticulous care of personal property, responding excessively to praise.

Traits considered characteristic of extroversion are not being hurt easily, seldom daydreaming, making friends easily, being the "life of the party," being free from excessive worrying, laughing frequently and easily, preferring oral reports rather than written reports, accepting orders from others as a matter of course, preferring work involving social contacts rather than confining details, avoiding indulgence in self-pity, being a good loser.

Some psychologists have tried to break down introversion-extroversion into several independent traits, such as social introversion-extroversion, emotional introversion-extroversion, and intellectual introversion-extroversion. Other psychologists question whether we should even think of extroversion and introversion as extremes of the same dimension of personality. For instance, there is some evidence that extroversion and introversion may be expressed differently in men and women. Certainly the two terms must be used with great care.

Neo-Freudian theories. Several psychologists have accepted some of Freud's basic psychoanalytic concepts but developed personality theories that place more emphasis than Freud's did on man's relationship to his social environment. Such theorists are sometimes called neo-Freudians. One of the earliest was Alfred Adler (1870–1937). In contrast to Freud's belief that man is motivated by inborn tendencies, Adler believed that man is motivated by external sources—urges arising from within the social environment.

Others include psychoanalysts Karen Horney ('hȯr-nī) and Erich Fromm, and the American psychiatrist Harry Stack Sullivan, all of whom stressed the importance of social situations and factors external to man himself in developing personality. For instance, Harry Stack Sullivan (1892–1949) thought that personality cannot be isolated from interpersonal situations, from contacts with other people. These are the only aspects that can be adequately studied. He believed that it is through personal interactions with significant persons in our environment that learning occurs and our personality develops.

Experimental theories. Several men prominent in personality theory have attempted to reconcile Freudian theory with learning theory. Both theories emphasize the reduction of tension and the importance of early training in determining later behaviors. However, Freud's original theories were very subjective, and learning theory is highly objective. Therefore some psychologists have been concerned with devising ways in which Freudian theory can be experimentally tested. Experimental theorists develop and explain their personality theories in terms of learning concepts, which can be measured. They stress such terms as drive, cue, response, and reinforcement. Drives make the organism act, cues suggest which behavior is appropriate in the situation, response is the behavior itself, and reinforcement strengthens the connection between the cue and the response by reducing the tension created by drives. Freud's concepts are translated into these terms, which can be objectively and consistently measured.

Some of the psychologists involved in the experimental approach to personality stress the importance of social behavior. They have criticized earlier studies that dealt primarily with nonhuman subjects and investigated human behavior in isolated rather than in social situations. For example, a paper-and-pencil questionnaire does not examine social situations between persons, nor does learning a list of nonsense syllables. These psychologists usually study persons interacting with one another in an experiment.

The organismic approach. Other personality theorists take the organismic approach, which focuses on the total combination of forces that interact to form personality. These theorists believe that the organism follows an orderly process in the unfolding of potential abilities. Everyone has a drive toward SELF-ACTUALIZATION, the constant striving of the individual to make potential abilities real ones. This need will vary from one person to another, since different people have different potential abilities.

The American psychologist Carl Rogers uses this approach in his theory of personality, which stresses the importance of the self. Rogers maintains that knowing only about external stimuli is not sufficient for understanding personality. It is necessary to know how the stimuli are perceived and interpreted by the person. Through the interaction of the person and his environment the individual develops a self-concept—what he believes is true about himself. Both the organism (the whole organized experience of a person) and his self-concept work toward actualization. When a person's experiences are inconsistent with his self-concept—for instance, if a person who thinks of himself as a good athlete is told by the coach that he is uncoordinated—then he may feel threatened and resort to defense mechanisms. When the individual perceives his own behavior clearly, so that his self-concept is in line with his experiences, there will be positive growth.

Another psychologist who uses the organismic approach and the concept of self-actualization in his personality theory is Abraham Maslow. Maslow has established a hierarchy of needs (shown on this page), based on the belief that a man's inborn needs are arranged in an order of priority. As the needs on lower levels—such as physiological needs—are satisfied, the person becomes freer to deal with needs on a higher level. For example, if an individual has not eaten in several days, his need for food may take precedence over safety needs—he will probably risk being shot or put in jail to steal food. If all physiological and safety needs are satisfied, the person can then direct his full energies toward satisfying his need for love and affec-

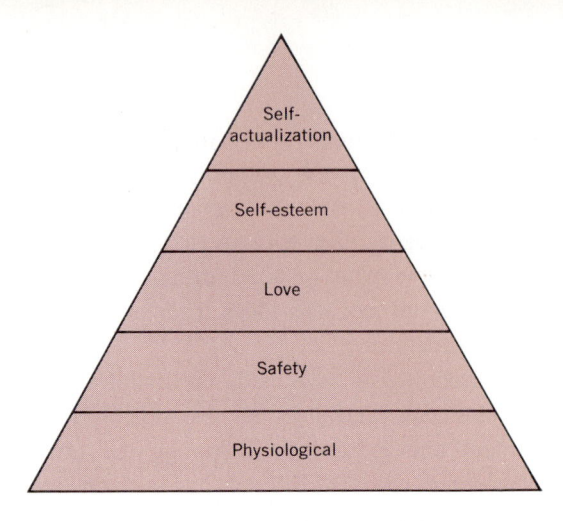

MASLOW'S HIERARCHY OF NEEDS
(Self-actualization / Self-esteem / Love / Safety / Physiological)

tion, the next level of need in the hierarchy. As the person satisfies needs, he moves toward the ultimate goal of self-actualization, or the need to develop his full potentialities.

Body-type theories. Many efforts have been made to relate an individual's personality to the structure of his body. One well-known theory is W. H. Sheldon's classification of body types. Sheldon rated individuals on the basis of three basic body types, shown on the right. He then found a relationship between each body type and certain personality traits. The *endomorph,* who has a round, soft body, is sociable, conventional, loves to eat, and seeks bodily comforts. The *mesomorph,* who is very muscular, likes strenuous exercise and is adventurous, energetic, and direct. The *ectomorph,* who has a thin, linear physique, is sensitive, shy, given to worry, and fearful of groups. Since few, if any, individuals can be classified in only one of these categories, Sheldon developed a scale for classifying the degree of endomorphism, mesomorphism, and ectomorphism in each person.

What are some criticisms of these different personality theories? Each of the theories of personality that we have just discussed has certain shortcomings. No one personality theory is accepted by all psychologists, although some psychologists accept various parts of different theories. The trait approach has been criticized for having traits, derived from paper-and-pencil tests, that are not related closely enough with specific behavior to allow for adequate prediction of individual behavior. It is especially difficult to use the trait theory to predict individual behavior in different situations. One problem is that specific labels, such as "anxiety," obtained from one test may not have exactly the same meaning on a different test or questionnaire.

And to have value for individual prediction of behavior there must be consistency in the measurement.

A serious criticism of any simple classification scheme, such as the introvert-extrovert theory, is that it tends to make us believe that persons can be separated into definite types or classes—that a person is in one class or another, and there is no overlapping. Actually, behavior is very complex. No matter how the psychologist measures individuals, he will not find any completely and clearly separable types.

Today it is not considered scientific to think of individuals as belonging in separate classes of introverts and extroverts. We can just as easily and more scientifically think of them as being distributed by small degrees along a curve, like the one shown on this page, where there are no definite categories or boundaries. How introverted or extroverted we are can be judged from our relative position on the curve. If we have more internally oriented habits and fewer socially centered habits than most persons, we would be to the left of the center (the mean, or average). If we have more socially centered habits and fewer self-oriented habits than most persons, we would be to the right of the average. How far from the average we are is determined by what proportion of our habits are internally oriented or externally oriented, and by the degree to which we exhibit the habits.

Those personality theories, known as neo-Freudian, that emphasize the importance of the social environment have been criticized as being too idealistic. Such theories suggest that if we just improved the social environment, we would have fewer problems. Yet man has been trying to do this for thousands of years and has succeeded only in creating imperfect social systems, in which violence, crime, and wars still occur. Another criticism of such theories is that they fail to state the specific means by which society molds its members. For example, exactly how do we learn to be members of a society? What specific role does learning play in the development of members within a society?

Experimental theorists are criticized primarily for examining small bits of behavior and failing to develop principles that relate the isolated behaviors to one another in some meaningful way. They are also criticized for putting too much emphasis on environmental forces in the shaping of personality. To some psychologists this outlook makes humans similar to puppets, whose strings are pulled by the environment.

Criticisms of the organismic or self-actualization approach center around the subjective terminology used in such theories. Also, critics take issue with the organismic view that "You can best understand an individual's behavior by using his frame of reference." The problem is that only the specific individual can ever really know how he perceives the world, and under some conditions may not even be aware of his interpretations of a situation.

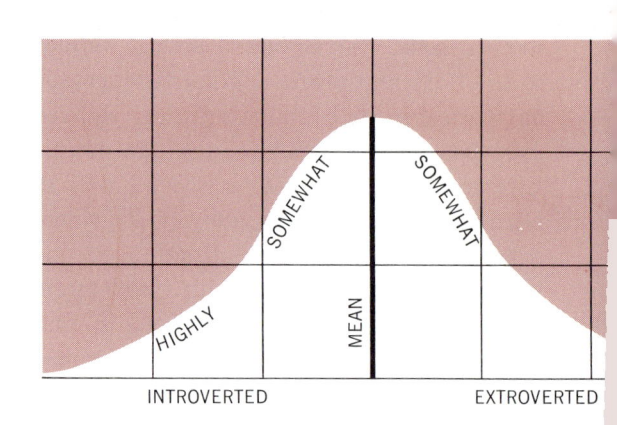

The attempts to relate body type and personality have not been generally accepted by psychologists. Efforts to relate these two variables have assumed that the biological aspects of an individual determine his psychological characteristics. Physique and personality may be closely related, but most psychologists question whether there is a causal relationship between them—whether physique *determines* personality traits. Perhaps, instead, society plays an important role in the development of temperamental traits. For example, we may expect the fat person to be jolly, and his awareness of this may lead him to fulfill the expected role.

Scientific Techniques for Measuring Personality

Some psychologists prefer to speak of evaluation rather than measurement of personality, especially when the individual is being considered in a broad social setting. Sometimes the term "assessment" is used for any procedure designed to describe an individual's characteristic behavior. But whatever terms they use to describe the process, psychologists employ similar techniques in their efforts to measure personality. The five techniques that they use most widely—ratings, inventories, interviewing, behavior sampling, and projective techniques—are discussed below.

1. Ratings

RATING refers to assigning a rank or a score to an individual. This method of measuring personality is often used in business and in schools.

An executive may be asked to rate the salesmen under his supervision on such personality traits as friendliness, courtesy, and honesty. Managers in industry may rate the men working under their supervision. By this means, the men with the most promising personalities can be selected for and promoted to those positions in which a pleasing personality is especially desirable.

In many schools the development of desirable student personalities is recognized as being as important as, or more important than, developing skill in solving quadratic equations, conjugating French verbs, or knowing outstanding dates in history. It is much easier to measure ability in algebra, French, and history than it is to measure personality patterns. Yet schools often do the best they can to measure personality by having each teacher rate his students on selected personality traits.

The order-of-merit method of rating. There are a number of techniques for rating. One is known as the ORDER-OF-MERIT METHOD. In using this technique the raters assign numbers, beginning with 1, to the persons they are rating. Suppose you are trying to find the most courteous person in the class. Each one who is judging the group will assign a number to each member of the group. Suppose Judge A decides from his knowledge of the behavior of Henry Smith that Henry is the most courteous boy in the class—then he will assign Henry the number 1. If he thinks Mary Jones is the next most courteous person in the class, he will assign her the number 2, and so forth.

This technique is easy to use if you write the name of each person on a separate slip. Then you can sort and re-sort the slips until you have them in the correct order from highest to lowest, according to the best of your ability to judge. Put a 1 on the highest slip, a 2 on the second, and so on. Several judges rank the group. The rating of each individual on each trait is the average of all his scores on that trait. Such a technique can be used only where the group to be rated is relatively small.

| Always follows others | Rather tends to follow others | Average | Rather tends to be a leader | Always is a leader |

(check mark above "Average" / "Rather tends to be a leader" area)

A graphic rating scale. Another rating technique makes use of a GRAPHIC RATING SCALE. For each trait considered, a line is drawn. The rater indicates on the line where he thinks the given individual stands. For example, suppose you are going to rate a person on leadership. The total line represents the range from never being a leader to always being a leader. It helps to put short descriptive phrases under parts of the line, as shown in the illustration at the top of this page. The check mark in the illustration would indicate that the rater believed the person he was rating was slightly above the average in leadership.

Sometimes the line is divided into a number of compartments, as shown in the illustration below. The rater does not indicate a point on a line but merely checks the compartment that fits best. Usually there are five or seven compartments. There are not very many persons who can judge accurately more than seven differences.

The foregoing two schemes for rating are not the only ones in use, but they illustrate the general method and are suitable for your use in class experiments.

What dangers must be guarded against in rating? Several precautions must be taken whenever an individual is called upon to rate others on traits of personality, regardless of which method is used.

First, be careful not to overrate. There is a tendency for people to overrate most persons on most traits. Psychologists speak of this tendency to overrate as the GENEROSITY ERROR. One of the authors of this text once made a study of the rating of 345 high school students. Their teachers rated these students each semester on ten personality traits. For example, one trait was appearance. The judgment of best in appearance was weighted 5, the next 4, and so on to 1 for the poorest in appearance. The average score should have been 3, but the psychologist found the average score to be 3.84. That is, the teachers were overrating the students in appearance. The same was true for all other traits. Possibly, in the traits rated, the students were above the average of the community as a whole, but the teachers had been told to rate on the basis of the high school population only.

Second, be careful of the HALO EFFECT. The word "halo" is used here in a technical sense, but it is related to the common use of the word meaning the circle of light around a saint's head in a picture. Psychologists use the term "halo effect" to describe the tendency to rate a person high on all traits because he makes a favorable general impression. The term also describes the tendency to rate some-

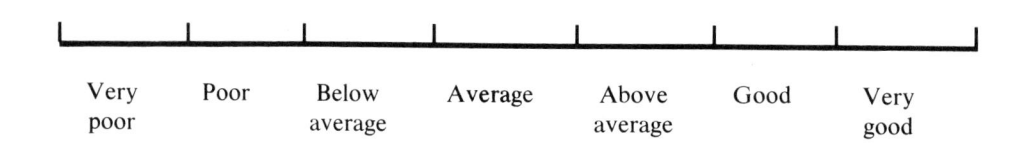

| Very poor | Poor | Below average | Average | Above average | Good | Very good |

126 UNDERSTANDING HUMAN BEHAVIOR

one low on all traits because he makes an unfavorable general impression. In short, the halo effect is the tendency of general impressions to spread to specific traits, or even the tendency of the impression made by one trait to spread to other traits.

For example, businessmen find it difficult to rate salesmen on specific personality traits without being influenced by their sales records. A man who has been bringing in large orders is very apt to be rated high in all personality traits. A man who has a poor sales record is very apt to be rated low in all personality traits. Although such high and low ratings may be justified, if the sales records were to get mixed up the ratings might be quite different.

Such a halo effect can be overcome, in part, by rating all individuals on one trait before going on to the next trait. For example, the business executive should rate all salesmen on initiative, then rate all of them on dependability, and so forth. He should not rate one man on all traits, then another on all traits. By concentrating on one trait at a time, the executive can make more accurate judgments.

Be careful also of a third error, the STEREOTYPE. We tend to apply to an individual the judgments we have previously formed of his racial, national, or social group. For example, we may have formed a stereotype judgment of the Chinese. If we meet a Chinese person, we are apt to assume that he "runs true to type." If we attempt to rate him, we may do so in terms of our prejudices and biases toward all Chinese rather than on the basis of his personal characteristics. When we have time to know him well before we attempt to rate him, we are likely to find that he does not conform to our previous stereotyped idea of Chinese people. Knowing of the error of the stereotype, a rater can be on his guard against it.

There is a fourth error to be guarded against in rating—the error of the TYPE, or PIGEONHOLE. We should be careful not to categorize—pigeonhole—people into a certain type. We should not rate individuals as the blond type or the brunette type, as the good type or the bad type, as an introvert or an extrovert. To do so would immediately introduce an error in our judgment.

Judging people on the basis of stereotypes is often inaccurate. For instance, you might think that these girls fit the stereotype of high school students. Actually, the girl in the center is Chris Evert, best known as a star tennis player.

Finally, there is the danger that when we rate another person, we may attribute to him our own characteristics, or their opposites. If we are very thrifty, we rate him as being very thrifty or else very wasteful. If we are very neat in dress, we are likely to regard him as similar to ourselves or very slovenly.

Rating is not a perfect measure of personality. If, however, the raters are trained in rating and if the technique is carefully developed, it is a useful psychological tool.

Regardless of the scheme of rating used, the one essential requirement is that those who do the rating must have had an opportunity to observe and know the individuals they are rating. Sometimes it is impossible to find enough judges who know the individuals to be rated and who are willing to take the time and effort necessary to rate them. How can psychologists get a measure of personality in such cases? The following method was devised for this situation.

2. Inventories

The word "inventory" is derived from the Latin word *inventarium* and means literally "to find out." Psychologists use the word to refer to a measuring device enabling us to find out about an individual's personality, and especially his ability to adjust to his environment.

The use of inventories to measure personality stems from studies made during World War I. The hundreds of thousands of men who entered the United States Army in 1917–18 differed greatly in their total personality patterns. Some fitted into army life easily. Others adjusted with some but not too much difficulty. Still others found it almost impossible to adjust to the army and the war. It was clearly necessary to find out which men would make good front-line fighters and which ones would not.

A committee went to work to devise a method for measuring personality on a large scale. From studies of those men who had difficulty in adjusting to army life, the committee made up a list of 116 questions. For example: "Can you stand pain quietly? Can you stand the sight of blood? Can you stand disgusting smells?" All questions were to be answered "Yes" or "No."

After the war the list was adapted for civilian use, and schools and businesses took up the inventory method.

How are inventories made up and scored?
Lists of inventory questions are known by various names: personality inventories, personality schedules, personality questionnaires. They are designed to measure various aspects of personality or the general adjustment of an individual to his environment. They are all based on a sampling—that is, from all the habits of overt action and thought that a person may have, one hundred to two hundred habits are selected to obtain a good cross-section of what all his habits are like.

So that inventories are easy to score, the answers are often given by drawing a circle around a "Yes," or a "No," or a "?" Then, by means of a scoring key, the answers are measured and a score is obtained.

Inventories were first developed as group measures of personality. In more recent years some personality inventories have been developed for administering to one individual at a time. In one of these individual inventories the psychologist gives the person being measured a large number of items similar to those found on group inventories. Each statement can be answered under three headings: "True," "False," "Cannot say." By using a scoring technique, the psychologist can tell a good deal about the individual's personality from the responses he files under each heading. Psychologists find individually administered inventories more valuable than group-administered inventories for the study of personality.

One of the objections to the inventory method is that the individual can quite often intentionally bias the results of an inventory. For example, an individual might be asked to answer either "True" or "False" to the following question: "Do you dislike your brother or sister?" Perhaps the individual actually dislikes his sister, but, believing that the answer "True" is socially unacceptable, he answers "False."

A device that has attempted to overcome this objection to inventories is the Edwards Personal Preference Schedule. In this inventory the individual has to choose between two statements, both of which are favorable, or both of which are unfavorable. For example, he may be asked to choose between the following:

A. I sometimes feel that I want to hurt others.
B. I feel inferior to others.

Another device used by some inventories is to include "lie" questions. One personality inventory contains fifteen questions to which the answers, if inconsistent with the large majority of other answers, indicate that the person taking the test is lying and cause the examiner to be suspicious of the scores on other parts of the inventory.

What are some cautions in using the results of personality inventories? Even trained psychologists must proceed cautiously with the results of personality inventories. It is easy to assume that an individual who scores high on some aspect, such as conformity, will behave according to his inventory score in actual situations. However, a number of studies have shown that this is not necessarily true. College students were given an inventory to measure conformity, but when later placed in an experimental situation designed to put them under social pressure to conform, their behavior showed little relationship to the scores they had made on the inventory.

When considering scores on inventories, remember that they are not like the scores on school tests. They do not represent right or wrong, they merely indicate the trend of the habits of action and thought of the individual. There is no such thing as a passing or failing grade. Inventories are of value in helping us to understand one personality as compared with the personalities of others, but they are not examinations on which anyone can be "flunked."

Even comparing the score of an individual with the scores made by others must be done with caution. What might appear to be an undesirable response for a person belonging to one social group might not be an undesirable response for a person belonging to a different social group. At one time several personality inventories were given to a group of Chinese students. A first glance at the data seemed to suggest that these Chinese individuals had undesirable traits of personality. One of the questions asked was, "Do you allow others to push ahead of you in line?" By American standards, since the person who permits others to crowd in ahead of him is considered to be too timid and submissive, the desirable answer is "No." By Chinese standards, the desirable answer is "Yes." In the traditional Chinese culture people gather around together and do not form lines as we do. The Chinese believe that if an individual crowds ahead, there must be a very special reason and deference should be given him.

Furthermore, inventories are measures of habits, and habits can be changed. We are not born with a fixed personality. Recent research has indicated that significant changes in habits and attitudes may continue to occur in the adult years of life. Such changes may even mean the difference between a personality that is pleasing and one that is not.

Scores on an inventory are of value only if the individual has answered the questions frankly and honestly. Even then, especially if he stops to think about his answers very long, he may indicate the kind of personality he would like to have rather than the kind of personality he does have at the time.

For all these reasons, when attempting to understand personality, it is not a good idea to use standardized inventory data alone. Personality inventories are crude measures at best. The data from such inventories should always be used in connection with other pertinent information about the person, and should be interpreted by a trained and qualified psychologist.

3. Interviewing

Sometimes interviewing is used as a technique for measuring personality. Many employers and personnel managers believe that they can size up the personality and other qualifications of an applicant for a job in just a few minutes by means of a personal interview. Something about an individual's personality can be learned from an interview. However, a general sizing up of a person in this way may give a far from valid impression of his personality.

Why is interviewing not always a valid measure? We noted certain precautions to be taken in rating individuals (pp. 126–28) and we need to take these same precautions when interviewing. The following experiment demonstrates that interviewing is not always a valid way of evaluating personality. Twelve sales managers in an automobile organization were

Do you think this is a valid interview? Interviewing is less reliable when no notes or recording devices are used and the results depend only on the interviewer's impressions.

asked to interview fifty-seven applicants for sales positions. These sales managers were accustomed to sizing up men and selecting those whose personalities indicated that they were suited for positions as salesmen. Each sales manager interviewed each one of the fifty-seven applicants. Then, without consulting anyone, he ranked the applicants in order of desirability for sales positions. That is, if a sales manager believed an applicant to be the best prospect of all, he gave the applicant a rank of 1. The applicant he judged to be the next best he gave a rank of 2, and so on down to a rank of 57.

When psychologists compared the rankings of the sales managers, they found many differences. For example, one applicant had been given the following rankings: 1, 2, 6, 9, 10, 16, 20, 21, 26, 28, 53, 57. One of the sales managers had thought him the best prospect, and another had thought him the worst —on the basis of the interview. Another applicant had been ranked 2, 4, 9, 13, 16, 16, 19, 28, 32, 33, 46, 55. Thus, one applicant might be judged very desirable by some sales managers, very undesirable by other sales managers, and intermediate in desirability by still others. Such sizing up of men, even by these experienced interviewers, did not give consistent results.

How has interviewing been improved? The principal difficulty with interviewing had been that so much depended on the judgment of the interviewer. Psychologists have found that judgments made following interviews become more valid if they are guided by the two previously discussed techniques for measuring personality—inventories and rating scales.

The interviewer may use a list of questions, some of which are similar to those asked on inventories. In a skillfully conducted interview these questions, which are given orally, may be answered more frankly and honestly than if they were merely printed questions to be answered by pencil marks. The interviewer can explain questions not fully understood and get more complete answers from the person being interviewed.

The interviewer may also use a rating scale to record his estimate of the degree to which the individual being interviewed has certain traits of personality. The rating scale is used during the interview or immediately following it. Judgments recorded while they are fresh are probably superior to those based on memory of past impressions.

Another procedure that produces more valid measures is to have several interviewers of an individual pool their findings. Also, it is helpful to recheck interviews. Rechecking has become possible in recent years with the improvement of tape-recording equipment. Tape recordings can be made of interviews and played back later so that interviewers can correct any wrong first impressions or note any points they missed during the original interview.

As commonly used (by personnel managers, for example), interviewing can scarcely be considered a scientific attempt to measure personality. However, interviewing by scientific methods is another matter. Interviews handled by well-trained interviewers who use modern techniques may be able to measure personality as well as, or even better than, ratings or inventories can.

We should add that interviews have another use besides measuring personality. They are sometimes valuable in the treatment of patients with emotional troubles. Psychoanalysts and clinical psychologists often use interviews for purposes of therapy.

4. Behavior Sampling

Behavior sampling is quite different from the three techniques just described. In this method no one's opinion is asked about another person, nor does the person answer questions about himself. Instead, a sampling of actual behavior is measured or recorded. To measure the characteristic of honesty in a person, a psychologist can set up a sample situation in which the person may be dishonest if he wishes. Then the extent of his honesty can be measured. For example, the person may be given a chance to steal a small amount of money under circumstances leading him to believe that no one will be able to detect that he has stolen. To measure the trait of leadership, the psychologist can create a sample situation in which an individual can demonstrate his ability to lead. The extent to which a person lies may be measured by counting the lies he tells in a given number of answers to questions.

How can cheating in schoolwork be measured? Cheating in schoolwork is measured by setting up an experimental situation in which students can cheat if they wish to do so. One favorite method is to give a test in some subject, collect the papers, and carefully make a record of right and wrong answers. The papers must be scored without indicating this on the papers in any way. The next day the teacher returns the papers to the class. The students then score their own papers, assuming that the teacher will collect them and record the marks in the grade book. Perhaps the teacher leaves the room for a few minutes, to give the students an opportunity to cheat. The student-scored papers are then collected. Whatever differences there are between the scores the students set down when marking the papers and the previous scores are a measure of cheating—unless there were actual errors in marking.

Other examples of behavior sampling. In one experiment junior high school students were used as subjects in a study to measure "finking"—in this case, telling on a classmate who had "stolen" some money from the teacher's desk. When the teacher left the room a classmate, who knew about the purposes of the experiment, walked up to the teacher's desk and said, "Hey, look! How about that!" and took seventy-five cents in change from the desk. After a short period of time, each student was called from the room and asked three questions about the "theft": (1) Do you know whether someone took change from Mrs. X's desk today? (2) Do you know who took it? and (3) If so, who took it? During the interrogations half the subjects were asked the questions while the "thief" was present and half were asked the questions when he was absent. Significantly fewer subjects reported any knowledge of the theft when the "thief" was absent than when he was present. The authors of the study believe that the subjects interpreted the absence of the "thief" during their interrogation as an indication that other evidence was not available about the theft, and so many of them kept quiet. If the subjects had been asked on a paper-and-pencil test before the experiment if they would report a theft, do you think their responses would have been any different from their actual behavior?

Behavior sampling is used to help predict how a person will react in a similar situation to the one being tested. One police academy found behavior sampling useful for the training of police. Behavioral samples were used

If you found a stamped, addressed envelope on the street that appeared to contain a half-dollar, would you open it or mail it?

to simulate a police patrol and a missing-person investigation. The results of these samples—how the individuals reacted in these two situations—were found to predict future success in police work.

Other types of behavior sampling include graphology and voice printing. Graphology, the assessing of personality by handwriting analysis, has recently been studied scientifically using stricter controls than in the past. Newer techniques for objectively measuring the speed and pressure of writing are now available. However, the results of such studies are usually so general that they cannot be applied to predicting what a given individual will do in a particular situation.

The recently discovered technique of voice printing has caused a few psychologists to reconsider a possible relationship between voice and personality. Voice printing is based on the fact that an individual speaking a given word has characteristic patterns that are unique to that person. For example, voice printing has been used in the identification of criminals, where voice prints of different suspects were compared to a recording of the voice of the known criminal. However, relationships between voice patterns and personality have yet to be scientifically established.

What caution is needed in interpreting behavior samplings? Behavior samplings are valuable in the scientific measurement of personality, but they must not be interpreted too broadly. Although psychologists strive for samplings that are representative of a person's behavior—that is, whether the person would behave similarly in a similar situation—you cannot assume that because a trait is shown in one situation, it will necessarily be shown in all situations. Students who cheat in schoolwork may not cheat in athletic contests. Classmates who "fink" in one case may not do so under different circumstances. However, such traits are usually representative enough so that behavior samplings can be of considerable value in studying personality.

5. Projective Techniques

PROJECTION is the process whereby an individual attributes elements in his own personality to other persons or objects in his environment. It is mainly the undesirable elements of his personality that he tends to project. For example, the student who is careless in his work may say that the teacher is so careless that she cannot teach him anything. He projects a trait of his own personality into the personality of the teacher. The individual who is dishonest tends to project this trait into the personality of others. He is likely to say, "Everybody is dishonest."

An individual is not aware of the fact that he is projecting his own characteristics to others. The careless student does not realize that he is attributing carelessness to his teacher because he himself is careless. The person who says that everyone is dishonest is not aware of the fact that he is seeing his own dishonesty reflected.

At one time a psychologist asked some college students to adjust a spot of light so that it appeared to be equal to the size of a penny, nickel, dime, or quarter. There were no coins present, so that the students had to adjust the light according to their remembered impressions of the sizes of these coins. Their adjustments of the light spots were quite accurate; they made a spot of light about the right size for a penny, nickel, dime, and quarter. Then the students were hypnotized and told that they were very poor, that it was very difficult for them to secure money, and so on. While hypnotized, they were again asked to adjust the size of the spot of light so that it appeared to be equal to the sizes of the various coins. In their "poor" state the students' adjustments of the light spots were consistently larger than in the normal waking state. Again they were hypnotized, but this time they were told that they were rich, that there was more than enough money for their every need, and so on. And again they were asked to adjust the spot of light until it appeared to be equal to the sizes of the coins. In the "rich" state their light adjustments were consistently smaller than in the normal waking state. How these students perceived the spots of light depended on their wants, needs, interests, attitudes, and values at the time they adjusted the light.

Inkblot tests. Projection can be demonstrated by a simple experiment. Place several drops of ink on a sheet of paper and fold the paper in half. The ink will blot and give an irregular but symmetrical design. Show your inkblot to a friend and ask him to tell you what he sees. Then show the blot to several others and ask them what they see. You will probably find that different persons interpret the inkblot in quite different ways. An individual who has had much experience with animals may see some kind of animal in a given blot. An individual who has studied designing may see a basic pattern for wallpaper in the same inkblot. What anyone sees in the inkblot depends to some extent on his own capacities and experiences. What he sees is, in reality, a projection of his own thoughts.

A Swiss psychiatrist, Hermann Rorschach ('rȯr-shäk), developed an inkblot test that some psychologists find very useful in studying personality. The individual whose per-

Look at this inkblot carefully. What do you see? Why do you think you interpreted it as you did? Psychologists use standardized inkblots to study personality.

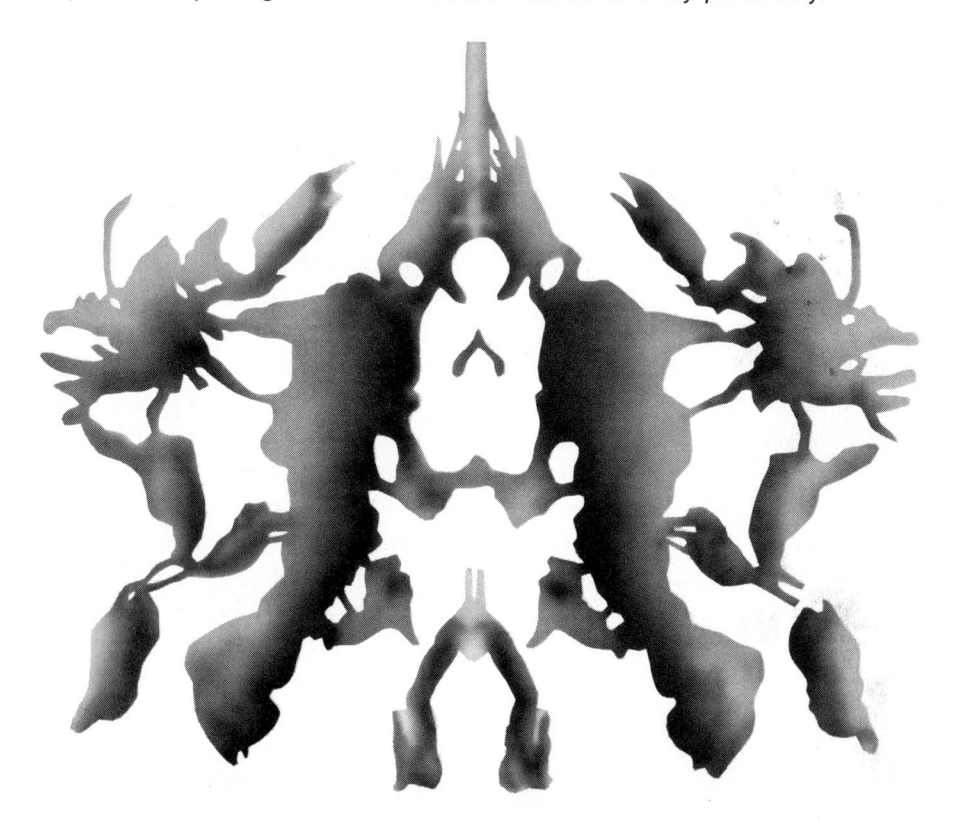

sonality pattern is being studied is shown a series of ten standardized blots, one at a time. He is asked to respond by telling and describing the things and ideas that each inkblot suggests to him.

Although the administering and scoring of this test are standardized, a difficulty arises in the interpretation of the responses. The lack of objective ways of interpreting responses has led to disagreement among some psychologists as to the validity of this test for indicating personality.

One attempt made to utilize some of the hypotheses underlying the Rorschach test, and at the same time provide an objective comparison of scores, is the Holtzman Inkblot Test, which uses forty-five inkblots. Whereas an unlimited number of responses are allowed on the Rorschach test, on this test the subject is allowed only one response per card and the response is scored objectively. The score of the individual can be compared directly with the responses of one or more norm groups (comparison groups). For example, the score of a college student can be compared with those of other college students or of a known group of mentally ill persons.

Some attempts have been made to modify the individual Rorschach test so that it could be used as a group test, but such group forms have not proved very successful.

Other projective techniques. Some psychologists use pictures of clouds and ask individuals to describe what they see in the clouds. Other psychologists use series of rather vague pictures involving persons, animals, and objects. They instruct their subjects to tell stories suggested by the pictures. Sometimes the psychologist merely begins telling a story without a picture and then asks the subject to complete the story. The themes of these stories and the characters involved reveal to the psychologist a great deal about the personalities of the individuals telling the stories. For example, suppose a boy tells a story in which the hero, who is so small that he has difficulty in defending himself, suddenly learns how to fight and goes about knocking down boys twice his size. The psychologist would have reason to believe that the teller of this story felt himself to be inferior. In his story he was projecting this feeling of inferiority onto the hero. Also, he was expressing his own desire to be superior.

Sometimes children are given toys to play with as they wish. During the play a psychologist observes many elements involved in the personality of the child. For example, suppose the child builds a house with a fence around it and says, "This is my house and I am building a high fence around it so that other kids can't come in and bother me." The psychologist will have reason to believe that the child is introverted.

Some recent research with semi-projective tests of personality involved adolescents who were asked to place circles, representing themselves, in relation to other circles that represented friends, teachers, and parents. As part of the test they were later asked to rank the circles representing themselves and others in order of importance. In comparison to a control group of randomly selected persons of the same age, it was found that adolescents with behavior problems tended to show a higher degree of self-concern, a lower interest in others, a low level of self-esteem, and little identification with friends, teachers, and groups.

Still other types of projective techniques are used by psychologists. For instance, individuals may be asked to draw pictures and tell the stories behind the pictures. In other cases the individual is given a background picture, such as a living room, a forest, an attic, a schoolroom, or a street scene. These pictures contain no people, but the individual is given cutout figures of men, women, and children of various races, animals, and so on. He is then asked to place these figures on the background pictures and tell the stories of the pictures. Finger painting has also been used as a projective technique. Or the first part of sentences may be given and the individual is asked to complete the sentences. Dreams have been studied as projections. Whatever the specific technique, all projective techniques give the individual a great deal of freedom in expressing himself.

How do projective techniques measure personality? Can projective techniques actually tell how much of a certain trait there is in an individual's personality? At present, projective techniques are more useful for finding the kind of personality traits someone has than for measuring their intensity. For the clinical psychologist treating personality maladjustments, it may be enough to know the quality of a person's traits. It is better, however, to know the quality and to be able to measure quantity.

Psychologists are developing various schemes to measure the replies to projective tests. Inkblots, pictures, and toy arrangements have been used with thousands of persons. Psychologists have found that a large number of people tend to give the same response. This response can be taken as a rough sort of "normal," or average, answer (although it should not be inferred that there are right or wrong answers to projective tests). We can then compare any individual's test with these "normal" answers. Thus, we can roughly measure how an individual compares with other persons.

There is another way of measuring replies to projective tests. A psychologist can count the number of times that one thought shows up in stories. Suppose that in nine out of ten stories John Doe expresses a feeling of inferiority. But Richard Roe expresses inferiority in only one out of ten stories. How often a certain feeling or attitude is expressed is a measure of the extent of each person's feeling, say, of inferiority.

In scoring responses to inkblots the psychologist may obtain measures of quantity by several means. He may calculate the percentage of responses concerned with the blots as a whole. Then he may calculate the percentage of responses concerned with details to be seen within the blots. He may count the responses indicating movement of the figures in the blots and the responses based on the seeing of the colored parts of the blots. Then he may compute the ratio of one total to the other. He may note whether responses are original or popular—for example, whether they are such as occur only once in every one hundred records, or once in every six records. The interpretation of the scores is much more difficult than the scoring itself.

What cautions must be considered in using and interpreting projective tests? Of all the tests given by trained psychologists, projective tests are perhaps the most difficult to administer, score, and interpret. For example, it usually takes a minimum of one year of graduate school training to qualify for administering and interpreting the Rorschach test. To complete a Rorschach record on one individual may require several hours of the psychologist's time.

Another problem is that sometimes projective tests are scored and interpreted in different ways by different psychologists. As yet, there is no universal agreement regarding the interpretation of specific responses on some projective tests, such as the Rorschach.

Terms to Know

behavior sampling	introvert	primary trait
ectomorph	mesomorph	projection
endomorph	order-of-merit rating	projective technique
extrovert	ordinal position	rating
generosity error	organismic approach	self-actualization
graphic rating scale	personality	stereotype
halo effect	pigeonhole error	trait

Topics to Think About

1. In competitions such as those to select a "Miss" city, state, or America, personality as well as appearance and achievement are considered. Suppose you were one of the judges in such a contest. How would you evaluate the personality of each girl?

2. If a psychologist asked your permission to measure your personality and indicated that he would use only one measuring instrument, which one would you prefer he use: an ink blot test, a personality inventory, an interview, a rating scale, or a behavior sampling? Why? (Actually, a psychologist would not be willing to evaluate your personality on the basis of just one such measuring technique.)

3. Suppose you were blindfolded and then were introduced to five strangers, after which you were given an opportunity to talk with each one on a specific topic. How well do you think you could evaluate their personalities on the basis of voice quality alone?

4. Do you think you have a normal personality? What is normal? How would you go about determining if your personality is normal?

5. If you had your choice, and to some extent you do have a choice, would you prefer to be an introvert or an extrovert?

6. Imagine and describe what the world would be like if everyone's personality were exactly the same.

Suggestions for Activities

1. Select a specific trait, such as shyness, and list behaviors that to you would describe or illustrate that particular trait. Compare your list to the behavior lists of other students. Can you see why personality inventories need to be standardized?

2. Write a brief autobiography, stressing the events in your life that you believe have especially influenced the development of your personality.

3. Select a child you know very well. With permission of his or her parents, but without the child's knowledge, observe the child's behavior, take notes, and then try to describe his or her personality from your first observation. Observe the behavior of the child several additional times. At the end of all the observations, describe what you believe to be the personality of the child. Did any of your original beliefs about the child change? Did you notice any personality "traits" you were not aware of at first?

4. Have friends write a paragraph on the personality traits they associate with a very muscular individual. Do they agree on traits? Could all muscular persons have similar personalities?

5. Choose a personality trait, such as aggressiveness or femininity, and compare the behavior characteristics associated with it in our society and in some other country, such as China or Mexico. How similar or different are the characteristics? Are there any traits with the same meaning in every society?

6. If possible, take and score one of the commercially available personality inventories, for example, the Gordon Personal Profile and Gordon Personal Inventory (published by Harcourt Brace Jovanovich). To what extent do you think it gives a true picture of your personality?

7. Assume that you are a school counselor and that a student has been referred to you. You wish to assess the personality of this student. List and describe which method or methods you would use. What would help you decide which method or methods to use?

8. Have someone in your class "lose" a number of notes or letters around the school. The notes or letters should be sealed in some way and should bear the names and locker numbers of members of your class. How many of the total "lost" are turned over to the addressees? Have they been opened?

9. Sometimes it is said that an author "writes himself into his work." Write down your impression of the personality of some author, such as Ernest Hemingway, whose works you have studied in an English course. Then check biographical and autobiographical material to learn to what extent the author seems to have projected himself into his writings.

10. Make a list of ten individuals you know. They may be younger, the same age, or older than you. Rate these persons on a five-point scale, according to whether you believe they are very meek (a rating of 1) to very aggressive (a rating of 5). A rating of 3 would mean that they are moderately aggressive-meek, and the numbers 2 and 4 would represent intermediate ranks between a rating of 1 and 3, and 3 and 5. Also, rate each person on a five-point scale for sociability (1 means withdrawn, likes to be by himself, 3 is moderately sociable, and 5 means very outgoing and sociable); intelligence; masculinity-femininity; and honesty. After you have rated each person on each of the five traits, determine every person's birth order—whether he or she is an only child, first-born, second-born, and so on.

Make a table to show the relationship, if any, between birth order and ratings. Compile data from several other students into one table or chart. Then answer the following questions: Did you find any relationship between ratings and birth order? What are the major drawbacks of using your rating of the persons?

11. Fold a sheet of white paper, open it, place two or three drops of black ink near the crease, and fold it over again. Have several persons describe the inkblot that you have made. What do they see in it? Are there individual differences? (Of course, you are not prepared to attempt a personality analysis. Furthermore, you must remember that your inkblot is not a standardized one.)

12. Using an overhead projector, display a homemade inkblot on a screen for one minute and have others write down what they see. Their papers should not include their names but should indicate whether the individual is male or female. Collect all the papers and divide them into two stacks, one for males and the other for females. Are there any differences between male and female responses? Can you see what others saw in the inkblot?

13. Find a picture showing several children, preferably children of both sexes. Show the picture to a number of children. Ask them to tell you about the picture—what has happened in the past, what the children are thinking about, what is going to happen in the future. Are there marked individual differences in the reactions of the children to whom you show your picture? Is there any evidence that a given child is identifying himself with a child in the picture? (You cannot make an analysis of personality on the basis of just one nonstandardized picture. You will, however, gain some idea of how individual differences may be tested by such techniques.)

14. Consult your local police department to see if someone in the department would be willing to be interviewed on what procedures they use to handle individuals with different behavioral traits. Do they handle all individuals in the same manner or do they take into account individual differences?

Suggestions for Further Reading

Hilgard, E. R., R. C. Atkinson, and Rita Atkinson, *Introduction to Psychology,* 5th ed., Harcourt Brace Jovanovich. See Chapter 17, "Theories of Personality," and Chapter 18, "Personality Assessment."

Kagan, Jerome, *Personality Development,* Harcourt Brace Jovanovich. A paperback that covers the development of personality from birth through adolescence.

Kagan, J., M. M. Haith, and Catherine Caldwell (eds.), *Psychology: Adapted Readings,* Harcourt Brace Jovanovich. See Selection 27, "The What and Why of Personality Assessment."

Kagan, J., and E. Havemann, *Psychology: An Introduction,* 2nd ed., Harcourt Brace Jovanovich. Chapter 12 goes into the details of personality theory.

Psychology Today: An Introduction, CRM Books. See Chapter 24, "Measurement of Personality," and Chapter 25, "Theories of Personality."

Ruch, Floyd L., and Philip G. Zimbardo, *Psychology and Life,* 8th ed., Scott, Foresman. See Chapter 11, "Personality: The Psychology of the Individual."

Wertheimer, M., *et al., Psychology: A Brief Introduction,* Scott, Foresman. See pages 169–82, 184–86, on how personality is described, how attributes are distributed, and statistical measurements.

chapter 6
How Behavior Develops

EACH PERSON at birth is almost totally helpless. As his processes of learning, thinking, and personality develop, he grows into adulthood. Do you know some of the patterns of development that he follows? In this chapter we will discuss some of the psychological factors that take place during the early years and some of the characteristic physical, emotional, social, and mental changes that occur in each individual. By becoming familiar with different factors associated with and influencing development, you can better appreciate how man's behavior, his actions and attitudes, are shaped.

Development

Every field of psychology could be headed by the terms "growth and development," because all areas of behavior—perception, learning, motivation, intelligence, personality, and so on—are occurring at different stages of development. For example, an individual's perception is not the same during infancy, childhood, adolescence, and adulthood. By studying how changes occur at the different stages of development we can better understand perception at each level.

By studying the various areas of development we can also learn what patterns of behavior usually develop, and thus establish standards for comparing behavior. Once we have standards of behavior for various age groups, we have a general idea of what to expect of the individual. And when we know what behavior to expect, we can help prepare the individual for the next step in his development. For example, if we know in advance that the usual pattern of behavior is for the average child to walk alone and without support at about fourteen months of age, we are able to provide him with ample opportunity to begin to learn this motor task a little before

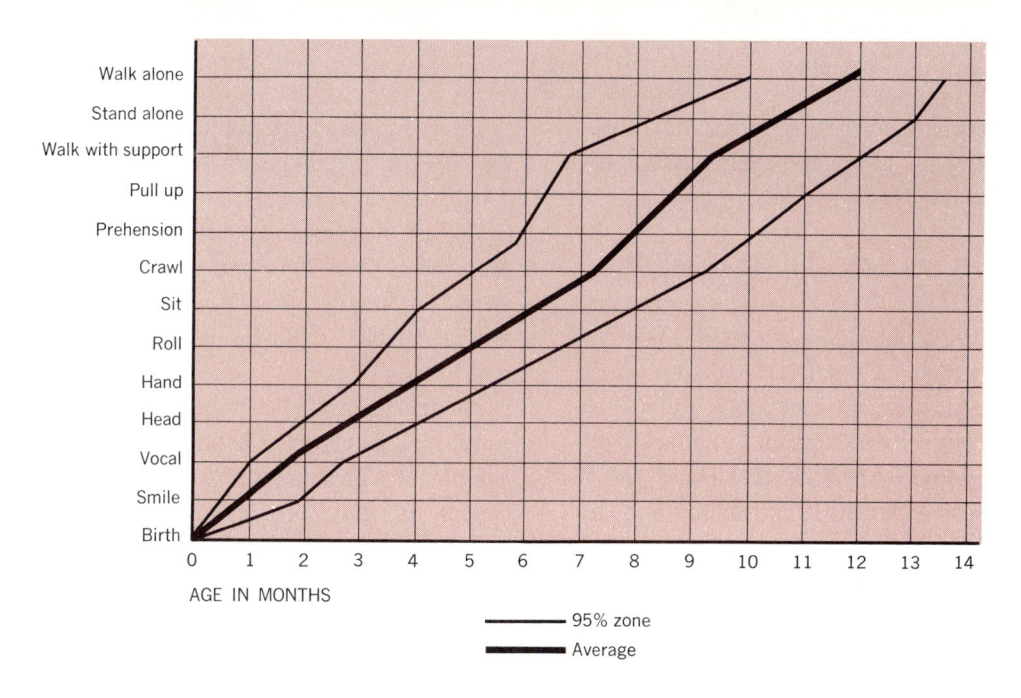

A development graph of the first year. The thick line shows the average age for these achievements; the thin lines indicate the age span of 95 percent of the babies.

fourteen months. In this way the child can be given a chance to develop at his own rate with adequate preparation. Or, in the area of intellectual development, by knowing when a mental trait, such as learning to tell time, begins to develop, we can assign the child tasks related to this trait and thus help him in the process of achieving his potential ability. If, however, we expect too little of a child, or too much, we could easily upset his developmental schedule.

Nevertheless, we should always remember that each person is an individual with his own developmental schedule and pattern. Also, only experts in this field, such as psychologists and psychiatrists, are qualified to make interpretative judgments about whether the individual is developing faster or slower than the average person in his age group.

How is maturation related to development?
To understand human development, it is important to see its relationship to maturation. MATURATION is the potential development of the individual as set by heredity. No individual can develop a specific trait until he is physiologically ready to develop that trait. For example, regardless of how hard you try to teach him, no baby can learn to walk before his muscles and neurons have developed that control his walking. The readiness of various parts of the body to perform more complex movements is determined by the degree of maturation of these parts.

Maturation is necessary not only for physical and motor development but also for the development of mental traits. For instance, it is a waste of time to try to teach a child to read if he is not mature enough for it. Remember, though, that some individuals develop faster and some more slowly than others. Not all children are at the same level of maturation at the same age. Since new evidence from psychologists on the individual's readiness to learn is constantly being discovered, the future should bring an increased understanding of how maturation relates to development.

Some general principles of development. Perhaps the most important single statement that can be made about development is that development follows a predictable pattern. One illustration of such a predictable pattern is the early physical development of infants. In babies development spreads downward from the head, which develops first, to the feet. If you observe a newborn infant you will notice that he develops control of his eyes first, then learns to turn his head, then his trunk, and finally gains control over his legs and can walk. In babies, development also proceeds outward from the central axis of the body to the wrists and fingers. The newborn baby first moves his arms in a very general way, then begins to control his elbows and hands, and finally his specific finger movements. These are two patterns of physical development in infants that are predictable.

Another principle of development is that the individual first develops general responses and then proceeds to specific responses. This principle becomes evident if you watch a very young baby trying to reach for a toy. His efforts seem to involve using his entire body. When you observe the same baby a few months afterward, you will see him use more specific parts of his body to reach the toy. Later on, he will be even more specific in his responses and will use only those parts of his body actually needed to obtain the toy.

A third characteristic of development is that it is a continuous process. The expression "stages of development" incorrectly implies that developmental tasks have a definite starting and stopping point. There is no one specific point at which a task suddenly appears or disappears. Some behavior may seem to appear all at once, but, in fact, this behavior has been developing slowly for some time. This is true of all developmental tasks. Nevertheless, it is convenient to group the occurrence of various developmental changes into stages as long as you remember that there are no specific dividing lines between these stages.

A fourth principle of development is that some individuals have a different rate of development. The pattern of development is similar for most people, but the amount of time required in developing may vary in different individuals. If there is some prenatal (before birth) or natal damage of the central nervous system or glands, it can cause a faster or slower rate of development, depending on the specific type of damage and when it takes place. For example, improper functioning of the pituitary gland can cause a noticeable change in the rate of development. When the gland secretes too little, the individual may develop as a miniature but normally proportioned adult. When the pituitary secretes too much, the individual may develop as an unusually tall adult. It should be noted in passing that not only can the rate of physical development differ among individuals but also that different parts of the body can develop at different rates.

Another characteristic of development is that each stage has unique features. Each stage is expressed differently, depending on the society and the period of development involved. For instance, the so-called rebellion period of adolescence is a feature of our own society and culture that is not found in most other societies.

A final characteristic is that early development is more important than later development. For example, consider the theoretical isolation of an individual at various periods of his development. Compare the effects on intelligence of isolating a child for a year between his first and second birthdays and isolating the same person for a year at the age of twenty. Although the latter isolation would certainly influence the person's development, the earlier isolation period would have a much greater and more lasting effect.

How do psychologists study development of the individual? One of the oldest methods of studying behavior and development is that of observation. In the beginning this method was used mainly by unskilled persons, without the benefit of controlled experimental conditions, and therefore it yielded inconsistent results. However, modern methods of observing behavior make use of more standardized procedures and produce more objective, unbiased results.

One of the best-known American psychologists to study behavior through observation was Arnold Gesell (1880–1961). He developed not only specific techniques but also a special room for observing the behavior of infants and small children. (See photograph on this page.) This room was dome-shaped with transparent walls. It was located inside a larger room from which skilled observers could watch what the children were doing. Children within the smaller room could not see the observers through the transparent walls, because the outer room was darkened and the smaller room well lit. Tape recorders, still cameras, and movie cameras were installed in the smaller room to provide a permanent record of the children's behavior. By observing a large number of individuals at different age levels, Gesell was able to establish norms of behavior.

Another means of studying the behavior and development of the individual is through the LONGITUDINAL METHOD, which involves selecting a group of individuals and studying

Gesell's one-way-vision observation dome (above) provides many advantages for studying behavior. How many can you list?

the development of their behavior over a considerable period of time. In some longitudinal studies individuals have been observed from birth to adulthood. The method has the following limitations, however: (1) it is time-consuming; (2) it can be very expensive; (3) it must face the difficulty of maintaining contact with the same group over a period of time, since some individuals may move to another location during the study; and (4) the individuals chosen for study may not be a representative sample of their age group. Nevertheless, the longitudinal method has the important advantage of providing psychologists with information on specific changes in behavior and development.

The CROSS-SECTIONAL METHOD selects different individuals of different ages in order to study groups at various age levels simultaneously. For example, different groups of three-, four-, five-, and six-year-old children can be selected and studied at the same time. This method has the major advantage of reducing the amount of time necessary for the study. However, it shares one of the limitations of the longitudinal method—the difficulty and necessity of selecting groups that are representative of their age levels. If the groups are not representative, norms of behavior cannot be established that are valid for the age levels involved.

In addition to the different methods to be used, the choice of subjects is an essential part of the study of development. The study of animals has the advantage that animals can be subjected to certain controlled conditions of deprivation, such as isolation, to determine the effects on their behavior and development. Animals can be experimentally deprived of any combination of their senses, or can be constrained in certain motor areas, to see what the effects are on development. In one experiment chimpanzees were reared in isolation and later allowed to mix socially with other chimpanzees. It was found that their motor activities were normal but that they were socially inept at getting along with the other chimpanzees.

For both ethical and moral reasons, it is obvious that human beings cannot be treated as animals. Nevertheless, it is also clear that psychologists are ethically able to study human beings while using enough experimental controls to be consistent. With identical twins, for instance, the hereditary factors are thought to be the same so that it is possible to control and study certain environmental factors to see their influence on the individual's development.

Physical Development

PHYSICAL DEVELOPMENT is the growth of an individual's body. As you can imagine, it has a considerable effect on the thoughts and behavior of persons.

How does body development affect the individual? A child who develops physically faster than the average for his age will be able to do things better and more quickly than others of his age group. His superior physical capabilities will influence his popularity, which could be increased by his achievements or decreased if he became a bully. The individual has the choice of using his greater strength to help others, to be sought after by his fellow playmates because he can run faster and hit harder, or to force others to obey him. How he is accepted by others will have an effect on what he thinks of himself. Inadequate physical development may cause others to tease the person and thereby affect his adjustment to the world.

From these few examples it is clear that physical development does play an important role in how the person sees himself and how others see him. Remember, however, that there is a considerable amount of variation within any age group. The figures given in this chapter represent the average for each age level. The simple fact that certain individuals are taller or shorter than the average for their age group should never be taken as a sign that they are not accepted by the group or will not be liked for their good qualities.

The development of height and weight. The two most frequently cited examples of an individual's physical growth are height and weight. Both height and weight have a developmental pattern of increasing in spurts, with the greatest percentage of growth in the earliest stages.

The greatest rate of growth in height for both sexes takes place during the preschool years. Tremendous growth occurs during the first year, when the average increase is 50

In a gathering of boys and girls who are between the ages of eleven and thirteen there is usually a great variety of growth patterns for height and weight. Girls are often taller than boys at that age, although the situation is reversed several years later.

percent. At the end of the third year, the average person is half as tall as he will be as an adult. By the fifth year he is twice as tall as he was at birth.

Girls grow faster in height than boys until the puberty stage, when the average male catches up with and passes the female. By the time he reaches adulthood the average male will be approximatey 4 to 5 inches taller than the female.

The general principles regarding rate of development of height also apply to weight. The largest percentage increase in weight will occur during the first five years of life. By age five the average person will weigh about five times what he weighed at birth. During the next seven years his weight will more than double.

The average newborn male baby is slightly heavier than the female. The female will equal and then surpass the male in weight at about ten years of age, but the male will catch up at about age fourteen and remain heavier than the female throughout life.

During adulthood the individual will gain weight. As the person approaches the middle-age period, an excessive amount of fat may accumulate. Later, however, as the individual reaches old age, he will lose weight, largely because of loss of body fluids and the various chemical changes associated with advanced age. Of course, at every age, exercise, a proper diet, and good psychological adjustment all play important roles in keeping the individual trim and fit.

There is usually a relationship between an individual's weight and his psychological adjustment. People with anxiety, guilt, and other disturbing feelings sometimes have a tendency to overeat and become overweight. Have you ever noticed how you frequently become hungry before and during exams or when watching your favorite team play ball? Observe the large amount of food consumed at ball games. It is not true, however, that every overweight person is distressed. Some people have glandular trouble that results in an overweight condition; others develop habits of overeating from their parents.

How do physical defects affect the individual? Physical defects are caused by such factors as heredity, an accident that may occur before, during, or after birth, and psychological factors. Most defects stem from physical causes, although some physical defects, such as stuttering, have a psychological basis. Usually those individuals who stutter do so only when they are anxious, frightened, worried, or similarly upset. Stuttering seems to be characteristic of civilized societies, since it does not usually exist in the more primitive societies. Surprisingly, slightly more than 85 percent of all American children stutter before they are three years old. As the child grows up and adapts increasingly to his home environment, his stuttering usually disappears.

The effect of physical defects on the individual will depend on the type of defect, when it occurs, how others regard it, and how the individual himself sees it. If the defect is a serious one, such as amputation of an arm or leg, the effect on the individual will be greater than with a less serious defect. If the physical defect occurs early in life, thereby giving the person a longer period of time to adjust, it will not affect him as much as if it occurs during the teens. The attitude and behavior of his parents, siblings, playmates, and teachers will significantly influence the person's own viewpoint of his defect. Probably, though, the most important single factor is the individual's own attitude toward his defect. A relatively minor defect that the person regards as a major catastrophe can seriously affect his psychological adjustment.

Actually, an individual's attitude toward himself is largely determined by how others react to him. In one study the researchers attempted to determine how people react toward a handicapped person. Each subject in the experiment was confronted by another person, who was really a confederate of the experimenter. The confederate appeared before each subject in one of four conditions: (1) in a wheelchair with apparently one leg missing and willing to talk about his handicap; (2) in the wheelchair with only one leg but not willing to talk about his handicap; (3) limping or with a built-up shoe and willing to talk about his handicap; and (4) limping but not willing to talk about his handicap. While the "handicapped" person was presumably attempting to learn a task, the subject was to administer a shock to him. The subject could set the intensity of the shock from light to painful on a ten-position button. He could administer the shock for as long as he wished, although he could only guess at the exact duration. (Of course, the confederate received no real shock, but acted as if he did.) The results of the study showed no differences in the intensity of shocks administered to the confederate in the four situations. However, there were differences in the duration of the shocks, which was much less for wheelchair than for limping confederates. Since the subjects knew the intensity of the shocks that they administered but were not fully aware of the duration of the shocks, evidently people behave differently toward handicapped individuals only when they are not fully aware of what they are doing.

You should remember that your behavior toward a handicapped individual will play a part in how he regards himself. It is a sign of your personal adjustment when you react toward a handicapped individual with friendliness instead of pity. Some people make fun of handicapped individuals as a way of boosting themselves. If you criticize and find fault with others, ask yourself why you do it.

Motor Development

MOTOR DEVELOPMENT is development of control over the muscles of the body. It follows the same general principles of development stated at the beginning of this chapter, which are that development has a predictable pattern, proceeds from general to specific responses, is a continuous process, involves different rates of development, has unique features for each stage, and is more important early in life than it is later on.

Motor development is a very important area in the total development of an individual. It is related to good physical and mental health, socialization, and the development of the person's concept of himself. If the motor development of an individual is slower than that of his age group, he may not be invited to participate in games and activities as much as the more fully developed person. As a result, he may decide that he does not want to join in. By not trying to participate, he will miss the exercise and practice necessary for better physical development and motor coordination.

Motor development influences the socialization of the individual. The newborn infant is totally dependent on others. He cannot move to others; they must move toward him. As he develops control over motor activities, he can crawl, walk, and eventually run to others. The development of the motor skills required in locomotion allows an individual to increase the number of people, events, and situations with which he comes in contact.

A person's motor development is also very important in developing his self-concept. At various stages of life motor development contributes to the individual's growing awareness of himself as an independent person. The young child gains a feeling of independence when he learns to do things for himself. A simple act such as learning to tie a knot in his shoelaces is a rewarding experience for him because it means that he no longer has to depend on someone else.

Competitive athletes, such as this downhill ski racer, develop their motor abilities far more than the average person does.

The way that others behave toward him affects the individual as he forms his own concept of himself. But the biggest factor is how the individual regards himself, not how others see him. He reacts to how he thinks others see him. If discrepancies or differences exist between how he believes others see him and the way that they actually do see him, the individual will be frustrated. An awkward person who believes that he has very good coordination will encounter frustration. Similarly, an individual who thinks that he is a very careful person but constantly falls down because of a lack of coordination is faced with a discrepancy between his actual behavior and his self-concept. The more discrepancies that exist between what is actually true about ourselves and what we think is true, the more frustrated we will be.

The sequence of motor development in a baby. Motor development in the head region takes place at a very rapid rate after birth. The newborn baby can hold his head up for a short period of time, although it is not until about the sixth month that he can hold it up while lying down. Control over eye movements occurs within the first few months. By the third month the baby is capable of performing fairly complex eye movements, such as remaining focused on a moving object as it goes across his field of vision. Babies can perform a type of smile (a reflex) within the first two weeks after birth, although smiling as a specific response to stimulation by another person does not occur until about the third month.

Since the sequence of physical development proceeds from the head downward, the trunk area develops next. After the baby has learned to control his head movements, he can learn to turn over completely. Learning to turn over is a gradual response, in which the baby first turns over from his side to his back, then turns from back to side, and eventually succeeds in making a complete turn. He cannot sit without support until he has full control over his trunk, which does not occur in the average baby until about the tenth month.

In accordance with the sequence of physical development proceeding from the body's central axis to the arms and hands, the average baby will make some general responses to an object placed in front of him by the third month. The baby is able to see the object before he has the coordination to reach it. He will not be able to grasp objects until about the fourth month. In picking up objects the thumb must work in coordination with and opposition to fingers, which occurs about the ninth month.

Most individuals are physically ready to walk between nine and fifteen months of age, but they usually progress through a crawling, creeping, and standing-alone stage before actually walking. Most babies walk within one month after they reach the standing-alone stage.

Characteristics of motor development in childhood, adolescence, and old age. Motor development in early and late childhood increases more slowly than in the period immediately after birth, but it does continue to increase. There is a popular misconception that during adolescence individuals are awkward and clumsy. On the contrary, many studies have shown that during this time motor coordination shows significant increases. Instead, the concept of awkwardness in adolescence seems to be due to the individual's lack of assurance toward himself and his abilities. It arises from his self-concept rather than from any lack of motor control. During adolescence the individual tries out various patterns of behavior and sometimes seems to give the appearance of a lack of coordination.

The development of an individual's motor abilities generally increases until approximately the early to middle twenties. There is a slight decline until the age of fifty and more of a decline to age sixty-five, after which it becomes considerably more rapid. Employers and industries have long used this decline in later years to support the idea of retirement.

Yet by setting an age for retirement they are overlooking individual differences, which are very large within any age group. Some older individuals maintain a high level of performance at the age of seventy.

Differences in the motor abilities of males and females. In general, there are no significant differences between the development of motor skills in males and females in the early years. Differences in motor skills begin to appear at about five years of age. From that time on, boys start to become more efficient in those tasks that require strength, endurance, and speed. The differences become more noticeable during and after puberty, when muscular growth increases considerably more for boys than for girls. On the other hand, girls from about the age of five onward show a superior ability in tasks that require very precise muscle movements, such as finger dexterity. For instance, as a hobby some girls make tiny, intricate designs in needlepoint or embroider complex patterns with great ease. These differences between boys and girls increase as they grow older.

Language Development

Verbalization is the major form of communication between humans, although it is not the only form of communication. We also communicate by facial expression, such as smiling or frowning, and by other behaviors, such as crying. Verbal communication itself has many facets. Even the same words spoken by the same person may have different meanings, such as "I love you," and "I love you?"

How does language develop? There are many theories regarding the origins of language and no one theory has gained complete acceptance. However, it is agreed that reinforcement and punishment play a vital role in the

All infants make similar sounds. The language that this baby learns to speak depends largely on which of her sounds are reinforced.

development of language. We know that newborn infants make a variety of sounds. The initial babblings of infants from different countries cannot be distinguished from one another. Then operant conditioning takes place. The child probably produces a sound that is interpreted by his parents as being similar to one that the parents desire, such as "mama" or "dada." Reinforcement of such a sound is usually immediate and increases the probability that it will occur again.

The average infant makes his first sound in relation to a specific object at about ten months of age, although there is a wide variation among individuals. He then begins to put words together into incomplete sentences. By the age of fifteen months the average child can use a vocabulary of about fifteen words. When he is six years old he can understand the meaning of about 8,000 words. By the time an individual is twenty years old he can understand approximately 50,000 words and can accurately use about 10,000 words.

Deafness can play an important role in the development of language. Therefore, it is important to discover deafness, or signs of it, as early as possible. Two methods of studying a subject's reactions to sounds offer hope in the early detection of deafness. One method is to measure the brain responses of infants exposed to sounds. The other method, especially useful for subjects who are too young to respond to ordinary procedures, is to measure the effects of sound on the heartbeats of newborn infants. The data that result from these procedures are then presented and analyzed by computers for evidence of deafness.

How can we study language? One interesting way of studying language involves the rating of a single word on the basis of several dimensions. This is called the SEMANTIC DIFFERENTIAL, or the study of the differences in the meanings of words as used by different people. According to one theory, words can be classified by three dimensions: (1) value (good-bad, beautiful-ugly, pleasant-unpleasant); (2) potency (strong-weak, masculine-feminine, hard-soft); and (3) activity (fast-slow, active-passive).

An example of how one word was evaluated according to these dimensions is shown in the graph on this page. The data indicate that there is considerable agreement on how male and female college students rate the word "pastel," although the males assigned it a slightly lower value, rated it slightly higher in potency, and saw it as somewhat more active than the females.

It has been found that approximately 50 percent of the differences in meanings between different words can be accounted for in terms of these three dimensions, which seem to occur in the major Indo-European and Oriental languages. This technique is also used to study semantic differences among various cultures.

Emotional Development

EMOTIONAL DEVELOPMENT involves the individual's awareness and expression of an affective experience, which might be pleasurable or not pleasurable, mild or intense. Emotions are something we all have. The kinds of emo-

A semantic differential rating of the word "pastel" by male and female college students

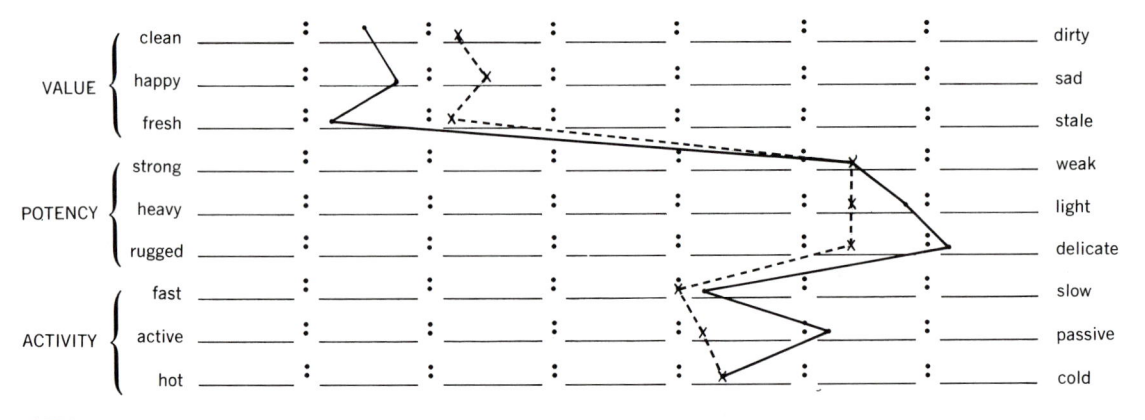

VALUE	clean		dirty
	happy		sad
	fresh		stale
POTENCY	strong		weak
	heavy		light
	rugged		delicate
ACTIVITY	fast		slow
	active		passive
	hot		cold

Men ✕–✕–✕   Women ●——●

150

tions we feel play a large part in how we get along with others and how well we get along with ourselves. An individual whose life is dominated by unpleasant emotions will be an unhappy person. Those people for whom the majority of emotions are pleasant will lead relatively happy lives.

Just as important as the kinds of emotions an individual feels is the way in which he handles his emotions. Two individuals can have the same physiological emotional condition, but one may handle it in an acceptable fashion and the other may not. For example, one student may become angry with his teacher and express his anger in words, whereas another student may become angry and smash a window, throw books on the floor, or perform some other unsuitable act to get rid of the anger.

Emotions involve physiological changes in the body, such as the secretion of adrenalin into the bloodstream, which can be partially counteracted by exercise. The next time you become angry, try running or some other form of strenuous exercise and see how long the anger lasts.

What emotions are present at birth? No specific emotions can be determined in the newborn infant. The only discernible emotion observed is a general state of excitement, which diffuses into distress and delight shortly after birth. Although distress appears a little before delight, both are present by the end

Approximate ages when emotions emerge during the first two years of life

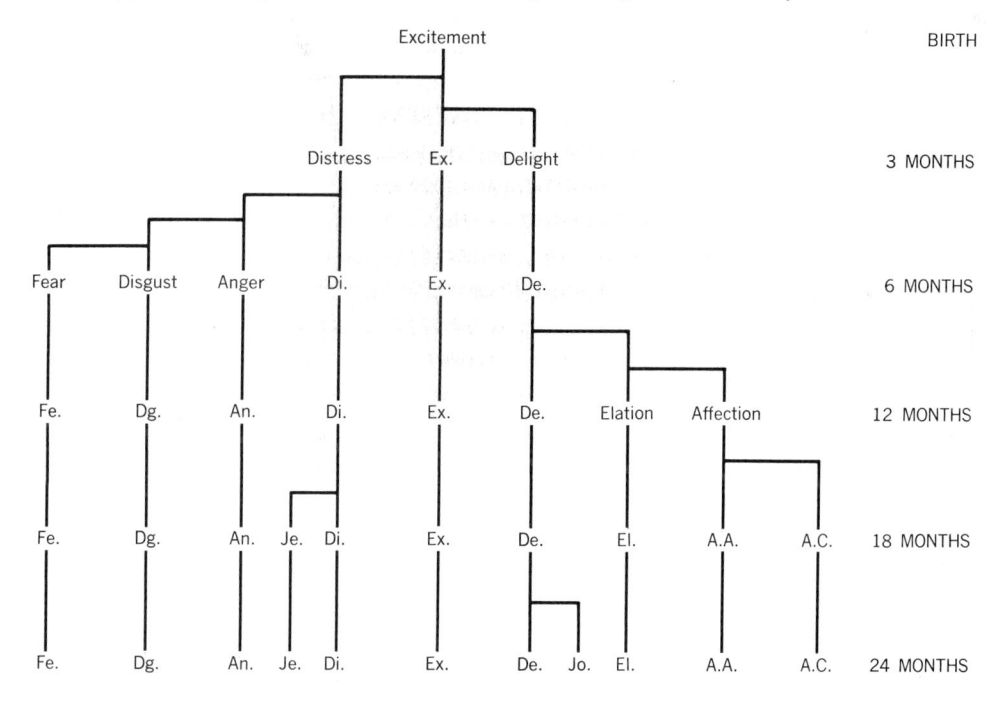

Excitement	BIRTH
Distress, Ex., Delight	3 MONTHS
Fear, Disgust, Anger, Di., Ex., De.	6 MONTHS
Fe., Dg., An., Di., Ex., De., Elation, Affection	12 MONTHS
Fe., Dg., An., Je., Di., Ex., De., El., A.A., A.C.	18 MONTHS
Fe., Dg., An., Je., Di., Ex., De., Jo., El., A.A., A.C.	24 MONTHS

*A.A. affection for adults   Dg. disgust   Fe. fear
A.C. affection for children   Di. distress   Je. jealousy
An. anger   El. elation   Jo. joy
De. delight   Ex. excitment

151

of the third month. The former is characterized by muscular tension and crying; the latter by muscular relaxation and smiling. By the sixth month fear, disgust, and anger appear, and by the end of the first year elation and affection are present.

When young children become angry, they are likely to show overt aggressive or hostile behavior. As they grow older they soon learn that this type of behavior is not socially acceptable and begin to hide it. The overt behavior eventually will become hidden and be manifested in pouting, which may continue even after the person reaches adulthood.

In middle age the male becomes less aggressive and hostile than he was earlier, which is usually attributed to a decline in physical strength. This change is more noticeable in the later years of life, when a man becomes considerably less able to defend himself physically. The emotions that were evoked by distress early in life, such as grief, self-pity, and boredom, seem to take on a more personal character in later years. His emotions are more related to himself as an individual and less involved with the social world around him.

Are emotions learned? It was once thought that some emotions were innate, or present at birth. These emotions were believed to be fear, rage, and love. Fear could be elicited by a sudden loud noise or loss of support, rage by restriction of body movement, and love by stroking and petting the infant. More recently, however, several studies have shown that newborn infants do not display specific emotions.

One of the best-known experiments on innate emotions was conducted by the psychologist John B. Watson. He selected a baby who was referred to as Albert. Since Albert was reared primarily in a hospital nursery (his mother worked in the same hospital), his life had remained more sheltered and restricted than the early lives of most children. Therefore, he had less opportunity than most babies to have learned emotions.

As part of the experiment Watson presented Albert with several objects, among which was a white rat. Little Albert showed no initial fear response to any of the objects, including the white rat. Watson then presented the white rat to Albert accompanied by a loud sudden noise that frightened Albert. This procedure was repeated several times. Eventually, whenever he saw the white rat, Albert showed fear. He had learned to associate the sudden loud noise with the white rat. This is a clear example of how an emotion can be learned through classical conditioning.

There was another interesting outcome of the experiment. Albert had learned to fear not only the white rat but also anything that resembled it, such as a white rabbit or a Santa Claus mask with a white beard, even though these things had not been associated with the noise or with the rat during the experiment. In other words, Albert had generalized fear from the rat to other things. However, Watson was able to recondition Albert so that the baby no longer feared the rat, by keeping him in the presence of the rat while Albert performed a pleasant task, such as eating.

Many times we dislike something or someone but do not know why. An individual who dislikes or is uneasy in the presence of someone with a mustache, for example, may have had some earlier unhappy experience with a man who wore a mustache. Later, he may generalize from that one person to all similar individuals. This may be one way in which individuals develop prejudices against an entire ethnic group.

Although all emotions are probably learned, they are not learned exclusively from personal experiences. Much emotional learning occurs by imitation of the behavior and acceptance of the attitudes of others as thoroughly as if the emotion had been experienced by the individual himself. Some young children hate spinach and other types of food, but on examination it sometimes turns out that they have never tried the food. They have learned not to like it from others. Would you eat fried snake meat or chocolate-covered ants? Probably not, even though you may never have tried them, and even though some people in other countries consider them great delicacies. You learn emotions from the people around you—your parents, siblings, friends, and teachers.

Some common emotions. Everyone shows fear, love, anxiety, worry, anger, or jealousy, although different people show varying amounts of each emotion at different times. The young infant probably fears nothing until his mental development increases to the point where he recognizes the potential danger of an object, event, or situation, such as patting a horse that could bite him. Most children fear specific things, such as snakes, spiders, or worms. During the preadolescent period, the child comes to have more generalized fear, such as worry and anxiety.

Although an individual can probably learn to fear anything, he usually follows a pattern of fears that changes with the different stages of life. Young children fear such things as strange people, unfamiliar animals and objects, and the dark. Ironically, the young child shows more fear than he did as a baby or will show later in life. This is probably because a baby has no understanding of danger, and an older child is able to separate real and imagined dangers more fully. The older child's increase in reasoning can differentiate the real from the unreal and dissolve some fears that were due to ignorance.

The number of fears diminishes after the child enters school. Perhaps the increase in the socialization process as a result of going to school helps the child overcome fears, especially when he learns from his schoolmates that some of his fears have no basis. Also, there is a change in the type of fear. The child shifts his emphasis from fears of tangible things to imaginary fears.

As the individual grows older, he begins to develop fears involving social situations and things he cannot understand at the time, such as thunder and lightning and death. The high school student develops a fear of failing courses, or being "different." As an adult, the person begins to fear loss of security and, especially in the case of males, sexual inadequacy. In old age there is an increase in the fear of death, losing a job, and financial problems.

Social Development

SOCIAL DEVELOPMENT involves learning to act and live in a culture or society as a member of that society. Sometimes it necessitates learning to inhibit your impulses. At other times it requires doing things that you may not like. An individual becomes a sociable person through associations with other people, from whom he learns cultural habits, mores, and what is right and wrong in that society.

When does social behavior appear? Social behavior first appears early in life, when the average baby is about two months old. The baby will cry when an adult leaves him and smile when the person returns. Children under one year of age will pay attention to the presence of another child, but they usually do not interact with two children at the same time until about thirty months of age.

Two of the most obvious social traits that appear in preschool children are dominance and submissiveness. To determine which children are primarily dominant and which are submissive, observe their behavior in a group. As the members of the group change and new members are added, however, some previously dominant children may become submissive, and some submissive children may become dominant.

During the preschool years the child will undergo three stages of interaction with adults: (1) dependence, (2) resistance, and (3) cooperation. Early in life the child passively accepts his dependence on adults. At two years of age he reaches a stage of resistance and rebels against adult standards. This is sometimes called the "I, me, mine" or "Let me do it!" stage. This stage occurs when the child begins to realize that he is a separate individual with certain rights and privileges. It can be a very confusing time of life, for the child must learn that although he does have rights, he also must have limits placed on his behavior. In the third stage the child becomes more cooperative and friendly as he begins to accept the limits imposed on him.

Social changes during the early school years. During the early school years, during grades 1 to 6, several social situations arise that were present to a small degree before but now begin to change the child. As the child enters school he is confronted with conflicting ideas and attitudes to a larger degree than in the past. Meeting new people, being exposed to the educational process, and having to leave home for a large amount of time each day bring about confusing situations for the child. It is at about this point that children begin to develop a disregard for adult standards and adopt those of the peer group. These attitudes increase and reach a peak in

At the age of two a child may rebel against adults and try to do things for himself.

the adolescent period, which occurs at the junior and senior high school level.

During the preschool years and up to about the second grade, the child disregards the sex of playmates. Then, at about the age of eight, males start to choose males and females to choose females. Between this age level and the puberty stage the two sexes develop disrespect, even hostility, for each other, preferring to associate with members of their own sex. Since girls reach the pubertal stage of development about one to two years earlier than males, during their early teens girls will begin to develop an interest in boys that will not be returned until the boys are some two or three years older. The earlier attraction of girls toward boys is probably one major reason that some girls in their early teens date boys who are two or three years older. At this stage, boys their own age are simply not interested in girls.

The desire of individuals to associate with members of their own sex during the early school years leads to the formation of gangs and cliques, but such social behavior is primarily for fun-and-games type of activities. These associations do not have the organization or leaders that gangs have during the adolescent period.

Some characteristics of the social behavior of adolescents. The adolescent period is the time when the individual grows out of childhood into adulthood—usually referred to as the teen years. It is characterized by the individual's striving to be independent from the home but recognizing that complete independence is impossible at this time. The individual rebels. Sometimes he chooses to rebel over minor things, such as how late he can stay out at night. Parents often fail to recognize their children's growing need for independence. Adolescents often fail to recognize that their parents are trying to protect them. When neither parent nor offspring recognizes the other's point of view, both are destined to experience frustration.

One of the most characteristic social developments during this period is the development of heterosexual interests. Generally, the individual passes through a hero-worship stage, then the so-called puppy-love stage, and finally the more intense romantic-love stage.

The first stage, which occurs in the early teens, is characterized by a strong attraction toward someone of the same or opposite sex and is based primarily on great admiration of the person. This person, who is usually older, may be a movie or television star, athletic hero, singer, or a successful person in some other area.

Individuals move out of this stage into the puppy-love stage during junior high school and early senior high school years. The affection then turns from an older person to a member of the opposite sex close to the individual's own age. In female behavior this new interest is shown when girls begin to use make-up, which is one way of making themselves more attractive to the opposite sex, as well as a way to conform to the standards of their age group. In a male this new interest can be seen by an increased desire to show that he is a man, which may cause him to start shaving before his beard has really grown.

The last stage, romantic love, starts in late adolescence and is a more intense, stable, and mature affection. The person's interest in other members of the opposite sex decreases as attention is focused primarily on one individual.

Characteristics of social development in adulthood and old age. The years beyond the teens to the late sixties are chiefly concerned with finding and keeping a job, getting married, and raising a family.

Marriage represents the culmination of the development of heterosexual interests. With marriage comes the responsibility of a spouse and a family. Marriage often means the end of an individual's membership in some of his former social groups, but it also usually leads to participation with new groups, such as other married couples of about the same age. The level of happiness changes during the course of married life, depending to some degree on the circumstances and expectations of the people involved.

As the individual approaches old age, he experiences changes in his physiological, emotional, and mental development. He feels more and more alone. The employed individual begins to fear losing his job and having to retire. When a person has worked long and hard at a job and suddenly finds himself with his time completely free, he may enjoy it very much—at least at first. Doing nothing can be very boring, however, especially if you have been forced to retire. Thus, it is important that individuals prepare themselves for retirement by learning new things and developing some interesting hobby.

A wife usually outlives her husband by several years, which makes old age an even more trying time for many women. The life expectancy for women in the United States is about seventy-five years, compared to about sixty-eight for men.

How Personality Develops

Each individual has a personality. PERSONALITY is the unique organization of an individual's characteristics of adjustment that sets him apart from other individuals. Although individuals' personalities may differ greatly, they have some similar developmental patterns.

The word "personality" closely resembles the Latin word *persona,* which means a mask. In earlier times a persona was a mask that actors wore on the stage so that the audience could tell what part the actors were playing or what emotion they were displaying. If the actor wanted to show joy or happiness, for

For centuries masks have been used in plays to portray certain personalities and the emotions connected with them. Here masks are worn in a performance of Oepidus Rex.

instance, he wore a mask with a smile. Thus, personality is something that each individual shows to other people so they can tell what kind of person he is. There are, however, deeper underlying aspects of an individual's personality that others do not see. In fact, there are parts of his personality that the individual may not be aware of himself. Because of the complex nature of these underlying aspects of personality, only the more obvious parts of personality will be discussed in this section.

How does self-concept affect personality? The self-concept is the core or center of personality. It includes everything that the individual believes about himself. Do you think that you are honest or a cheat, tall or short, smart or dumb? Your self-concept, or ego, provides you with the answer. It also includes what you assume other people think of you. The development of the ego occurs during the first few years of life, when the child reaches the "I, me, mine" stage.

The individual's self-concept governs to a large extent how he behaves. There is a strong tendency to do things that agree with, support, or reinforce the ego. If you see yourself as an honest person (if honesty is part of your self-concept), the chances are you will not cheat on an exam when given the opportunity, since you are honest and you believe that honest people do not cheat.

Formation of the ego involves learning, whether from the attitudes of others or from personal experiences. Parents are the first and most important factor in the development of the child's ego. If parents consistently tell their son, "You are a failure," they are very likely to convince him that this is true. The child may develop the attitude that he cannot do anything well. This attitude becomes part of his self-concept.

Our self-concept is learned not only from parents but also from everyone with whom we come in contact—teachers, peer groups, siblings, and other relatives. Anyone or anything that disagrees with our self-concept will cause us to defend our ego. If you believe that you are very smart and someone tells you that you are stupid, your self-concept will be disturbed, and you will probably want to contradict the person. Not every self-concept necessarily agrees with cultural values. For example, a person who sees himself as the best hubcap stealer in the world will be angry or hurt if you say he is not a good hubcap stealer. The point is that, regardless of the values on which the self-concept is based, the self-concept is defended when contradictory statements occur between what the person believes and what others tell him, or what his own behavior tells him, is true.

The individual who has an inaccurate self-concept is more unhappy, tense, and worried than someone whose self-concept is accurate. When you constantly have to defend your self-concept against others or against your own contradictory behavior you have little time to do anything else. On the other hand, a well-adjusted individual has the ability to change his self-concept throughout life. He can do this even in a case where his self-concept was once true but is true no longer, now that he is older. For example, as the fast, well-coordinated young person eventually reaches middle age, his abilities based on speed and coordination begin to decrease and he cannot keep up the pace of his earlier days. To be accurate, his self-concept must change, too.

How much does personality change? Surprisingly, the basic personality structure of the individual is laid down before he enters school. After he enters school his personality changes very little, although specific ways of behaving or responding may change as he grows older. Unless he undergoes strong emotional shock or psychotherapy, however, his pattern of responding will not change very much during the rest of his life. In general, as the individual grows older, his personality becomes more stable, and significant changes are harder to make. This does not mean that the individual's personality is fixed at any single period of life. It merely means that personality remains much the same after the first few years of life.

One study of individuals from birth to age fifteen indicated that general ways of behaving in a situation changed very little during those fifteen years. The baby who showed fear and screamed when he was a year old, showed fear and ran away at the age of two. Although there was a modification in the specific response because the child had learned to run, the general pattern of behavior was the same.

Mental Development

Another fundamental aspect of human development is the development of an individual's mental abilities. It is important because it has such a decisive effect on the individual's total development. MENTAL DEVELOPMENT refers to the increase and decline of the traits and abilities that comprise an individual's intelligence.

Some problems in studying the development of mental abilities. It is very difficult to determine specific mental traits in infants. At present, measuring the intelligence of babies relies heavily on the measurement of motor abilities, which have a small but positive correlation with intelligence scores later in life. Measuring mental abilities is further complicated by the problem of comparing the results of different intelligence tests, since not all intelligence tests measure precisely the same things. Therefore, some changes may show up in specific mental traits simply because different tests were used at the various age levels. Another factor complicating the description of intelligence over a long period of time is that a longitudinal study over a period of sixty-five years takes exactly that long to make. To avoid waiting so long for conclusions, psychologists have turned to cross-sectional studies for much of the data on this subject. This section will emphasize the aspects of mental growth that psychologists agree upon most.

When do mental traits appear, develop, and decline? One of the first mental abilities that appears in babies is memory. The baby learns that certain faces, such as those of his parents, are associated with pleasant things. Learning plays a major role in the baby's mental development, as it does in other areas of development.

Some other mental traits may exist within the individual but do not show up in his behavior because he lacks the physical growth to express them. For example, the mental ability to solve the problem of getting from one place to another and then returning to the same place by another route might be present, but the behavior cannot occur until the individual has been able to learn to crawl.

One study involving infants from two to eleven weeks of age found that the infants made an avoidance response to the shadow of an object that was coming directly toward them, but not to the shadow if it was on a path that would miss them. Evidently at a very early age individuals have the mental ability to distinguish between objects that are and objects that are not on a collision path with them. And in another study it was shown that, even minutes after birth, human

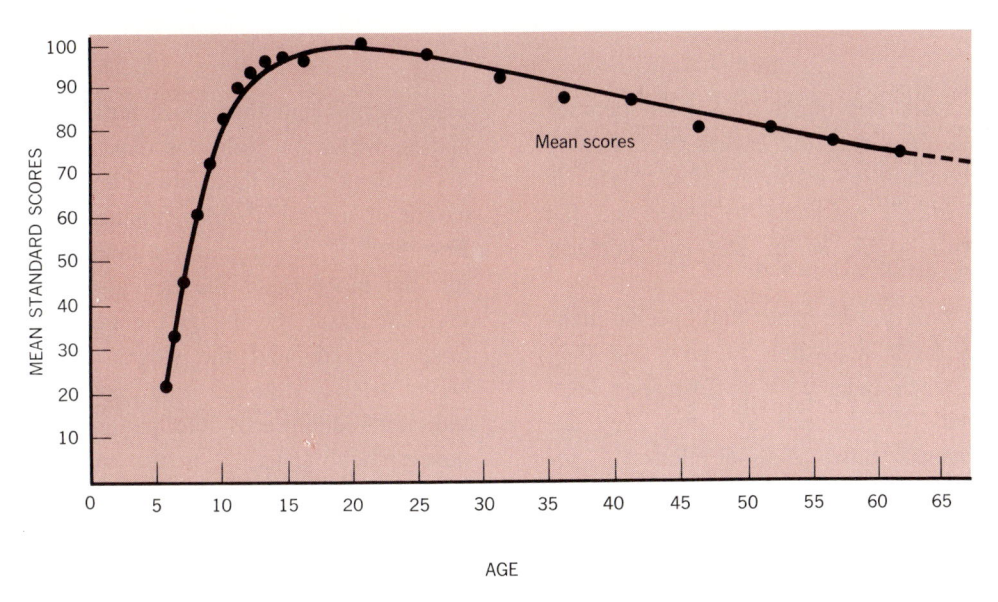

Changes in intelligence scores between the ages of seven and sixty-five

infants have the ability to relate their eye movements to the location of certain sounds. Other infants, as young as thirty days of age, became visibly distressed when their mother's voice came over a loudspeaker located at some place other than where their mother was standing.

Regardless of when mental traits appear, once they have appeared they continue to grow rapidly until the average individual reaches his early twenties. As he passes through the twenties, some mental traits will hold up well, while others will begin a fast decline. However, each mental trait will eventually decline in the individual. The following summary list can be used as a general guide:

1. Verbal ability increases until the early thirties, although it increases less rapidly in the middle and late twenties.

2. Perception of spatial relations (of visual form relationships) significantly slows down in the early twenties, levels off in the late twenties, and begins to decline sharply in the early thirties.

3. Reasoning ability begins to decline in the late teens or early twenties.

4. Numerical ability increases to the middle forties and then declines.

5. Word fluency rises until the early thirties, declines for a few years, rises, and then begins a continuous decline in the early forties.

Generally, the earliest and fastest decline of abilities after early adulthood occurs in the areas of intelligence involving speed in solving problems and abstract reasoning. Those abilities that rely primarily on verbal skills, previous experience, and judgment decline more slowly and later in life.

The increase and decline of mental traits differ according to the composite intelligence score of the individual. Those who are above average will have a sharper rise in the development of mental traits, and their abilities will increase or hold up longer than for the average person. For those below average intellectual ability, the development of traits will reach a peak sooner and more slowly, and will decline faster.

This does not mean that older persons know less than they did earlier or that they do not continue to learn. What decreases is the individual's readiness to learn and the speed with which he or she can perform tasks.

In summary, remember that specific mental traits differ according to how fast they develop, when their peak performance level is reached, and the rate at which they decline. Overall intellectual development increases for the average person until about the twenties. It begins to decline slowly up to the early thirties and then more rapidly until the sixties, when the decline is most rapid. Also, do not forget that there are differences in the extent of mental abilities among individuals. For instance, the higher the intellectual ability, the more rapid the development of individual traits, the higher the peak performance reached, and the slower the decline. Nevertheless, although there are important individual differences, the pattern of mental development generally is the same. This is true of all the areas of development discussed in this chapter.

Terms to Know

cross-sectional method
ego
emotional development
language development

longitudinal method
maturation
mental development
motor development
personality

physical development
self-concept
semantic differential
social development

Topics to Think About

1. Suppose that when you have children, one of your children has a "temper tantrum." How would you handle such behavior?

2. You often hear it said that girls and women talk much more than boys and men. Is there any justification for this statement? If so can you give an explanation?

3. Why do so many people look down on those who have a physical defect of some kind? Does the age of the individual expressing contempt for handicapped persons have anything to do with whether or not he looks down on them?

4. At what age should most men retire from active vocational life? Should the age be the same for women? Should there be a specific retirement age at all? What would happen if there were no set retirement age?

5. What would be the effect on society if medical science were able to make the life expectancy of men equal to that of women?

6. In the United States the average life expectancy at birth is about seventy years. In some countries life expectancy is around thirty-five years. Consider the differences in development between seventy-year-old individuals and people in their thirties. How would the problems of these two life expectancy groups differ?

7. Sometimes we have heard it said that "he (or she) never really grew up." What does this mean?

8. Are cliques contrary to the general principles of democracy?

Suggestions for Activities

1. Assume that you have discovered an individual twelve years of age, who has been reared by wolves since shortly after birth and appears to have average intelligence. Describe the procedures you would use in helping the person become "socialized." How would you teach the person your language?

2. Try to remember how you developed in height in elementary school and even further back, if possible. Perhaps your parents kept a "baby book" that would have a record of your height at different ages. Describe in a report this area of development and if you felt, at different ages, that you were above or below average in developing. What effect might your feelings at that time have had on your present self-concept? Has your study of psychology helped you in evaluating your present self-concept?

3. Imagine that you personally have developed a physical handicap and write a report on how you would react and adjust to it. Be as honest as you can in describing the handicap and how you would feel about it.

4. If you have a tape recorder or one is available, record the voices and speech of children of different age groups. For example, record children whose ages range from one to five years. What changes can you detect in the number of words used at each age level? in the structure of sentences? in the level of difficulty of words used? What other changes do you find?

5. Obtain some old movies of friends or movies of your own family. By watching the movies, can you detect any differences in motor activities, such as running and jumping? Can you find any examples to illustrate any of the principles of development in this chapter?

6. If you have identical twins in your school whom you know personally, describe your observations of the twins, such as similarity of clothing, interests, courses taken in school, and attendance at social events. Be sure that you have the consent of the twins and that no embarrassment to them will result. Do the twins agree or disagree in these areas? Stress any differences you might find.

7. If you have an opporunity to do so, with the parents' consent, pick up a small child to whom you are a stranger. Does the child cry or try to escape? Do reactions to strangers vary with age? If you do not have an opportunity to carry out this activity yourself, you may observe others picking up children to whom they are strangers. For example, as part of the baptismal service in some churches, the clergyman takes a child in his arms. Do children of various ages react differently in this strange situation?

8. Select any two beliefs, interests, or attitudes that you have and try to determine how they came about. When did they originate and how did they develop?

9. Select five things that you are afraid of. Describe your feelings about each one. To what extent, if any, have these fears changed your behavior? Has your study of psychology helped you understand some of your fears? Compare your list with the fears of other students. Is there any agreement?

10. There is growing concern over the use of toys that might be dangerous in some way to young children and babies. Survey several local toy shops that sell toys for babies or young children and look for toys that might have some potential danger to a child. Bring your list to class and discuss what toys you found that might be dangerous. How might you modify these toys to make them safe for babies or children?

Suggestions for Further Reading

Fraiberg, S., *The Magic Years*, Scribner. A paperback that describes emotional development in children.

Hilgard, E. R., R. C. Atkinson, and Rita Atkinson, *Introduction to Psychology*, 5th ed., Harcourt Brace Jovanovich. See Chapter 3, "Infancy and Childhood," and pages 342–45 on emotional development.

Kagan, J., M. M. Haith, and Catherine Caldwell (eds.), *Psychology: Adapted Readings*, Harcourt Brace Jovanovich. See Selection 19, "Motives and Behavior in the Young Child: Hostility and Affiliation"; Selection 20, "How Emotions are Labeled"; Selection 31, "Teddy and Larry: A Comparison of an Institutionalized and a Family-raised Infant"; and Selection 32, "Birth to Maturity."

Kagan, J., and E. Havemann, *Psychology: An Introduction*, 2nd ed., Harcourt Brace Jovanovich. You will find especially interesting Chapter 15, the authors' discussion of three different patterns of personality that exist among infants and what effects these differences have on later life. The chapter considers development from birth to ten years of age.

Lovell, K., and David Elkind (eds.), *An Introduction to Human Development*, Scott, Foresman. A paperback that covers development in the areas of physiology, logical thought, perception, language, and personality.

Meyer, W. J., *Developmental Psychology*, Center for Applied Research in Education. A short book dealing with general principles of behavior development.

Ruch, Floyd L., and Philip G. Zimbardo, *Psychology and Life*, 8th ed., Scott, Foresman. See Chapter 4, "Developmental Processes."

Wertheimer, M., *et al.*, *Psychology: A Brief Introduction*, Scott, Foresman. See pages 114–20, 126–30, 196–99, on the developmental aspects of adapting to the environment, interaction with other people, language development, and age differences.

chapter 7
Measuring Intellectual Ability

WHEN PSYCHOLOGISTS first began to develop tests, they were primarily interested in measuring intellectual ability. Today intelligence is still one of the most frequently measured attributes of human organisms. Over the years research on intellectual ability has answered many questions, but it has also raised many additional questions, as yet unanswered. Perhaps one day some of you will provide answers to those questions.

The Meaning of Intelligence

It is very difficult to give a satisfactory definition of intelligence. Nevertheless, we can say that INTELLIGENCE is the ability of an organism to adapt itself adequately to the new as well as the old situations in the environment. An individual is intelligent to the extent that he can quickly and successfully adjust to situations on the basis of his past learning and his present grasp of the problems he encounters. One psychologist has described intelligence as "the ability to see what ought to be done and how to do it." Adjusting to the environment is the primary general characteristic.

To make a successful adjustment to American society—to live in what we call comfort—it is usually necessary to be able to earn money. But the signs of intelligence and a successful adjustment in one society do not necessarily apply to some other society. For example, to a Pygmy, hunting skill might be more valuable than a million dollars. A Pygmy may have intelligently fitted himself for living in his environment without even knowing what money is.

The highly intelligent person is able to assimilate and retain many facts. Yet it is possible to be a "walking encyclopedia" and still not be very successful in adjusting to new situations. The highly intelligent person not only retains many facts, he also manipulates them and his ideas about them to come up with new solutions to his problems. There is much more to intelligent behavior than appears in one glance at our definition of intelligence. (See pages 188–89.)

How many factors make up intelligence? When items from various tests of intelligence are treated statistically, intelligence can be broken down into a number of factors. There are two main theories of identifying factors of intelligence. The psychologist L. L. Thurstone has classified the ways of being intelligent into seven primary factors. Another psychologist, J. P. Guilford, has broken down intelligence into 120 factors, and holds out the possibility of an even higher number.

Thurstone's studies led him to identify the following seven primary abilities:

   1. *Space factor*—the ability to visualize flat figures and objects, to see the relationships of forms, as in drawings that illustrate three dimensions.

   2. *Number factor*—the ability to do numerical tasks and arithmetic problems, an ability needed, for example, in accounting.

   3. *Verbal comprehension factor*—the ability to understand words, to comprehend and interpret verbal passages.

   4. *Verbal fluency factor*—the ability to express yourself orally or in writing, to think of appropriate words rapidly.

   5. *Memory factor*—the ability to recall learned materials, to remember facts of all kinds with ease.

   6. *Reasoning factor*—the ability to figure out a general rule on the basis of presented data.

Would architects rate high in the space factor of intelligence? Drafting the plans of a building to scale requires the ability to visualize the relationships of forms.

   7. *Perceptual factor*—the ability to grasp visual details and determine similarities and differences between pictures.

Originally some psychologists thought that these seven primary factors were independent of one another, that they were separate fundamental elements of intelligence. However, more recent evidence indicates that these factors are related to each other and therefore are not independent elements, although it is possible that the factors are primary ones but the tests presently available to measure the factors are not pure enough to adequately isolate the factors.

The other major theory that separates intelligence into factors is Guilford's. Guilford developed a structural model of the intellect, which has 120 factors. So far, more than eighty of the 120 single factors of intellectual functioning have been demonstrated through testing.

Older tests of intelligence have placed emphasis on factual data, in which there is one correct answer to a question. Guilford has broadened the concept of intelligence by including divergent thinking, in which the individual is to give the widest possible range of answers. For example, one question might be "What uses can you think of for a straight pin?" An answer might include "to hold two items together, to bend it and use as a fish hook, to clean in small cracks," and so on. By designing tests for this kind of thinking Guilford has increased our understanding of the range of intellectual abilities.

Some useful applications of recognizing factors in intelligence. All too often it has been assumed that a child who is "bright" in some ways must be bright in all ways, or that a child dull in some ways must be dull in all ways. These are wrong assumptions. In actual fact, a child may be high in one factor of intelligence, yet low in another. It is well known, for example, that some children can do well in arts and crafts but have great difficulty in other subjects because they cannot read efficiently. Eventually teachers may be able to fit their methods of teaching to each child's ability in certain factors of intelligence. However, we must not completely overlook the possibility of a general factor—that is, a general intellectual ability.

Knowledge of factors of intelligence may be of value to young people in selecting a lifework. For example, students of superior ability in the verbal factors would probably do well to consider writing or journalism. Students superior in the visualizing (space) and reasoning factors might well consider engineering or work in the physical sciences. However, in our present state of knowledge there are no tests that can tell a young person exactly what vocation he should choose. Many of the factors involved cannot be measured by present tests.

Another great advantage in recognizing the various factors in intelligence has to do with personality development. It may be that many children fail in schoolwork, become discouraged, and develop feelings of inferiority because they are forced to try to succeed in the wrong field. They should be given an opportunity to excel in the field of their greatest ability.

The major drawback to any factor theory of intelligence is that it does not account for the way in which the different factors interact with one another. Perhaps the best position that educators can take is to assume that possibly every intellectual factor can be developed by learning.

Individual Tests of Intelligence

Measurement is a very important part of scientific study. Psychologists have devoted years of work to devising tests to measure intelligence.

How did intelligence tests originate? A number of attempts were made to arrive at measures of general intelligence before a really workable test was devised. Intelligence tests in the form generally used today have developed from the work of Alfred Binet (bi-'nā), a French physician and psychologist. Binet,

These are similar to items on the 1960 Revised Stanford-Binet that are used to test the intelligence of young children. A child is asked to perform various tasks and answer questions.

with the assistance of another French psychologist, Theodore Simon (sē-'mon), published his first measure of intelligence in 1905. This test consisted of thirty tasks to be performed by children. These were simple tasks that the children would be likely to know from their everyday experiences without formal teaching, not the kinds of tasks that the children were required to learn in school.

Binet and Simon made two important revisions of this test. In both revisions they arranged the tasks in groups from age three to adulthood. To select the tasks to be assigned to each age group, Binet and Simon did not depend on their own judgment of what children of a given age should be able to do. Rather, they tested a large number of children on all tasks in their list. If at least half of presumably normal children at a given age passed a task, the task was considered to be correctly placed for that age. For example, they found that about one-half of all children five years of age could count four coins, that most children four years of age could not do so, and that the task was too easy for most children six years of age. Thus, they concluded that the task was suitable for testing five-year-olds.

Some individual intelligence tests for Americans. American psychologists soon became very interested in the work of Binet, and they began using the Binet-Simon tests with American children. These tests were translated from French into English and adjusted to fit the conditions of American life.

One of a number of American psychologists who became involved in the problem of the measurement of intelligence was Lewis M. Terman of Stanford University. In 1916 he published the *Stanford Revision of the Binet-Simon Test*. This test consisted of ninety items arranged by years, covering a range from three years of age to superior-adult ability. The *Stanford Revision* has been used extensively in schools and psychological clinics in America. Two revisions of it, made in 1937 and 1960, are known as the *Revised Stanford-Binet*.

Three other individual tests of intelligence widely used in the United States are the *Wechsler Preschool and Primary Scale of Intelligence* (WPPSI), the *Wechsler Intelligence Scale for Children* (WISC), and the *Wechsler Adult Intelligence Scale* (WAIS). All three tests are composed of two parts: one section on verbal ability and the other on performance. A measure of intellectual ability is obtained for each part individually. The total score is then based on a composite score of the two parts combined. The WPPSI is designed to measure the intelligence of individuals from four to six and one-half years of age; the WISC measures individuals who are two through fifteen years of age; and the WAIS measures individuals who are sixteen years of age and older. One difference between these tests and the *Revised Stanford-Binet* is that on the *Revised Stanford-Binet* items measuring different factors (such as verbal and numerical ability) are mixed together within any single age grouping, whereas on the Wechsler tests all similar items are under one heading, in an order starting with easy questions and proceeding to very difficult ones.

In conclusion, it should be stated that psychologists quite often obtain important information about an individual from an intelligence test in addition to his score. For example, on one of the timed sections of the WAIS the tasks are arranged in order of difficulty. The last series of tasks become very difficult and can be frustrating for the individuals working on them. While administering the WAIS, one psychologist, to learn more about the subject's behavior, permitted him to continue past the time limit for solving one task (without informing the subject or giving him credit for anything done in the extra time). The individual finally became so frustrated that he picked up the blocks used in the problem and threw them against the wall, shouting "No one can do this!" On the other hand, another subject, faced with the same problem and allowed to work well past the time limit, was also unsuccessful in solving the problem, but showed seemingly endless persistence in continuing to work on it. Given this information, which of the two subjects would you recommend for college, all other things being equal between them?

Performance tests of intelligence. Sometimes psychologists wish to determine the intelligence of someone who has a different cultural background, is handicapped by a lack of understanding of the English language, or is too young to know the language, such as an infant. Performance tests, occasionally known as "nonverbal" tests, are designed to be administered to these persons. Such tests are usually of the form-board or picture-completion type. The form board consists of a board with recesses into which the individual must insert variously shaped forms. The picture-completion test is one in which the person must select certain parts that will complete a picture. Actually, performance test results relate less closely than verbal test results to combined verbal and performance test results. Most psychologists prefer to use tests that measure both verbal and performance aspects of intelligence.

One factor on the *Wechsler* and *Revised Stanford-Binet* tests is auditory memory. Testing auditory memory is also useful for measuring individuals who do not speak the English language. A performance test requires

A nonverbal performance test of intelligence is useful for testing individuals who have difficulty with verbal tests.

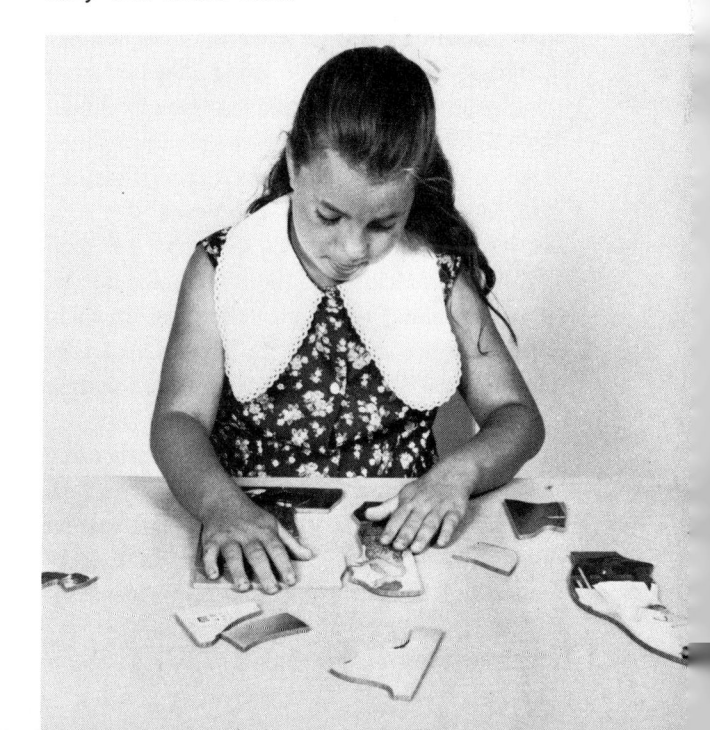

little or no verbal instruction by the person administering it. For example, the examiner can tap on a desk three times with a pencil, as the subject listens and watches. Then the examiner hands the pencil to the subject and indicates that he is to repeat the same tapping. After the subject repeats the same number of taps, the examiner repeats the taps but lengthens the number of digits presented. For example, he may tap three times, pause, then tap two more times (3-2). The number of digits presented can be lengthened to make any combination of numbers, although the digit 5 is usually the highest tapped out. Each digit can be reused, however, so that the length of one series can be quite long (1-4-3-2-2-5). Notice that it makes no difference what language the subject uses for the digits, as long as he repeats the same number of taps as the examiner in the same order.

Group Tests of Intelligence

All the measuring devices mentioned so far have been individual tests; that is, the examiner gives the test to one individual at a time. Obviously, any extensive program of individual testing requires many trained clinical psychologists and a great deal of time and money.

During World War I the army was faced with the problem of testing the intelligence of many thousands of men. There was work in the army that could be done by men of very low general intelligence, other work for men of very high general intelligence, and all kinds of jobs between these extremes that required men of all degrees of intelligence. In the rush of war, there was not enough time, nor were there enough trained psychologists, to give individual tests to all the men. A group of psychologists was called together to construct group tests of intelligence.

In all, 1,726,966 enlisted men and officers were tested during World War I. After the war the large-scale intelligence testing in the army came to a close for a time. However, the foundation had been laid, and work in group intelligence testing continued in other fields, especially in the schools.

How do schools use group intelligence tests? Schools have used group intelligence tests quite extensively since the 1920's. You have probably taken at least one of these tests some time during your school career. School officials use these test scores to get a rough measure of each student's intellectual ability. Sometimes they then group students into fast, average, and slow learning sections and adjust instructional methods accordingly. Although much can be said for this educational practice, teaching and learning involve so many variables that sectioning on the basis of group intelligence test scores alone may lead to situations that do not serve the best interest of individual children. For all children presenting unusual problems, group intelligence tests should be followed by individual tests, administered and interpreted by trained psychologists.

Group intelligence tests for school use have certain advantages over individual intelligence tests. There are not enough trained psychologists to enable schools to give each child an individual test. Also, the cost per student would be prohibitive for most schools. Group intelligence tests can be administered and scored by school administrators and classroom teachers who are not trained psychologists and who are already salaried employees of the school system. A large number of children can be tested at one time, and their papers can be scored easily, often by a machine.

Offsetting these advantages is the fact that a group test may not give a very valid measure of a given child's intellectual ability. He may be emotionally upset or not feeling well at the time the test is administered, he may fail to understand directions, or he may not be motivated to do his best. In some cases children have achieved high scores because they have managed to copy from the papers of other children! The trained psychologist administering an individual test can avoid such conditions.

As you can see, from the practical point of view of the school, group intelligence tests have many advantages. From the point of view of the individual child needing guidance and assistance, they may have some disadvantages.

No psychologist claims that his test, whether an individual or group test, is a perfect measure of general intelligence or of any factor in intelligence. Yet tests are accurate enough to give a mathematical measure. They enable the psychologist to express an individual's intelligence by a number.

One word of caution about intelligence tests and the measurements they give. Such tests are very valuable in the hands of a trained psychologist, but they should never be used or interpreted by untrained individuals.

The Intelligence Quotient (IQ)

A term often used to give a mathematical measure of intelligence is the "intelligence quotient," or IQ. There are many misconceptions about an IQ. Actually, an INTELLIGENCE QUOTIENT is merely the ratio between a person's mental age and his chronological age. It is expressed by the following formula:

$$\text{Intelligence quotient} = \frac{\text{mental age}}{\text{chronological age}} \times 100$$

$$IQ = \frac{MA}{CA} \times 100$$

An individual's MENTAL AGE (MA) is his present level of mental functioning, as determined by his scores on a standardized test of intelligence. If a child's performance on a mental ability test is equal to the performance of children exactly five years old—if he can do the tasks that most children five years of age can do and no more—he is said to have a mental age of five years. A child may have a mental age of five years and have a chronological age of four or six years. An individual's CHRONOLOGICAL AGE (CA) is the number of years, months, and days since his birth, usually rounded to the nearest month when used in computing the IQ. The intelligence quotient is a convenient way to express the ratio between mental age and chronological age, and thus show the rate of intellectual growth.

Strictly speaking, the term "IQ" applies only to individual tests of the Binet type. However, a number of group tests also indicate a score somewhat comparable to an IQ.

How is an IQ calculated? Suppose an intelligence test shows that a child can do what the average child eight years of age can do. That is, he has a mental age of eight years. Furthermore, suppose that his chronological age is also eight years. That is, it is just eight years since he was born. To find his intelligence quotient, divide his mental age by his chronological age and multiply by 100, as follows:

$$IQ = \frac{MA}{CA} \times 100 = \frac{8}{8} \times 100 = 100$$

(The 100 in the formula is simply for the purpose of enabling psychologists to express an IQ without using a decimal point—merely a matter of convenience.)

Now suppose an intelligence test given to a child indicates that he can do what the average child six years of age can do. That is, his MA is six years. However, his birth records shows that he is chronologically eight years of age. His intelligence quotient would be computed as follows:

$$IQ = \frac{MA}{CA} \times 100 = \frac{6}{8} \times 100 = 75$$

To sum up, if a person can do less on an intelligence test than the average person of his chronological age, he has an IQ below 100. If he can do more than the average person of his chronological age, he has an IQ above 100. Remember that MA shows the present level of intellectual functioning, while IQ shows the rate of intellectual development.

Although the concept of the IQ is often useful in measuring the intellectual ability of children, as a measure of adult ability it is subject to various errors and is approximate only. For example, an individual's chronological age continues to change, although his mental age becomes relatively stable during later years. Therefore, the method of computing IQ just described is no longer useful, because it presumes that both chronological age and mental age as measured by tests are continuing to grow. Then, too, adults are usually tested for ability in specific fields rather than for the general ability that tests designed for children measure. For these reasons, psychologists have refined their methods of computing the IQ. In fact, in the latest (1960) revision of the Stanford-Binet, special statistical adjustments (rather than the ratio of MA to CA) are employed to determine a person's IQ.

Some tests of intelligence now use a multi-media approach. They may include slides shown on a screen, a tape recording, and films, as well as verbal material and a test booklet to answer.

A more recent and well-established method of calculating IQ results is the DEVIATION IQ, which is used on the Wechsler tests. This method of computing an IQ places emphasis on comparing a person's ability with people of his own chronological age. The score on a test for a given individual is compared to the average score of a large number of persons who represent that particular group.

There are also two new ways of measuring IQ currently being investigated. One of these is a multi-media approach, which gives instructions through the use of films, slides, and tapes. Test booklets use cartoons, geometric shapes, and other visual forms. The test yields thirty-five scores that are estimates of language development, the specific style of response used by the subject, and ability to form concepts, solve problems, and do logical thinking. Preliminary findings indicate that results of these tests are valid for different ethnic groups.

A second approach under investigation now involves calculating IQ by measuring electrical brain waves. In this method a light is flashed in the eyes of a subject. The changes in brain waves are then recorded and analyzed by a computer. The speed at which the brain waves change is the measure of intelligence—the faster the change, the higher the IQ. The results seem to correlate well, although not completely, with standard IQ scores. This method has the advantage of not being culturally biased toward any particular group, such as white middle-class children, since it measures physical, not cultural or emotional factors.

Does the IQ remain stable through life? The IQ of an individual tends to remain approximately stable—that is, approximately the same—throughout his life. Suppose a child whose chronological age is three takes an intelligence test and shows a mental age of three. In other words, his IQ is 100. When he is five, tests show that his mental age is five —his IQ is again 100. When tested at age ten, he also shows an IQ of 100. In such a case the IQ is considered stable—it has remained the same. Actually, such a close correspondence in IQ from year to year is rare. But in the majority of cases the IQ does not vary more than about five points above or below its average value from year to year.

There is considerable evidence that tests of babies and preschool children do not predict later intelligence test scores very well. During an individual's early years, test results indicate that the IQ may vary considerably rather than remain stable. However, the variation may be due in part to the inadequacy of the tests used to measure intelligence during the very early years of life.

Although the intelligence tests for older children and adults produce more stable IQ's than do tests for very young children, the IQ's of adults also change somewhat, in many cases becoming higher. We have spoken of the group tests of intellectual ability that were developed and administered during World War I (p. 168). Thirty years after they had taken one of the army tests, a group of 127 men took the same test again. The results showed that the group had increased their scores over the period of thirty years. These were college-trained men who, as a consequence of their training, had tended to live in challenging environments. But there is some evidence that even retarded individuals improve in intelligence test scores as they grow older, providing they live in an environment that is challenging to them.

There is even evidence that a change in motivation of a person taking an intelligence test can produce some change in IQ. One scientist says that students are not likely to exert their full powers in a test conducted merely for research purposes. He has found that when a student's acceptance at some school or university depends on his intelligence test score, the score may rise ten IQ points higher than when the student takes the test merely for a research study.

One way of viewing intelligence is to consider that there are two aspects—the innate potential, and the observable aspects. Intelligence tests deal with the observable aspects, the level of performance or comprehension at a given point in the development of the individual. The innate potential aspect of intelligence does not change in a person, unless he has some organic difficulty. The observable levels of intelligence, on the other hand, do change.

How much of intelligence is inherited? Many people believe that intelligence is primarily inherited. One psychologist has stated that he believes 80 percent of intelligence within a family group is due to heredity. However, there are serious considerations to take into account in interpreting the results of such studies. It is necessary to examine the populations involved in the studies, the specific intelligence tests used, and the statistical assumptions made by the investigator.

Several recent studies have indicated that little or no difference in intelligence and academic achievement test scores exists between minority and white students when social and environmental factors are taken into account. Some of the socioeconomic factors that were taken into account in these studies were the amount of space in the home, whether the mother expected her children to go beyond high school, whether the father had more than nine years of schooling, if English was spoken all the time or most of the time in the home, whether the setting was rural or urban, and the geographical location. One psychologist has proposed that formulas be developed to translate IQ's in terms of the home and community so that all IQ's would be comparable.

Mental maturity. As a person grows up, he continues to learn more and more about how to adjust himself to his surroundings. Thus, he is able to do (let us say) eight-year-old work at age eight, ten-year-old work at age ten, and twelve-year-old work at age twelve. His IQ remains constant because each year he is able to answer more questions on an intelligence test. That is, his mental age keeps up with his chronological age.

Psychologists have said there comes a time, however, when he is no longer able to improve appreciably in his ability to answer questions on an intelligence test. When a person ceases to improve his score as he grows older, we say he has reached intellectual or MENTAL MATURITY. Some psychologists have placed this age as early as sixteen or even thirteen, some as late as the mid-twenties.

Of course, the idea of mental maturity does not imply that an individual cannot learn after reaching such maturity. He may show great improvement in his ability to answer questions in specific fields, such as science, language, history, finance, and business administration. Also, some factors of intellectual ability tend to remain relatively high as an individual grows older, whereas ability in other factors tends to decline.

There is no simple answer to the question of what age individuals achieve mental maturity. The age seems to differ greatly from individual to individual, although it is probably later in life for persons of superior ability than for persons of quite limited ability.

The classification of IQ's. Sometimes it is convenient to apply descriptive terms to IQ ranges. One classification is given in the table on this page. You will note that in this classification IQ's from 90 to 109 are described as average, or normal. Nearly half of all individuals tested (actually 46½ percent) have IQ's in this range. Although it is not indicated in the table, we know that about one-third of all persons have IQ's between 100 and 116, and that about one-third have IQ's between 84 and 100.

Descriptive Classification of Intelligence Quotients

IQ	DESCRIPTION
180 and above	Genius
140–179	Very superior, or gifted
120–139	Superior
110–119	High average
90–109	Average, or normal
80–89	Low normal, or dull
70–79	Borderline
Below 70	Mentally retarded

It is necessary to be very cautious in using a descriptive classification of IQ's. Such classification schemes are quite arbitrary. Psychologists are not agreed on the descriptive terms to be used. Furthermore, the IQ is, at best, a rough measure of intelligence. It certainly would be unscientific to say that an individual with an IQ of 110 is of high average intelligence, while an individual with an IQ of 109 is of only average intelligence. Such a strict classification of intellectual abilities would fail to take account of social elements such as home, school, and community. These elements are not adequately measured by present intelligence tests. Furthermore, it would not take account of the fact that an individual may vary somewhat in his test score from one testing to another.

Measures of intelligence are valuable, but much harm can be done by persons who try to classify individuals strictly on the basis of such measures alone. No one should be either alarmed or discouraged if he finds that his IQ is not as high as he might have hoped. Remember that many elements besides IQ contribute to success and happiness.

Practical Applications of Intelligence Tests

The development of intelligence tests led overoptimistic persons to believe that a simple method had been found for fitting everyone into a suitable place in life. Actually, human beings are far too complicated for any simple procedure in arranging their lives. Nevertheless, on the basis of intelligence tests, many sound suggestions can be made for school and adult living.

How schools use intelligence tests. Some schoolwork requires greater ability (either in general intelligence or in specific factors) than other schoolwork. To give a child of high intellectual ability work requiring very little such ability is as great a mistake as to give a child of low intellectual ability work requiring high ability. In neither case are the children happy in their work. Children need to be classified so that they may be given suitable schoolwork. Some modern group tests are so constructed that they measure not only general intelligence but also factors in intelligence. For example, verbal and nonverbal factors may be measured. The development of group intelligence tests such as these has made it possible to test and consequently to classify many children at one time and at relatively little cost to the schools. Today many elementary schools, high schools, and colleges give some kind of individual or group intelligence test as a regular part of the school's duties.

A psychologist is often called on to advise parents and teachers about the school possibilities of particular children. Children with IQ's below 50 will probably never be able to do even first-grade work satisfactorily in traditional schools. Those with IQ's in the 50's may be able to do schoolwork through the second grade but probably can go no further. Children with IQ's from 60 to 65 are also very limited in their scholastic ability. No matter how long they stay in school, they usually cannot do satisfactory work beyond the third grade. Children with IQ's in the 70's cannot satisfactorily do higher than about fourth- or fifth-grade work. Those with IQ's in the 80's can probably complete the seventh and perhaps the eighth grade. Pupils with IQ's from 90 to 110 or above can do high school work, although those near the 90 mark have some difficulty. Individuals with IQ's of 115 and above can do college work satisfactorily. There is also evidence that students with IQ's in the neighborhood of 100 can do acceptable college work, especially for the first year or two, depending on the standards of the college and the willingness of the student to work hard.

What is the relation between IQ's and school grades? What is the relationship between intelligence, as measured by intelligence tests, and ability to be educated, as measured by subject matter tests and school marks? In the elementary school, psychologists have found a close relationship between achievement in classwork and intelligence test scores. This means that, by giving an intelligence test early in the school life of a child or early in a school year, the teacher will be able to predict with considerable accuracy the quality of work the child will be able to do. Teachers recognize, of course, that factors other than intelligence are involved in schoolwork. Furthermore, predictions of school success should never be made on the basis of a single intelligence test score, especially a score from a group test.

Prediction of school achievement from intelligence test scores is less certain at the high school level than at the elementary school level. There are two reasons for this. One is that students of low intelligence usually drop out of school at the first opportunity. Consequently, high school students form a

Schools can make use of intelligence tests by giving school readiness examinations, to help judge if a child is ready to start school.

more homogeneous group than do elementary school students. That is, there is less range in intellectual ability within the group. The majority of students at the high school level are of average or higher intellectual ability. Thus, it is harder to distinguish between them and harder to predict that one will do better than another.

A second reason for the lower relationship in predicting school achievement at the high school level than at the elementary school level is that more factors are involved in high school achievement. In elementary schools all students must learn basic facts and skills. The subjects studied are much the same for everyone. But high school students have some opportunity to choose the subjects they wish to study. Consequently, interest plays a greater part in determining achievement than it does at the elementary level. The high school student has more opportunities for social life than the elementary school student. If the high school student indulges in too much social life, his school success will not be very closely related to his intellectual ability. High school students often have jobs outside school hours. If these jobs take time that should be devoted to study, the relationship between school success and intelligence will be less.

At the college level, the relationship between achievement in classwork and intelligence test scores is even less. The college group is even more homogeneous in intellectual ability than the high school group. Many persons not in the upper levels of intelligence do not attempt to go to college. Also, college students have much more freedom than high school students. If a college student does not wish to study, he does not have to do so. In many cases the college student lives away from home. If he has not learned to take care of himself, he may indulge in excessive social activities or just plain loafing, because his parents are not present to make him study. Furthermore, students differ in the way they respond to the stress of college examinations. There is evidence that students who have records of good marks show a decrease in quality of work under such pressure. Perhaps, at least to some extent, some students obtain poor marks because of the stressful nature of college examinations rather than because of a lack of intellectual ability. All such factors tend to reduce the relationship between intellectual ability and school achievement.

Intelligence tests have proved to be of great value in helping teachers and administrators in their tremendously important task of guiding students. In some cases too much confidence has been placed in the score on a single test. Sometimes teachers and administrators have failed to recognize the importance for school success of the various factors in intelligence and of elements other than intellectual ability. Nevertheless, when properly used, intelligence tests are one of the major contributions of psychologists to the work of the schools.

Intelligence tests and jobs. Business executives sometimes ask psychologists to help them by devising and giving intelligence tests to their employees and to applicants for positions. In most cases of industrial intelligence testing, group tests are used. Although applicants may be tested one at a time as they appear, for convenience they are given group tests rather than individual tests.

One psychologist gave intelligence tests to a group of clerical workers. He compared their scores with the percentage of turnover for a period of thirty months. (*Turnover* is the rate at which employees leave jobs and are replaced by others.) The clerical work was graded into five degrees of difficulty.

Turnover for Various Grades of Clerical Workers of High and Low Intelligence Test Scores

GRADE OF WORK	PERCENT TURNOVER FOR INTELLIGENCE TEST SCORES OF 80 POINTS OR LESS	PERCENT TURNOVER FOR INTELLIGENCE TEST SCORES OF 110 POINTS OR MORE
A	37	100
B	62	100
C	50	72
D	58	53
E	66	41

Grade A was the lowest grade, the work consisting simply of opening mail. Grade B work required more ability than Grade A work, Grade C required more than Grade B, and so on up to Grade E. The individuals in Grade E work were private secretaries with very responsible positions. The percentage of turnover for each grade of work was computed for individuals who had test scores of 80 points or less and for those who had scores of 110 points or more. (Note that these scores are not IQ's.) The table above gives the results.

As you can see, persons of low intellectual ability tended to remain in the lower-grade jobs, but persons of high intellectual ability quit these jobs. On the other hand, persons of low intellectual ability tended not to remain in the higher-grade jobs, whereas those of high intellectual ability tended to keep the more difficult jobs.

It must be admitted, however, that quite a number of studies have shown very little, if any, relationship between general intelligence and degree of proficiency or success in particular jobs. There seems to be much waste of intellectual ability in industry. The student of superior ability should resolve not to permit himself to be kept in a job that does not challenge his intellectual ability.

What is the relation of intelligence to vocations? Many studies have shown that on the average, men engaged in the professions tend to have higher intelligence test scores than men in clerical and business positions. In turn, clerical workers and businessmen tend to have higher scores than skilled laborers. Skilled laborers tend to have higher scores than semiskilled laborers. The lowest average scores are made by unskilled laborers. This relationship of intelligence to vocation was first noted during World War I, when soldiers were classified according to their vocations in civilian life, and intelligence test scores for each vocation were assembled. This relationship was found to hold true in many studies made since then.

There is a relationship between the kind of work a person can do successfully and his ability as measured by intelligence tests. Yet always remember that many elements other than general intelligence are involved in success in any vocation. An individual may be appreciably below the test score average for a given vocation, but if he is sufficiently enthusiastic and willing to work hard, he can be reasonably successful. There are elements other than intellectual ability to consider when selecting your lifework.

Mental Retardation

The table on page 173 indicates that individuals with IQ's below 70 are often spoken of as being mentally retarded. Measurement of the IQ alone, however, is insufficient to determine whether or not a person is mentally retarded. In fact, psychologists often try to get away from this tendency to think of mental retardation in terms of IQ. Social factors are very important in determining whether or not a given person should be classified as retarded. Nevertheless, IQ's are helpful in making a diagnosis and will be considered, along with social factors, in our study of mental retardation.

Mental retardation is a great social problem. It has been estimated that about 3 percent of the population of the United States is mentally retarded. Some are being cared for and trained in special institutions for the retarded. Still other mentally retarded persons may be found in prisons, reformatories, hospitals, and social welfare institutions. However, the great majority of mentally retarded individuals are not institutionalized.

There are four commonly described levels of mental retardation: mild, moderate, severe, and profound. People have social contacts with some higher-level retarded persons nearly every day without recognizing them as retarded.

Severely and profoundly retarded persons. In your everyday experiences you probably seldom see a severely or profoundly retarded individual. These persons are nearly always cared for in special institutions. It is estimated that they constitute only a tiny fraction of all mentally retarded individuals. Some are so low in intellectual ability that they cannot understand the most simple statements or utter simple words. Often they cannot wash and dress themselves. Some cannot learn to

Severely retarded individuals are not able to take care of themselves. Usually they require custodial care, since they need someone to dress them, feed them, and help them with other essential activities.

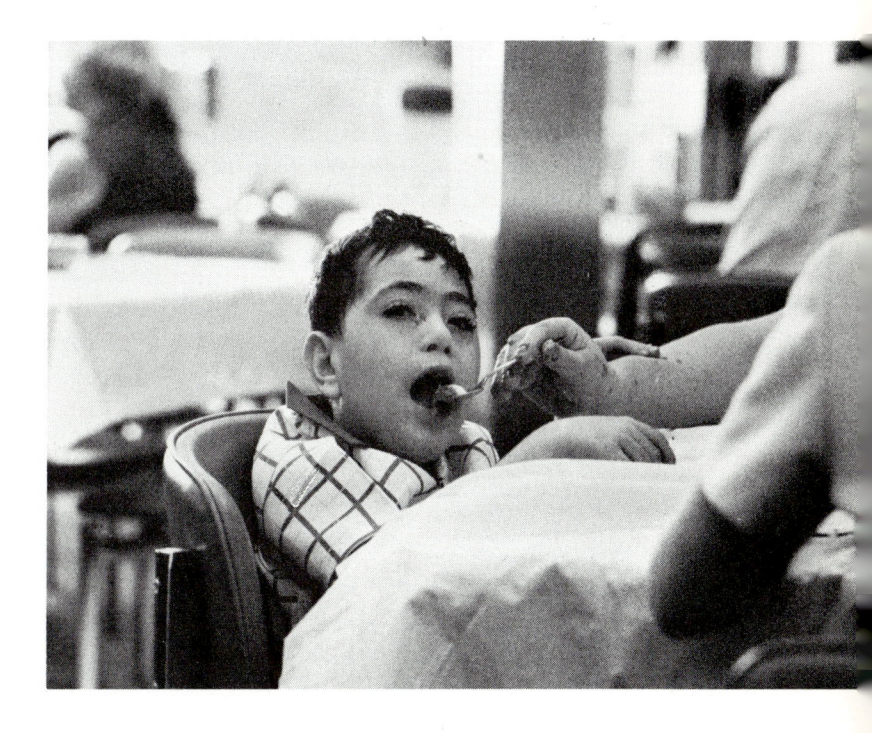

eat and drink or take care of their other bodily needs without assistance. If permitted to be out of institutions, they would not know enough to avoid the ordinary dangers of life. If able to walk, they would be likely to walk directly in front of speeding cars. They are custodial cases, they must be cared for by others, and no amount of training will make independent, self-supporting citizens of them.

Profoundly retarded persons—those individuals whose IQ is below 20—show practically no response to stimulation from their environment. Severely retarded persons, with IQ's between about 20 and 35, have about the same intellectual ability as a normal three-year-old child. Even though the individual may be an adult twenty or twenty-five years of age, he can do no better on an intelligence test than a normal child who is just learning to talk well.

Moderately retarded persons. Moderately retarded persons have more ability to adjust to life than do severely and profoundly retarded individuals. They are, however, unable to respond in any satisfactory way to the teaching of ordinary school subjects. In special schools for the training of the retarded they can be taught to take care of themselves to a certain extent (to avoid the common dangers of life, to feed, dress, and wash themselves), and to help in the work of the institution (to polish floors, make beds, set tables, help in a laundry, and perform other simple routine

Many individuals who are mildly retarded are educable—they can learn certain simple skills that may enable them to support themselves. In the training school shown below, a mildly retarded person is being taught the fundamentals of a printing press.

tasks). But they must have someone watch over them all the time and tell them just how and when to do things.

After a period of training, some are able to return to their homes, provided the parents are willing to assume the responsibility of supervising their activities. They may help with tasks in the home or do other useful work under supervision. They seldom, however, can be entirely self-supporting.

In terms of IQ, moderately retarded individuals range from about 36 to 52. As adults, their mental ages range from about four years to about seven years. More individuals are moderately retarded than are severely retarded, but the moderately retarded still constitute only a small percentage of all mentally retarded persons.

Mildly retarded persons. Persons who have IQ's ranging from about 53 to 69 are usually considered mildly retarded. The great majority of all mentally retarded persons are in this group. Many of them are not in institutions but live in the community. The mental ages of adult mildly retarded persons are usually between eight and twelve years.

Mildly retarded children are unable to progress normally in ordinary schools. In special ungraded classes, and after much time and effort, they may learn to read, to write or print, and to do simple arithmetic problems. Ordinarily, they are not able to progress much beyond the level of the third grade, no matter how long they remain in school. However, mildly retarded persons can be trained so that they can take their places in society as self-supporting citizens. They are capable of earning their living as domestic servants, farm workers (not farmers), day laborers, routine factory workers, and so on. Unfortunately people do not always give the mentally retarded a fair chance to earn a living.

Some adults with IQ's in the 60's are able to make their way in their home communities, though they are probably thought of as dull or "odd." Other persons with IQ's in the 70's have to be removed from the community and placed in institutions. Why must one individual be institutionalized when he has a higher IQ than an individual who is not institutionalized? Much depends on emotional stability. Some mildly retarded persons are well behaved, fairly industrious, and inoffensive, while others are easily upset and are constantly getting into social trouble. The well behaved have adjusted sufficiently to remain in the community. For the sake of the society, however, the less well controlled individuals must be placed in institutions.

How well a mildly retarded individual adjusts socially depends a great deal on how much love, care, and help he receives at home. Members of the family can also assist him with regard to the law. Sometimes mildly retarded persons get into trouble with the law because they do not understand certain moral and legal obligations or foresee the consequences of their actions.

What can mentally retarded persons learn? In recent years educators have become more aware of the possibilities of providing special classes for the mentally retarded.

Classes for mildly retarded individuals deal primarily with the programs emphasizing social skills, the use of money, and the development of simple occupational skills. Such classes are designed for the mentally retarded who are *educable*. These persons are capable of learning some of the simple processes involved in such subjects as reading and arithmetic.

Classes for the moderately retarded have more limited objectives, although as adults these persons can be taught to take care of themselves and to work in unskilled or semi-skilled occupations with supervision.

The severely retarded can be taught, as adults, to maintain some self-care under constant supervision. That is, they are *trainable*. Some experimental data from recent studies indicate that operant conditioning procedures are useful in training the severely retarded.

The profoundly retarded may develop some motor and speech abilities, but they are incapable of self-help and need complete care and supervision, even in adult life.

Today more emphasis is being placed on formulating new educative programs that make appropriate use of principles of learning to enable mentally retarded persons to become active, productive members of society. There are many programs of education and training specifically designed to help such persons care for themselves and, if possible, obtain work in various service occupations. Some products today are made entirely by mentally retarded persons. When they are hired, mentally retarded individuals usually have excellent attendance and production records. The majority of those who eventually do not continue at a job have dropped out because of their inability to cope with the social, personal, and interpersonal problems that arise in any employment situation. This is very understandable, since most mentally retarded persons who are employed have never worked before and are unaccustomed to the fast-moving world of business. Training and educating programs have as their goal to equip more mentally retarded individuals to lead more constructive lives in the community.

What causes mental retardation? Why are millions of Americans mentally retarded? At the present time there are more than 100 known or suspected causes of mental retardation, yet it is very difficult and sometimes impossible to determine the precise causes in a specific case. Although mental retardation does run in families, and many medical men and psychologists believe that heredity is the basic factor in causing mental retardation, there are other known causes. Some of these other causes involve environmental factors.

Injury before, during, or shortly after birth is responsible for some cases of retardation. Toxic agents, such as carbon monoxide and lead, may bring about brain damage in an unborn child. Biochemical factors, genetic-chromosomal factors, and premature birth cause some of the other cases of mental retardation. If, early in her pregnancy, the mother develops a syphilitic or other infection, such as measles, she might have a retarded child. Also, certain glandular deficiencies are present in some mentally retarded persons. Yet, despite all these possible causes, in many instances the specific cause of mental retardation is unknown.

Recent studies have indicated a relationship between malnutrition and intelligence. In a series of studies with animals it has been shown that early malnutrition produces a permanent reduction in brain size. The earlier the malnutrition, the more severe the damage and the more difficult it is to correct, if at all possible. Research with human beings has produced similar results. Children exposed to severe early malnutrition show deficiencies in language development, perception, and short-term memory. In one study it was found that malnourished children admitted to a hospital under six months of age did not improve their test scores, even after 220 days of treatment. The most crucial factor seems to be the age at which malnutrition occurs, with the degree and duration of the malnutrition also being important.

Mental retardation, especially at the severe and moderate levels, may appear in any family, even though there are no known cases of it in the family history. The presence of such a child in an otherwise normal family is tragic, but the child should never be considered a disgrace. If some member of the family is blind, deaf, or crippled, he is not considered a disgrace—he is helped and treated with sympathy. The same kind of understanding must be given to an individual who is mentally retarded.

Can mental retardation be cured? Although much can be done through training retarded persons, there is at present no known way of "curing" those who have serious brain damage. Drugs, individual psychotherapy, and special education programs are useful in helping the mentally retarded to make a better adjustment in their social life, but these procedures are not designed to cure the disorder. Administration of thyroxin (the active hormone of the thyroid gland) has produced, in some cases, significant improvement of a specific type of mental retardation (cretinism). Also, surgical techniques have been devised for treating hydrocephalus, a condition in which an abnormal amount of fluid in the cavities of the brain results in an extremely large head. Special diets have brought about an improvement of some cases of phenylketonuria (fen'əl-kē-tōn-yur'ē-ə), which is caused by the lack of a certain chemical substance in the body. Vitamin therapy has improved the mental functioning of children who suffer from malnutrition. Early diagnosis is extremely important if treatment is to be of maximum value in those cases where a treatment exists that can help.

Superior Intelligence

Individuals of very superior intelligence are correctly termed abnormal, as are mentally retarded persons. The "gifted" are above the average, while the mentally retarded are below the average. Psychologists make even less attempt to classify persons of very superior intelligence than they make to classify mentally retarded persons. The term GIFTED is often applied, however, to the five or six persons in a thousand who have IQ's of 140 or more. At the far reaches of this group is the one person in a million with an IQ of 180 or more, who is spoken of as a GENIUS.

Recently there has been a trend away from using the term "genius." Instead, emphasis is being put on the terms "gifted" and "creative." Psychologists today are interested in determining what background factors are

Benjamin Franklin was a person of superior intelligence. Inventing bifocal eyeglasses was only one of his many accomplishments.

MEASURING INTELLECTUAL ABILITY **181**

associated with gifted and creative persons, and what present conditions stimulate their development.

Intellectually gifted children. Just as mental retardation is often apparent very early in life, so is intellectual superiority. Studies that have been made of the early lives of men who have become prominent indicate that in many cases these persons showed remarkable intellectual ability as children. For example, Charles Dickens was reading such books as *Robinson Crusoe, Don Quixote,* and *The Vicar of Wakefield* before he was seven years old.

The Swiss psychologist Jean Piaget, at the age of ten, wrote a short article that was published in a natural history journal. In his early teens he began a series of authoritative articles on local mollusks, and at nineteen he wrote a philosophical novel that was later published.

Sir Francis Galton, a nineteenth-century English scientist of great brilliance, could pick out and name the capital letters when he was twelve months old. He could identify both capitals and lowercase letters at the age of eighteen months. By the age of thirty months he read a book, and at three years he could sign his name. The day before his fifth birthday, Francis wrote the following letter to his sister:

> My dear Adele:
> I am 4 years old and I can read any English book. I can say all the Latin Substantives and Adjectives and active verbs besides 52 lines of Latin poetry. I can cast up any sum in addition and can multiply by 2, 3, 4, 5, 6, 7, 8, 9, 10, 11.
> I can also say the pence table. I read French a little and I know the clock.
> *Francis Galton*
> Febuary 15, 1827

Perhaps this letter shows a bit of childish bragging. Francis himself realized that he might have overstated his ability a bit, for in the original letter he crossed out the 9 and 11 in the list of numbers he could multiply by. Nevertheless, we must recognize that Galton was a genius. Compare this letter with one "written" by an average child at about the time of his fifth birthday. It is true that Galton misspelled "February," but high school students have often made the same error. If Galton could have been tested by modern means, his IQ would probably have been about 200.

One of the authors once tested one six-year-old boy with an IQ of 175. At the age of six he was collecting butterflies, mounting them in a professional collection box, and labeling them with their Latin names, entirely on his own. He was also in his first year of studying Spanish, learning it from his seven-year-old sister. The sister, who had an IQ of 176, was in her second year of Spanish, studying on her own with the aid of Spanish phonograph records.

Is the gifted child superior in all ways? Children of very superior intelligence are popularly supposed to be frail, sickly, maladjusted in schoolwork, and hard to get along with. Lewis M. Terman, with other psychologists' cooperation, made an extensive study of one thousand children of very superior intelligence. Terman found that, as a rule, mentally superior children are also physically superior. For example, he found that on the average they are taller and heavier and have greater lung capacity, greater width of shoulders, and greater muscular strength than other children of their ages. Sometimes it is said that children of very superior intelligence do not do well in schoolwork, or possibly do well in only one subject. Terman found that 85 percent of his superior group were further along in school than most children of their ages. None of the superior group were held back in school. Their schoolwork tended to be of superior quality in all lines of study rather than in just one line. The superior children read on a wide range of topics, especially on science, history, travel, biography, informational fiction, poetry, and drama. As a rule, their social interests were normal, and their fellow students and friends did not think them peculiar.

Sometimes it is said that children of very superior intelligence do not live up to the promise of their childhood and become inferior in ability, and even mentally ill, as they mature. Terman kept in touch with individuals of this superior group and found that they continued to be superior as they grew older. Many of them entered the professions. They went far in formal education, 48 percent of the men and 27 percent of the women obtaining advanced academic degrees (higher than the bachelor's degree). They wrote books and magazine articles. They married and evidently lived happily, since their divorce rate was lower than the national average. The percentage who became mentally ill was lower than for the population as a whole. They made good, or at least comfortable, salaries.

Unfortunately, society often does not pay as much attention to its very superior children and adults as it does to mentally retarded persons. In many schools superior children are forced to waste a good deal of time while the remainder of the class catches up with them. They are often much more neglected (in terms of their potentialities) than are dull children. In adult life superior individuals often have to spend a large part of their time in relatively trivial tasks to make a living, rather than using this time to do work more in keeping with their abilities and more profitable for the society.

Do students of superior ability live up to their potential? In one research study high school students of above average intellectual ability (all with IQ's over 110) were studied to find out if their school achievements were as high as could be reasonably expected of them. They were divided into two groups on the basis of their high school records. One group was designated as "underachievers" because each member had a grade-point average below the average of his class. The other group was designated as "achievers" because each member had a grade-point average above the class average. More boys than girls were classified as underachievers.

Following the division of students into these two groups, their academic records were traced from the time each had entered the first grade. Data for the boys indicated that the underachievers (as compared with the achievers) had been obtaining grades below their ability since the first grade. Data for the girls indicated that the underachievers (as compared with the achievers) had been obtaining grades significantly below their ability level since the ninth grade and had tended to do so since the sixth grade.

In another research study female college students who earned higher grades than might be expected of them in terms of their intellectual abilities were compared with students who earned grades lower than might be expected of them. The overachievers were found to have stronger motivation for studying than the underachievers, tended to be more self-confident, and had a greater capacity for working under pressure. The underachievers showed a marked tendency to procrastinate, to rely on external pressures to make them complete their assignments, and to be critical of educational methods.

According to most studies of underachievement and overachievement, approximately 10 to 15 percent of a school population is underachieving, although the specific percentage depends largely on what method is used to select individuals as underachievers. From the data just given on underachievers, however, do not assume that underachievement *causes* the various tendencies mentioned. There is a relationship between underachievement and certain tendencies, but not necessarily a causal one. What does seem apparent is that individuals who come from homes that stimulate them to achieve, to be motivated, and to continue their education have distinct advantages in our society over those individuals who come from homes where this stimulation is lacking.

Criticisms of Tests

In the early part of the 1960's several public attacks were launched against tests. These attacks were concerned with discrimination of tests against minority groups, the legitimacy of tests (since they select individuals with specific talents), invasion of privacy, and secrecy of test scores. Intelligence tests received their share of the criticisms.

Suppose, for example, someone gave you an intelligence test based on a culture that was unfamiliar to you. Would you consider it fair? A test made up of questions such as those below would be easy for some Americans but difficult for the majority, who are not members of the subculture.

_____1. A "handkerchief head" is: (a) a cool cat; (b) a porter; (c) an Uncle Tom; (d) a hoddi; (e) a preacher.
_____2. Which word is most out of place here? (a) splib; (b) blood; (c) black; (d) spook; (e) gray.
_____3. A "gas head" is a person who has a: (a) fast-moving car; (b) stable of lace; (c) process; (d) habit of stealing cars; (e) long jail record for arson.
_____4. "Bo Diddley" is a: (a) game for children; (b) down-home cheap wine; (c) new dance; (d) down-home singer; (e) Moejoe call.
_____5. If a man is called a "blood" then he is a: (a) Negro; (b) Mexican-American; (c) fighter; (d) hungry hemophile; (e) Redman or Indian.

(*The answers are on page 187.*)

Furthermore, individuals in some cultures or subcultures do not place much emphasis on speed, which is an important factor on some tests. Such differences in cultural backgrounds can significantly influence the results of tests, especially intelligence tests. As a result of these criticisms, psychologists, and others, are studying new approaches to measuring intelligence that reduce or eliminate the effects of cultural differences on the test results.

It is true that tests discriminate *between* persons. That is exactly what they are intended to do. They are not, however, designed to discriminate *against* individuals. Neither are test results meant to be used as the sole source of information on an individual. They are designed to provide supplementary data about a person, to be used together with other data. Furthermore, the fact is often overlooked that test results provide objective data about a person which, when properly used, can help overcome discrimination.

When is the use of tests legitimate? In recent years the United States Supreme Court ruled that tests may be required of a person if the test results are specifically related to the requirements of the job being applied for. However, the Court's decision prohibited an employer "... from requiring a high school education or passing of a standardized general intelligence test as a condition of employment in or transfer to jobs when neither standard is shown to be significantly related to successful job performance. . . ."

Do tests really invade privacy? One way to answer this question is to consider the purpose of the test. If the purpose of the test is to help the person better understand his abilities, interests, personality, needs, aptitudes, and other pertinent factors, then the test is not so much an invasion of privacy as a positive effort to enable the individual to plan his life and avoid failure.

Should test scores be kept secret? This question, like the others, is a complex one. Certainly a person's intelligence test scores, for instance, should not be posted on the nearest bulletin board. Test scores should not be used by anyone to intentionally hurt someone else in any way. Most people do not know how to interpret test results accurately and are not always aware of the limitations of tests. However, shouldn't test scores be given to those who are interested in helping the person? If you were a medical doctor and knew that a patient had a severe heart ailment, would you tell the patient about the trouble, knowing from past experience that telling him might increase the probability of his having a heart attack? Instead, might not you give the information to someone else who was in a position to help the patient? In principle, the same aspects apply to the use of test results.

Like many other things, such as guns, tests are neither good nor bad in themselves. A gun can be used to murder a fellow human being, or to kill a rabid fox about to bite a child. Test results can be used to intentionally prevent an individual from obtaining employment, or to place a person in a position where he stands a better chance for success.

Terms to Know

chronological age
deviation IQ
educable
genius
gifted

intelligence
intelligence quotient
mental age
mental maturity
mild retardation

moderate retardation
primary mental abilities
profound retardation
severe retardation
trainable

Topics to Think About

1. The term IQ has become so popular that it has lost much of its technical value. Can you suggest a better way of expressing a person's intellectual ability?

2. Have you ever had a job for which you honestly believed you had too much intellectual ability? too little intellectual ability? What made you think so—what was your basis for judging your ability in relation to the job?

3. Imagine that you are a psychologist living with some primitive peoples, for example, deep in the jungles of South America or in the bush section of Australia, and you wish to measure their intellectual ability. What kind of test would you use? What questions would you include? How long would the test be?

4. How would our society and the individuals in it benefit if we knew all the factors and processes involved in intelligence?

5. With improved nutrition and improved social conditions, do you think that mental retardation as we know it today would disappear from our society? Why or why not?

6. As schools develop better methods for teaching children of superior intellectual ability, do you think that the number of geniuses will increase?

7. In industry modern computers have taken over many of the more routine and monotonous tasks formerly performed by persons of average, below-average, or even above-average, intellectual ability. What is to be the role of these displaced individuals in our society?

Suggestions for Activities

1. There are some persons who are very opposed to the use of standardized tests, especially intelligence tests. Survey a number of individuals in your community to see how many are opposed to the use of tests in different situations, such as in schools and industries. Also, contact the personnel managers of several large industries to find out what kinds of tests they use for employment purposes and how they use the results of their tests.

2. Review the seven primary factors of intelligence given in this chapter. Consult references listed for further information on these factors. Make up a short test consisting of two or three items for each factor, which you believe might measure the factors. Remember, however, that your "test" is not really an intelligence test and may not measure the factors. Nevertheless, try out your questions on several persons just to note individual differences in responses.

3. If your school has a counselor, psychologist, or guidance teacher, make an appointment and ask what tests are given in your school and how the results are used in the school. Ask particularly about intelligence tests.

4. Call or write to your local and state health departments to see to what extent, if any, there are individuals within your area and state who might be suffering from malnutrition. Such data are sometimes difficult to obtain. Then try to get similar data for the nation as a whole and compare with your data. Are the figures for your community and state higher or lower than for the whole country? Why do you think this is so?

5. There is a growing tendency to hire the mentally retarded to perform worthwhile business activities. Survey your local businesses, or call your chamber of commerce, to determine which businesses in your community either do or would hire such persons. Report your findings to the class.

6. Find out if your city or town has special education programs for the mentally retarded. If possible, determine what criteria are used in selecting individuals to participate in the programs. Also, you might wish to find out what training or care for the mentally retarded your state provides.

7. If it can be arranged, visit a school for the mentally retarded to see how these people are cared for and trained.

8. Write a theme on the life of some great scientist or other person who can be classed as a genius. Note especially evidences of superior intellectual ability in childhood.

9. Write a frank evaluation of yourself as a student. Do you believe that you are an underachiever or an overachiever? Are you "in a rut"? Do you like to study (most of the time)? Do your teachers have to use pressure in order to get you to study? Are you self-confident? Do you tend to procrastinate? Are you frequently critical of the school in general and of certain teachers? Do you "fold" on examinations so that you don't do as well as you are capable of doing? You may have taken one or more group intelligence tests, or even an individual test, although probably you were not told your score. Do you think such tests really measured your potentialities?

Suggestions for Further Reading

Byrne, Katharine M., and John Byrne, *You and Your Abilities,* Science Research Associates. A Guidance Series Booklet written for students in grades 9–12.

Gage, N. L., "Replies to Shockley, Page, and Jensen: The Causes of Race Differences in IQ." *Phi Delta Kappan,* Vol. 53 (1972), pages 422–27.

Hilgard, E. R., R. C. Atkinson, and Rita Atkinson, *Introduction to Psychology,* 5th ed., Harcourt Brace Jovanovich. See pages 360–80 on tests of general intelligence and the extremes of intelligence.

Kagan, J., M. M. Haith, and Catherine Caldwell (eds.), *Psychology: Adapted Readings,* Harcourt Brace Jovanovich. See Selection 28, "Mental Growth and Personality Development," and Selection 29, "The Discovery and Encouragement of Exceptional Talent."

Kagan, J., and E. Havemann, *Psychology: An Introduction,* 2nd ed., Harcourt Brace Jovanovich. Chapter 14 treats in detail the requirements for a test of intellectual ability and the meaning of intellectual ability.

Psychology Today: An Introduction, CRM Books. See Chapter 23, "Individual Differences and Their Measurement."

The answers to the questions on page 184 are: 1. (c); 2. (e); 3. (c); 4. (d); 5. (a).

WHAT IS INTELLIGENCE?

Suppose you were assigned the project of finding a way to measure intelligence in human beings. How would you begin? What would you measure? What is intelligence?

David Wechsler, a major contributor to the development of intelligence tests, has defined intelligence as "the aggregate or global capacity of the individual to act purposefully, to think rationally, and to deal effectively with his environment." This definition emphasizes that intelligence is not just the sum of abilities, it involves the number and quality of abilities and how they function together. This definition also recognizes that other factors, such as motivation, enter into intelligent behavior. How would you define intelligence?

Psychologists do not all agree on what intelligence is. Neither do they agree on the best way to measure it. Most conventional intelligence tests try to determine an individual's IQ on the basis of the proportion of right and wrong answers made by the individual as compared to the answers of others of the same age group. However, a new kind of intelligence test is being devised that focuses on the kinds of incorrect answers a person makes. This test is based on the theories of Jean Piaget, the famous Swiss psychologist, who sees a child's mental development as evolving through four different stages. The purpose of the test is to find out the stage of a person's intellectual development through determining the underlying structure of intelligence. By pursuing the reasons why a child gives the answers that he does, the test can discover the structure and quality of his or her reasoning processes. Such a test would analyze a child's concepts of causality; space; conservation; numbers and classification; and time, movement, and speed. The child's understanding of these concepts would indicate what stage of development he is in.

Just as there is disagreement among psychologists over how to measure intelligence, so also there is disagreement over what determines intelligence—whether heredity or environment plays the more important role. One of the most controversial persons on this subject is the psychologist Arthur Robert Jensen. Whereas psychologists such as B. F. Skinner stress the role of the environment in determining IQ, Jensen emphasizes the importance of heredity. Jensen agrees with others that learning (environment) influences IQ, but he focuses on the differences found in the rates and readiness to learn, which he attributes to heredity. Jensen points out that a young child who copies figures at a certain level of performance cannot improve his performance as much by intense practice and instruction as he can by simply growing up for an additional year. There is an innate growth rate that no amount of environmental influences will increase.

Although other psychologists strongly disagree with him, Jensen's research has led him to hypothesize that blacks as a group are genetically inferior to whites in some kinds of intelligence. He thinks that several hundred years of slavery may have had a crippling genetic effect on blacks. His views have stirred heated controversy. They have caused his life to be threatened, his colleagues to criticize him, and his college classes to be picketed. Nevertheless, Jensen continues with his line of research. In a forthcoming book he discounts the idea that malnutrition, an environmental factor, has a detrimental effect on IQ. He is presently engaged in many projects, one of which is the development of a new and simple way to measure IQ—a reaction time test that measures a person's reaction in thousandths of a second.

The search for finding better ways to understand intelligence continues. Undoubtedly great strides will be made during your lifetime. Your children's generation may be taking a completely new type of intelligence test, based on theories of intelligence that do not exist today.

unit 4
PATTERNS OF BEHAVIOR

chapter 8   Heredity and environment

chapter 9   Biological influences on behavior

chapter 10   Getting to know your environment

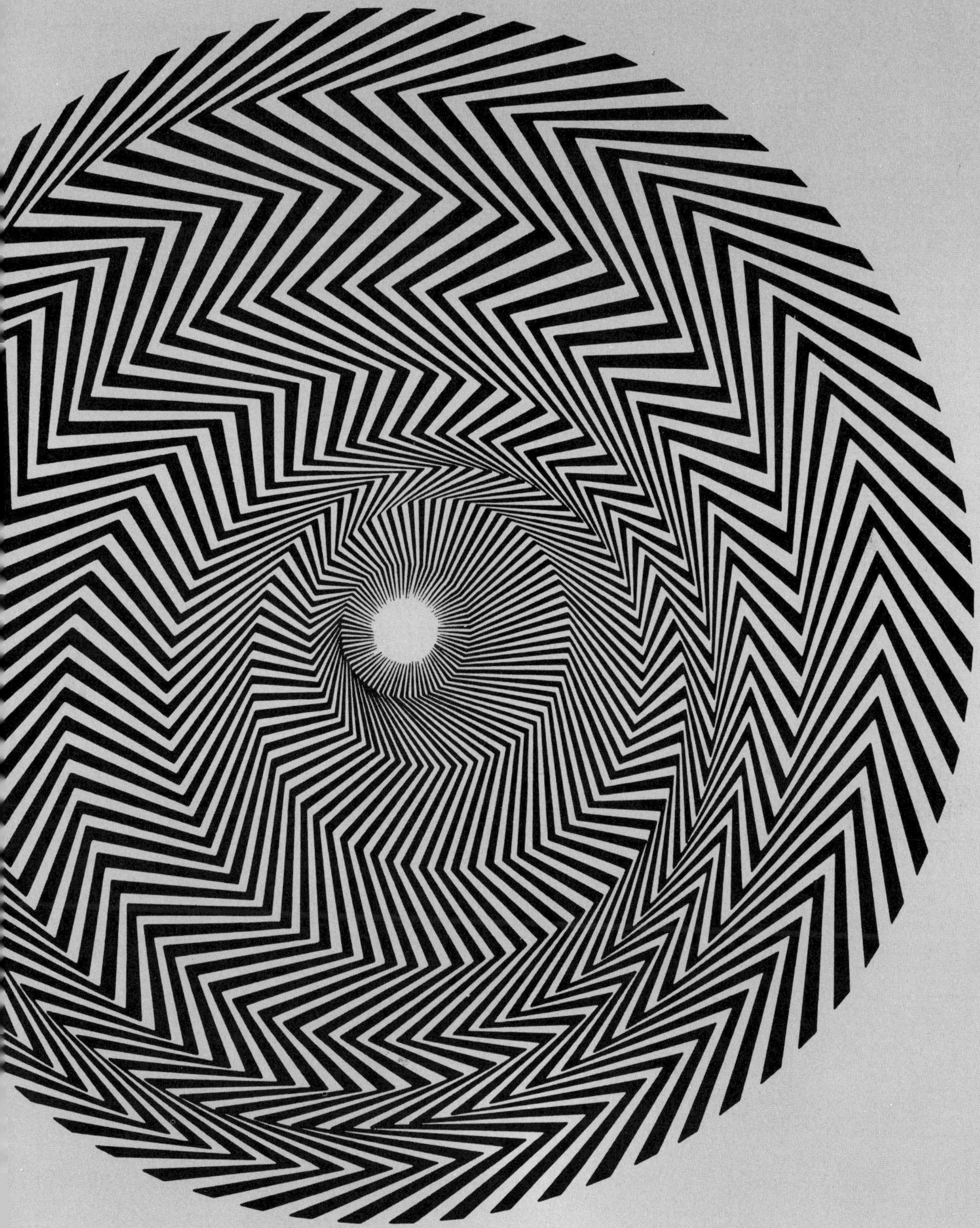

chapter 8
Heredity and Environment

TO WHAT EXTENT does your heredity influence your behavior? How does the environment affect your behavior? Sometimes people mistakenly try to explain all behavior in terms of either heredity or environment. Consider, for instance, the explanations of Billy's parents.

Billy has been warned repeatedly about his misconduct in school. The teacher decides to ask Billy's mother to come in and talk over the situation with her in an effort to arrive at an understanding of—and with—Billy. During the conference the mother admits that Billy's behavior is not what she would like it to be. She then confides to the teacher, "Poor boy, he comes by it naturally—everyone on his father's side of the family is like that." If Billy's father comes to school, he might say, "Oh, yes! We know Billy could be better. Unfortunately, Billy's friends act the same way, and Billy acquires all his bad habits from them." One parent accounts for Billy's present behavior by his heredity, the other by his environment.

Actually, both heredity and environment play a part in the behavior of an individual. As a result of research in recent years, we know that much, but far from all, behavior formerly attributed to heredity can be better explained by environmental influences. Nevertheless, the development of an individual must be understood in terms of both biological factors and external forces, conditions, and influences.

Both these elements start having an effect at the time of conception. Hereditary influences are determined at that time. The environment of the body of the mother-to-be also influences the life of the embryo and fetus. Before discussing the effects of environment, though, let's first look at the process of heredity.

Inherited Characteristics

Often it is said of a child, "He is the very picture of his father (or mother)." This remark implies that in some way he has inherited outstanding physical features from one side of his family or the other. How does this inheritance take place?

Dominant and recessive characteristics. Gregor Mendel, a nineteenth-century abbot, did much to create scientific interest in the biological facts of heredity. He referred to the separate features of parents as UNIT CHARACTERS. Mendel said that unit characters are passed on to children independently and as wholes, sometimes becoming apparent in the first generation, sometimes not appearing until later generations. Characteristics that appear in all individuals of the first generation of descendants are said to be DOMINANT CHARACTERISTICS. Those that are latent and do not appear in the first generation of descendants, although they may appear in subsequent generations, are said to be RECESSIVE CHARACTERISTICS. A few dominant and recessive characteristics in man are as follows:

DOMINANT	RECESSIVE
Brown eyes	Blue eyes
Curly hair	Straight hair
Dark hair	Light hair
Dark skin	Light skin

Chromosomes and genes. Most cells of the body contain rod-shaped "colored bodies" called CHROMOSOMES. There is evidence that 46 chromosomes exist in each human cell. These chromosomes are in pairs. Prior to fertilization, by a special process of cell division the number of chromosomes in the egg and sperm cells segregate so that one of each pair finds itself in different daughter cells. The result is that each sperm and each egg contains 23 chromosomes. When the sperm fertilizes the egg, the fertilized egg contains 46 chromosomes, or 23 pairs.

Each new cell in the human species normally contains 46 chromosomes. In other species the number of chromosomes in each cell is different from the number in the human species. For example, the crayfish has 100 pairs; the moth, 31 pairs; the salamander, 14 pairs; the mosquito, 6 pairs. Recent investigations have revealed that approximately 95 percent of all mongoloids have 47 chromosomes instead of the usual 46. Thus, a study of chromosomes as they relate to mongolism suggests that possession of an extra chromosome may even be responsible for this type of mental retardation. There has been some discussion, although no conclusive proof, of a relationship between an abnormal chromosome structure (an extra Y chromosome) and the likelihood of that person developing into a criminal. Some data suggest that extreme tallness is associated with an extra Y chromosome. Chromosomes often provide an explanation of some physical irregularity present at birth.

For a while heredity was understood in terms of combinations of the chromosomes. Now, however, scientists speak of tiny parts within each chromosome called GENES. In the human species there are probably at least a thousand genes in each of the 46 chromosomes. An individual's genetic make-up for any characteristic is called a genotype. A GENOTYPE refers either to the sum of all the biological characteristics that an individual is capable of transmitting to his or her offspring, or to a single such characteristic. Thus, if one parent contributes a gene for blue eyes and the other parent contributes a gene for brown eyes, the fertilized egg contains blue-brown

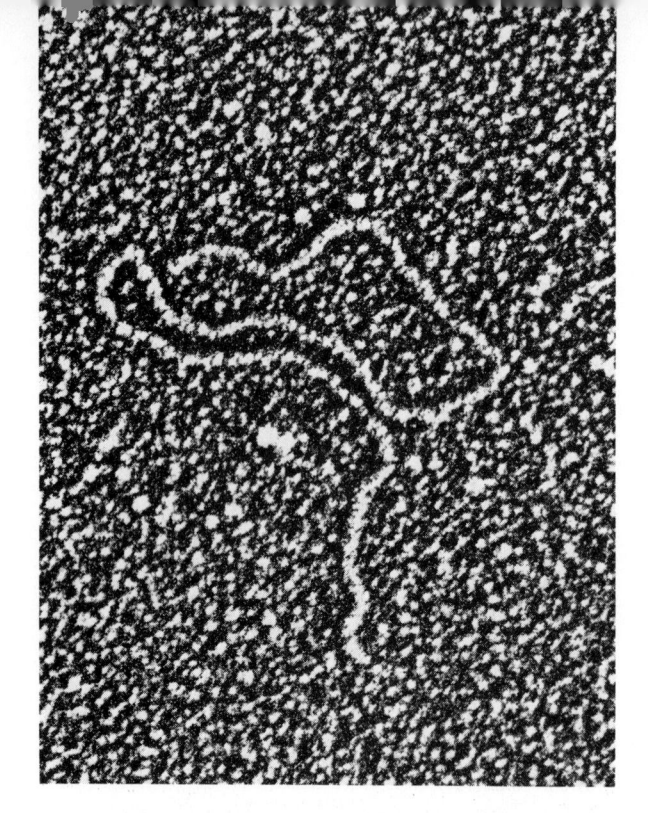

This is a single gene—the first one to be isolated and photographed under such high magnification. It is 55 millionths of an inch long.

as a genotype for eye color. The actual, observable characteristic that an individual manifests is called a PHENOTYPE (ˈfē-nə-tīp). Thus, although an individual's genotype for eye color is blue-brown, his actual eye color or phenotype will be brown. If the pair of genes an individual receives from his parents differ, the one that always wins out (and therefore becomes the phenotype) is said to be dominant, and the one that does not show is said to be recessive.

How do genes determine your biological development? In recent years new evidence has been discovered on genes and the specific procedures of how a single cell ultimately develops into an extremely complex adult being. The primary chemical that seems to be the basis for all genetic action is called DNA (deoxyribonucleic acid). This substance is found in the nucleus of every cell in all living organisms. DNA is responsible for forming another similar chemical known as RNA (ribonucleic acid). DNA gives special "hereditary instructions" for the cellular development of the organism, and these instructions are partially carried out by RNA. What results is the development of all the cells of the body, some of which make up the hands, others the brain, still others the nerves, and so on. If the instructions are not obeyed, the result may be a deformed arm, green rather than blue eyes, mental deficiency, or death.

Of special interest to psychologists is the fact that RNA seems to play a role in memory, as suggested by the following experiment. Rats were conditioned to go to a food cup whenever a click was sounded. Then RNA from these trained rats was injected into the brains of untrained rats. The untrained rats now showed a significant tendency to go to the food cup when a click was sounded, even though they themselves had not been conditioned to the sound.

Attempts to repeat RNA experiments have not always been successful. There is much for psychologists and biologists to learn about DNA and RNA, but further research may do much to change some of our present ideas about the processes of heredity. The potential importance of the discovery of both DNA and RNA is that once we know how these substances give instructions and how the instructions are carried out, we may be able to correct faulty growth in mankind. We may, for instance, eventually be able to correct inherited abnormalities.

Each human father has genes that can combine in several million different ways, as does each mother. The genes of both can be combined theoretically in more than one hundred thousand billion different ways. Unless you are an identical twin, probably no other person in the world has or ever had your genetic make-up. No one exactly like you will ever read the words on this or any other page with precisely the same background that you have. In other words, you are literally a unique individual. The biological and environmental factors that have combined to make you a unique person are so complex as to be almost unbelievable.

Do you inherit characteristics from your parents or from remote ancestors? Strictly speaking, you do not inherit tallness, musical ability, or any other specific trait from your parents. Parents merely pass on to their children some of those characteristics that they received from their parents, and so on, back through all the generations of life. The genes within the chromosomes within the reproductive cells are not believed to be changed by the individual carrying them. Instead, parents transmit to their children, unchanged, genes that they have inherited from their own parents.

A characteristic acquired by parents themselves and not possessed by preceding generations is not transmitted by heredity. A man and his wife may have spent years studying music, yet their child will not know one note from another—unless he is taught, just as other children are taught whose parents were not musicians. One biologist cut off the tails of mice for twenty generations, yet each new litter of mice appeared with full-length tails. For generations, Chinese women bound their feet; but each baby—girl or boy—was born with normal feet.

If you look like your mother or your father it is because you both have a common ancestry rather than because your parent in some way reproduces his appearance in you. We can say that a child inherits characteristics from his parents only if we mean that

Assume that the figure below represents a hypothetical family's genetic make-up for hair color. Assume, too, that black represents the dominant gene, dark hair, and that grey represents the recessive gene, light hair. What, then, is the genotype for hair color for each member of the family? What is the phenotype for each? (The answers are given on page 196.)

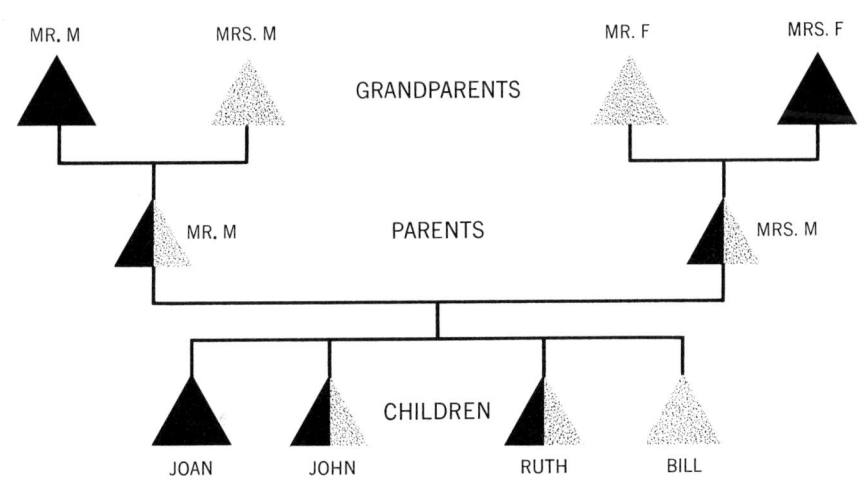

MR. M   MRS. M   GRANDPARENTS   MR. F   MRS. F

MR. M   PARENTS   MRS. M

CHILDREN

JOAN   JOHN   RUTH   BILL

the parents were the immediate carriers of the characteristics of their ancestors.

Some Studies of Heredity

Although for humanitarian reasons we cannot carry out experiments on human heredity, we can do so with animals. We can also learn something about human heredity by studying family histories.

The results of animal experiments. First, let us look at an experiment with subhuman animals. One psychologist took 142 rats at random and set them the task of learning to run through a maze to secure food. He found that the rats differed greatly in ability, just as human beings differ in ability. Some rats entered as few as seven or eight blind alleys. Others, with no greater opportunity to make errors, made as many as 214 entrances into blind alleys. Thus, it seemed that some rats were more intelligent than others.

The psychologist segregated the bright rats and let them mate and then permitted the mediocre and dull rats to mate. This selective breeding went on for eight generations. Descendants of the original bright rats always bred with other descendants of the original bright rats; dull and mediocre rats always bred with other descendants of the original dull and mediocre rats. By the end of the eight generations, there was practically no overlapping of the two lines of descendants so far as ability to learn a maze was concerned. That is, the descendants of the original bright rats were very bright; the descendants of the dull and mediocre rats varied from mediocre to very dull. The dullest of the bright group was about as bright as the brightest of the dull group.

Next, the bright and the dull rats were mated. The offspring, when tested in the maze, showed a distribution much like that with which the experiment began—there were some dull rats and some bright rats, while most of the rats were in between the two extremes.

This experiment is very impressive, but the data must be interpreted with caution. Further experimentation with the two strains of rats revealed that the bright rats were much more active than the dull rats, thus achieving higher scores. Possibly it was this capacity for activity that was transmitted from one generation to the next rather than a general intellectual ability. Furthermore, several recent studies have suggested that in some cases differences in intelligence formerly attributed to heredity may have been due to the bias of the experimenter.

In a college class in experimental psychology students were told about the experiment described above. Then half of the students were given a dull strain of rats and half were given a bright strain of rats. The rats were placed on a simple two-branch maze. They were to learn to go to the darker branch of the maze, which half of the time was on the left side and half of the time was on the right side. Each of the sixty rats was given ten trials every day for five days. The rats from the dull group had an average of 1.5 daily correct responses, whereas the rats from the bright group averaged 2.3 daily correct responses. Also, the dull rats refused to move away from the starting position in 29 percent of the trials, while the bright rats refused to start only 11 percent of the time. Of the rats that started,

---

Answers to problem on page 195 (genotypes precede phenotypes): Grandparents—Mr. M and Mrs. F, dark-dark, dark; Mrs. M and Mr. F, light-light, light. Parents—Mr. M and Mrs. M, dark-light, dark. Children—Joan, dark-dark, dark; John and Ruth, dark-light, dark; Bill, light-light, light.

196 PATTERNS OF BEHAVIOR

the dull rats ran slower than the bright rats.

Afterward, the students were asked to rate their rats and their own attitudes toward the rats. Those students with bright rats rated their rats smarter, more pleasant, and more likable than did the students with dull rats. Also, the students with bright rats were more relaxed, handled their rats more often, and were more gentle with their rats than were students with dull rats.

Actually, the students had been misled. The two groups of rats had not been bred for brightness and dullness. They were just ordinary laboratory rats of the same strain and had been labeled as dull or bright arbitrarily. Students who thought their rats were dull were not as "nice" to their rats as were students who thought their rats were bright. Were the intelligence test results of the rats due primarily to heredity or environment?

A similar situation was found in an experiment with human beings, in which 256 teachers-in-training were asked to score the papers on a new test of "learning readiness." The teachers were told that children who scored high on intelligence tests and reading tests tended to score high on this new test. Each child's IQ and reading level was provided on the front of his reading-readiness test booklet. Some of these scores were high and some were low, but all were fictitious. It was found that when the teachers believed they were scoring the new tests of children with high IQ and reading level scores, they tended to give the children much more benefit of the doubt on uncertain answers than when scoring the papers of children with low previous scores.

This study suggests that when examiners must judge subjectively scored questions on tests, individuals who are giving good responses to most questions tend to be given the benefit of the doubt, whereas individuals who are not doing well on many questions are likely not to be given the benefit of the doubt. Although individually administered tests of intellectual ability are scored quite objectively, there are some questions in which the examiner must use his subjective judgment as to the correctness or incorrectness of an answer. In the past some of the results of intelligence tests may have been influenced by the environment—by the examiner's subjective judgments.

Such experiments do not rule out the possibility that brightness or dullness is inherited, for there is considerable evidence that learning capacities are inherited to some extent. But they do suggest that we need further careful experimentation on the subject.

Studies of human families. Breeding experiments, such as those with rats, cannot be carried out with human beings. But it is possible to learn something about heredity in humans by working backward and studying family trees.

At first glance, tracings of family trees seem to indicate that heredity plays a very important part in the development of any individual. It was found, for instance, that when one or both parents were considered mentally retarded, they tended to produce a larger percentage of mentally retarded children than would be expected in the general population. Conversely, family trees of unusually intelligent couples showed a large number of descendants who became top public officials, college professors, lawyers, physicians, and clergymen.

Although heredity is important, these studies are no longer accepted as scientific evidence today. The men making these studies were not always as scientific as they should have been in collecting their evidence, often depending on hearsay rather than on carefully

Above are three generations of the Ford family, Henry Ford (left), Edsel, and Henry II (right). The Fords have been a successful family in America since the beginning of this century. How much of their success do you think is due to heredity?

collected facts. Also, they had a tendency to omit cases that did not prove their point. For example, all undesirable members of a family with some history of mental retardation were noted with care, but not so much attention was paid to the normal or superior members of the family. Finally, these studies did not take into account the influence of environment. That is, the children of unusually bright or unusually dull parents grew up in that particular environment. Would the results have been the same if, in some way, exceptionally intelligent children could have been raised in the homes of mentally retarded families? There are too many uncontrolled variables in the tracing of family trees for the results to be of scientific value.

Practical applications for controlling heredity. In a province in northern Italy there existed for many years an excessive number of mentally retarded persons. Then, beginning in 1890, these mentally retarded persons were prevented from marrying. Within twenty years this form of mental retardation had almost disappeared from the province.

EUGENICS (yù-'jen-iks) is the science that deals with methods for improving the hereditary qualities of a species, especially of the human species. One method that some eugenicists advocate is the method described above —that of preventing defective people from reproducing. Some states in the United States now have laws providing for the sterilization of certain defective people, so that they cannot reproduce. Others interested in eugenics try to educate the public to the value of choosing marriage partners with good hereditary background. Eugenics is a controversial subject—one in which legal, social, and religious as well as scientific attitudes enter.

Some aspects of heredity are beyond the control of eugenics. For instance, some married couples of normal or superior intelligence may produce a mentally retarded child, since many defective characteristics are recessive. Eugenics could not control these cases. Also, in most cases eugenicists cannot control the environment of human beings, and we cannot be sure to what extent defective characteristics are hereditary unless we are able to control environmental factors.

Much research in the area of human heredity still needs to be done. Perhaps some of you will be geneticists and will contribute to this research.

Heredity and Maturation

A study of heredity must include a study of a process that is determined by heredity—maturation. You are undoubtedly aware of changes in a human being that result from physical growth and development. This process of physical growth and development of an organism over a period of time is called MATURATION.

Maturation is not the same as learning, since changes due to maturation are determined by heredity. For example, a newborn baby cannot learn to walk, no matter how much instruction he is given. Only when his body structure has developed sufficiently due to maturation can he be taught to walk.

Different species of animals have different rates of maturation as a result of heredity. An eight-week-old puppy can run about, eat from a dish, and do most of the things he will do as a grown dog. An eight-week-old baby, on the other hand, is still quite helpless and could not survive if he were not cared for. Dogs mature more rapidly than do human beings—but their capacity for development is far more limited.

The effect of maturation on learning. How do organisms such as salamanders "learn" to swim? In one experiment a large group of salamander eggs was divided into two groups. One group served as a control for the experiment. The eggs of this group were placed in ordinary water and permitted to develop as they normally do in nature. The other group of eggs served as the experimental group. These eggs were placed in a drug solution that did not interfere with the normal processes of growth but did paralyze the animals so that they could not move. The control group developed the usual swimming ability. After these salamanders had been swimming for five days, the ones that had been in the drug solution were removed and placed in ordinary water. Within thirty minutes they were able to swim about with as much ease as the members of the control group that had had five days' practice. Apparently the development of a salamander's ability to swim depends on maturation rather than on practice or learning.

Why did it take these experimental salamanders about thirty minutes to develop swimming? Why didn't they swim as soon as they were placed in ordinary water? What effect did the drug have? To answer these questions, the experimenters placed in the drug solution other animals that had been raised in ordinary water and had developed normal swimming. Of course, they now became motionless. After twenty-four hours in the drug solution, they were put back in ordinary water. It took them up to thirty minutes to regain swimming ability.

Maturation and human learning. The following experiment on maturation and learning involved identical twin babies. Since identical twins result from the same ovum and sperm, they have the same heredity. At the age of forty-six weeks one of the twin girls was given an opportunity to climb a set of stairs. She did not climb any of them. She was then given training in climbing stairs, and after four weeks of such training she was able to climb the stairs without assistance. The other twin was not given any experience with stairs until she was fifty-three weeks of age. In her first test at this age she climbed the stairs unaided in 45 seconds. After two weeks of training, this twin, who had had no training until she was fifty-three weeks of age, was actually climbing stairs better than her twin, who had had five weeks of training.

Another study of twins (originally thought to be identical twins, but later discovered not to be) also investigated the influence of maturation vs. environment on learning. Twin boys, Johnny and Jimmy, were placed under very different environmental conditions at the age of twenty days and were used as experimental subjects until they were about two years of age. Johnny was given training in such acts as diving, swimming, roller skating, and use of language. By the age of eight months he swam 7 feet. At eighteen months he swam 50 feet. At fifteen months he would dive headfirst from a springboard 5 feet above the water. Before most children can walk, Johnny

A certain amount of maturation is necessary before such activities as high jumping can be done. Once maturation has taken place, then the amount of training and practice becomes very important in determining how fast an individual learns to high-jump and how proficient he becomes.

200 PATTERNS OF BEHAVIOR

was learning to roller skate, and before he was two years of age, he was quite a proficient skater. Johnny was trained largely on the sink-or-swim basis. That is, he was made to face hardships in the hope that he would be bold and self-reliant.

Jimmy had no such special training and could not perform the same acts as Johnny. Furthermore, Jimmy would not even attempt these acts. That Jimmy was more timid than Johnny may well be explained by the difference in their training.

In any case, the training given Johnny did not make him permanently superior to Jimmy in such behavior as crawling and creeping, sitting up, and reaching and grasping objects. Maturation in itself seemed to produce these activities. Training did make Johnny superior to Jimmy in the less essential skills, such as swimming, diving, and skating. However, later, when Jimmy was given an opportunity to learn these activities, he usually acquired them more easily than had Johnny at an earlier age, since he was more mature when he undertook the learning.

We will consider just one more illustration of the effects of maturation. Traditionally, Hopi Indian babies are attached to cradle boards for most of their first nine months of life and so have very little opportunity to exercise the muscles to be used later in walking. Some Hopi Indians, however, allow their babies to move about freely, unconfined by cradle boards. In one study it was found that both Hopi babies raised in the traditional way and Hopi babies who moved about "learned" to walk at almost exactly the same age (about fifteen months).

Can maturation guarantee learning? The importance of maturation is receiving more and more attention in modern education. For example, at what age should a child be taught to read? The answer depends in part on the degree of maturation of the child. Some children are ready to read at an earlier age than other children because of their more rapid biological growth rate. The answer also depends on environmental forces. Children do not suddenly mature into being able to read without training. The child growing up in a home where there is a good deal of reading and other broadening experiences will wish to learn to read at an earlier age than a child growing up in a home where reading is neglected and where life is very monotonous. Learning to read is influenced partly by the processes of maturation and partly by environmental influences.

In general we can say that human learning cannot be accounted for solely in terms of maturation, but learning does take place most efficiently when the environmental stimulation is keyed to the degree of maturation of the individual. A child can learn to read most efficiently if he is given instruction in reading at a time when he has achieved a sufficient degree of maturation.

Imprinting. Have you ever seen baby chicks following their mother around the barnyard? Perhaps you assumed that such following was "natural," without realizing that it involved a very interesting relationship between maturation and learning. Psychologists use the word IMPRINTING to refer to a special kind of very rapid learning that takes place in some animals—notably birds—at an early stage of their development. Imprinting does not occur because of a specific reward or reinforcement. It can take place only at the time that maturation makes it possible. In imprinting, an animal is presented with a large moving object at the appropriate time, and he quickly learns to follow it. Such learning is relatively insusceptible to forgetting or extinction.

"They think I'm their mother."

As early as 1873, it was noted that incubator-hatched chicks tended to follow the first large moving object they saw—in this case, a scientist—and would have nothing to do with their mother when she appeared later on. In one experiment the scientist imprinted a group of goslings on himself and imprinted another group of goslings on their mother. All of the goslings were placed together under a box while the mother goose and the scientist stood nearby. When the mother started to walk away so did the scientist, but in a different direction. The box was lifted. The goslings imprinted on their mother followed her, and the goslings imprinted on the scientist followed him.

Imprinting varies with the age of the animal and the conditions of the imprinting. For example, with ducklings the tendency to follow is strongest when imprinting occurs thirteen to sixteen hours after hatching. Merely allowing the bird to see a large moving object does not necessarily produce imprinting. The young bird must spend effort to stay near its object. In one experiment ducklings were imprinted on a large wooden decoy duck that moved mechanically around a circular track. Those required to walk only a few feet showed less strength of imprinting than those required to walk 100 feet.

Wouldn't it make an interesting experiment for a fair or other exhibit to imprint baby chicks on a mother duck and to imprint ducklings on a hen? Such a demonstration might be quite disturbing to people who had thought it was "natural" for baby chicks to follow a hen and for ducklings to follow a duck.

Influences of the Environment Before Birth

For nine months after conception the child lives in the limited environment of the mother's body. What are some influences of that environment on the development of the child?

There is a common superstition that the thoughts of a pregnant woman affect the unborn baby that she is carrying in her body. It is said that if the mother reads good literature, the child will have literary ability; if the mother reads crime stories and sees crime films, the child is likely to become a criminal. It is sometimes said that if the mother looks intently at strawberries, the child will be born with a red spot, which—by a stretch of the imagination—may appear to be a picture of a strawberry. All these ideas are groundless. Scientists know that there is absolutely no connection between the nervous system of the mother and the nervous system of the fetus developing in her body.

Some maternal influences. Although the blood of the mother does not flow through the veins of the child, some things do pass from the mother to the child. Disease germs, such as those of diphtheria, typhoid, and syphilis, may succeed in passing from the body of the mother to the body of the child. Some biologists believe that if the mother worries a great deal or has a severe emotional shock, the chemicals formed in her body as a result of this worry or shock may be carried to and affect her unborn child. There is evidence that experiences of aggression and induced seizures of female mice before or during pregnancy can cause changes in the behavior and physiology of their offspring, and that these effects may persist for several generations.

Of course, the health of the mother affects the health of the developing child. If the mother damages her health—by excessive use of alcohol, for example—the child is affected. Poisons in the mother's system or narcotics like opium or morphine in excessive doses may also cause damage to the child.

Such influences as these are due to environment, not to heredity. They may affect the child during the nine months before his birth, whereas his heredity was complete at conception.

The influence of prenatal malnutrition. The evidence is mounting that malnutrition during pregnancy has undesirable influences on the later development of the offspring. Malnourished pregnant rats in an experimental group have been found to have offspring with a reduced number of brain cells as compared to the offspring of rats that had adequate nourishment during pregnancy. Even though the offspring were fed adequately after birth, their brain cells did not increase to a normal number. There is even some evidence that protein-calorie deficiency in an infant female rat may affect the development of her offspring years later. It may be that a history of malnourishment for several generations will have an influence on later generations, an influence that in the past we have assumed to be due to a simple chromosome-gene heredity of some kind.

The evidence is growing that malnutrition affects the development of unborn children. One study found that the offspring of undernourished, poor human mothers were, at birth, 15 percent smaller in body weight than children from wealthy homes. Furthermore, some of their organs were abnormally small. For example, the average weight of the thymus gland of children in poor families was only 66 percent of the normal weight for that gland. Since the thymus gland seems to be related to both growth and immunity, these children were starting off life at a disadvantage.

Influences of the Environment After Birth

We have noted that malnourishment before birth has an adverse influence on the developing animal or child. What about the effects of malnourishment after birth?

Effects of malnourishment in young animals. There is evidence for both rats and pigs that undernourishment during the first 21 days after birth results in a permanent reduction in brain weight and some degeneration within brain cells. Furthermore, the earlier the malnutrition occurs, the greater the effect and the less likelihood there is of recovery when adequate nourishment is supplied.

Malnutrition is followed by changes in the behavior of animals. For example, after only four days of restricted diet, rats developed trembling of their heads and forepaws, and puppies became very irritable. Rats that were on food deprivation during the weaning period did not explore their environment as much as rats on a normal diet, so they did not learn as much from their environment. In some ways, then, the food-deprived rats could be considered less intelligent than the rats on a sufficient diet.

Effects of malnourishment in human infants. Although scientists do not conduct experiments on the effects of food deprivation on human infants for humanitarian reasons, unfortunately society gives us many cases that can be studied. Recent studies indicate that malnutrition, especially during the first year of life, results in children with smaller heads, and presumably even smaller brains, than children on an adequate diet. Even though later these children are given an adequate diet, they have lower intelligence test scores than children who have not suffered malnutrition early in life. They tend to be especially retarded in language development. As in the case of animals, the earlier in life the malnutrition occurs, the greater is the retardation.

What can be done about the effects of malnutrition on children? Supplementing the diet of malnourished pregnant mothers with vitamins has reduced the effects of malnutrition on their children. In one research study mothers from a nutritionally poor environment were given vitamin supplementation during pregnancy. The children they bore had an average IQ eight points higher than the children of other mothers from a similar poor nutritional environment who received no vitamin supplementation.

But what about the children born of malnourished mothers who did not receive a vitamin-enriched diet during pregnancy? Can we improve the intellectual ability of malnourished children by giving them more nutritional food? In one piece of research nutritional therapy was given to four groups of children. The children all ranged in age from two to ten years. One group consisted of well-nourished but intellectually retarded children. A second group consisted of well-nourished and intellectually normal children. A dietary improvement for these two well-nourished groups produced relatively little change in IQ. On the other hand, the third group consisted of malnourished but intellectually retarded children, and the fourth group of malnourished and intellectually normal children. Following a period of dietary improvement, the originally malnourished retarded children gained ten points in IQ and the originally malnourished normal children gained eighteen points. Nutritional therapy did make a difference.

Nevertheless, we must always remember that prevention is better and more certain

Can any society afford to have malnourished children, who have lower IQ's and less healthy bodies than well-nourished children?

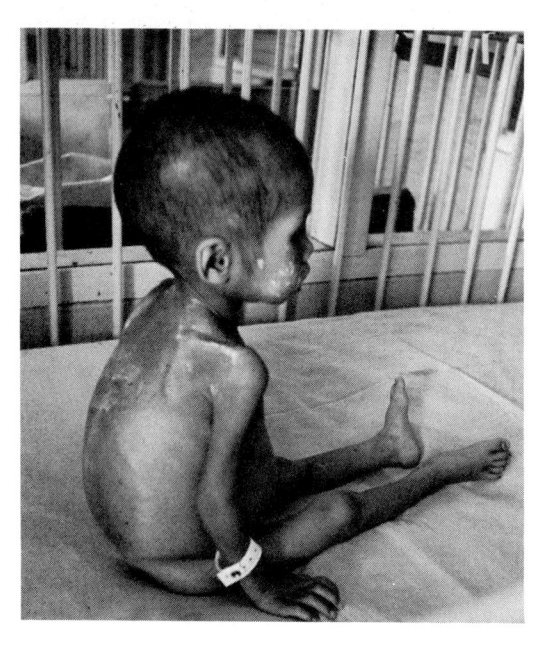

than cure. We must decrease the number of malnourished women who will have offspring with inferior bodies, including inferior brains. We must not have malnourished children growing up in our society. Something can be done to prevent malnutrition. What can you do to help improve our environment so that there is enough nourishing food for everyone?

Changes in the home environment can result in a change in IQ. In one case a study was made of twenty-six children in an orphanage. This particular orphanage was conducted with little thought for the welfare of the children. There was overcrowding, those in charge were not trained for the work, play and study equipment was lacking or very poor, and the children received very little individual attention. On entering the orphanage the children all had IQ's of 80 or above, the average IQ being 90. After these children had lived in the undesirable environment for less than two years, their average IQ dropped 16 points, to 74. An IQ of 74 is not so far above what is generally considered mental retardation, yet none of these children had given indications of mental retardation before living in the orphanage.

A limited environment affects the IQ. There is a growing concern for individuals who are born and grow up in culturally limited environments that do not offer the usual sensory stimulation. Recent studies suggest that adequate and early sensory stimulation is necessary for adequate intellectual development. In one study a group of black boys fifteen months of age, with limited environments, were given special tutoring for the next twenty-one months. The boys were tutored for one hour a day, five days a week. The special tutoring consisted of talking with the boys, reading to them, giving them experiences with books and puzzles, taking them on special trips and walks, and helping them with their emotional or behavioral problems. A control group of similar age, background, and IQ did not receive any tutoring. At the close of the study, the average IQ of the tutored boys was higher than the average IQ of the boys in the control group. When the amount of tutoring was decreased, the IQ's of the tutored group decreased, although their IQ's were still higher after tutoring than those of the control group. The data suggest the value of providing a more stimulating environment for children with limited cultural experiences.

The following study of children in five radically different home and community environments also indicates that a limited environment has an effect on IQ. These children lived in five "hollows" in a mountainous section of Virginia.

One hollow consisted of a few scattered families living in an area so isolated that it did not even have a road to the outside world. There was neither a school nor a church, and none of the citizens could read or write.

A second hollow was connected with the outside world by a rocky mountain trail. Occasionally the townspeople held meetings in a combined church and schoolhouse, and a few of the men could read and write.

A third hollow could be reached by automobile, although the road was very poor. There was a combined church and school, and a general store that contained the post office. The people of this community did most of their buying from mail-order catalogues.

A fourth hollow could be reached by a fair road connecting with a state highway. There was daily mail service. About 75 percent of the people could read, and they kept in touch with events through the newspapers. There was an organized school in session seven months out of the year.

The fifth community was on a hard-surfaced road. There was a modern school. The people kept up with current events through various mass media as well as automobile travel. This community was a rather typical small American town.

When the children in these five communities were given intelligence tests, it was found that there was a direct relationship between scores and the conditions under which the children lived. The more isolated the hollow, the lower the intelligence test scores. Since the children in the remote hollows were from the same general ancestral background as the children living in the fifth community, limitations of the environment—lack of schools, books, social life, and so forth—seemed the most plausible explanation.

How do race and socioeconomic conditions affect intelligence test scores? Perhaps you have heard that black children do not have as high IQ's, on the average, as white children. There are statistical studies to verify this statement. However, this is not the same as saying that black children are not as innately intelligent as white children. Most of our present-day intelligence tests were developed and standardized on white middle-class children, and so they tend to be biased against black children, although we do not yet know the extent of such bias. We do know that many black children grow up under poor socioeconomic conditions.

The Society for the Psychological Study of Social Issues, a Division of the American Psychological Association, has gone on record as saying,

> We believe that a more accurate understanding of the contribution of heredity to intelligence will be possible only when social conditions for all races are equal and when this situation has existed for several generations. We maintain that the racism and discrimination in our country impose an immeasurable burden upon the black person. Social inequalities deprive large numbers of black people of social, economic, and educational advantages available to a great majority of the white population.

Interaction of Heredity and Environment

Over the years psychologists have made studies in which they have tried to answer the question, "Which is more important, heredity or environment?" Today psychologists concentrate more on finding an answer to the question, "How do heredity and environment interact?"

Motivation. Psychologists who study motivation can tell us a great deal about the influences of heredity and environment on an individual. Motivation refers to the regulation of behavior that satisfies needs and leads toward goals. By studying motivation, psychologists can understand something of the conditions that predispose individuals to one kind of behavior instead of another. How an individual behaves is determined partly by biological drives and partly by social considerations.

All men, as well as lower animals, have certain biological drives based on their inherited structures. Biological drives that motivate man are the drives for nourishment, water, oxygen, elimination, and reproduction. Man is also motivated to keep his body at a comfortable temperature and to provide it with sleep and rest. The biological drives help man and lower animals maintain their bodies in a state of equilibrium.

How an individual satisfies these drives depends on his learning from his social environment. For example, an individual who is

This girl practicing to be a successful singer shows how heredity and environment interact. She is motivated to sing partly because she inherited a good vocal apparatus and partly because her environment has been conducive to a musical career.

motivated by hunger may work for the money with which to buy food, or he may steal to eat. He may eat his food according to accepted rules of table etiquette, or he may stuff it into his mouth. He may insist that his meat be well cooked, or he may prefer to eat it raw.

Man is also motivated by psychological and social drives. For example, he has the need for the security found in group living. Man forms social groups varying from the family to international organizations. The infant's group living is limited to the mother and other individuals in the family circle. These individuals satisfy the infant's early biological needs. But soon he learns to value companionship even when it is not necessary to satisfy his biological needs. It is not necessary to think of our desire for group living as inborn or inherited. Rather, we can think of it as learned behavior, growing out of a period of dependence through which we all pass.

Interaction of heredity and environment in an experiment with rats. This experiment used rats that had been bred for brightness and dullness over thirteen generations. The bright and dull rats that resulted were raised under three different environmental conditions: restricted, neutral, and enriched. For the restricted environment, cages were covered with wire mesh and contained only a source of food and a source of water. The neutral environment consisted of the usual rat laboratory cages, from which the rats could observe activities in the laboratory. The cages with an enriched environment contained marbles, bells, swings, mirrors, tunnels, and other small objects. Half of the rats placed in each environment were bright and half were dull. The rats were kept in their respective restricted, neutral, and enriched environments for forty days after weaning. Then all of the rats were tested in a maze and a record was kept of how many errors they made. The more errors they made, the lower was their learning ability. The results are shown in the graph on this page.

You can see that in each of the two extreme environmental conditions, the restricted and enriched, the performances of the bright and dull rats were quite similar. Also, both bright and dull rats made many more errors in the restricted environment than in the enriched environment. These data suggest that any hereditary differences between the bright and dull rats were overshadowed by environmental influences. It was only in the neutral environment that heredity seemed to play a major role, the bright rats making far fewer errors than the dull rats. In general, it seems that the restricted environment lessened the learning ability of the bright rats whereas the enriched environment aided learning for the dull rats. If our objective was to develop a society of bright rats, we would need both to breed for brightness and to provide an enriched environment.

Although we cannot carry out similar experiments with human children, we can learn something about the interaction of heredity and environment in man through studies of twins.

Studies of heredity and environment involving twins. Psychologists find it useful to study IDENTICAL TWINS, who come from a single fertilized cell. Since identical twins have the same heredity, whatever differences appear in them must be due to the influence of environment. Remember, however, that the heredity of FRATERNAL TWINS, children of the same parents who happen to be conceived and born at about the same time, is no more alike than other children of the same parents.

A number of scientific studies have been made of twins. In general, it has been found that identical twins are much more alike than fraternal twins and that in many cases fraternal twins are more alike than siblings (children of the same parents regardless of age or sex) who are not twins.

In IQ, pairs of identical twins tend to differ, on the average, about 5 points. Pairs of fraternal twins differ about 9 points, while other siblings differ about 11 points. Unrelated pairs of individuals selected at random tend to differ about 15 points.

In most cases identical twins live in very similar environments. Once in a while, however, it does happen that identical twins are separated early in life and grow up in quite different environments. Scientists succeeded in

The number of errors made by rats raised under three different environmental conditions

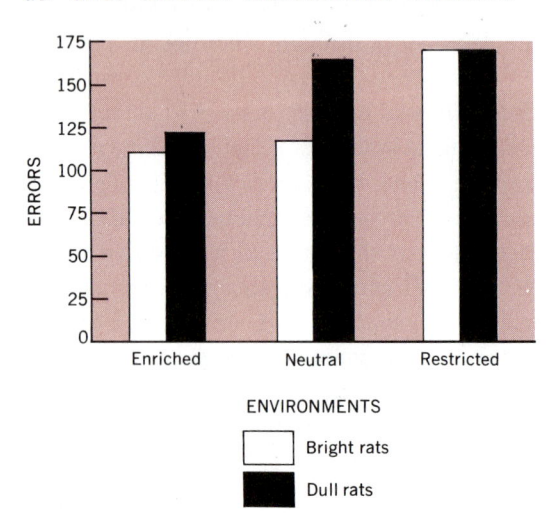

finding nineteen pairs of identical twins who had been separated early in life and who were at least twelve years of age when studied. Thus, there had been a considerable length of time in which environment had had a chance to play its part in their development. Here was an opportunity to study the effects of different environments with individuals having the same heredity. In several cases the twins grew up in total ignorance of each other's existence.

The average difference between the IQ's of these nineteen pairs of twins was 8.2, as against about 5 for identical twins living together. Consider, however, that the difference of 8.2 points for all pairs of identical twins reared apart is less than that usually found between nontwin siblings living in the same home environments (11 points). Certainly it is less than the 15 points found on the average for unrelated individuals living in different home environments. This study seems to suggest that heredity is an important factor in the development of the individual, regardless of the influences of the environment.

Another study of identical twins raised in separate homes indicates the importance of environmental factors. Case studies were made of identical twin boys born in a mountain village in Tennessee, whose mother died at the time they were born. The paternal grandparents adopted one, known in psychological writings as R. The maternal grandparents adopted the other, known as J. The grandparents who took J were industrious and gave him many advantages. There were books in the home and J developed a taste for good literature. He graduated from high school and became an engineer.

The grandparents who took R were rather shiftless. The grandfather tried blacksmithing, working on the railroad, and coal mining, but he did not stick to any kind of work. R attended school for eight grades but was not interested in schoolwork. Something of his environment can be seen from the fact that in the community in which he lived school was in session for only five months of the year. After leaving school, R found employment of various kinds, but he seemed to avoid all work as much as possible. At the age of twenty-seven, J's IQ was found to be 96 and R's 77 (Stanford-Binet).

As a result of their studies of twins, some psychologists have concluded tentatively that physical characteristics are least likely to be affected by environment; that intelligence, as measured by the IQ, is more likely to be affected; that education and achievement are still more likely to be affected; and that personality is most likely to be affected.

Psychologists have also related the studies of twins to the question of differences in intellectual ability of blacks and whites. The Society for the Psychological Study of Social Issues has issued a statement saying,

> ...we find that observed racial differences in intelligence can be attributed to environmental factors. Thus, identical twins reared in different environments can show differences in intelligence test scores which are fully comparable to the differences found between racial groups.

How do heredity and environment interact? To help answer this question, compare an individual with a rectangle. Which is the more important factor in a rectangle, its base or its altitude? Obviously we cannot have a rectangle without both base and altitude. Neither can we have an individual without both heredity and environment. Did you ever see an individual without any environment? Did you ever see an individual who did not have ancestors?

We might represent an individual by a four-sided figure, with heredity as the base and environment as the altitude, as in the figure above. Although we cannot have a rectangle without both a base and an altitude, the base and the altitude can vary in length. A rectangle may have a narrow base and a high altitude, or a wide base and a low altitude, as shown in the figure at the bottom of this page.

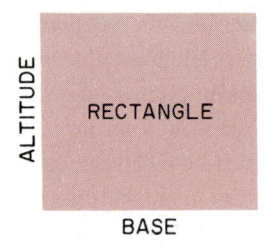

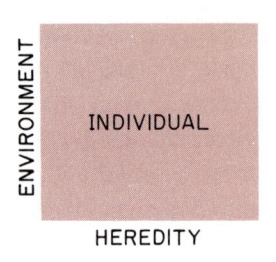

An individual may have an inferior heredity and a superior environment, or an individual may have a superior heredity and an inferior environment. Suppose there are two individuals with approximately equally good heredity. One is placed in a rich cultural environment, the other in a poor cultural environment. The resulting total individuals will be quite different. Or suppose two individuals with considerably different heredities are placed in approximately the same environments. The total individuals developing will be quite different, owing to the factor of heredity.

Psychologists do not know enough about either heredity or environment to speak in terms of specific measurable units. Hence, it is not possible to say that one individual's environment is three times as good as another's or that one individual's heredity is twice as good as another's. Neither can it be said that as a result of both heredity and environment one individual is, for example, three times as capable as another. Individuals cannot be appraised by a geometric formula. The analogy to rectangles suggests, however, the related contributions of heredity and environment to the development of the individual.

Go back to the case of Billy, who misbehaved in school (p. 192). Was that misbehavior due to heredity or environment? Perhaps Billy inherited a small body; he is shorter and weighs less than the other boys his age. Perhaps where Billy lives, the larger boys make fun of him and make him feel inferior. Billy does not wish to be the subject

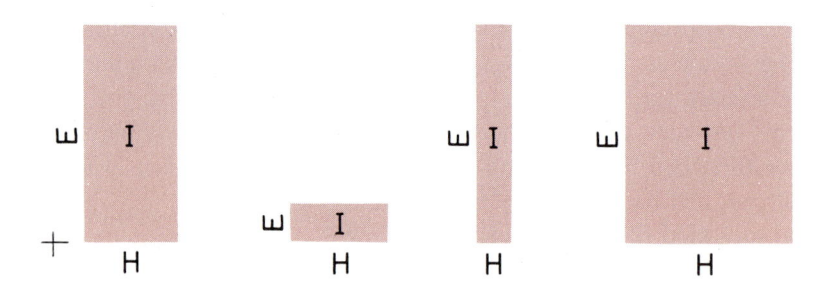

210 PATTERNS OF BEHAVIOR

of jokes about his size, does not wish to feel inferior. He believes that by misbehaving in school he will cause the other children to think that he is tough. If Billy's heredity had been different, he might not have had a small body and would not have been the subject of jokes about his size. If Billy's heredity had been the same but he had lived in a community where other children did not make fun of him, his misbehavior might not have developed. In effect, his present behavior is to be understood in terms of both his heredity and his environment. Heredity and environment always interact. (See pp. 264–65.)

Terms to Know

chromosome
DNA (deoxyribonucleic acid)
dominant characteristic
eugenics
fraternal twin

gene
genotype
identical twin
imprinting
maturation

motivation
phenotype
recessive characteristic
RNA (ribonucleic acid)
unit character

Topics to Think About

1. What are your dominant and recessive characteristics? To what extent do you think they have influenced your life?

2. Suppose some day you should wish to adopt a child five or six years of age. Which factor would you give greater consideration to: his or her heredity, or the early home or institutional care of the child? Why?

3. Should we attempt through legislation to reduce the number of children born to parents of limited intellectual ability, or should we attempt to provide a richer environment for whatever children are born to parents of limited intellectual ability?

4. What would you do to improve our environment so that human beings born 100 years from now will be superior to human beings living today?

5. One survey of more than 170 psychology texts written in this century revealed that unpleasant emotions were mentioned twice as often as pleasant emotions. Another survey of 500 psychology journal articles on emotion showed that 80 percent dealt with unpleasant emotions and only 20 percent dealt with pleasant ones. In contrast, a study of literary sources found that almost 75 percent of the references were to pleasant emotions and only 25 percent to unpleasant ones. Why do you think there was such a discrepancy between what concerns psychologists and what concerns literary writers? Would data such as these prove that psychologists are really morbidly concerned with only the negative side of life?

Suggestions for Activities

1. Hold a debate in which one team takes the viewpoint that environment is the major consideration in the development of the individual, and another team takes the view that heredity is of primary importance in the development of a person. The debate can be made more interesting by having students take the side that they don't agree with.

2. Write a history of your family. The history should include such physical characteristics as height, weight, eye color, hair color, and possibly body build. Also, include records of the vocational activities, social achievements (for example, public offices held), religious affiliation and activities, travel experiences, homes lived in, military service, schools attended, and so on. There may be stories of personal happenings that you will wish to include. In writing your history you will need to confer with your parents, grandparents, aunts and uncles, and other relatives. There may be family records that you can refer to. You may wish to consult official public documents. Pictures of living members of the family should be included and also, if available, pictures of members of the family no longer living. Your history will be of value to you now as you study the influences of heredity and environment. In time, it may become a valuable document in the family archives.

3. If you live in a large city, or when you visit one, travel through one or more areas of homes belonging to people in the higher socioeconomic levels. Then travel through the poorer areas of the city. Contrast the homes, schools, churches and synagogues, stores, and recreational facilities. Is there a difference in the personal appearances of the children and adults that you see on the streets? To what extent do you think the adult lives of the children will be influenced by their environments? You may wish to take some pictures to illustrate your report, but take care not to offend anyone, especially in the poorer districts.

4. Find and bring to class any family albums that may be available. Can you trace any physical characteristics from these pictures?

5. Visit a farm or zoo and observe the behavior of young animals, especially of the bird family. Do you note any indications of imprinting? Are there any of the young of one species being cared for by mothers of another species? If you live on a farm, you might try to imprint ducklings or chicks on some animal other than their mother or on some large moving object.

6. If possible, contact a medical doctor; a psychologist; and a priest, pastor, or rabbi, and have each talk with your class on the question, "Should eugenics be applied to human subjects? Why or why not?"

7. Educators often use what is called the "lock step" procedure in education. That is, almost all persons of similar chronological ages enter school together. Many school districts use the month of November, or some other month close to November, as the latest month in which an individual can have a birthdate and enter the first grade as a five-year-old. Form a panel of students to discuss the ways in which the "lock step" process in education violates principles of individual differences in terms of heredity and environmental influences.

Suggestions for Further Reading

Hilgard, E. R., R. C. Atkinson, and Rita Atkinson, *Introduction to Psychology,* 5th ed., Harcourt Brace Jovanovich. See Chapter 12, "Physiological Background of Motivation"; Chapter 13, "Human Motivation"; and Chapter 16, "Behavior Genetics."

Kagan, J., M. M. Haith, and Catherine Caldwell (eds.), *Psychology: Adapted Readings,* Harcourt Brace Jovanovich. See Selection 17, "Environmental Stimulation of the Reproductive System of the Female Ring Dove," and Selection 18, "The Study of Motivation."

Mead, Margaret, *New Lives for Old,* New American Library (Mentor Books). This book describes the effects of environmental influences on a primitive people.

Wertheimer, M., *et al., Psychology: A Brief Introduction,* Scott, Foresman. See pages 186–91, 204–08, 217–19, 222–24, on the heredity-environment problem and how it is studied, fitting human qualifications to the environment, creating environments that fit human capacities, and how people are different but share the same environment.

chapter 9
Biological Influences on Behavior

As you know, psychologists are interested in the relationship between an organism and its environment. The activities of a person's body affect how he responds to his environment and what his behavior will be. Therefore, it is important to have some knowledge of how the body functions.

Your body is very complex, and the operations of all parts are related. Anything that affects one part of your body affects all parts. Suppose you run a mile. You run with your legs, but are your legs the only parts of you that tire? After running, can you lift heavy weights just as easily as you could lift them before you ran the mile? Does your heart beat at the same rate it did before you ran? Is your breathing the same as before? Of course, your entire body has been affected. How?

Much of the unification of our bodily activity occurs through the circulation of the blood. When you run, fatigue chemicals are formed in the muscles of your legs. They are carried to all parts of your body through the bloodstream. Your whole body becomes tired.

Other factors in the unification of bodily activity are the nervous systems and the glands. You may have learned something about the nervous systems and glands in elementary school. Or perhaps you have studied about the parts of the body and their functioning in a biology course in high school. A study of psychology will also give you some fundamental knowledge on how the human body functions.

The Nervous Systems

The nervous systems are major regulators of the body's activities, and therefore of behavior.

The central and peripheral nervous systems. We can divide the nerve structure of the body into two main divisions—the central nervous system and the peripheral nervous system. The CENTRAL NERVOUS SYSTEM is made up of the brain and the spinal cord. The PERIPHERAL NERVOUS SYSTEM consists of nerve fibers running to and from the central nervous system. The central and peripheral nervous systems act as connecting and coordinating systems between the sense organs and the muscles and glands. You start to unscrew a hot lamp bulb. A "message" is carried to the brain and out to a muscle. Instantly you jerk your hand away from the hot bulb. The illustration on this page will help you recall the important parts of the central and peripheral nervous systems.

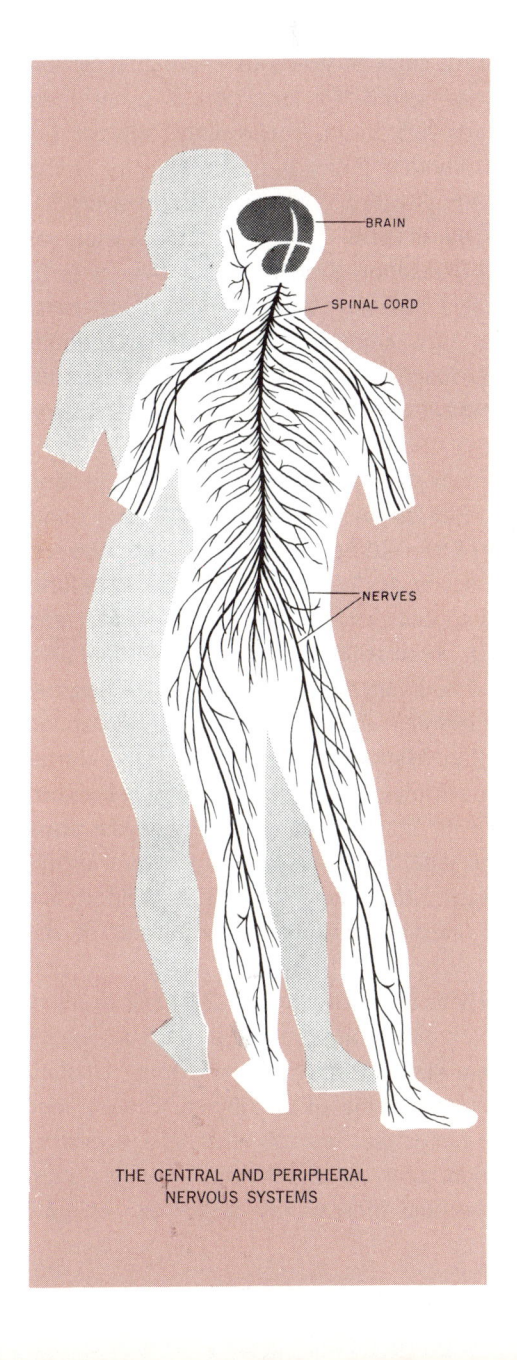

The autonomic nervous system. In terms of function, a part of the central and peripheral nervous systems regulates the activities of the vital organs. We call the part of the nervous systems that performs this regulating function the AUTONOMIC NERVOUS SYSTEM. It acts somewhat, but not entirely, independently of the central nervous system. Ordinarily we are not aware of its activities. It regulates the activity of those organs necessary for life and reproduction, namely, the lungs, the stomach, the intestines, the heart, the liver, the eliminative organs, and the reproductive organs.

Under most circumstances we cannot voluntarily control the activities regulated by the autonomic nervous system. However, we do have temporary control over a few activities, such as breathing, which we can voluntarily regulate for a short period of time. Also,

THE CENTRAL AND PERIPHERAL NERVOUS SYSTEMS

The central and peripheral nervous systems are something like a telephone system. If you want some flowers delivered, you can go to a telephone and dial your florist. The message is carried through the exchange office and out to your florist. Soon the flowers are on the way to you. Although the human body is much more complex than a telephone system, the process is somewhat similar. When a sense organ is stimulated, a nerve impulse passes along the peripheral nerves to the central nervous system. The brain and spinal cord then send nerve impulses back out to the organ.

BIOLOGICAL INFLUENCES ON BEHAVIOR

several activities regulated by the autonomic nervous system have been controlled by man through the use of learning procedures.

Reaction Time

Men and women engaged in scientific research have made extensive studies of the nervous systems of men and other organisms. Psychologists, in particular, have done much experimental work in the measurement of reaction time. REACTION TIME refers to the interval of time between the onset of a stimulus and the beginning of the observer's overt response. It is a measure of the time required for a nerve impulse to travel from a sense organ to the brain and then to a muscle.

How fast are your reactions in automobile driving? Suppose that a traffic signal turns red, or a car suddenly turns out from a side street, or a child runs out into the road in front of you. How long will it take you to release your foot from the accelerator pedal and apply the brake pedal? One way to find out is to test your reactions under simulated driving conditions. The person being tested sits in a seat similar to the seat of a car. In front of him are a steering wheel and brake and accelerator pedals, just as they are found in an automobile. Through the windshield he can see a traffic light. He is told to take hold of the steering wheel, put his foot on the accelerator pedal, and "drive along" until the traffic signal turns red. Then he is to put on the brake as quickly as possible. A recording instrument indicates the time required.

The average reaction time for getting the foot pressed against the brake pedal is about .45 second. The reaction time is much longer if the driver is not concentrating on his driving. If a person is concentrating his attention on the steering wheel rather than on the foot pedal, his reaction time is lengthened by between .10 and .15 second.

The factors affecting reaction time. There are wide variations in reaction time for each individual. The reaction time may even vary for the same individual, depending on the combination of factors and on the type of situation. One such factor is the specific sense involved, such as vision or hearing. Reaction time for sound, for example, is faster than that for light, and, surprisingly, slowest for pain. Another factor is the complexity of the stimulus situation. For example, in everyday life, where there is reaction to a variety of stimuli, reaction time is slower than it is in typical laboratory experiments, where most stimuli are controlled. Similarity of stimuli affects reaction time, in that the closer stimuli resemble each other, the longer the reaction time.

Other factors act to lessen the reaction time. For instance, as the strength and duration of the stimulus increases, the reaction time becomes shorter. The reaction time also tends to decrease with increased practice and strong motivation. Reaction time shortens, too, if the individual is prepared to react—for example, a runner starting at the sound of a gun. Have you ever noticed that a starter at a track meet usually varies the time between "On your mark . . . get set . . ." and the firing of the gun? If the warning time were always the same, the runners might respond to the time interval and not to the sound of the gun.

There are many factors that tend to make reaction time longer, such as fatigue, length of time vigilance has occurred, drugs, alcohol, and the smoking of marijuana. Finally, one more factor that has the effect of lengthening reaction time is acceleration. Acceleration has become increasingly important not only

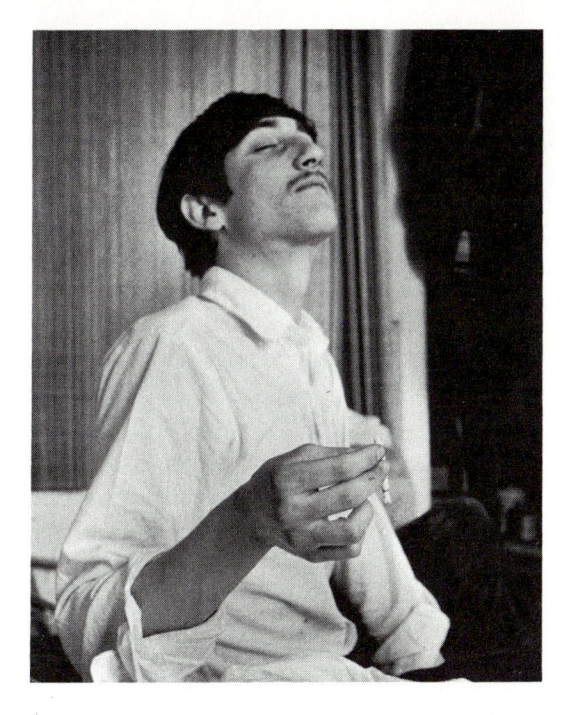

When an individual smokes marijuana, his reaction time becomes lengthened considerably.

for aircraft pilots, as the speed of aircraft grows ever faster, but also for astronauts. When a vehicle suddenly changes direction at high speed, or changes from a stationary to a moving state, as when astronauts take off from the launching pad, reaction time slows down.

The Brain

We mentioned earlier that the brain is an important part of the central nervous system. The brain plays an essential role in the behavior of an organism.

How do scientists study the role of the brain in behavior? The relationship of the activity of the brain to behavior has fascinated philosophers and scientists for many years. Today three principal techniques are used in studying this relationship. One technique involves direct stimulation of specific areas of the brain. Such stimulation can be given by implanting electrodes in the brain. The scientist then passes a very weak electrical current through specific areas of the brain and notes the effect on behavior. For example, he can elicit drinking and eating behavior in rats by sending an electrical current through the CORTEX—the outer layer of the cerebrum—of their brains. The stimulation of the brain can also be accomplished by injecting drugs through tiny tubes implanted in specific areas of the brain.

Another technique for studying the relationship between the functioning of the brain and behavior is through a study of the effects of brain lesions. A BRAIN LESION refers to the destruction of part of the brain through surgery, accident, or disease. With animals, the experimenter may destroy specific parts of the brain to study the effects of such destruction on behavior. With human subjects, the scientist can use only those cases in which brain surgery is necessary for medical reasons, or there has been a brain-damaging accident, or disease has destroyed part of the brain.

A third technique for the study of the relationship between brain activity and behavior is by means of the EEG. These initials refer to an instrument called an ELECTROENCEPHALOGRAPH, which is used to record a person's brain wave pattern on a chart. The record made by the instrument is called an ELECTROENCEPHALOGRAM. When electrodes from the EEG are placed on a person's scalp over various parts of the cortex, the instrument makes a recording of the electrochemical changes that constitute his brain activity. The recordings change as the activity of the individual changes. The record is different when the person sleeps than when he is awake. It changes when he is performing arithmetical calculations and then tries to remember something.

Is there any relation between brain size and intelligence? Can a person's intelligence be judged from the size of his brain? To find out, students of anatomy have examined the brains of deceased individuals.

It has been found that on the average the brains of adult men weigh about 48 ounces, while the brains of adult women weigh about 44 ounces. From this particular scientific fact some men have jumped to the conclusion that men must be more intelligent than women. However, many studies of intelligence, as measured by tests, school marks, and success in life show that on the average women are just as intelligent as men. It is the quality of brain structure that is important, rather than the quantity. Why should anyone expect the brain of a woman to weigh as much as the brain of a man? The average weight of women is less than the average total weight of men. The weight of a woman's brain is as great in proportion to total body weight as the weight of a man's brain.

Some animals have more brain than man. An elephant's brain weighs about 10 pounds and a whale's brain weighs about 14 pounds. However, the brains of elephants and whales weigh far less than the brains of men in proportion to total body weight. Furthermore, man's brain, especially the cerebrum (see diagram on p. 220), is more highly developed than the brain of any other species.

Are the brains of very intelligent persons heavier than the brains of mentally retarded persons? The heaviest brain ever found was that of a moderately retarded individual, a London newsboy, whose brain weighed 80 ounces (almost twice as much as the average). The lightest brain ever found was also that of a moderately retarded person. Individuals differ in the sizes of their brains, but size in itself cannot be taken as a measure of an individual's intellectual ability.

Nevertheless, on the average the brains of civilized races are somewhat heavier than those of primitive races. It has been found that the brain weight of individuals who are intelligent enough to live normal social and economic lives is slightly heavier than the average brain weight of those individuals who are so lacking in intellectual ability that they must be cared for in institutions.

Experiments with animals have indicated that changes in the environment can affect the size of the brain. In one study scientists raised rats under two experimental conditions. Some of the rats were raised under conditions in which they could do little except sit in their cages or move about in them. Other rats were placed in cages in which they could climb about on ladders and play with a variety of objects, which were changed daily. The rats reared in the enriched environment had heavier brains and thicker cortices (outer layers of the cerebrums) than the rats reared in an impoverished environment. Moreover, the brain weight increase was not due to increase in general body weight. Might we find someday that human children living in enriched environments had heavier brains than children living in impoverished environments?

Is there a relation between kinds of thinking and specific parts of the brain? Surgeons have found that if parts of the cortex are stimulated with a very mild electric current, specific muscular contractions will occur. If one particular spot is stimulated, the toes will be moved. Stimulation of another spot produces movement of the forearm, stimulation of still another spot produces movement of the neck, and so on. Also, sensations are known to be rather definitely localized in the brain. For example, an area at the back of the cerebrum functions in vision; an area on each side is related to hearing, as shown on page 219.

Not only are sensory processes related to particular parts of the brain but also the individual nerve cells, or neurons, within certain areas of the brain have specific functions. In one study neurobiologists inserted electrodes into individual neurons in the cerebral cortices of cats and monkeys. The animals were exposed to projections of different light shapes, and the electrical impulses of individual neurons in their brains were recorded. The neurobiologists found that there were patterns of neuron responses. Each pattern of neurons was set to respond to specific angles, sizes, shapes, colors, or movements and to occur in a hierarchical order. Similar experiments are being performed in the areas of touch and hearing.

Although some areas of the cerebral cortex are known to be related to sensory processes and other areas to motor activities, nearly three-fourths of the human cortex has no known specific function. The complicated processes of thinking seem to be spread over much of the cerebrum in areas sometimes referred to as association areas. These areas seem to be related to the storage of information and the relationship between stored information and incoming stimulation.

In some cases destruction of parts of the human cortex does not seem to result in a loss of general intellectual ability. Studies have been made in which general intelligence tests are administered to individuals both before and after brain surgery. In most instances the tests did not show a loss of intellectual ability.

This is not the case in some animal experiments, however. In one experiment monkeys watched food being placed in one or the other of two cups. Then both cups were hidden behind a screen. After several minutes these monkeys could still remember which cup contained the food. But after a brain lesion operation on the frontal lobes of their brains, monkeys could not remember which cup contained the food if the delay in uncovering the cups was more than a second or two.

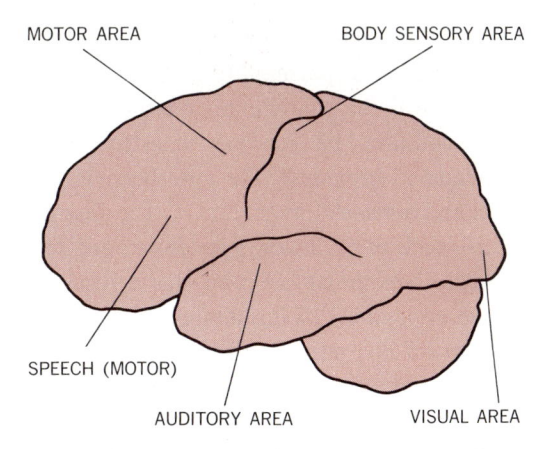

Some of the localized functions that are found in the cortex of the human brain.

A number of experiments performed in recent years on rats, porpoises, and other animals indicate that there are "pleasure" and "pain" areas in the brain. When electrical stimulation of the "pleasure" area was used as the only reward for behavioral responses, stimulation resulted in the learning of the responses. Rats have been taught to reduce their heartbeats by 20 percent through this method. Each time their heart rate dropped to a predetermined level, the rats were rewarded with an electrical impulse through an electrode planted in the pleasure area of their brains. Other rats learned to blush in one ear and not the other.

Is there a relation between personality and the brain? There is evidence of a relationship between personality changes and some areas of the brain. If the cortex in one frontal lobe becomes diseased or is removed, no marked change in personality occurs. If both frontal lobes are destroyed, however, very considerable alteration in personality may result. The behavior of the individual often becomes rather childish—he becomes boastful about his imagined greatness. He may become immoral and antisocial in general. Other changes occur—such as an increase in temper and less control of emotional behavior—as a result of disease or removal of the temporal lobes (see diagram on this page). Disorders or destruction of other lobes of the brain do not result in such personality changes, however.

The EEG is being used to study the relationship between activity of the cortex and personality. There is some evidence that many —but not all—children showing socially undesirable behavior have abnormal patterns of activity in the cortex. Adult criminals and some persons with severe mental disorders often show abnormal patterns, also.

The EEG permits us to study the *alpha waves* in our brains, which influence our behavior. Some research has indicated that the brain can only perceive stimuli during each alpha wave. An alpha wave has a frequency of approximately ten pulsations per second while an individual is awake. When a person is relaxed, the alpha wave is less noticeable, and when he is asleep, it disappears entirely. Individuals have been taught to control the appearance and disappearance of alpha waves, enabling themselves to voluntarily have periods of relaxation. At least one business is looking into the possibility of using alpha wave training methods to reduce the tensions of their executives and help them be more creative.

Convulsive Disorders

Psychologists use the term CONVULSIVE DISORDERS to refer to those disorders popularly spoken of as epilepsy. One way a doctor discovers that his patient has some disturbance of a convulsive nature is through the EEG. The brain wave patterns of a person having an epileptic seizure are quite different from the patterns of that person at other times. Even when an epileptic person is not having an epileptic seizure, his EEG record often

The human brain

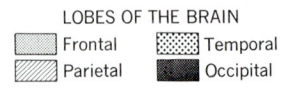

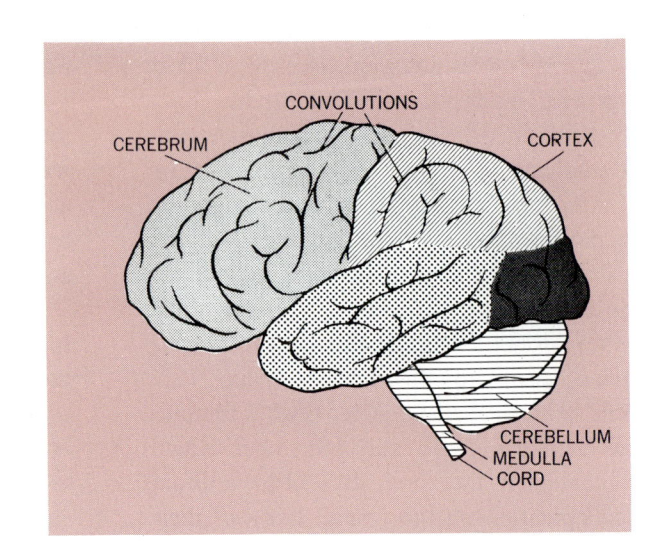

LOBES OF THE BRAIN
Frontal   Temporal
Parietal Occipital

PATTERNS OF BEHAVIOR

differs from the records of persons not subject to this illness. About 10 percent of the population show brain wave patterns that suggest they are more susceptible to seizures than those with normal EEG patterns.

Types of convulsive disorders. For practical purposes, convulsive disorders are usually described under one of four classifications (although they can be classified according to the area of the brain most involved).

1. *Grand mal* ('gran 'mäl). More than half of all convulsive disorders exist in this form. Grand mal, which is French for "great illness," has very pronounced symptoms. Historically, this form of seizure has been known as the "falling sickness." The person loses consciousness and falls, usually with a cry or a moan. His muscles become stiff, and he may bite his tongue or cheek as the muscles stiffen. At first he may be pale, and then his face will become flushed. The pupils of his eyes dilate. The skin may become blue or slightly purple. This stage usually lasts about half a minute. Then the individual begins a violent jerking of his arms, head, jaws, and trunk. Many times there is a frothing at the mouth, which is caused simply by air being forced through the saliva. The patient may cough and grunt. Sometimes he loses control of the bowels and bladder. This stage may last for only part of a minute, or it may last as long as from five to ten minutes.

After this phase the individual goes into a stuporous sleep lasting several hours. On awakening, he may feel fatigued and complain of a headache, but he does not remember anything about his behavior or thoughts during the seizure. In fact, on regaining consciousness he may resume a conversation at the exact point at which it was interrupted by the seizure.

2. *Petit mal* (pə-'tē 'mäl). The term means "little illness," and the symptoms of the petit mal are much more mild than for the grand mal. The individual may become dizzy. He may lose consciousness for a few seconds. There may be a slight trembling. Sometimes the eyes appear to be staring vacantly. He seldom falls. In fact, his friends may not be aware that he has had a seizure. They may note only that he paused in his conversation or that he stopped momentarily in his work.

3. *Jacksonian.* This form of convulsive disorder is much like the grand mal except that the attack begins in one part of the body, or with a feeling of numbness or tingling, and then spreads over the entire side of the body. The patient often does not lose consciousness until the attack has affected a considerable part of his body.

4. *Psychomotor.* In the psychomotor form of convulsive disorder the person loses consciousness but continues with the activity in which he has been engaged and appears to be conscious. The attacks usually do not last more than a few minutes, yet they can last for several days. Patients have been known to harm themselves or to commit vicious crimes while having a psychomotor attack. Later they remembered nothing of the incident, with the possible exception of a vague feeling that they had done something terrible. A person having a psychomotor attack should not be forcibly restrained unless absolutely necessary for safety, since to do so may increase the severity of the seizure.

Convulsive seizures are sometimes preceded by hallucinations of light, sounds, tastes, or smells. These are imaginary sensations—no stimuli for them exist outside the person. Such a hallucination at the beginning of an attack is spoken of as an AURA.

Causes of convulsive disorders. The causes of the convulsive disorders just described are not known definitely. There are evidences of various physiological disturbances. As we noted earlier, the brain wave patterns of persons having convulsive disorders are distinctive. We are not sure to what extent heredity is a factor in convulsive disorders, but in many cases it probably only predisposes a person toward the illness. Brain injuries occurring before, during, or after birth, or an infection following such diseases as measles or encephalitis, may be factors in producing convulsive seizures.

Psychological studies of people with convulsive disorders have shown that there is no typical personality structure. Most persons with convulsive disorders have normal intellectual ability, and some famous persons have been included in this group—Julius Caesar, Lord Byron, Alexander the Great, Guy de Maupassant, Paganini, and Van Gogh. In one study of 95 college students with convulsive disorders, it was found that 70 percent of them were capable of doing successful college work. It is true, however, that in some cases persons with convulsive disorders may show mental deterioration. One reason for mental deterioration has been the necessary anti-convulsive drugs given to some such persons. But when anti-convulsive drugs are combined with chemical and vitamin therapy, there is improvement in the conditions of patients.

At least 70 percent of persons suffering from some form of convulsive disorder display their first symptoms before they are twenty years of age. EEG patterns are used to help determine whether patients who have not had a seizure in several years should continue treatment. With adequate modern medical and social care, probably about 80 percent of persons with convulsive seizures can lead relatively normal lives.

How can you help a person displaying convulsive behavior? You should always treat such persons with genuine sympathy. If you should encounter persons with the characteristics described on page 221, you should recognize such behavior as a symptom of a disorder, and should not consider their acts as personal offenses. Because of their condition, such persons may have special problems in their school and college studies.

Adults subject to convulsive seizures often have difficulty in finding jobs because of popular prejudice against them. Generally they cannot drive cars safely, although on the approval of a physician and under certain medical conditions, some persons having convulsive disorders can obtain a driver's license. There are, however, many jobs that they can do as well, and as safely, as anyone else.

Basically, you can help individuals with

One way of determining if an individual is subject to convulsive disorders is to tape EEG electrodes to the person's head, as shown here, and record the brain wave patterns.

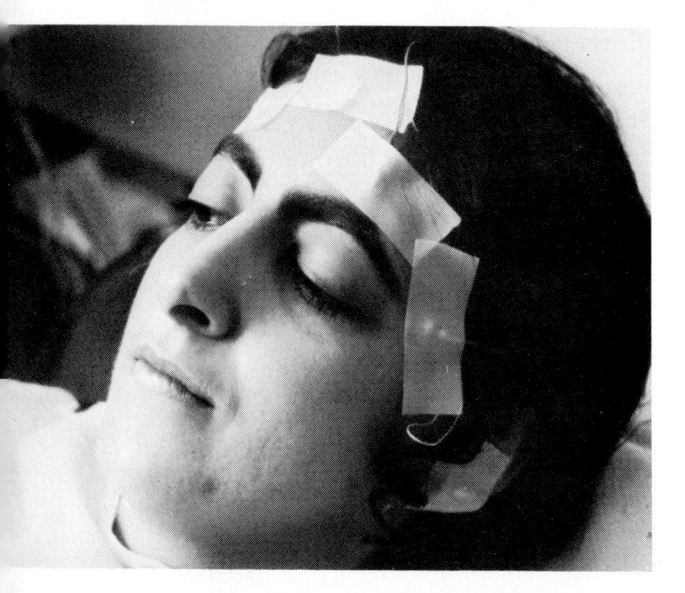

convulsive disorders by thinking of them and treating them as normal people who have a special problem of adjustment.

Glands

At the beginning of this chapter we spoke of the glands as being a factor in the unification of bodily activity. There are two kinds of glands in the body—duct glands and ductless glands.

Duct glands. These glands empty their contents through small openings, or ducts, onto the surface of the body or into body cavities. Since duct glands do not secrete their products directly into the bloodstream, they are often spoken of as glands of external secretion, or exocrine glands. On a warm day you become aware of your sweat glands, which are important in eliminating fatigue products from the body. Whenever you get a tiny object in your eye, you become aware of your tear glands. When you put food in your mouth, or sometimes when you just think about food, the salivary glands pour saliva into the mouth cavity. After food is swallowed, the contents of other duct glands are poured into the stomach and small intestine so that the food may be digested.

Ductless glands. Although the duct glands are very important, psychologists are more interested in the ductless glands. Ductless glands have no openings or ducts through which they can pour their contents. Because they secrete their products directly into the bloodstream, they are sometimes referred to as glands of internal secretion, or endocrine glands. The chemical substances they produce are known as hormones, which are absorbed directly into the bloodstream. Of the ductless glands shown in the illustration on this page,

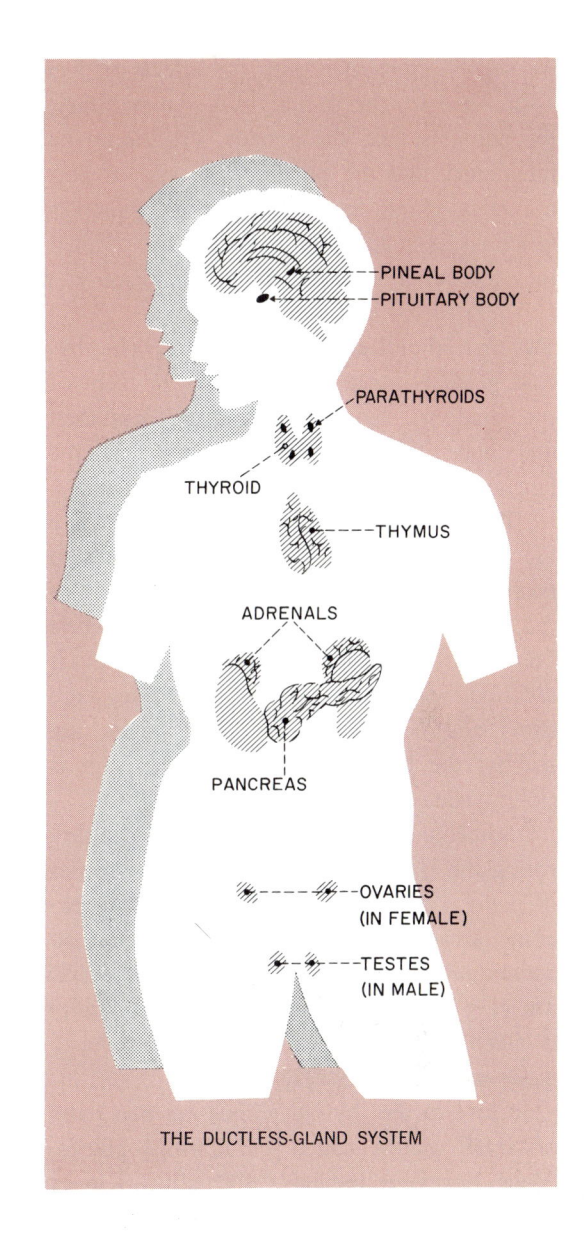

THE DUCTLESS-GLAND SYSTEM

The ductless, or endocrine, glands (above) are studied by psychologists because these glands are important regulators of the body and their activity has a considerable influence on behavior. Psychologists examine the relationship between biological factors, such as these glands, and social factors to help understand an individual's total personality.

BIOLOGICAL INFLUENCES ON BEHAVIOR

we will be concerned with the effects of five—the thyroid, the parathyroid, the pituitary, the adrenals, and the gonads. (It should be mentioned that the pancreas is only in part a ductless gland; another part of the pancreas functions as a duct gland, pouring its product into the small intestine to aid digestion.)

The thyroid and parathyroid glands. The thyroid gland is located in the neck in front of the windpipe. Normally it weighs less than an ounce. One important element in the hormone produced by this gland is iodine.

If the thyroid gland becomes underactive (in hypothyroidism), the individual tends to become lazy and dull. If the underactivity of the gland dates from infancy, a condition known as *cretinism* results. The cretin is dwarfed, with a thickset body. The legs are short and bowed, the feet and hands are stubby, the hair is coarse, and the skin is sickly yellow.

Sometimes there is overactivity of the thyroid gland (hyperthyroidism) as in some cases of *goiter* (ˈgȯit-ər), when the gland may become greatly enlarged and very prominent. Individuals suffering from hyperthyroidism are very restless and excitable, have difficulty in sleeping, tend to be irritable, and seem to work with untiring energy.

Close to the thyroid glands are two pairs of small glands called parathyroid glands. Their hormone regulates the utilization of calcium in the body. Where there is a lack of this hormone, a condition known as *tetany* occurs. It is characterized by intermittent, involuntary muscle twitching and spasms.

The pituitary gland. The pituitary gland is attached to the underside of the brain. Part of this gland has great influence on bodily growth. If there is overactivity of the gland in childhood, *giantism* results. There is a record of one young man who at the age of nineteen years was 8 feet 6 inches tall and was still growing at the rate of 2 inches a year. He weighed 435 pounds and wore size 36 shoes. For a time he played basketball. "But it's too easy," he said. "I'd stand down near the net, someone would throw me the ball, and I'd drop it in. I don't think the other teams liked it much." At birth he was of normal size (8½ pounds); it was a hyperpituitary condition that produced his great height. A skillful surgeon can remove some of the excess glandular substance and so prevent giantism if the hyperpituitary condition is discovered early and is promptly brought to his attention.

In a case of underactivity of part of the pituitary gland in childhood, the individual becomes a dwarf or midget. Many dwarfs or midgets, unlike cretins, have well-proportioned or reasonably well-proportioned bodies. Administration of pituitary extract to an afflicted child will do much to promote normal growth. In one case an infantile, emaciated eighteen-year-old boy was treated with pituitary extract. He had not grown for eight years. Yet within four and a half months after treatment began he had matured sexually and had grown two inches taller.

The adrenal gland. Located near each kidney is a small gland called the adrenal gland. It is composed of two parts and really should be thought of as two separate glands, although it is usually referred to as one.

One psychologist tells the story of a young woman who was a musician. She was very fond of her piano. It was a heavy piano, which she could not move. Whenever she wanted to dust behind the piano, she had to have someone move it for her. One day the house caught fire. No one else was at home, and it seemed that her piano was going to burn. In her excitement she moved the piano across the room and out the door to safety. Had she been pretending when she required someone to move the piano for her on cleaning days? No, under the excitement and fear of the fire she was able to do something that she actually could not do under normal conditions. Activity of the adrenal glands was in part responsible for the change.

Under the excitement of anger or fear, one part of the adrenal gland becomes quite active. As it releases its hormone, adrenalin, into the bloodstream, a number of changes take place in the body: the heartbeat increases, the stomach temporarily ceases activity, the pupils of the eyes become dilated, the blood coagulates easily, the individual may perspire freely, feelings of fatigue vanish, breathing is speeded up. All these bodily changes help prepare an individual for short-time emergency activity.

The hormone cortisone, produced by the other part of the adrenal gland, helps the individual resist infection. Also, it seems to play an important part in preparing the individual for long-continued muscular activity. If the amount of the hormone produced is very small, blood circulation is impaired, sex activities decrease, the individual becomes weak. Death follows unless the hormone is administered artificially.

If an excess of this hormone is produced, the individual shows increased sexual development, regardless of how young he is. An excess may also produce masculine characteristics in a woman.

The gonads. Sometimes called the sex, or puberty, glands, the gonads supply the sperm and egg cells for reproduction. In addition, they produce hormones that have an important effect on the personality development of the individual. Although the sex hormones are present in childhood, production of the hormone is increased during adolescence, causing the development of the biologically mature man and woman. The behavior of a male horse that has had its gonads removed is quite different from that of a stallion. If the gonads are removed from female animals, male characteristics often develop. For example, if the ovaries are removed from ducks and pheasants, the birds soon develop the characteristic male plumage.

In this brief discussion of the ductless glands you have seen that particular glands produce particular effects on individuals. But remember that the glands interact on one another. Furthermore, the glands are only part of the total individual. In organisms as complex as human beings, social factors as well as physiological factors are important in development.

Has man's changing environment affected glandular activity? To study the effects of environment on glands, one psychologist compared domesticated Norway rats from his laboratory colony, which had been in existence for over thirty-six years, with wild Norway rats trapped in alleys and yards. After making a careful comparative study of his domesticated and wild rats he reached these tentative conclusions: (1) The adrenal glands in domesticated rats are smaller and less effective than in wild rats. (2) The thyroid glands are less active in domesticated than in wild rats. (3) The gonads develop earlier, function with greater regularity, and cause a much greater fertility in domesticated than in wild rats.

It might be added that he found the brains of domesticated rats smaller in weight than the brains of wild rats. He believed that the brains of domesticated rats function less effectively because these rats are more subject to convulsions than are wild rats.

The psychologist reporting the above comparison raises the question, "To what extent has civilization brought about changes in man parallel to those produced in the rat by domestication?" He points out that today great physical energy is not needed. In many ways man lives in a very "soft" environment. The psychologist concluded his report with the questions "Where are we going? What is our destiny?"

Emotional Behavior

Suppose one morning an impressive legal-size envelope arrives in the mail. You open it—and learn that an uncle you never knew has left you $10,000 in his will. Would you be happily excited? Would your heart beat faster? Would you rush about, telling your friends?

If you were driving a car and some careless driver almost hit you, would you gasp? do some rapid and forceful turning of the wheel and jamming down of the brake pedal? be angry? Unprepared-for experiences are likely to produce emotional disturbances.

Usually emotional disturbances have survival value. They enable the individual to run away from danger or to fight against that which threatens him. If the emotional disturbance is too intense, he may "freeze" in his tracks, he may be too frightened to run or fight. In some animals such paralysis may have survival value because by remaining motionless the animal may escape the notice of his enemies. Such paralysis in man might have value in certain war situations or in jungle travel, but ordinarily he is more likely to survive if he runs from or fights back against some physical danger.

Everyone experiences emotion. Some persons express their emotional states more noticeably than others.

How many ways of expressing emotion can you count in this picture? You can see the varied physical aspects of emotional behavior. You can also see how differently one group of people can react to the same situation.

An emotional state. Think about some emotional experience that you have had recently. Did your heart pound so loudly that you thought others could hear it? Did you gasp? Did you become nauseated? Did you break out in a cold sweat? No doubt you were aware of some of these symptoms.

Emotional states involve the entire body. We know that the autonomic nervous system, the glands, and the viscera (stomach, lungs, heart, and other internal organs) are involved in emotional behavior. A part of the brain called the hypothalamus is involved in emotional states. The cerebral cortex is also involved. We think about our emotional experiences and so prolong them. On the other hand, there is evidence that the cerebral cortex inhibits the intensity of emotional expressions, for in an animal whose cerebral cortex has been removed, emotional states are more intense than before such surgery. As you can see, an EMOTIONAL STATE involves widespread physiological changes that are either pleasant or unpleasant to the individual experiencing it.

How can emotional states be studied scientifically? It is difficult to produce genuine emotional states in the laboratory. An experimenter may say to his subject, "Be afraid now." In order to cooperate in the experiment, the subject may try to be afraid, but he is not actually afraid. On the other hand, the psychologist cannot be present with his measuring instruments when someone is having a narrow escape from an accident on the highway. A young man cannot be connected with scientific instruments while he sincerely proposes marriage to a girl. It is possible, however, to set up some laboratory situations in which an individual may actually experience an emotional state.

To obtain a genuine emotional response, it is essential that the subject being experimented on be unprepared for what happens to him. Sometimes a gun is fired behind his back, or he is given an unexpected electrical shock, or he is stuck with a pin, or he is told funny stories—while he incorrectly believes that the experiment has not actually begun.

One psychologist produced an emotional state in his subjects by requiring each subject to sit alone in a dark room for a considerable amount of time. Then suddenly and unexpectedly his chair fell backward through an arc of about 60 degrees. The complete falling of the chair was prevented by a powerful door check. The subject was not hurt, but he was frightened. He screamed, struggled to escape, and called for help. He had a genuine emotional experience.

Another psychologist used a rather unique method for measuring his subjects' fear of small animals, such as snakes, spiders, and rats. He seated his subjects at the end of a conveyor belt that brought the feared animals closer and closer to them. The subjects could control the approach of the animals by pressing buttons that started and stopped the conveyor. Physiological reactions were monitored in a separate room. The psychologist found that there was a distinct difference between the subjects' verbal reports about the feared animals and their actual laboratory behavior as shown by physiological responses.

Measuring emotional states. From experience you know that under emotional excitement of any kind your breathing rhythm is different from its usual rhythm. The next time you see an exciting motion picture, notice how those about you gasp and hold their breath at the critical moments. In the laboratory breathing is measured by means of specially designed instruments, which make a record of breathing rate and pattern on a revolving drum.

Using these recording instruments, one psychologist found that at the blast of an auto horn, sounded suddenly while his subjects were seated quietly before instruments, breathing was momentarily checked. Then breathing was resumed at a rate greater than normal, and was also deepened.

Have you ever had a narrow escape and, after the danger had passed, noticed how rapidly your heart was beating? In the laboratory the rate of the pulse is measured by sensitive electronic instruments and records of the rate of beat are made.

Under one emotion-producing situation or another, a person may have "goose-flesh," turn pale, experience a feeling of either warmth or coldness, have a tingling sensation in the skin. Psychologists measure skin changes under emotion-producing conditions by means of a technique known as the GALVANIC SKIN RESPONSE, or GSR. In this technique two electrodes are pressed against the skin. One electrode may be placed on the left hand and the other on the right. Then a very weak electric current (2 to 3½ volts) is passed through the body. Under some conditions more resistance is offered to the passage of this current than under other conditions. When a person is asleep, resistance is great, whereas just following vigorous exercise resistance is much reduced. Under emotional excitement the amount of resistance offered to the passage of an electric current is reduced, due partly to increased sweat secretion. The amount of electricity passing through a given circuit is measured with an instrument called a GALVANOMETER. Using this instrument, one psychologist secured the record shown on this page. In this case a decrease in resistance, indicated by a rise in the line, resulted from the emotion-producing stimulus of an unexpected scream. Following this decreased resistance, which began soon after the scream, there was a gradual return toward normal.

Another method for measuring emotional states requires that the subjects fantasize an emotion and express it by pressing a button with the fingertip. The pressing of the button yields a record of the vertical and horizontal pressures exerted on the button. These pressures are then analyzed by a computer. By having subjects imagine such emotions as love, hate, joy, and anger, one scientist was able to report that individuals from different cultural backgrounds showed similar shapes of emotions. For example, the shape of love was the same for individuals from the United States, Japan, and Bali.

The lie detector. The best-known application of measuring emotional states is the lie detector. As you have seen, emotions are to be explained largely in terms of physiological changes. Telling a lie is usually an emotional experience. The lie detector merely measures some of the physiological changes that take place in an individual under the emotional stress of lying.

Some lie detectors measure three physiological factors: blood pressure, pulse, and breathing. Blood pressure seems to be an especially sensitive indicator of the emotional

This is the record of a galvanic skin response following an emotion-producing scream.

state produced by lying. It has been found that blood pressure will usually rise 8 millimeters or more under the emotional stress of lying. Not only is the rate of breathing affected but also the pattern of breathing is often changed when a person tells a lie. Under normal conditions the ratio of inspiration to expiration is about one to two—inspiration takes about half as long as expiration. When a person tells a lie, the inspiration-expiration ratio tends to decrease—the person takes relatively less time for inspiration and more for expiration.

Some lie detectors measure changes in the skin resistance offered to the passage of a weak electric current—the galvanic skin response. Police may use a modern instrument combining the features of the two kinds of lie detectors just mentioned.

Can the lie detector be wrong? Can a person fool the lie detector? In the great majority of cases the answer is "No." Can a criminal practice so that his blood pressure, rate of heartbeat, and breathing will not change when he tells a lie? No, because such physiological changes take place regardless of any desire to prevent them. It is true that to some extent a person can learn to voluntarily control specific physiological reactions. For instance, an individual can control his breathing. But a person cannot control all the physiological reactions associated with lie detection so that these reactions remain normal. And the mere fact that a suspect held his breath or breathed abnormally would lead the police officer to suspect that he was trying to hide a lie.

The lie detector is a very valuable instrument in the hands of the police. Law-enforcement authorities cannot be 100 percent sure of results with it. When used by a qualified person, however, lie detectors are accurate about 75 percent of the time. That is, they will accurately detect lying in about three out of four individuals.

Pupillometrics. PUPILLOMETRICS (pyü-pəl-ō-'me-triks) is a new method used in measuring physiological changes during emotion, based on the principle that the pupil of the eye enlarges when a person receives a pleasant stimulus and contracts when he receives an unpleasant stimulus. An instrument has been developed that records the changes in the pupil of a subject as stimuli are presented. Eventually, pupillometrics may make it possible to present a potential patient for psychotherapy with a series of pictures showing unpleasant situations and, by observing his pupil, determine which picture evokes an unpleasant emotion in the subject. The method has a distinct advantage over galvanic skin response and most other physiological measures of emotion because the pupil contracts and dilates to more specific emotions, unpleasant and pleasant, respectively, whereas other physiological measures indicate only that an emotion has occurred.

How do emotions affect digestion? Perhaps after some intense emotional experience you have noticed that your stomach is upset. Psychologists have found that under emotion-producing situations, normal digestive processes are interrupted. For example, a cat may be placed under a fluoroscope so that its stomach movements can be seen and studied. Before being placed on the machine, the cat is given food containing a substance that shows up on the fluoroscope. Under normal conditions, churning movements of the stomach are seen. A dog is brought into the room and permitted to bark at the cat. Presumably, the cat is having an emotional experience. Its fur stands on end, it arches its back, it spits. The fluoroscope shows that the churning

A tense, emotion-filled situation can produce worry and fear, which can affect digestion, as in the case of this young boy. An argument between his parents is worrying him and causing him to lose his appetite.

movements of its stomach stop. Even though the dog is taken from the room, the churning movements are not likely to begin again for about fifteen minutes.

Uncertainty and fear may result in ulcers, not only for human beings but also for laboratory animals. For example, in one experiment two groups of rats were used. For one group, every time a light was turned on the rats were given an electric shock, but when a buzzer was sounded, they were never shocked. For the other group, half the number of times the light was turned on the animals were shocked, and half the time when the buzzer sounded they were shocked. Both groups received the same total amount of stimulation from light, buzzer, and shock. For rats of the first group, the shock was predictable. They learned when it was going to occur. For the rats in the second group, the shock was unpredictable—they could not learn when it was going to occur. This second group developed significantly more ulcers than the first group.

Instincts, or Species-Specific Behavior

In an earlier day, and even to many people today, much of both human and animal behavior is accounted for by something called "instinct." In fact, some people say that animals cannot really think at all, that they do everything by instinct. Other people attribute such human activities as mother love, competition, self-preservation, and war to instincts. They assume that these kinds of behavior are inborn in all human beings and do not have to be learned.

Some years ago psychologists believed that they had discerned a number of human instincts, among them the mating, maternal, acquisitive (acquiring possessions), gregarious (being with other people), manipulative (using the hands to make things), and play instincts. But modern psychologists believe that more accurate explanations can be found for behavior, especially human behavior. So much of what man does depends on learning that it seems best not to call any of his behavior instinctive.

What do psychologists now mean by instinct? If they use the term "instinct" at all, psychologists apply it to certain behavior of lower animals, not to human beings. Psychologists define INSTINCT as a complex, organized, unlearned behavior pattern that applies to all members of the species. To be an instinct the behavior of a given species must be found in all members of that species studied under experimental conditions. The nest-building of certain species of birds is an example. The behavior may not appear at birth, but as the organism matures, the pattern appears in practically complete form with no learning and little, if any, stimulation.

In our definition of instinct the term "complex" means that the behavior pattern has no simple explanation. As an example, one type of behavior that is often called instinctive is the reflex. A REFLEX is an automatic unlearned response, such as removing your finger from a hot stove. This type of behavior does not meet all our criteria for instinctive behavior. The reflexive type of behavior has a comparatively simple explanation. For example, when you put your finger on a hot stove, by the time you feel the pain and begin to think about removing your finger, your muscles have already started the process of removing your finger from the stove because the "message" from the burned finger is sent to the brain and appropriate muscles at the same time. "Organized" means that each part of the behavior of the organism is related to the other parts. That is, it is not haphazard, or random, behavior. "Unlearned" means that the behavioral response is innate or inborn. The words "behavior" and "pattern" mean that the response must be observable and measurable and that it recurs, always in much the same way.

As a modern substitute for the often misused word "instinct," many psychologists prefer to use the term SPECIES-SPECIFIC BEHAVIOR.

Examples of instinctive, or species-specific, behavior. Mud-dauber wasps construct curious little clay nests, or brooders, provisioned with live but paralyzed spiders for their young. The builders do not learn from older wasps how to fashion and stock their nests, for each generation dies before the succeeding generation comes out of the nest. By some means of heredity, this complex pattern of behavior is passed on from one generation to another.

Orioles build distinctive hanging nests, even though they have been raised in isolation from other orioles. It is true that the nests may vary slightly depending on what nest-building material is available, but the general pattern of the nest is very characteristic of the species. Also, many fish construct nests in which to lay their eggs, but no two species make exactly the same kind of nest.

Another example of species-specific behavior is shown in an experiment in which ducks were reared in isolation to prevent their learning any behavior from other ducks. When the ducks were still young, one was taken to a field and put into a small cage. A cardboard cutout of a chicken hawk and a duck in flight was arranged on a pole so that when it revolved, the shadow of the cardboard would pass over the duck's cage. Whenever the experimenter passed the shadow of the chicken hawk over the cage, the little duck became very frightened. When the shadow of a duck passed over, the duckling was calm. It instinctively knew the difference between the shadow of a chicken hawk, which represented a potential danger to the duck, and the shadow of another duck.

Can species-specific behavior be altered? An experiment with moths suggests that sometimes species-specific behavior can be altered. There is a moth that lays its eggs on hackberry leaves. Each generation of females selects hackberry leaves on which to deposit their eggs, even though leaves of other kinds are just as available. An experimenter found, however, that if he transferred the eggs from hackberry to apple leaves, the larvae still developed normally. Then when the adult females that spent their larval stage on apple leaves were given a choice of leaves on which to deposit their eggs, a high proportion of them selected apple leaves in preference to hackberry leaves. Thus, the experimenter was able to alter species-specific behavior in one generation.

Other explanations for some behavior popularly called instinctive. Experiments have shown that some behavior labeled instinctive can be explained in other terms. For example, many people would say that cats instinctively kill mice. If this were true, cats would kill mice, without training or experience in doing so, in 100 percent of their opportunities. A psychologist put this hypothesis to a test. Fifty-nine kittens were divided into three approximately equal groups. The kittens in one group lived alone and were kept from any possible contact with rats or mice. Later, when released in a cage with mice, 45 percent of the kittens killed mice. The kittens of the second group were raised in a cage with their mother and every fourth day saw their mother kill a rat or a mouse. When these kittens were released in a cage with mice, 85.7 percent of them killed the rodents. The kittens of the third group were raised in a cage with a rodent and never saw one killed by an adult cat. When the kittens of this third group were later placed in a cage with mice, only 16.7 percent of them killed mice.

It is clear that in no group did 100 percent of the kittens kill mice. In fact, in some cases the mice may have died because the kittens played too roughly with them rather than as a consequence of intentional killing. The evidence seems to indicate that kittens do not have an instinctive tendency to kill mice. But because of their speed, their claws, and their size, they may rather easily learn to do so. For instance, the kittens that saw their mother kill mice were efficient in their mouse killing.

Studies with other animals suggest that some behavior commonly said to be instinctive might be explained better in terms of the body structure of the animal and in terms of learning. For example, you may have noticed that when horses are caught out in a field during a storm, they "instinctively" turn tail to the storm. People familiar with the habits of buffaloes report that these animals "instinctively" face a storm when caught out in the open. Is there some better explanation of such behavior than to say that it is instinctive? Colts, because of their structure, probably learn very early in life that it is more comfortable to turn tail to a storm than to have the storm beating in their faces. On the other hand, baby buffaloes, with their heavy coats of matted hair on head and shoulders, probably learn very early in life that it is more

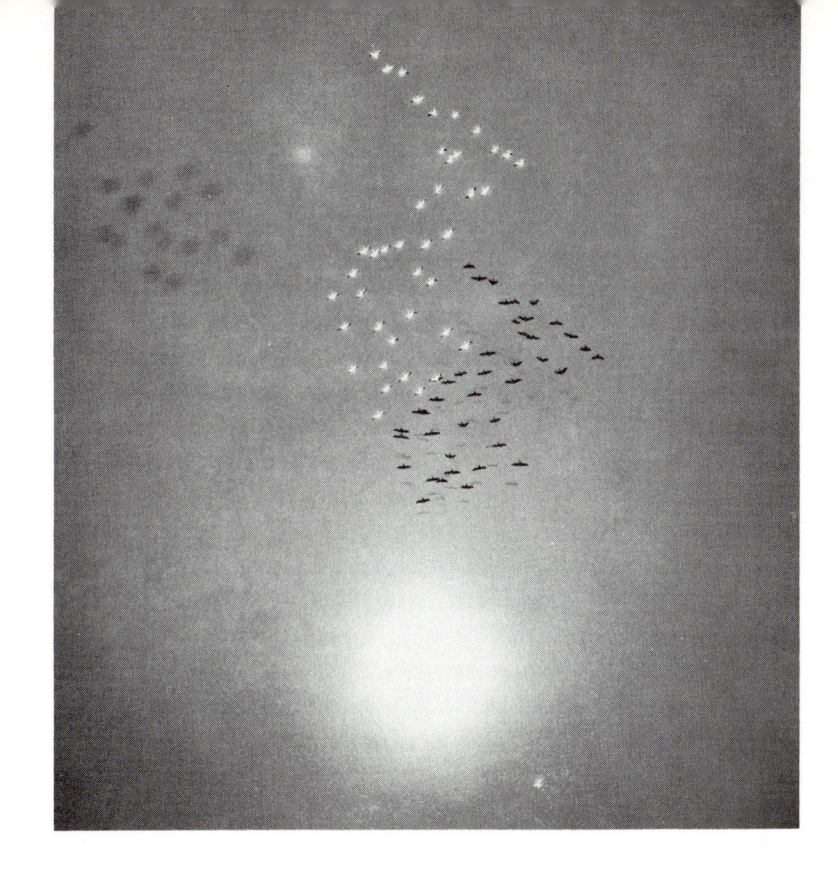

Is the migratory behavior of birds a species-specific behavior? Or is it partially learned? Psychologists are now studying how much birds use the sun and moon rather than their instincts for navigation in their migratory flights.

comfortable to face a storm than to turn tail to it. However, not all animal behavior has been explained in such simple terms of structure and learning.

For many years scientists have been fascinated by the navigating ability of migratory birds. At one time they were satisfied just to label this behavior instinctive. Today we have some evidence that birds use the sun in navigation, although we are still not sure exactly how they use it. It is known that birds flying over unfamiliar territory are less accurate in their flight on cloudy days than on sunny days. Other evidence indicates that birds use the stars in navigation. One scientist found that on clear nights caged migratory birds pointed themselves in the direction in which their species would normally migrate. On cloudy nights they did not point themselves so distinctly. In another phase of the experiment the scientist took birds to a planetarium in which images of stars could be projected on the inside of a large dome. After some short exploratory flights, the birds took off in the direction normally followed by their species, which was indicated by the artificial position of the stars in the planetarium.

To sum up, scientists have shown that much behavior once called instinctive can be explained in terms of learning. But many questions, such as how birds navigate, remain to be answered. In our present state of knowledge it is best to be cautious in using words like instinct. You might question the scientific background of anyone explaining human behavior in terms of "human instincts."

The Effect of Sleep on Behavior

The final biological influence on behavior that we will consider in this chapter is the ef-

BIOLOGICAL INFLUENCES ON BEHAVIOR 233

fect of sleep on human behavior. The amount of sleep we get often influences how we act.

How important is sleep? In many cases production in an industrial plant tends to be low on Monday. By Tuesday or Wednesday workers seem to be "warmed up," with production at a maximum for the week. Possibly the low production on Monday can be explained by the hypothesis that Saturday and Sunday nights may be spent in prolonged and tiring entertainment. The resulting loss of sleep shows up in inefficient production on Monday.

Various tests indicate that loss of sleep is followed by inefficient performance, although highly motivated individuals can do remarkably well following periods of continued wakefulness, even in work involving concentration. There is evidence, however, that efficiency of work is maintained only through the expenditure of a great amount of energy.

A person may lose sleep in two ways. He may go without any sleep for a long period, or he may sleep much less than usual for a period of several nights. In one experiment subjects were kept awake continuously for 72 hours. They were under constant medical supervision during this dangerous experiment, but even with this precaution some fainted at the conclusion of the experiment. Again, subjects reduced the amount of their sleep from about 8 hours to about 5 hours a night for a period of five nights. In both cases the subjects were given various tests before and after the periods of no sleep or reduced sleep.

Intelligence test scores dropped 24.5 percent following a period of 72 hours without sleep but dropped only 14.9 percent following five nights with only 5 hours' sleep each night. The corresponding percentages for decrease in ability to solve addition problems were 13.8 and 3.1 percent, respectively. How much the individual swayed forward and backward when trying to stand still was measured. After 72 hours without sleep, there was a 51.8 percent loss in control of bodily swaying. After five nights of 5 hours' sleep each, there was a loss of only 6.1 percent.

When it is absolutely impossible to get normal amounts of sleep, studies have indicated that it is better to take a number of short naps than to try to use all available sleeping time in one period.

The different stages of sleep. At one time EEG records alone were used to determine whether or not the subject was asleep and how deeply he was sleeping. Today psychologists use an electroencephalograph together with several different methods to determine the depth of sleep. One method employs noises of graded intensities, assuming that the louder the noise needed to awaken the subject, the deeper is his sleep. Other methods use different kinds of sensory stimulation, such as pressure or electrical shock. Sometimes, though, as a result of using different methods to determine the depth of sleep, different research studies may produce what appear to be contrasting results.

The EEG and new methods have enabled psychologists to learn more about sleep in the last twenty years than they had learned throughout history to that time. They now know that man does not sleep uninterruptedly throughout the night. Psychologists now speak of four stages of sleep. Stages 1 and 2 indicate a light sleep, and Stages 3 and 4 represent deeper sleep.

The general pattern of sleep, which varies not only for the same individual from one night to the next but also from one individual to another, is that sleep occurs in cycles. The individual goes from an awake state into Stage 1, then into Stages 2 and 3, and finally into Stage 4, the deepest stage of sleep. As individuals fall asleep, they progress rapidly through the different stages, reaching Stage 4 in about forty-five minutes. After spending about fifteen to twenty minutes in Stage 4, they go, either directly or indirectly, back to Stage 1 or 2, and begin the second cycle of sleep. Most individuals have at least four or five cycles each night. With each succeeding cycle, the individual spends less and less time in deep sleep and more and more time in lighter sleep.

One study has found that all stages of sleep are present in every subject to some degree. Also, each subject appears to have certain overall amounts of various stages of sleep, although the amounts differ from one subject to another. Stage 4 sleep occurs primarily in the first third of the night and dreaming becomes predominant in the last third of the night.

How do we know when a subject is dreaming? Stage 1 sleep, which is the lightest sleep according to EEG records, is most often associated with subjects having rapid eye movements (REMs). REMs seem to indicate that an individual is dreaming. Even those individuals who deny that they dream quite frequently report dreaming if they are awakened when they are having rapid eye movements. On the other hand, individuals who are awakened while not having rapid eye movements rarely report dreaming. This stage of sleep—Stage 1 with REMs—is called PARADOXICAL SLEEP because the person is supposed to be in the lightest sleep at Stage 1, and yet when he is having REMs he is harder to arouse, indicating deeper sleep.

Dreams may last from a few minutes to more than an hour, with the average dream period extending about twenty-five minutes. This finding is contrary to beliefs held by some psychologists only a few years ago, when dreams were thought to last only a few seconds. It is a good example of how new evidence changes ideas and concepts and therefore why scientists must be willing to remain flexible in their thinking.

Are dreams necessary? In one experiment subjects were deprived of their dreams by awakening them during REMs. It was found that when they were allowed to sleep later they dreamed longer—sometimes twice as long as their normal dreaming. It has also been found that those deprived of dreams have temporary changes in behavior during their waking hours, such as greater irritability, difficulty in concentrating, and some memory

Donald Duck looks as if he is sound asleep, but actually he is having rapid eye movements. He is in Stage 1 of sleep and is dreaming, according to his EEG record (shown below).

BIOLOGICAL INFLUENCES ON BEHAVIOR

lapses. These changes disappear, however, when the subjects are allowed to sleep undisturbed, during which time they dream more frequently. It is as if they were trying to catch up on their dreaming. Perhaps you are wondering whether the disturbance of sleep and not the disturbance of dreams might have produced these data. Experimenters eliminated this possibility by awakening subjects during periods of no REMs, which resulted in no increase in dreams or changes in behavior.

In one experiment subjects were deprived of Stage 4 and REM sleep by an electrical shock administered to their feet at the onset of each of these stages. It was found that a stronger stimulus was required to eliminate Stage 4 sleep than was needed for REM sleep. However, Stage 4 showed a much more rapid recovery rate than REM sleep. Finally, differences were noted in the behavioral after-effects of subjects deprived of Stage 4 and REM sleep. Individuals deprived of Stage 4 developed behavior similar to that found at the onset of depression, whereas those deprived of REM sleep had psychological profiles indicating considerable anxiety.

The evidence available today indicates that dreams seem necessary for sleep, and that probably everyone does dream, although not everybody remembers his dreams. It is interesting to note that cats have REMs when they are asleep, during which time movements of their whiskers and tails occur. Also, monkeys have REMs when they are asleep. What do you suppose cats and monkeys dream about?

Terms to Know

alpha wave
aura
autonomic nervous system
brain lesion
central nervous system
convulsive disorders
cortex
duct (exocrine) glands
ductless (endocrine) glands
electroencephalogram
electroencephalograph (EEG)
emotional state
galvanic skin response (GSR)
galvanometer
grand mal
instinct
Jacksonian convulsive disorder
paradoxical sleep
peripheral nervous system
petit mal
psychomotor convulsive disorder
pupillometrics
rapid eye movements (REMs)
reaction time
reflex
species-specific behavior

Topics to Think About

1. Would you be willing to ride in a car if you knew that the driver was subject to convulsive attacks? If so, under what circumstances?

2. What would be the advantages and disadvantages if a person never had to sleep?

3. Has a dream ever influenced your life? In what way?

4. If there were no advertising of any kind for cigarettes, cigars, or chewing tobacco, to what extent do you think people would continue to use these products?

5. Do you experience any degree of fear when driving in fast and heavy traffic? If so, what indications are there that you are experiencing fear?

6. We have not discussed the effect of caffeine on the body, but do you think that children should drink coffee? What about high school students? individuals of college age? middle-aged adults? old people?

7. The Food and Drug Administration removes harmful drugs from the market. Yet it permits the sale of alcoholic beverages, and every year tens of thousands of people are killed by intoxicated drivers. Why do we permit the legal sale of alcohol? How would you define a "harmful" drug?

Suggestions for Activities

1. Secure data from your local police officials on reaction time for drivers and stopping distances for motor vehicles. A motor club may be able to furnish this material, too. Make graphs showing these data.

2. Take the pulse of a friend under normal conditions. When he is very excited, take it again and note the difference. You may find it necessary to produce the excitement—for example, by making a sudden loud noise.

3. Ask a few of the oldest persons you know to tell you about the days when alcoholic beverages were sold in saloons. Also, ask them to tell you about the days when there was national prohibition of the selling of alcoholic beverages.

4. If you are a candid-camera fan, take some unposed pictures of persons in various emotional states. For example, at athletic contests when the home team is winning and when it is losing. Cover all such pictures except for the face. Or, if you have facilities for enlarging pictures, include just the faces of some individuals. Then show the photographs to friends and have them say what emotion they think was being expressed. It is easy to make errors in judging emotional states from facial expressions when the environmental situation is not known.

5. Select some pictures that are likely to arouse pleasant emotions, and others that are likely to arouse unpleasant emotions. A photograph of an automobile accident from a newspaper might represent the unpleasant picture. A pleasant picture might be of a person whom your potential subject likes. Shuffle the pictures without letting anyone see them and then ask your subject to look at them one at a time—for about fifteen seconds each. Without seeing which picture the subject is looking at, watch the pupil of one eye. Do you notice any difference in pupil size when the subject looks at the automobile accident? at the picture of the person whom the subject likes? Remember that this may

not work, as the difference in pupil size may be very small. Looking at the pupil through a magnifying glass might help. Also, be sure that you do nothing that would embarrass anyone, especially your subject.

6. Ask your parents or friends who have not studied psychology to name both "human instincts" and instincts that only animals have. Make lists of these "instincts" and, in class, compare them with the lists obtained by others and with the textbook material on species-specific behavior.

7. Observe and report on what seems to be instinctive behavior in your pet dog or cat or in wild creatures. If possible, include very young animals in your observations. Can much of this behavior be explained in terms of learning?

Suggestions for Further Reading

Hilgard, E. R., R. C. Atkinson, and Rita Atkinson, *Introduction to Psychology,* 5th ed., Harcourt Brace Jovanovich. See Chapter 2, "The Behaving Organism"; pages 82–87, on bodily changes during adolescence; pages 162–72, on varieties of waking states, and sleeping and dreaming; pages 178–80, meditation and self-induced alterations of consciousness; and pages 334–42, on the physiology of emotion.

Kagan, J., M. M. Haith, and Catherine Caldwell (eds.), *Psychology: Adapted Readings,* Harcourt Brace Jovanovich. See Selection 6, "The Interpretive Cortex"; Selection 16, "The Effects of Hemisphere Deconnection on Conscious Awareness"; and Selection 26, "Treatment of Insomnia by Relaxation Training."

Kagan, J., and E. Havemann, *Psychology: An Introduction,* 2nd ed., Harcourt Brace Jovanovich. Chapters 8, 9, and 10 give a broader coverage than your textbook of such topics as genes, the effects of glands and the nervous systems on behavior, bodily changes during emotional states, and biological drives.

Psychology Today: An Introduction, CRM Books. See Chapter 9, "Behavior Genetics," pages 163–73, a full description of heredity and genetic action.

Ruch, Floyd L., and Philip G. Zimbardo, *Psychology and Life,* 8th ed., Scott, Foresman. See Chapter 3, "The Physiological Bases of Behavior."

Wertheimer, M., et al., *Psychology: A Brief Introduction,* Scott, Foresman. See pages 50–61, 191–94 on hunger, sex, activity, EEG, sleeping and dreaming, and sensory deprivation.

chapter 10

Getting to Know Your Environment

MAN COMES to know the environment through his sense organs. Although modern civilized man has the same sense organs that his distant ancestors had, today he must learn to live in an environment where there are many sights, sounds, odors, tastes, and other sensory stimulations that were unknown to early man. As he explores space, modern man must learn through his senses to live in an environment quite different from that on earth.

Perhaps you have been told that man has five senses: those of seeing, hearing, touch, smell, and taste. But we probably have at least eleven senses, and maybe more.

A person's senses are capable of responding to very weak stimulation. For example, the average person is so sensitive to light that he can see the glare of a match at a distance of about thirty miles on a clear dark night. In a quiet room he can hear the ticking of a tiny clock at a distance of twenty feet. The sense of touch is such that a person can detect the wing of a fly falling on his cheek. He can smell a single drop of perfume when it is diffused into a six-room apartment. Taste is so well defined that a person can detect a teaspoon of sugar stirred into two gallons of water. Before examing these senses, though, we will consider the topic of attention and the sorts of things that attract our senses.

Attention

We are constantly bombarded by stimuli, from birth until death, even when we are asleep. A STIMULUS is an energy or energy change acting on a sense organ and exciting it. Since it is impossible to react to all stimuli in our environment at any given moment, we must become selective as to which stimuli gain our attention. For example, as you read this page

Manufacturers of mouthwashes attempt to gain the attention of customers by the size, shape, and color of their bottles and packaging. They may also offer as an added stimulus the bonus of a free gift with the purchase of their product.

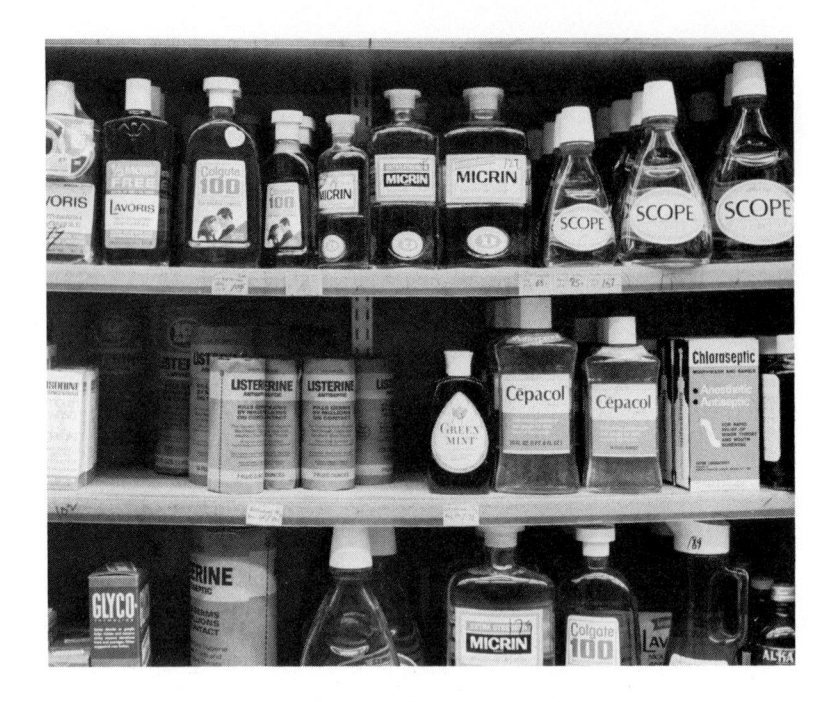

stop for a moment, close your eyes, and concentrate on the different ways that you are being stimulated, such as by sounds and by the feel of your clothes. Were you aware of all these stimuli before you stopped to focus on them?

In this case, you deliberately decided to pay attention to stimuli. But sometimes stimuli intrude on you. If someone nearby mentions your name while you are talking to another person, you will probably become aware that your name has been spoken and will pay attention to what that speaker is saying. The various factors that make us pay attention to stimuli can be divided into two classes: characteristics of the stimulus, and characteristics of the individual.

Characteristics of stimuli that gain our attention. There are several major characteristics of stimuli that make us pay attention to them: intensity, size, contrast, movement, changes, novelty, and repetition. Any of these characteristics, or a combination of them, will result in our paying more attention to one specific stimulus than to others.

Manufacturers of such goods as soap, pens, and processed food are very concerned with making us aware of their particular product. They try to make use of these characteristics—by, for instance, using intense and novel colors for their product or packaging—to get us to pay attention to their product rather than to competing products.

On board submarines it is often necessary to gain everyone's attention immediately. One method of gaining such attention is to do the unexpected—to precede an important announcement with a recorded female voice saying, "Now hear this" several times.

Characteristics of the individual that influence what gains his attention. Another factor associated with reacting to a stimulus is the condition of the individual at that time. For example, if you are hungry and looking for a place to eat, a lighted sign of a restaurant on a dark road is much more likely to draw your attention than if you are not hungry.

The needs, attitudes, expectancies, motives, and past experiences of an individual play a large role in determining which stimuli that person will pay attention to. A person interested in birds will attend more to sounds of birds on a camping trip than the person who is indifferent to birds. If you look through a book trying to locate a specific picture or diagram, you will pass over many other illustrations but will give immediate attention to the correct one.

The following study demonstrates how the condition of the individual influences his perception. The subjects were deprived of food and water for differing lengths of time. They were shown pictures of foods and liquids for fifteen seconds under a standard illumination. The light was then turned off for ten seconds. Next, the subjects were asked to turn the light on the picture and adjust a brightness control so that the lighting of the picture looked the same as at the original showing. It was found that as deprivation time increased, the subjects used less light to make the picture look like the original brightness.

Maintaining attention. Not only is gaining our attention important, but maintaining that attention is also important. Once our attention is focused on a particular stimulus, the manipulation of the stimulus characteristics that originally made us pay attention to it can also be used to hold our attention. We hear a siren and pay attention to it for a moment. Our attention is maintained if the sound of the siren continues with changes in pitch, loudness, and duration.

Can we pay attention to two stimuli presented at the same time? This question has been studied by presenting two different messages to a subject through earphones placed over his head. One message is fed into the left ear and another message is fed into the right ear. The experimenter asks the subject to pay attention to the message being received by, say, the left ear. At the conclusion, the experimenter can check on his subject's attention by asking him to repeat the message to which he was told to attend, as well as the message that was fed into his other ear. How much the subject remembers has a lot to do with how difficult and how familiar each message is. In general, however, while there is some recall of the unattended message, it is far less than the recall of the attended one.

If a student is attending to an attractive girl or handsome boy while the teacher is explaining something important to the class, how much do you think will be remembered of what the teacher said?

Sensation and Perception

Look at the figure below. What does this simple drawing represent? Decide for yourself. Now check with others in the class and see whether you all agree. Unless some have seen

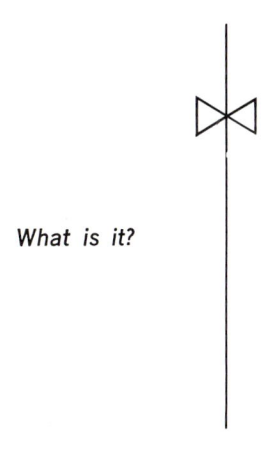

What is it?

GETTING TO KNOW YOUR ENVIRONMENT **241**

the figure before, each student will probably explain the drawing in a different way. One may say that it represents a pinwheel, another may think that it represents a butterfly on a stalk, another may guess that it is an axe, and still another may see it as a pyramid looking at itself in a mirror.

Why does one student interpret the drawing as a pinwheel and another see it as a butterfly? The only explanation can be in terms of the previous experiences of the individuals. Perhaps the first person had a pinwheel as a child, while the second recently walked through a field in which there were butterflies. The third person may have chopped wood recently. Actually the drawing is intended to suggest a man with a bow tie stuck in elevator doors. You may want to think up pictures of your own and try them out on your friends.

When you looked at the drawing on page 241, your eyes were stimulated by light. Thus, you had a visual sensation. The word SENSATION is used by psychologists to refer to the physiological arousal of a sense organ by a stimulus. Psychologists use the word PERCEPTION to refer to sensation plus meaning. When you looked at the figure on page 241, you interpreted it—you put meaning into it—according to your previous experiences. Sensation and perception are both factors in the process of getting to know your environment.

Thresholds. An additional concept that psychologists use in studying the senses is ABSOLUTE THRESHOLD, which is the minimum amount of stimulus that a subject can detect, such as the lowest sounds that a person can hear.

In some studies it is important to know how much a stimulus must be changed before the subject is aware that the stimulus has been changed. The amount of change necessary for a subject to notice the change in stimulation, such as the change of a sound, is known as a DIFFERENCE THRESHOLD. The difference threshold is the amount of change necessary to detect a JUST-NOTICEABLE-DIFFERENCE 50 percent of the time.

Psychologists use the concept of just-noticeable-difference (j.n.d.) to determine the ability of an individual to distinguish between two stimuli. A single stimulus, such as a violin note, is presented to a subject and then is changed by a very small amount. The minimum amount of change in the stimulus necessary for the subject to be able to detect it is called the just-noticeable-difference.

Subliminal perception. We have said that perception refers to sensation plus the way in which we interpret the sensation. Stimuli may be so weak that we are not aware of the sensations that they are arousing. Yet our perception of them may influence our thought or overt behavior. This perception of sensation aroused by stimuli that are too weak to be specifically reported by an individual is called SUBLIMINAL PERCEPTION.

Although psychologists have studied subliminal perception for many years, the public became keenly interested in it a few years ago when a report claimed that such phrases as "Eat Popcorn" and "Drink Brand X" (a soft drink) had been flashed on the screen during a film showing in a theater. As a result, the report said, popcorn sales increased 50 percent and sales of the soft drink increased 18 percent. It was said, on the basis of some very questionable and incomplete data, that the phrases were flashed on the screen for only 1/3000 second so that the audience was not aware of seeing them. Nevertheless, because of the rise in sales, the members of the audience were thought to have perceived them.

Some advertising men anticipated that

this report might be the basis of a whole new field for their efforts. Other individuals were quite alarmed by the report. They saw in it possibilities for dangerous social controls. They feared, for instance, that elections might be controlled by one political party flashing "Vote Republican" or "Vote Democratic" on the television screen during campaign years for subliminal lengths of time.

There are many variables that must be taken into account for successful subliminal stimulation, such as the strength of the stimulus itself, the speed at which the stimulus is given, the nature of the stimulation immediately following the subliminal stimulation, and the general train of thought in which the viewer has been engaged. Also, the number of times that an individual is exposed to the stimulus makes a difference. In one experiment subjects were exposed to a picture of a pen pointing to a knee for 1/1000 second. An exposure of this length is so brief that most subjects say they do not see anything. Yet when required to report whatever word they thought of after the exposure, the subjects tended to give words that were associated with the picture in some way. However, subjects who were exposed to the same picture for a considerably longer (1/30 second) period of time responded with fewer related words than did subjects exposed to the picture for only 1/1000 second. Possibly they were nearer to actual perception and so realized their uncertainties. Further presentations at 1/1000 second produced even fewer responses, suggesting that if subliminal effects occur at all, they are more likely to occur in a first exposure than in a later exposure.

In general, psychologists seriously question the effectiveness of subliminal stimulation to influence behavior under most conditions. Certainly, it seems that stimulation of which we are aware is more effective in influencing behavior than is subliminal stimulation. At any rate, much more research is needed before we can speak authoritatively on possibilities of and conditions for subliminal stimulation.

Vision

Although psychologists have studied many aspects of vision, we will discuss only what color is, how we perceive depth, and how optical illusions occur.

The physical nature of color. Three basic terms are used in describing colors: hue, brightness, and saturation.

HUE refers to the quality of redness, blueness, yellowness, or greenness that differentiates one color from another. It is what most people commonly call color. Sunlight can be broken up into different hues, as, for example, in a rainbow. The complete arrangement of hues visible to the human eye is called the VISIBLE SPECTRUM. Arranged according to wavelengths, the spectrum has red on one end and violet on the other, as shown on page 248. In the spectrum red shades off into orange, which shades into yellow, and then green, blue, and violet. There are no sharp dividing lines between the colors in the visible spectrum. As many as 150 distinct hues can be observed. These hues can also be thought of as arranged around a circle, as illustrated on page 248. Purple is indicated on the circle, although purple is not a color of the spectrum. However, because it can be formed by mixing red and blue lights, which are on the spectrum, it is included in the color circle.

BRIGHTNESS refers to the sensation of lightness or darkness of any color or gray. Note in the picture of the color solid on page 250 that the vertical axis runs from white at the top to black at the bottom. Between

An artist's palette often contains a wide range of hues. The artist can increase or decrease the brightness of his colors by adding white or black. He can also change saturation.

the black and white poles of a color solid are shades of gray. As hues approach white at the top of the color solid, they become progressively lighter. The lighter the color, the brighter it is. You can see how red (on the left) increases in brightness—becomes lighter—as it moves up toward white at the top of the axis and decreases in brightness—becomes darker—as it moves down toward black at the bottom of the axis.

SATURATION refers to the purity of a hue. Look again at the picture of the color solid and note how saturation is represented on it. As a hue runs from the outermost point on the color solid toward the center, it progressively loses its purity and becomes grayer. We say that it has become less saturated.

Notice how red diminishes in its amount of redness, or saturation, as it approaches the vertical axis.

An example will help explain saturation still further. A seamstress makes a dress and puts away scraps of the material for use as patches. The dress is damaged in wear, and the scraps of cloth are brought out to patch with. But the scraps no longer match the dress. The dress has been exposed to sunlight and washing. It has faded, while the scrap that was packed away in the dark is as fresh as when new. In technical terms, the faded dress is less saturated than the scrap.

Color combinations. Colors that are opposite each other on the color circle are said to be COMPLEMENTARY. When mixed together, they give gray. Does this seem strange? Would you mix blue and yellow paint to form gray? Of course, that would give green paint, but mixing paint is somewhat different from mixing light. In this discussion of color we are mixing lights, not pigments. To mix light, disks of colored paper are placed on a wheel and the wheel is rotated rapidly, or else different colored lights are projected on the same area on a screen.

When two colors on the color circle are mixed together but are not opposite each other, the resulting hue will be between the two hues. The hue will be closest to that color which has the greater proportion in the mixture. As an example, if you were to mix yellow and red, the result would be orange. If yellow made up 60 percent of the mixture and red 40 percent, the saturation would be more yellow than red.

In many cases it is necessary to use two colors together, as in advertisements, in school colors, and in clothes. As a rule, a combination of two colors is pleasing if the colors are complementary. Blue and an orange-yellow

244 PATTERNS OF BEHAVIOR

would make pleasing school colors; so would red and blue-green, or blue-purple and yellow-green (see p. 248). If three colors are to be together, a simple rule can be followed. Select colors that are equidistant on the color wheel. A triangle of equal sides inscribed in the circle will give you a pleasing combination of three colors.

Saturation must be considered when choosing pleasing color combinations. As a rule, red and yellow are said to be too close together on the color wheel to give a pleasing combination. If, however, both the red and the yellow are of very weak saturation (pastel tints), they may give a pleasing effect when used together. Such rules are only true in general, though, and colors that please one person will not necessarily be liked by someone else.

Some practical applications of color. A number of years ago a large mail-order house included in its catalogue two different pages on which skirts were advertised. The skirts on the two pages were identical in style and were practically the same in price and quality. One page presented the skirts in black, white, and intermediate grays; the other page showed the skirts in colors. It costs far more to print a page in color than to print it in black, gray, and white. Do sales justify the additional expense? The orders from the page in color were ten times as great as the orders from the page in black, white, and gray. There is a record of one company that increased its sales of a given product 1000 percent merely by changing the color of the wrapper.

There are many other practical applications of color. For instance, color may determine how often a room is used. One manufacturer decorated the cafeteria in his plant in light blue, a favorite color of Americans. Nevertheless, the employees complained that the room was cold. Many insisted that they needed to wear their coats while eating. The thermometer showed that the room was at a comfortable temperature. Then the manufacturer had the room trimmed in orange and had orange slipcovers placed on the chairs. The employees no longer complained of the cold and no longer wore coats while eating. The thermometer indicated that the temperature was the same as before. In another industry, the walls of the recreation room were painted oyster white. The room was seldom used by the employees until it was repainted in a soft rose.

Color blindness, or color weakness. We have been assuming that any person who is not completely blind can see colors as well as any other person. Unfortunately, this is not true. There are some persons who cannot distinguish all the colors that most of us can distinguish. Popularly, such persons are said to be colorblind, although more strictly they should be said to be color weak, or color deficient.

Two common kinds of color blindness are total color blindness and red-green color blindness. Those persons who are only red-green colorblind can still distinguish blue and yellow. To the totally colorblind person the world appears like a black-and-white snapshot or an uncolored film. To the red-green colorblind person, a scene wholly in blue and yellow would appear just the same as to a person who is not colorblind. Red and green, however, would appear to him as a dull yellow-gray. Very few persons are totally colorblind. Interestingly enough, there are a few individuals who are colorblind in one eye but have normal color vision in the other eye.

Color blindness is inherited and is related to sex. It is generally estimated that from 6 to

8 percent of men are colorblind to some extent. Practically no women are colorblind, yet colorblindness is inherited through the female side of the family. Thus, a colorblind man will have a daughter who has normal vision, but his grandson (not granddaughter) may be colorblind.

One of the tests usually given to applicants for driving licenses, as well as to railroad employees and airplane pilots, is a test for color blindness. Such tests often consist of numbers, letters, or curved pathways differing in color or shade from the background on which they are printed. For example, there may be a number made up of faint gray dots on a background of red and purple dots (see p. 247). The person with normal vision can observe the numeral without difficulty, but the colorblind individual is unable to distinguish the gray numeral from the red background.

How do we perceive distance and depth? Although we are able to perceive depth as well as length and width when we use only one eye (monocular vision), our perception of depth is improved by looking at any object with both eyes (binocular vision). Using both eyes when looking at an object gives you a cue to the distance of the object, because you have two retinal images. Each eye has a slightly different view of the scene, which is called RETINAL DISPARITY.

We perceive space by using cues in our environment to achieve an awareness of distance and depth. One of the ways in which we perceive distance and depth is the movements of our eye muscles. When our eyes follow a moving object, certain muscles cause the lens of the eyes to become flatter as the object moves into the distance or to bulge outward when the object comes close. One movement of eye muscles can be easily demonstrated by holding a finger at arm's length and moving it slowly toward your nose. Your pupils will converge, or come closer together. This cue to distance is called CONVERGENCE.

If one object blocks the view of another it is assumed that the object blocking the view is closer than the one behind it. This cue is known as INTERPOSITION.

Another cue is that of movement. If we move, those objects near us seem to move past us, while those at a distance seem to remain still or to move by us much more slowly. For example, when you are riding in a car, the edge of the road seems to go by very fast, whereas objects in the distance seem to stand still or to move very slowly.

Other cues are linear and atmospheric perspective. In LINEAR PERSPECTIVE objects appear to be closer together the farther away they are. For example, railroad tracks seem to meet in the distance, and telephone poles seem to get closer together the more distant they are. In ATMOSPHERIC PERSPECTIVE objects that are blurred or hazy from smoke or dust in the air appear to be farther away than objects that can be seen clearly.

The perception of light or texture also helps us determine distance and depth. For instance, the effect of light, including the casting of shadows, is a cue for judging depth. If the texture of an object can be seen clearly, the object appears to be closer than when its texture cannot be as distinctly defined.

Another cue involves using standards or familiar objects to judge distance. If a close friend of yours were standing beside a stranger, and you knew the height of your friend, your guess of the stranger's height would probably be much closer to his actual height than if he were standing alone, since you have a standard by which to compare heights. If you are unfamiliar with an object and have no standard of comparison close to it, it is very difficult to judge its size or dis-

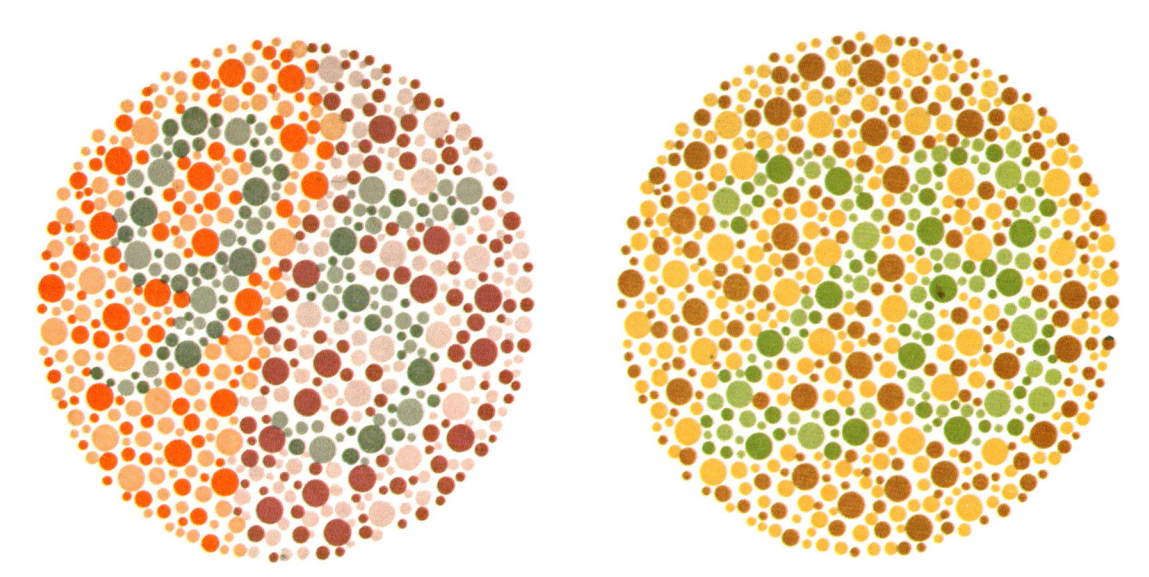

What numbers do you see inside the two circles above? These two plates are part of the Dvorine Pseudo-Isochromatic series of color blindness tests. The circle on the left is a test for red-green blindness. Some people can see no numbers, some can see only the number five, others see only the number nine. If you have normal vision, you can see the number ninety-five. The plate on the right also tests whether a person is red-green blind. A colorblind person cannot see the green numbers in the circle. A person with normal vision can read the number twenty-eight.

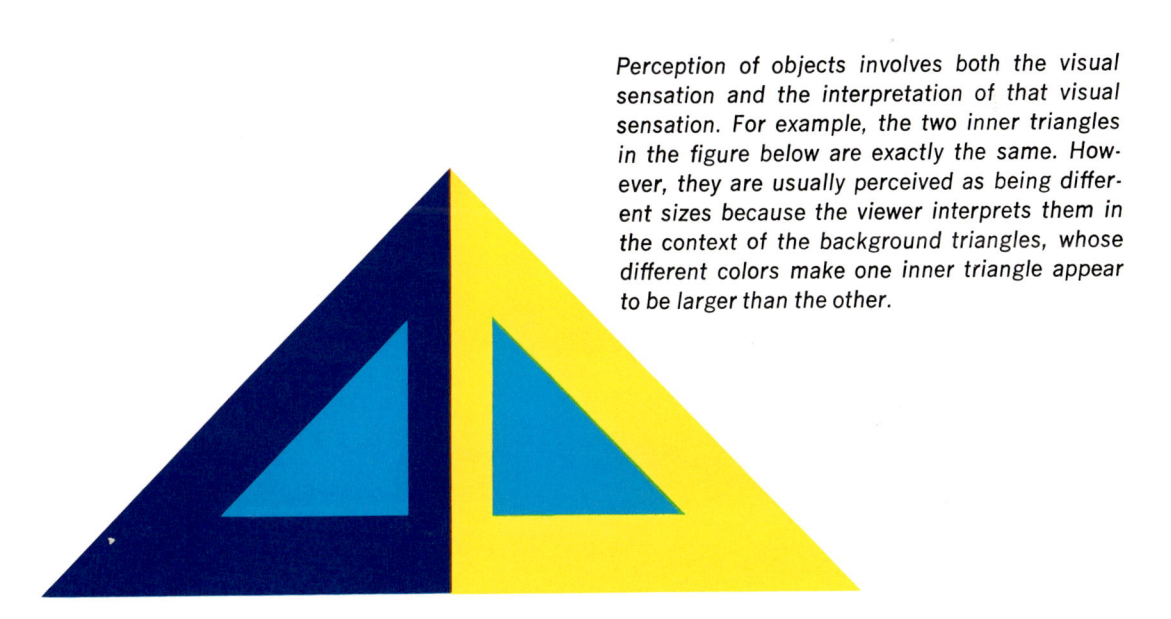

Perception of objects involves both the visual sensation and the interpretation of that visual sensation. For example, the two inner triangles in the figure below are exactly the same. However, they are usually perceived as being different sizes because the viewer interprets them in the context of the background triangles, whose different colors make one inner triangle appear to be larger than the other.

247

Colors produced by light waves may be arranged according to the length of the light waves, as in the solar spectrum above, or may be arranged around the circumference of a circle to form a color wheel, as shown below. The solar spectrum results when sunlight is sent through a prism. The colors of the spectrum are in the same order as can be seen in a rainbow. When color light waves are arranged in a circle, those colors opposite each other, known as complementary colors, will mix into a neutral gray. Some colors—certain purples and reds—do not exist on the spectrum, but are included in the color circle because they can be produced by mixing spectral lights.

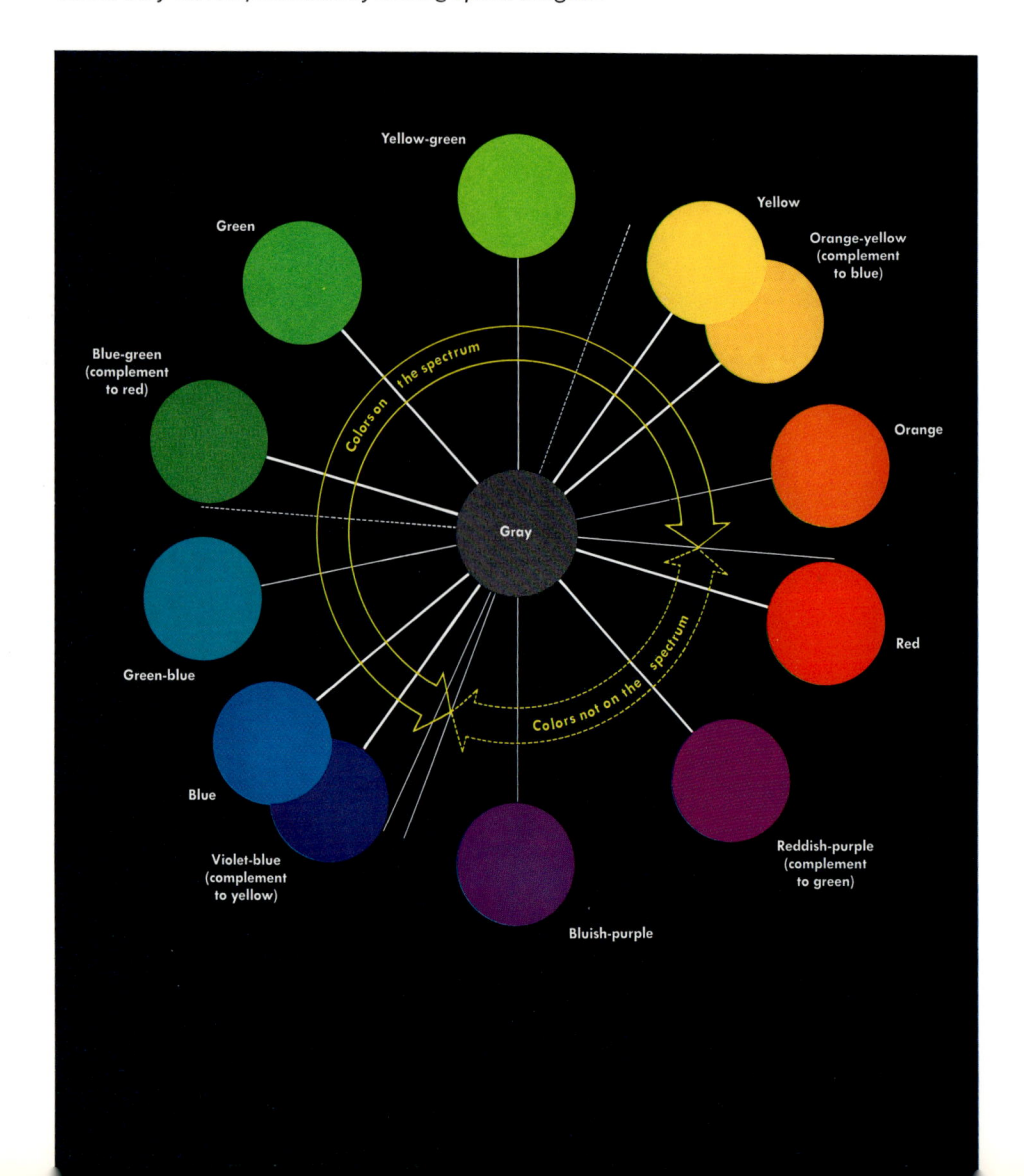

248

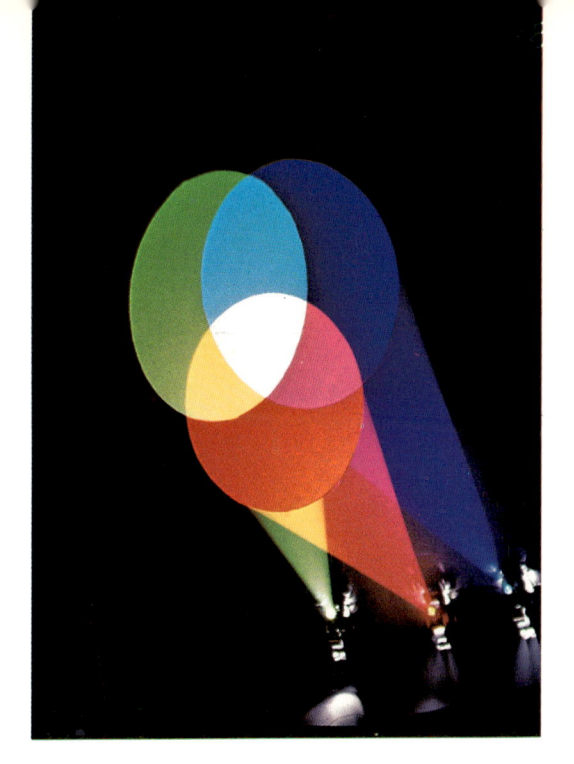

In a mixture of color wave lengths (above), the lights of two noncomplementary colors can be combined to produce a third color. For instance, red and green fuse into yellow. The three colors overlap in the middle to make white.

In a mixture of color pigments (above), pigments or color filters are used. Here yellow and blue produce green (such a mixture of color wave lengths would produce gray). The three primary colors overlap in the center to make black.

The mixing of color light waves can be studied by putting discs of several different colors on the shaft of a small electric motor (right), and rotating them. As the speed of the rotation is increased, the colors seem to blend into one—sometimes gray and sometimes a hue, depending on what colors the discs are. These yellow and blue discs would merge into gray.

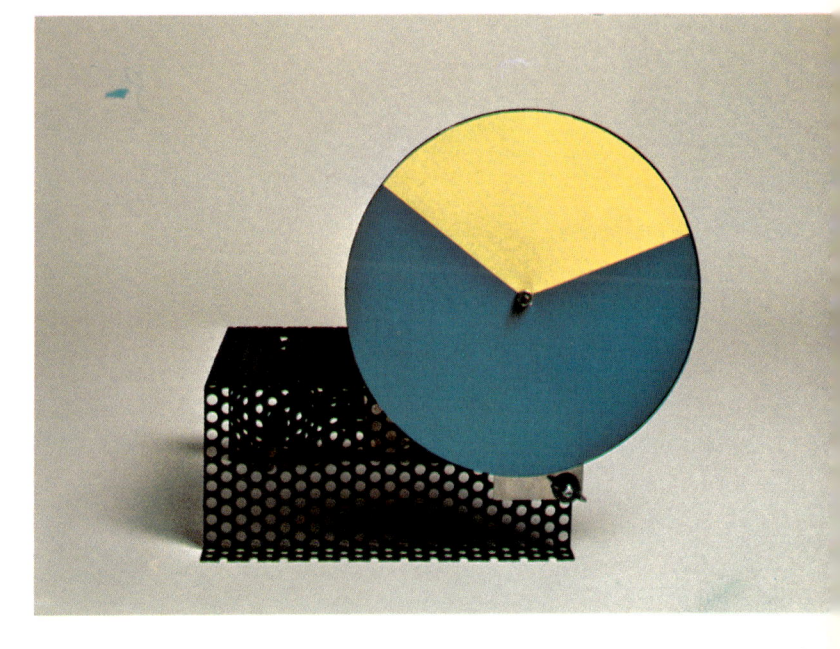

249

The color solid—or color cone—above illustrates the three dimensions of color: hue, brightness (along the vertical axis), and saturation (along the radius). A vertical slice from the color solid for the hue red shows the brightness range vertically, from light at the top to dark at the bottom, and gives the saturation range horizontally, running from "pure" red on the outside to gray at the center.

Stare fixedly at the dot inside the blue circle (below, left) for about 20 seconds. Then shift your gaze to the dot in the middle of the gray square. What do you see? Repeat the same procedure with the dot inside the yellow circle. What color is the afterimage in the gray square? Repeat both procedures. Is the afterimage clearer?

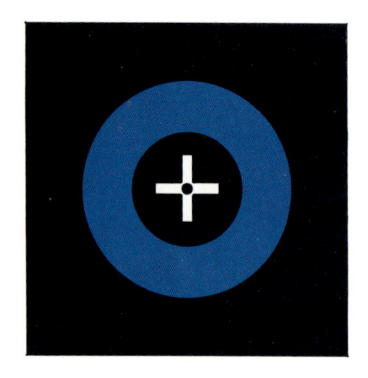

How many different cues to distance and depth can you detect in this picture? What about linear perspective? What about interposition? Do you notice any others?

tance accurately. For example, you would find it very difficult to guess the distance or size of a wire with the sky as a background unless you could determine its texture or use other cues.

Artists quite often use most of these cues to give depth to their paintings. The next time you look at a painting, try to determine the cues used by the artist to give you the perception of depth and distance.

Are these spatial cues learned or innate? At the present time we cannot adequately answer this question. However, interesting experiments have been performed in recent years which suggest that there may be some innate patterning of the brain for depth perception.

Several studies have been performed with varying species of young organisms, using a "visual cliff." This apparatus consists of a large piece of heavy glass several feet off the floor. A textured piece of linoleum is glued directly underneath one end of the glass. Beneath the other end of the glass the linoleum drops away abruptly and levels off several feet below, to give the appearance of a cliff. Viewed from above, one area is seen as a shallow area, while another appears to be a deep valley.

When infants of six to fourteen months of age were placed on the glass, almost all of them refused to cross the deep end, even when called by their mothers on the other side. The infants would cross the shallow end very readily. Some infants would pat the sheet of glass over the deep end but still would not cross, refusing to believe their sense of touch. They preferred to rely more on their sense of vision than on touch. Studies such as this

This infant perceives that one end of the "visual cliff" drops off several feet and he refuses to move onto that end, although he can feel that it is covered by a glass surface.

have been performed with chickens, goats, lambs, and kittens, with approximately the same results. Rats, which depend a good deal on touch with their whiskers, will cross the cliff side if they can first feel the glass with their whiskers. If, however, the glass over the deep end is dropped several inches so that the rat, who stays on a platform or shelf above, cannot touch the glass with his whiskers, he will cross only the shallow side. The studies seem to indicate that the perception of certain depth scenes, such as a "visual cliff," is present early in life. But at this time we do not know which cues the subjects under study used to perceive depth.

Optical illusions. Sometimes we make mistakes in our perceptions. False perceptions of stimuli of any kind are referred to as ILLUSIONS. If the false perception is in the field of vision, it is called an OPTICAL ILLUSION.

On the top of page 253 are two horizontal lines, exactly equal in length. The images of these two horizontal lines are equal, but we perceive one as longer than the other. Why? One explanation is that we do not restrict our attention to the horizontal lines themselves. Instead, we look at the entire figures. One entire figure is longer than the other, and we interpret this to mean that one horizontal line is longer than the other.

What is the difference between an illusion and a hallucination? As we have just seen, an illusion is a false perception of an external stimulus. On the other hand, a faulty senselike perception for which there is no external stimulus is called a HALLUCINATION.

Suppose a person is walking along the street and "sees" a snake on the sidewalk. Such an experience may be either an illusion or a hallucination. If a branch has fallen off a tree and the person mistakes it for a snake, he is having an illusion. If there is no branch, or no other object that might be mistaken for a snake, the person is having a hallucination.

Some practical uses of illusions. Every day we see examples of practical applications of illusions. Much of our clothing is selected with the intention of giving impressions that are not exactly in harmony with actuality. A person who wishes that he or she were not quite so tall can wear clothing in which lines run horizontally, whereas a person who wishes he or she were taller can wear clothing in which the lines run vertically. Light-colored clothing tends to produce the illusion that a person is sturdier and larger than is actually the

252 PATTERNS OF BEHAVIOR

case, whereas dark clothing tends to give the impression that a person is smaller.

Military camouflage is simply a matter of illusion. A tank or a soldier's uniform is covered with spotches of color so that the enemy perceives the tank or soldier as part of the landscape.

The illusion of stroboscopic motion. The ordinary movie and television pictures are optical illusions. They are a series of still pictures thrown on the screen with a very brief interval of time between them. The rate at which each picture is flicked on and off the screen is so rapid that you do not perceive the separate pictures but experience the illusion of motion.

Advertisers often use the illusion of motion to attract our attention. For example, you may have seen a neon sign of a dog running. First the dog is shown with his legs in one position. Then the light in these legs is turned off and the light in another set of legs is turned on. The dog appears to be running, although of course it is an optical illusion. Other electrically operated signs give the illusions of wheels turning, arrows flying, and liquids pouring. Such illusions as those just mentioned are spoken of as STROBOSCOPIC MOTION—apparent motion due to successive presentation of stimuli.

A very simple form of stroboscopic motion is sometimes referred to as the *phi phenomenon,* or perceived movement between successive presentations of separate points of light. You can demonstrate this phenomenon by arranging two stationary lights side by side. Turn off one and then immediately turn on the other. Do you perceive the spot of light moving from the first position to the second position?

Hearing

There is a great deal of interesting and technical material on the subject of hearing, but here we will limit ourselves to a brief discussion of what we hear, known as sound, and to three interesting aspects of hearing: perception of space, the problem of noise, and deafness.

Which of these figures is tallest? Which is shortest? How is this illusion created?

What are pitch, loudness, and timbre? Sound may be discussed in terms of pitch, loudness, and timbre. Some sounds are of high pitch, others of low pitch. We can distinguish between the pitch of a cornet and the pitch of a bass horn. A sound with a clearly marked pitch is called a TONE.

The PITCH of a tone is determined by the rate or frequency of vibration of the sound wave. The greater the frequency of vibration, the higher the pitch of the tone. And conversely, the lesser the frequency of vibration, the lower the tone.

Although sound can carry through such substances as water and metal, most sound waves that we hear travel through the air. Man cannot hear all the vibrations that reach his ear but is limited to those from about 20 to about 20,000 hertz (vibrations per second). Some individuals cannot hear sounds above 15,000 to 16,000 hertz. As a person grows older, the pitch of the tones he hears is not so high as the pitch he could hear in his youth. On the other hand, there is some evidence that older people lose their hearing partially because of the culture in which Americans and Europeans live. Tests for the hearing of individuals in a primitive culture have shown that these individuals tend not to lose their hearing for higher frequencies as much as Americans and Europeans do. Our loss of hearing such frequencies in later years may be due in part to the rather noisy environment in which we live.

In the case of animals, dogs can hear sounds above 25,000 hertz. Bats are able to hear sounds of 40,000 to 50,000 hertz. Yet turtles' ears are highly sensitive only to waves ranging from about 100 to 700 hertz. They cannot normally hear above 3000 hertz.

Perhaps you are wondering how we know what sounds animals can hear. The range of hearing (for frequency) is determined by presenting a tone of a specified frequency to an animal, rewarding him for responding to the sound, then presenting a tone of a slightly higher frequency and rewarding him for his response to that. This procedure is continued until the animal no longer responds to the frequency. The same steps are used to determine the lowest level of hearing except that the tone is presented in decreasing stages until the animal no longer responds.

The LOUDNESS of a tone is determined primarily by the height, or amplitude, of the vibrations of the sound wave. The greater the amplitude of the waves, the louder is the sound.

Suppose you are blindfolded. You hear middle C produced by a violin, a cornet, and a human voice. Suppose further that this is a carefully controlled experiment. The three sounds are of exactly the same pitch. Could you distinguish the sources of the three sounds?

The distinctive quality of tones is known as TIMBRE and depends primarily on the overtone pattern of the sound waves. The human voice, most musical instruments, and other sources of sound give off overtones as well as their fundamental tone. For example, when a tone is played on a violin, you hear not only the fundamental tone but also a number of overtones. The human voice is very rich in overtones. Were it not for the differing overtones in the voices of our friends, we could not tell one voice from another. In fact, each individual has a characteristic voice sound pattern that usually identifies him even if he attempts to conceal or change his voice sound.

Can we perceive space through hearing? Just as having two eyes gives us some cues for space perception, so also having two ears separated by the width of the head gives us additional cues for space perception. Sounds

PITCH
determined by the frequency of vibration

LOUDNESS
determined by the amplitude of the vibrations

TIMBRE
determined by the overtone pattern of the vibrations

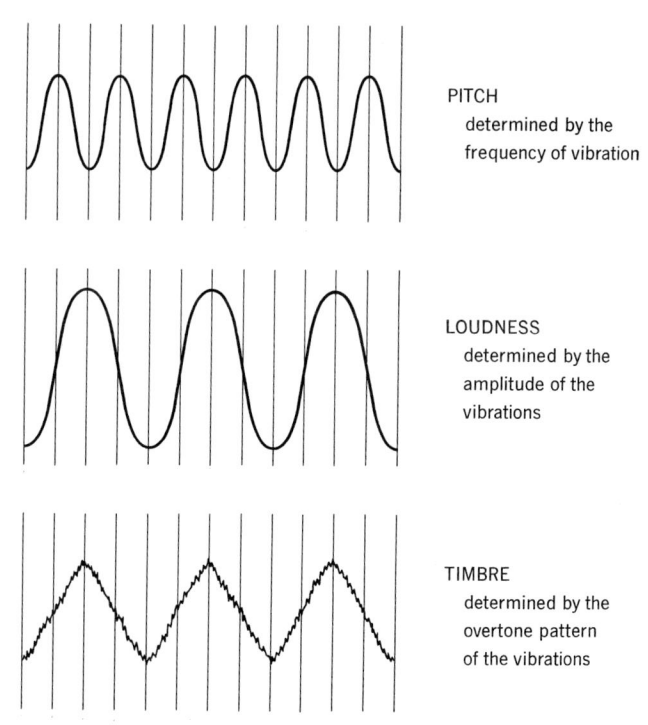

In this graphic comparison of the properties of sound waves, pitch is represented by the frequency of the waves, loudness by the height of the waves, and timbre by the complexity of the wave pattern.

from one side or the other reach our two ears at different times. Although the difference is less than .001 second, it enables us to perceive the direction of sounds in space. Sounds coming from one side or the other are louder in the ear closer to the source of sound. Another factor in auditory space perception is that the timbre of tones in the two ears is different. In going around the head from one ear to the other, tones lose some of their overtones and this provides a cue to direction in space.

What is the difference between music and noise? Both music and noise are produced by vibrations in the air. In many cases it is difficult to distinguish between the two. The sounds made by a modern dance orchestra may be music to the dancers and a horrible noise to the musician trained in classical music. The sounds from a typical apartment house full of radios, televisions, stereo sets, and tape decks all playing at top volume would be classed as noise, although each of the sets in itself might be playing music. In general, noises produce unpleasant experiences, whereas music produces pleasant experiences. The sensation of noise is stimulated by sound waves of irregular and unrelated frequencies. In other words, noise differs from tone in that noise has no clearly defined pitch.

Noise is a serious social problem, especially in thickly settled communities. In pro-

GETTING TO KNOW YOUR ENVIRONMENT 255

gressive cities definite campaigns to reduce noise are under way. In some cities it is against the law to sound an automobile horn except in an emergency. In most cities it is against the law to drive a car without a muffler on it. Police action may be brought against persons who insist on playing their radios, televisions, records, or tapes at full blast during all hours of the day and night. There is even some evidence that damage to hearing may result from repeated attendance at places where extremely loud music is played.

It has been found that noise is especially annoying when it is unexpected, when it spreads and reverberates, when it is judged to be unnecessary, and when it indicates malfunctioning of mechanical equipment. Irregular, variable sounds are more annoying than steady ones. High-pitched sounds tend to be more annoying than low-pitched sounds.

Intensive noise, even when it has no apparent effect on efficiency of performance, tends to produce discomfort, irritability, and distraction. Loud or intermittent sounds tend to produce changes in blood pressure, gastric secretion, pulse rate, perspiration of the palms, respiration, muscle tension, and EEG recordings. Reduction of noise is not only a matter of personal comfort and health, it is also a matter of dollars-and-cents efficiency.

Deafness. There are varying degrees and kinds of deafness. Some persons are tone deaf. They can hear sounds but they have very poor pitch discrimination. If you play two notes on the piano they will be unable to tell which note is the higher one. They can appreciate the rhythm in music even though they cannot appreciate the melody. Obviously, such persons could not become great musicians. Also, they would find it practically impossible to acquire correct intonation in a foreign language.

The word "deafness" is used most commonly to refer to the condition of persons who are "hard of hearing"—that is, those who cannot detect faint sounds that can be heard easily by persons of normal hearing ability. This deafness may be for the whole range of pitch, or it may be limited to particular parts of the total range of sounds. Old persons are often unable to hear either high-pitched or low-pitched sounds. At one time the hearing of over a million persons was tested. It was

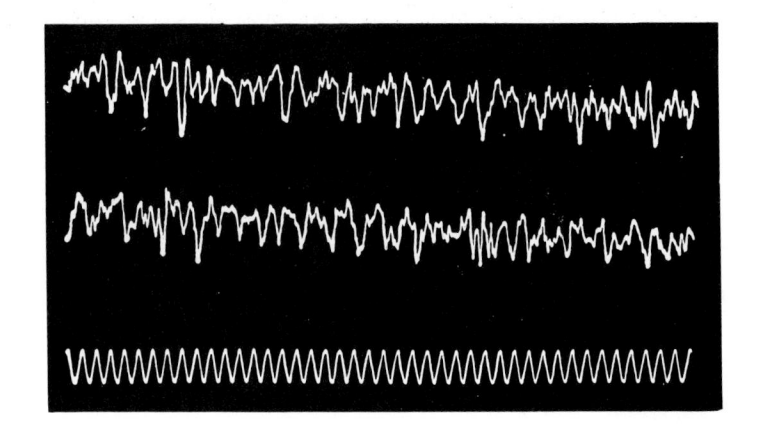

The sound waves of street noises (top and middle) and of a pure tone (bottom)

found that 1 out of 25 persons had difficulty in hearing in auditoriums; 1 in 125 had trouble in hearing face-to-face conversation; 1 in 400 had difficulty in hearing over the telephone.

We all sympathize with the person who is blind, but we are not always so considerate of the person who is deaf. Blindness can be recognized quite easily. Yet the fact of another's deafness may not impress itself on a person who has normal hearing ability. The associates of a deaf person may think that he is ignoring them when he does not enter into their conversation. Or they may think that he is not very intelligent, because he does not respond to their questions. If he does respond, his answer may be confused because he did not hear all of the question clearly.

It is necessary to raise your voice in talking to individuals who are hard of hearing. This attracts the attention of everyone in the room, both to the speaker and to the deaf person. They both feel conspicuous.

Fortunately, there are ways in which a deaf person can overcome his handicap to a great extent. Persons who are hard of hearing often make excellent typists, printers, and machinists. They can concentrate on their work in a quiet world of their own. For social contacts they can use modern hearing aids which, with the new microelectronic circuits available today, can be worn almost without detection. The person who is completely deaf can broaden his social field by learning lip reading. He can understand what is being said from the lip movements of the speaker.

Other Sense Fields

We will not go into detail concerning other sense fields. Nevertheless, a few comments about these other fields may stimulate you to read more about them.

Smell. Of course, man has a sense of smell, although it is not as keen as in some animals. A good bloodhound, for example, can trace a person for miles by the faint odor remaining on the trail.

Our sense of smell comes from receptors in the upper part of the nose, which are easily stimulated by gases. There have been various attempts to classify the odors that we sense. One classification suggests that there are six fundamental odors: spicy, burnt, resinous, flowery, fruity, and putrid. Most persons consider some of these odors to be pleasing and others displeasing. Another classification system suggests only four primary odors: acid (vinegar), burnt (roast coffee), fragrant (musk), caprylic (goaty).

Taste. For most people taste is primarily a means of getting enjoyment from the environment. Taste is related to the sense of smell, and much of the taste of food is really the smell of that food. You have probably noticed that when you have a cold, your appreciation of taste is greatly diminished.

A substance must be in liquid form to be tasted. The liquid is supplied either by the substance itself or by the saliva. Wipe the surface of your tongue dry with a clean cloth, and then place a lump of sugar or salt on the tip of the tongue. You will not be able to taste it until enough saliva forms to produce a solution of sugar or salt, which seeps down to the taste buds below the surface of the tongue. Insoluble substances cannot be tasted.

There are about 245 taste buds located mainly on the top and sides of the tongue. These taste buds can be divided into four specific classes: sweet, sour, bitter, and salty. That is, there are four primary taste sensations. Taste buds at the tip of the tongue are especially sensitive to sweet solutions, those along the sides are especially sensitive to sour solu-

A potter uses the skin senses, particularly the skin receptors for pressure. The potter molds the shape of an object by the amount of pressure he or she applies to the clay.

tions, and those at the back of the tongue are especially sensitive to bitter solutions. Taste buds especially sensitive to salt solutions are located on the tip and sides of the tongue.

Taste buds are made up of taste cells, which vary in their responsiveness to the four basic taste qualities. For example, some taste cells respond to sugar and salt, while other cells may respond only to salt. Since the cells of a taste bud vary in sensitivity, some doubt exists over whether there are specific taste buds for any particular taste quality. There is no simple explanation of taste.

In one experiment a group of subjects ate what normally would have been a delicious meal. However, tinted lights were used so that the meat looked green, the milk appeared to be blue, and the potatoes were red. Many of the subjects felt ill while eating the meal and some stated that the food "just didn't taste right."

The skin senses. There are four kinds of skin receptors—those sensitive to cold, warmth, pain, and pressure. The various types of skin receptors can be demonstrated by touching the skin with such instruments as cooled or warmed nails, needles, and bristles. You can easily demonstrate these skin senses for yourself. For example, a number of points on the skin can be touched with a nail (not very sharp), which has been placed in cold water for a while. As some spots are touched a sensation of cold will be produced, while other spots will merely yield a pressure sensation. Certain spots respond to low and high temperatures but not to intermediate temperatures (an intermediate temperature is the approximate temperature of the skin under normal conditions). Although there are only four primary skin sensations, our daily experiences of touch are always complex. Experiences such as tickle, smoothness, roughness, and wetness involve combinations of the primary skin sensations.

The sense of pressure is especially valuable to a blind person who seeks to overcome his visual handicap. The blind person is able to read by his sense of pressure as he moves his fingers across a page of Braille, a system of raised dots. There is a record of a blind and deaf woman who had so learned to use her sense of pressure that she could recognize, a year later, the hand of a person with whom she had shaken hands once.

Kinesthetic sense. The kinesthetic sense, or the muscle, tendon, and joint sense, is important in determining body movement and position. A person can determine the position of parts of his body without the use of his eyes. This can easily be demonstrated by having someone place your arm in a specific position while you are blindfolded or have your eyes closed. You will find that you will have no trouble in recognizing the position in which your arm has been placed.

Equilibrium. The sense of equilibrium tells an individual where his body is in space. It is governed by the inner ear (part of the auditory system), and is used to aid the person in maintaining body position. It is this sense that, when disturbed, produces "motion sickness."

Sensory Deprivation

Now that you have learned something of the senses and their importance, what is the result of depriving an organism of its senses? This may become a very practical problem in the years ahead as man travels further and further into space. His trip is going to take a long time, and on the way his sensory experiences are going to be very limited. At first thought it might seem that the trip would be a very restful and pleasant experience with no annoying sights, noises, or odors. However, we do have experimental evidence suggesting that the experience may be far from pleasant unless research can alter these conditions.

Students were hired to take part in an experiment in which each one was confined for several days and nights in a small soundproof room. Each one wore frosted glass goggles so that he could not distinguish patterns, even though there was some light in the room. His hands and arms were covered so that he had very little perception through touch. He lay on his bed and did as little as possible. Such sensory deprivation proved to be very disturbing to the students. They complained of being unable to concentrate, their ability to solve simple problems declined, they became bored, and they imagined that they saw and heard things. Some became so confused that they had difficulty in finding their way home after they left the laboratory.

In another experiment sixteen subjects were placed on air mattresses in a dark soundproof chamber. They even wore earmuffs to deaden whatever sounds any of them might make in the chamber. All remained in the room for one week. The only intrusions were for tests made within the chamber, which lasted about forty-five minutes each. What was the effect of such prolonged sensory deprivation? Most subjects had visual hallucinations, such as flashes of light, dim glowing lights, and flickering lights. These hallucinations ranged in length from a few seconds to as long as fifteen minutes. Several subjects had auditory hallucinations, such as howling dogs, a ringing alarm clock, and the sound of a typewriter. Two tactual-kinesthetic hallucinations were reported—one of cold steel pressing on the body and the other of someone trying to pull the mattress out from under the subject. On being released from the chamber, the subjects found that their visual sensory images were more vivid than before their period of sensory deprivation. Some reported that they had become especially sensitive to sounds, and that previously unpleasant sounds now seemed pleasant. After the first day out of the isolation chamber, however, most of these perceptual changes disappeared.

In still another experiment subjects were placed in a limited isolation room with low-level and diffused light stimulation. They, too, had visual hallucinations. Some thought that pictures were being projected on the goggles they wore. Some had difficulty in distinguishing between whether they were asleep or

A prisoner who is kept in an isolation cell has very little sensory stimulation. If he remains isolated for a long period of time, he may become disoriented and begin to have hallucinations.

awake. After removal of the goggles and moving to a normal-environment room, nearly all the subjects reported perceptual distortions. For some, still objects seemed to move or change size and shape. For others, flat surfaces appeared curved.

Sensory deprivation is one technique of brainwashing. Prisoners are isolated in dark rooms with a minimum of stimulation. In time, many of them will agree to almost any suggestion and will even confess to crimes they did not commit in order to be relieved from the horror of sensory and social deprivation.

There is experimental evidence that sensory deprivation results in retardation of learning. We know that persons deprived of vision or hearing are handicapped in their learning. If a person is deprived of both these senses, learning becomes a difficult process because most of it must come through the sense of touch.

Several studies of sensory deprivation have been made with animals as subjects. The results of such studies with dogs indicate that when they are deprived of normal stimulation early in life, the dogs later have great difficulty in learning to avoid painful stimuli or objects that are associated with painful stimuli.

The evidence presently available seems to indicate that early, and especially prolonged, sensory deprivation does influence the normal development of the individual. Also, there is evidence that early and a wide variety of sensory stimulation experiences contribute to a higher level of coordination and development in an individual. After four days, infants in an experimental group who were subjected to an enriched environment of sensory stimulations responded longer and more often to stimulating objects than did infants in a control group who received no special stimulation. Yet sensory stimulation should not be forced on an individual. Much additional data need to be gathered before we can adequately begin to understand the full effects and meaning of sensory deprivation.

Terms to Know

absolute threshold	illusion	retinal disparity
atmospheric perspective	interposition	saturation
binocular vision	just-noticeable-difference	sensation
brightness	kinesthetic sense	skin senses
color blindness (weakness)	linear perspective	stimulus
complementary colors	loudness	stroboscopic motion
convergence	monocular vision	subliminal perception
difference threshold	optical illusion	taste buds
equilibrium sense	perception	timbre
hallucination	phi phenomenon	tone
hue	pitch	visible spectrum

Topics to Think About

1. Which of your senses do you consider to be the most important to you, the one you would like to lose least? Why that one?

2. In your own experience, under what conditions does time "fly" and when does time "drag"? What senses are involved in your perception of time when it seems to pass quickly or very slowly?

3. If you ever go to the moon or some planet, how will your sensory experiences there probably differ from those you have had on earth? Can you imagine any sensory experiences that you have not had but would like to have?

4. Have you ever slept on a waterbed? If so, how were the sensory experiences different from those you have when you sleep on a traditional kind of mattress?

5. If air and water pollution keep on increasing, how do you think our sensory processes may be affected in the future?

6. Imagine yourself alone in an isolation room in a situation of as complete sensory deprivation as possible. How long do you think you could stand it? What measures would you take—for instance, what would you think about—to help retain good mental health? What sense would you miss the most?

Suggestions for Activities

1. Try spending one hour with a blindfold over your eyes. What sensory experiences do you notice that you are usually unaware of?

2. Secure two focusing floodlights or slide projectors. Over the lens of one place a yellow filter (yellow cellophane will do) so that you can project a yellow circle of light on a white screen, such as a movie screen. Over the other floodlight place a blue filter so that you can project a blue circle of light on the same screen. Now move the projectors so that the two circles of light overlap. You have added light waves. What is the result? Next, use only one floodlight or projector. Place both the yellow and blue filters over the lens and project on the screen. You have subtracted light waves. What is the result? Is there any relation to the mixing of paints?

3. Using sheets of colored paper, cut out one 6-inch square each of red, yellow, blue, and green. Mount these on a piece of white paper so that they are about 2 inches apart. Late some afternoon, place the large sheet of paper containing the colored squares in the sunlight. At about ten-minute intervals while the sun is going down, look at the squares one at a time. Do you notice any change in the saturation of the colors? Does one color seem to remain clearer than the others as the sun goes down? As illumination decreases, the cones (the parts of the retina of the eye responsible for our seeing colors) do not receive enough light to be stimulated. Sensitivity to red is lost first, then yellow, blue, and finally green.

4. Cut a hole about an inch in diameter in the center of a piece of white cardboard. Under this hole you can place pieces of paper of various colors, especially red, green, blue, and yellow. Gaze at one such color fixedly for about forty seconds, trying not to blink or change your focus. Have someone tell you when the time is up and then shift your gaze to any place on the white cardboard. Is the color of the afterimage the same as the one at which you had been gazing? If not, can you find it on the color circle on page 248? What term is used to apply to such colors? Rest your eyes for several minutes and then try gazing at another color.

5. Probably you have heard of absolute pitch, which is the ability to name correctly a particular tone that is sung or played, without directly comparing it with any heard tone, or the ability to sing a required tone without a reference tone being given. If you know someone, possibly a musician, who seems to have absolute pitch, have him or her give a demonstration in class. Can the individual offer any explanation of this rather unusual ability? At what age in life did the person first realize that he or she possessed this ability? Has the ability changed in any way over the years?

6. To demonstrate perception with both eyes as opposed to perception with only one eye, try the following. Select a room that has a number of obstacles in it, close one eye, and walk around the room between the obstacles. Most people find it more difficult to thread their way through the room with one eye than when they use both eyes. Your two eyes give you stereoscopic vision, or a three-dimensional perception of space. (Of course, in using both eyes, you also have a wider field of vision.)

7. Secure two or three paintings, including one landscape, from the art department, or bring some prints or paintings from home. What cues have the artists used to create the perception of depth?

8. Have you ever had difficulty in seeing objects when you first enter a darkened movie theater but found that later you could see them without difficulty? Your eyes had become adapted to the dim illumination. You can easily demonstrate visual adaption to different amounts of light by closing one eye for about ten or fifteen minutes before entering a dimly lit room. When you enter the room, keep your eye closed for a minute longer. The room will appear dark when you use the eye that you kept open. Then open your closed eye, and close the one that you kept open. Can you see more clearly?

9. Try this simple demonstration of stroboscopic motion. Hold your forefinger at arm's length and focus on it. Alternately close your right and left eyes without moving your finger. Do you have a perception of motion, although there is no actual movement of the stimulus object?

10. To demonstrate body adaptation to temperature, place three bowls in a row. Pour very warm but not scalding water in one bowl, pour very cold water in another bowl, and water at about body temperature in the third bowl. Place and keep one hand in the bowl of very warm water and the other in the bowl of cold water for several minutes. Then put both hands in the water that is at body temperature. Does this water feel warm to one hand and cold to the other? For several minutes keep both hands in this body temperature water. What happens?

Suggestions for Further Reading

Buddenbrock, Wolfgang von, *The Senses,* University of Michigan Press. This book deals with the functioning of eight senses in man and other organisms.

Gregg, J. R., *The Sportsman's Eye: How to Make Better Use of Your Eyes in the Outdoors,* N.Y.: Winchester. An illustrated 210-page book written by a professionally trained optometrist who is also an enthusiastic sportsman. Discusses such topics as visual capacities of game animals, contact lenses, gunsights, binoculars, golfing, fishing, skin diving, and skiing.

Hilgard, E. R., R. C. Atkinson, and Rita Atkinson, *Introduction to Psychology,* 5th ed., Harcourt Brace Jovanovich. See Chapter 5, "Sensory Processes," and pages 135–56, on perception.

Kagan, J., M. M. Haith, and Catherine Caldwell (eds.), *Psychology: Adapted Readings,* Harcourt Brace Jovanovich. See Selection 9, "Sensory Deprivation: A Case Analysis"; Selection 10, "The Role of Movement in the Development of Visually Guided Behavior"; and Selection 11, "Cultural Differences in the Perception of Geometric Illusions."

Kagan, J., and E. Havemann, *Psychology: An Introduction,* 2nd ed., Harcourt Brace Jovanovich. The authors of this textbook devote Chapters 6 and 7 to the psychology of getting in touch with the environment. If you find the topics of sensation and perception especially interesting, you will enjoy the greater details given in this book.

Ruch, Floyd, L., and Philip G. Zimbardo, *Psychology and Life,* 8th ed., Scott, Foresman. See Chapter 7, "Awareness of the World We Live In."

Wertheimer, M., et al., *Psychology: A Brief Introduction,* Scott, Foresman. See Chapter 2, "How We Get Information About Our Environment." This chapter contains some duplication of your textbook, but also has some new material on sensation and perception.

THE WORK OF DR. ANASTASI

Which is more important in an individual's life, heredity or environment—nature or nurture? And how do you find out? What tests do you construct to measure the relative importance of heredity and environment?

Dr. Anne Anastasi, head of the psychology department at Fordham University, is one of America's leading authorities on constructing and interpreting psychological tests to determine the influence of heredity and environment on individuals. When Dr. Anastasi was of high school age, she had no intention of becoming a psychologist. In elementary school her main interest was mathematics. Even during vacations she entertained herself by making up numerical games. She planned to major in mathematics at college. Then, during her sophomore year at college, she took a course in developmental psychology. An article on using mathematical procedures to determine the factors in intellectual ability made her realize that she could combine her love of mathematics with her new interest in psychology. She decided to major in psychology.

Since then, Dr. Anastasi has conducted many studies on the psychology of individual differences, both on her own and together with her psychologist husband. She has applied statistical techniques and scientific methodology to the construction of various psychological tests, and has come out with some unexpected results.

In one study Dr. Anastasi measured the language abilities of Puerto Rican children living in New York who heard one language spoken in their homes and another language spoken at school. She found that the children learned neither language fully—they were handicapped in both languages. Did this mean that Puerto Rican children were intellectually duller than children coming from homes in which the same language is spoken in the home and at school? Not at all. Dr. Anastasi also studied the spontaneous speech of Puerto Rican preschool children under circumstances in which they were free to use a combination of English and Spanish. She found that these children showed superior linguistic ability as measured, for example, by sentence length and sentence structure.

In another long-term research project Dr. Anastasi investigated the effect of environmental experiences on the development of creative thinking in children and adolescents. First, she measured the personal characteristics and background experiences of high school students with above-average ability in creative thinking. Next, she studied the home environment and child-rearing practices of elementary school children, since these environmental factors are related to creative ability. Then she developed a program for training elementary school children in creative thinking. Dr. Anastasi's research has indicated that creative attitudes and creative achievement can be improved significantly by providing a school program that gives children appropriate experiences. In other words, the environment can substantially increase an individual's ability to think creatively.

In her research Dr. Anastasi has focused on the recognition of individual differences and the encouragement of whatever maximum use an individual can make of his particular abilities. She believes that an individual's environmental differences influence not only his general intellectual development but also specific areas of his abilities.

How much do you think the environment can increase or decrease your abilities? What role do you think heredity plays in determining your abilities?

unit 5

EMOTIONAL AND BEHAVIORAL ADJUSTMENTS

chapter 11   Facing frustration and conflict

chapter 12   Some emotional problems of adolescents

chapter 13   Behavior disorders and their treatment

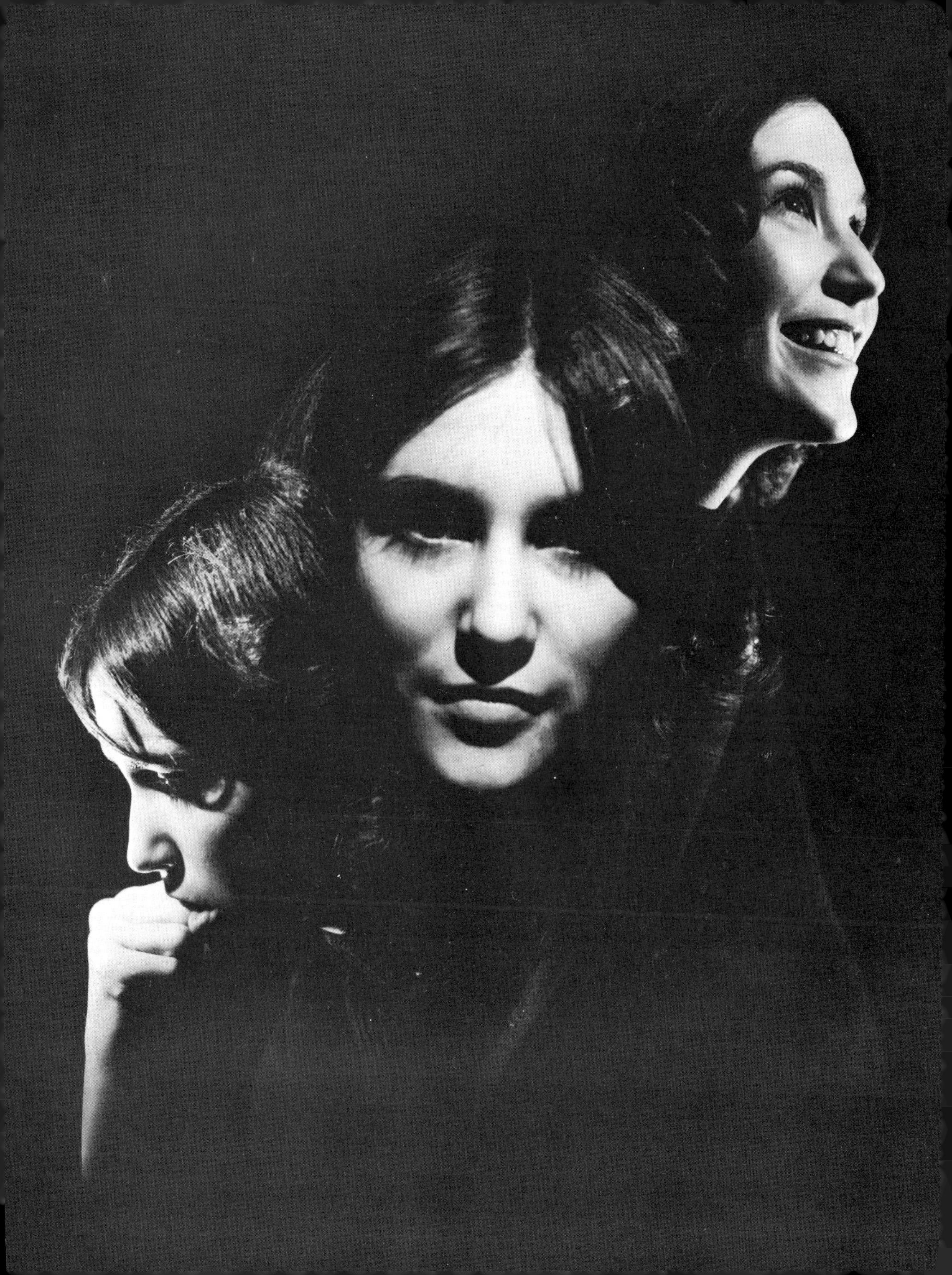

chapter 11
Facing Frustration and Conflict

THIS UNIT DISCUSSES the emotional and other behavioral adjustments that individuals must make in order to live in society. An emotionally healthy person is well adjusted to his social environment, both from his own point of view and from the point of view of others. He is able to live with his fellowmen without undue stresses, strains, and conflicts. He finds life satisfying and pleasant most of the time. He lives in such a way as to make life satisfying and pleasant for others.

High school students, like everyone else, face many problems that make it difficult to achieve a balanced adjustment. In fact, because you are changing so rapidly and are approaching adult status, you seem to encounter difficult situations rather frequently. You run head-on into many frustrating circumstances and situations involving conflict. As a result, you may become emotionally upset. You must learn how to deal with your emotional reactions.

Frustration and Conflict

A person is said to be frustrated whenever any of his goal-directed activities are slowed up, rendered difficult, or made impossible. Our society is so complex and our goals are so elaborate that most persons experience many frustrating situations. An individual must learn that he cannot always have what he wants when he wants it. Each of us develops characteristic patterns of responding to frustrating situations, and sometimes these patterns indicate poor adjustment.

What are some reactions to a frustrating situation? One classic study was concerned with the effects of frustration on the behavior of preschool children. The children were invited to enter a room where there were toys with some parts missing. The children did

Suppose you must catch the 10:57 a.m. train to keep a long-standing dentist appointment. You leave the house in time, but there is unexpected traffic on the way. Then you can't find a parking place. As you reach the platform, the train begins to pull out. You run after it . . . but you are too late. How do you react to this frustrating situation?

play with these defective toys, however, and seemed to enjoy themselves. During this time, skilled observers rated each child according to the constructiveness of his play activities. The children were then allowed to enter the other side of the room, which had been blocked from view by a screen. In this side of the room the children found much more attractive and interesting toys. They were allowed to play with these toys for a short period of time, after which they were returned to the other side of the room and separated from these new toys by a wire screen. They could now see the new toys but could not reach them because of the physical barrier. The children experienced frustration.

Observers again rated the children according to the constructiveness of their play. The level of constructiveness was now much lower for the children as a group. Some of the children attacked the wire screen, others asked for help from adults, some tried to leave the room, some showed regressive behavior, such as whining like younger children, and others went back to playing with toys from which parts were missing. On the other hand, a few of the children showed an increase in constructive play. These are some of the ways in which individuals may react to a frustrating situation.

What are some frustrating situations in everyday life? There are many kinds of frustrating situations. Our physical environment often places obstacles in our paths as we work toward goals. Perhaps, since you are going to

FACING FRUSTRATION AND CONFLICT **269**

have a very full and energy-consuming day tomorrow, you decide to go to bed early and get plenty of sleep. But the neighbors have a big party that lasts far into the night, and the noise makes sleep impossible. Or for a week you have planned a picnic, but on the big day it rains. Perhaps you are in a hurry to get to a football game, but heavy traffic allows you only to inch along. Undoubtedly you can think of many other examples.

Frustration also may come from social regulations and conditions. Perhaps you would like to take a particular course, yet school regulations forbid it. Possibly you would like to marry at once and establish a home of your own, but social pressures and economic factors may prevent your taking such steps. You may wish to get a full-time job and make enough money to buy a new car, more clothes, a television set of your own, but social pressure dictates that you remain in school. You would like to travel extensively and have many new experiences, but parents, schools, and financial problems keep you at home doing the usual things.

Frustration may be a consequence of personal limitations, too. A boy who wishes to play basketball is too short to meet the coach's requirements. A girl who wants to be a fashion model just doesn't meet the usual qualifications. A student who wants to attend a certain college with very high entrance requirements and limited enrollment does not have the grades to compete successfully with other applicants.

Young people have to face many frustrating situations, from difficulties in learning that prevent you from achieving certain goals in school, to circumstances that may keep you from being popular, to physical handicaps that limit your activities, to environmental factors that hinder you.

Frustration tolerance. Psychologists use the term FRUSTRATION TOLERANCE to indicate the ability of an individual to withstand frustration without becoming maladjusted or unduly upset emotionally. When a turtle meets a situation with which it cannot cope, it withdraws into its shell. When a person encounters a frustrating situation, he may "withdraw into his shell"—he may not be able to tolerate the frustration. On the other hand, a well-adjusted person accepts frustration as one of the realities of life. He may have to readjust his goals and his plans for achieving these goals, but he does not feel that everything is hopeless. He may begin by tolerating little frustrations without becoming upset—a shoestring breaks when he is in a hurry. Frustrating situations do not seem to be so frustrating when you realize that they are quite normal.

Conflicting situations can cause frustration. Sometimes frustration results not so much from being prevented from doing something as from having to choose between alternatives. Conflict is often very frustrating. In such a simple matter as buying an article at a store, you often have to decide between the expensive and the inexpensive, between the good looking article of poor quality and the less attractive article of good quality. The frustration occurs because if you have to choose between one of two articles, the purchase of one becomes a barrier to purchasing the other.

Many young persons are faced with making the decision between early marriage and continued schooling. There is a conflict, and the decision may be very difficult. Popularly such conflict is expressed by the saying "You can't have your cake and eat it too."

Young persons of late high school and early college age are faced with many other conflicts. They must decide whether to go on with formal schooling or not go on, whether to leave home in order to get a good job elsewhere or to remain at home and accept an inferior job, whether to go along with the crowd using drugs or not to go along, whether to act like a child or to act like an adult, and so on. There are many situations that require decisions.

Psychologists often speak of three kinds of conflicting situations: approach-approach, avoidance-avoidance, and approach-avoidance.

Approach-approach conflicts. When you are faced with two attractive choices that are mutually exclusive, you are torn between them. Both are positively attractive. You would like to do both, but you can't. This is called an APPROACH-APPROACH CONFLICT. Such a conflict can be diagrammed as shown below.

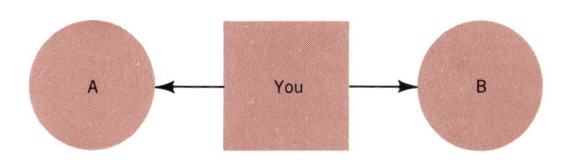

A ← You → B

Both choices A and B are equally desirable

There is the story of the donkey standing halfway between two very attractive bales of hay, but in this approach-approach conflict he starved to death because he couldn't decide which way to go. A boy knows two very attractive girls. He would like to take both of them to the dance next Saturday, but two girls with one boy is just not accepted behavior for such an event. Since he can't decide which one to approach, he stays home alone the night of the dance. A girl wishes to buy a new dress for a party and finds two that are equally attractive in design, quality, and price. Since she can't decide which one to buy, she doesn't buy either.

Actually, in everyday life, circumstances intervene that often cause us to make a decision. Probably the donkey would have moved around a bit and as he moved nearer one bale of hay, that bale would have seemed more attractive. He would have approached it and feasted instead of starved. The boy might just have happened to meet one of the two girls in the hall, stopped to talk a minute, mentioned the dance, and his whole problem would have been solved. If she said "Yes," the conflict was over. If she said, "No," the conflict was likewise over, because now he could approach the other girl for a date. The girl trying to buy a new dress might have been influenced by the saleswoman who merely said, "You look very nice in that one." In many approach-approach conflicts we waver back and forth for a short time and then make a decision.

In one experiment rats were taught to receive food placed at one end of an alley. The rats were put into a harness, which was attached to a spring scale so that the pull on the harness could be measured in grams. The rats could be stopped at any point in the alley—either close to the place of reward or far from it. It was found that the closer the rats came to the place where they had been rewarded (approach behavior), the harder they pulled. This increase in the strength of the pull toward an attractive goal the nearer the subject gets to the goal is spoken of as the APPROACH GRADIENT. Once an approach has been decided on, the strength of the approach increases in direct relation to the nearness of the goal. Data from this experiment are

FACING FRUSTRATION AND CONFLICT 271

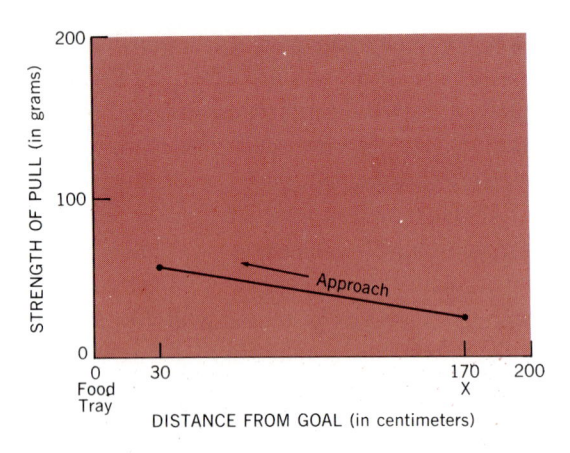

A graph illustrating the approach gradient, in which the strength of the rat's pull increases as the rat gets nearer to the food tray

shown in the graph above, in which the rat was placed at point X.

Avoidance-avoidance conflicts. When you are presented with two alternatives that are equally unattractive, you are facing an AVOIDANCE-AVOIDANCE CONFLICT. To use the popular expression, you find yourself "between the devil and the deep blue sea." Such a conflict can be diagrammed in the following way:

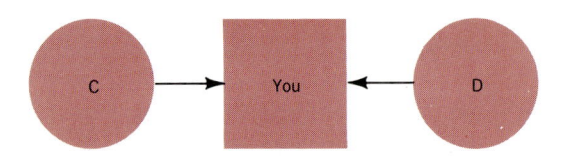

Both choices C and D are equally undesirable

As a student you may be faced with the unpleasant thought of having to study for an examination on an evening when there is a special program on television. An equally unpleasant thought is that if you don't study you may fail the exam, fail the course, and fail to graduate. You would like to avoid both situations—studying and failing the exam. Maybe you go to your room and sit down to study but cannot keep from thinking about what you are missing, so you go to the living room and watch the television program. However, you cannot enjoy the program because you keep thinking about the possibility of failing. Back you go to your room and open the book—then back to the living room. Such wavering is very unpleasant. You would like to "leave the field"—to use a psychological expression. You decide to take a walk, you drift off into a daydream, you remember a task around the house that needs your attention. You try to avoid both the thought of study and the thought of failing.

In another experiment using rats in a harness (so that the strength of their pull could be measured), the rats were given a shock at one end of an alley. In this experiment the rats pulled away from the point of shock (avoidance behavior). The closer to the shock point, the harder they pulled away; the farther away from the shock point, the less hard they pulled away. This decrease in the strength of the pull the farther away the subject gets from an undesirable situation is spoken of as the AVOIDANCE GRADIENT. The strength of avoidance behavior seems to increase as the subject gets nearer and nearer to the situation he seeks to avoid. Data from this experiment are illustrated in the graph at the top of page 273. The rat was placed at point Y.

You will note that in the graphs of the two experiments with rats (pp. 272 and 273), the avoidance gradient is much steeper (indicated by the slope of the line) than the approach gradient. What conclusions can you draw from this fact?

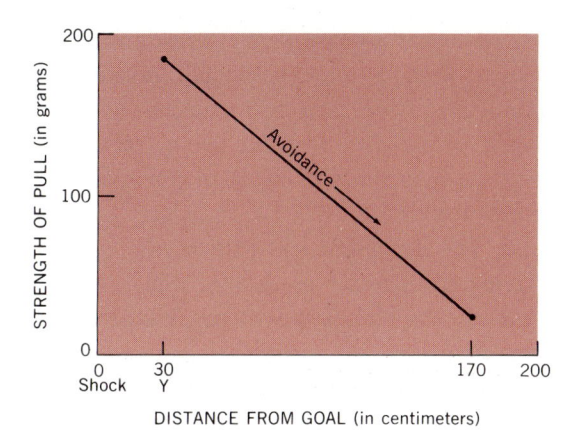

A graph showing the avoidance gradient, in which the strength of the rat's pull lessens as the rat gets farther away from the shock

Approach-avoidance conflicts. Sometimes you are attracted by certain aspects of a situation, and at the same time you are repelled by other aspects. This is APPROACH-AVOIDANCE CONFLICT. Such a conflict can be diagrammed as follows:

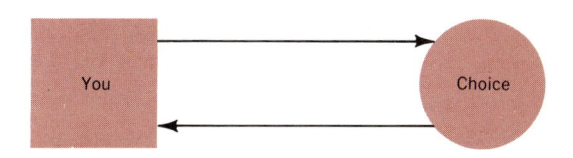

The choice has both desirable and undesirable aspects

You would like to approach a particular goal, but at the same time you would like to avoid it. It has both positive and negative value for you. You are pulled in opposite directions, liking and disliking at the same time. For example, you are at the beach, and a swim with your friends seems most attractive. You run down to the water's edge and a small wave covers your feet. The water is terribly cold. A swim suddenly seems like something to avoid rather than something to approach. You run back up the beach. Your friends call. You approach the water again, but it hasn't warmed up. You run back up the beach, and so on. You are faced with an approach-avoidance conflict.

Perhaps you are trying to decide whether or not to apply for admission to college. You have heard a great deal about the pleasures and advantages of college life, and you would like to approach it. However, you have heard of the long hours of study, of difficult examinations, and of the high expense involved. You would like to avoid these unpleasant features.

Suppose a rat learns to obtain food from a tray and then is given an electrical shock whenever it approaches the tray. It will have an approach-avoidance conflict. If we combine the two previous graphs, and place the approach gradient line and the avoidance gradient line in the same graph, as shown below, we find that the point of greatest conflict is where the lines cross. If the rat is placed to the right of the intersection of lines, it will probably pull toward the tray. If placed to the

The point of wavering for a rat in an approach-avoidance conflict

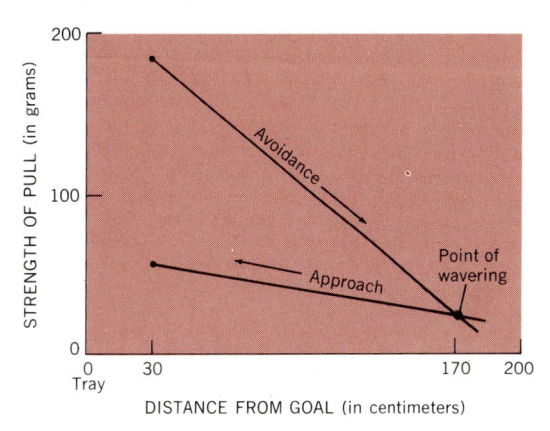

FACING FRUSTRATION AND CONFLICT

left of the intersection, it is likely to pull away from the tray, because avoidance in this case is stronger than attraction. If the rat is at the point of intersection, it is likely to remain there wavering for some time.

Do you find that in an approach-avoidance conflict you usually try harder to avoid an undesirable situation than to approach a desirable situation? The answer depends a great deal on how close you are to the situation, but do you reach a point of intersection where you waver back and forth?

Actually, approach-avoidance conflicts are often more complex than we have indicated so far. There is usually more than one aspect of a situation that makes it an approach or avoidance situation, and sometimes there are four or five. Suppose a young woman, Mary, is seriously considering marriage, but finds herself in the predicament of being "in love" with two men. One man, Harry, is physically very attractive, but Mary has found that he is also very selfish and would probably be a self-centered and inconsiderate partner for life. She has an approach-avoidance conflict when she thinks of Harry in terms of marriage. On the other hand, Bill, the other man with whom Mary is "in love," is not nearly as physically attractive as Harry, but he is kind and thoughtful and would probably be very considerate as a partner for life. Mary has an approach-avoidance conflict when she thinks of Bill in terms of marriage. We can diagram this situation in the following way:

A *double approach-avoidance conflict*

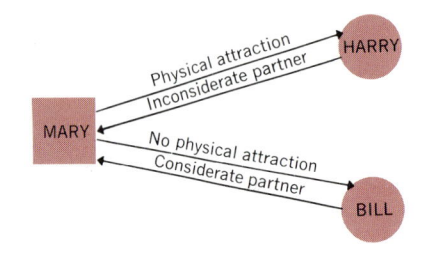

Mary has a very difficult decision to make. Unlike rats in an experiment, though, she can have more than two choices. She can begin dating Jim with an eye to marriage. But she may run into an approach-avoidance conflict with Jim. She becomes very fond of him, but finds that she dislikes the idea of having his parents as in-laws. She can add several more men friends as possible prospects for marriage. At first she had a simple approach-avoidance conflict, now she has a complex approach-avoidance conflict.

Which of the three kinds of conflict are easiest to solve? To find out, two psychologists had seventy college students use the maze shown on page 275. The college students were led to believe that the maze was simply a technique for measuring reaction time. They were told to move with a pencil from the starting point (X) to either goal. The goals were to be thought of as cities. At each city there was a red light and a white light that the experimenter could turn on and off.

Each subject was asked to imagine that whenever the red light was turned on, an atomic bomb would be dropped on that city. Therefore, he was to move away from that city as quickly as possible. Whenever the white light was turned on at a city, he would receive a million dollars if he reached the city quickly enough. Of course, he was to move toward that city as quickly as possible. To be sure that the subject started away from or toward a city, he was asked to imagine that an atomic bomb would be dropped at the starting point (X) shortly after either light at either city was turned on. All areas outside the pathways were regarded as quicksand.

The subjects were given trials with either the red or the white light turned on at only one city. There was no conflict. These situations provided control data for the other parts of the experiment.

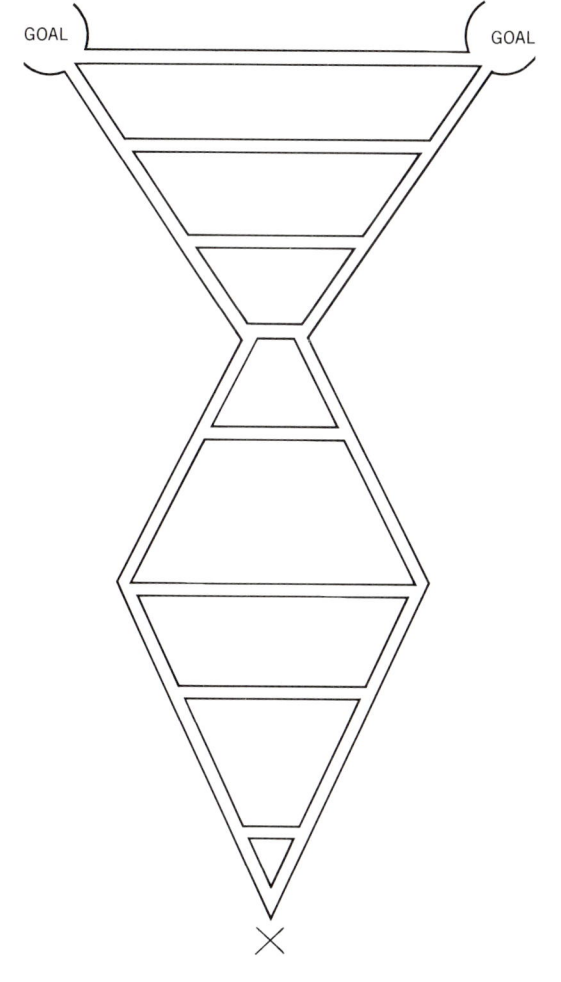

The maze used for testing responses to three types of conflict situations

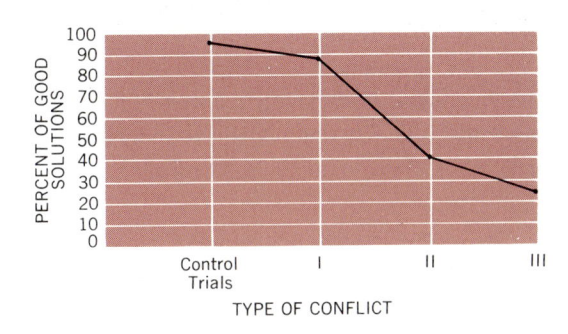

The relationship of good solutions to the type of conflict encountered by the subjects

Unknown in advance to the subjects, on the twenty-first, thirty-second, and forty-third trials, one of the following three conflict situations was presented.

Type I. Approach-approach: white lights were turned on in both cities.

Type II. Approach-avoidance: a red light and a white light were turned on in one city.

Type III. Avoidance-avoidance: red lights were turned on in both cities.

The psychologists determined the percentage of good solutions for each type of conflict situation on the basis of the quality of the responses as well as the speed of the responses. Responses were classified under such headings as going directly and without detour to the goal, stopping at some point along the way, moving through one or more of the crossways. The results are presented in the graph on this page.

As can be seen from the graph, good solutions were easiest in approach-approach conflict situations. Good solutions were most difficult in avoidance-avoidance conflicts, and nearly as difficult in approach-avoidance conflicts.

Life is full of conflicting situations, and many times a person is at least temporarily frustrated. How will he respond to such conflict? By highly emotional but ineffective behavior? Conflicts are unpleasant, but a well-adjusted individual can take them in his stride.

Desirable Ways of Responding to Frustration and Conflict

When a person is frustrated or runs into conflicts, he may become quite aggressive. He may respond either by trying to do something to his environment to change it so that he can achieve his goals or by adjusting his goals to

FACING FRUSTRATION AND CONFLICT 275

the environment. Below are a number of suggestions that you may wish to consider as you meet frustrations and conflicts in your life.

Tackle the problem even though it appears almost hopeless. It takes determination to pitch into a problem that seems almost hopeless. At one time a psychologist developed a kind of test of "spunk," or determination. The individual being tested was asked to stand on a small platform with his heels off the floor. The apparatus was so made that when the individual's heels touched the floor, a bell rang and the test was stopped. Although you might think that standing on the balls of your feet would require a great deal of physical strength, this is not the case. The test depends far more on the ability to endure discomfort in order to make a good score. It was found that a group of normal young persons could remain off their heels from 12 minutes to 2½ hours, with an average of 36 minutes. They had determination. A group of delinquent boys from a reform school were tested with the same apparatus. Their time ranged from 2½ minutes to 53 minutes, with an average of 15 minutes. They lacked the determination to endure discomfort to achieve a goal.

Ask other people for help. Asking for help is a satisfactory way of responding to a difficulty, providing you only ask for help and do not ask someone else to solve your problem for you.

Your family is an ever-ready source of help. You may feel that your parents do not understand you and are the cause of most of your frustrations. Nevertheless, in the great majority of cases they are both ready and anxious to help you. In one study in which high school students were asked where they turned for help in overcoming obstacles, 37 percent said that they turned to their families for help in cases where the problem involved conflict with family standards.

You may feel frustrated in your social life because you do not know how to act in accordance with accepted social rules. Of the high school students mentioned above, 67 percent found their schools a source of help in learning social techniques.

If you feel blocked in reaching your goals because of health or physical development, you can turn to your family physician, school health department, or community health center for help.

Your friends and classmates are a potential source of help. They are near your own age and so may have insights that an older person might not have. A give-and-take discussion may indicate that your frustrations and conflicts are shared by others. You may be able to help one another.

Work with others. Many jobs or decisions are just too big for one person. If he attempts them by himself, he soon feels frustrated and develops feelings of inferiority. Working with others on a common problem is not a way of running away from the problem. Frequently it is a way of attacking the problem in an efficient way. Good athletic teams consist of individuals who have learned to work together when faced with opposition.

The student who is having difficulty in some school subject may help solve his problem by working with another student—provided they work together rather than gossip together. A person who is shy may find working on a committee a pleasant way to overcome this difficulty.

Search for a better way to meet the problem. Suppose you are looking for an office job. Such a job will probably require skill in typing, but suppose you have no training in typing. Perhaps you have access to a typewriter and have spent many hours practicing on it. You have become quite proficient as a two-finger typist, but such typing is not likely to meet job requirements. You will be frustrated in getting a job. You can exercise your determination and pound the typewriter hour after hour, but you will find it very difficult to become an efficient typist. A better way to meet your problem would be to learn the conventional method of typing, perhaps by taking a typing course.

Suppose you are having difficulty with your schoolwork. You can spend long hours studying (and it does take time to study), but that may not be the answer to your problem. Perhaps you need to increase your study efficiency, and thereby overcome your frustration. You might try talking with each of your teachers to learn the best way to study for each course.

Know when to be flexible. Giving up whenever you are frustrated in reaching a goal is not a sign of being well adjusted, but neither is there any virtue in carrying out a poor decision. Suppose you have decided to get a job as soon as you graduate from high school rather than go to college. That may have been a wise decision. On the other hand, you may have made this decision when you were emotionally upset as the result of a poor grade or a "bawling out" at home. One night on a date you may have felt you were in love and decided to get married as soon as you graduate from high school. That may have been a wise decision or a foolish one. Decisions made

One of the ways to deal with frustration, such as the frustration of missing a train, is to plan ahead so that you can arrive at the station with plenty of time to spare, and thus avoid the frustrating situation.

FACING FRUSTRATION AND CONFLICT **277**

under emotional stress are seldom made with due consideration for both sides of a problem. If you make a decision when you are emotionally upset, you will be wise to reconsider it objectively after you have calmed down. You will then be able to think of all possibilities with a problem-solving attitude and so make a wiser decision.

In the past you may have made a decision with great care and in the light of all known facts. Today, new evidence may be available, so that you will need to change or alter your decision. You may have decided not to go to college, but college aptitude test scores and an offer of a scholarship may indicate that you should reverse your decision. On the other hand, you may have decided to go to college on the basis of limited information about social activities and athletic teams. After you have the facts from your school counselor concerning your interests, aptitudes, and abilities, you may wish to reverse your decision.

A wise man often changes his plans. A foolish man may never change his plans, or he may change them with every passing fancy.

Consider alternatives. Sometimes frustrations cannot be overcome directly. You may have to detour. Under proper control, making a detour—compensating—may be the best possible solution to frustration. We will examine this topic of compensation in the next section.

Adjustment Mechanisms

We have considered desirable ways of responding to frustrations and conflicts. Now we will turn to other ways of responding to frustrations and conflicts, known as adjustment mechanisms. ADJUSTMENT MECHANISMS are ways of behaving that help satisfy needs, reduce anxiety from frustration, and protect the individual's self-esteem. Some of these ways may be either desirable or undesirable, depending on how and to what degree they are used.

Compensation. Psychologists use the word COMPENSATION to refer to an attempt to make up for a deficiency in one field by expending extra effort and energy over a prolonged period in order to excel in some other field. A person may consciously set out to compensate for some deficiency, or he may compensate without being aware that he is doing so.

Compensation can be a very desirable way of meeting frustrations. It may lead toward good mental health. It may even result in constructive activities that leave a person better off than before he experienced frustration. A member of a high school football team was crippled in an automobile accident, with the result that he could never play football or any other strenuous game again. He might have compensated by becoming a ping-pong player, but even in this relatively mild game his physical deficiency would have meant a very hard uphill fight and one probably not worth the price. His interests were in athletics, and he did not wish to change his interests just because he could no longer play strenuous games. While still in high school, he became the sports reporter for the school paper. After graduation he worked his way up as a reporter on a city newspaper. He is now a successful sportscaster on a television program. He has many friends among sports fans. Once in a while his most intimate friends hear him say, "Gee, I wish I could get out there and play myself," but he knows and admits that he cannot play. He has compensated for his physical handicap in a desirable way.

Compensation can also be used in an undesirable way. For instance, after his automobile accident, this same fellow might have decided that since he couldn't play, he would make money out of sports by gambling. He could have gone in for "fixing" games so that the player or team on which he bet would be sure to win. He would have compensated for his deficiency, but at the expense of becoming dishonest, losing friends, and degrading the activity that he was most interested in.

A student may realize and admit that even though he tries very hard, he just can't be a superior student. He may compensate by becoming superior in some other field in which he does have ability. For example, a girl was just getting by in most subjects in high school in spite of her best efforts. For a while she did become very much interested in the chemistry course when the teacher talked about and demonstrated chemical processes involved in photography. In fact, the girl made a B in chemistry for that grading period, and B's were scarce on her record. She began developing and printing pictures at home. She borrowed and studied library books on photography. She joined a local camera club. Several of her pictures were published in the school annual, and one appeared in the local Sunday newspaper. She had compensated for her lack of general scholastic ability. She had developed an interesting and, possibly, a profitable hobby.

Compensation for none-too-good schoolwork might have taken an undesirable turn. According to records in the guidance office this girl possessed only average intellectual ability, and her school record seemed to bear out test scores. In spite of this, she might have set out to prove to herself that she was a genius. She might even have said that in chemistry the teacher and the textbook were all wrong. In that case she would not have learned the things she found so useful in photography. Belittling others is a common but unfortunate kind of compensation.

There are many ways in which a person can compensate. The person who is not very attractive physically can compensate by being very friendly and helpful. The student who does not do well in vocational subjects may compensate by doing well in the more academic subjects, and vice versa. The person who, for some reason, is unable to have children of his or her own may compensate by being a Scout leader or playground supervisor caring for other people's children. The person who is unable to travel can compensate by reading books and magazines about travel. Undoubtedly you can make a long list of ways in which an individual can compensate for feelings of frustration and inferiority.

Overcompensation. When a person compensates excessively, to the extent of more than balancing his feelings of inferiority, guilt, or inadequacy, he is OVERCOMPENSATING. The shy student may try so hard to compensate for his lack of social life that he studies excessively, even to the point of not getting sufficient healthful exercise and eliminating what little social life he did have. The poor student may try so hard to compensate for his lack of scholastic ability that he joins every available club or other social organization. He is out every night. His schoolwork drops still lower. Both the student who studies almost all the time and the student who engages in excessive social activity may be overcompensating for their respective deficiencies.

Did you ever hear a boy say, "I'm the dumbest person in school," or a girl say, "All the other girls are so much prettier than I am"? Did they expect you to agree with them? Did they want you to say, "I'd hate

This little boy is demonstrating his identification with his father by literally trying to fill his father's boots.

to see them come any dumber," or "I can't imagine anyone uglier than you"? On the contrary, they hoped you would say, "Oh, you're one of the smartest boys in school," or "I think you're the prettiest girl in the whole world." Self-repudiation, that is, "running yourself down," often indicates overcompensation.

Identification. The word IDENTIFICATION refers to the process of imitating or closely affiliating with the behavior of other individuals or groups. Small boys identify with their fathers; little girls identify with their mothers. Later, they may identify with their teachers or with the heroes or heroines in films, plays, or television programs. By putting themselves, in imagination, in the place of an older and admired person, they can achieve some vicarious satisfaction.

As we become more mature, we tend to identify ourselves with organizations rather than with individuals. A person may join a club, lodge, or other social group because, by so doing, he can enjoy the social life and do his part in carrying out the worthwhile objectives of the organization. On the other hand, he may identify with an organization for the feeling of superiority such membership gives him rather than for the good he can do for the organization. A student may join a school club only because it is the largest or most popular club in school. A high school graduate may choose a college because it has a very good football team and he can say, *"We* are the strongest team in the league" (even though he may not play and takes physical education only because it is required).

We all do a certain amount of identifying, but the person who finds himself deriving too much glory from the accomplishments of another, or who finds himself joining organizations solely for the prestige he will derive from membership, should strive for more personal success.

Projection. Have you ever attributed your own emotions and intentions to someone else? When a person perceives in other people certain traits or motives in which he feels himself to be inferior, he is demonstrating PROJECTION. He may blame others for his shortcomings or difficulties, or he may attribute to others his own unacceptable desires. A student yields to the temptation of cheating on an examination. To relieve his feeling of guilt, he says, "Everybody else in the class cheats. I even saw Evelyn cheating and she is on the honor roll." He had arranged to have a neighbor drop a slip containing the most important answers so that he could pick it up. But to minimize his guilt, he says, "When Evelyn borrowed a pencil during the exam, I'm sure she looked at my paper." An irritable person may accuse others of being irritable. An impolite person may accuse other people of rudeness.

We may gain a bit of temporary relief from our feelings of frustration and inferiority when we project our traits and motives onto others, but the person striving to become well-adjusted tries to correct his faults rather than to see them in others.

Stereotyped behavior. When faced by frustrating or conflicting situations, some individuals respond simply by continuing in a blind way with their past behavior patterns, making no attempt to adjust to new conditions. A person has difficulty in being socially accepted, possibly because of the careless way in which he dresses. Instead of trying to learn why he is not readily accepted, he goes ahead doggedly trying to enter social groups without improving his appearance. A student has difficulty with a particular kind of algebra problem. Instead of trying to work out a new plan of attack, he plunges ahead with the same incorrect approach time after time.

Psychologists use the term STEREOTYPED BEHAVIOR to refer to inflexible behavior, behavior that is not altered by circumstances.

Repression. One way of getting around frustrations and conflicts is to "forget" them. We do forget many things, but when we "forget" because the original thoughts are painful to us, we are demonstrating REPRESSION rather than true forgetting. Psychologists often use the term in a very special and technical way. For our purposes, however, we can say that repression is selective forgetting. We "forget" that which is unpleasant for us to remember.

Perhaps you have had some very embarrassing experience in the classroom. For weeks you were kidded about the unfortunate incident. Life became rather unhappy. You might say to yourself, "I'll just forget the incident." If by "forget" you meant that you were going to try to think of other things and take the kidding good-naturedly, you were making a good adjustment. If, without saying "I'll forget," you began to avoid situations that reminded you of the unfortunate incident, you were repressing your thoughts of the incident.

Probably we all repress some undesirable thoughts, but with some persons such "forgetting" becomes extreme. They repress whole areas—perhaps many years—of their earlier lives because of certain painful experiences that occurred to them then.

Regression. Sometimes an individual, when faced with personal problems, tries to evade unpleasant facts or responsibilities, to run away from the situation. He may regress, or return to earlier ways of behaving, to avoid present problems. REGRESSION is the escaping of present problems by returning to earlier-known ways of meeting frustrations. Older children sometimes become infantile in their behavior when they find the problems of an older child too difficult to face with comfort. Sometimes "tired businessmen" run away from their jobs and behave in a very childish manner at conventions or school reunions. Adolescents may resort to childish temper tantrums and fights rather than attacking their problems.

Occasional temporary regressions are not abnormal. However, persons who run away from their frustrations to the extent that they show regressive behavior full time may need to be institutionalized.

Procrastination. Another very common way of escaping problems is by PROCRASTINATION, or delay. By putting off a task, the individual gets temporary relief from a distressful situation. For the time being, he escapes an unpleasant task.

A person is especially likely to procrastinate if he has very high ambitions but feels inferior. He is not willing to test his strength because of fear of failure. For example, a high school senior said that he was very anxious to enter a certain college. Going to this college was a "must" on his list of ambitions. The college provided a very helpful scholarship, and several seniors were applying for it. This boy said, "I just have to win that scholarship," yet he also realized that someone else might win it. He put off filling out the necessary application blank. Finally, he filled out the blank and sent it in—two days after the deadline for applications. Of course, he didn't win the scholarship, but he could say, "I'd probably have received the scholarship if I had sent the application blank in on time." Instead of facing a possible failure, he had run away from any possibility of success.

The student who puts off doing an assignment, such as writing a paper, escapes, for a time, what seems to be an unpleasant task. The longer the task is put off, the more unpleasant it becomes. In the meantime, he rushes from one activity to another. He says, "I just don't have time to write that paper." Finally, and at the last minute, he hurriedly gathers some material and writes the paper. Of course, the grade on the paper is poor. He claims, "I wouldn't have had the poorest grade in the class if I had had enough time to work on the paper." He ignores the fact that he had done many other things while putting off the writing of the paper. He kids himself into believing he would have had a good paper if he had had more time, but in reality he had been running away from the task so that he would have an excuse for his failure.

It has been said that "procrastination is the art of keeping up with yesterday." Probably everyone gets behind in some of his work at times. Sometimes it is not his fault. But the person who is generally behind in much of his work should ask himself, "Basically, why do I procrastinate? What am I trying to run away from?" An honest answer to these questions may aid him in becoming a well-adjusted individual.

Displaced aggression. Perhaps you have run into some difficulty at school. You were not prepared for class and so the teacher gave you an extra assignment to complete. You had planned to go to a movie. Now your plans have been upset. As you come home, your dog runs out to meet you, wagging his tail. Instead of patting him, you kick the dog. You were angry at the teacher, but you could not give direct expression to your hostility by kicking the teacher, so instead you kicked your poor dog. A workman is bawled out by his boss in front of others. He feels like striking the boss, but that direct aggressive behavior would mean the loss of his job. He goes home and growls and snaps at his wife and children instead. A child is happily playing with his toys when he is told to put them away and go to bed. He is frustrated, but what can he do to his parents? He kicks the toys all over the floor and may even break some of them.

All of the situations described above are examples of DISPLACED AGGRESSION, or the transfer of hostility from the actual source of frustration to some innocent person or object. Popularly, displaced aggression is spoken of as "blowing off steam."

This individual is displacing his aggression from its real source onto a wastepaper basket.

Letting someone else decide for you. Making a decision is often difficult and even painful. To avoid such difficulty, you can ask a friend for the answer to your problem. You might ask him, "What would you do if you were in my place?" But how does he know what he would do if he were in your place? Both his heredity and his environment are different from yours. His hopes and aspirations are different. Your friend can give you information and even make recommendations, but all too often when you ask for advice, you are really asking for a ready-made solution to your problem. You are not facing your own problem. You are escaping. Or, instead of asking a friend to solve your problem, you may put the burden on mere chance. You flip a coin, refusing to face the problem yourself.

Rationalization. Instead of actively attacking or plainly running away from his problems, a person may try to "explain" what he has done. He may rationalize. By RATIONALIZATION psychologists mean the kind of thinking people do when they explain their behavior in terms of socially approved and high-sounding reasons instead of real reasons. Unlike projection, in which the individual places blame for his shortcoming on another person or persons, rationalization does not necessarily involve another person. An individual often rationalizes his behavior by blaming an object or a set of circumstances.

Rationalizing is not the same as lying. The person who does the rationalizing deceives himself first and others (maybe) afterward. He is not willing to admit that he is wrong. Instead, he fools himself into accepting some explanation for his behavior that will save his "face," or pride.

The student who has neglected his work finds he has received failing or poor marks. He feels that it will be necessary to explain these low marks to parents and friends. The real reason for his negligence is not a good one and will not be approved by his parents and friends. He "reasons out" more acceptable explanations for his low marks. He says, "I did the work all right, but the questions on the test were very unfair," or "My classes are so dull that I can't possibly pay attention." By such defenses as these, he saves his pride in his own eyes, and he may even fool a few friends. But many persons will recognize immediately that he is rationalizing and is unwilling to face the truth.

A man may stress the importance of honesty to his children. Then in his business he has a chance to make a profitable deal, providing he tells an outright lie or raises a false implication about the merchandise he is offering. He completes the dishonest transaction. Later a friend may accuse him of not living up to the principles he taught his children, or he may be troubled by questioning thoughts of his own. He is not willing to admit to himself or to others that he has been dishonest, for dishonesty is not approved by society. Possibly he rationalizes by saying, "Business is business. Anyone else would have done the same thing. The customer knew, or should have known, what he was buying. Anyway, I gave no written guarantee."

We must be careful not to condemn too freely in our thoughts the person we know to be rationalizing. Just as none of us is in perfect physical health, none of us is completely well adjusted. We all rationalize.

We can get a better understanding of rationalization by noting two forms it often takes, "sour grapes" and "sweet lemons."

The "sour-grapes" rationalization. The name *sour grapes* is given to the form of rationalization in which a person says that he does not want something that he cannot have. By finding fault with the unattainable object, a person makes it seem less appealing to himself. The term comes from the fable of the fox and the grapes—a fable attributed to Aesop, who lived twenty-five hundred years ago. The fox, unable to reach the grapes he desired, declared that they were sour. Maybe some of his fox friends believed that he didn't want the grapes. Probably most of them knew very well that he was rationalizing.

Have you ever known a case like the following? A student works hard, hoping to receive grades that will put him on the Honor Roll. Yet he fails to make it by a narrow margin. He says, "I didn't care to get on the Honor Roll anyway. Only bookworms get on the Honor Roll." Instead of admitting that he was sorry that he did not succeed and resolving to work even harder the next time, he tried to save his pride by presenting himself and any of his friends who would listen with a sour-grapes rationalization.

A boy asks a girl to go to a party with him. For some reason she does not accept his invitation. Her refusal hurts his pride. Perhaps other fellows hear about it and tease him about having been turned down. Instead of admitting his situation and, perhaps, asking another girl, he says, "I didn't really want to go to that party anyway. Besides, I wouldn't want to be seen with her. She is too short" (or tall, or fat, or skinny)—and so on.

The "sweet-lemon" rationalization. Psychologists have given the name *sweet lemon* to the form of rationalization in which a person says that what he has (but doesn't really want) is just what he wants. The lemon is sour, but if we put sugar on it we may be able to take it with a fair degree of grace. If we add enough sugar, we may be able to make it appear to others and to ourselves that a lemon is exactly what we want.

If, on a blind date, a girl finds that she does not particularly like the boy, she may say to a friend, "He may *appear* to talk only about himself, but actually he is a very thoughtful and considerate person." In truth, she is unhappy with the date, but by putting enough "sugar" on her disappointment she is able to stand the failure a bit more easily. Just possibly she is able to fool some of her friends.

The person who drives an out-of-date car says, "I wouldn't trade this old bus for any of the new models. I wouldn't accept a new model as a gift." In spite of this statement he enters an advertising contest in which the prize is a latest-model car. If he should win the contest, would he refuse to accept the car?

Can rationalization be constructive? Under some circumstances rationalization may be helpful in providing a measure of relief from disappointment. Suppose a student has striven hard to be elected to the position of editor of the school annual or some other school publication. Only one person can be given this honor. An unsuccessful candidate may be keenly disappointed. In his effort to console himself he may think, "Well, the job probably would be a lot of trouble anyway; I'd have to sit up nights working at it." By looking at that side of the picture for a little while, he may succeed in overcoming his disappointment, or at least in greatly lessening it. Finding relief from disappointment in that way may not be undesirable. It may even be helpful, provided a person (1) keeps such thoughts to himself, (2) recognizes that he is only consoling himself, and (3) resolves to try for success in some other field of endeavor.

Both sour-grapes and sweet-lemon rationalizations indicate that an individual is unwilling to face the unpleasant realities of life. Although the sweet-lemon rationalization is

Drawing by Joseph Farris, © 1971, The New Yorker Magazine, Inc.

"Perk up! Think of all that interest piling up at six per cent per annum from day of deposit, compounded quarterly."

probably more desirable than the sour-grapes rationalization, friends tire of sweet lemons as well as sour grapes.

The individual who is striving to become well adjusted will take into account as many of his rationalizations as possible. He will face reality, even though that reality is sometimes unpleasant, rather than excuse himself by offering plausible explanations for his conduct.

How do groups and nations rationalize? Social groups as well as individuals devise and accept rationalized explanations for their behavior.

Under the ancient law of Moses, a goat was selected, over whose head the high priest confessed the sins of his people. Then the "scapegoat" was driven into the wilderness, bearing with it, symbolically, all those sins. Today we refer to any individual or group blamed for the misdeeds or mistakes of others

FACING FRUSTRATION AND CONFLICT 285

as a SCAPEGOAT. If civil authorities are unable to cope with the problems in a community, they do not like to admit their failure. They find it easy to place the blame on some powerless minority group. This or that "element" becomes the scapegoat.

Wartime produces many good illustrations of group rationalization. Most persons do not believe in killing other persons. Therefore, for a country to be led into war, the people must be taught to rationalize performing acts of death and destruction. History is full of such instances.

When a national leader is unable to cope with economic and social problems, he may not dare to admit his failure. He rationalizes, and influences the public to rationalize with him.

Cognitive Dissonance

Closely related to rationalization is a kind of thinking process that psychologists speak of as COGNITIVE DISSONANCE. In cognitive dissonance the individual is faced with a lack of agreement between his various thoughts and beliefs, or between his thoughts and overt behavior. This lack of harmony can produce discomfort and frustration. Therefore, the individual tries to alter his thoughts or actions in order to reduce the dissonance.

You may be familiar with the word "dissonance" in connection with music. We say that dissonant sounds are harsh, that they jar us, and we may find them unpleasant. Similarly, our thinking may become harsh, jarring, and unpleasant to us. We feel uncomfortable when we find ourselves thinking or acting in a way that seems inconsistent with information we have about ourselves and our environment. In cognitive dissonance a person realizes that his thinking is inconsistent and he tries to do something about it. He may change his thinking so that it is more consonant and pleasant.

A few examples of studies dealing with cognitive dissonance will help to clarify this concept.

Cognitive dissonance as related to smoking behavior. Cigarette smokers enjoy smoking. On the other hand, they realize there is considerable evidence that smoking is harmful to a person's health. To smoke or not to smoke, that is the question. There is cognitive dissonance.

In one study (made in the 1950's) smokers and nonsmokers were asked to express their opinions on the relationship between smoking and lung cancer. Only 7 percent of heavy smokers expressed the opinion that a relationship between smoking and lung cancer had been proved. Of the nonsmokers, 29 percent believed that a relationship had been proved. The opinions of light and moderate smokers fell between those of heavy smokers and the nonsmokers.

A person who enjoys smoking and yet has reason to believe smoking is harmful to his health is disturbed by the cognitive dissonance, or inconsistency, in his thinking. Therefore, he tends to reject information indicating that smoking is harmful in order to reduce the dissonance. (It should be added that the above data must be taken with "a grain of salt." We do not know how many of the nonsmokers might have liked to smoke but did not do so because thhey believed smoking cigarettes would be harmful to their health.)

Cognitive dissonance using children as subjects. A psychologist secured data on cognitive dissonance from eighty-three boys in the second to fourth grades of school. He did not tell the boys about the true nature of the experiment, but simply informed them that

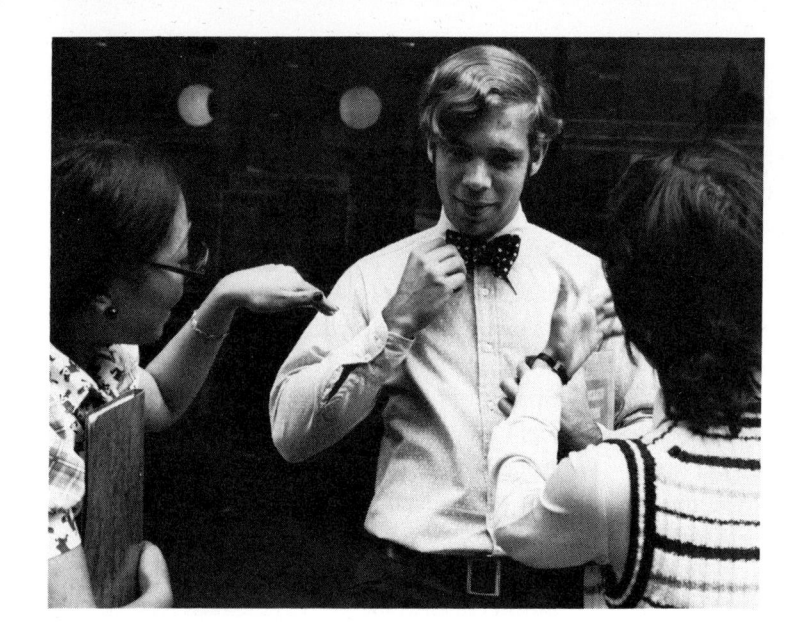

These girls are complimenting the boy on his bow tie, but what do they really think of it? Have you ever felt compelled to compliment a person on something that you didn't like? How did you resolve the disharmony between what you said and what you really thought?

the study concerned their preferences among various toys—a cheap plastic submarine, an extremely expensive battery-operated robot, a child's baseball glove, an unloaded toy rifle, and a toy tractor. The subjects were asked to indicate on a rating scale their liking for each of the toys. The robot was rated as the most attractive toy by far. The boys were then told that they could not play with the robot while the experimenter was either out of the room or busy working at something else in the room.

Some of the boys worked under conditions of a mild threat: "Do not play with the robot. It is wrong to play with the robot." Others worked under conditions of a severe threat: "If you play with the robot I'll be very angry and will have to do something about it." The boys who did not play with the robot were given a second opportunity to play with it several weeks later, but with the original threats removed. It was found that the subjects who resisted temptation under mild threat were less likely to play with the robot in the second session than were those who had resisted temptation under severe threat. Since all the boys wanted to play with the robot, and fewer of them did so after a mild threat, more cognitive dissonance—or lack of agreement between their desires and their actions—had been produced by a mild threat than by a severe threat.

Remember that we have cognitive dissonance only when we have to make a decision about our thinking or overt behavior. There would be no problem of dissonance if everyone were forced by law to, say, smoke two packs of cigarettes each day (although some people might disagree with the law!).

Ways of reducing cognitive dissonance or justifying the disharmony. In this study the psychologist gave his subjects, who were college students, as dull and boring a task to do as he could devise. On the table in front of the subject were rows of blocks. The subject was asked to go through the rows of blocks, giving each block a quarter of a turn. As soon as he had turned all of the blocks he was to begin again, turning every block another quarter turn.

After the subject had completed this seemingly pointless task, a favor was asked of him. Would he please tell the next subject for the experiment, who was waiting in another room, that the experiment was very interesting and even exciting? Unknown to the subject who had just completed his dull block-turning task, the person in the waiting room was actually an accomplice of the psychologist. When told how interesting the experiment was, the accomplice said that he had a friend who had participated in the same experiment and this friend had said that the experiment was extremely dull and boring. Of course, the subject denied this, insisting that the experiment was very interesting. Obviously, he was saying something that was contrary to what he really thought. He was experiencing cognitive dissonance.

Then the factor of justification was introduced into the experiment. The psychologist offered each member of one group of subjects a dollar to help out in the experiment by telling the person in the waiting room that the experiment was interesting and enjoyable. Each member of another group was offered twenty dollars for telling the same lie. Later, all the subjects were asked to indicate how interesting and enjoyable they really found the experiment to be.

Which group do you think would be more likely to develop a belief that the routine turning of the blocks was really interesting and enjoyable? Wouldn't it be the group who was paid twenty dollars for telling an obvious lie rather than the group who was paid only one dollar? No, the data indicate that those who received only one dollar had less justification for telling a falsehood, and therefore had more cognitive dissonance than did those who received the twenty dollars. Members of the one-dollar group reduced their dissonance by actually coming to believe that the experiment was interesting and enjoyable. To members of the twenty-dollar group, the financial reward was sufficiently high to justify their inconsistent thinking so they didn't have to change their attitudes toward the dull and boring task.

Have you ever found yourself accepting ideas that you knew were inconsistent with what you believed? Do you ever find yourself believing that things you do are right even though there is evidence to the contrary? You are not alone in these endeavors, in trying to make dissonant thinking seem to be consonant thinking. But now that you know something of the theory of cognitive dissonance and have evidence concerning it, will you be a bit more careful of such thinking in the future?

Having investigated the sources of frustration and conflict, and the different ways that people react to such situations, we will turn to some specific emotional problems that young people, in particular, face.

Terms to Know

adjustment mechanism
approach-approach conflict
approach gradient
approach-avoidance conflict
avoidance-avoidance conflict
avoidance gradient
cognitive dissonance

compensation
displaced aggression
frustration tolerance
identification
overcompensation
procrastination
projection

rationalization
regression
repression
scapegoat
sour-grapes rationalization
stereotyped behavior
sweet-lemon rationalization

Topics to Think About

1. In your dating activities you may face situations in which conflicts arise. Which conflict situations do you find the easiest to meet: approach-approach, approach-avoidance, or avoidance-avoidance? Why? Which are the most difficult to meet? Why?

2. How important has identification been in shaping your values and behavior? Think about the people or organizations that you have identified with over the years. How much influence have they had on your life?

3. Do you wish to decide for yourself everything that will affect your future, or do you wish to have others, such as your parents or friends, make some decisions for you? Do you think that you rely too much on others to make decisions for you? Or do you make too many decisions on your own without consulting others for advice?

4. What is the most frustrating experience that you can remember in your life? How did you react to it? Did you resort to one or more of the adjustment mechanisms?

5. If you smoke, or use alcoholic beverages or nonmedical drugs regularly, and are being perfectly honest with yourself, have you caught yourself rationalizing about the effects of the habit on your health?

6. Suppose you were a policeman or a policewoman in a large city with a high crime rate, and you had to face many tense and frustrating situations. Under what circumstances do you think you would find it most difficult to control your emotions? What methods would you use to help yourself maintain your self-control?

7. Have you ever made someone else a scapegoat for your own misdeeds or mistakes? Why did you do it? If the circumstances were to repeat themselves, would you do it again, or would you react differently?

Suggestions for Activities

1. Happiness depends not on the absence of conflicts but on how well you resolve conflicts. Often it is helpful to make a simple analysis of conflicts so that they can be faced more objectively. For a few days, jot down the nature of conflicting situations that you encounter and try to classify these conflicts as approach-approach, approach-avoidance, or avoidance-avoidance. Perhaps some of your conflicts are related to school situations and are common to a number of students. If they are not too personal, discuss them in class or in small groups. Does such a group approach help you with your individual conflicts? Does classifying them help?

2. You may wish to write a report for English or history class in which you portray the life of some person whose life seemed to be largely spent in compensating for a handicap, for example, Napoleon, Helen Keller, Thomas Edison, Demosthenes, Theodore Roosevelt. Your report may be based on some character in literature—for example, in Shakespeare's *Richard III,* Gloucester compensates for a deformed and stunted body by shrewd striving for power.

3. For a period of one or two weeks, take notes on frustrating situations that you experience, both those in which you are prevented from doing something you wish to do and those in which you are faced with a conflict. Such situations may involve schoolwork, dates, home activities, recreational activities, and so on. Draw up a four-column chart with the following headings: "Situation," "Desirable Response," "Questionable Response," "Undesirable Response." Down the side of the page, under the heading "Situation," list the experiences that you have found frustrating—or conflicting. Then, for each situation, indicate how you responded to it, classifying your response under the heading that best describes it. For those situations responded to in questionable or undesirable ways, indicate in red ink under "Desirable Response" how you might better have met the situation.

4. While watching sports events, such as boxing, wrestling, and auto racing, some individuals become very excited. If you have a chance to attend or watch such sports events (perhaps on television, or in movies), observe the people in the audience. What evidence can you find that they are identifying with the players?

5. For at least a week, check newspapers for items suggesting group rationalizations. Are there evidences of scapegoats? Examples of group rationalizations are especially easy to locate during the campaigns that precede a political election.

6. For one week, listen for and jot down apparent rationalizations that you hear. Some may be given by your friends or relatives, some may be overheard in the conversations of strangers, some may be detected in your own conversations. As far as you can judge, which ones are "sour grapes" and which ones are "sweet lemons"? Are there more "sour grapes" than "sweet lemons," or the other way around?

7. If you have an opportunity to play individually with a number of small children of approximately the same age, think up some "game" that you believe would be very dull for them. For example, play that it is "lots of fun" to make four-block piles of blocks. Be sure to have plenty of blocks and allow enough time for the game to become quite boring for them, and probably for you. Play with only one child at a time so there will be no competition, and do not build blocks yourself except in the beginning to show the child how to play the game. Tell some children that they will receive "pay," such as ten candy bars. Tell other children that they will receive "pay" of one candy bar for playing the same game. After the time is up, ask each child how much he or she enjoyed the game, and why. Other students should carry out this activity with a number of children of other ages. Then compare the results. Do older children seem to demonstrate more cognitive dissonance than younger children?

Suggestions for Further Reading

Bergler, Edmund, *Tensions Can Be Reduced to Nuisances: A Technique for Not-Too-Neurotic People,* Collier. An interestingly written set of ways to reduce tensions for those who worry too much.

Hilgard, E. R., R. C. Atkinson, and Rita Atkinson, *Introduction to Psychology,* 5th ed., Harcourt Brace Jovanovich. See Chapter 19, "Conflict and Adjustment."

Janis, Irving L., *Stress and Frustration,* Harcourt Brace Jovanovich. A paperback that stresses man's struggle to cope with stress, the role of learning in helping to meet stressful situations, adaptive personality changes, aggression, and how people of different ages cope with grief.

Kagan, J., and E. Havemann, *Psychology: An Introduction,* 2nd ed., Harcourt Brace Jovanovich. See Chapter 11, pages 369–87, on frustrations and conflict, and the various defense mechanisms that people use to cope with frustration and conflict.

Mahl, George F., *Psychological Conflict and Defense,* Harcourt Brace Jovanovich. A paperback that covers such topics as the types of conflict, projection, overreactions, and interference with defenses. It is psychoanalytically oriented.

Parks, G., *The Learning Tree,* Fawcett. A paperback that contains the biography of a black adolescent who grew up in a small Kansas town.

Ruch, Floyd L., and Philip G. Zimbardo, *Psychology and Life,* 8th ed., Scott, Foresman. See Chapter 10, "The Cognitive Control of Behavior."

Wertheimer, M., *et al., Psychology: A Brief Introduction,* Scott, Foresman. See pages 66–67, conflicts in thinking and ways of avoiding.

chapter 12
Some Emotional Problems of Adolescents

BECAUSE SOCIETY often fails to recognize the physical and social maturation of adolescents and because adolescents often fail to recognize that they are not completely mature, young people may have more intense emotional problems than do persons in earlier and later periods of life. Since the number of possible emotional experiences is enormous, only a few emotional problems that have been shown to be rather common during adolescence will be discussed in this chapter: feelings of inferiority, daydreaming, thrill-seeking, family conflicts, dating and love, and assuming the roles of men and women.

Inferiority

Psychologists use the word FEELINGS to refer to the pleasantness or unpleasantness of emotional experiences. They use the term AFFECTIVE EXPERIENCE to refer not only to the pleasantness or unpleasantness of an emotional experience but to the intensity of the experience. An affective experience may range from a very mild one to a very intense one. Psychologists might speak of affective experiences of inferiority, but here we will use the more popular term, "feelings of inferiority." Although persons of all ages often believe that they are inferior to others in some ways, such "feelings" are likely to be more common in young people than in children or older adults.

Are feelings of inferiority abnormal? A feeling that you are inferior to other individuals in certain areas is normal, and is desirable from the point of view of mental health. We should all feel inferior to some persons in some ways. If you were invited to go into the prize ring with a professional boxer, no doubt you would and should feel inferior. On the other hand, the boxer might well be and feel inferior to you in certain other areas. A well-adjusted person is not disturbed by the fact that he is inferior to others in some ways.

Feelings of inferiority are characterized by a general feeling of worthlessness. Popularly, feelings of inferiority are often referred to as an "inferiority complex." As the individual looks about at his associates, he feels that he compares very unfavorably with them. Actually the comparison may mean only that

Physical abnormalities need not cause feelings of inferiority. Michael Dunn (below) has used his size to advantage as an actor. He played the dwarf in the movie "Ship of Fools."

he or she is different from others. As you know from studying psychology, individuals differ in many ways, but all too often adolescents fail to recognize this and feel that to be different is to be regarded unfavorably. As an individual becomes still more mature, he has less tendency to be bothered by the fact that he is different. In fact, he may recognize that he is making his most worthwhile contribution to society by being different from others in certain ways.

It is not uncommon for anyone to feel rather worthless at times, but for well-adjusted persons such a feeling is temporary. The adolescent is especially likely to feel temporarily worthless as he tries to make the transition between childhood and full adulthood. Basically, the young man or woman is asking, "Who am I?" or "What is my role in society?" In a relatively few years he or she will be established in adult life, will have a job, will probably be married and have a family, and will be participating in worthwhile community activities. He or she will feel worthwhile rather than worthless. If, however, the feelings of inferiority—of worthlessness—continue throughout life, the individual is not well adjusted.

Should physical abnormalities cause feelings of inferiority? In many cases a physical defect may serve as a foundation for excessive feelings of inferiority. The individual who has crossed eyes, a harelip, a hunched back, defective hearing, or who is crippled, does have a physical defect. That is a fact, but it is not a fact that an obvious physical defect leads to inferior attainments in all fields of endeavor. If possible, the defect should be corrected. If it cannot be corrected, the individual must face his situation squarely. He must recognize that he is not the only individual who has some physical defect. He must

SOME EMOTIONAL PROBLEMS OF ADOLESCENTS

realize that others have succeeded in spite of physical handicaps. He must understand that although he happens to be inferior in one physical way, he may be outstanding in other ways.

Sometimes there is no defective physical structure but merely an unusual physical development. A boy may happen to be of very small physical stature. Although he may not be able to make a varsity athletic team, he need not feel excessively inferior. One high school student, who described himself as a "runt," desired to play football, which was out of the question. Nevertheless, he went out for football practice. He listened to all the coach's instructions. He studied rule books and books on techniques of playing. He became a local authority on football. Members of the team came to him for advice on the interpretation of rules. He planned some of the plays the team used. Whenever the coach could not be present at practice, this "runt" took charge. At the end of the season he was awarded an honorary athletic letter and was recognized as the one individual who had done most to ensure success for the team. Because he was physically small, he might have felt inferior to others, but he didn't. He chose a special field in which he could be superior.

Often high school students are unnecessarily concerned about what seems to them to be abnormal physical development. An individual who is smaller or larger than his classmates at one time may not always be so. During late elementary or high school years, most individuals take a rather sudden spurt in growth. A girl may gain her full height before some of the boys in her class catch up with or surpass her in size. A boy may be slow in growing. Neither boys nor girls should worry about differences in height.

Not every student can play on the varsity team, but every student can find some extracurricular activity in which he can excel. He may play in the band, he may be on the debating team, he may work on the school paper or yearbook.

How important are good looks? Sometimes girls feel that they are not attractive unless they resemble movie actresses or television stars. They forget that make-up artists and good photographers can work marvels and that these stars may not be so glamorous in private life.

The fact is, however, that some girls are too thin, too tall, too short, or too heavy to resemble the actresses they would like to resemble. Should this make them feel inferior in every way? No doubt they are superior to their film or television idols in many ways. Certainly in social adjustment and true happiness they may become greatly superior to some highly publicized stars. The girl who does not have the particular qualities of a film star should do all that she can to make herself attractive in her own right and in conformity with her own general personality pattern. She should strive to excel in some field or fields in which stunning or exotic or borrowed looks are not a necessity.

Some people delight in referring to companions by such nicknames as "Skinny," "Fatty," "Shorty," and so on. They say, "Oh, he doesn't mind being called 'Shorty.' " Possibly the person who is of short stature does not resent being called "Shorty." On the other hand, he may dislike the nickname more than anyone realizes. Such a nickname may tend to encourage feelings of inferiority. Those who apply uncomplimentary nicknames to others may be trying to make themselves feel superior by calling attention to inferiorities in others; they may be trying to cover their own feelings of inferiority. Persons who are thoughtful of others very seldom use taunting nicknames.

Members of Aspira (above) help prevent any feelings of inferiority among Puerto Ricans due to social prejudice by improving educational opportunities for Puerto Rican youths.

How does clothing affect feelings of inferiority? Clothing, as well as physical structure, has much to do with appearance. It is not strictly true that "clothes make the man." Nevertheless, clothing often does serve as a basis for excessive feelings of inferiority—or for feelings of self-confidence.

In choosing clothes, you may wish to follow these two fundamental principles: (1) clothing should be somewhat similar to that worn by most members of the social group to which you belong, and (2) there should be some element of individuality expressed in your clothing. Note that cost is not a necessary factor in either of these fundamental principles of dress. Sometimes young persons feel inferior because their clothing has not cost as much as the clothes worn by some of their companions. Such a feeling is unwarranted so long as the clothing has been chosen in accordance with the two basic principles listed above. Persons suffering from excessive feelings of inferiority tend to overdress. Those persons who do not feel inferior tend to dress in conformity with the standards set by their social group. Clothing may be formal or extremely casual. It may be quite different from clothing worn by the previous generation, but may resemble clothing worn by earlier generations or by persons of very different cultures.

Social prejudices can cause feelings of inferiority. Excessive feelings of inferiority may develop from social factors. In one study of college students it was found that 32 percent of the inferiority disturbances were attributed to social causes. Prejudices often develop against particular social groups. If a person happens to belong to a group against which prejudices have been formed, there is danger that he will develop excessive feelings of inferiority. Members of religious groups that happen to be in the minority anywhere and members of some nationalities (especially in time of war) must be constantly on guard not to develop feelings of inferiority that may spread to all their activities. They must face the unfortunate fact that unjust prejudices exist. Also, they can contribute and achieve much and even win great acclaim in spite of the handicaps that such prejudices impose.

Young persons may develop feelings of inferiority because they are not familiar with accepted forms of etiquette. Fortunately, the remedy in such cases is simple. High school and college libraries and public libraries contain books that tell how to act in various social situations. Time spent in studying such books, followed by practice of the principles they lay down, may bring an end to such feelings.

Should poor school marks be taken as a proof of inferiority? Sometimes students develop a feeling that they are inferior in every way if they cannot make high marks in all school subjects. Of course, relatively few individuals can earn the highest marks. If, despite doing his best, a student finds that he is not at the top in school marks, there is no need for a galling feeling of inferiority. There are many fields of human endeavor other than schoolwork in which he can be superior.

Sometimes college freshmen develop excessive feelings of inferiority because they are no longer the "bright and shining lights" that they were in their local high schools. They may give up and leave college. Probably the trouble is not that they are actually inferior as students. Competition is keener in college than in high school because high school students with the lowest grades tend not to go to college. Students who fail to recognize this fact may become emotionally disturbed in trying to meet the new demands and standards of college work. Poor adjustment rather than lack of ability may be responsible for their failure in college.

What are the symptoms of excessive feelings of inferiority? If we are able to recognize symptoms of excessive feelings of inferiority in ourselves, we can start to improve our outlook. If we recognize symptoms of excessive feelings of inferiority in our friends, we can do much to help them. The following are outstanding and common symptoms of excessive feelings of inferiority.

1. Seclusiveness and avoidance of social contacts

2. Envy of the social attainments and possessions of others

3. Excessive sensitivity to criticism (may even apply general social criticism to himself)

4. The frequent use of the phrases "I never had a chance" or "Other people always get the breaks"

5. Frequent pointing out of real or imaginary faults of others

6. Resentment on not winning in competitive games; charging unfairness on the part of the opponent or officials

7. Over-responsiveness to flattery and compliments

8. Excessive self-consciousness if required to appear before a group

9. Fear of attempting any activity in which success is not certain

10. Bullying younger or smaller persons (an attempt to secure a temporary feeling of superiority)

11. Boasting about personal accomplishments (another attempt to secure a temporary feeling of superiority)

12. Talking in a loud and impressive tone of voice to attract attention

13. Wearing flashy clothing or unusual hair styles to attract attention

14. Awkwardness and lack of poise in social situations

15. Resentment at any expression of social authority on the part of others

16. Girl wishing she had been born a boy because girls never have a chance; boy wishing he had been born a girl because girls have all the chances

17. Perfectionistic behavior—doing a given bit of work over and over again, even after it has been done as well as possible; a vain striving after unattainable perfection

18. Excessive compensating behavior, such as the student who studies excessively because he feels inferior in athletics or the athlete who trains excessively because he feels inferior in classroom work. However, compensating behavior may be highly desirable. Much of the great literary and scientific progress of the world has been accomplished by individuals who were compensating for feelings of inferiority. If a person is happy in his work, such compensation shows a desirable adjustment to life.

Daydreaming

Excessive feelings of inferiority may be followed by daydreaming, although not all daydreaming is a way of compensating or an escape from reality.

How common is daydreaming? A psychologist questioned a group of college students about their habits of daydreaming. He found that only about 2 percent reported no recent daydreams. Approximately half the group reported that within the past month they had had repeated daydreams. Another psychologist asked college students whether or not they daydreamed frequently. Sixty-nine percent responded in the affirmative. In still another case a psychologist questioned 1475 persons, ranging in age from seven to twenty-one and beyond. All but two or three of this large group reported daydreaming.

Daydreaming during adolescence is normal, as long as the individual does not spend too much time in daydreaming.

When does daydreaming become undesirable? Imagination may be very constructive and helpful to a young person, but sometimes imagination takes nonconstructive forms. The wishful-thinking kind of daydream is often a reaction to feelings of frustration. Instead of leading to action, such daydreams become ends in themselves. The individual is so satisfied with daydreaming that he is a major-league baseball player that he does not bother to go out for his school baseball team. Content with imagining that he is a talented actor, he does not try out for a part in his school play. He daydreams that he is very popular and has dozens and dozens of friends. His visions are so satisfying that he does not feel it necessary to develop a pleasing personality in order to win and hold real friends.

We will give special attention to two forms that daydreaming often takes, to help enable you to evaluate your own daydreams.

The "conquering hero" daydream. Psychologists give the name "conquering hero" to daydreams in which the individual imagines himself performing great deeds while an appreciative audience applauds. A boy wishes to become a great musician. One day his music teacher criticizes his playing technique. Instead of going to the work of practicing to correct the error, he indulges in a wishful daydream.

He imagines himself practicing his music lesson. A world-famous musician happens to be in town, and while strolling down the street this great musician hears the sweet strains of our hero's music practice. Recognizing talent immediately, he rushes to the door and asks to see the budding musical genius. The great musician is so charmed by the technique that he arranges to give free lessons.

In a short time our hero finds himself on the concert stage. An audience is held spellbound by his playing. He studies under other great masters and becomes famous all over America and throughout the world.

Finally he decides to give his home town a break. He returns home for a visit. The whole town is waiting at the airport to greet him. The high school band is playing as the plane rolls to a stop. As he steps out, photographic bulbs flash and television cameras grind. He glances over the applauding crowd and notes his former music teacher, the one who had had the nerve to criticize his technique. He generously bestows a forced smile on this amateur musician. The "conquering hero" has come home.

His beautiful daydream is so satisfying that our hero feels it unnecessary to practice his music. As a result, at the next lesson his technique is poorer than before. Instead of practicing, he indulges in the daydream again and again. Finally he ceases taking music lessons. He drops out of the high school band. His musical career is ended, except in his daydreams, where he imagines the musician he wishes he might be—and never will be.

To take another example, the daydreamer may see herself walking down the aisle toward a handsome young man while the organ plays a wedding march. She has "conquered" in matters of love. Such a dream may be so pleasant that the dreamer does not bother to make social contacts that might eventually lead to a happy marriage.

The "suffering hero" daydream. All daydream heroes are not conquering heroes. Sometimes they are suffering heroes. The daydream takes the form of self-pity, from which the sufferer derives considerable satisfaction.

A high school girl once related the following daydream. In the elementary school that she attended the teacher made pupils stand on their chairs as punishment for misconduct. The other children were permitted to laugh at the child being punished. (The teacher who used this form of punishment certainly did not know very much about educational psychology.)

Evidently our heroine was not a model pupil from the teacher's point of view, for frequently she had to undergo the humiliating and tiresome experience of standing on her chair. She came to think of herself as a martyr suffering under the tyranny of the teacher. In her daydreams the chair on which she was standing suddenly broke. She fell to the floor. Her leg was broken. The teacher cried, "Oh, you poor little thing!" Then our heroine was picked up tenderly and taken home. A physician set the leg and chastised the teacher for making children stand on their chairs. Each day for weeks the teacher brought our suffering heroine candy and flowers. The other school children sent her presents. Everyone showered her with sympathy.

Perhaps a young man has had a misunderstanding with his girl friend. Of course, this is a very unpleasant experience. In his daydream he sees her crossing a street. A speeding car is bearing down on her, but she does not see it. Our hero dashes into the street and shoves her to one side just in time, but alas, too late for himself! The car strikes him. An ambulance comes. He sees the girl wringing her hands in agony as he is gently placed in the ambulance and rushed to the hospital. Hours later he is in a hospital room filled with flowers (most of them from the girl friend), but he is not long for this world. Our "suffering hero" has given his all for a girl who did not appreciate him until it was too late. The daydream is so painfully pleasant that he does not bother either to correct the misunderstanding or to find a new girl friend.

In these illustrations the daydreamers invent their own dreams. Some persons do not bother to invent dreams of their own but use ready-made daydreams. They take a story from a thrilling film, novel, or love-story magazine and identify themselves with the hero or heroine of the romantic tale.

How useful are daydreams? Daydreams that lead to action can be very useful. In many ways daydreaming is a form of planning. The high school student may daydream about his later college, vocational, marital, and social successes. As long as he works toward the fulfillment of these successes, his daydreams are contructive.

"Suffering hero" daydreams, however, are not constructive. Some persons derive so much enjoyment from being suffering heroes in their daydreams that they go on to actual suffering, although not as heroes. Young persons have been known to inflict injury on themselves and even to attempt suicide to arouse sympathy. When such a thing does happen, instead of becoming a hero, the individual is more likely to arouse pity.

From the point of view of behavioral adjustment the "conquering hero" daydream is more wholesome than the "suffering hero" daydream. However, the conquering hero must continually check on himself by asking, "Is this daydreaming an end in itself, or is it leading me to action that will make me the successful person I dream of being?"

Thrills and Thrill-Seeking

Young persons often find life very thrilling. Older persons often wish that they could return to the thrilling days of youth. Thrilling situations are noted for arousing emotions. They can also lead to emotional problems during adolescence.

What makes a situation thrilling? The basic characteristic of a thrill is suspense. In a thrilling situation there is a possibility of danger or risk, but at the same time there is a chance of escape or winning—of coming out ahead. For the most part, suspense results in a rather sudden, intense, and pleasant emotional experience. We sometimes take deliberate chances in order to have the resulting pleasant emotional experience. A person may go to a race and be thrilled while watching a reckless driver because there is a chance that the driver might be killed or injured, but there is also a chance that he might come through his reckless driving alive and uninjured. A well-adjusted person who knew with certainty that the driver was going to be killed would find the race horrifying, not thrilling.

Taking a chance. As used popularly, the word "chance" implies an agency of some kind that unpredictably governs the course of events. It is a kind of "fate." We have an automobile accident. We say that it was a matter of chance. If we had taken another road, or started five minutes earlier or later, the accident would not have happened. Of course this is true, yet there is the possibility that if

299

we had taken the other road or started earlier or later, we might have had a more serious accident. Often "chance" is used to rationalize carelessness or bad planning.

"Chance" has another meaning. It is the theoretical probability of some occurrence, mathematically calculated in the light of related past experiences. It denotes a calculated risk. On the basis of carefully collected data, the actuary is able to compute just what the mathematical probability is that a given individual will live to a certain age. Life insurance rates are based on such chance. Accident insurance is also based on calculated chance. Driving at excessively high speed may be thrilling for a driver or those watching him, but the event is not thrilling to the automobile and life insurance companies. The driver is just a cold statistic on which they have calculated.

Here Evel Knievel jumps his motorcycle 100 feet in the air between two ramps. Would the event be as thrilling if there were no risk?

Why do people take chances? People take chances on events that they cannot control or do not try to control. Scientific experiments, including those in psychology, are very interesting, but the scientist would not ordinarily say that he is thrilled by his experiments. He takes every precaution to control as many factors as possible (except the independent variable). As little as possible is left to chance. The child playing with his toy chemistry set is probably much more thrilled as he dumps the contents of one bottle into another than is the research chemist at work in his laboratory.

In many ordinary events of life there are so many factors we do not know how to control that outcomes are often thought of as chance events. Young people are often willing to take chances in such life situations. Perhaps you feel that if you make a mistake, you have plenty of time to try again, at which time you will control factors you did not control the first time. This is often true, although there are cases in which the taking of the chance proves to be a fatal error. Perhaps you take a chance because you have not yet had enough experience to realize the possible and even probable outcomes of certain factors involved in the risk. Perhaps, as we saw earlier in this chapter, you take chances because you have been made to feel inferior. If you take a chance and win, you can feel superior.

Slow, steady progress is made by persons who calculate the risk as carefully as possible and plan accordingly. It must be admitted, however, that sometimes progress is furthered by those who are willing to take a chance involving quite a number of uncertain factors. Early in the morning on May 20, 1927, a young man started out to fly across the Atlantic. He had prepared for the trip, but, nevertheless, he knew there were chances of failure. Although he had studied weather conditions, sometimes storms developed unexpectedly. Other pilots at the same field were not willing to take the chance that day. This particular young pilot had a good engine, which had been carefully tested, yet sometimes even the best of engines break down. He was a well-trained pilot, but he had with him no copilot to take over in case of personal emergency. This young pilot might have gone down in mid-ocean, but Charles Lindbergh took a chance and won, and the civilized world was thrilled. He won, and aviation advanced.

For ages man has dreamed of traveling to the moon, but the odds against such a trip were very great. With the development of scientific knowledge and space exploration, the risk became less. Yet in spite of all precautions there was a chance that things could go wrong. Finally, successful trips were made around the moon. Then man actually walked and traveled by vehicle on the moon's surface. Chances had been taken. People all over the world were thrilled.

The person who never experiences thrilling situations is not enjoying good mental health. Life involves taking chances. Some of the chances can be calculated or estimated in advance. Some situations involve so many variables that we speak of luck. If we are lucky and win, we are pleasantly thrilled. A person should do what he can to control as many variables in his life as possible, but he should not worry about losing or be too depressed if he does lose. If he has controlled as many variables as possible, he can enjoy the thrills that accompany successes.

Now we will consider a form of chance-taking, a means of securing a thrill, in which many young persons—and older ones, too—engage. We will discuss gambling.

Why do people gamble? If asked why they gamble, most persons would probably say that they gamble in the hope of winning money or other prizes—that is, in the hope of increasing their income. Gambling may take the form of trying to get something expensive at a low price.

Young persons often feel the need for more income than they have so that they can expand their social activities or obtain much-desired possessions. Gambling looks to them like an easy solution to the problem. The young person may not know how to manage such income as he has and may waste much of his money. In the hope of recovering his losses, he may resort to gambling.

Gambling is partly a matter of thrill. No one gambles on an event if the outcome is absolutely certain. No one would put a nickel in a slot machine if he knew for sure that he would lose it, although the chances of doing so are always great. In case he does hit the jackpot, he is thrilled (and probably puts the money right back in the machine and loses it).

You do not buy "bargains" if you are sure that the quality is poor, but you will be quite thrilled if you do succeed in buying at a low cost something which may have a much higher value. We all tend to feel that there is a chance we may be lucky.

In one experiment 344 students were given four tests in different subject-matter fields. A gambling score was computed by permitting each student to ask for 2, 3, or 4 points for each question answered correctly. Twice the number asked was deducted if the question was answered incorrectly. Boys consistently had higher gambling scores than girls. But both sexes tended to gamble more on unfamiliar than on familiar material, hoping for an improbable lucky guess.

Gambling may give a person a temporary feeling of superiority. When others watch him play, he hopes that they are admiring his daring. In case he wins, he enjoys the admiration and envy of his companions. The purchase of a bargain gives the buyer an opportunity to feel superior. He feels that he is a clever buyer.

Pure gambling is the betting of money or something else of value on an outcome governed purely by chance. Betting on the throw of a pair of dice may be pure gambling. We know from the mathematics of chance that certain combinations can be expected to appear a given percentage of the time in a large number of throws of the dice.

Much gambling involves both chance and intellectual cleverness or manual skill. Some people bet on basketball games. Elements of chance or luck are involved, but they are also betting on their cleverness in observing the abilities shown by the two teams in past games. An individual may bet on his skill in playing such a game as billiards, or he may bet on the outcome of a game of cards.

A person who bets his money on pure gambling schemes will neither lose nor win money in the long run, according to mathematical probability. In professional gambling the bettor usually has less than a 50–50 chance of winning. In most gambling establishments the management knows exactly its mathematical advantage and how much it will earn in the long run. Records are kept so that if there is a deviation from the expectancy of chance, the odds can be corrected. If a player cares to do so, he can calculate his chance of losing.

Even in gambling that seems to be based on skill, such as tossing pennies into a bowl, operators of gambling establishments make sure that they will win. Is there much thrill involved in gambling where the player is sure to lose in the long run?

Although compulsive gambling does not have the physiological involvement of alcohol and drugs, it is really a kind of addiction. The compulsive gambler refuses to face the reality of the odds that are against him. He is constantly tense, even though he is able to keep a "poker face." He does not seem to be able to quit when he is ahead.

Gambling is learned behavior, involving intermittent reinforcement (reward given at uneven intervals), and learning by such reinforcement is very resistant to extinction.

Family Conflicts

A common source of emotional difficulties for many adolescents may be found in the family. Since there are dangers of conflict in any social situation, it is not surprising to find some conflicts developing within home circles. Nevertheless, the majority of young people seem to get along fairly well with their parents, brothers, and sisters.

Subjects on which adolescents and their parents disagree. A number of studies have been made of the sources of conflict between high school students and their parents. Since most of the studies are in rather close agreement, only one will be mentioned in detail.

In a nationwide survey high school students were asked to indicate the ways in which they disagreed with their parents. Some of the data are indicated in the table on page 303. Are some of these problems similar to yours? Are there other problems that you would like to add to the list? How do you account for the difference in percentages for boys and girls? Don't overlook the fact that for none of the circumstances mentioned did as many as one-fifth of all the boys and girls come into conflict with their parents.

Why do adolescents "fight" with their brothers and sisters? Psychologists use the term SIBLING RIVALRY to refer to the inability of one child to share affection with his or her brothers and sisters. There is competition between a given child and his siblings for material things, such as toys. More important, there is competition for the time, praise, and attention of the parents and other relatives. Probably the child is not aware of this competition as such, but once in a while a direct conflict flares up. There is a fight.

If you have brothers and sisters, you have probably had some spats with them. Perhaps you have felt guilty following such emotional upsets. You know that, basically, you loved them, but.... As with other human relations, your adjustment with your siblings will be helped if you stop to consider some of the psychological factors that may be involved.

Just now, you are trying to establish your place in life as an adult. Because you may feel insecure at this time, rivalry with your siblings may increase. It is comforting to know that as you grow older, there will probably be less conflict with your brothers and sisters and more open affection for them. At one time a group of college students was asked, "Do you have any conflicts with a brother or sister now?" Less than a third of them said, "Yes." Don't you think far more than a third had such conflicts when they were younger? Don't you think even fewer of them will have conflicts as they become still older and establish homes of their own?

Percentage of Adolescents Who Reported the Following Sources of Conflict with Their Parents

SOURCE OF CONFLICT	PERCENT OF BOYS	PERCENT OF GIRLS	TOTAL
Parents too strict about my going out at night	16%	19%	18%
Parents too strict about family car	24	9	16
Family always worried about money	15	15	15
Parents too strict about dating	8	17	13
Parents interfere in my choice of friends	10	15	13
Parents nag about studying	16	10	13
Parents hate to admit I'm sometimes right	13	13	13
Parents too strict about dates on school nights	10	13	12
Wish parents would treat me like a grown-up	10	14	12
Parents interfere with spending money I earn	15	7	11
Parents play favorites	8	12	10

Most older persons have a great deal to contribute. A grandmother, for instance, can bring her grandchild to the park for an afternoon. She can take care of him, and they can have an enjoyable time together.

Why is old age often a personal problem for young people? Many young people are faced with the problem of having grandparents or other older persons in their homes. This may or may not cause difficulty in family adjustments. The older people may do much to help in the work of the home. On the other hand, they may cause conflicts. In one study of 193 men and women with a median age of seventy-four years, it was found that one-third expected their grown, married children to obey them. Thirty percent believed that they should interfere in the training of their grandchildren. The grandchildren were placed in the difficult position of wishing to please their parents and their grandparents. The parents were placed in the difficult position of wishing to please their parents and their children. Such difficulties can result in emotional disturbances.

The older person in the home may present financial problems. The family budget may have to be stretched to include food, clothing, and medical care for the older members. This means less money for the younger members of the family, which may become a source of tension.

How can you assist the older person? It is very important to make older persons feel wanted and useful. As a child, if you ever felt unwanted and in the way, you have some idea of how older people feel. Old people do not wish to sit around and do nothing but rest. They can and should do useful work, even though they can't do it with your speed and accuracy. You will be helping the grandparents in your home if you remind them of what they can do rather than of what they cannot do.

Basically, the greatest thing you can do for older persons is to show them your love and approval. Most of your adventures are still to come; most of theirs are behind them.

Dating and Romantic Love

Probably any dates that you may have are affective experiences. They may range anywhere from mildly to intensely pleasant or anywhere from mildly to intensely unpleasant. Romantic love is a pleasant, usually ardent, emotional state.

No doubt you have had older adults talk to you, formally or informally, about dating and romantic love, and have participated in group discussions of these topics. We will not duplicate such material here but will consider aspects of these topics from the psychologist's point of view.

Dating. Some young people begin dating while still in elementary school or junior high school. The practice becomes more and more common in high school and in the years immediately following high school. Then marriage follows for most people. According to the love stories in many popular magazines, novels, films, and television programs, dating is practiced by all young people. According to popular fiction, there are amusing and sometimes confusing incidents, but, on the whole, everyone is having a marvelous time. There is factual evidence to the contrary, however. Dating can involve disturbing emotional problems.

What does dating accomplish? From the psychologist's viewpoint, a good deal of the behavior involved in dating and romantic love can be explained in terms of a learning process (although biological factors also enter in). Two individuals meet on a date. They mutually reinforce each other's behavior. They "fall in love." Dating can provide an opportunity for two individuals to learn to love each other.

There are a variety of dating customs in which individuals can learn to love. In some parts of the world chaperoned dating is still the accepted custom. A parent, some other older relative of the girl, or a trusted friend of the family usually accompanies the couple whenever they go out together. Within these dating customs young people learn to love each other, to marry, and to raise a family.

There is a reason behind customs that put restrictions on dating. For quite a few years parents have made decisions affecting the behavior of their children and then assisted their children in making their own decisions. Most parents believe that such assistance should not suddenly come to an end when their sons and daughters begin dating, even though their adolescent offspring often do not appreciate this assistance when it comes in the form of restrictions.

Customs of dating have changed greatly in the United States during the past century, especially in recent years. You might ask your parents, grandparents, or other older married persons what dating was like when they were your age. If views that seemed modern to them seem dated to you, remember that someday your adolescent children will probably resist your attempts to assist them and will consider you old-fashioned.

How would you like to have an electronic computer arrange a date for you? We usually think of the high school and college student as having many opportunities to meet members of the other sex and to arrange dates with more or less ease. In very large high schools and universities, although there are many members of the opposite sex in attendance, social contacts leading to dating may be more limited than in smaller schools. After graduation from school or college, the meeting of suitable dating partners often becomes a difficult problem. Dating clubs under various names are formed and sometimes requests for dating partners are placed in the "personal" columns of newspapers.

Today the electronic computer can be used for matching dating partners. For example, in one instance over 300 couples were formed for a university dance by matching the characteristics each individual considered most desirable in the other sex with individuals who possessed such characteristics. Most of the male students considered the physical attractiveness of women to be very important. The female students sought socially desirable qualities, such as the same race and religion. Also, the women were more interested than the men in high scholastic ability and stylish clothing.

Following the dates, the students were asked how satisfied they were with their computer-selected partners. Female students were less satisfied than male students. For example, 51.6 percent of the women said that their computer-selected dates had absolutely no romantic attraction for them. On the other hand, only 37.8 percent of the men said that their partners had absolutely no romantic attraction for them and they would not enjoy additional dates with that person.

Are you surprised that the computer technique of arranging dates was so inefficient? Perhaps not enough truly basic characteristics were fed into the computer. Or perhaps both the men and the women did not find the computer-arranged dates as exciting as dates made in the usual way—maybe the computer-arranged dates did not begin with as much physiological arousal. Also, the evaluations of the selected partners were made after just one date. Had the couples agreed to have a number of dates with the computer-selected partner there might have been more opportunity for learning to like or love each other.

If your school system has computer services, would you favor trying out matching for dates on the basis of data fed into the computer? Or, lacking computer facilities, how would you feel about matching partners objectively on the basis of information recorded on cards by a disinterested person who would not know the names of the persons at the time of matching?

Are boy-girl relationships changing? A common parental lecture often begins with, "Now when I was your age...." Are patterns of boy-girl relationships really changing, as parents imply? Fortunately we do have some data on this topic. Back in 1942, students in grades six, nine, and twelve were asked to indicate whom they would select as a companion in nine different social relationships: (1) to occupy the next seat in class, (2) to attend a movie, (3) to go for a walk, (4) to go skating, (5) to make a model of something, (6) to play outdoors, (7) to play indoor games, (8) to study schoolwork, (9) to read for fun. The survey was repeated twenty-three years later in 1965, using the same questions. Part of the data are given in the table below.

Percentage of Boys and Girls in Three Grades Who Chose the Other Sex as Desired Companions

	GRADES 6	9	12
Boys choosing girls			
1942	45%	72%	75%
1965	49	80	91
Girls choosing boys			
1942	39	60	63
1965	53	73	83

Reading the table horizontally, you can see that interest in the companionship of the other sex increased as students became more mature. Comparing the 1942 and 1965 percentages for both sexes and for all three grades, you will note that in each combination students were more sex conscious in 1965 than in 1942. Your parents might be interested in the comparison.

Do you think data collected today would be different from data collected in 1965? Why not make a survey in your school system, or at least the twelfth grade of your high school?

Some characteristics of romantic love. How does a person know that he is in love? Although there is no simple answer, a person romantically in love usually displays most of the following characteristics.

1. There is a strong physical attraction.

2. The individual believes that this love is forever; it is the "real thing" at last.

3. Blissful daydreaming about the loved one is common.

4. The individual is willing to make any sacrifice to win the love of the beloved. He or she is willing to reform, to turn over a new leaf.

5. The beloved is idealized. He or she is thought to be incapable of any but the most noble thoughts and deeds. There tends to be a complete glossing over of any faults or deficiencies that the beloved may have.

6. Jealousy is often present. In one study of adolescents in love, 34 percent of the sources of their conflicts were found to be matters of jealousy or possessiveness.

7. Separation or anything else that interferes with the romance is very painful to the lovers.

8. There may be some quarreling. If lovers learn to quarrel, they will probably continue to do so after marriage. An occasional spat, however, should not be taken too seriously.

9. In our culture the boy tends to dominate the courting situation, while the girl displays a certain amount of coyness and reserve. There are indications, however, that girls are beginning to play a more active role in courtship, and in some cases are taking the initiative.

These two people seem to be romantically in love. Have you ever been in love? How did you know that you were? Did you experience any characteristics of romantic love not listed here?

Physiology and love. We have said that psychologists tend to explain romantic love largely as a learning experience. Recently psychologists have begun to study romantic love in terms of physiology as well as in terms of learning.

A leading psychologist has suggested that there are two basic components of any emotion, including romantic love: (1) physiological arousal, and (2) interpretation of such arousal. Neither one alone is sufficient to produce emotion, such as the emotional experience that we call romantic love. Undifferentiated physiological responses seem to determine the intensity of an emotional experience. But the quality—which emotion it is—seems to be determined by thought processes, by the individual's interpretation of the physiological processes taking place in the body.

This relationship between physiological responses and the interpretation of them was tested in an experiment in which subjects were given an injection of "Suproxin." The subjects were told that Suproxin was being used in an experiment to test the effect of the drug on vision. One group of subjects was actually given an injection of Suproxin, a fictitious name for an adrenalinelike drug that tends to bring about such physiological changes as increased heart rate, a flushed feeling, increased rate of breathing, and tremor. A control group of subjects, who also thought they were getting Suproxin, was given a placebo instead—they received a nondrug that produced no physiological arousal.

The subjects who actually received Suproxin were then divided into three subgroups. For one subgroup, the psychologist explained the bodily reactions to be expected from the adrenalinelike injection. Another subgroup was told that the drug would have no noticeable side effect on their bodies. A third subgroup was told that the drug would produce such side effects as numbness, a slight headache, and itching.

While the subjects waited in a room for the Suproxin to take effect, they met another student who apparently was going to participate in the same experiment. In reality, the other student was a confederate of the experimenter. For half of the subjects he acted very happy, and for the other half he acted as though he were very irritated and angry. Members of the first subgroup, to whom the true effects of the drug had been explained, later reported that they had been neither happy nor angry as a consequence of the behavior of the confederate. Members of the two subgroups who had been given the Suproxin but had been given no explanation of its effects or had been given an incorrect explanation were asked to report how they felt after being in the room with the confederate student. Those who were in the room when the confederate played an angry role reported that they had become angry as a consequence of the Suproxin. Those who were in the room with the confederate when he played a happy role reported that they felt happy as a consequence of the Suproxin. Thus individuals with the same physiological arousal reported happiness or anger, depending on the social situation and their interpretation of that situation.

It should be added that members of the control group who were given a placebo were subjected to the confederate who played a happy role for half of them and an angry role for half of them. They reported that they were neither happy nor angry as a result of the behavior of the confederate. It would seem, then, that both physiological arousal and interpretation of that arousal are essential to an emotional experience.

In another experiment involving physiological arousal and thought processes, male subjects were told that they would soon receive three "pretty stiff" electrical shocks. A bit later the experimenter told half of the group that an error had been made in explaining the experimental procedure and that they would not be given any shocks. Nothing was said about a shock to a third group of men, the control group. Next, each of the men in the three groups was introduced to a young woman and soon after was asked to indicate how much he liked her. Both those who expected to be given an electrical shock and those who thought an error had been made and they would not be shocked after all indicated a greater liking for the young woman than did the men in the control group. Evidently the physiological arousal resulting from fear and the physiological arousal resulting from relief from fear both increased the interpretation of attractiveness, as compared to the control group.

Would you agree that romantic love is more likely if an individual has been aroused by either anger and fear or by excitement and joy than if he or she has not been physiologically aroused at all? According to the studies just mentioned, physiological arousal, whether negative or positive, is an important part of producing an emotion such as romantic love. Some girls believe that the path to romance is best achieved by playing hard-to-get. Such rejection produces physiological arousal and so may intensify the boy's love. Other girls believe that the path to romance is best achieved by being friendly and affectionate. Here again there is physiological arousal and so there may be an intensification of the boy's love. Some boys will be attracted by one emotional technique and some by the other technique, depending on the general personality of the boy. Some boys may not be aroused by either technique.

Love at first sight. Occasionally a man and woman do seem to "fall in love" the first time they meet. Perhaps at the time of their first meeting each had recently been physiologically aroused by experiences leading to an emotional state such as anger, fear, or happiness. Each interpreted the physiological condition of his or her body as love. Then they continued to meet each other and thus reinforced each other's romantic behavior.

Probably most adults have had several experiences of falling in love at first sight. Each of us builds up ideals in connection with romantic love, and when we meet someone of the other sex, we measure that person in terms of our ideals. If this first rough measure shows that the person does not meet our ideals, we do not continue our relationship with him or her, and the process of reinforcement does not go on with that person. If the person continues to hold some attraction, we may learn to love him or her. Later we may look back on the beginning of the relationship as love at first sight.

Assuming the Roles of Men and Women

As we go through life we assume many roles. The word ROLE refers to the kind of behavior that society expects of an individual in a particular social situation. The doctor acts more or less as other doctors do, the housewife acts as she thinks most housewives do, the student tries to behave as he thinks typical students behave. Under a variety of circumstances, we each assume roles that we believe appropriate to our particular sex.

The learning of what is considered appropriate behavior for one's own sex helps to reduce anxiety for an individual because it enables him or her to know what to do under certain social conditions and even to know what to say at certain times. This feeling of security is especially important during adolescence.

What determines the male and female roles in a society? The roles that men and women in a society are expected to assume are determined in part by biological differences and in part by the culture. In the course of social development men have tended to do work requiring muscular strength, and women have tended to do work related to the home and the care of children. This division of roles reflects biological differences.

Cultural influences are especially important in determining the roles of each of the sexes. For example, although the woman is traditionally the homemaker, the man has traditionally assumed the more dominant role in the home. In our culture, man tends to dominate in other social situations as well. For instance, in the job world men often get better positions and better pay than do equally competent women.

From early in life into adult years there is a tendency for individuals in our society to prefer activities that are considered masculine. By the time children are in kindergarten and for the next few grades, boys show a much stronger preference for masculine than for feminine things. Furthermore, most girls show a greater preference for masculine than for feminine things. One study found that between 60 and 70 percent of the girls in the first four grades of school said they would rather work with building tools than with cooking and baking utensils.

In considering what is appropriate male behavior and what is appropriate female behavior we are likely to think in terms of our own society. It is important to remember that appropriate male and female behavior differs from one culture to another. In a well-known anthropological study of tribes in New Guinea, three quite different sex roles were found. In one tribe the behavior of men and women was much more similar than in our culture, and resembled our traditional concept of feminine behavior. Both sexes were gentle, mild, passive, and much interested in family life. In another tribe the behavior of both men and women was similar, and took the form of what we tend to call masculine behavior. Both sexes often displayed violent and aggressive behavior. In a third tribe, the sexes played dissimilar roles but it was the men who usually cared for the children and were submissive, whereas the women were quite aggressive and usually handled the business affairs.

Also, what is considered appropriate masculine and what is considered appropriate feminine hair styles and clothing differ from one culture to another, and from one period of time to another within the same culture. Should women or men have long hair? Should men or women, or both, wear pants? Should men or women wear lace and brightly colored clothing? You might examine illustrated history and travel books to compare the various styles for each sex at different periods in the past and at the present.

What changes are taking place in masculine and feminine roles? In spite of what has been said about the traditional roles of men and women in our society, there is evidence that within the past generation many changes have taken place in what is considered masculine and what is considered feminine behavior. The roles of the two sexes are tending to converge. Some schools now offer courses in cooking and child care for boys, and courses in home repairs for girls. Husbands often help with such household duties as dishwashing and housecleaning, especially if their wives hold jobs outside the home.

Today many women resent what they believe to be their inferior and subordinate roles as compared to men. One psychologist speaks

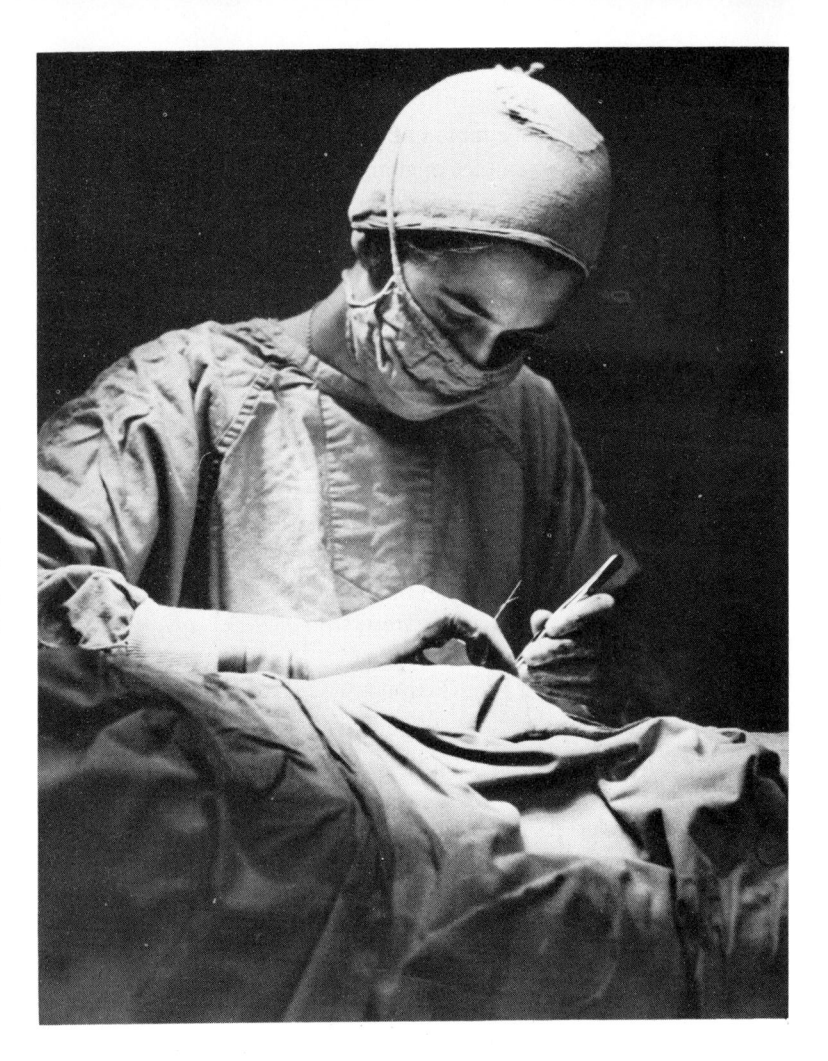

Masculine and feminine roles are changing. More women are demanding an equal right to enter many professions, such as surgery, that traditionally have been monopolized by men.

of the dehumanization of women, caused by men who consider them only as sex objects. Many women are organizing in an effort to gain equal recognition, and equal compensation, with men in business and in the professions. Some women prefer the title "Ms.," which refers to both single and married women, just as the title "Mr." refers to both single and married men.

In some societies that we may call primitive, the role of women is clearly defined in terms of marriage and the bearing of and caring for children. In our society the feminine role is less clearly defined, although to some people the woman who does not choose to marry is looked down upon, as is the woman who marries but for one reason or another does not have children. However, we know that the desire for children is not universal among women and that some women who have children resent them. There are also some individuals who believe that with the population explosion in the world today those women who do not have children may be doing society a service.

Although little girls often prefer "masculine" toys, they are still likely to be given dolls and domestic toys in preparation for their assumed traditional roles as mothers and housekeepers. Yet as they go through school

SOME EMOTIONAL PROBLEMS OF ADOLESCENTS

they learn of many jobs that appeal to them and may even seem quite glamorous. As the girls achieve maturity they may face a conflict between a desire for homemaking and a desire for a career in business or in a profession. Some women can do both successfully, although in the past cultural attitudes have often made it difficult for them to do so.

Especially for girls who have a more than average amount of formal schooling, a new feminine role seems to be emerging. Some women marry and have their children while still in their twenties, and are soon free to take a full- or part-time job. Some go back to college or a university, at least on a part-time basis, and work toward an undergraduate or graduate degree after their children are born. Others work and have children later.

Hopefully feelings of hostility between the sexes have not developed as a result of this discussion of male and female roles in our society. The discussion should lead instead to a better understanding of your own role and the role of the opposite sex. Perhaps as a result of the discussion you may wish to help promote attitudes favorable to equality of the sexes. What do you think should be the roles of men and women in our society?

Terms to Know

affective experience
chance
"conquering-hero" daydream
feelings
feelings of inferiority
role
romantic love
sibling rivalry
"suffering-hero" daydream

Topics to Think About

1. If you had to change roles with the opposite sex, what activities or behaviors would you like the most? Which ones would you like the least?

2. Suppose your right arm (or left arm, if you are left-handed) had to be amputated at the shoulder. In what ways would you overcome this physical handicap?

3. If you could choose the number, sex, and ages of your siblings, or to have none, what would you choose? Why?

4. What is your favorite daydream? Is it a "conquering-hero" or a "suffering-hero" daydream? What does it do for you?

5. Which do you find more thrilling, a game of chance that is based primarily on mathematical probability, such as the roulette wheel, or a form of gambling that involves skill also, such as poker? Why?

6. Should girls take the lead in asking for dates? If so, should they insist on paying for all, or at least half, of the expenses involved?

7. What is your idea of romantic love? Can you trace back to how you developed your views? Have they changed much in the past few years? If so, in what ways?

Suggestions for Activities

1. How do your problems compare with those of other young people? There are checklists or inventories that will assist you in answering this question. The following are recommended:

The Bell Adjustment Inventory (Student Form), Consulting Psychologists Press, 577 College Avenue, Palo Alto, Calif. 94306.

Elias Gabriel, *The Family Adjustment Test,* Psychometric Affiliates, Chicago Plaza, Brookport, Illinois 62910.

Mooney Problem Checklist (Level H is for senior high school), The Psychological Corporation, 304 East 45th Street, New York, N.Y. 10017.

Have your teacher order, as publishers do not sell directly to students.

2. Make a three-column table. In the first column jot down circumstances under which you feel inferior or ill at ease. In the second column indicate as frankly as you can why you feel inferior under each of these circumstances. In the third column indicate what you can do to overcome the feeling of inferiority in each case. If there is a handicap that cannot be overcome, indicate how you can compensate by superior achievement under other circumstances. Keep this information private.

3. On the basis of material in this chapter and other material brought out in class discussion, make up a list of complaints you have concerning family conflicts. Each member of the class should indicate on an unsigned slip which statements apply to him or her (√), do not apply (X), or possibly do not apply (?). You may wish to have the lists mimeographed in order to make a survey of the entire school. Each sheet should have a place for the respondent to indicate the sex and grade level, but with no names. The data so obtained can serve as a basis for class discussion and as a help in individual problem solving.

4. Assign a few students to participate in a role-playing situation concerned with some emotional problem common to many high school students—for example, the problem of where a girl should go on a date and what time she should be home. There might be four actors assigned to the roles of daughter, boyfriend, father, mother. Each actor should express himself as he would if he were actually in the situation and should react to the others not as actors, but as real-life characters in the situation. For example, the girl would try to think of the other actors as my father, my mother, my boyfriend. As the drama unfolds without script, or practice, are frustrations and conflicts brought into the open and frankly discussed? Are helpful suggestions made?

Some or all of the remainder of the class can make an interaction diagram for further study. In the example suggested, make four squares on a sheet of paper and label each with one of the roles. Every time one of the actors speaks to another actor, draw a line between the appropriate squares and indicate by an arrowhead the direction of the remark. For instance, in the illustration on page 314 the daughter addressed her remarks to her boyfriend twice, and he spoke to her once. She spoke to her father once, and her mother spoke to her three times. If you repeat the drama using four different actors, you will be able to make some very interesting comparisons.

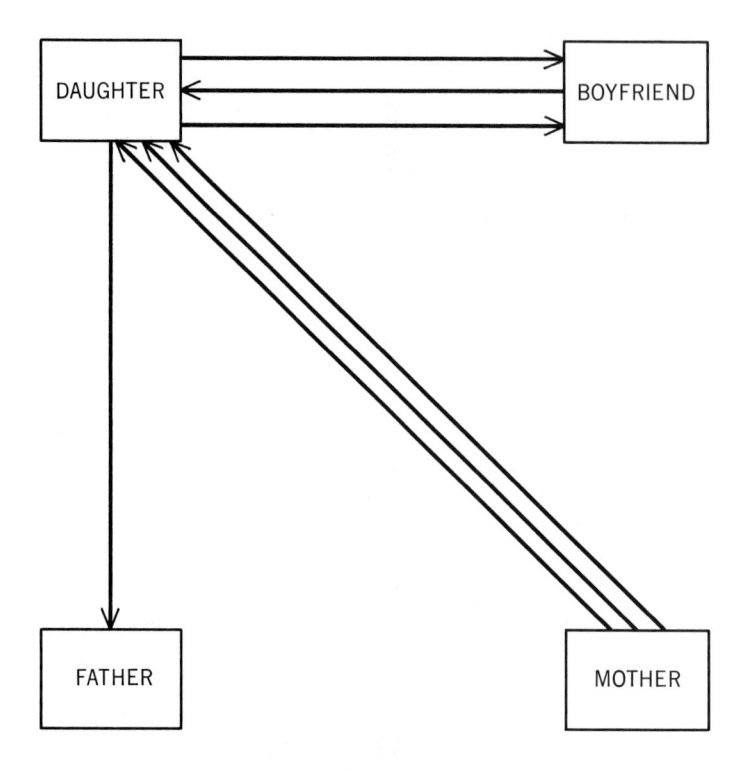

5. Some students might volunteer to ask their parents, or preferably their grandparents, about the rules they had to follow on dates. Compare these with the present-day variety of rules. Is there more or less freedom today in rules of dating? In what other areas of behavior are the young people of today given more freedom than their parents or grandparents?

6. If there are students in your school from another country, perhaps they would be willing to describe dating practices in their country, which might be quite different from those you follow. If no such persons are available, perhaps several students would volunteer to describe the rules for dating that their parents require them to follow, such as how late they are allowed to stay out during week nights and weekends; if they can travel to another city without permission from their parents, and if so, how far away from home; whether they have their own cars or how often they can borrow the family car for dating; and how frequently they can date.

7. The extent to which individuals look into each other's eyes has interested man for generations. Persons in love derive a great deal of pleasure from looking into each other's eyes. You might observe some couples who are engaged, or appear to be in love, and note how much time they spend looking into each other's eyes as they carry on a conversation. For a control, observe males and females who are friends, but are not in love, as they carry on a conversation. Then compare the amount of time these two groups spent looking into each other's eyes to the total time they spent in conversation. Do persons in love spend more time than others in gazing into each other's eyes?

Suggestions for Further Reading

Axline, Virginia, *Dibs: In Search of Self,* Houghton Mifflin (paperback, Ballantine). During his first years of life, Dibs was deprived of love but with help was able to overcome this handicap. Students report it is difficult to put this book aside once they have begun to read it, and they see in Dibs some of their own problems.

Hilgard, E. R., R. C. Atkinson, and Rita Atkinson, *Introduction to Psychology,* 5th ed., Harcourt Brace Jovanovich. See pages 87–94, the role of the adolescent; pages 95–112, the adult years; and pages 345–352, emotion and motivation.

Jenkins, Gladys G., and Joy Neuman, *How to Live with Parents,* Science Research Associates. A Guidance Series Booklet written for students in grades 9–12.

Kagan, J., M. M. Haith, and Catherine Caldwell (eds.), *Psychology: Adapted Readings,* Harcourt Brace Jovanovich. See Selection 21, "Fear in Sports Parachutists."

Ullman, Frances, *Getting Along with Brothers and Sisters,* Science Research Associates. A Guidance Series Booklet especially written for high school students.

Voeks, Virginia, *On Becoming an Educated Person,* 2nd ed., Saunders. Some college students suggest that this book should be required reading for all high school students planning to go to college. "It would save them a lot of time, tears, and traumatic experiences."

chapter 13
Behavior Disorders and Their Treatment

DID YOU EVER open a popular book on medicine, or even a book from a doctor's library, and discover that you had some of the symptoms of whatever disease was described on that page? Although the chances were very remote that you had that disease, you may have become unnecessarily concerned about your symptoms. Only your physician is in a position to determine whether or not you have the symptoms of a given illness. There is danger that as you read the symptoms of behavior disorders in this book and elsewhere, you will become unnecessarily and falsely alarmed. Don't try to diagnose yourself on the subject of behavior disorders! If you really believe that you are not in good mental health, go to a person trained to diagnose and treat such illness. You might consult your family doctor. If you really have a behavior disorder, he may diagnose and treat your difficulty, or he may suggest that you see a psychiatrist or clinical psychologist.

Behavior Disorders in Our Society

Most people have outbursts of emotions and yet they are still considered to be well adjusted, just as most people who are usually in good physical health develop colds, sore throats, headaches, and backaches at times during their life. Nevertheless, some individuals do develop behavior disorders and need to undergo treatment.

What is a behavior disorder? Perhaps the best way to answer this question is first to determine what is considered normal and abnormal behavior. We can define normal behavior in several ways: (1) statistically; (2) according to socially approved ways of behaving; and (3) by degree of individual impairment.

Defining normal behavior on a statistical basis means that if a large majority of persons exhibit that behavior, it is considered normal. However, a statistical definition alone is inadequate for our purposes since it means that a person with a high IQ would be abnormal, as would a tall or a short person. We must consider something in addition to a statistical definition because abnormal behavior is more than just the behavior of a minority number of people—it implies some degree of maladjustment. Furthermore, a statistical definition incorrectly suggests that there is a distinct dividing line between normal and abnormal behavior.

The society in which the person lives also may define normal and abnormal behavior. That is, if a majority of people in a specific society perform a certain behavior, it may be called normal. The society may label "abnormal" certain behavior that few of its members display. The disadvantage of this definition is that what is considered normal behavior will differ from society to society. What is looked upon as appropriate and sometimes even desirable behavior in one society may be condemned in another. There is no universal agreement that what one society does should occur in all societies.

Probably the most useful way of defining normal behavior, and thereby understanding the meaning of abnormal behavior and behavior disorders, is to consider the degree of impairment that the behavior has on the individual. For example, whether certain behavior is normal or abnormal might be determined by how much the behavior hinders persons from meeting everyday responsibilities, keeps them from developing their abilities, and causes harm to them or others.

Although it is difficult to draw a sharp line, psychologists sometimes speak of two kinds of behavior disorders: organic and functional. ORGANIC DISORDERS are those which can be attributed to known psychological causes, such as disease or injury to the nervous system, malfunctioning of glands, or toxic conditions in the body. FUNCTIONAL DISORDERS are those for which there are no clearly defined physiological causes. (There is, however, increasing evidence that chemical imbalances in the body may be involved in what had previously been thought of as functional disorders.) The so-called functional disorders are generally said to account for at least 95 percent of all mental illness cases.

How widespread are behavior disorders? It is difficult to determine the exact number of mentally ill persons in the United States, but it is estimated that at least one person in every ten has some form of mental disorder that requires psychiatric treatment. At least 50 percent of all general medical and surgical cases treated by private physicians and hospitals have a mental illness complication.

Where are all the persons with behavior disorders cared for? Many of them are in mental hospitals, although the number of patients in mental hospitals is decreasing, partially because of better techniques of treatment, such as the use of new drugs. A large number are being treated at mental health clinics. Also, some mentally ill persons are cared for, often inadequately, in prisons, infirmaries, nursing homes, their own homes, the homes of relatives, and various other institutions.

Mental illness occurs at all ages. Each year behavioral disorders are being detected and treated in very young children, as well as in thousands of adolescents. During World War II, one out of every eight men examined for the draft was not admitted to military service because he was not in sufficiently good mental health to adjust to military life.

What has been done to attack the problem of behavior disorders? With so many persons not enjoying good mental health, the need to remedy the social and personal problems of behavior disorders has become increasingly evident. Here we will look briefly at what some individuals and groups have done and are continuing to do to solve these serious problems.

In the earlier days of our country, conditions in "insane asylums" were very bad. Pioneer work in improving conditions was done between 1840 and 1881 by a schoolteacher, Dorothea Dix. She visited jails, asylums, and poorhouses and taught a Sunday school class in a women's prison. Shocked at the deplorable conditions she found, she determined to campaign for improvement. Through her efforts public interest was aroused and millions of dollars were raised to build suitable hospitals. A resolution presented by Congress in 1901 described her as "among the noblest examples of humanity in all history."

Another important figure was Clifford Beers, a man who experienced mental illness himself. On recovering, he determined to help others. In a famous book, *A Mind That Found Itself,* he described his own behavior disorder and the undesirable treatment he received in three typical institutions of that day. Beers succeeded in arousing the interest and assistance of many public-spirited citizens, including some professional men.

In 1909 Clifford Beers founded the National Committee for Mental Hygiene, an organization that has done much to promote mental health in the United States and even in other countries. It has now merged with other organizations to form the National Association for Mental Health. The purpose of this association is "to bring some few central truths of mental health to the attention of every person in the country; to see that psychiatric services are available at whatever level needed—mental hospitals, clinics, psychiatrically oriented teachers; to facilitate research on the whole problem of improving emotional health."

Other organizations such as the American Psychological Association, the American Psychiatric Association, and the American Psychoanalytic Association are attacking the problem of behavior disorders on a national level. There are state and local organizations for laymen and for professional workers that strive for the improvement of mental health.

Interest in mental hygiene and realization of the need for it have become so great that the United States Government has accepted responsibility for combating behavior disorders in the nation. In 1946 the National Mental Health Act was passed, the purpose of which is to reduce the amount of mental illness and give every citizen an opportunity to enjoy the best possible mental health. The United States Public Health Service, in carrying out the provisions of the National Health Act, is assisting the various states with their programs of mental hygiene, is sponsoring research into the basic problems of behavior disorders, and is assisting in the training of professional workers.

There has been a tremendous improvement in the handling of emotionally disturbed persons over the past few years. Many mental hospitals have increased their facilities to meet the recreational, educational, vocational, and therapeutic needs of patients. They now offer a larger variety of recreational activities and course work, which can be applied toward obtaining a high school or college diploma. They also help patients find a job after their release. In addition, the growth of mental health clinics in many communities has reduced the necessity of an individual becoming a patient in a mental hospital.

In modern psychiatric centers the bars are gone from the windows, the grounds are landscaped, and the treatment is more efficient than in the mental hospitals of 100 years ago.

Greater emphasis today is being placed on the early detection and prevention of behavior disorders. Attention has turned to emotional disorders in young children, recognizing that such disorders are likely to continue if not treated. There have been nationwide studies, campaigns, and community health programs to detect, and hopefully ultimately prevent, environmental conditions that give rise to behavior disorders in the lower socioeconomic classes. Although tremendous strides have been taken recently, the problems of behavior disorders are far from being solved.

There is a great need for trained individuals to work in hospitals and clinics. State and county hospitals need psychiatric aides to provide care and companionship for patients, recreational therapists to teach patients how to enjoy life through play, and occupational therapists to teach patients how to make and create something of their own and so relieve restlessness and discouragement. There is a great need for both men and women psychiatric social workers. Obviously, many clinical psychologists and psychiatrists are also needed.

Some of you may want to attack the problem of behavior disorders by serving as unpaid volunteer part-time workers in our hospitals and clinics; others may want to serve as salaried full-time workers. Some state hospitals will hire high school or college students for part-time work with mental patients. The basic need in attacking the problem of behavior disorders is for experimentation and research. For those of you with the desire and ability to be scientists, it is a great field of opportunity. Each of such professions as psychology, sociology, medicine, and pharmacology has highly trained men and women doing research in an attempt to bring about a better understanding of behavior disorders. As more and more research is done and brought together, great forward strides in diagnosis and therapy should result.

Neurotic Behavior

A neurotic (or psychoneurotic) person is one who is suffering from a mild form of behavior disorder and often requires professional help. In recent years there has been a growing tendency to avoid speaking of neurotic behavior as a form of mental illness. Nevertheless, we will discuss such behavior in this chapter, although it is not possible to describe all types of neuroses here.

The term NEUROSIS refers to certain kinds of maladjusted behavior most commonly characterized by anxiety and tension. The neurotic individual is restless and uneasy. He anticipates the future with considerable fear. Anxiety and tension are common among many persons. When they build up rather suddenly and last but a short time, that is popularly called "nervousness." The term "neurosis" is reserved for the case in which the anxiety and tension are chronic, or long-lasting.

What are the symptoms of neurosis? Although anxiety is the most prominent symptom of neurosis, there are others. Some neurotic people cannot seem to sit still; they fidget. They may show spasmodic twitchings of the face or other parts of the body, known as TICS. For example, they may grimace or blink the eyelids more frequently and rapidly than necessary. They may bite their nails, drum on the table with their fingers, tap on the floor with their feet, rub their hands together, or twist part of their clothing. At any sharp noise they are likely to jump violently. They may be very annoyed by any continuous noise, such as that of a running motor. They go around "with a chip on their shoulders" and make cutting remarks. If another driver puts a slight dent in the fender of such a person's car, the latter becomes emotionally upset and may cry or fume.

The neurotic person worries a great deal and lives in some dread of the future. He may be easily moved to tears. He may have a PHOBIA, an exaggerated and apparently unreasonable fear of a specific object or situation. He may have a fear of high places (acrophobia), or a fear of closed or confined places (claustrophobia). Often he does not get a normal amount of sleep. The term OBSESSIVE-COMPULSIVE refers to the behavior of neurotic persons beset by morbid, fixed, haunting ideas, such as the repeated memory of a near drowning.

The neurotic person often shows an exaggerated anxiety about his health and delights in telling friends about his pains. He complains of being tired much of the time, even when he has done practically no work. He may complain of stomach trouble and express a dislike for many foods. An individual who is preoccupied with bodily ailments and who exaggerates every trifling symptom is known as a HYPOCHONDRIAC.

Often the neurotic person doubts his own ability and finds it difficult to make decisions. For example, there is a record of a high school boy who had considerable difficulty with his schoolwork. He constantly felt uncertain about whether he understood what he read. If he came across a word and was not absolutely certain of the exact meaning, he looked it up in the dictionary. Then he would look up definitions of words within that definition—and then definitions of words within those definitions. At times it took him a half-hour to read one page. Of course, careful reading is a sign of a good student, and he should look up in a dictionary words with which he is not familiar. The point is that this boy doubted his own ability and could not decide what he really knew and what he did not know.

Although neurotics have symptoms that vary widely, and not all neurotic symptoms are found in any one case, neurotic persons do have some common symptoms. The symptoms shared by most neurotic individuals are feeling inadequate, tense, irritable, self-centered, and generally dissatisfied with their role in life, being rigid in their thinking, not realizing the inadequacy of their own nonintegrated behavior, and being unable to withstand much stress without becoming emotionally disturbed.

An obsessive-compulsive neurotic may have an irresistible urge to wash his or her hands. Such persons compulsively wash their hands at every opportunity, perhaps unconsciously attempting to cleanse themselves of unacceptable thoughts or overt behavior.

Such inadequate ways of behaving may lead to physical symptoms, such as high blood pressure. These physical symptoms may then cause the individual to worry, which could cause the physical symptoms to become more pronounced, thereby causing more worry, and so on. This situation is sometimes called a "vicious circle." If the symptoms release the individual from some unpleasant task, such as housework, a job, or schoolwork, they may promote the development of a neurotic illness still further.

What are the causes of neuroses? The words "neurosis" and "nervousness" may suggest to you some damage to or malfunctioning of the nerves, but such is not necessarily the case. Neurotic behavior is generally believed to be based on faulty emotional habits and attitudes rather than on organic disturbances. It is a problem of inadequate adjustment. In other words, a neurosis is a functional disorder. Nevertheless, physiological factors may contribute to the development of a neurosis. The human body is a very complicated organism, and all its parts interact. Sometimes one or more of the glands do not function properly, which may result in the development of neurotic patterns. The thyroid gland especially seems to be related to neurotic behavior.

If a person has some chronic physical disorder, such as arthritis, appendicitis, gallstones, or an abscessed tooth, he may show many of the symptoms that have been described. Have you noticed how easily you become irritated when you have a cinder in your eye? Anything that disturbs the smooth and orderly functioning of the body tends to produce anxiety and tension. A physician should make a careful check of the neurotic person and do what he can to correct any physical defects he may find.

Many times no physiological disturbance can be found in a neurotic person. His trouble usually stems from habits of thought rather than physical defects. He worries about things that cannot be helped. He is overconcerned with unimportant details. He tries to realize his ambitions in too short a time. He may even worry about the possibility of developing a severe mental disorder, although neuroses seldom develop into severe illnesses.

We will now examine four types of neurotic behavior: conversion reaction, dissociative reactions, anxiety reactions, and psychosomatic disorders.

BEHAVIOR DISORDERS AND THEIR TREATMENT **321**

Conversion reaction. Though less common today than earlier in the century, an especially interesting form of neurotic behavior is CONVERSION REACTION (or conversion hysteria), so-called because the individual's psychological disturbances are "converted" into bodily disturbances. For example, some soldiers in a war became "paralyzed" in their right hands. Being paralyzed, they could not shoot a gun. Hence, they had to leave the battlefront. When they were out of danger, the paralysis rapidly disappeared. Had these soldiers pretended to be paralyzed? In most cases, probably not. They were faced with a tremendous conflict: they wished to be brave soldiers, but at the same time they did not wish to die in battle. A soldier who is paralyzed cannot go into battle, nor can he be considered a coward.

Conversion reaction may take almost any form: jerking of various parts of the body, blindness, pains in various places, loss of sensitivity in various parts of the body, loss of speech, and so on.

Conversion reaction is probably learned behavior. Perhaps at some time an individual was faced with an unpleasant task and happened to develop a stomach ache, thus evading the task. Having a stomach ache was rewarded by getting out of something unpleasant. This may have happened several times. Soon the individual developed a stomach ache whenever he was faced with an unpleasant task, although he was not aware that the learning process had taken place.

Dissociative reactions. A DISSOCIATIVE REACTION is one in which the individual views parts of his activities as separate from his own personality. It represents an extreme form of repression. We will discuss only three dissociative reactions, although there are others, such as stupors and dream states.

One dissociative reaction is AMNESIA (am-'nē-zhə), or loss of memory. In general, such memory lapses occur in the area of the personal aspects of an individual's life. An individual may forget that he is married, has children, owns a home, and has a job, but he usually does not forget how to use a knife and fork, make change for a dollar, or correctly identify colors. In brain-damage cases, amnesia may represent actual permanent loss of memory.

A second dissociative reaction, FUGUE ('fyūg), occurs when the individual not only has amnesia but also engages in actual flight away from his usual geographical location. This condition applies to the individual who suddenly "wakes up" in a strange place, not knowing who he is or how he came to be there. Usually the person does not remember what has happened during his fugue, or flight away from home.

A third dissociative reaction, MULTIPLE PERSONALITY, involves the development of two or more usually independent and separate personalities within the same person. It occurs rarely. The most famous recent case is the one on which the movie *Three Faces of Eve* was based. The multiple-personality reaction attempts to satisfy opposite desires by developing two separate personalities, which possibly enable the person to avoid the guilt and confusion that would be present if only one personality existed. At some time we all have an impulse to act contrary to our usual behavior, but the neurotic develops inappropriate ways of handling such impulses.

Anxiety reactions. The main symptom of this neurotic behavior disorder is chronic, acute, diffuse anxiety. The anxiety may be "free-floating"—not attached to any specific object, event, or situation—or it may be "bound"

—attached to a specific object, event, or situation. Acute anxiety may suddenly appear and last for several hours or days, although the reason for the anxiety is often not readily observed or known.

An anxiety neurotic may find some relief from anxiety by becoming excessively concerned with his physical well-being through imaginary physical illnesses, or by exaggerating minor ailments, as in the case of the hypochondriac. By doing so he becomes occupied with thinking about his physical condition, which may reduce his awareness of the anxiety. He may also gain sympathy from others. Some neurotics constantly complain of being fatigued and unable to sleep, although there is nothing medically wrong with them. Such persons quite often have enough energy to perform those activities which they like, but use the symptoms to avoid those they do not like.

Psychosomatic disorders. In some cases individuals develop organic ailments attributed to emotional and other psychological causes. Such ailments often include actual damage to body tissue. These disorders are described as PSYCHOSOMATIC. Emotional factors, such as worry and anxiety, are known to be related to such ailments as high blood pressure, migraine headaches, ulcers, some skin diseases, asthma, and obesity (excessive overweight). Any treatment that helps to relieve emotional tensions also helps to relieve the organic damage, and, conversely, treatment that improves organic damage may alleviate emotional stress.

There is evidence from the laboratory as well as from clinical cases that emotional stress and peptic ulcers are related. In one experiment rats were kept in a cage for thirty days under stressful conditions. Food and water were available, but the floor around the food and water was kept constantly charged with electricity, except every forty-eighth hour, when the current was turned off. A rat could satisfy its hunger and thirst only by enduring shock, except for the one hour in forty-eight. The rat was faced with the conflict between desire for food and water and the desire to escape shock. Six of the nine rats subjected to this experimental procedure developed peptic ulcers. Of course, there was a control group of rats. Food and water were available to these rats for only one hour in forty-eight, but they were not subjected to shock at any time —they faced no conflict. These rats developed no ulcers.

In another experiment monkeys were used as subjects. One monkey was designated an "executive" monkey—he was responsible for what happened to another monkey. Both mon-

In this experiment of emotional stress and ulcers, only the "executive" monkey (on the left) could press a lever and prevent a shock to both animals. Under tension to perform, the "executive" monkey alone developed ulcers.

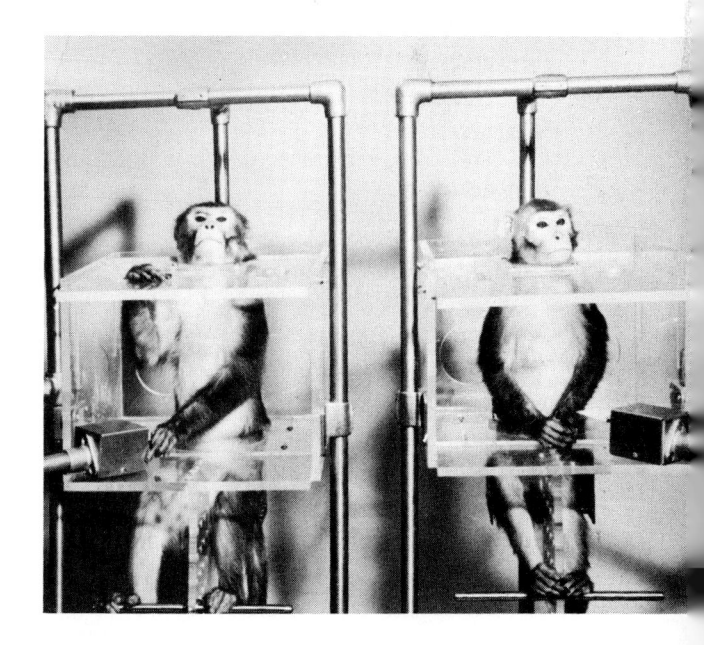

keys were placed in an apparatus where they could be given electric shocks every twenty seconds. However, both monkeys could avoid the shock if the "executive" monkey pressed a lever when a red warning light flashed. After twenty-three days of the experiment the "executive" monkey died, although he seemed to have been in good health at the beginning of the experiment. A postmortem examination revealed that he had a large ulcer. The other monkey remained in good health. In a second experiment the "executive" monkey did not die, but he did develop ulcers while his nonexecutive partner did not. The monkey receiving the shock without having control over decisions may have resigned himself to the fact that there was nothing he could do to prevent the shock, while the "executive" monkey had to keep making decisions.

It has been estimated that approximately half of all patients under a physician's care have illnesses precipitated by emotional stress, or psychosomatic illnesses.

Psychosis

Having briefly examined some mild behavior disorders known as neuroses, we will now discuss more severe forms of behavior disorders. As we consider the different forms of neuroses and psychoses, remember that it is often very difficult to distinguish between the different classifications, and psychologists do not always agree in diagnosing specific cases. Psychologists are much more interested in preventing and treating neuroses and psychoses than in attempting to classify individuals into categories.

What is a psychosis? Psychologists use the word PSYCHOSIS for any severe behavior disorder. A psychosis may be either functional or organic, although the incidence of functional psychosis far outnumbers that of organic psychosis.

A person suffering from psychosis is a *psychotic* patient. Sometimes psychotic persons are referred to popularly as "lunatics." This word is derived from the Latin word *luna,* meaning moon. Psychotic persons were formerly supposed to act in an unusually strange manner at the time of a full moon. Such words as "lunatic," "crazy," and "maniac" are not used in modern psychological literature.

In legal circles the word "insanity" is used to refer to "any form of mental disorder which renders the individual incompetent to act in accordance with the legal and conventional standards of his social environment." A person is legally insane if he has been declared so by the courts. "Insanity" and "insane," therefore, are legal terms rather than psychological ones.

Some common misconceptions about psychosis. Probably because of the popular association of psychosis with evil spirits and sin for many years, some persons still consider it a disgrace if anyone in the family is or ever has been psychotic. At one time a psychologist overheard two women talking about another woman in the community who had just died. He was surprised to hear one of the women say that it was very fortunate that their neighbor had died. Then in a whisper (a true gossip's "whisper," which is loud enough to be heard through the wooden partition between a barbershop and a beauty parlor) she said, "Oh, it would have been such a disgrace to her family if she had lived. It wasn't generally known, but I was told in strict confidence—I just must tell you—that she was off in her head! The members of the family were afraid that they would have to put her in an insane asylum if she lived. It is so fortunate for the family that they have been mercifully spared that awful disgrace."

Is it a disgrace if one of our friends develops cancer, tuberculosis, or any other disease and has to be sent to a hospital for treatment? Quite the contrary. We are sorry for him and do everything we can to cheer him and help his family in their time of difficulty. From the psychological point of view, the person suffering from the form of abnormal personality development called psychosis is just as much in need of skillful, painstaking care as the person who is suffering from cancer.

There have been a number of experiments performed on the relationship between a person having a stigma, such as a behavior disorder, and the reactions of others toward him. Although the data are not conclusive at the present time, some evidence indicates that subjects sometimes punish more severely (an electrical shock of longer duration) those who have a stigma than those who don't. When the subject closely identifies with the stigmatized person, he is less likely to inflict pain on the person.

A common misconception about psychotic persons is that they are dangerous. As a matter of fact, the great majority of psychotic individuals are not dangerous. One may walk through most mental hospital wards in perfect safety.

One further misconception about mental illness is that it cannot be cured. If their illnesses are caught in time, however, between 70 and 80 percent of all mental patients can be released and can make a satisfactory adjustment to life. In some disorders the recovery rate is higher than 90 percent.

On what basis is a person judged psychotic? There is no simple criterion that can be used to determine whether or not a given individual has a psychosis. Of course, the technical problems of diagnosis must be left to the clinical psychologist or psychiatrist. We may note, however, that it is often necessary to study an individual in terms of his social environment. An individual who is not considered to have a psychosis in one environment might be considered to have one in another environment. Also, the criteria for what is considered to be psychotic behavior can change from time to time in the same society.

Ordinarily, if an individual talks about how much he hates certain other persons and how he would like to kill them, he is considered psychotic. His behavior is abnormal, and he is placed in a mental hospital for treatment. But suppose that war is declared. The great majority of persons begin talking about how much they hate the people who live in the enemy country. They are anxious to kill those people. If they are unusually successful in doing so, they are known as heroes and are decorated with medals. Are they psychotic? We do not speak of them as being psychotic, for they are doing the normal thing. That is, they are doing what is socially accepted at the time. If, after the war, some of these persons continue to hate and kill, we place them in either mental hospitals or prisons. The behavior that was considered normal during wartime is now abnormal.

Despite the lack of absolute criteria, there are some variables that are used to diagnose psychoses. A psychotic person may have a HALLUCINATION, a faulty, senselike perception for which there is no external stimulus. For example, in an auditory hallucination, the most frequent type, the person hears voices speaking to him, although no real voices or other sounds are present. Other hallucinations may involve visions of persons long since dead or the touch of someone's hand on the individual's shoulder, although no one is near

"NOW THAT YOU'VE HAD YOUR FUN, WHAT DID YOU DO WITH THE REAL DR. PRANSTON? I PENETRATED YOUR DISGUISE THE MOMENT I WALKED IN!"

him. Another factor used in diagnosing psychotics is the presence of DELUSIONS, false beliefs that the person vigorously defends despite substantial evidence that his beliefs cannot possibly be true. A third indication of psychosis is the person's lack of contact with reality, which may include disorientation in time, place, identity, or the season of the year. Other diagnostic indications are extremes of depression or excitement; motor disturbances, such as rigid postures; apathy; extreme hostility; and conceptual disorganization—confused ideas about people or objects.

In recent years attention has been given to the possibilities of diagnosis by computers. Such diagnosis consists of collecting an enormous amount of data on symptoms of disorders and storing this information in a computer. Data are then collected on a given patient and fed into the computer, which compares the patient's symptoms to the extensive data already in its storage unit and comes out with a report on the disorder. These procedures, which are being used with some of the major medical diseases, are being investigated for their effectiveness with psychotic disorders.

In summary, diagnosis of a mental disorder is based on medical criteria, psychological elements, and also sociological factors, such as the family and community setting where the disorder may have originated.

Functional Psychoses

It has already been pointed out that there are many more cases of functional psychoses than of organic psychoses. Although organic factors are usually involved in a functional psychosis, the basic difficulty nevertheless seems to be an unsatisfactory adjustment to the environment. In this section we will examine these severe mental disorders, which include manic-depressive behavior, schizophrenia, and paranoid reactions.

What are some suggested causes of functional psychosis? Inheritance has often been suggested as the cause of severe mental disorders, but in most cases there is no conclusive evidence to support the suggestion.

Popularly, it is believed that disappointment in love, a death in the family, a great financial loss, or family discord will cause functional psychosis. At some time in their lives, most persons go through such periods of emotional stress without having to be committed to mental hospitals. An emotional situation might help to bring on psychosis in the case of a poorly adjusted person, but the emotional situation does not, in itself, cause the functional psychosis.

Some authorities believe that the pace of our modern life is responsible for a tremendous amount of psychosis. They believe that our constant rushing to catch buses, trains, and airplanes, our high-speed automobile driving, honking horns, blaring television sets, and shrieking sirens all tend to produce functional psychosis. We are occasionally advised to return to a primitive state, where everything is supposed to be peaceful and quiet.

There is evidence, however, of psychosis among primitive peoples. In fact, primitive peoples have many causes for worry and dread that we do not have. Since they know nothing of modern medicine, they are constantly in dread of sudden sickness and death. There is ever present the fear of offending evil spirits or of being a victim of black magic. Conditions of modern life cannot be held as the cause of all functional psychosis, although we might possibly reduce the number of persons who become psychotic by lessening some of the strain of modern life.

What do psychologists think are the causes of functional psychosis? Psychologists find that roots of functional psychosis often go back to childhood. The child (or adult) who learns to pout and have temper tantrums may be more likely to become a manic-depressive patient than the individual who learns to face life more calmly. The child who never has an opportunity to play with other children, or who is never permitted to make decisions for himself, or who is always protected from the hard realities of life is in danger of developing an abnormal personality pattern. He may become so abnormal as to be classed as schizophrenic. The case of the individual who develops the habit of sidestepping the conflicts and problems of life by drifting into a world of daydreaming may someday be diagnosed as having paranoid reactions.

The characteristics of manic-depressive behavior. The term MANIC-DEPRESSIVE is applied to a form of functional psychosis that is characterized by periods of excitement and periods of depression. "Manic" refers to the excited and excessively active periods. "Depressive" refers to the periods of unpleasant thoughts and inactivity.

At one time the patient will show manic behavior. For example, he may sing, shout, or move about rapidly. He may talk almost continuously. Sometimes he becomes so excited and active that he may destroy furniture or injure his fellow patients unless care is taken to prevent such destruction and injury.

This phase of behavior will pass, and his behavior may be quite normal for a while. Then he may become depressed. During this

This drawing of a swan was done by a manic-depressive patient when he was in a period of elation—when he was feeling manic.

phase of his behavior, which usually lasts longer, he becomes quite sad and dejected. He feels that he is just about the most miserable person on earth. He may refuse food because he feels that he is too unworthy to live. He may even attempt suicide.

In time he will become quite normal again. Later he may have another manic phase and still later another depressive phase. These periods may continue to alternate, although not necessarily at regular intervals nor following the same pattern. Actually, only 15 to 25 percent of manic-depressives show definite cycles of manic and depressive behavior. Most so-called manic-depressives are either manic or depressive.

Persons who often show these extreme forms of excitement or depression, or who alternate between the two, are unusual—that is, abnormal. Do persons who are not patients in mental hospitals ever show similar behavior? We all have times when we feel full of pep and enthusiasm and other times when we have the blues. Some persons seem to have more pep than others, some seem to be more subject to the blues, and some alternate between these moods. Having occasional spells of the blues or of excitement does not mean that a person is psychotic.

There is reason to believe that the cycles of the manic-depressive are related to physiological cycles. The exact cause of manic-depressive psychosis is not known, although some scientists believe that it is genetically caused, since it tends to run in families. There is evidence that some cases of manic-depressive illness can be inherited through a genetic defect. Psychological theories emphasize that the manic-depressive usually has a background of high achievement standards, and extreme feelings of guilt and worthlessness if his goals are not obtained. He has an inflexible conscience that prevents open expression of hostility and anger, so that these emotions are often turned inward.

The number of manic-depressive persons being admitted into public mental hospitals has been decreasing recently, but the explanation could be that more manic-depressive patients may now be going to out-patient clinics or private hospitals. Their chances of being discharged from the hospital and returning to normal home and community life are quite good. With modern treatment the recovery rate of manic-depressives is higher than 90 percent, although three out of four patients will have recurring attacks.

The characteristics of schizophrenia. The term SCHIZOPHRENIA (skit-sə-'frē-nē-ə) literally means "split mind." The layman often speaks of "split personality" in referring to this form of mental illness. Formerly schizophrenia was referred to as "dementia praecox" (di-'men-chə 'prē-käks), a term literally meaning "mental deterioration in youth." This term, now obsolete, was inaccurate, because most cases of schizophrenia develop during adulthood rather than during childhood or adolescence.

The major symptoms of this disorder include withdrawal from reality, disturbances in emotions and thought, delusions, hallucinations, bizarre behavior, and disorientation as to identity or time. Remember, though, that no one person exhibits all of these symptoms.

The American Psychiatric Association lists ten major forms of schizophrenia. We will describe briefly four of the most important: simple, hebephrenic, catatonic, and paranoid. *Simple schizophrenia* is a disorder characterized by apathy, indifference, and mental deterioration. *Hebephrenic schizophrenia* is typified by silliness and regressive behavior, which may result in childish giggling over trivial situations. *Catatonic schizophrenia* is less common than other forms, although it has perhaps the most dramatic symptoms. Such a person is extremely negative, quite often doing exactly the opposite of what is requested of him. Perhaps the most significant behavior is a state of catatonia, or muscular rigidity. The patient may remain in a fixed position for several hours. The *paranoid schizophrenic* has delusions of grandeur, thinking, for instance, that he is a millionaire, or delusions of persecution that people are "out to get him."

We do not know for certain whether or not schizophrenia is inheritable. Schizophrenia is often found in members of the same family, but this may be due to environment as well as to heredity. The child living in a home where either of the parents is developing a schizophrenic psychosis is living in an environment likely to result in his own withdrawal from reality and his own disorientation. Yet a growing number of scientists are beginning to attribute schizophrenia to a chemical imbalance of the body, which affects messages carried to the brain and results in sensory disturbances. Some of these scientists suspect that the defective body chemistry may be the result of heredity.

Although schizophrenia is classified as a functional disorder, there is increasing evidence of a physiological basis for schizophrenia. In one study a substance called taraxein was found in the blood of schizophrenic patients. This substance was injected into nonpsychotic volunteers, who developed temporary symptoms similar to schizophrenia. But at present it is not known which occurs first, taraxein or schizophrenia. Also, there is the possibility that other factors could be causing both of these variables. Further scientific evidence is needed before definite conclusions can be drawn.

Approximately half of all patients in hospitals for the permanent care of behavior disorders are diagnosed as schizophrenic. The chances of recovery from this form of psychosis are not as good as for manic-depressive psychosis. Figures from mental hospitals differ, depending on the treatments used and the conditions under which patients are discharged. With modern treatment, however, more than one-half of first-admission schizophrenics are discharged in less than six months after admission, and nearly all are discharged within the first year.

Paranoid reactions. Psychotic persons who suffer from persistent, systematized delusions are said to show PARANOID REACTIONS. We have just seen that such delusions are characteristic of some schizophrenic patients. In fact, most hospital patients displaying paranoid reactions are classified as schizophrenics. The primary difference between a paranoid schizophrenic person and a person with paranoid reactions is that the paranoid-reaction psychotic devises elaborate descriptions and justifications of his delusions.

The delusions that characterize paranoid reactions may take the form of delusions of grandeur. The individual may believe that he

This series of cat portraits, drawn by an artist who developed schizophrenia, shows the progressive stages of the behavior disorder. You can see the artist's increasing withdrawal from reality by the deterioration of structure in these pictures.

is a great author, a multimillionaire, a world-famous physician, a great inventor, a member of a royal family, and so on. Accompanying the delusions of grandeur there are often delusions of persecution. The patient talks about how his enemies are plotting against him, how scheming persons are trying to steal his money, how others have copied his ideas for inventions. He often insists that his enemies have succeeded in having him unjustly confined in the hospital. Frequently there are delusions of reference. Even the most trivial incidents take on a personal reference. Whenever he sees two persons talking, he is sure that they are talking about him. A nurse or doctor may happen to make some slight gesture, but the patient insists that this hand movement is a signal to his enemies. If his place at the table in the hospital is changed, he thinks that it has been changed because the food being served at the new place is poisoned.

A brief review of a case history will serve to illustrate a paranoid reaction. A patient in a mental hospital believes that he is a general in the army—although in actuality he never rose above the rank of private first class. Each morning he writes out the orders of the day for the army. Parts of these orders are in code so that enemy agents cannot read them. The patient is a college graduate, keeps up on current events, and talks in an interesting manner. He gives very logical-sounding explanations. The cottage in which he lives is his office, the other patients in the cottage are members of his military staff, the entire hospital is an army post, and all the patients are soldiers or nurses. He reports that the President of the United States makes frequent reference to him in press releases, although not by name.

Organic Psychoses

The psychoses we will discuss in this section —paresis, senile psychosis, and alcoholic psychosis—are organic because they result from damage to the central nervous system. You may read of other ways of classifying the psychoses mentioned in this section. Instead of being categorized as functional or organic, psychoses are sometimes classified as either acute or chronic. ACUTE brain disorders include temporary and reversible brain tissue impairment, such as is found in drug, poison, and alcohol intoxication and in certain circulatory disturbances. Acute psychosis usually has a fairly rapid onset and lasts a comparatively short amount of time. CHRONIC brain disorders are those psychoses which involve relatively fixed brain tissue damage, such as those caused by the process of aging or by permanent head injury. Chronic psychosis is usually of lengthy duration and uncertain recovery.

Paresis. PARESIS (pə-rē'səs) is the name given to the form of psychosis caused by syphilitic infection of the brain. The term "paresis" is the one most frequently used in psychological literature. This form of psychosis is sometimes, however, referred to as "softening of the brain," or "progressive general paralysis." Do not assume that "paralysis" and "paresis" are synonymous, though. Many persons have paralysis who are not suffering from paresis.

Not everyone who has syphilis becomes a paretic. In fact, of all those who contract syphilis, only about 5 percent become paretics. Syphilis may destroy any part of the body, but if the brain is the part destroyed, paresis results. When the brains of paretics are examined after death, the destruction of brain tissue can be plainly seen.

Paretics often show paranoid reactions. They may also display a false sense of well-being. They tend to look at the world through rose-colored glasses. For example, they might make the most rash and foolhardy investments because they feel sure that everything will turn out perfectly.

The paretic walks with a characteristic shuffling gait. His speech is disturbed, he mixes up his words and syllables, has a faulty memory, and becomes indifferent to social proprieties, with a resulting vulgarity.

Within the past thirty years, medical science has made great strides in the effective treatment of syphilis. If the patient is treated by modern methods, he has a very good chance of recovery.

Senile psychosis. An organic psychosis that sometimes affects old people is called SENILE PSYCHOSIS. The term "senility" is applied to the general deterioration that often accompanies old age. Old persons frequently show a breakdown in the functioning of their bodies, and have many pains and discomforts. The brain, as well as other parts of the body, does not always function as efficiently as in earlier days. There may be cerebral arteriosclerosis, a thickening and hardening of the wall of the arteries resulting in a decreased circulation of blood in the brain.

If a large blood vessel bursts in the brain, the elderly person is said to have had a stroke. Following this bursting of the blood vessel, he may be paralyzed or he may become unconscious. In severe cases death may follow. If only a tiny capillary in the brain bursts, the brain is not damaged to a great extent, but the old person may show confusion in his thinking. He may not be able to recall recent past experiences, and may become angry easily. Often his behavior is childish, and it is said that he is in his second childhood.

Such paranoid reactions as delusions of persecution may develop. The elderly person may believe that his relatives and friends are mistreating him, that they are whispering unpleasant things about him. He may even believe that they are trying to kill him to get his money. Of course, the very ones that he believes are plotting against him may be the ones who love him most and who would do everything in their power to help him.

Alcoholic psychosis. With the use of alcohol an individual becomes less inhibited. Activities that would have seemed wrong before drinking seem all right following the drinking. Alcohol produces a false feeling of well-being and efficiency, but actually it is a depressant rather than a stimulant. The user becomes less alert, responds more slowly, and is less dependable. After drinking more alcohol, the individual's speech, motor coordination, and vision become disturbed. His thinking becomes confused. Still later, the user enters a stuporous state and may become unconscious, or "pass out."

To determine whether or not an individual is drunk, generally the amount of alcohol consumed is not as important as the concentration of alcohol in the blood stream. Fortunately most individuals pass out before they consume enough alcohol to kill them. Individuals usually pass out when the concentration of alcohol reaches a 0.50 percent concentration level. A concentration level higher than 0.55 percent is considered lethal.

The person who uses excessive amounts of alcohol over a long period of time is likely to show general physiological deterioration. Alcoholic psychosis is likely to occur in persons who have been chronic alcoholics for a number of years. Unfortunately, alcoholic psychosis seems to be increasing in recent years. Here are some mental illnesses that are fundamentally alcoholic in origin.

1. Delirium tremens. Delirium tremens is found in a small percentage of those who have engaged in heavy drinking for a long period of time. Trembling of the hands and other parts of the body is apparent. The individual is apprehensive, confused about time and place, restless, and irritable. He often suffers from insomnia. He has vivid hallucinations: "pink elephants" or other large animals, snakes, rats, bugs of all kinds.

2. Acute hallucinosis. This alcoholic illness resembles delirium tremens in many ways but is characterized by auditory hallucinations.

As a person drinks more and more alcohol, he has trouble with his motor coordination, his speech and gestures become less controlled, and eventually, he passes out.

The patient hears voices talking about him, calling him names, and accusing him of all kinds of crimes. The voices threaten him with horrible punishment. He may become terror-stricken and scream for help. He may arm himself for a fight, or he may attempt suicide.

3. *Korsakoff's psychosis.* This mental illness occurs in older alcoholics, often after approximately twenty-five years of chronic alcoholism. The outstanding symptom is inability to remember previous experiences, especially recent ones. The patient is unable to recall eating a meal, even though he has just left the table. He may have just talked to someone but doesn't remember the person at all a minute after the individual has left the room. The patient often fills in the gaps in his recall with fanciful tales that may sound quite plausible until the facts are checked.

4. *Pathological intoxication.* Unlike the previous forms of alcoholic illness, pathological intoxication may follow the consumption of only a very small quantity of alcohol. It is especially likely to occur if the user is very tired or emotionally upset. The patient may become violently angry and brutal. He may kill, rob, burn, or commit other crimes. He may commit suicide.

What can be done to help the alcoholic? Alcoholism is one of the most serious health problems facing us today, yet there is no generally accepted technique for treating it. We have almost no special hospitals for the treatment of alcoholics. General hospitals usually offer treatment for severe cases only, and their treatment is of short duration. In most communities the alcoholic goes to jail instead of to a hospital. Yet jails have neither the equipment nor the professional staff to care for alcoholics. The drunk is sobered up, but he is not treated.

Alcoholism is generally a symptom of a basic personality maladjustment. It is a result rather than a cause of the individual's difficulties. When we treat just the alcoholism, we are treating the symptom rather than the illness. The alcoholic is cured only when he learns to meet life's responsibilities and difficulties by attacking them rather than turning to alcohol.

One organization designed to help alcoholics is Alcoholics Anonymous, started by two men who had helped themselves and each other to recover from alcoholism, and decided that they wanted to assist others. Although individual help is given, Alcoholics Anonymous essentially conducts a form of group therapy. Meetings are held in which individuals can have social life and entertainment without going to a bar. Also, at these meetings problems of the alcoholic are discussed. Persons who have been "through the mill" tell of their experiences and how they have been helped. The alcoholic is made to feel that he is not alone with his problems, that he is a member of an important group, that he will be more successful if he attacks his problems than if he runs away from them. Reports indicate that treatment by Alcoholics Anonymous is effective, sooner or later, in about three-fourths of the cases who come for help. It works only when the individual is willing to admit that he has been escaping his problems by means of alcohol and desires to be helped. An individual must avoid alcoholic beverages completely once he has been treated, because taking even one drink is likely to cause alcoholism to recur.

Some alcoholics have been successfully treated with emetine, a nausea-producing drug. After taking emetine, they become nauseated when they drink alcohol. Eventually the nauseous feeling recurs whenever they see or smell alcohol, even though they have stopped taking the drug. What was once an approach response to alcohol becomes an avoidance response.

Although progress is being made, more research on alcoholism is needed. The alcoholic needs help rather than condemnation. Some large business concerns have psychiatric programs designed to help their alcoholic employees. In alcoholism, as elsewhere, prevention is better than cure.

Personality Disorders

There are many people in and out of mental hospitals who suffer from personality disorders. They do not show the same disturbances as psychotics in thoughts or bizarre behavior. Nor do they display much anxiety or feelings of distress. Their main problem is the development of personality trait patterns that deviate significantly from accepted social behavior.

One type of disorder is the *schizoid personality*. Such a person is characterized by emotional coldness and detachment, avoidance of competition, and fear. The *paranoid personality* is similar to the schizoid, except that it includes strong feelings of being persecuted. Nevertheless, neither of these is psychotic, because their contact with reality is significantly better than in psychoses.

The *sociopathic personality* is characterized by violations of the rules, laws, and mores of the society in which it is found. Many chronic criminals have sociopathic personalities. They have little or no feelings of guilt over their behavior, are usually very good at explaining their actions, and are convinced that their behavior is completely justified. The "con man" is an example of this disorder. Superficially he is usually a good talker and very convincing. Other aspects of the sociopathic personality include impulsive behavior, irresponsibility toward others, and sometimes even acts of violence and murder.

Treatment of Behavior Disorders

Some of the forms of treatment discussed here are used predominantly in mental hospitals; others are used in clinics or by psychiatrists or psychologists outside of hospitals. There are many procedures available for treating behavior disorders, and new forms of treatment are being developed all the time.

Procedures emphasizing physical treatment. One of the major forms of helping persons with behavior disorders is *drug therapy*. Although drug therapy treats the symptoms, not the causes, of disorders, the alleviation of symptoms sometimes makes it possible for the patient to break a vicious circle. The husband who, through the use of tranquilizing drugs, no longer feels as much anxiety may begin to treat his wife better, who in turn begins to show more love and affection toward her husband. Drug therapy has been successful in treating schizophrenic patients by helping them to establish better contact with reality. Drugs are also helpful in treating manic-depressive psychoses. The use of drugs has significantly reduced the number of patients in mental hospitals.

Another new program of treatment embehavior disorders is *electroconvulsive therapy* (ECT), which consists of sending a mild electric current through certain areas of the brain. In electric shock treatment the length and severity of the current can be controlled so that the patient feels no pain from the shock, but he usually awakens with a headache and becomes apprehensive when approached for additional shock treatments. In treating some disorders of extremely depressed individuals with ECT, recovery is higher than 90 percent. Such treatment has shortened the recovery time for neurotic and psychotic de-

The number of patients in state and county mental hospitals has been decreasing every year since the introduction of the extensive use of certain drugs in treating behavior disorders.

pressive disorders from several years to a few months.

Procedures emphasizing the social environment. *Environmental therapy* is designed to make the mental hospital more like the real world outside the hospital. Modern hospitals have parties, dances, provide movies, games, bus trips, recreational facilities, opportunities to learn worthwhile occupational skills, and other activities designed to make the patient more aware of and encourage him to participate in social activities. This is in contrast to the older concept of mental hospitals that were considered insane asylums mainly for custodial care. Although some primitive mental hospitals still exist with overcrowding, unsanitary conditions, and inadequate treatment for patients, there has been considerable improvement in many mental hospitals. Where inadequate conditions do exist, it is usually because of a lack of money and public interest.

While great strides are being made inside mental hospitals, there are many new developments in treatment outside as well. One such program calls for community resource centers. The idea is to provide help with a variety of problems at one location and at minimal cost. Basically, psychological services would be included in such centers, but additional services would also be offered. In addition to physical and mental health services there would be referral services to social agencies, professional advice on financial and budgeting matters, legal aid, and help with educational and occupational problems. Most problems of persons do not occur in isolation, but in conjunction with many other problems. For example, the husband who is suffering from anxiety over bills and a fear of developing ulcers could obtain psychological help, medical assistance, legal aid, and help with budgeting his income, all in one place. These centers are based on the premise that individuals react as total organisms and that what upsets one aspect of the person also has an effect on other aspects.

Another new program of treatment emphasizing environment is called the *T-group* or *sensitivity-training group*. It brings people together in a social setting to develop trust, mutual communication, and exposure of feelings and thoughts, to ease fears of being isolated, and to develop the feeling that others do care. Such procedures are based on the assumption that behavior disorders arise in the social environment and can be more adequately treated within a social framework.

Procedures emphasizing individual treatment. One such procedure is PSYCHOTHERAPY, which attempts to determine the problems of the patient and ways of solving them through a complex process involving a verbal exchange between the psychotherapist and the patient. It is usually used in conjunction with other data, such as the person's life history, and both physical and psychological examinations.

Psychotherapy may take several forms, one of them being *supportive therapy,* which is arranged to give support to the patient while he faces a crisis. This type of therapy does not bring about permanent changes in personality, but does aid the person while he is undergoing some crisis. *Psychoanalysis,* originated by Freud, is designed to help the patient achieve an understanding and acceptance of underlying mechanisms involved in adjustment. In psychoanalysis the therapist interprets and evaluates the patient's feelings. In *client-centered therapy,* another form of psychotherapy, the major emphasis is on placing the patient in a warm, psychologically permissive environmental atmosphere so that he can discuss his potential abilities, problems, and solutions to problems without fear of condemnation.

Psychotherapy is used mainly in the treatment of less severe behavior disorders, such as neuroses, because results are faster and better than with psychotic persons, and because there is a scarcity of trained psychotherapists. By treating primarily neurotic behavior, psychotherapy has proven valuable in preventing the development of more severe disorders.

One technique employed by some psychotherapists is *psychodrama,* which permits patients to act out their problems by playing roles in realistic situations. Aside from providing the therapist with information about the patient, it has the added benefit of allowing the patient to act out his emotions rather than verbalizing them. He may play the part of a disturbed father, a child, or any other of a variety of roles that are related to his emotional problems.

Another technique used by many psychotherapists is *group therapy,* in which patients meet together to talk over their problems. Each person learns that others have problems, too, and together they work out solutions.

In a group therapy session, one individual may try to communicate her feelings about someone or something, while the other members listen and then react to her and her problems.

There are also several innovative techniques currently being developed and tested in the area of psychotherapy. One of them uses a computer as a psychotherapist. The computer is programmed to react to several hundred key words, such as "mother," "father," and "hate." The patient types his feelings on a typewriter that is attached to a computer, and the computer reacts by typing a reply. For example, the patient may type "I dislike my mother," and the computer may answer "Why do you dislike your mother?"

Treatments emphasizing conditioning procedures. One of the most promising new techniques of treating behavior disorders is called BEHAVIOR MODIFICATION. This type of treatment is based on the premise that the symptoms accompanying a behavior disorder are learned and can therefore be unlearned. The extinction of an undesirable behavior can be accomplished by either weakening the undesirable response through punishment, or by strengthening a response that is incompatible with the original behavior. Therapists using behavior modification techniques are not concerned with underlying causes of the behavior disorder, such as unconscious anxiety. They believe that the behavior itself is the source of the person's trouble, and that extinguishing the undesirable behavior will result in improved adjustment of the individual and acceptance of him by others. Behavior modification procedures have been criticized for treating symptoms, not causes. However, one study reported that out of 249 patients treated by these procedures, only four acquired new symptoms.

One type of behavior modification, known as *counter-conditioning,* uses classical and operant conditioning procedures to cause the subject to avoid an event, object, or situation, or to develop desirable ways of behaving.

Classical conditioning procedures have been used successfully to cause people to give up a harmful habit by associating the habit with an unpleasant experience, such as becoming nauseated (induced by emetine or some other drug). Soon the individual feels nauseous whenever he begins returning to the habit. It is similar to a situation where someone eats too much of a particular food, becomes very sick, and afterward finds that he has a strong tendency to avoid even thinking about that food, much less eating it. When the purpose of the counter-conditioning is to make the person avoid something, it is usually called *aversive therapy.*

When the purpose of the counter-conditioning is to make the person feel more comfortable in the presence of something he dislikes, it is called *desensitization.* Desensitization is a useful procedure for treating phobias, hypochondria, psychosomatic illness, and stuttering, all of which involve anxiety. It reduces the anxiety under controlled conditions. In one case a man became very anxious when he had a pain in the middle of his chest—he imagined that he was having a heart attack. No amount of assurance from medical doctors was sufficient to reduce the anxiety. Then he was placed in a desensitization program and was taught to relax. He was asked to imagine a pain in the lower right part of his abdomen, which produced much less anxiety than when he imagined pain in the middle of his chest. Gradually he was asked to imagine pain closer and closer to the middle of his chest, each time relaxing his muscles. Eventually he could imagine heart pain with no anxiety.

Behavior modification programs also use operant conditioning procedures to change undesirable behavior or strengthen desirable responses. In applying operant conditioning procedures it is necessary to arrange reinforcement so that it occurs in a lifelike situation.

One method used in mental hospitals today consists of reinforcing desirable behavior through the use of "money," such as plastic tokens, which can be earned and spent by the patient. For example, a patient who does not usually keep his room clean may be given tokens for keeping it clean. He may receive other tokens for taking his medicine, delivering a message, or performing a certain amount of work. The "money" he earns can be spent for extra servings of food, watching television for an extra hour, and so on. Token economy programs have also been used with some success with juvenile delinquents and in classroom activities for emotionally disturbed children.

How effective are the many forms of treatment? The majority of patients are cured by the treatment procedures they receive. Some individuals state that anyone who has had a behavior disorder and has been cured may become disturbed again. In some cases, this is true. But when you go to the doctor with a sore throat and he cures it, does he guarantee that you will never have a sore throat again? Of course not. The doctor cures your sore throat and prescribes certain preventive measures to enable you to better avoid having another sore throat. It is the same with behavior disorders. The psychologist cannot guarantee that the individual will not become emotionally disturbed again any more than your medical doctor can guarantee that you will never have a sore throat again.

Whatever the therapeutic technique used, the objective is to enable as many patients as possible to be effective members of their communities and to take their places in society.

Much can now be done to cure, or at least improve, persons with behavior disorders. In the future, as research leads the way, more and better treatments will be possible. The best treatment, however, is still prevention. How are you striving to maintain good mental health?

Terms to Know

acute hallucinosis
acute psychosis
alcoholic psychosis
amnesia
anxiety reactions
aversive therapy
behavior disorder
behavior modification
catatonic schizo-
   phrenia
chronic psychosis
client-centered
   therapy
conversion reaction
counter-conditioning
delirium tremens
delusion
desensitization

dissociative reaction
drug therapy
electroconvulsive therapy
   (ECT)
environmental therapy
fugue
functional disorder
group therapy
hallucination
hebephrenic schizophrenia
hypochondriac
Korsakoff's psychosis
manic-depressive
multiple personality
neurosis
obsessive-compulsive
organic disorder
paranoid personality
paranoid reactions

paranoid schizophrenia
paresis
pathological intoxication
phobia
psychoanalysis
psychodrama
psychosis
psychosomatic disorder
psychotherapy
senile psychosis
sensitivity-training
   group
schizoid personality
schizophrenia
simple schizophrenia
sociopathic personality
supportive therapy
tic

Topics to Think About

1. In what ways would you change our society so that we might have fewer neurotics? Do you think that reducing the tensions and fast pace of life in our society would help reduce the amount of neurotic behavior?

2. Suppose that some day you are admitted to a mental hospital for therapy. How would you like to be treated by the hospital personnel? How would you like to be treated by the members of your family when they come to visit you?

3. As a child, did you ever feel that you just had to step on every crack in the sidewalk or touch every telephone pole? Did other children make a game of this kind of activity? What is the difference between this kind of activity and neurotic obsessive-compulsive behavior?

4. Suppose you were going to pursue a career in treating behavior disorders. Would you be more interested in a medical approach, researching chemical imbalances in the body and using drug therapy, or would you emphasize a psychoanalytical approach, investigating the unconscious as the basis of behavior disorders? Why?

5. If you have had any experience with psychotherapy or psychiatric care, what aspect of it did you feel was most beneficial? Would you recommend such procedures to others with similiar problems? If not, why not, and what would you recommend?

6. Some people feel that everyone in our society could gain from the experience of group therapy or sensitivity training. Do you agree or disagree? Why?

7. Assume that you have all the money you want to spend on improving mental health in your state. How would you spend the money?

Suggestions for Activities

1. It is difficult for some people to begin psychotherapy, especially with a complete stranger, because of their shyness in front of another person. To get an idea of how they feel, have a friend give you a sealed list of ten emotionally invoking words, such as, "boy," "mother," "blood," and so on. Do not look at the list until you are in a place where you are completely alone and cannot be overheard. Open the list of words and as you read each word say aloud the first thing you think of. How do you feel? Do you feel embarrassed? How would you feel if someone else had been in the room?

2. There seem to be many common expressions that suggest that some of our organic processes are related to emotional and other psychological causes. For example, when we become irritated or angry with someone, we say, "You give me a pain in the neck!" If we have a very frightening experience, we say, "I was so scared that my flesh fairly crawled!" For a few days note and jot down such

expressions as you hear them. Bring your notes to class and make up a list of "psychosomatic" expressions. (Classes report that they can gather lists of twenty or more such expressions without much difficulty.)

3. Visit a drugstore to look over the "nerve" and sleep-inducing preparations available without prescription. If you have studied chemistry, you will be interested in reading the labels. Are such preparations a satisfactory answer to the problems of "nervous" people?

4. Write a theme on the behavior of some well-known person in history whose reactions were so unusual that he might be called psychotic. You might consider such figures as Caligula (a Roman Emperor), Ivan the Terrible (a Czar of Russia), Napoleon, and Hitler.

5. Check the telephone directory or look under "Personal" in the classified advertisements of your newspaper to find out if the services of Alcoholics Anonymous are available in your community. A member of this organization might be willing and glad to speak to your class.

6. Form a debate team on the issue "Public drunkenness is a crime," vs. "Public drunkenness is an illness." Include in the debate any differences between the two viewpoints in possible treatment that might be used.

7. If it can be arranged, visit a mental hospital to see how patients are cared for. Although in most cases you will not be able to tell by looking at patients, a doctor or a psychiatric aide may be able to point out patients with one psychosis or another.

8. Look in your local telephone directory for the address of a mental health organization in your area. If you find such an organization, make contact and ask about the organization's activities. For instance, they may have volunteer groups that visit patients in mental hospitals. You might report on their activities to the class. Quite often volunteer groups take small gifts to patients. Maybe you could organize some activity in your school (with permission) to help raise money to purchase small gifts or items that patients need. (These gifts need be nothing more than a bar of soap, colorful ribbon, a tie, and so on.) You might even be able to help start a patient on the road to recovery by your activities.

9. In cooperation with your teacher, ask several students in your class to volunteer for this activity. You should have volunteers who are not afraid to talk in front of the class. Before the designated period for this activity, your group should meet with the teacher and work out details.

During the class period the teacher, or someone designated by the teacher, acts as an interviewer, and each student in turn portrays the symptoms of a particular neurosis or psychosis. The interview procedures consist of asking questions, to which the student volunteers give answers that are characteristic of a particular behavior disorder. The volunteers should not attempt to memorize specific words or statements, but they must be familiar with the symptoms of the disorder. The class diagnoses on a sheet of paper each "case" as it is portrayed.

After all cases have been completed, class members compare diagnoses and discuss cases on which class members disagree. This allows students to become aware of some of the problems involved in diagnosing behavior disorders.

10. Rehearse a hypothetical therapy situation with another student that the two of you (one as the therapist and one as the patient) will perform in front of the class. The mock therapy session might involve such subjects as a threatened suicide, marital problems, a school problem, and so on. During the therapy session, and by prearrangement, stop the session five times, for about one minute each time, and have students write down what they would do next if they were the therapist.

After the session is completed, have class members compare notes on what they wrote down. Discuss points on which a large number of class members disagree. This activity gives the class a chance to discover how a therapist might feel in a real situation.

Suggestions for Further Reading

Beers, Clifford W., *A Mind That Found Itself,* rev. ed., Doubleday. The autobiography of a man who was mentally ill and who set out to improve conditions in mental hospitals. This book created widespread interest in mental hygiene.

Capote, Truman, *In Cold Blood,* New American Library. A detailed account of the behavior of two sociopathic personalities.

Fried, Barbara, *Who's Afraid: A Phobic's Handbook,* McGraw-Hill. Many phobias are discussed in this 92-page book, together with suggestions for possible "cures."

Green, Hannah, *I Never Promised You a Rose Garden,* Holt, Rinehart & Winston (paperback, Signet). A true story about an adolescent girl's struggle with mental illness.

Hilgard, E. R., R. C. Atkinson, and Rita Atkinson, *Introduction to Psychology,* 5th ed., Harcourt Brace Jovanovich. See Chapter 20, "Behavior Disorders"; and Chapter 21, "Psychotherapy and Related Techniques."

Josselyn, Irene M., *Emotional Problems of Illness,* Science Research Associates. A Guidance Series Booklet written for high school students that describes the various kinds of emotions that are prevalent in behavioral disorders.

Kafka, Franz, *The Trial,* Knopf. A novel about a paranoid's inability to grasp reality and his tendency to interpret all events as persecution.

Kagan, J., M. M. Haith, and Catherine Caldwell (eds.), *Psychology: Adapted Readings,* Harcourt Brace Jovanovich. See Selection 22, "Psychoanalytic Notes on a Case of Paranoia"; Selection 23, "The Ghost of the Weed Garden: A Study of a Chronic Schizophrenic"; Selection 24, "A Sociopsychological Investigation of Suicide"; and Selection 25, "Behavior Modification in a Mental Hospital."

Piersall, Jim, with Al Hirschberg, *Fear Strikes Out: The Jim Piersall Story,* Little, Brown. The story of a player for the Boston Red Sox who entered a mental hospital for treatment and later returned to his job as a big-league baseball player.

Ruch, Floyd L., and Philip G. Zimbardo, *Psychology and Life,* 8th ed., Scott, Foresman. See Chapter 14, "Deviance, Pathology, and Madness"; and Chapter 15, "The Therapeutic Modification of Behavior."

DR. CLARK AND SOCIAL BEHAVIOR DISORDERS

Is there any way to cure man's inhumanity to other human beings?

Dr. Kenneth B. Clark, a noted psychologist and former president of the American Psychological Association, has spoken out repeatedly against the inhumanity and cruelty that exists in our society. He has expressed the need for social justice, for correcting the behavior of insensitive members of society who destroy other human beings. He has called on psychologists and other social scientists to recognize their responsibilities and work toward ending the conditions and cruel practices that dehumanize mankind.

Much of Dr. Clark's research has been in the area of minority group status and desegregation problems. Some of his studies include the effects of racism on black children. Dr. Clark has also studied the dehumanizing effects on blacks of being raised in a Negro ghetto. In his book *Dark Ghetto*, he describes the behavior patterns and deviations that can result from confinement in a slum area, with little hope of economic mobility. For instance, the ghetto of Harlem has higher rates of juvenile delinquency, narcotic addiction, illegitimacy, and homicide than the rest of New York City.

Dr. Clark feels that crime there is more a reflection of the sickness of the ghetto than the result of purely individual motivation. He attributes the emotional ill health among blacks living in Harlem—the personality problems and psychological imbalances and patterns of violence—to American racism.

Dr. Clark has given a good deal of thought to the social behavior disorders that exist in our society. He concludes that with the modern nuclear weaponry now available, we are in a position to destroy mankind through the misuse of social power. Therefore, we must find some way to control human cruelty and destructiveness. In a speech to members of the American Psychological Association, he suggested that we turn to the physical and biological sciences to find some kind of biochemical medication that would control the behavior of persons with destructive tendencies. Drugs that can exhilarate or depress the emotions already exist. Dr. Clark stated that we now need a medicine that can control the irrational aggressive tendencies of people, especially leaders who can start wars, if the human species is to survive. Since doctors use medicines to overcome and even prevent disease, he recommended that appropriate medication should be used to reduce human hostilities, violence, and cruelty, and bring about psychological health.

Do you agree or disagree with Dr. Clark? Some psychologists, although recognizing his point of view and his right to express his ideas, have strongly disagreed with him. They have foreseen that a number of problems might arise. For instance, who is to decide to whom medication to reduce aggressiveness is to be given? Even if it were generally agreed that some of our social problems could be solved through medication administered to aggressive leaders, would the leaders be willing to take the medicine? Would those suggesting medication to reduce aggressiveness and violence in others become aggressive themselves if their suggestions were not followed?

Suppose you could do something to curb the aggressive tendencies of some world leaders today. Would you be justified in using your power? Would *you* become aggressive to prevent aggression?

unit 6

SMALL GROUPS

chapter 14   The family group

chapter 15   The peer group

chapter 16   Behavior in small groups

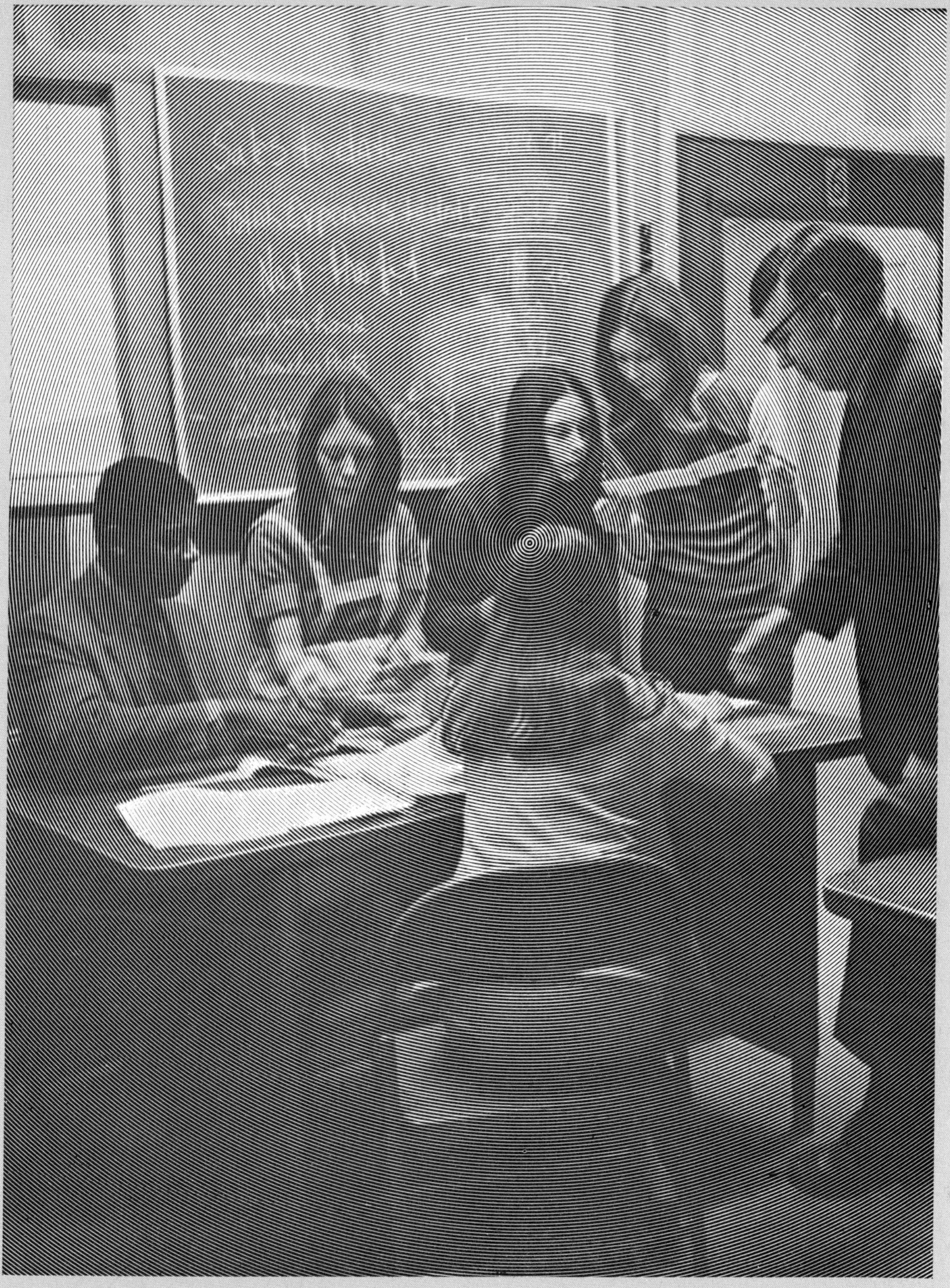

chapter 14

The Family Group

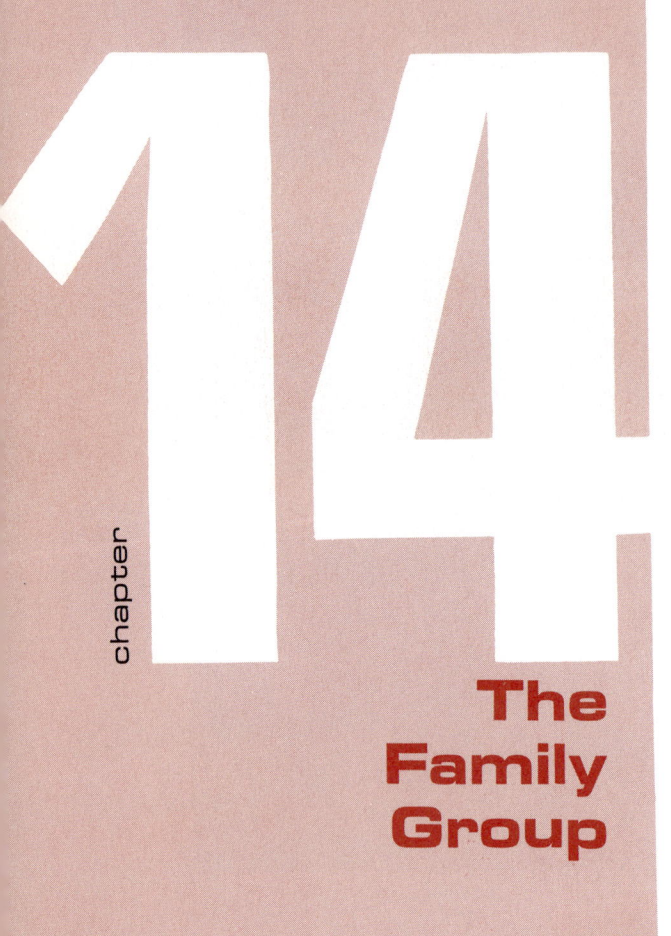

YOU ARE SPENDING, and will spend, much of your life as a member of small social groups. For most Americans, the family is the small group within which most of their behavior is centered. When they are children, their lives usually revolve around their parental homes. Later, if they become parents, their lives usually center around their own families.

The Family

To most of us a family means a father, a mother, and their children living together as a small social group. In some other societies, a family means something quite different.

What constitutes a family? In India, the Hindu family includes grandparents as an integral part of family life, not just as people to be sheltered and cared for in their old age. Nursing homes and other homes for the aged are unknown. The grandparents, their children, and their grandchildren all participate in family plans and activities, each according to his abilities.

In Uganda, Africa, there are examples of a more "extended" family than the Hindus. There the children regard uncles on the father's side as having the same relationship to them as their actual father. They look upon maternal aunts as mothers, along with their biological mother. The children grow up experiencing a great deal of love and security. As adults, they know that in case of sickness or unemployment their extended family will see that they have food and shelter.

A still different family situation is formed on a kibbutz in Israel. The Hebrew word "kibbutz" means a group. The kibbutzim of Israel are social groups, or communal farms. The people in these groups reject the importance of private property, private business, and child rearing by single family units. The emphasis in raising children is on the peer group rather than on the family. Children live apart from their parents in their own quarters, where they sleep, eat, play, and are educated. Parents may visit with their children every day and children may visit with their parents, sometimes sleeping at home. Although not family-centered, this kind of communal life does not mean that all family ties are broken. Parents and their children become friends and companions with a maximum of love and a minimum of punishing and discipline.

Social groups also exist in America in which children are a part of groups larger than the usual American family. For example, in Iowa there are seven villages in which members of a religious group known as the Amana Church Society have lived since 1855. In the early days of this society the homes did not contain kitchens or dining rooms because a single family did not eat together as a unit. Instead, members of the community ate in a common dining hall. Just as some women were assigned the task of securing, preparing, and serving the food, other women were responsible for taking care of the children of the community while their mothers and fathers were busy working at various tasks.

Today in America many mothers no longer limit their activities to homemaking and caring for children. Even very young children may be turned over to babysitters for a number of hours each working day. Other children may be cared for by trained persons in nurseries or day-care centers.

How are American families structured? Although there are some American families in

The structure of family life in our society is changing. The advent of community day-care centers has helped free women with young children to work during the day, while the children, such as those below, are taught and cared for in day-care centers.

which one of the parents autocratically rules the family group, more typically the group operates as a somewhat democratic unit. Many families have meetings in which family problems are discussed and solutions reached. Each member has a right to express his or her ideas, including grievances, and to influence discussions about various family activities.

There are those who point out that modern life, especially urban living, tends to disrupt family structure. In addition to his job, the father may belong to various clubs, such as business and golf clubs, and spend relatively little time with his family. The mother may be employed, belong to a bridge club, or be active in civic and welfare improvement organizations, and so have little time for the family. Aside from their school activities, the children may be busy as members of clubs, music organizations, athletic teams, and so on. For them home is only a place to eat and sleep. The family may be essentially a group of independent individuals rather than a social unit.

On the other hand, there is some evidence that families are beginning to function more as social units than in the past. The total number of hours in a week that a father and mother must spend at a job is decreasing, giving them more time to function in the family. Our private, city, state, and national parks provide many opportunities for families to picnic and camp as units. Transportation companies offer special rates so that the whole family can afford to travel together. Even large cities can be thought of as composed of subcommunities that can and do strengthen family structure. Many urban housing developments now provide swimming pools and other recreational facilities for families.

What do you think? Would you say that family structure is being disrupted or strengthened at the present time?

Marriage

Although marriage is not a state of continuous bliss, many couples are happy together and have made a successful marital adjustment. What is involved in a successful marriage?

Some characteristics of a happy and successful marriage. Obtaining accurate research data is sometimes difficult because of the many variables involved. Nevertheless, over the years certain basic elements found in most successful and happy marriages have emerged.

1. Persons who have had happy childhoods are more likely to have happier marriages than are those who have had unhappy childhoods. Unusual emotional disturbances in childhood tend to be related to later unsatisfactory adjustment in marriage.

2. Individuals coming from homes in which the parents were happily married are more likely to succeed in their marriages than are individuals from homes in which the parents quarreled frequently and were unhappy together. The children of happily married parents know from experience that marital problems can be solved satisfactorily. They are not so likely to give up and feel that their problems of marital adjustment are hopelessly difficult. Furthermore, the happiness of the parents is reflected in the happiness of their children, and this happiness in itself is a factor in successful marital adjustment.

3. The newly married couple tends to have more difficult problems of adjustment if a child is conceived immediately after marriage. The divorce rate for couples who conceive their first child days after marrying is much higher than for couples who delay the first conception a few months to a year. The divorce rate is even higher for those whose first child is conceived before marriage.

4. The age at which individuals marry is related to success in marriage. The divorce rate is higher for those who marry before the age of twenty-one years than for those who marry after this age. At one time a psychologist administered a battery of tests to 300 engaged couples and after nearly twenty years was able to retest all of these couples again. He found that of the original 300 engaged couples, 278 had married and only 39 (14 percent) had terminated their marriages by divorce. Of the marriages that lasted, one characteristic was that the couples had not married while in their teens. At the time of the original testing with the psychologist, the average age of the men was 26.7 years and the average age of the women was 24.7 years. Nearly 90 percent of these men and women were between twenty-one and thirty when first tested.

The above data were published over twenty years ago. Do you think that conditions are different today? If so, why?

5. There is a direct relationship between desire for children and success in marital adjustment. A study of 526 married couples to determine the relationships between desire for children, having children, and marital adjustment found that there was a good marital adjustment among couples who had one or more children and desired them. Perhaps you will be surprised to learn that there was an even better marital adjustment among couples who had no children but desired them. Children can bring many problems into the home that may put a strain on marital adjustment. The adjustment was less good among couples who had no children and did not desire any, and also among couples who had children but did not want them.

6. Having friends is related to happiness in marriage. Those who learn to have pleasant social relationships with members of both sexes are the same ones who learn how to make their marriages successful. For example, the same study of 526 married couples just mentioned produced these findings: Of the husbands who reported that they had a few or almost no men friends, only 30.8 percent had made a good adjustment. On the other hand, the men who reported having several men friends were more successful in their marital adjustment—47 percent had made good adjustments. Of the husbands who reported that they had almost no women friends, 33.3 percent were found to have good marital adjustments, whereas 51.8 percent of men who had several women as friends had good marital adjustments.

Similarly, wives who had almost no friends of either sex were less well adjusted in their marriage than wives who had more friends.

7. The individual who has known cuddling and other bodily affection in babyhood is more likely to be emotionally responsive in marital life than is the individual who was not given such affection in babyhood. There is evidence that children reared from birth in orphanages where they received little cuddling and attention during the first two years of life were later less responsive to affection than were children placed in the orphanage after they were two years of age. Remember, though, that bodily affection is one, but only one, factor in marital success.

This matter of cuddling and affection in babyhood brings up an interesting question in our society. Should fathers cuddle their small sons? Some fathers believe that caressing and cuddling their sons is inappropriate, although it is quite all right for mothers to caress and cuddle their small daughters. You can probably think of some reasons for this view. Do you believe that there should be a difference?

The amount of affection a youngster receives—how much cuddling and love he gets—is related to the child's future marital happiness.

The importance of the father in the development of children and the success of marriage is sometimes overlooked. One research study examined preadolescent boys attending a city recreation center. Half the boys were from homes in which the father was regularly present as a member of the family group. The other half were from homes in which the father was absent from the home because of death, divorce, desertion, and so on. Observers noted the behavior of all the boys. The boys from homes in which the father was not present sought more attention and help from other boys than did those from homes having fathers present. Also, boys whose fathers left the family circle before the boys were five years of age had more difficulty in learning characteristically masculine behavior than did boys whose fathers were around during these years.

In another study, male college students responded to an antisocial behavior scale. Some of the men came from homes where the fathers were away in military service when their sons were one to four years of age. The other men had been in homes where their fathers were present when they were one to four years old. The men from homes in which the father was absent indicated more participation in antisocial activities than did the others.

It seems that the presence of both fathers and mothers is needed, when possible, for the most successful marriages in terms of their own lives and the lives of their children.

Some other factors related to marital adjustment. Without going into detail, we can list some other factors that have been found to be related to marital happiness.

Cooperative attitude
Respect for each other's individuality
Self-confidence
Health
Economic sufficiency (not necessarily wealth)
Wholesome sex education in childhood and absence of degrading sex attitudes
Wholesome sex harmony between husband and wife
Lack of conflict with the mother or father
Attachment to the parents and to brothers and sisters
Firm but not harsh discipline in childhood
Parental approval of the marriage
Similarity of religious belief, ethnic background, amount of formal education, intellectual ability, and socioeconomic class

What are some of the problems between married people? There are joys in marriage, but there are duties and responsibilities as well. Sometimes there are financial problems; sooner or later there is bound to be sickness; there are sometimes disagreements.

The marriage ceremony does not miraculously make two individuals with different heredities and environments into one personality. After the ceremony they still have their individual likes and dislikes. In one study, some engaged men and women were measured on 38 aspects of personality. The records were kept, and twenty years later the measurements were repeated for 116 of the couples who had married and continued to live together as husband and wife. In general, there had been little tendency, with the passing of the years, for the husbands to become more like their wives or for the wives to become more like their husbands. In fact, for 21 of the 38 aspects of personality, the differences were slightly greater after twenty years.

It is not necessarily undesirable for married persons to disagree. In fact, disagreement on some topics seems to be necessary if there is to be a high degree of marital happiness. Disagreement is dangerous only when it results in quarreling or in the giving up by one person of any attempt to understand the other's point of view.

Unfortunately, marriage sometimes results in unhappiness instead of happiness. Is there any basic cause for unhappy marriages? Many factors enter into the problem, but the following study offers us some clues. One psychologist asked a group of men to indicate the things they disliked about their wives, and gave the wives an opportunity to indicate what they did not like about their husbands. The ten principle grievances, arranged in order of seriousness, are indicated in the table on this page. You will notice that "selfish and inconsiderate" stands high on both lists and that selfishness and inconsiderateness exist in most of the other grievances listed. It is difficult for a marriage to be happy if the scope of an individual's love does not expand beyond the selfish love characteristic of children.

The Ten Most Serious Grievances of Some Married Persons

HUSBANDS' COMPLAINTS REGARDING WIVES	RANK FOR SERIOUSNESS	WIVES' COMPLAINTS REGARDING HUSBANDS
Nags me	1	Selfish and inconsiderate
Not affectionate	2	Unsuccessful in business
Selfish and inconsiderate	3	Untruthful
Complains too much	4	Complains too much
Interferes with my hobbies	5	Does not show his affection
Slovenly in appearance	6	Does not talk things over
Quick-tempered	7	Harsh with children
Interferes with my discipline	8	Touchy
Conceited	9	No interest in children
Insincere	10	Not interested in home

How do marriage counselors help in promoting successful and happy marriages? Many couples seek professional advice from a marriage counselor. Such a person may be a psychologist who has specialized in helping individuals make decisions about the personal problems that have arisen in the course of their courtship or marriage. Or he may be a clergyman, sociologist, psychiatrist, or social worker who is specially trained for this work.

Couples who go to a marriage counselor for premarital counseling often get a head start toward a successful and happy marriage. The counselor will probably give the young couple information about marital problems, listen to their specific problems, suggest several possible solutions, and in many cases reassure them if he thinks such reinforcement is justified. In the light of his knowledge about marital problems, he helps to make decisions about compatibility. But even the best marriage counselor cannot guarantee a marriage without serious personal problems.

Some problems of individual adjustment are almost certain to arise after marriage. These problems may become difficult to solve because they are so emotionally involved that communication between the husband and wife breaks down. Each argues with the other, trying to defend his or her own behavior rather than objectively discussing their problems. Here is where a marriage counselor can provide valuable assistance. One study of married couples who were having difficulties in adjusting to each other found that of those who experienced the least amount of discord and quarreling, 83 percent discussed their marital problems rather than arguing. On the other hand, only 29 percent of those who had the greatest amount of discord and quarreling really discussed their mutual problems. Although they thought that they were discussing their problems, professional evaluation indicated that they tended to resort to arguing.

What is family therapy? So important is the family group that today there is increasing attention being given to family therapy. The father, mother, a child, or an adolescent may have personal and social problems so great that professional help is needed. A therapist meets with the entire family because he recognizes that the problems of one member probably reflect the problems of one or more of the other members in the family. All members of the family are encouraged to express their attitudes and even their gripes toward the other members. Thus, mutual understanding develops and the problems of one or more members of the family can be solved.

Love Between Children and Parents

Where does it come from? How does it develop?

Filial love. Is FILIAL LOVE—the love of children for their parents—"natural" or learned? It is true that the great majority of children love their parents more than they love any other adults in the world. But this love does not exist because of some kind of inherited force that makes children love those who gave them birth as much as because the children have learned to love their parents.

The human baby comes into the world a very helpless creature. He can take food if it is presented to him, but he cannot go about seeking his food. He needs to be kept warm. Who usually supplies the infant with food, clothing, and shelter? Of course, the parents are usually the ones who take care of the baby. This care goes on for years, during which time the child learns to love his parents.

Can a child love his foster parents as much as his biological parents? Suppose that very soon after birth an infant is adopted by

Here a father communicates his love for his young child. There is no inherent reason for mothers to love their children more than fathers do, although circumstances may allow mothers to spend more time with their children.

strangers who care for the child as if he were their own. Certainly the child can learn to love them as much, and as "naturally," as he would his biological parents.

Take the case of a girl who had been adopted as an infant. For years she did not know that she was an adopted child. The foster parents did not tell her, because of the mistaken fear that she would not love them if she knew. Then one day the neighbors felt it their duty to tell the girl that she was "merely" an adopted child. The girl did not believe them and ran to the house to ask her foster parents whether or not she was an adopted child. Although they feared that she would no longer love them, the foster parents told her the truth. She immediately made this significant statement, "Oh, I love you more than ever now, because you have done so much for me and have loved me even though I was not your own child." Actually, psychologically speaking, she *was* their own child.

Parental love. The love of parents for their children is spoken of as PARENTAL LOVE. Usually parents look forward to the coming of an infant. During the months of waiting for its birth, they are preparing to love it. They are overjoyed when it finally arrives. If they have not seen other newborn infants, the parents may be disappointed at first in the appearance of their newborn child. But a newborn baby loses his wrinkles and red face fairly soon after birth. And as they care for him, they learn to love him more and more.

Sometimes people speak of "mother love" as though it were something a mother experiences merely because she is a mother. The mother plays a very important role in the life of the child both before and after birth. It is during this long period that she normally learns to love the child. There is no reason, however, to think the mother has any more "natural" love for the children in the home than the father has—except insofar as the mother may have more opportunity to care for, and so learn to love, the children.

A psychologist reports that at one time he

was on the witness stand in a divorce case. Because the intellectual ability of the child involved was thought to be unusual, the child's intelligence became a factor in determining whether the mother or the father should receive custody of the child. Therefore, the psychologist had been asked to administer an intelligence test and to interpret the results. Following the psychologist's technical report, the lawyer for the mother asked, "In your opinion as a psychologist, isn't it true that a mother naturally has more love for a child to whom she has given birth than does the father?" Through this question the lawyer assumed he would increase his client's chances of receiving the care of the child. He quickly dismissed the psychologist as a witness when the psychologist stated that in his opinion the mere physiological processes of motherhood would not in themselves cause the mother to have any more love than the father had for the child, since love was fundamentally a matter of learning.

Do parents always love their children? Occasionally, married persons do not want children in the home. They may think that children are a source of annoyance or a financial burden. Their love for any children born to them is quite limited. Their attitudes toward children prevent them from learning to love their children.

To give another example of absence of parental love—the father and mother of an illegitimate child are biologically his parents, but often they do not want to love the child born to them. In fact, they may abandon the child or put him up for adoption as soon as possible.

Just as children can love foster parents as much as their biological parents, so also can parents love adopted children as much as their own offspring. Suppose that in a hospital each of two babies was given to the parents of the other. (Hospitals are very careful to prevent this kind of accident.) Wouldn't the two sets of parents learn to love the children who were not biologically their own?

Children

Most of you will marry and have children. If you are to be good parents, you must be prepared to apply principles of mental hygiene in the training of your children. Probably at present you have many opportunities to be with children in your home, in your friends' homes, and in other social situations. Possibly you take care of children while their parents are away. What better time than now to learn how to guide children so that they will grow into well-adjusted and happy adults?

There are many areas in which a child's behavior needs guidance and in which a greater knowledge of how to guide his behavior can be helpful. We will limit ourselves to considering only six topics: children's conscience, lying, cheating, discipline, fear, and television watching.

The Development of Conscience in Children

If an individual engages in undesirable activities such as cheating, lying, or delinquent behavior, he is likely to say that his conscience "hurts." What is a conscience? In psychological terms CONSCIENCE is the ongoing process of an individual's approving or disapproving of his own present behavior or proposed future behavior in terms of his standards of what is right and what is wrong.

How does conscience develop in a child? Certainly the beginnings of conscience are in the home, where even the young child learns what is considered wrong or undesirable behavior and what is considered right or desirable behavior. A leading child psychologist has suggested that two basic factors are involved in the child's development of conscience: (1) identification, and (2) dependency.

As a rule, the child wishes to be like his parents. He identifies himself with them. What the parents do is considered by the child as a good thing for him or her to do. In his play the child copies what his mother and father do and often wishes to dress like the parent of the same sex. Many young children delight in literally trying to walk in their parent's shoes. If the parents make a practice of attending religious services regularly, the child is likely to consider this a good thing to do. He may play-act the service at home. If the parents are friendly with their neighbors and occasionally do things to help them, the child will probably consider such behavior to be right and desirable. He will try to be friendly and helpful "just like Mommy and Daddy."

Although children identify with both parents if both parents are present in the home, at an early age boys begin to identify especially with the father and girls begin to identify with the mother. In one study thirty-one children between the ages of three and five were permitted to play with dolls representing both sexes and then were engaged in conversation to determine their parental orientation. All of the children identified more closely with the like-sex parent than with the opposite-sex parent—boys tended to identify with the father and girls tended to identify with the mother. This trend was especially strong in the case of the boys. Furthermore, the older boys in the group identified with their fathers to a greater extent than did younger boys, which suggests that this identification increases with the years.

The other major factor in the development of conscience is dependency. In addition to depending on parents for food, clothing, and shelter, the child must depend on his parents for learning what is considered right and wrong behavior. The child keeps the pet dog's water dish filled at all times. Parents reinforce this behavior by an affectionate gesture or by saying something positive like "good work." The child quickly learns that such behavior is good or right behavior according to his parents' social standards. If the child pulls the dog's hair, the parents explain to him that such behavior is undesirable because it brings pain to the animal. The child may be scolded. If he pulls the dog's hair again, or even plans to pull it, the child's conscience will "hurt."

The fact that a child develops conscience by identifying with and depending on his parents places a great deal of responsibility on parents. Many psychologists believe that the development of a mature conscience is closely related to the affection that a child receives from his parents during the early years of childhood.

What kind of behavior makes your conscience "hurt?" Your answer to this question will depend on how your conscience developed. Let's consider how some high school students determined when their consciences bothered them.

One study involved asking fifteen-year-old boys and girls how they recognized having a good conscience and how they recognized having a bad conscience. It was reported that a good conscience was accompanied by a feeling of peace, happiness, and satisfaction, whereas a bad conscience was accompanied by feelings of regret, self-condemnation, guilt, and even fear. Further questioning revealed that a good conscience usually went hand-in-hand with normal social behavior, but a bad conscience was often accompanied by withdrawal from social contacts, bad temper, and irritability.

Conscience is frequently considered in terms of religious standards. Back in 1949 a survey was made of the faith of 3676 high school students in the Los Angeles public schools. The results indicated that 36 percent attended religious services regularly, 52 percent attended irregularly, and only 12 percent rarely or never attended. Why did so many students attend religious services, at least to some extent? Did their consciences "hurt" if they did not go? Pressure to attend because of their own conscience was reported by 23 percent of the students. Do you think that data on attendance at religious services would be different if a survey were made in your high school today? What percentage of students in your school would report that their consciences "hurt" if they did not go?

The Problem of Lying

Although most people agree that children should be guided so that they will tell the truth and become honest, studies show that many children and adults do not tell the truth. Apparently their consciences do not disturb them enough to prevent them from lying.

What is lying? Dictionaries usually define LYING as telling falsehoods with the intent to deceive. Children often define lying simply as saying something for which they will be punished. Unfortunately, children are often punished for lying when they are not telling untruths with an intent to deceive. The child may say something he believes is true but which is untrue. At this early age of learning he may be confusing fact with that which is not fact. Perhaps he confuses a fairy tale with reality. He may tell an imaginative story that adults interpret as a lie—although they would not condemn an equally imaginative story told by an adult fiction writer. As a general rule, we can say that up to about the age of four the untruths of children are not lies—that is, their tales do not involve deliberate intent to deceive.

Even adults are not always truthful. We do not frown strongly upon a lie that is told to protect a friend. Many of us may tell "cultural" lies. For example, a girl may say that she is going to be busy on a certain evening rather than tell a boy the truth—that she does not wish to have a date with him. Adults must appreciate the difficulty children experience in learning to distinguish between

This child is engrossed in the fairy tale her father is reading to her. Occasionally children confuse fairy tales with reality and tell stories without intending to deceive, or lie.

truthfulness and untruthfulness. They must not overlook children's lies in the sense of pretending not to notice them. On the other hand, they must look for the basic causes for any lies their children may tell. A lie may be a consequence of the social immaturity of a child, or it may be a symptom of a basic problem of adjustment.

Why do children tell lies? The child may tell a tall tale, which is obviously untruthful, to attract attention to himself. Such a lie should be regarded as a symptom of feelings of inferiority. Instead of being punished, the child should be helped to find other ways of satisfying his desire for approval and recognition.

The child may lie because an adult suggests the lie to him. The mother may say, "You did well on that test today, didn't you? Because if you didn't...!" The child may have made a poor grade on the test, but how can he answer the question truthfully when it is phrased in such a way? Sometimes children lie because adults force them to give an immediate answer, whereas the children might give truthful answers if they had enough time to think them out.

The child may purposely tell an untruth in self-defense. The child who has accidentally broken a dish is asked whether or not he did so. He may know from past experience that he will be punished for breaking the dish if he tells the truth. Therefore, he lies. In such a case the fault is more with the parents' methods of child guidance than with the child.

Selfishness is often the basic motive for lying. The child may lie to protect himself at the expense of others. He may say that a brother or sister broke the dish that he actually had broken. Possibly his lie is an attempt to get revenge on the brother or sister for something displeasing they may have done to him.

Among young children there is a tendency to escape from a very unpleasant situation by denying that it ever existed. They lie about an event, trying to make it not so by saying it is not so. Sometimes adults show similar behavior on receiving very bad news. They may say, "Oh, no! it can't be true."

When under emotional stress, the child may even convince himself, at least for the moment, that his statement is true, although adults call it a lie. Often, however, when adults make similar untrue statements they call it rationalizing, not lying.

The Problem of Cheating

Cheating among children is not unusual. Sometimes children cheat as a kind of thrilling sport. "Getting away with it" is a game. If they win, the other children will look up to them as being clever.

Do children learn to cheat? Most children are not specifically and directly taught to cheat. In fact, most children are probably taught that cheating is wrong. But psychologists have found that there is often little relationship between moral knowledge and moral conduct. Unfortunately, the child may readily learn to cheat from the example of adults and other children. A psychologist asked 376 children in the primary grades, "Do the boys and girls often try to cheat you?" Of the boys, 42 percent replied in the affirmative. Of the girls, 33 percent replied in the affirmative. Then the children were asked, "Is it all right to cheat if no one sees you?" Nine percent of the boys and 12 percent of the girls answered yes. In other words, one child out of ten thought that it was all right to cheat if no one observed that he was cheating. Obviously, ways must be found for children to develop attitudes that are favorable toward honesty and unfavorable toward dishonesty. Situations must be provided that will give children an opportunity to feel secure and successful without having to resort to dishonesty in an effort to achieve their goals.

Cheating in school. Cheating does not disappear with the passing of childhood. You may know of instances of cheating in high school. In some high schools a teacher who has several sections of the same course will give an examination in each of the classes on the same day. The students in the ten o'clock class ask the students in the previous class what questions were asked. The same thing happens for subsequent classes. This gives the students in later classes some advantage, even though the teacher may not ask exactly the same questions in all classes. Isn't this a form of cheating?

If we see someone stealing, offering a bribe, or using his social position to secure some special privilege, we are likely to become infuriated. If we know that a small child cheats in school, we are quick to condemn him. Yet if we see someone cheating on a high school test or know that a student hands in another student's report as though it were his own, we hesitate to report the incident or even to reprimand the cheater. Indirectly we are offering our approval of cheating even though we do not cheat ourselves.

What is the attitude of high school students toward cheating? At one time high school students were questioned about their attitudes toward cheating in school work. Expressing their attitudes orally in an informal group discussion, 60 percent of them said that cheating was seriously wrong, while 33 percent condoned some cheating because they thought school marks were more important than honesty in schoolwork. Also, 33 percent said they thought cheating was all right if the person was not caught. Only 11 percent of the students felt that those who cheated were looked down on by other students. (The percentages total more than 100 because students were free to express their opinions on more than one view.)

Would a student cheat himself? To find out if students would cheat themselves when studying programmed books by choosing to look at the answers before responding to the questions, one psychologist had some college freshmen study a programmed book requiring about six and one-half hours to complete. With the book they were given an appendix that listed one or more acceptable answers for each frame in the program. Needless to say, they were instructed to complete each lesson before they compared their responses with those in the appendix. Two of the answers in the appendix were entirely unrelated to the corresponding items in the book. Of the fifty-two students who answered all of the items in the lessons, thirteen turned in answers that included these unrelated and completely inappropriate answers. In other words, 25 percent of the students had used the answers in the appendix and had cheated themselves. These students had significantly lower scores on a test covering the material in the programmed book than those who had completed the lessons as instructed.

What can be done about cheating? Most students who cheat do so to raise their school marks (although students who admitted to cheating in surveys had poorer final marks than noncheaters). In one study 36 percent of the students said that cheating was one way of getting revenge for poor teaching, although this may have been a rationalization on their part. Yet even if there is no cheating, marks, as they are given in many schools to-

change	1. *Learning* is a *relatively permanent change* in *behavior* that occurs as the result of *practice*. Thus learning is not a behavior —it is a _____ in behavior.
permanent	2. Learning is a relatively _____ change in behavior. This excludes temporary states such as fatigue or adaptation.
practice	3. Learning occurs as a result of _____. The idea here is to exclude from the definition of learning anything that has to do with maturation.
relatively change, behavior practice	4. Therefore we say that learning is a _____ permanent _____ in _____ that occurs as the result of _____.

It is very easy to look at the answers and cheat yourself when using a programmed book, such as the excerpt above. To make the best use of it, however, you should cover up the left column until after you have filled in the blanks on the right.

day, may be inaccurate measurements of actual student accomplishment. In time various mechanical aids and new teaching methods may free teachers from having to spend so much of their time teaching facts and then basing students' marks on the learning of these facts. Teachers may eventually be free to guide students mainly in the areas of creative thinking and the development of social values. Under these conditions students could compete with their own previous records rather than with the records of other students. In fact, in some schools traditional marking systems have already disappeared. Relieved of the pressure of competitive marks, isn't it possible that someday students may no longer cheat in school?

Probably in a relatively few years you will be parents and will have children in school. How will you react to any known cases of cheating by your children?

The Problem of Discipline

As you guide your children for living in the small social group of your family, and as you prepare them for living in larger social groups, you will probably use some disciplinary measures. The problem of discipline must be faced by everyone who is responsible for guiding a child's behavior. Many persons use the words "discipline" and "punishment" interchangeably. We will use DISCIPLINE to mean the entire program of adapting the child to social life. Punishment may occasionally be necessary in this program, but it plays only a minor and an emergency role.

What is the purpose of discipline? The ultimate goal of discipline is the achievement of self-control or self-discipline. A well-adjusted adult does not have to be told what to do and when to do it. He disciplines himself. The child can learn self-discipline only through experience with self-discipline. If an adult controls a child's behavior by telling him exactly what to do on all occasions, the adult may secure what seems at the time to be faultless behavior from the child. Yet that child is not learning self-control. Discipline should be a matter of guidance, or leadership, and should rely on example rather than coercion.

We may think that a child should pick up his playthings. We would achieve this result by commanding the child to pick up his toys and then rewarding him with candy for doing so—or spanking him if he does not comply. But if we always use such methods, how will the child learn self-regulation? On the other hand, we can suggest to the child that he is old enough now to take care of his own possessions. We could mention how much neater the room will be after he picks up his toys. We might suggest that he take the responsibility for putting his toys away each evening now that he is so grown-up. The child who is disciplined by being trained to accept his little responsibilities is being prepared for a responsible adulthood.

Discipline must be consistent. One fundamental principle of discipline is that treatment of the child be consistent. If one day we permit him to scatter his toys all over the floor and the next day we forbid him to do so, how can we expect him to know what is desirable behavior?

When told not to take his toys out of the toy chest, the child will probably ask, "Why?" This is a perfectly reasonable question. Yet many children receive the answer, "Never mind why. Do as you are told!" The adult has a reason for telling the child not to scatter his toys around on a particular day. Perhaps friends are coming, and the house should be neat and orderly. Why not take time to explain this reason to the child? The explanation may take just a little more time than the command "Do as you are told!" but it will help to prepare the child for a responsible adulthood.

When two or more adults share the responsibility of training a child, they must be careful to keep this joint training consistent. If the father says, "You may ride your tricycle around the block," and the mother says, "Don't ride your tricycle around the block," how can the child be expected to know what he is to do? The child will soon learn to take advantage of such disagreement. Adults engaged jointly in the serious business of training children must have frequent conferences and agree on fundamental principles of discipline.

Should you use reward or punishment? First of all, prevention of socially undesirable behavior is easier and more effective than the attempted correction of such behavior after it has developed. It is much easier to remove car keys when leaving the car than it is to punish a thief who steals the car with keys left in it. Providing little sticks to play with is much better than punishing the child for playing with matches.

But if it is necessary to use reward or punishment, it is usually better to use reward rather than punishment. Consider the following experiment, which bears out this principle. A psychologist had four groups of school children work on a series of tests in arithmetic addition for five consecutive days. The groups, designated as first, second, third, and fourth, were equal in ability at the beginning of the experiment. To all four groups of children praise was a form of reward and a reprimand was a form of punishment. Each day the first group was called to the front of the room, and the members were publicly praised for their work. The second group was called to the front of the room each day and the members were publicly reprimanded for poor work. The third group was ignored, although the members were in the same room and could hear the others being praised or reproved. The fourth group served as a control. They were in another room and could hear neither the praise nor the reproof.

The results of the experiment are shown in the graph on this page. You can see that at first, reward and punishment were equally effective in producing desired school activity. After the first session, however, punishment lost its effect, whereas reward continued to be effective. As for the ignored group, they seem to have profited slightly by hearing others praised or reproved. They may have been trying to attract some attention to themselves by showing improvement.

Extrinsic rewards. An EXTRINSIC REWARD is an artificial one, not directly or logically associated with the behavior being rewarded. Should extrinsic rewards be used in child training? Should we promise to give Johnny a quarter if he will eat his spinach? Or promise Betty a new doll if she will hang up her clothes every day? Such artificial rewards must be used sparingly. Any reward loses its value if given frequently and for too little achievement.

It is true that artificial rewards produce temporarily desirable behavior. Johnny eats his spinach and Betty hangs up her clothes. In the long run, however, the results of using rewards of this kind may be quite undesirable. The giving of paper stars, buttons, and merit cards is a less objectionable form of rewarding children than that of bribing them with quarters or presents. The star, button, or card has value only in that it is related to desirable behavior; it may help the child to recognize the value of social approval. A child who does

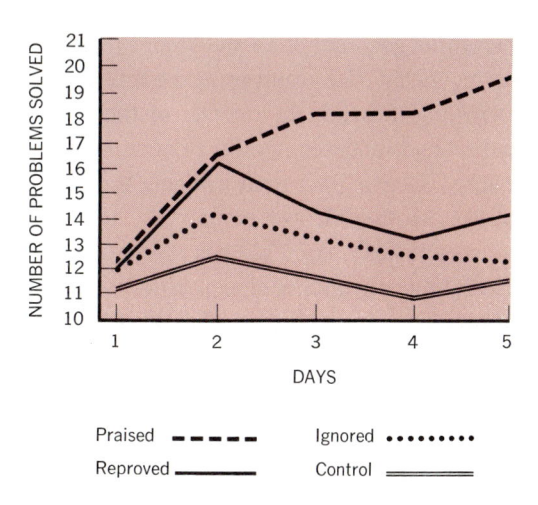

The relative effects of reward, punishment, and indifference on efficiency

not feel the need for learning the alphabet may learn it in order to have a star placed after his name on a school chart. Along with the alphabet, the child learns that even though a task may be unpleasant, it can be satisfying if it brings the approval of his parents, teacher, and classmates.

When giving artificial rewards to children, the adult dispensing them should try to help the children understand the social value of the behavior being rewarded. The adult should distinguish between the social value and the actual worth of the artificial rewards by themselves.

Intrinsic rewards. An INTRINSIC REWARD is logically associated with the behavior being rewarded. It is better to train a child to work for intrinsic rewards than for extrinsic rewards and, whenever possible, intrinsic rewards should be substituted for artificial ones. Johnny is interested in growing up to be big and strong like his father, or like his favorite television personality. If we explain to Johnny that eating a good breakfast will help him to achieve this goal and if we weigh and measure him frequently, with appropriate comments on his growing muscles, the quarter or the paper star becomes unnecessary or at most supplementary. Betty is interested in being a woman just like Mother. If we explain to her that Mother puts her own clothes away and if occasionally we comment on how grownup Betty is getting to be, a new doll or an award button will not be necessary.

Artificial punishment. Should Johnny be spanked if he does not eat his spinach? Should Betty be slapped if she does not hang up her clothes? For many adults, the answer to these questions seems to be, "Yes, it works." Or they quote, "Spare the rod and spoil the child." Yet psychological experiments have indicated that the effectiveness of ARTIFICIAL PUNISHMENT—punishment that is not a direct or logical outcome of the behavior being punished—is uncertain. Artificial punishment only sometimes extinguishes behavior, while reward usually reinforces behavior. In general, punishment merely suppresses behavior but does not result in the desired unlearning. The use of punishment alone shows the individual what *not* to do, but it does not show him the correct behavior, or what he is supposed to do.

Since artificial punishments are not always very effective, why are they used so frequently? Perhaps the answer lies in the effect that punishment has upon parents or other adults, rather than in the permanent effects of punishment upon children. When a child does something that the adult does not approve of and is punished immediately, the child ceases his undesirable behavior for the time being. That is, the adult's action is immediately reinforced by the end of the child's annoying behavior. The adult quickly learns that he can operate on the environment to bring about a desired result by punishing the child.

Despite the disadvantages of artificial punishment, there are some occasions when it must be used with children. Although punishment should be the logical consequence of the undesirable act, which artificial punishment is not, logical punishment can hardly be arranged in many cases. And at times the logical punishment itself is undesirable. For example, the logical consequence of playing in the street is injury or death in traffic, a very undesirable punishment. It may be necessary to use some form of artificial punishment temporarily as a deterrent, especially with very young children.

How should corporal punishment be administered? If artificial corporal punishments, such as spankings, must be used, they should not be administered while the adult is angry. Punishment should be only for the purpose of producing socially desirable behavior on the part of the child. Punishment administered in anger is usually more severe than is necessary for learning purposes. When we are angry, we do not realize our own strength.

Another guideline is that punishment should be administered immediately following the undesirable behavior. Nevertheless, it is better not to punish immediately if the adult cannot control his anger.

An even better rule is that a child should be punished at the beginning of undesired behavior rather than after the behavior has been completed. Many children like to poke wires or other metal objects into electric outlets. Why not? They see their parents plug in lamps, the vacuum cleaner, and the television. Yet poking a wire into an outlet can be dangerous to the child. It is better psychologically, as well as for his safety, to punish the child as he prepares to poke the wire into the outlet rather than after he has done so.

If corporal punishment for undesirable behavior seems necessary, the punishment can be made more effective if, as soon as possible, some similar but desirable behavior can be reinforced. If we punish a child for putting a wire into an electric outlet, it would be more effective if he then began putting pegs into his pegboard, for which he would immediately get a pat on the back or some other reinforcement.

The Problem of Fear

Children are afraid more often than adults realize. A psychologist questioned some children in primary grades and found that 31 percent of the boys and 49 percent of the girls admitted that they were often afraid of things. Probably even more of the children than would admit it were frequently afraid.

Are fears learned? Is it "just natural" for children to be afraid of the dark, of dead animals, of white rats, or of a policeman? To the contrary, the evidence indicates that such fears are learned.

The snake, in particular, has earned a reputation as an object of people's fears. Do children have an unlearned fear of snakes? Do they show signs of fear the very first time they see a snake? We have laboratory evidence that even adult chimpanzees fear snakes the first time they see one. The chimpanzees tested had been raised from birth in a laboratory, where it was known that they had never seen a snake before. Human children often show fear of a snake the first time they see one, too.

However, not all babies fear snakes on first exposure. An infant chimpanzee that is frequently exposed to snakelike objects from birth does not show fear the first time it sees an actual snake. Children whose parents are fond of snakes and keep them as pets throughout the life of the child do not show fear of

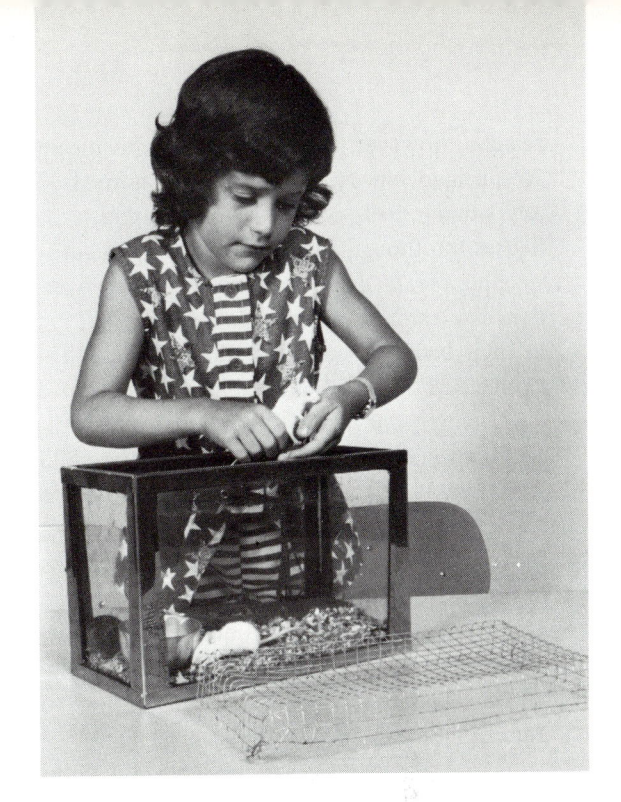

Although some women are afraid of mice, this girl is not the least bit frightened. Fears of animals such as mice are learned. Children brought up with pet mice show no fear of them.

snakes. Perhaps it is the strangeness and the sudden slithering movements of the snake that make some human and chimpanzee babies afraid of them, not the fact that the organism is a snake. Since fear of snakes does not usually develop until a child is two or three years of age, the child by then has had many opportunities to learn to be afraid of similar strange objects and creatures.

Children learn to fear other things besides snakes. Death is a concept that a child finds almost impossible to comprehend. Therefore, he easily learns to fear death. Many children have a fear of dying by the age of five. Perhaps a grandparent, other relative, or playmate died following an illness or an accident. To soften the fact of death, the parents may tell the child that the deceased is asleep. The child soon

THE FAMILY GROUP **363**

realizes, however, that the person who meant so much to him is not around anymore. Is it any wonder that some children become terrified at the thought of going to bed at night if sleeping means death to them? Is it any wonder that some children want a light left on in their bedroom so that if they awaken they can be sure at once that they are not "asleep"?

Children can learn to be afraid of fear itself. Especially in the case of boys, the child who is experiencing fear is told, "Don't be afraid. Be brave. Act like a man." Since he is anxious to become a man, being afraid means to him that he is not masculine and so he fears being afraid. Unfortunately, he does not know that brave soldiers in combat are often quite afraid, show their fear, and are willing to admit that they are afraid.

There are certain situations that a child must learn to fear for his own safety. A child must learn to be careful of moving cars. He must learn that under some circumstances fire is dangerous. He must learn that some substances are unsafe to eat. He must have wholesome fears of those dangers everyone must face. This does not mean, of course, that he ought to be terrified by every situation.

What causes fear in children? One source of fear in children is the sensation of falling. Sudden removal of bodily support produces an emotional reaction in very young infants that is usually interpreted as fear. If an infant is accidentally dropped he will show a fear reaction, even though he lands quite safely on a nice soft mattress. An infant held in an elevator that begins a very rapid descent will probably cry in fear.

A loud noise will also cause a fear reaction in infants. An infant may be quite happy in his crib, he may even be asleep, but if he hears a pan drop or some other loud noise, he will probably start crying.

The suddenness with which a child is stimulated seems to be related to fear. In fact, the suddenness of a noise seems to be more important than the loudness of the noise in causing fear.

Another source of fear is the strangeness of a situation, especially if the situation occurs rather suddenly. Many a carefully planned Christmas festivity for a child has been spoiled by the sudden appearance of a strange man with a strange white beard, wearing a red suit and shouting "Ho! Ho! Ho!"

The older a child becomes, the better he is able to differentiate between the familiar and the strange. As he comes to recognize what is strange to him, the child becomes more likely to react to strangeness by crying or some other expression of fear.

If there is any great discrepancy between what a person expects and what actually happens, fear is likely to occur. A child expectantly waiting for his mother to walk through the door sees a dog come running out instead. Although the child is not ordinarily afraid of dogs, there may well be a fear reaction.

Of course, the most common source of human fears seems to depend on learned expectancies of distress or pain, which begin developing in childhood.

How can adults counteract the fear experiences of children? Adults cannot prevent every unfortunate experience from taking place, but they can help a child to face fearful experiences as part of life. Some children are afraid because of a personal fear-producing experience. For example, the child who has been hurt in an automobile accident may generalize his fear and become afraid of cars. When a child has a fear experience, adults should not exclaim "Oh!" and "Ah!" and "Poor darling!" They should remove the danger, care for the child if he has been injured, and assure him that he is safe.

In counteracting unfortunate fear experiences, adults should apply their knowledge of conditioning. If the child has been burned on the stove, he should then have pleasant experiences with the stove—possibly he could watch his mother cook something that he especially likes. If he has learned to be afraid of dogs, an adult may help by playing with a puppy in his presence and encouraging, but not forcing, him to pat the puppy. The child who has learned to be afraid of automobiles may be taken for a short ride under as pleasant circumstances as possible, probably in the company of other children who are not afraid.

The child should have opportunities to become acquainted with feared situations on his own, free from compulsion or enticement by adults. He should be able to approach and retreat from the fear-producing situation at his own will. As the child gradually moves closer and closer to the fear-producing situation without showing fear, extinction of that fear takes place.

A very basic way of dealing with children's fears is to help the children develop skills that will enable them to cope with possible fearful situations. Parents who teach or otherwise provide instruction in swimming and water safety may not only be counteracting unfortunate past experiences, they are also preventing future unfortunate experiences in the water.

This young girl is unfamiliar with ponies and has some fear in being so close to one. However, by reassuring her, showing her how to approach the animal, and praising her for doing so, her father can help the child overcome her fear.

Adults may unintentionally teach or increase a child's fears. Most of the fears that children have are the result of teaching by adults and other children. Sometimes this teaching is not intended by the adult. Perhaps an adult is unreasonably afraid of snakes, even harmless little ones. If, while with a child, he sees a garter snake and shows an exaggerated fear, the child will learn to have the same unreasonable fear. Adults should strive not to show their unreasonable fears in the presence of children.

If we force a child to participate in a feared situation, we are forcing the child to practice an undesirable response that is likely to become even more undesirable. Sometimes well-meaning parents coax their two- or three-year-old children far into the surf. Sooner or later the children are knocked down by big waves and become terrified of the water. Wise parents let their children play along the beach where the water is only a few inches deep, for a whole day if necessary. Later, they will find their children plunging fearlessly into the surf.

Adults are often tempted to steer the child away from all experiences that have frightened the child in the past. This, however, would prevent the child from learning how to meet such situations when they recur. To direct the child away from all possible fear-producing situations or to shield him carefully from any mention of fear-producing situations assumes that he will forget his fears over a period of time. Yet studies have shown that the passing of time in itself does not necessarily insure forgetting. In fact, the fears may become intensified.

Fear is an undesirable means of discipline. In far too many cases the teaching of fears is intentional. If parents do not want a child to disturb things in a room, they may tell him that it is dark in the room and that a bogeyman will get him if he goes into it. The child may be told that a policeman will come and take him away if he does not behave, or that a doctor will cut off the child's ears. Lies and threats may stop undesirable behavior, at least until the child recognizes them for what they are. But such a cure is worse than the disease.

Fear should never be used as a means of discipline. To instill unnecessary and unreasonable fears in a child is to prepare him for a maladjusted and unhappy adult life. We cannot expect a timid child to grow into a self-confident adult. It is true that by a long and careful period of training many childhood fears can be overcome. But it is best to remember the principle that prevention is better than cure.

Television Watching

One very important area of family behavior is that of watching television programs. Most of the activities in which children participate, such as school classes, school athletic events, scouting, and even many religious activities, are not centered around the home. Other than mealtimes, watching television is often one of the few occasions when the family is together as a group.

How common is television watching? It has been estimated that about 98 percent of American homes have television sets. In the average home the set is turned on more than six hours a day, seven days a week, and even more frequently during the winter months. The typical American child spends 3000 hours watching television before he begins his formal schooling. Although this is equivalent to about three usual school years in the primary grades, probably very little of the television-watching time is devoted to programs of any real educational value, and some may be positively harmful. Approximately eight violent episodes per hour are shown on television, and about 97 percent of the cartoons for children contain acts of violence.

What are some results of television watching on children? We know that the same program will have different effects on different children. For instance, children who have few friends tend to daydream more about a program after seeing it than do children who have a more adequate social life. Also, after watching a given program, boys tend to remember the fight scenes in which the male hero of the program participated, whereas girls tend to remember the romantic scenes involving the heroine of the program.

A number of research studies have been done on the influence of television on children. In one study the children were divided into two groups, those spending an unusually large amount of time watching television (heavy viewers) and those spending relatively little time watching television (light viewers). Also, the IQ's for all the children were secured and the children were divided into three groups: those having low IQ's, those having middle IQ's, and those having high IQ's. A third variable in this study was that some of the children were in the sixth grade and some were in the tenth grade. The data are summarized in the table on this page.

You will note that the percentage of light viewers increases between the sixth and tenth grades, with the greatest increase in the high IQ group. The percentage of heavy viewers decreases between the sixth and tenth grades, especially in the high IQ group. Did the amount of television that you watched increase or decrease between the sixth and tenth grades?

A report from the United States Surgeon General's office concluded that under some circumstances watching violence on television can cause persons to act aggressively. According to this report, which is a summary of several dozen research projects and other data, impressionable young children who rely on television watching for a great deal of their knowledge about the world are probably the ones most influenced by watching violence on television. Although the data are not conclusive, evidence does indicate a slight relationship between seeing violence and aggressive behavior.

Perhaps what is involved is not so much

Percentages of Sixth- and Tenth-Grade Children of Differing Intellectual Abilities Considered as Light and Heavy Television Viewers

	LOW IQ	MIDDLE IQ	HIGH IQ
Light viewers			
6th grade	24%	27%	36%
10th grade	33	49	70
Heavy viewers			
6th grade	76	73	64
10th grade	67	51	30

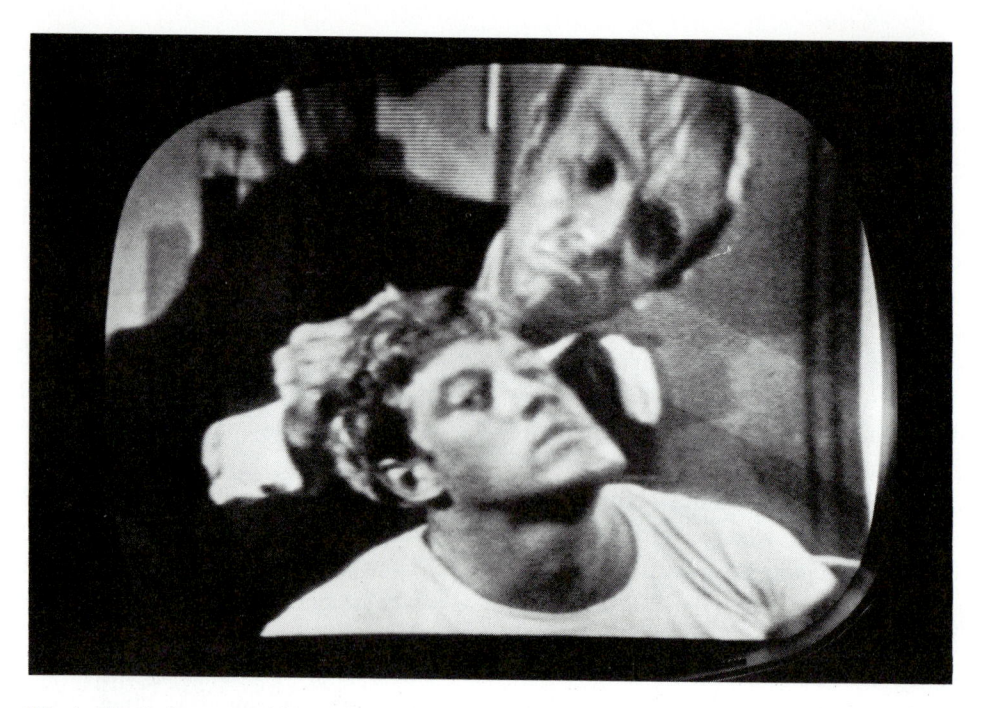

What effect does watching aggression and violence on television have on the viewer? How many of the programs that you watch include violence? How does it affect you?

that viewing violence causes aggressive behavior as that it sometimes shows how to be aggressive or perform antisocial acts. For example, several years ago a television drama entitled "The Doomsday Flight" portrayed an individual who placed a bomb on an airplane and then repeatedly telephoned the airline about the bomb. Within twenty-four hours airlines had received four real telephone calls, and by the end of the next week eight bomb threats had been made to them. Over the past few years there have been many attempts to "skyjack" airplanes (to steal planes, and occasionally even bail out in midair afterward), some of which seem to be carbon copies of previous attempts broadcast over television. Perhaps what is mainly being learned from observing violence on television is the methods to be used in antisocial acts.

We have now considered behavior in a very basic small group, the family. In the next chapter we will examine some fundamental aspects of behavior in a slightly larger group, the peer group.

➤ Terms to Know

artificial punishment	extrinsic reward	intrinsic reward
conscience	family therapy	lying
discipline	filial love	parental love

Topics to Think About

1. If you had your choice, would you like to live as a member of a close family group consisting of grandparents, parents, and children of your generation, or would you rather live in a family group consisting only of parents and children, away from all other relatives? What would be the advantages and disadvantages of each arrangement?

2. Who should be the "boss" in a family, the mother or the father? Why?

3. Would you like to have your children spend most of their time in a kibbutz or some other social group for children rather than living in a house or apartment with their parents? Consider this question from the point of view of the child, the parent, and the society.

4. What do you think are the ideal circumstances within a family for rearing children?

5. Would you "spoil" your children? But first, what do you mean by "spoil"? What about the old saying, "Spare the rod and spoil the child"? When would you resort to punishment? What kind of punishment would you use?

6. Do you remember ever lying to your parents? What was the reaction of your parents? How would you treat a child who lied to you?

7. How much would you permit your children to watch television? Would you permit viewing some programs and prohibit viewing other programs, or would you give your children free choice as to quantity and quality? If the first, on what basis would you select programs for them to watch?

Suggestions for Activities

1. Read several autobiographies or biographies that describe the childhood of the person and take notes on the development of the individual's conscience—what influences were brought to bear on him; what values were stressed, and how; and how the person's conscience affected his behavior. Compare the influence of conscience on the person's behavior in each of the books.

2. As a class, make a collection of valentines as well as of cards such as are often sent to parents on Mother's Day and Father's Day. Compare the concept of love that is presented in them. Do any of them suggest that love is a learning process? Which kind of card stresses most the pleasures connected with love?

3. Analyze some current popular love songs. If available, compare these songs with love songs written twenty to thirty or more years ago. How do popular songs describe love? Is the emphasis on physical attraction? Do the songs suggest basic characteristics necessary for a happy married life? Is there any difference between what is emphasized now and what was emphasized thirty years ago? If so, what are the differences?

4. Note and record the kinds of disciplinary measures used by parents. These records can be compiled merely by observing parents with their children at social gatherings or in such public places as stores. Do parents suggest some fearful outcome if the child does not behave? Do they suggest that the child will not be loved if he does not do as the parents wish? Is ridicule used? Is there corporal punishment or threat of such punishment? Is there any indication that the children return to the forbidden behavior soon after such techniques are used? Which is the more common method of discipline—punishment or reward? Compare your findings with those of your classmates.

5. Make a list of fears you had when you were a small child. Do you know the circumstances under which at least some of these fears developed? What efforts did your parents make to counteract these fears? If you find that your children have such fears, how will you attempt to counteract them?

6. Watch some of the television programs that are so popular with children. If possible, watch a program with a child so that you can note his reactions. A few days after watching the program, ask the child to tell you about it. What does he remember most?

7. Survey the parents in your community on whether or not they feel any regulations should be imposed on television programs that show violence, and if so, what regulations they would want. Then survey children on the same subject. Are there differences between the two groups? Is there any agreement within each group?

Suggestions for Further Reading

Kelley, Robert K., *Courtship, Marriage, and the Family,* Harcourt Brace Jovanovich. A college textbook that explores courtship patterns in America, early adjustments in marriage, and the development of family life.

Ruch, Floyd L., and Philip G. Zimbardo, *Psychology and Life,* 8th ed., Scott, Foresman. See Chapter 9, "The Motivation of Behavior," and pages 366–69, "The Maternal Drive and 'Contact Comfort.'"

Schramm, Wilbur L., J. Lyle, and E. B. Parker, *Television in the Lives of Our Children,* Stanford University Press. A description of some of the effects of television on youngsters.

Sears, Robert R., E. E. Maccoby, and H. Levin, *Patterns of Child Rearing,* Harper & Row. A report on child-rearing practices as determined by interviews with mothers. It examines child-training procedures and the effects of different procedures on the child.

Sorenson, Herbert, Marguerite Malm, and G. A. Forehand, *Psychology for Living,* 3rd ed., McGraw-Hill. A high school psychology textbook with an emphasis on adjustment. See Chapter 5, "An Effective Marital Relationship," for information on marital expectations and family pitfalls.

Wertheimer, M., et al., *Psychology: A Brief Introduction,* Scott, Foresman. See pages 64–66, 68–72, on social motives, development of fears, and how bodily contact reduces fear.

chapter 15
The Peer Group

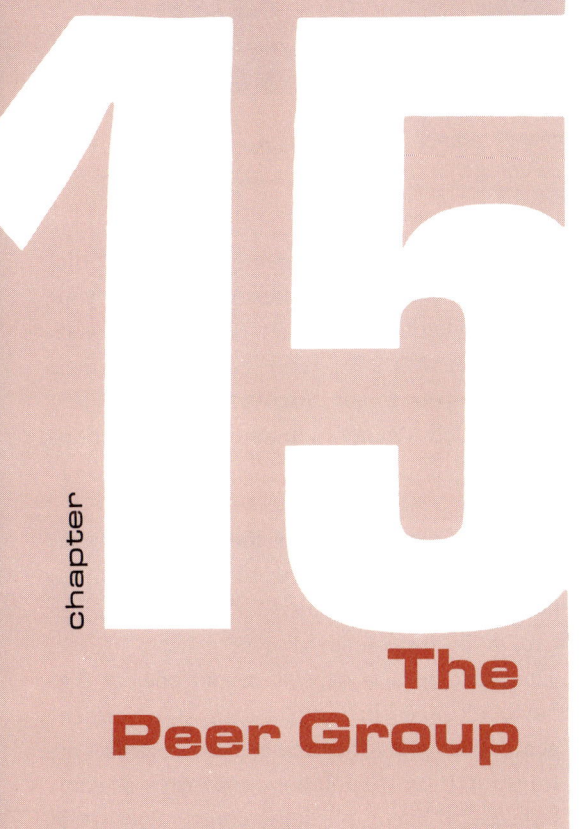

THE PEER GROUP plays a vital role in a person's social and emotional development. A PEER GROUP consists of individuals who are approximately the same age and have about the same status. It is the medium through which the individual practices social skills and develops beliefs about himself and others. The child wants to be accepted by members of his own age and sex, and at times the views of his peers are more important to him than those of his own parents.

Although each individual has a peer group, regardless of his age, we will emphasize the roles and influences of the peer group on young people.

The Generation Gap

The GENERATION GAP involves differences between the values, beliefs, and attitudes of one generation and those of another. It is usually associated with the differences between parents and their offspring.

There are a number of studies that show disagreements between parents and offspring. For example, in one study of the differences between college-age students and their fathers, conducted in the mid-1960's, the following results were found:

	STUDENTS	FATHERS
Repelled by long hair	7%	32%
U.S. should not be in Vietnam	78	46
Opposed to marijuana	21	92
Approved of interracial marriage	61	18

From the above data it is obvious that differences do exist in the attitudes of the students and their fathers in these areas.

One superficial evidence of a generation gap is the difference in appearance, in clothing and hair styles, between young people and an older generation.

Young people today feel that the generation gap also includes a "communications gap," which is a lack of adequate communication and understanding between themselves and not only their parents but also older people in general.

Is today's generation gap unique? Contrary to the opinion of some, the generation gap is not of recent origin. For example, one of the reasons that some of the early Pilgrims came to this country was to remove their children from what they considered to be the disrupting influences of other youths. The parents feared that their children were being drawn away from the traditional religious beliefs. A much earlier example is provided by Socrates, who lived over two thousand years ago. He stated that the youth of his day did not obey their parents and were discourteous to adults. Perhaps if you asked your parents whether or not they had disagreements in values, attitudes, and beliefs with their parents, you might discover that they also experienced a generation and communications gap.

What are some causes of the current generation gap? Although it would be difficult to determine specific causes of the generation gap, it is possible to discuss general causes. There are several aspects of our society that have resulted in emphasizing the present generation gap. The tremendous increases in transportation, population, and ways of communication have partially contributed. It is so easy, compared to earlier days, for the youth of today to gather in groups or talk over the phone. And they have more time to do so than their parents had when they were children. Since young people now have many means at their disposal for reaching and communicating with one another, they can exchange views and develop mutual values more easily than in the past.

Another factor in creating today's generation gap is the difference in the economic experiences of the generations. Some parents of today were born prior to and during the Depression of the 1930's, and were deprived of many things. Many of them resolved to work harder so that their children would not suffer such deprivations. With the greater affluence of the 1960's and 1970's in our society, though, some young people no longer find the values of hard work and acquiring material goods so important.

Another possible reason for the present gap is the tremendous amount of information and knowledge that is available today and is constantly accelerating. Some of this information helps to increase the differences between the generations. In the past, many parents emphasized repression of behavior. Now parents are more exposed to books and articles advocating freedom of expression and little restriction of their children's behavior. There is a difference in values and methods of upbringing between generations. In addition, children now learn about subjects, such as psychology, that often were not studied when their parents were in school. Other subjects, such as math and foreign languages, are taught in a new way. Some of the knowledge learned by parents is now out of date. As a result, the younger generation and their parents may have difficulty in understanding and communicating with one another on various topics.

Although today's parents lived under the threat of the Depression and World War II, the younger generation has grown up in a world that offers threats of much greater proportions, such as a nuclear war. The younger generation looks at the problems of crime, drugs, nuclear weapons, and so on, that they must help to solve, and some blame the older generation for creating them. Of course, the older generation also inherited problems, as has each generation. The major difficulty seems to be that each succeeding generation inherits problems of much vaster proportions. And these problems cannot be ignored. Anyone who believes that he has no role in helping to solve the problems, because he did not create them, is in the same situation as the man who watches the forest fire approach his home and does nothing, because he did not start the fire.

One other factor that influences the dissonance between adults and younger people is the fact that our society has no clear division between childhood and acceptance as an adult. In societies in which the individual is formally recognized at a given time—say, at an initiation ceremony—as an adult, the person is more likely to identify with the values and beliefs of adults. But in our society an individual often gradually progresses from childhood to adulthood without specific delineations of the divisions between being a child, a young person, and an adult. The result is that instead of looking forward to a specific time when they will be recognized as adults, young people often develop a different set of values and beliefs.

Some parents are quite disturbed when their offspring obey the standards of the peer group more than those of their own parents. In one study of high school girls it was found that the girls had a tendency to comply with their peers on issues that the peers believed important, and to comply with the parents on issues that the parents thought important.

BERRY'S WORLD

"Your mother and I know how it is, son—and we hope you will be able to find yourself soon!"

© 1970 by NEA, Inc.

However, the more important the girl personally felt the issue to be, the more likely she was to rely on her parents' judgment.

In conclusion, it should be added that there are some people today who do not believe that a gap of any type exists between the older and younger generations; or if one does exist, it is no worse than any that might have existed in earlier times. We would probably all agree that if there were more communication, patience, and understanding of one another, this world would be a much better place in which to live. Actually, by applying what we learn from the field of psychology, each of us can improve conditions and make the world around us a better place.

Peer-Group Influence

The time in his life when an individual directs his social attention to people other than members of his peer group is as an infant. As the individual progresses from infancy to adulthood, the influences of the peer group can have as much or more influence than his own parents, depending on the specific behavior involved.

Why is the peer group such a great influence on young people? One reason is that the peer group provides an atmosphere in which the younger person can find secure relationships with others of his own age. The first friendships are usually developed within the family group. Then the support of his contemporaries helps the individual make a transition from parental control to more self-control. To some extent, the peer group takes over the control of behavior. For example, parents may overlook selfcenteredness in their offspring, but it may not be tolerated in the peer group. The peer group can often cause an individual to change his behavior.

Another reason why the influence of peers is so important is that they help the individual obtain an evaluation of himself. The first evaluations of behavior are usually made within the family, which sometimes gives individuals a biased and inaccurate picture of their abilities, skills, values, and attitudes. For example, a child with a higher than average mechanical ability may have siblings who have even more ability in this area. When he compares himself to his siblings, he may develop the belief that his mechanical ability is inferior. When he later compares his ability to those in his peer group, some of whom have less than average ability, he can reevaluate himself and arrive at a more accurate assessment. Or, if a child has higher intellectual ability than his siblings, he may discover that he doesn't do as well as he had expected when he later compares his ability to his peers. An individual needs to evaluate himself and his degrees of competence in different areas with persons of his own age and sex.

A third reason for the influence of the peer group is the opportunity it gives an individual to identify with ROLE MODELS, or persons who provide examples for behavior that another individual might copy. Some peers command more respect than others, and achieve positions of leadership. The individual who needs a model to develop certain behaviors can find appropriate models from the peer group. It is because of this fact that parents are often particular about what peer group they will allow their children to associate with.

Peers also provide a social setting in which social behavior can be developed. The family unit with two or three children begins the process of social development, which is carried further by the peer group. It is within the peer group that individuals develop, for better or worse, certain roles, such as clown, athlete, or rebel. The individual cast in a role has a tendency to play out the behavior expected of him because it gives him acceptance and special recognition.

A final reason for the importance of peer influences is that in the peer group an individual can gain acceptance of any feelings of rebellion against authority or against society itself, including its values, procedures, attitudes, beliefs, and customs. The individual feels secure in discussing feelings of hostility, lack of trust in authority, sex, and other topics with his peers. Perhaps the person feels less guilty about his own feelings when he discovers that similar feelings are shared by his peers.

How does the peer group affect the individual's attitude toward school? As we have said, the peer group is very influential in helping the individual form attitudes. For example, lower-class boys are typically less interested in school than middle-class boys. Yet the influence of the peer group is such that lower-class boys who associate with a peer group of middle-class boys show an interest in school, and middle-class boys who associate with boys in a lower socioeconomic class develop unfavorable attitudes toward school.

In our society it is common for some students to criticize our educational institutions. If a student wishes to gain acceptance by those of his peer group who criticize schools, then he must join them in their attitudes. As the student becomes more critical of school, he may develop the idea that school is really worthless and this may, in turn, cause a poorer

Individuals learn much of their behavior from members of their peer group. They may develop new interests through friends. They may also learn new skills, such as playing the guitar.

adjustment to school. Eventually he may interpret his poor adjustment as proof that his attitudes toward school were originally correct.

It is difficult for a student to like school if he is unpopular with his peers. Good grades or acceptance by teachers is not adequate compensation. Some groups who may find it difficult to obtain acceptance from fellow students are those who belong to a religious or racial minority in the school, the physically handicapped, lower-class individuals in a middle-class school, and those who deviate considerably from the norm in classroom achievement.

A number of studies have been made on the relationship between a student's self-concept and acceptance by peers, and his success or failure in school. There is some evidence of a high relationship between negative self-feelings and academic failure of black children. Yet other studies have found relationships between positive self-feelings and low achievement of black students.

Also under investigation have been the views that students and their peers have of themselves when the students are of different races and socioeconomic backgrounds. One study examined the perception of self and peers among deprived black and economically advantaged white fifth-graders. The black subjects were from a school with 90 percent black enrollment and the white students were from a school with a predominantly white population. All subjects were administered standardized tests to determine their self-concepts in the areas of self-rejection, parental approval, rejection by authority, defensiveness, and social and self-acceptance. They were also given tests to determine peer-concepts in the areas of evaluation, potency, and activity. When all the factors for all students were compared, no significant differences were found between the two groups, indicating that there was a great deal of similarity in the way these two groups perceived themselves and their classmates.

Friendship

Most individuals develop friendships with one or more members of their peer group. A FRIENDSHIP may be defined as a pleasant relationship between two persons based on mutually reinforced behavior. It develops through learning experiences, which involve reward and punishment. A friendship grows when the pleasant experiences between two persons are mutually rewarding. Friendship puts stress on emotion rather than on rational analysis and accumulation of knowledge (although knowing facts about a given person and deciding to be friendly with him or her often helps in forming friendships). Friendships formed in high school may be of short duration or last a lifetime, but whatever the length, the affection involved distinguishes friendship from casual relationships.

Learning about friendship from experiments with animals. Like any other kind of behavior, friendship can be studied experimentally. Although we usually think of friendship as referring only to a human relationship, we can gain some understanding of friendship by studying animal behavior under experimentally controlled conditions.

In one experiment puppies were reared in isolation. No puppy had an opportunity to play with or even fight with any other puppy. Furthermore, none had social contacts with human beings (although, of course, food and water were placed in each cage). Later, as mature dogs, because they had not had an opportunity to learn to be friendly, these animals were unable to interact socially with other dogs or to respond affectionately to human beings. This experiment suggests that friendly behavior is behavior that is learned as animals—and human beings—mature.

Some very interesting work conducted with monkeys further indicates how important it is for young animals to receive attention and affection. A psychologist, Dr. Harry Harlow, used artificial objects as *surrogate,* or substitute, mothers to take the place of the monkeys' real mothers. One surrogate mother was made from a block of wood, covered first with sponge rubber and then with terry cloth. Another surrogate mother was made of uncovered wire mesh. Both artificial mothers were warmed by a heat source, and both contained a bottle arranged so that an infant monkey could nurse from it.

Then baby monkeys, one by one, were placed in a cubicle with two surrogate mothers.

It was clear that they preferred the cloth-covered mother, because they spent far more time clinging to her than to the other artificial mother. When confronted with fear-producing stimuli, the infant monkeys showed a marked tendency to run to the cloth-covered mother rather than to the wire-mesh mother. As Dr. Harlow stated, "The wire mother is biologically adequate but psychologically inept." (Recently he has found some evidence that it was the olfactory cues—the smell—rather than the cloth that the infant monkeys were responding to. A cloth surrogate mother absorbs more of the smell of monkeys than a wire surrogate. When the cloth on the surrogate is changed frequently, there is a significant reduction in the amount of time an infant spends on a cloth surrogate.)

Other experiments with surrogate mothers

When frightened by something and in need of comfort, the infant monkey would rush toward and cling to the terry-cloth surrogate mother.

THE PEER GROUP 377

indicate that infant monkeys prefer a rocking mother to a stationary one. They also prefer a slightly heated (7° above room temperature) surrogate to a colder (5° below room temperature) one. In fact, when an infant monkey was first exposed to a "warm" mother for four weeks, it later avoided a "cold" mother entirely. An infant initially exposed to a cold mother avoided the surrogate and later failed to develop as much contact with a warm mother as did the infant first exposed to a warm surrogate. Apparently the infant reared with a cold mother developed adverse reactions to mothers in general.

Two months later these infant monkeys were exposed to a fear stimulus. The infants raised with a warm mother ran to their surrogate and hung on, but the infants raised with a cold surrogate ran to a corner of the cage.

Another variable studied was the reactions of infant monkeys to the face of the surrogate. One infant was reared with a surrogate mother whose face was a round wooden ball, to which the infant adapted. When the infant was three months old, a more appropriate face was placed on the surrogate mother. The baby monkey took one look, screamed, and fled to the rear of the cage. After several days, the infant solved the problem by turning the new face 180 degrees so that the back of the head showed, which looked like a round wooden ball. When the psychologist continued to turn the face around, the infant eventually detached the head, rolling it into a corner and abandoning it entirely. In the words of the psychologist, the infant monkey "had lived with and loved a faceless mother, but she could not love a two-faced mother."

Some of the monkeys that were reared by surrogate mothers have been studied as they matured. It was found that, as adults, they failed to develop healthy, friendly relationships with other monkeys. Mating behavior was not normal, although some of the females did have infants. These females were not very good mothers: they showed little affection for their babies. In fact, they avoided their offspring, pushed them away, and some even beat their infants or crushed them against the floor. They displayed what we would consider to be abnormal behavior in human beings. Instead of caring for their babies, the mothers would sit in their cages all day staring into space and would pay little, if any, attention to other living creatures. If approached by other monkeys or human beings, they would sometimes go into frenzies of rage so great that they would injure themselves. Their pattern of behavior suggests that in order to have friendly relationships monkeys, and perhaps human beings, too, need affection in the early stages of development. (See pages 424–25.)

Learning about friendship from experiments with human infants. Scientists cannot duplicate with human subjects the complete isolation they can impose on animals in an experiment, nor can they raise human infants with wood or wire-mesh surrogate mothers. But they can study certain infants who have received very little maternal care. For example, during a war some infants are left without a family when their parents and other relatives are killed. These infants are usually sent to orphan homes, but with so many of them and so few people to tend to them, they may receive only the most essential care. In these orphan homes no one has time to cuddle the infants, fondle them, or sing to them. Babies growing up under such institutional care often develop slowly, both in bodily growth and intellectual functioning, and fail to show normal affectionate behavior.

Scientists are sometimes able to provide improved living conditions for a selected number of such infants. In one experimental study a child psychologist selected sixteen babies for special "mothering" care. These babies were not only bathed, diapered, and fed, but also they were soothed when they cried, they were held and played with, and they were responded to when they smiled or vocalized. This special care was provided 7½ hours a day, five days a week, over a period of eight weeks. Although the other babies were not neglected in any way, they received only the essential care they had always been given. Since they were not given special mothering care, they served as a control group.

Before, during, and after the period of experimentation, the babies were given various tests. So that the test scores would not be influenced by the attitude of the experimenter, the same person did not administer the tests and also do the experimental mothering.

One of the tests administered was for social responsiveness. In it the examiner performed a variety of acts, such as smiling and frowning at the baby and calling and talking to him. Before the eight-week experimental period began, experimental and control groups had been practically equal in scores on this test. When retested afterward, the experimental babies had scores indicating much more responsiveness than was the case for the control babies. In other words, after eight weeks the experimental group had become more friendly babies.

At the time these data were first published, many child psychologists believed that the children simply showed the need for and advantages of "mothering." A year later the children were retested. The experimental and control groups were now indistinguishable. Apparently the advantages of early stimulation were not maintained over the period of a year. The evidence also suggests that institutionalization did not have a lasting adverse effect on the behavior of the children, for the control group did not show the apathy or attention-seeking behavior often considered to be characteristic of institutionalized children. We do not yet have data, however, concerning the adult behavior of these individuals.

Another research project had somewhat similar results. Two groups of infants three months of age were used. One group consisted of infants who were being raised in an institution. The other group consisted of infants who were being raised by their parents in homes of high socioeconomic status. There were some marked differences in the environments of the two groups. For example, the own-home infants were played with by their parents seven times as often as the institutionalized infants. Yet tests revealed that the institutionalized infants actually smiled and vocalized more and, in general, were more responsive than the own-home infants.

Why these unexpected findings? We do not know for certain. Perhaps the institutionalized infants learned that they could get more attention by cooing and gurgling than was the case for own-home infants. Perhaps the fact that a number of persons cared for the institutionalized infants provided greater stimulation than in the case of the homes where just one person, the mother, provided most of the stimulation. At any rate, it seems that friendly babies need some sort of stimulating environment in which to grow up, and in our society this stimulation is usually accompanied by displays of affection.

How do friendships develop in childhood and adolescence? Friendships develop partly as a result of contact with an increasing number of other individuals of about the same age. As babies mature and become children, their social contacts expand. They change from playing alone to playing with one other child, to playing with two other children, and then to playing with three or more children. They establish contact with the children in the neighborhood. When they go to school, they have the opportunity to meet many more children. As they become adolescents and enter junior and senior high schools, their range of acquaintances expands even further. They often join various clubs and other social groups.

Along with contact, another basic factor in the development of friendships is propinquity—the nearness in time and place that makes social contacts possible.

But why do individuals develop friendships with certain individuals and not with others? To answer this question, one investigator measured friendships of children whose ages averaged three and a half years. Since these children were in a nursery school, it was easy to observe their social contacts with their peers. A count was kept of the number of times each child was with every other child, which was considered a measure of the degree of friendship. The most interesting finding was that at this early age children tended to form their strongest friendships with other children of their own sex.

As children grow older, the basis for forming friendships broadens. In one study second-graders were asked to choose phrases that described their best friends. They tended to stress such phrases as "has lots of money to spend," "is good-looking," "has a nice home." When a group of sixth-graders was asked to describe their best friends, they tended to stress aspects of personality such as friendliness, cheerfulness, tidiness, and cleanliness.

In general, as children grow older they tend to quarrel less with their friends, although there is a difference between the two sexes—girls are less quarrelsome than boys and they have fewer outbursts of anger. At any given age during childhood, girls have more friends than boys.

As boys and girls approach adolescence, they tend to become more stable in their friendships. In one research study children and adolescents were asked to indicate the names of their best friends. When they were asked to do so again two weeks later, 40 percent of the girls eleven years of age chose the same best friend, but more than 60 percent of the girls fifteen years of age chose the same best friend. For boys, the corresponding percentages were 50 and 60. Friendships were found to become more permanent as the adolescents increased in age. The oldest age studied in this particular research project was eighteen years.

To summarize, as children grow older they tend to develop friendships in ever-widening social circles, they have more friends, they quarrel less with their friends, they shift the basis for forming friendships from superficial physical and social aspects to deeper aspects of personality, and their friendships become more stable. As children become adolescents, friendships include members of both sexes rather than remaining limited to mostly one sex.

How much of friendship is learned? Although affection may be partly a matter of maturation, the relationship of the individuals for whom we develop an affection and whom we call friends is determined mainly by conditioning. In infancy and babyhood our parents were instrumental in satisfying our physiological needs for food, drink, and bodily care, and as a result we developed affection for them. When we grew older, other adults and children satisfied our physical needs and our needs for companionship. In our experiences outside the home, we learned that interaction with some children and adults brought re-

As children, our friends and activities tend to be with members of our own sex. However, by the time we reach middle adolescence, we spend more of our leisure time with persons of both sexes than with individuals of our own sex.

wards and satisfactions of various kinds, and so we tended to seek reinforcement from them. If we had contacts with children, especially older children, who pushed or bossed us around or with adults who teased us, we soon learned to avoid them. We learned to form friendships with some children and adults and not with others.

Even though, as we have seen, friendships tend to become more stable as we grow older, we do continue to make new friends, and some who have been close friends may become mere acquaintances. Lack of contact with close friends or the sheer physical unavailability of friends we used to see frequently but who are no longer in the vicinity is a major factor in dissolution of friendships. High school and college class reunions are a lot of fun for a short period of time, but after an hour or two of pleasant exchange of memories, individuals often find that there is little left to talk about. Perhaps their needs have changed, and the individuals no longer find the old friendships as mutually satisfying as they once were. If one or the other of a pair of friends gets little, if any, satisfaction from the friendship, or finds it frustrating because of quarrels or differences in social standards, their friendship is not likely to continue.

Popularity

Although popularity and friendship are related, the personality traits associated with popularity are not necessarily the same as those that usually win friends. Some persons may strive so hard to be popular that they actually lose friends.

A person is said to be POPULAR if he or she has many admirers, or is esteemed by many individuals who feel that the person has a pleasing personality. Too often we compare ourselves with a few persons who are outstandingly popular and fail to consider that most persons we know probably have no more friends or admirers than we have.

What is the price of popularity? Individuals who conform to the norms of their peer group tend to become popular with most of the members. However, a person may deliberately choose not to be popular in a specific group whose social behavior is contrary to his beliefs. For example, he may not try to be popular in a group that professes religious or political beliefs contrary to his own.

Is popularity worth the cost of denying or even changing your own socially acceptable beliefs, sometimes for less desirable ways of behaving? There are usually many groups you can join whose social behavior is acceptable to you and agrees with your own values.

How is athletic ability related to popularity? Among adolescents, athletic ability seems to be a major factor in determining an individual's (particularly a boy's) popularity. On the other hand, studiousness seems to have only a small positive relationship to popularity and in some schools may even tend to make a person unpopular. When there is such unpopularity, though, envy could well be the cause of it.

Some adults condemn students for this frivolous popularity of athletes. If, however, they glance through a newspaper, listen to a radio, or watch television, they will notice that adolescents reflect the attitudes of adults on this subject. Mass media give far more time and space to major-league baseball, golf, and football than to the scholarly, creative activities of scientists, artists, and literary persons.

Eleventh-grade students in a big-city high school were asked to express their attitudes toward eight hypothetical students with various combinations of athletic ability, brilliance (intellectual ability) and studiousness. The range of possible scores on the scale of acceptability (popularity) was from positive 46 to negative 46. There were 305 girls and 310 boys participating in the research. Their average ratings for various combinations of hypothetical students appear in the table on this page. You can see the rank order for girls and boys differs only slightly.

Average Ratings on Social Acceptability for Eight Hypothetical Students

COMBINATION OF TRAITS	GIRLS	BOYS
Brilliant, nonstudious, athletic	31.36	25.28
Average, nonstudious, athletic	29.04	23.14
Average, studious, athletic	26.10	22.27
Brilliant, studious, athletic	23.66	23.83
Brilliant, nonstudious, nonathletic	14.27	9.24
Average, nonstudious, nonathletic	10.68	10.61
Average, studious, nonathletic	8.86	8.02
Brilliant, studious, nonathletic	1.58	2.83

Both boys and girls consistently rated athletes higher than nonathletes in social acceptability (popularity). Students who themselves had good scholastic records placed about the same value on athletic popularity as did students with lower scholastic records. Athletes are popular regardless of whether they are considered to be of high or average intellectual ability and whether they are considered to be studious or nonstudious.

At this point you may wish to consider two questions for discussion. Do some students become athletes because they are popular, or do they become popular because they are athletes? Do some individuals become studious because they are not very popular, trying to obtain recognition through academic channels, or do they become less popular as a result of their studiousness?

Some basic elements of a pleasing personality. Psychological research suggests that individuals who are highly popular with the members of one group are likely to be popular with members of other groups. This finding indicates that there are common requirements for popularity among various groups. Popularity has traits that can be described and that pertain to popular members. Popular individuals have developed social skills and likable characteristics, so that they can recruit friends from a wide range of acquaintances.

How can a person acquire these characteristics and become more popular? There are no special social tricks to developing a pleasing personality. The development of a truly pleasing personality is the work of a lifetime. Yet it is worthwhile to think about the following basic elements:

1. *Sincerity.* Being sincere includes striving for genuine friendships rather than developing acquaintances for selfish purposes, such as to get on the team or be accepted into a club.

2. *A basic guiding philosophy.* The person who has no basic guiding philosophy is less likely to attract friends and is often undependable. On the other hand, the person who develops definite and essentially worthy ideals that he upholds is usually admired.

The individual seeking to develop the qualities of a pleasing personality must begin with a concern for the general good as the foundation of his personality, using honesty as the cornerstone. He must be persistent, develop a responsibility to himself and any task he undertakes, and live up to his own standards, which must become part of his life plan. Some persons find a basic guiding philosophy of life in their religion.

3. *Unselfishness.* It is necessary to be of help to others. At times a person must be willing to sacrifice his own comfort and wishes for those of others, without expecting favors in return.

4. *A tendency to look for good in people.* It is quite easy to find fault with people and to see how they do not live up to our standards, just as we ourselves often fail to do our best. But most people do have some admirable qualities. It is necessary to look for the good in others.

5. *Cheerfulness.* Most people like to see others smile. Happiness is contagious. If you can relate humorous incidents so that people will enjoy hearing them, you should do so, but do not force yourself on others. Develop a healthy sense of humor. Learn to laugh at jokes on yourself. The person who can comfort, encourage, and make others happy by actions and words is a cheerful person.

One way to become popular and well-liked is to pay close attention when friends are talking to you and respond sincerely when they ask your advice.

6. *Control of emotions and moods.* Learn to control—but not repress—your emotions. Learn not to "fly off the handle" easily. A person who consistently overreacts to a situation by giving free vent to his emotion, such as going into raptures of joy over the least bit of good news, is likely to repel rather than attract others. On the other hand, the person who shows neither pleasant nor unpleasant emotional reactions is likely to be considered dull and uninteresting.

Remember that others are not always in the same mood you are, and may not wish to share your mood of the moment.

7. *Self-respect.* For others to respect you, you must respect yourself and consider yourself a worthwhile person. Make a list of your good points, of things that you can do well, of ways in which you excel—but keep this list to yourself. People will be attracted to you if you respect yourself, but not if you brag about yourself.

Leadership in Peer Groups

In a group of peers, usually one person stands out as a leader. A leader is an individual who exerts great influence on his group. He initiates, organizes, and directs group activity. He guides the thinking of his group and plays a major role in formulating goals and in inspiring the members to work toward these goals.

A true leader is responsible to those both within his group and those outside it. He must lead the members of his group toward goals that are consistent with their own welfare. But he must also see that these goals and the way in which the group works toward them do not run counter to the welfare of those outside the group. For example, a leader in school athletics strives to produce a winning team, but he does not recommend shady practices that might bring victory but would also bring dishonor to the school.

Why do some persons wish to be leaders? People become leaders for a variety of reasons. The individual who leads because he has the characteristics of leadership behavior is probably enjoying good social adjustment. But some individuals strive to achieve a position of leadership because, whether they realize it or not, they feel inferior and wish to be a leader to bolster their self-esteem. They want to acquire followers so that they will feel less inadequate. These individuals are probably not well adjusted. They may not have many friends or be very popular.

Different kinds of leaders. One psychologist has suggested that there are two basic kinds of leaders. (1) The individual who leads the group in accomplishing whatever tasks it has set for itself or in solving whatever problems are at hand. He is able to guide the group's thinking because of his superior ideas and carefully thought-out plans, and his willingness to work himself. (2) The individual who handles social-emotional problems of his group with relative ease. He tends to have a pleasing personality and to be popular with members of the group. He is able to settle arguments tactfully between members of the group or between cliques in the group. At times he may even be able to prevent the group from disbanding. In rather rare cases an individual may be a leader in both task accomplishment and in handling social-emotional problems.

Another way of classifying leaders is in terms of how they achieve their positions of leadership. In some groups a leader emerges from the group itself, informally or by election. For other groups a leader is appointed or imposed upon the group by those higher in authority.

Leadership depends not only on the characteristics of the individual but on the group of which he is a member and the circumstances within the group at any given time. Although we cannot speak of only one type of leader, we can consider some of the generally recognized characteristics of many leaders and how they perform.

Some functions that leaders perform. Psychologists have suggested that leaders serve a great many different functions in the group. Some of these leadership functions are as follows:

1. Executive
2. Planner
3. Policymaker
4. Expert
5. External group representative
6. Controller of group relations
7. Purveyor of punishments and rewards
8. Arbitrator and mediator
9. Exemplar, or model
10. Substitute for individual responsibility
11. Ideologist
12. Father figure
13. Scapegoat

Of course, not all leaders carry out all these functions in a given group, and the relative importance of each function may vary from group to group. You may wish to relate the functions just listed to the activities of certain leaders in your school or in large business organizations.

Is there a specific kind of personality for leadership? Research on the subject indicates that the following aspects of personality are related to leadership: (1) intellectual ability, (2) good personal adjustment, (3) extroversion, (4) dominance, (5) a tendency not to be conservative, and (6) sensitivity to interpersonal relationships.

Related to the above aspects of personality, but deserving special mention, is the characteristic of verbal activity. People who talk quite freely in a group are more likely to be chosen as leaders than those who are relatively quiet. Communication is very essential for effective group behavior, and the individual who communicates freely is likely to be chosen as a leader, even though his ideas may not be the best in the group.

Leadership is always relative to the situation. The same individual may be a leader in one social group and a follower in another social group. Or, as group goals change, an individual may alternate between the role of leader and follower in the same group. Nevertheless, one research study reported high leadership ratings for the same person when placed in groups that were confronted with different tasks. It would seem that those persons accustomed to being leaders in one group may show leadership tendencies in various groups.

Are physiological processes related to leadership? If we are ill or recovering from an illness, or if we always seem to be very tired, we are likely to welcome a role as a follower in a group rather than as a leader of that group. Psychologists and physiologists do not have much evidence concerning a relationship between the physiology of the body and leadership, but several experiments with monkeys offer some interesting data.

In a colony of monkeys one monkey usually emerges as aggressive and dominant. He is the boss of the colony. In one experiment a "boss" monkey had an area of the brain (between the top of the brain stem and the cortex) electrically stimulated. During this stimulation he lost his aggressiveness. The other monkeys soon roamed about freely in the cage, no longer recognizing him as boss. Then, when the electrical stimulation was

In this experiment a psychologist electrically controls the behavior of a wild bull. As the bull charges him (left), the psychologist uses a radio transmitter to send a mild current to the electrodes planted in the bull's brain, and the bull stops short (right).

turned off, the "boss" returned to his aggressive behavior and resumed his role as leader.

In another experiment the same general area of the brain of a "boss" monkey was altered surgically. Following the surgery, this "boss" monkey became fearful and submissive. All of the other monkeys in his group now dominated him. We must be careful not to jump to conclusions, but we should take note of any experimental or clinical evidence indicating a relationship between physiology and leadership in the years to come.

Is leadership in high school related to leadership later in life? In one research study the leadership qualities of 956 Air Force cadets were compared with their participation in high school extracurricular or cocurricular activities. Each cadet indicated the high school activities in which he had engaged: football, basketball, track, debating team, chorus or glee club, science club, hobby or interest club, student government, or class office. A measure of leadership was obtained by asking each man to rank every other man in his group on the basis of leadership potential.

Positive, but small, relationships were found between leadership potential and most major sports and athletic honors. That is, there was some tendency for men with high school athletic records to be considered leaders in the Air Force school. Participation or honors in nonathletic activities were less predictive.

The researchers then studied whether the size of the high school that the cadets had attended was related to their leadership ability. They found that, for the most part, participation in activities in large and small high schools was about equally related to cadet leadership, although there were the following exceptions. In small high schools being a member of the debating team was positively related to cadet leadership to a greater extent than it was in large high schools. Being an officer or a member of the student government was positively related to leadership for cadets from large high schools but not for those from small schools.

Some activities that you might expect to show a positive relationship with leadership later in life were found to show no relationship whatsoever. Some of these activities were president of an interest club, hobby club, language club, or science club, or being editor of the school newspaper or yearbook. Why are these activities not related to leadership? We do not know. Possibly students with relatively low leadership ability go into such activities. Then too, leadership is relative to the situation. For example, the leader in a high school science club may have achieved that position because of above-average knowledge in science, a factor which may not necessarily make him stand out as a leader in a group of men preparing for careers in aviation.

Remember also that we have been considering only one kind of adult leadership—military leadership. Adult leaders in other areas may have somewhat different characteristics, and may show a closer relationship to leadership ability in high school.

Democratic leaders, autocratic leaders, and laissez-faire leaders. How do these three kinds of leaders differ? A democratic leader works with his group. Although at times he may have special guidance responsibilities, he generally participates as a member of the group. He may suggest certain policies, but he welcomes and appreciates contributions by the other members.

The autocratic leader, on the other hand, directs the operation of his group with a firm hand. He formulates policies and gives detailed and frequent directions, but he is essentially outside the group and neither asks for nor welcomes suggestions from the members.

A third kind of leader, the laissez-faire (le-sā-'fer) leader, is not really a moving force in his group. He is a leader who tends to stand by passively without exerting much influence on his group, although he is willing to give information or help if asked for such assistance.

In one well-known investigation the behavior of boys was studied in three kinds of social climates. The boys were formed into clubs, those in the various clubs being matched so that they were as nearly alike as possible. They worked under adult leaders who played the roles of democratic, autocratic, and laissez-faire leaders.

Under democratic leadership the boys showed initiative in making plans. They worked happily and vigorously, used their time to good advantage, were friendly toward one another and toward the leader, and worked well even when the leader left the room.

Under autocratic leadership there was much hostility. Certain boys became scapegoats. The boys worked, but the work was done apathetically—that is, with little enthusiasm. Work stopped and aggression broke out whenever the leader left the room.

Under laissez-faire leadership group interest lagged. Individuals tended to work for themselves rather than for the group.

When the boys were asked which kind of leader they liked best, they indicated that they much preferred the democratic kind of leader.

Can techniques of leadership be learned? Psychologists cannot accept the popular view that some persons are "born leaders," in the sense that they inherit qualities of leadership. Techniques of leadership are learned. This learning may begin very early in life and continue for many years without a conscious effort on the part of the individual. If, however, a person is not a leader but aspires to be one, he can deliberately undertake to develop qualities of leadership. He can do much to develop a strong and healthy body. He can set himself the task of developing skills that win him the deserved respect of others.

Two psychologists asked themselves the question: "Can social leadership be improved by instruction in its technique?" To find out, they had students in a high school rate each other on leadership. Next, they divided the students into two groups. The groups were so selected that they were equal to each other in leadership qualities as indicated by the ratings. In a series of eleven conferences held during the seven months that followed, the students in one group were instructed in the qualities and techniques of leadership. Students in the other group were given no such training. At the end of the seven months, the students again rated one another on leadership. This time the mean rating of those students who had had training in qualities and techniques of leadership was appreciably higher than the mean rating of those who had not had this training.

One of the techniques that has proved effective in training for leadership is *role playing*. In this technique a situation is outlined, and individuals take on the roles of the people who would be involved in it. Without rehearsing or using a prepared script, the role players act as people in a real-life situation, assuming their feelings, attitudes, and characteristics. For example, one way of training supervisors for business is to have the trainees act out certain situations involving interpersonal relationships between supervisors and those under them. One trainee assumes the part of a supervisor, and the others play the parts of workers under him. Not only does the individual playing the role of a supervisor learn how to handle the problems of those under his supervision,

A democratic leader encourages other members of the group to express their ideas, listens to them, and takes their ideas and interests into account in making decisions.

but those playing the roles of the nonsupervisory personnel learn to understand something of the feelings and attitudes of the employees whom they will be supervising.

Teachers are in positions of leadership. Sometimes part of the training for teaching consists in having some prospective teacher act out the role of a teacher while others assume the roles of students. Such role playing is very likely to give prospective teachers a new insight into problems of student-teacher relationships and thus make them better leaders.

Leaders are needed. There is evidence that persons can be trained for positions of leadership. Do not forget, however, that everyone is a follower in many situations. Psychologists need to study the characteristics of good followers as well as those of good leaders.

Do people think less of an individual if he is not a leader? Most individuals in most situations are followers rather than leaders. Furthermore, most individuals show at least one of the functions of leadership in small groups or subgroups. Since practically everyone is a follower, and many followers qualify as partial leaders, statistically speaking there is no justification for looking down on those who are regarded as followers rather than leaders.

The relatively few studies done on followership seem to bear out the fact that individuals are not thought any less of for being followers. At one time each Naval cadet graduating from Officer Candidate School was asked to nominate three of his classmates whom he considered the best-qualified men to lead a special military mission. Then each cadet was asked to think of himself as the leader for the mission and to choose the three cadets he would want to be part of his unit. Finally, each cadet was asked to name his three best friends. The results showed that each cadet tended to choose the same individuals to be his leaders and his followers. There was no indication of looking down on followers, even in this group of men specially trained to be leaders. Also, friendship was not the chief factor in choosing either leaders or followers. A man might consider another man as one of his best friends without thinking of him either as a leader or as a follower. It would also seem that the selection of leaders and followers was not a matter of mere popularity.

We can conclude from this chapter that an individual is influenced by his peers in many ways and has a variety of roles in a peer group, including those of friend, being popular, and being a leader or follower.

Terms to Know

autocratic leader
democratic leader
friendship
generation gap
laissez-faire leader
peer group
popularity
role model
role playing
surrogate mother

Topics to Think About

1. If you should suddenly find yourself living in a foreign country, one in which you could not speak the language, how would you go about establishing social relationships with those of your own age?

2. What do you think are the biggest problems between generations—for instance, between you and your parents? Can you think of ways to help solve these problems?

3. As you have learned, some societies have definite initiation ceremonies at which young people assume full adult rights and responsibilities. Can you suggest some such ceremony for our society? Would this ceremony make the transition from youth to adulthood easier than it is now?

4. If all human beings in our society over twenty-five years of age were to suddenly disappear, how well do you think you and your peers would solve the problems faced by our society today? What would you change first?

5. What would be the possible benefits and problems of intentionally seeking the development of more friendly relationships with individuals outside your peer group?

6. What characteristics do you have that might reduce your popularity with your peers? If you wish to change these characteristics, what can you do to correct them?

7. What kind of leaders are each of the following: the President of the United States, governor of your state, and mayor of your town or city? To what extent does he or she lead, and to what extent follow, the expressed wishes of groups of constituents? To what extent does he or she seek the advice of individuals with special knowledge and skills?

Suggestions for Activities

1. List five individuals, other than your parents, who have had the most significant positive influences on your ideas, attitudes, personality, and behaviors. List five individuals who have had the most significant negative influences on you. Do not let anyone else see your list. Then classify each individual (using symbols, *not* names) under one of the following categories: "younger person," "peer group," and "adult." Compare your category results with other class members, possibly combining data for all class members. Which age group has the largest number of positive influences? negative influences?

2. Select several topics, such as dating, marriage, prejudice, drugs, and recreation. Make a list of questions associated with each topic, such as "What time should a high school student be home from a date?" Write your reactions to each question. Then interview your parents, and, if possible, your grandparents or elderly persons, asking them how they would answer each of your questions. In what areas is there agreement between the different age groups? In which areas is there disagreement? What do you suppose would be answers given by children of elementary school age when they grow up?

3. Decide who are your present three best friends. Hand in an unsigned slip of paper on which you have written your own sex, the sex of each friend, and how far each lives from your home. Then determine the sex and the distances of friends for the class as a whole. Are there any sex differences? Think back to your childhood at the time just before you started going to school or kindergarten. Did your three best friends at that time live closer to your home than do your current friends? You may wish to secure similar data for your last year in elementary school. At that time did your friends live farther from your home than they did before you started going to school? How do present distances compare with either of the previous periods in your life? Do you think the next five years will bring any great differences?

4. Indicate, on an unsigned piece of paper, how long you have known each of your three best friends and how long each has been one of your best friends. You may wish to secure similar data from your own experiences when you were in some specific grade in elementary school, or you may wish to secure such data from some group of children in elementary school at the present time. Statistical treatment of the data should provide interesting information on the stability of friendships.

5. In class discussion or a written report analyze a friendship as portrayed in some literary work. What factors contribute to the friendship, and what causes friendship to dissolve?

6. Discuss steps that are being taken to promote friendliness among nations and among citizens of different nations. You may be able to arrange correspondence with students in some other country.

7. Make a list of characteristics of several young men who are leaders in your class social activities. Do the same for young women. Make similar lists for persons who hold an office by virtue of outstanding ability along some line. Are there outstanding differences between the characteristics of social leaders and of those who hold office because of their ability? Are there sex differences? For your own sex, which characteristics apply to you personally?

8. If a business leader or military officer is willing, have him speak to the class about his experiences in leading other men.

9. Have a few selected students act out a spontaneous play in which one person assumes the role of leader and the others the roles of followers. Have another group of students do the same, but this second group should not have seen the play by the first group. Were there differences in qualities of leadership and followership? Were there evidences of democratic, autocratic, or laissez-faire leadership?

Suggestions for Further Reading

Hilgard, E. R., R. C. Atkinson, and Rita Atkinson, *Introduction to Psychology*, 5th ed., Harcourt Brace Jovanovich. See pages 512–23, "Attraction Between Persons."

Menninger, William C., *Making and Keeping Friends*, Science Research Associates. A Guidance Series Booklet written for high school students that covers ways of behaving and attitudes that can be developed to make and keep friends.

Northway, May, *What Is Popularity?* Science Research Associates. A Guidance Series Booklet that discusses the meaning of popularity and mentions ways in which a person can become more popular.

Seidman, Jerome (ed.), *The Adolescent: A Book of Readings*, rev. ed., Holt Rinehart & Winston. See pages 605–17, "Children's Attitudes Toward Peers and Parents as Revealed by Sentence Completion."

Shacter, Helen, *Getting Along with Others*, Science Research Associates. A booklet written for high school students that includes many useful principles and procedures in developing ways of behaving that will help you become a more sociable person.

Wertheimer, M., et al., *Psychology: A Brief Introduction*, Scott, Foresman. See pages 131–46 and pages 166–68 on how groups are formed and studied, influences of the group on the individual, and individual differences in leadership.

Wrenn, C. Gilbert, *How To Increase Your Self-Confidence*, Science Research Associates. A Guidance Series Booklet that is of special interest to adolescents lacking self-confidence.

chapter 16

Behavior in Small Groups

HAVING CONSIDERED how individuals behave as members of two specific small groups, the family and the peer group, we will now turn to GROUP DYNAMICS, or the way small groups form and function and the interpersonal relationships that develop between individuals within the group. Because many high school classes are examples of small groups, special attention will be given to the high school classroom.

This chapter also goes into how psychologists investigate small-group behavior. Since the problems of society as a whole are so complex, it is often difficult, if not seemingly impossible, to study them in a thoroughly scientific manner. Therefore, many times psychologists study social problems by using small groups for their research.

The Composition of Small Groups

A SMALL GROUP is an aggregate, or collective unit, of individuals in which face-to-face relationships exist among the members. It may be as small as only two persons. No maximum figure can be set for how large it may be, although some psychologists limit most small groups to between fifteen and twenty persons. Groups larger than this tend to break up into subgroups. To be considered a small group, the actual number of individuals is not so important as the rule that the members must be able to engage in direct personal relations at any given time.

Some examples of small groups. The family is a small group. Many high school classes also fit our description of a small group, as do such groups as camera, athletic, foreign language, mathematics, and music clubs. Although religious memberships are often too large to qualify as small groups, within any given church or synagogue there are likely to be small group organizations for certain age levels or for individuals with special interests. Within a community, persons interested in bridge, bowling, dancing, camping, social welfare work, and various hobbies may meet together in small groups. Thus, many of our social activities and many of our individual interests are centered in small groups.

Small groups have existed throughout history and in some cases have developed into institutions. Our early American history provides one example. In the New England colonies functions of local government were often carried out in a small group—the town meeting. As our country has increased in population, we have had to turn to small representative groups to perform many government functions. Such small groups as committees, councils, and panels have now replaced the town meetings and have become an essential part of our government.

How are small groups classified? Although there are a number of ways to classify small groups, we will consider only two basic categories. One category is task-oriented or interaction-oriented groups, which are categorized according to the purpose for forming the groups. The other category is inclusive or exclusive groups, which are classified according to how membership is determined.

Task-oriented and interaction-oriented groups. These small groups are classified by the purpose for which the individuals have come together. In a TASK-ORIENTED GROUP the pri-

One example of a task-oriented small group is the Price Commission (below), set up by President Nixon in November 1971. This seven-member group was appointed to perform the specific job of restraining inflationary price and rent increases.

mary purpose is to perform a specific job or task. One example is the small production unit in an industrial plant. This unit's job is to turn out a specific product that meets the required standards for quality and quantity. Since the men or women in the small group are there to put out a product, they are generally not involved in the larger problems of the plant's management, design, or sales promotion. Their orientation is toward their specific production task.

In a high school, a small club may be formed to provide the band with instruments. Except in a general way, the members of this small group are not concerned with the larger problems of music education or school administration. They are a task-oriented group whose purpose is the specific job of providing musical instruments.

In an INTERACTION-ORIENTED GROUP the primary purpose is to provide opportunity for social contacts or interaction. For example, the small production group in a plant may form a bowling team whose orientation and activities have nothing to do with production. The purpose of the bowling team is to provide wholesome social recreation for its members. In other words, the group is an interaction-oriented group. Or, to take another example, high school students may form a small music club because they want to talk with one another about music, listen to recordings, and dance to different kinds of music.

Of course, many small groups are task-oriented and interaction-oriented. The men and women in the plant production unit may work together more efficiently because of their interaction as a bowling team, and their bowling team may be better as a result of their work contacts. The high school music club may both provide the band with instruments and have a very enjoyable social experience. A group undertaking the task of helping underprivileged children in the community could formulate their plans at a dinner meeting, or enjoy social contact at a fund-raising dance.

Inclusive and exclusive groups. Another way of classifying groups is in terms of how the group's membership is determined. In an INCLUSIVE GROUP the members derive satisfaction from expanding their activities and trying to include more people. Another characteristic is that the group generally emphasizes the individual equality of its members.

The high school group whose original aim was to supply instruments for the band may decide to raise enough money to finance the band's trip to some music festival, parade, or athletic event. Along with such an increase in the group's activities there is usually a tendency to increase the size of the group. As a result, some of the new members may be more interested in the general welfare of the school than they are in music. The basis of the group may begin to change. Inclusive small groups have a tendency to grow into larger groups, thus losing some of the purpose and intimacy of a small group.

In an EXCLUSIVE GROUP the members derive satisfaction from their feeling of status and importance, which comes from not permitting some would-be members to join, or else permitting them to join only if they meet certain requirements. College fraternities and sororities are examples of exclusive groups, as are community groups such as literary societies, businessmen's clubs, garden clubs, music organizations, and country clubs. The members of exclusive groups usually derive a great deal of satisfaction from the feeling that they belong to elite groups.

Exclusive groups frequently emphasize initiation and other ceremonies. At such ceremonies the members may go through elaborate rituals dressed in special costumes. Prior to initiation, candidates for membership may have to undergo certain trying experiences. In one experiment sixty-three college women were considered for membership in a discussion group. Of this number, twenty-one had to undergo what was called a "severe" initiation—they had to take an embarrassment test. This test consisted of reading aloud a list of words generally regarded to be in very poor taste. Another group of twenty-one women had to undergo what was called a "mild" initiation. They, too, were required to read material aloud, but their words were more acceptable and in better taste. The third group of twenty-one women served as a control group. They did not have to read any material aloud to become members of the discussion group. Later, after all sixty-three women were members of the discussion group, they were asked to indicate on a scale how highly they would rate the group. The women who had experienced the severe initiation rated the discussion group significantly more attractive than did the groups who went through a mild initiation or no initiation. In fact, there was no appreciable difference between the ratings of women who underwent a mild initiation and those who had no initiation. Perhaps those women who had experienced the severe initiation felt that undergoing and passing a difficult test for membership had made their membership in the group more valuable.

Members of certain exclusive groups often wear special pins or other jewelry to indicate their membership. This use of jewelry fits into a concept known as the FIGURE-GROUND RELATIONSHIP, which is the perception of a stimulus or stimuli as having a definite shape against a formless background, such as an airplane against the sky, or a black dot in the middle of a white sheet of paper. According to this concept, members of an exlusive group tend to think of themselves as being the main

This drawing illustrates the figure-ground relationship—the white vase stands out against a black background. Can you also see two faces in profile against a white background? An exclusive group tends to see itself as the figure against a formless background.

figure, whereas all nonmembers constitute the background. Wearing the group's jewelry helps members to promote this figure-ground concept.

Exclusive groups may present some problems in a democratic society. Although they often serve the useful purpose of preserving valuable traditions and maintaining long-established, desirable forms of social behavior, exclusive groups are sometimes based on autocratic standards and prejudice. In some cases, these groups assume that certain individuals are better than others through birth, regardless of how meager their own achievements and how great the achievements of nonmembers.

The Size and Efficiency of Small Groups

The size of work groups will vary from group to group, depending in part on whether the group is task-oriented or interaction-oriented and whether the group is inclusive or exclusive. The group's size will also depend on the degree of maturity of its members. In general, as persons become more mature they can more effectively participate in larger groups.

Does work production increase as the size of a group increases? At first it might seem that the answer is a simple yes, since the more members there are in a group, the greater the background of information and the larger the number of ideas that can be presented. Also, in a big group there will be more members to carry out the jobs that the group undertakes, so that presumably the larger the membership, the more they can accomplish. Idea production and work output of the group do not, however, automatically increase with an increase in group size. Idea productivity often accelerates more slowly as the size of the group grows. That is, with each increase in the size of the group there is a progressively smaller increase in the number of ideas presented and the amount of work accomplished.

This relationship between size of the group and production of ideas is linked to problems of communication. In very small groups there is usually enough time for each member to express his ideas and to provide the group with whatever special information he may have. As the size of the group increases, the time available for each member's participation decreases. In large groups much of the talking is done by relatively few persons, while the other members of the group spend much of their time in silence.

Should a small work group have an odd or even number of members? In the smallest group possible, a group of two members, each member usually has an opportunity to express his ideas. In fact, the two members will probably try to avoid any major disagreement. Agreement between two members has some advantages, but it can stifle the presentation of new ideas. If one member of the two-member group tends to be dominant and the other submissive, the submissive member may give up his good ideas and work efforts rather than disagree with the dominant member. Also, the submissive member cannot get support from anyone else.

In a group of three, the members tend to break up into a majority of two and a minority of one. The pair support each other, but the single member has no one to support him. Although the single member may have very good ideas and be willing to work hard, he is often dominated by the pair. As a result, he may not only begin to keep his ideas to himself but also begin to lose interest in the group work.

What happens in groups larger than two or three members? In groups of an even number there is always the possibility that exactly half of the group will disagree with the other half. If neither subgroup is willing to back down on its original position, any votes taken are likely to end in a tie. In odd-numbered groups, a disagreement will cause members to divide into a majority subgroup and a minority subgroup (or single individual), which means that votes cannot end in ties. Although the minority members may not like the majority decision, in groups based on democratic ideals the minority will nevertheless abide by it.

Many psychologists believe that the best size for a work committee or other work group is usually five. A group of five permits members to know each other personally. It ordinarily allows each member an opportunity to express his ideas and to feel that he is doing his part in the group, which is large enough to provide mutual stimulation. If there is a three-to-two difference of opinion, each of the two members of the minority group has the satisfaction of knowing that someone else sup-

Here the leader is having difficulty in gaining the attention and control of the group. Certain techniques, such as good organization beforehand, can be used to make a meeting go more smoothly.

ported his contribution to the group's work. Even in a four-to-one decision, the majority members may well accept parts of the ideas or activities suggested by the lone dissenting member.

Of course, under some circumstances small work groups of seven, nine, eleven, or more members can be very effective. As the size of the group increases, however, each member has more personal relationships to maintain in the group and less of his total time to devote to each of these important relationships.

Techniques that increase the efficiency of group work. There are ways to conduct a group meeting that increase its effectiveness, regardless of the group's size. With skill and planning, groups larger than five can also operate very efficiently.

A common difficulty with small group meetings is how to control the discussion so that members can contribute without monopolizing. Just trying to begin the meeting can be a problem. Did you ever attend a meeting in which most of the discussion was about everything except the subject matter for which the meeting was called? Before all the members of the group arrived, perhaps those present were talking about the latest popular records or the success of the basketball team. Such conversation often serves the useful purpose of establishing warm friendly relationships, but may cause the leader of the group some difficulty when he tries to get the meeting under way. When he finally says, "Don't you think it is time to get down to the business of the meeting," someone may respond, "That's a good idea because I have to leave early, but first, what did you think of the horror film on television last night?"

One way to promote an efficient meeting is to prepare an agenda and distribute it to the members before the meeting. Since the members will then know what work needs to be done in the meeting, the leader should find it easier to keep the discussion under reasonable control. An agenda helps to keep the meeting moving forward. It also helps prevent talkative and aggressive members from monopolizing the group's time with their pet ideas.

Another way in which the leader of the group can promote the efficiency of the meeting is to have all essential materials and information on hand before the meeting begins. A meeting that starts off with, "Jack, will you go find some more chairs, and Beth, will you go get some paper and a pencil so that you can take notes," shows a certain inefficiency and disorganization. Good techniques for controlling group behavior and conducting an efficient meeting are to hand out a mimeographed sheet of data, or other information, at the beginning of the meeting, or to open with a brief talk on the meeting's subject matter.

Even good small group meetings can become very boring if they are prolonged over a long period of time. A predetermined approximate time limit is very helpful. If the group cannot accomplish its work in a reasonably short amount of time, it should take a brief break or two, which might include some refreshments. Members who have disagreed with each other heatedly during a meeting may come to terms when they relax over a doughnut and a bottle of soda. Admittedly, it takes a good chairman to get the group back to work following a break.

Another technique for small groups is to seat them around a table or even in an open circle. Such seating arrangements promote a face-to-face relationship between members, which is an essential part of any small group.

In a small group there is a tendency to criticize the chairperson or whoever is leading the group. Sometimes rotating the leadership is an excellent technique for promoting the work of a small group. Each member is more likely to be involved in the group if he knows that at some point it will be his turn to run it. Furthermore, during his term as leader he will work better with the other members because he knows what it is like to be in their position.

These are only a few suggestions for increasing the efficiency of small group work. Through class or subgroup discussion you may think of many other techniques.

Belonging to Small Groups

Society is made up of many groups. Individuals join some groups and do not join other groups. What factors determine which groups they will join? Although the answer is not simple, the behavior of joining a group can be studied and analyzed and some of the factors determined. The following are several reasons why individuals join certain small groups:

1. *Pleasure from activities.* If an individual enjoys collecting stamps, he may well increase his enjoyment by joining a group of stamp collectors and learning some of the finer points of this activity. If an individual likes camping, he may increase his enjoyment of it by getting together with other local campers for meetings and weekend camping trips. If an individual gets pleasure from helping people in need, he may wish to join some religious or civic group that has been set up to aid needy families. Individuals can often accomplish more in groups than they could acting alone.

Joining a group whose members have similar goals has the advantage not only of serving as a creative outlet for the individual but also of perhaps leading to a vocation. The stamp collector may become so enthusiastic that he eventually achieves recognition in that field. In time, the camper may organize and lead camping expeditions. The person who enjoys helping the needy may become a professional social worker.

2. *A feeling of security.* There is often security in numbers. Individuals frequently feel more sure of themselves if they have other people to back them up. The soldier on combat duty derives some feeling of security from having his "buddies" near him. The physician knows that other doctors in the local medical association will stand behind him if he is unjustly accused of malpractice by an angry patient. The delinquent teen-ager is given some feeling of security by knowing that the members of his gang will help defend him in case he gets into a fight with a member of some unfriendly gang. Individuals can protect themselves better if they are in groups than if they are acting alone.

3. *Enhancement of status.* By joining a group whose members have similar interests, an individual may also gain social status. A citizen of limited formal education who is interested in historical events may gain status by becoming active in the local historical society. In this group he may associate with history teachers and other well-educated persons on an equal or even superior basis.

Sometimes an individual may join a group even though the goals of the group are quite different from his own goals. He joins this group or tries to join it for the prestige he feels membership will bring him, so that he can tell people he is a member of _____ club.

4. *For purposes of business.* Membership in such organizations as a bridge club, a golf club, a businessmen's association, or a civic improvement group will enable an individual to make social contacts that are likely to result in business contacts. The insurance salesman can say, "That was quite a game of golf we had this afternoon. By the way, did I understand you to say that you had no theft insurance? Perhaps I can be of assistance to you." A woman may enjoy the social life of a bridge club, but the next time she needs dental work she may well go to the dentist who has been her partner in several of the bridge tournaments.

Possibly you dislike the idea that people join social groups for business purposes. If you think about it, however, this system may be better than having business and professional contacts thrust upon the individual.

The disadvantages of belonging to small groups. Although probably our most interesting, pleasurable, and valuable activities are carried on in small groups, there can be some disadvantages to small-group membership. As you know, small groups can be very slow in reaching decisions and carrying out work projects. Many good ideas that are suggested in a group are lost because they are referred to a committee that never gets around to acting on them. There are two disadvantages in this case: the member who made the proposal may feel frustrated at what happened to his idea, and the group members lose the benefit of the good idea.

Small groups have other disadvantages with regard to getting their work done. Sometimes small groups spend too much time discussing minor problems and then carelessly rush through major decisions. Other times, when the group performs both a social and a work function, some members may be so interested in the social activity that they slow up the work activity. Another disadvantage is that in a small intimate group, members with divergent opinions may give in and agree with questionable suggestions to keep the peace. They thus permit the work of the group to be hampered rather than risk hurting someone's feelings.

Belonging to small groups can also have the disadvantage of encouraging individuals to be too one-sided. A person may become so wrapped up in the activity of a group that his other interests suffer. He may actively take part in only this one small group. Perhaps he is a coin collector. He talks about collecting rare coins all day long—at breakfast, lunch, and dinner as well as at coffee breaks on the job. Even when he plays bridge to please his wife, his casual conversation during the evening is mostly about his coin collection. He goes to religious services but greets his friends there with news of a rare coin he has just acquired. In short, he is not only a coin collector, he is also a bore.

An individual in a small group may become a bore in another way. He may use membership in a group as an outlet for his own pet ideas or peeves. He may bombard the group with his tirades against property, inheritance, income, and sales taxes. Or he may rant against certain ethnic or religious groups and try to persuade all the members that they should be as prejudiced as he is. (Of course, he doesn't believe that he is prejudiced.) Or, after the group has heard a formal presentation, he may use the question period to express his pet peeve or idea, even though his "question" basically is quite unrelated to what the speaker of the evening has said. He uses the group as a captive audience through which he tries to secure recognition for himself.

In this photography class on how to use a darkroom, there is only one enlarger so each person must spend time waiting to use the equipment. One disadvantage of a small group is that it may take longer to get something done than on your own.

Who belongs to groups? Despite some of the disadvantages of small-group membership, most people want to belong to small groups. We all belong to a number of informal or only slightly formal small groups, such as our families, school groups, and religious groups. Probably we belong to one or more rather formal groups in which the membership may be too large to fit our definition of a small group.

Adult membership in groups is, in fact, quite extensive. A few years ago surveys were made of adult social participation in a large American city—Detroit. About 80 percent of the adults interviewed belonged to some formal organized group. The two groups to which they belonged most frequently were churches and labor unions.

Of course, many individuals belong to organizations without being active in them. In Detroit only about a third, or slightly more, of the adult members interviewed attended meetings of their groups frequently. About a fourth indicated that they had attended no meetings of their groups during the previous three months.

There is evidence that the more formal education a person has the more likely he is to join groups and be active in them. In the Detroit survey only 52 percent of adults with six or fewer years of formal schooling belonged to organized groups, and only 2 percent of these adult members were very active in their groups. On the other hand, 78 percent of those who had attended college reported group membership, and 19 percent of these were very active.

Age is also related to group activity. As individuals mature, they tend to become more active in groups. Then, beginning in the fifties, individuals tend to become less active in groups. In the sixties, there is a marked decline in group activities.

Some Characteristics of Small Groups

Having discussed various aspects of small groups, we will now consider four specific characteristics: group cohesiveness, morale, atmosphere, and climate.

Group cohesiveness. GROUP COHESIVENESS is the mutual, overall attraction that each member feels toward other members of the group. This attraction is based on such factors as the extent to which the members have common goals and the extent to which the members feel that they share a common fate. Small military units often exhibit great cohesiveness because the members have the common goal of specific missions and feel that they all share a common fate.

How can cohesiveness be measured? Since behavior can be measured by psychologists, techniques have been developed for measuring group cohesiveness. One such technique is sociometry. SOCIOMETRY involves quantitative studies of how individuals perceive, feel, and think about the other members of their group. For example, each member of a group may be asked to indicate which of the members he would prefer to work with, serve on a committee with, or attend a social event with. From such data a diagram or chart, called a SOCIOGRAM, can be constructed, which illustrates these group relationships.

Suppose in a group of six individuals we ask each member to indicate secretly which one of the others he would most prefer to work with on a particular group task. Each circle represents a member of the group, and each arrow indicates a choice. A two-way arrow indicates a mutual choice: that is, both individuals prefer to work with each other. A sociogram of this information might look like the diagram on the top of page 403.

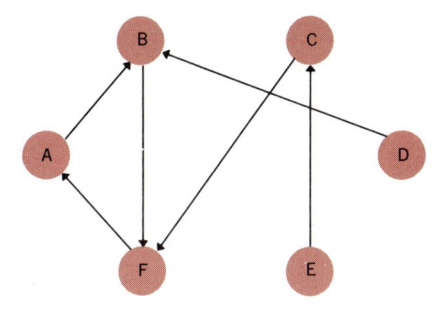

Another possibility would be a sociogram like the diagram that appears below. Which of the two groups is more cohesive? Is there any indication of cliques within either group?

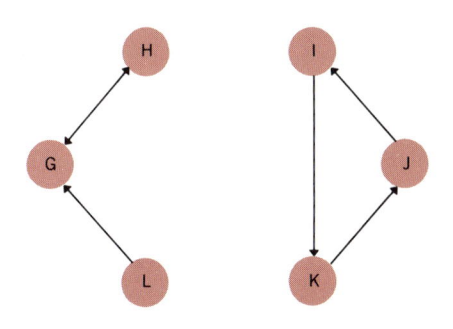

Instead of asking for just one preference, we might have asked members for their first, second, and third choices of partners for a group task. In that case, we might have used different kinds of lines to represent the various choices, such as: first – – – – –, second ─────, third . . . . We can also construct sociograms that include additional information about the group. For example, a square and a circle can be used to represent the two sexes. These symbols can be drawn with different colored pencils to indicate those who live geographically close together. The size of the square or circle might indicate the number of times an individual was chosen for a partner. Perhaps you can think of more methods to show different variables on a sociogram.

There are other ways, besides sociometry, to measure group cohesiveness. Psychologists have measured group cohesiveness by counting the number of times members used the word "we" rather than the personal pronoun "I." Group cohesiveness has also been measured by checking on the number of members who regularly attend group meetings, or even the number who pay their dues regularly.

Group morale. GROUP MORALE refers to the prevailing attitudes of the individuals in a group, to their loyalty toward the group, and to their willingness to participate in the group's work. Although the term "morale" is sometimes used interchangeably with the term "group cohesiveness," morale usually puts stress on the task orientation of the group. When we speak of the morale of military units, we are referring to their willingness to work together at an assignment, regardless of how unpleasant or dangerous it may be. When we speak of the morale of a student body, we mean the willingness of the students to work together on the tasks assigned to them, even though these tasks may be unpleasant.

How does individual morale affect group morale? Group morale is determined to a large extent by the morale of each individual in the group. When the morale of each individual is high, he is willing to fulfill his particular role in the group. If a student believes that his efforts in a school club will produce no worthwhile results, his morale is low. If morale is low among many of the individuals in a group, the group morale is likely to be low.

BEHAVIOR IN SMALL GROUPS

Group atmosphere. GROUP ATMOSPHERE is the general emotional state of a group at any given time. The atmosphere of a student group may be jovial at a party, sad after losing an important game to the traditional rival school, or hostile if school authorities decide to cancel an anticipated vacation. A classroom may have a happy atmosphere on a day when there is a lively discussion, and an unhappy atmosphere on the day of a difficult examination.

The group atmosphere among these students is one of slight nervousness, uneasiness, and anticipation, as they wait to begin writing a final examination for one of their courses.

Group climate. When a certain kind of atmosphere prevails in a group over a considerable period of time, we speak of GROUP CLIMATE. The climate in a classroom of students of superior ability and high ambition is likely to be quite different from the climate in a classroom of students of lesser ability who have indifferent attitudes toward their schoolwork. Sometimes the climates of early morning classes are quite different from the climates of classes meeting late in the afternoon.

Leaders can be an important factor in the development of group climates. For instance, there are differences of climate and behavior in groups under democratic, autocratic, and laissez-faire leadership.

How Roles Vary in Different Groups

If you will think about your behavior in the various groups to which you belong, you will realize that you act differently in each group. You play a different role in different groups.

To understand more about roles, remember that different actors play different roles in the theater. A part of an actor's role is determined by the script; a part of the role is determined by the personality of the actor himself.

What is an individual's role in a small group? The term "role" also has a dual meaning when applied to behavior in groups. ROLE refers both to the function and position of the individual in a group and to his expected behavior as a result of his personality. For example, one member of the group, Helen, might be elected or appointed to keep a record of the minutes of all meetings. Her role in the group would be that of secretary. Helen is also a very friendly girl. Without any formal recognition, she might assume the role of seeing that each person becomes acquainted with every other member of the group. The number of roles of an individual depends on the number of groups to which he belongs. You have one role in your family circle, another role in any school social club to which you belong, still another role in your classroom groups.

Although in most cases a person can adjust to his various roles without difficulty, occasionally there is conflict. The adolescent may find it difficult to follow the role of a growing child in his family and the role of a young adult outside the home. Even if no conflict exists between the roles, a person may be successful in one role and not in another. For example, a man may be very successful in his role as a businessman and unsuccessful in his role as a father.

Role changes as the individual matures. At one time your role was that of a small child in the family group. Then your role changed to that of a preadolescent, and now your role is that of an adolescent. Probably you will assume the role of husband or wife, of parent, and of grandparent. In kindergarten or first grade your school role was quite different from your role as a high school student. If you go on to college or graduate school your role will change still further. Your role as a full-time employee will be quite different from your role as a student or a part-time employee. If you become an employer, your role will be different from that of an employee.

There are two periods in life, adolescence and old age, in which it is especially difficult for the individual to adjust to his roles in groups. You are undoubtedly aware of some of the difficulties that adolescents encounter. There are also certain difficulties for individuals as they change from the role of active adulthood to the role of old age.

Individuals seek to satisfy certain desires through their roles in groups. One psychologist has suggested that an individual has three dominant purposes as he assumes group roles. One of these purposes, or desires, is for individual prominence and personal achievement. In our culture a person usually strives for some degree of success. He wishes to be recognized as a leader or as outstanding in at least one field. He wants to be personally creative.

A second desire is to help the group attain its goals. The individual wishes to play the role of assisting the group in achieving the goals that its members have set for the group.

The third desire is for sociability. The behavior of the individual will involve his or her wish to establish and maintain satisfying and happy relations with the other group members.

Probably when an individual joins a group he hopes to play all three of the above roles. He may find, however, that these roles conflict with one another. He may achieve prominence and personal achievement only at the expense of the goals of the group. He may have some difficulty in keeping up pleasant social relationships with individuals who are competing with him for personal achievement. Accomplishing the goals of the group may not allow much time for socializing. If socialization is stressed, there may be interference with the achievement of both individual and group goals. It takes a good deal of thought and effort for an individual to maintain satisfactory relationships as he undertakes to play these three roles in his groups.

Communication Within a Group

A dictionary of psychological terms defines COMMUNICATION as "transmitting, or trans-

Much communication can be carried on through the use of gestures, without a word being spoken. These two individuals exchange a greeting and communicate their feelings by using the gesture of the peace sign.

mitting and receiving, information, signals, or messages by means of gestures, words, or other symbols, from one organism to another." The organisms, or individuals, involved must be able to distinguish what is transmitted.

As the definition states, communication is not limited to words and sentences. In recent years research has shown that nonverbal communication is of great importance to man in his social relations and that verbal and nonverbal communications are closely related. One person can signal to another by such means as his posture, the direction of his gaze, physical proximity, nods of the head, pats on the back, caresses, and slaps. For general face-to-face communication in groups, some psychologists use the term INTERACTION.

Why is communication important in groups? Communication is essential to group behavior. You would not have a group situation if you had five soundproof and sightproof rooms in the same house, because you would have no communication among these individuals.

Some ways in which people communicate. One way that people communicate is through EMPATHY. In communicating with one other person you may attempt to place yourself in the other person's frame of reference. You may then unconsciously begin to mimic the nods, glances, frowns, and smiles of the other person. These empathic responses provide one form of communication between individuals.

Another way that people communicate is

through a special language. Have your parents ever complained that they cannot understand what you say when you are talking with your friends? Perhaps you have developed a special JARGON—that is, a language peculiar to your own group of friends that can be fully understood only by the members of the group. The special vocabulary could pertain to anything from popular music to cars to drugs.

Clubs and other social groups often have their secret language. They may also have "high signs" and special handshakes. All such behavior serves as communication.

Does the number of people in the group affect communication? Most people find it easier to communicate with one other person than with a small group of persons. Many people have an easier time talking to a small group than to a large group.

The same individual may even say one thing in a face-to-face situation involving only one person and another thing in a group situation. It is not unusual for a chairman to sound out the individuals on his committee only to find that in a group meeting they vote quite differently from their point of view during face-to-face communication.

Group communication can help the individual. Communication can help to clarify an individual's own thinking. When called on in class, a student will sometimes say, "I've got the idea in my head but I don't know how to say it." He probably does not have a very clear idea in his own head, but being required to communicate with others in the class may cause him to try to clarify the fuzziness of his thinking.

Perhaps you have begun work on what you thought would be an easy class report only to find that your ideas were not clear at all. By having to communicate the ideas, you were forced to look at them more carefully. Or maybe you had some ideas that had seemed very clear to you, yet when you heard them discussed in class you realized that your own thinking needed some clarification and revision. Group communication can help you know more precisely what you do think.

Feedback is important in small group communication. Feedback, or reinforcement, is very important in learning. An individual's learning is facilitated if he is informed how well he is doing. Such feedback for each member is given readily in small groups. There is also GROUP FEEDBACK, which informs the members of a group how well they are doing as a whole. Studies have been made to determine which is more effective, individual feedback or group feedback.

One investigation, using groups of seven men, provided feedback under two different conditions. In some groups each member was informed of the success or failure of the group as a whole. In other groups each member was informed of his own success or failure and that of every other member of the group, as well as the success or failure of the group as a whole. This second condition of reinforcement brought about the greater improvement in performance. In this case, individual feedback was very effective and group feedback was relatively ineffective.

On the other hand, there is evidence that group feedback is effective under some conditions. Groups of airmen were given favorable and unfavorable feedback on their performance in a simulated air defense maneuver. For some groups the feedback was related to the success of the group as a whole. For other groups feedback was related to the success of the individual members of the group. Here group reinforcement proved to be more effective than individual reinforcement.

Although further research is needed on the relative value of group and individual reinforcement, the evidence clearly indicates that some kind of feedback is very important in small-group communication.

Communication and status. STATUS is one's standing in a group. An individual's status, therefore, such as what office he holds, is always dependent on the other people in the group.

A person's status can influence what he communicates in a group and to whom he communicates it. A person of low status in a group often fails to communicate his ideas to a person of high status, especially if he thinks that the person of high status disagrees with him. A workman may fail to suggest improvements in work production methods because he feels that the boss of his small group does not approve of such suggestions.

On the other hand, a person of high status in a group may tend to force his ideas on those of lower status, even though he has ideas that are inferior to those of some persons whose status is lower. When the person of high status is very competent, though, his communication with those of lower status may result in very effective production.

Studying communication in a laboratory. Because communication within a group is so important, psychologists conduct scientific studies of communication. One of their techniques is to use a one-way laboratory for observing group behavior.

A one-way-vision and one-way-sound laboratory has a room containing what appear to be mirrors. Actually these mirrors are one-way-vision glass. From the dimly lighted area on the other side of the "mirrors," psychologists and students can observe what goes on in lighted rooms, but they themselves cannot be seen. In the lighted room microphones, probably concealed, carry the sound to speakers or headphones in the observation area, although what is said in the observation area cannot be heard on the other side of the mirrors. Also, the microphones may be connected to recording devices for future analysis of everything said in the group. Observers behind the one-way glass make notes on the group members in the lighted room, recording the reactions members have and the roles they play. The observers may make sociograms with arrows indicating all the communication of any individual with any other individual.

If your school does not have such a laboratory, you can make one by filling the upper half of a doorway with a screen wire and the lower half with a wood panel. You, in a dark room, can look through the screen at children in a well-lighted room without being seen.

Communication in a three-person group. Using a laboratory like the one just described, psychologists can study communication in a three-person group and diagram the directions of communication. In a group of two persons, the line of communication is very simple, A ↔ B. Adding even one person complicates the situation, as the diagrams on page 409 show. The arrows indicate the direction of communication from talker to listener.

The following experiment used five three-man groups. All five groups were given the task of reassembling into one list the words from three lists. Each of the three men in a group had one of the three lists and therefore had to communicate with the others to form the one list. Members of the groups could speak whenever they wished, but their speech would be carried by headphones only in the direction indicated by the arrows.

1.

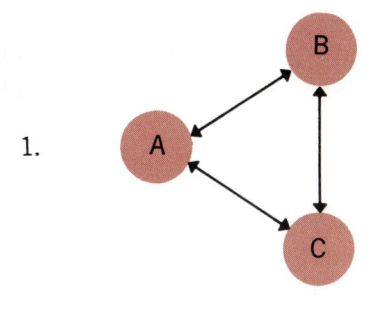

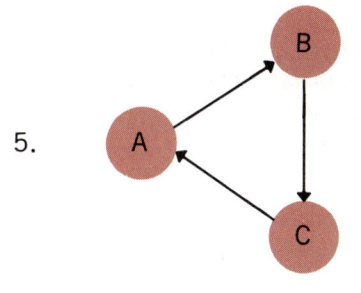

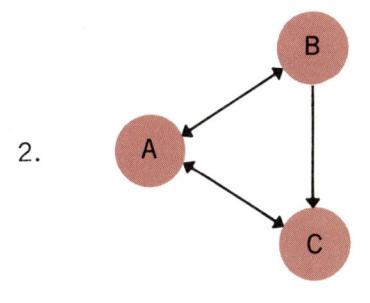

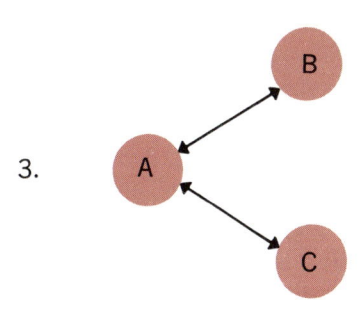

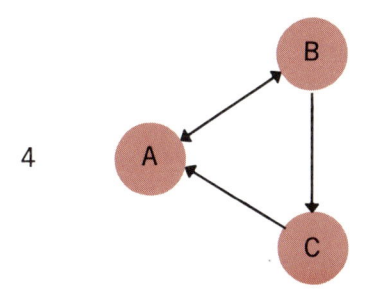

5.

2.

3.

4.

In Group 1, communication in all directions was perfectly free. In Group 2, there was a difficulty not found in either Group 1 or Group 3. B had a choice: he could communicate with either A or C or with both, but when he chose C instead of A, C had to waste time because he could not communicate directly with A. If B spoke to A and C at the same time, C had to tell A to tell B to keep quiet. Group 2 was slower in its work than either Group 1 or Group 3. In Group 5, there was no direct communication between any two members. If B wished to check on what C said, he had to go through A as an intermediary, which had the disadvantage of possible misunderstandings as well as loss of time. Group 5 was the least efficient of all the groups. Group 4 was the next least efficient. In general, it was found that when two members of a group could not communicate naturally, their communication through a third party was likely to act as a disturbance rather than as a help.

Communication in a four-person group. A group of four persons can communicate in more different patterns than three-person groups can. We might have a completely open communication system, in which each person

BEHAVIOR IN SMALL GROUPS **409**

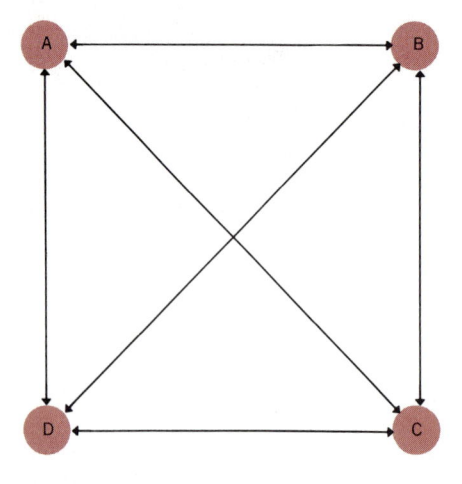

can communicate with every other person, as shown in the figure above. We can also have various combinations of partly closed channels, in which some persons cannot communicate with certain other persons in the four-person group.

Communication in a five-person group. Open or all-channel communication in a group of five individuals is much more complex than in a three-person group and more complicated than in a four-person group, as you can see from the diagram below.

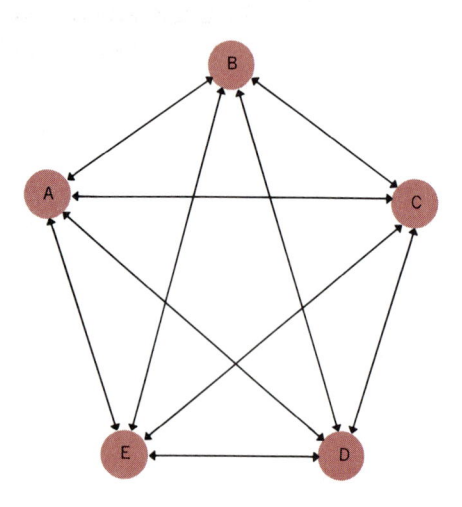

To study the effects of different patterns of communication, psychologists sometimes limit the lines of communication in various ways. In one well-known experiment a psychologist used 100 men college students as subjects, dividing them into twenty groups of five men each. These groups of five students were seated in the four different arrangements shown on page 411, and were tested under each of the four patterns of communication.

The students were seated in separate cubicles (although the experiment has been repeated without the use of cubicles). Each student could communicate only with those whose cubicles connected with his. In the circle arrangement, for instance, A could communicate with both B and E. In the chain pattern A could communicate only with B, although B could communicate with both A and C. Messages were passed through slots in the cubicle walls.

Each subject in a group was given a card on which appeared a set of five out of a possible six symbols. The six symbols used in this experiment were: ○ △ ◊ □ + *.

Each subject's card was different from the others in his group in that a different symbol was missing. Thus, in any set of five cards there was only one symbol in common. The subjects had to discover which symbol that was, by passing messages back and forth.

Each group was given fifteen trials on each pattern. It was found that the wheel pattern of communication was the most efficient one, as measured by the time required for solution and the number of errors. Next in efficiency was the Y pattern, followed by the chain pattern. Least efficient was the circle, although the difference between the circle and the wheel was not great.

After completing the communication-pattern part of the experiment, all subjects were given a questionnaire. One of the questions

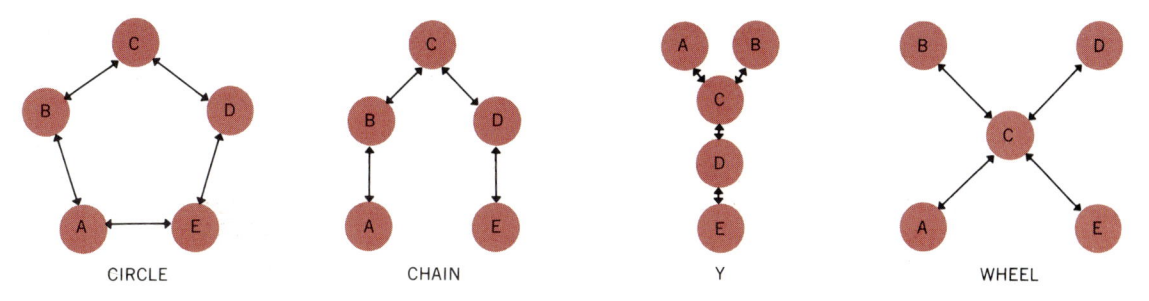

Four different seating arrangements by which groups can communicate

asked was, "Did your group have a leader? If so, who?" The student in the circle arrangement had a great deal of difficulty in answering this question and only about half were able to identify any leader. Those they did name as leaders were distributed among the five positions in the circle. On the other hand, almost all of the students in the wheel pattern of communication were able to identify a leader, and they unanimously selected the person at the center of the group (C). The chain and the Y groups fell between the the circle and the wheel patterns in ability to select a leader.

Although we must be careful not to jump to conclusions on the basis of the above experiment, it does seem that the individual whose position in a group gives him the most opportunity to communicate with others is likely to be thought of as a leader, regardless of his personality.

Another question asked of the subjects was, "How did you like your job in the group?" The order for enjoyment was: circle, chain, Y, wheel. Although some of the differences in enjoyment were not great, the circle members enjoyed their job to a significantly greater degree than the wheel members. Note that efficiency in the various communication patterns differed from the enjoyment patterns.

Still another question revealed that there was an increasing degree of satisfaction with the task as the experiment progressed for students in the circle pattern, but a decreasing satisfaction as the experiment progressed for those in the wheel pattern.

Communication in larger groups. You might try diagramming channels of communication for groups of six, seven, or ten persons. You will soon see why, for research purposes, it is often best to keep groups quite small.

To study communication in larger groups a psychologist may keep the four basic circle, chain, Y, and wheel patterns of communication but have more than five subjects. For example, he might wish to use a group of eight subjects, but limit the lines of communication for three of them. Various arrangements could be made, of which the patterns shown on the next page are but samples.

Note that some of the members of each group, three members in each of these cases, are on the fringes of the group. They are part of the group, but not part of the main pattern of communication. We might think of these three extra members in our modified arrangements as persons of lesser social status than those in the main pattern of communication. On the other hand, we might think of them as persons with special knowledge or skills who are called in as consultants to members of the main patterns of communication. We see such additional members in the functioning

BEHAVIOR IN SMALL GROUPS **411**

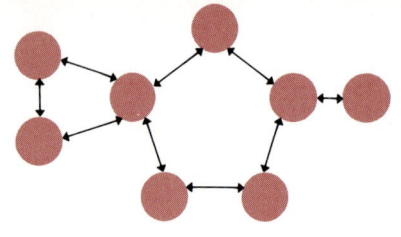

MODIFIED CIRCLE

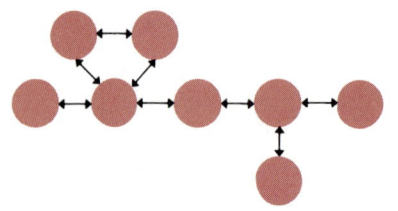

MODIFIED CHAIN

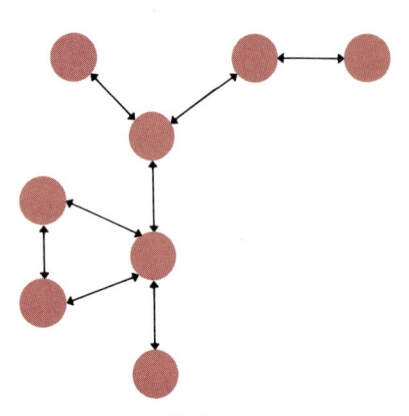

MODIFIED Y

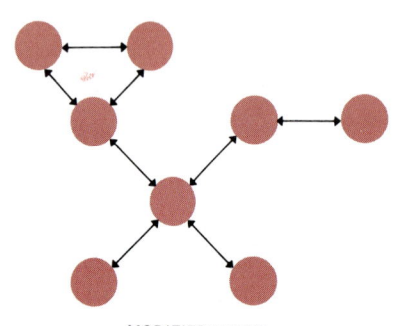

MODIFIED WHEEL

Modified arrangements of the four basic patterns of communication shown on the previous page. Here three of the eight subjects in each pattern have limited communication.

of committees or business organizations. Members of the committees or business organizations will do the eventual communicating and reaching of conclusions but, to aid them in making decisions, one or more members may consult with scientists, executives, and others with special knowledge and skills.

In groups of more than five persons we can also have modified all-channel patterns of communication. For example, the members of a congressional committee may consult with specialists at a meeting in which every member is free to speak out.

Which small-group pattern of communication is best? Too many variables are involved to answer this question unqualifiedly. However, we can make some tentative answers, especially for circle and wheel patterns.

In the experiment involving six symbols, the wheel was found to be the most efficient pattern of communication. However, the task was relatively simple. For more complex problems, the circle may prove to be more efficient than the wheel. One psychologist has suggested an explanation in terms of saturation. In the wheel pattern the central person (C) has to do most of the work—either by producing the solution to the problem or by relaying information. He may get fed up (saturated) with the task. It may be too much for him. Someone else may have to become the leader even though he is in a less favorable communication position, which would make the wheel pattern less efficient.

Other psychologists have suggested that the circle is more efficient than the wheel for complex problems because in the circle pattern each member receives information from two different sources, while in the wheel pattern each member—except (C)—receives information directly from only one person. The

412 SMALL GROUPS

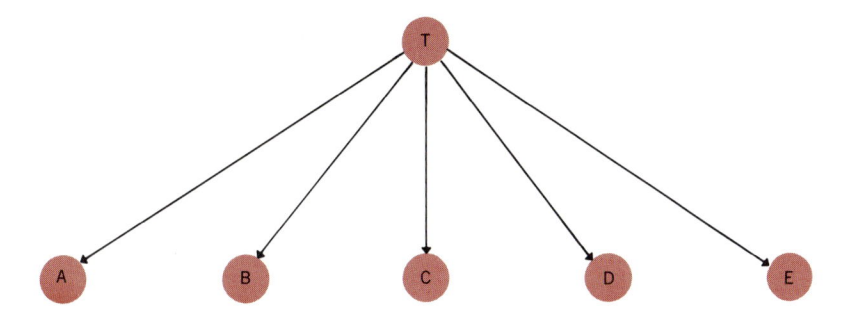

individual receiving information from two persons is more likely to discover errors than if he receives information from only one person. Furthermore, he has a better chance to solicit information from others.

Another factor to consider in deciding which pattern of communication is best is the amount of restriction of the members. All-channel communication is the least restricted of the patterns of communication we have discussed. Also, circle communication is less restricted than wheel communication. In our society most people seem to like to have some degree of independence. In the wheel pattern it may be that the central person (C) is thought of as having too much control, as being a possible dictator. The other individuals in the group may resent the limitations imposed on them by the central person.

One other factor that affects which small-group pattern is best is the size of the group. As we have noted earlier, the efficiency of small groups depends to a great extent on the size of the group.

The Classroom as a Small Group

Throughout this chapter references have been made to student groups. Now more specific consideration will be given to the classroom as a small group, since many high school classes fit within our definition of a small group. We will discuss some common techniques for guiding classroom behavior—techniques that can also be applied in other small groups.

The lecture method. Although not found regularly at the high school level, some high school teachers do occasionally use the lecture method of teaching. When it is used, students take notes on what the teacher says and eventually take an examination covering the material in the lectures. The flow of communication of the lecture method can be diagrammed as shown on this page, using an example of a class of only five students.

The question-answer method. Although used less today, question-and-answer was once a very common method of teaching. The teacher called on an individual student, the student responded, and then the teacher called on another student. We can diagram this kind of classroom situation as shown on page 414.

Although communication is limited in the question-answer method, there is more communication than in the lecture method.

Group-centered discussion. One possibility for group-centered discussion is all-channel group communication. In this free discussion method the teacher is simply a member of the group without any control of group behavior. Such free discussion, however, is rarely successful in the classroom. Aggressive or overly talkative students are likely to take up more than their share of communication time. They may antagonize other students. The discussion often becomes random, almost meaningless, and unproductive.

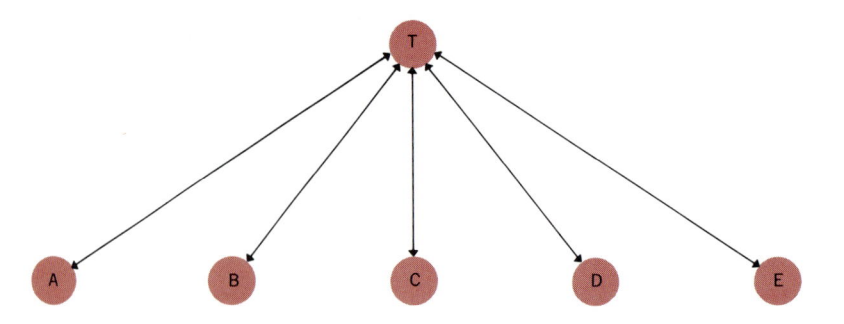

Therefore, the teacher is trained to guide classroom discussion. In a guided discussion situation the teacher suggests topics for discussion, assigns readings or directed observation, gives introductory lectures, and meets with individual members of the class in advance to plan the discussion period. During the discussion period the teacher serves as a member of the group, but only as a guiding member.

We can diagram a controlled discussion class period as follows:

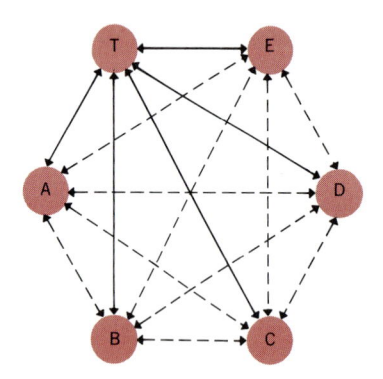

The lines indicating the teacher's communication with each student have been drawn as solid lines to show that the teacher is the guiding member of the group. The student-to-student communication lines are represented by broken lines.

Research studies have indicated that the discussion method of teaching is not necessarily the best method of teaching, particularly where the objective for a course is the mastery of information, as in some courses in mathematics, science, and foreign languages. On the other hand, students usually feel less emotional strain in discussion sessions than in sessions based on question-and-answer. Discussion methods of teaching seem to be especially effective for developing values and attitudes.

What happens when a student takes charge of class discussion? Sometimes a student is asked to be a guiding member of a group-centered discussion. He must, of course, make careful preparation for the meeting so that he can truly guide it. Are there any general rules that he should follow during the class discussion?

The author of a book devoted to learning through discussion has suggested ten rules of how a leader should behave in a group-centered discussion. These suggestions might be very helpful to you.

1. Do not argue.
2. Do not give advice.
3. Do not direct the discussion.
4. Do not force answers.
5. Do not take sides.
6. Listen rather than talk.
7. Try to understand why group members do not participate.
8. Try to grasp what lies behind what the speaker is saying.
9. Do not make moral judgments.
10. Above all, try to communicate to the speaker your appreciation of what he says and how he feels.

Buzz sessions. Some teachers use buzz sessions as a variation on group-centered discussions, especially in relatively large classes. The purpose of a buzz session is to encourage student involvement, interest, and enthusiasm. Have you ever noticed how passive and uninvolved some students become in large classes when the class is treated as a whole?

For a buzz session the whole class is divided into subgroups, which are usually from four to eight students in size. As a rule, the teacher arbitrarily divides the class on the basis of rows or seats rather than on the basis of abilities or friendships. Each subgroup then selects a member as recorder, or secretary. The subgroups may choose someone to act as their leader, especially if there are more than four or five individuals in the subgroup.

The teacher suggests a topic or question for discussion, and each of the subgroups begins to discuss it. Instead of the traditional quietness of a classroom, the room sounds like one big buzz. After a short period of time, usually five to ten minutes, the teacher calls the class together as a unit and asks each recorder (R) to report briefly on the discussion of his subgroup. The flow of communication can be diagrammed as shown on this page, using a class of fifteen students.

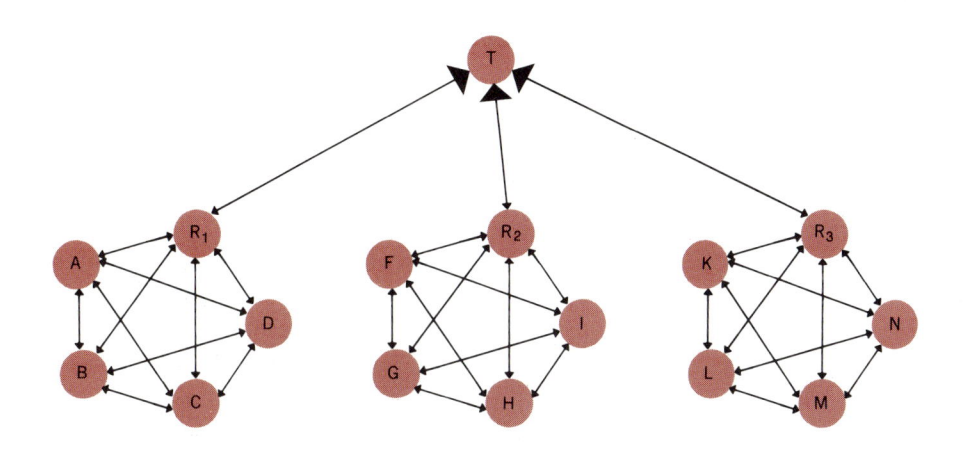

The heavy arrowheads indicate the flow of communication from the recorders to the teacher. After hearing his report, the teacher may ask the recorder to clarify a point or two. The light arrowheads indicate this possible flow of communication. Eventually the recorders, or even possibly the other members of each buzz group, may communicate very briefly with one another and with the teacher (although such a situation is not shown in the diagram).

Can buzz sessions make effective use of poor ideas? Even poor ideas may contribute something to a group discussion. In a large class it is inefficient if many students with poor ideas take time to present them. In the buzz subgroup, however, poor ideas may help the group to clarify its thinking and little class time is lost, because only the better ideas are reported to the teacher and to the class as a whole.

Are buzz sessions useful for teaching factual material? The buzz session, like free discussion, may well prove to be an ineffective way of learning factual material. Suppose your class is studying about operant conditioning. The teacher might suggest the question "Can a rat be taught to press a lever in order to secure food?" There is very little need to divide up into subgroups to discuss it, since many experiments have already answered this question in the affirmative. The time could be better spent in learning about the experiments. Or the teacher might ask, "Can high school students learn scientific facts by using programmed books?" Since there is scientific evidence that the answer is yes, the usefulness of a class buzz session on the question is limited.

On the other hand, the teacher might ask, "Do you find John Doe's *Programmed Learning of Psychology* a valuable book for use in your class?" For an evaluation of this controversial question, a buzz session can be a very effective learning technique.

A buzz session is not very useful for teaching factual material, which may need to be memorized more than discussed. On a subject in which there are differences of opinion, however, a buzz session can be very effective in evoking participation and varied responses from many students.

Role playing. Role playing can be used in the classroom as a small group technique for investigating certain problems of behavior by acting them out, followed by immediate analysis of the behavior. Role playing in the classroom is generally very stimulating to the students, and can be useful in understanding class interaction.

Sociodrama. A SOCIODRAMA is a spontaneously acted brief play involving only a few selected actors and presented for the purpose of assisting members of a group to analyze and understand some problem of interpersonal behavior. Unlike psychodrama, the players do not act out situations relating specifically to their own personal problems.

Although in a regular play directors need experience, in sociodrama students may act as directors. The teacher sometimes directs at first because he or she knows the necessary steps and procedures. There is no written play. Either the director or members of the class will choose some problem of interpersonal relations. For example, the problem might be "Why do parents usually object to late-hour parties following a dance?"

Next comes a decision on what setting the play should have. For the problem just suggested, the scene might be a home living-room in which parents and their adolescent child or children are discussing this problem. The scene might be expanded to include some friends of the parents and their adolescent children, although the number of actors should be kept low.

Casting is very important. Students are chosen for roles which it is hoped they will be able to play well. Certainly a student

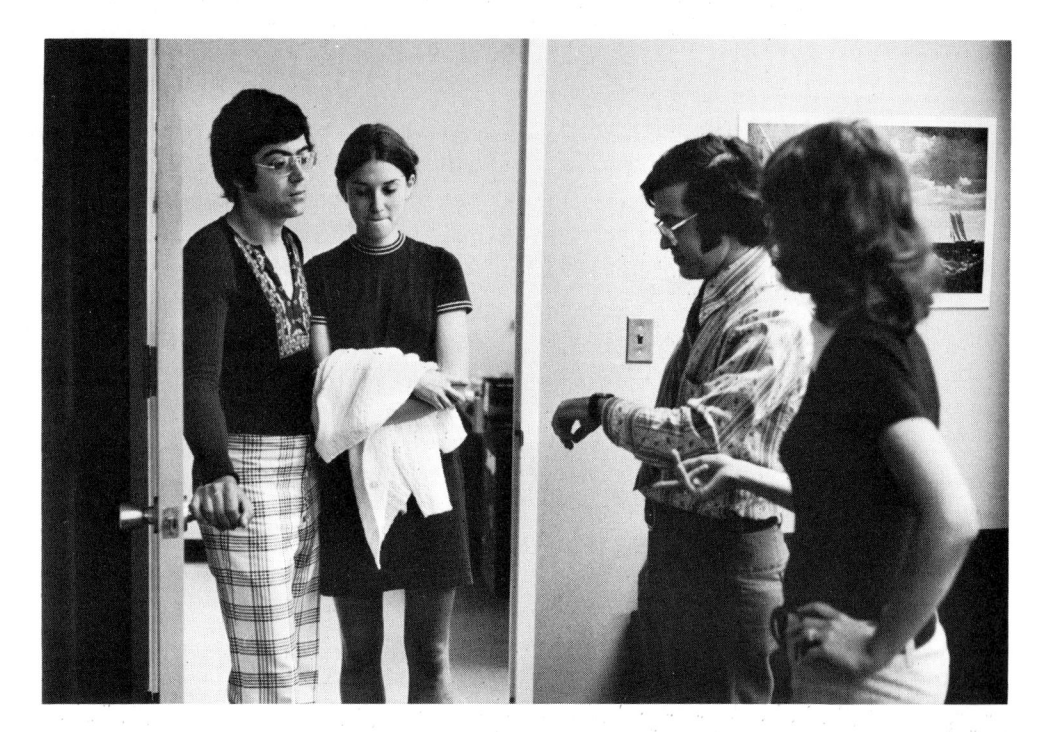

In this sociodrama the two individuals on the right act as parents who have been waiting for their daughter to arrive home from a date. The daughter and her boyfriend (on the left) come back late. What conversation do you suppose takes place?

should not be selected for a part that he will find embarrassing or threatening to him personally. Any unfavorable or unpopular roles in the play should be assigned to students who seem to be socially well adjusted and secure. Frequently, casting for sociodramas is done on a voluntary basis.

There should be simple props for the play. A few classroom chairs can serve as livingroom chairs. A lamp or two might be helpful for a livingroom scene. There can be a box to represent a television set. The director may assign some reading to the actors and even to the whole class to give them a background for the production of the play.

What happens in a sociodrama? To become relaxed, players often begin by talking about some irrelevant topic, such as the weather. At a signal from the director, the play itself begins. Using our example of late-hour parties, a student playing the role of a parent will launch into this topic, improvising his conversation probably on the basis of what he has heard at home. The other actors soon join in. The play will not be long. In fact, it may be quite short. It is up to the director to terminate the play whenever he believes that it has achieved its purpose.

When the play is over, the director will call on each member of the cast to give his or her reaction both to the role he played and to the roles of others. Then the discussion may be thrown open to the entire class. Sometimes the director asks each member of the class to write out his reaction to the play.

Following discussion, the players may reenact their roles, taking into account class comments, or they may exchange roles. For example, those having played the roles of

BEHAVIOR IN SMALL GROUPS 417

parents may now play the roles of teen-agers. A third possibility is for a new set of actors to repeat the play.

We have very little specific evidence on the value of role playing as a method of teaching factual material. Yet there is no doubt that occasional use of sociodrama has high interest value for students and that it is an effective way of studying group behavior.

Famous Studies of Behavior in Small Groups

Throughout this chapter, references have been made to scientific studies of small groups. In this last section we will focus on several well-known experiments. But first, to fully appreciate that these experiments present a true group effect rather than a pseudogroup effect, we will consider briefly what pseudogroup effects are.

Pseudogroup effects. PSEUDOGROUP EFFECTS refer to interpretations of data that falsely attribute certain results to group influence when no group communication actually took place. A true group influence is present only if there is communication between the group members. You should be aware of pseudogroup effects and the false impression of group behavior that statistics can sometimes convey.

For example, suppose you have an object whose exact weight you know. Suppose the object is in a small box but is relatively heavy in weight. You call the members of a group into the room one by one, ask each person to lift the box, and have each tell you exactly how much the box weighs. You make sure that the individuals who leave the room have no opportunity to communicate with the members of the group who have not yet lifted the box. No doubt some individuals will greatly overestimate and some will greatly underestimate the box's weight. Yet probably you will find that the mean or median weight is not very far from the actual weight. Furthermore, if you increase the size of the group, probably the average or median will come closer to the actual weight. It is a principle of statistics that when you increase the number of estimates, you reduce the variability of average estimates from the actual measure.

In this case, however, the improvement in average estimates would be a pseudogroup effect. There had been no opportunity for group communication. If you had selected just one individual to repeat his estimates of the weight of the box, you would have secured about the same results. (In order to rule out, as much as possible, the factor of remembering his early estimate, you would have to ask him to estimate the weights of quite a number of boxes and then use only the data from the same box that the group lifted.)

Other pseudogroup effects. Another example is a situation in which the group solution is based on information provided by one individual rather than on a joint group endeavor. Imagine presenting a small representative group from your school with a technical problem of some kind—perhaps a problem connected with electrical circuits. There may well be an individual in the group who knows a great deal about electrical circuits. He might be able to explain the basic principles to other members of the group in a short time. The group would then come up with a solution in far less time than the average time for individual solutions. You might be tempted to conclude that group behavior is more effective in solving this problem than individuals would be acting on their own.

However, you do not have a true group effect. In fact, you could have placed the individual members of the same group in separate soundproof booths and told each one to press a buzzer button as soon as he reached a solution. The first one to press the buzzer button with the solution would probably be the one individual who had a great deal of knowledge about electrical circuits. Indeed, his time would probably be shorter than the time for the group solution, when he had to explain the basic principles to other members of the group. When presented with a group solution, you should be aware of whether the solution is really the result of communication between group members or whether it is based on the behavior of one individual.

Notice that in the following studies the possibility of pseudogroup effects has been ruled out.

A study on how much group judgments influence individual judgments. This experiment examines what judgment an individual makes when confronted with an incorrect judgment by other members of his group. As part of an experiment, 123 college students were asked to participate in what they believed to be a simple study of visual judgments. In groups of seven to nine, they were shown a card on which there was a single vertical black line and another card on which there were three vertical black lines of various lengths. One of these three lines was the same length as the single line on the other card. The other two differed substantially.

Each student in turn was asked to report aloud which of the three lines he believed to be the same length as the reference line. Unknown to one student, the others in the group were directed to select an incorrect line and report it as being the same length as the single line on the other card. The one student who was not in on the scheme of the experiment was faced with a conflict—whether to report according to the evidence of his sense of sight or according to the opinions of his fellow students. To reduce suspicion, the students who knew about the real nature of the experiment gave correct responses the first few times and occasionally thereafter. Of the students who were not in on the experiment, about one-fourth were completely independent and never agreed with the erroneous judgments of the majority. On the other hand, some students went with the majority nearly all the time. When faced with the purposefully incorrect judgments of their fellow students, other individuals, on the average, gave 36.8 percent of their own judgments incorrectly. Although a person might really make a mistake in his judgment of the correct line, there was evidence that students did so in less than 1 percent of the judgments under ordinary conditions.

Does having an ally help the individual withstand group pressure? As part of the above experiment a partner was selected for each student unfamiliar with the experiment's real purpose. These partners had been instructed to indicate the correct lines on the first six trials, although the others in the group were indicating incorrect lines. With such support, most of the students who were unaware of the nature of the experiment usually resisted the pressure from the majority of the group. Then, following previous instructions, the partners switched over to agreeing with the incorrect answers of the majority. Immediately there was an abrupt increase in the errors of the uninformed students. Their allies had gone over to the other side.

Have you ever found yourself alone, or nearly alone, in a group discussion? Did you change your opinion so as to agree with the majority? Did having a friend who agreed with you make any difference? If the friend had to

In this visual-judgment problem the subject in the middle is beginning to feel the strain of disagreeing with the other two, who have been instructed to give wrong answers (top). Nevertheless, he decides to persist in his opinions (bottom).

leave the group, did you become less certain of your position? If he or she deserted you and agreed with the majority, did you stick to your original point of view, or did you give verbal assent to the majority point of view, even though it didn't seem right to you? The tendency to conform is very strong in our society.

How strong is conformity to group norms? Everyone is influenced in one way or another by what his associates are saying and doing. The contacts that members of a group have with one another generally result in the establishment of group norms. Rather than risk having others disapprove of him or even disagree with him, an individual may conform to the group standards. This tendency to conform has been demonstrated in the following well-known laboratory experiment.

Using the autokinetic illusion to indicate group influence. The apparent movement of a small fixed spot of light in an otherwise dark room is spoken of as the AUTOKINETIC ILLUSION, or EFFECT.

You can produce an autokinetic effect with a member of your family or a friend. First you have to have a completely darkened room —so dark that nothing in the room can be seen. Then arrange a light source so that only a very small point of light can be exposed in a fixed position. You can cover the source of light with heavy black paper and then punch a pinhole in the paper. The idea is that your subject can see nothing else except the point of light. Tell your subject that you will turn on the tiny spot of light which, in a few seconds, he will see move. As soon as he reports that the light has moved, turn off the light. Ask your subject to tell you as accurately as possible—to at least the nearest half-inch—how far the light has moved. Obviously, since the source of light is in a fixed position, your subject will be reporting an illusion.

In a classic experiment that involved autokinetic illusion and conformity, three isolated subjects each gave 100 judgments on the amount of apparent movement they saw. At first the judgments tended to vary. After a time, however, the judgments of length of movements tended to become fairly stable. It is true that the subjects' judgments differed from each other—one subject said the light generally moved about a half-inch, another said it moved about 2 inches, the third said the light generally moved about 7½ inches. Nevertheless, norms were established for each individual subject.

Next, the experiment was set up to study group influence. The subjects were placed in a dark room together. Each could hear the judgments made by the others. As a result, judgments tended to come together. By the end of the group session, the mean judgments for the three subjects were between 2 and 2½ inches. Two subjects had raised their estimates and one had lowered his estimate until their judgments achieved a level of conformity. Furthermore, when the subjects were put back in isolation after the group situations, they still tended to give group estimates. The conformity to group norms stayed with them, even in the absence of the physical presence of the group.

From these studies on the effects of group behavior on individuals, and considering the frequency with which we have contact with small groups, you can get some idea of how much influence small groups have on people's behavior.

Terms to Know

autokinetic illusion
communication
empathy
exclusive group
figure-ground relationship
group atmosphere
group climate
group cohesiveness

group dynamics
group feedback
group morale
inclusive group
interaction
interaction-oriented group
jargon
pseudogroup effect

role
sociodrama
sociogram
sociometry
small group
status
task-oriented group

Topics to Think About

1. In our democratic society would we be better off if we had fewer exclusive groups, or would society as a whole suffer from reduction in the number of such groups?

2. Do you personally prefer belonging to and being active in large groups or in small groups? Why?

3. Choose one of the small groups that you belong to. What can you do to promote group cohesiveness and morale within it? Would greater cohesiveness and morale improve the functioning of the group?

4. In any group that you belong to, which individuals do you like better, those who talk a great deal, or those who talk very little? Why?

5. If you were the manager of a large industrial plant, what procedures would you incorporate so that all personnel in the plant would be more highly motivated? Would you organize departments into large groups or small groups? Would you emphasize group feedback? What would you do to improve group atmosphere?

6. In election years, to what extent do those running for office try to communicate with the voters? Do you think communication increases or decreases after the election?

Suggestions for Activities

1. See if you can make a drawing of your own that illustrates the figure-ground relationship. When you look at it, you should be able to make the figures stand out against the background, but you should also be able to see the reverse: to perceive the background as predominant and see the figures as background. Your drawing should illustrate how exclusive groups are a matter of perception—how some people are perceived as being predominant and the rest, outside the group, are seen as background.

2. Try using a "candid camera," that is, a concealed-movie-camera technique, for observing communication through gestures. If you are photographing children, you must secure the consent of the parents before using the film in class. If you use high school students as subjects, their own consent should be sufficient. Do not, of course, show any films that might embarrass the subjects.

3. You can demonstrate communication with gestures by having one student try to communicate specific ideas to the class, using only gestures.

4. Try the old party game in which the members of the group are seated in a circle. One individual starts off by whispering some factual material to his neighbor on his left, that neighbor whispers what he heard to the person on his left, and so on around the circle. Communication is to be in a one-time, one-direction pattern—that is, no individual is permitted to ask for a repetition of what he has heard. How much is the material distorted by the time it has gone around the circle? Next, permit each individual to ask his neighbor for a repetition of what has been whispered, thus increasing the flow of communication. Under these conditions, how much of the original material is distorted by the time it has gone around the circle?

5. Present a sociodrama on some interaction-oriented group situation. The rest of the class should note the communication and interaction that takes place in the sociodrama. There can be a number of variations, such as having the actors change roles, having the drama reenacted after class discussion, or having a group that has been out of the room act out a drama on the same group situation.

6. Make a list of jargon, or current words with special meanings, in your high school. Your parents or grandparents may be able to give you some examples of the jargon used in their high school days. If, by magic, you and your parents or grandparents could be together as a group of adolescents, would there be some difficulty in communication, at least for a short time?

7. You may wish to experiment with the autokinetic illusion. Children make excellent subjects because they are not likely to suspect your basic objective. Have each one indicate the direction and distance of the "movement" of the point of light, taking care that he or she has no chance to communicate with the other children. Then bring the children together as a group so that each child has an opportunity to hear the judgments of the other children. Do the judgments become more uniform? Does the judgment of any one child seem to be especially influential? Does any child stick to his judgments regardless of what others say? You might start off by having one or two high school students, or even a teacher, give first judgments. Do the children tend to conform with the judgments given by older persons?

8. Organize a task-oriented group of three persons to perform some activity, such as writing a song, poem, or scene of a play. See what roles develop within the group and what interaction takes place. Make a sociogram of the communication that occurs.

Suggestions for Further Reading

Cartwright, Dorwin, and Alvin Zander (eds.), *Group Dynamics: Research and Theory,* Harper & Row. A book of readings that includes such topics as group cohesiveness, group pressures and standards, and individual motives and group goals.

Frisch, Karl von, *The Dancing Bees: An Account of the Life and Senses of the Honey Bee,* rev. ed., Harcourt Brace Jovanovich. This book covers in detail how bees communicate with one another to describe the location of food sources, and how bees function as a group.

Hare, Alexander Paul, *et al.* (eds.), *Small Groups: Studies in Social Interaction,* Knopf. A book of readings on the interaction of small groups.

Kagan, J., and E. Havemann, *Psychology: An Introduction,* 2nd ed., Harcourt Brace Jovanovich, Chapter 16. Note especially the material on group dynamics. Also, note the discussion of the *risky shift,* that is, the tendency of people to be more willing to undertake risks in decisions made in a group than in decisions made individually.

Psychology Today: An Introduction, CRM Books. See Chapter 32, "Small Groups," which discusses the formation of, leadership in, and relationship within, small groups.

Ruch, Floyd L., and Philip G. Zimbardo, *Psychology and Life,* 8th ed., Scott, Foresman. See Chapter 12, "The Social Bases of Behavior."

LOVE AND AGGRESSION

Love is a very important aspect of our behavior. Poets, philosophers, playwrights, and authors have been writing about it for thousands of years. However, it is only relatively recently that psychologists have been studying love from the scientific point of view.

The psychologist whose name stands out above all others in this field is Dr. Harry F. Harlow of the University of Wisconsin. As a beginning psychologist, he had noticed that the topic of love was not discussed in elementary psychology books, and decided to study affectional relationships under laboratory conditions. He settled on rhesus monkeys as subjects since they are primates, as is man, and they have a long period of development, as do human children.

Dr. Harlow raised some baby monkeys with their mothers and other baby monkeys only with members of their peer group to discover how essential the infant-mother affectional interaction was to the development of normal behavior personalities. The baby monkeys raised with their peer group were separated from their mothers a few hours after birth. None of them received any maternal care from its biological mother, although some had a surrogate wire or terry-cloth mother in their cages. Dr. Harlow found that the monkeys who received no mothering, but were raised with their peer group, developed normally in every way. The peer group interaction seemed to make up for the lack of mothering. Monkeys do have a need for some form of affectional system and social interaction, since other baby monkeys raised in isolation developed abnormally, but this need can be satisfied by love from either the mother or peers.

Do you think the same is true of human beings—that human babies need some form of affection for normal personality development, although not necessarily maternal care? Would babies brought up in a common nursery, free to play with their peers every day, be any less normal than babies raised with their parents?

Although Dr. Harlow is best known for his research on love, his work has caused him to become interested in other forms of behavior development, including aggression. For this research he again used rhesus monkeys. Because humans and monkeys have a similar kind of biological heritage, Dr. Harlow believed that he could learn something about human aggression by studying aggression in monkeys. By raising some monkeys in isolation, some in colonies with other monkeys, and some under both conditions at different times, he discovered that there were three phases that young monkeys go through. During the first phase, baby monkeys develop the capacity for affection. During the second, they learn to cope with fear. In the third phase, they discover how to control aggression.

If monkeys are isolated during any one of these phases, their development in that area is hampered. For instance, in one experiment the young monkeys were raised under normal conditions until just before the aggressive phase, and then were isolated. When they were returned to the normal monkey colony after the third phase was over, they displayed abnormally aggressive behavior. They became unusually violent—they had not learned to control their aggression.

This experiment suggests that the capacity for aggression is inborn, not learned. Instead, what must be learned is the ability to control aggressive tendencies. And this is learned through interaction with other monkeys during the appropriate time span.

Dr. Harlow concludes that aggressive behavior is probably still passed on from generation to generation as a part of man's biological heritage. Not everyone would agree with him that aggression is inborn in human beings, however. What do you think? Does aggression appear spontaneously in childhood? If children were isolated during the crucial phase so that they did not learn to control their aggressive tendencies through social interaction, would they show abnormally aggressive and violent behavior, as the monkeys did? Would there be less danger of war if individuals from different countries could have rather extensive social contacts at an early age?

chapter 17 Some social relationships

chapter 18 Psychology and problems of society

chapter 19 The world of work

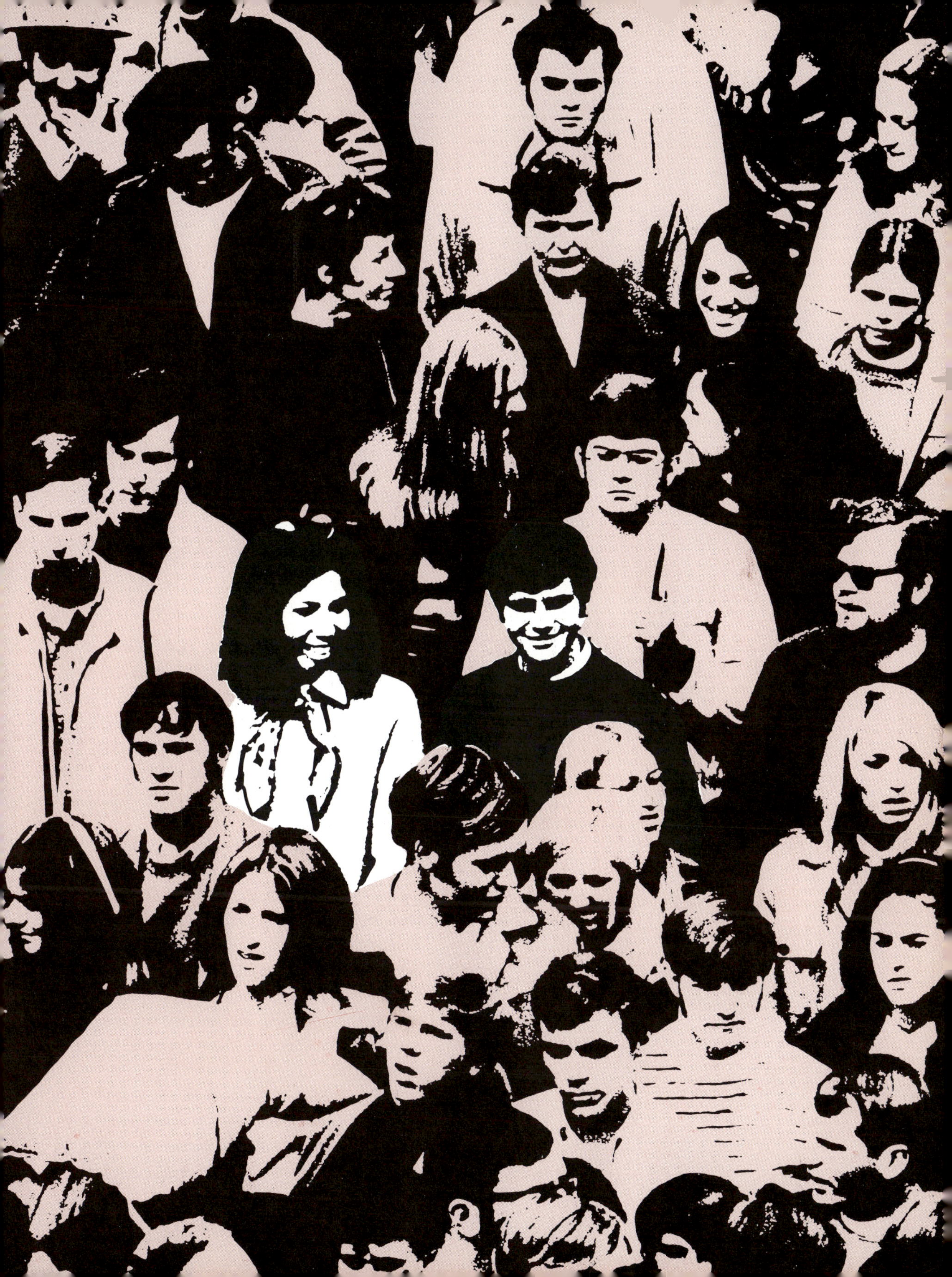

chapter 17
Some Social Relationships

IF YOU SAW a fellow human being across the street who was in obvious need of help, would you cross over and provide aid? Or would you try to ignore the situation and continue walking on your side of the street? Do you think that your relationships with others are governed more by competition or by cooperation? How can we increase cooperation between members of our society? We will consider these and other questions in this chapter on social relationships. After looking at some examples of man's inhumanity to his fellowmen, we will discuss some advantages and disadvantages of working with others—the dangers of threatening others, the effects of competition and rivalry, and how social cooperation works.

Would You Help a Person in Distress?

There are numerous cases, every day, of individuals in distress and in need of help. People react to such situations in a variety of ways. Some people ignore the situation and pass by, others stop and watch passively, still others actively provide aid. What do you think you would do in the following situations?

Some cases of failure to help. Returning home from work at 3:00 A.M., a woman was attacked on the street in front of her home. She screamed and made desperate pleas for help. Thirty-eight of her neighbors came to their windows and watched as the attacker took over a half-hour to murder her. Not one of her neighbors made any attempt to come to her aid. Not one of them even called the police.

A seventeen-year-old boy was stabbed on a subway. There were eleven other passengers in the car who watched as the boy bled to death. None came to his assistance, even though those who had stabbed him were no longer in the car.

Suppose the thirty-eight neighbors or the eleven passengers had been given a social attitude scale containing the question, "If you saw someone being attacked and murdered, would you do anything to help the person?" How do you think they would have answered the question? Yet when they had an opportunity to demonstrate their attitude in such a situation, they did nothing.

When one of the authors was a senior in high school, he went to a large city with his older brother. While walking back to their hotel one night he noticed what appeared to be a fight across the street. Several individuals were witnessing the situation. On closer inspection, the author discovered that one man was viciously kicking another man, who was lying on the sidewalk. Feeling compassion for the victim, the author started across the street to aid him in whatever way he could but was stopped by his brother, who explained that it would be dangerous to intervene. After a time the assailant stopped kicking the victim and went into a bar around the corner. The bystanders wandered over to the victim and then most of them left the scene. Some thirty minutes later the victim was still lying motionless on the sidewalk. Since evidently no one had called the police, the author did so. Shortly thereafter the police arrived and called an ambulance, which took the body away. Probably this tragedy could have been prevented if the bystanders had been willing to come to his aid. Ever since, the author has deeply regretted his failure to give help. What would you have done?

Various reactions to physical assault. The three cases just described were social incidents, not experiments. However, one experiment, using college psychology students as subjects, did investigate whether or not bystanders would come to the aid of a victim who was being physically assaulted. The college students were not told about the true nature of the experiment. Instead, they thought that the experiment was to study the effects of a program of psychodrama on college students of psychology.

A psychodrama was performed in front of the subjects. The actors were drama students who worked in pairs. Each pair began to disagree and then to argue. One appeared to lose his temper and slapped the other in the face. The actor who was slapped said, "Look, this is only acting.... You can't get away with hitting me like that." At this point they began to fight in a violent and extremely convincing manner.

A total of thirty-five subjects, seventeen men students and eighteen women students, thought the acting had turned into a real fight. Each of the thirty-five students saw one of the following four fight conditions: (1) one man beating up another man, (2) one woman beating up another woman, (3) a man beating up a woman, and (4) a woman beating up a man.

The results were that ten of the seventeen men subjects attempted to interfere in the fights, whereas only two of the eighteen women subjects attempted to interfere. All four of the men subjects who saw Fighting Condition One, in which both of the fighters were men, went to the aid of the victim. Four out of five men subjects went to the aid of the victim when one woman was beating up another woman. None of five men interfered in Condition Three, when a man was hitting a woman, although later some said, probably as a rationalization, "If he had hit her just one more time, I would have interfered." Two of three men subjects interfered when a woman was beating up a man. Of the women subjects, most did not interfere, regardless of the sex of the people fighting. One woman subject interfered when one woman was fighting another woman, and one woman subject interfered when a man was beating up a woman.

Does fear of physical injury keep bystanders from rendering help? One reason that an individual may not intervene in some emergency situation is because of fear of bodily harm. In the experiment just mentioned, for instance, students going to the aid of the victim might have received a few blows themselves. Would it make any difference if the situation involved little, if any, likelihood of harm befalling the person who attempted to help? Would it make a difference in whether or not a person offered help if he knew that other potential helpers were nearby?

Fifty-two college students taking an introductory course in psychology served as subjects in what they thought was an experiment on the topic of personal problems faced by college students. Each subject was alone in a laboratory cubicle. The subjects were divided so that they served under three experimental conditions: (1) believing that there was no other subject in a nearby cubicle, (2) believing that there was one other subject in a nearby cubicle, and (3) believing that there were four other subjects in nearby cubicles. The subjects were told that since any outsider might inhibit their responses to the topic of personal problems, even the experimenter would not listen to them communicate, but would later ask them to respond to a questionnaire. They were told that because the experimenter would not be present, a mechanical switching device would cut microphones on and off automatically. While the microphone of each subject was turned on for two minutes all other microphones would be turned off, so that no subject could talk to

If you were walking along and came upon this scene, what would you do? Would you stop and help the victim, or would you pass by? If you decide not to get involved, what reasons do you give to yourself for not offering any help?

Response of Subjects to an Epileptic Seizure Victim

NUMBER OF PERSONS INVOLVED	PERCENT OF SUBJECTS RESPONDING BY END OF THE SEIZURE	PERCENT OF SUBJECTS EVER RESPONDING	TIME IN SECONDS BEFORE RESPONDING
2 (Subject and victim)	85%	100%	52
3 (Subject, victim, and one other)	62	85	93
6 (Subject, victim, and four others)	31	62	166

any other subject. Actually, the voices of the other subjects were on prerecorded tapes.

The subjects were led to believe that one of their fellow students was subject to epileptic seizures with some resulting problems of personal and social adjustment. Each subject was a potential helper for this fellow student. Also, a person knowing that another individual is subject to epileptic seizures realizes that he is not going to be attacked if he goes to the aid of the individual.

The voice of the student supposedly subject to epileptic seizures was also on tape. During the time that his microphone was turned on, his voice became louder and louder, and eventually became quite incoherent. The victim stuttered and said, "... I'm gonna die-er-er, I'm gonna die-er-help-er-er-seizure-er." He choked, and then became quiet.

Data from the experiment are given in the table on this page. You can see that when an experimental subject believed he was the only one who could come to the aid of the victim he always offered help, and did so in less than a minute. If the subject thought that there was one other person who could go to the aid of the victim he was somewhat less certain to respond, and took longer to do so. If he thought that there were four other potential helpers he was still less likely to respond, and was even slower in responding. Nevertheless, even when a subject believed that there were four other persons who might go to the aid of the victim, nearly two out of three did attempt to offer help.

Do you have time to help a person in distress? We have just seen that an individual may fail to give help to a person in distress because he thinks someone else may do so. In our society we often rush from one activity to another, yet each of us would probably say that we consider helping our fellowmen more important than rushing from one appointment to another. But how would we behave if put to the test?

To investigate this question, forty volunteers from a theological seminary were used. These seminarians were preparing to become clergymen, devoting their lives to helping people in various ways. They were preparing to preach and practice the doctrine of brotherly love, and therefore were highly motivated to help their fellowmen, yet they were also a part of our ever-rushing society.

Unaware that they were serving as subjects in an experiment, the seminarians accepted an assignment to prepare a brief talk

Why do you think this man may be ignoring another human being in distress? Perhaps he is in a hurry. Perhaps he believes that the person is drunk and should be left alone to sleep it off. Should people feel no responsibility to help others?

and then record it. After preparing his talk, each student had to go down an alley between two buildings to where the recording would be made. Lying in the alley was a young man who was coughing and groaning. Evidently he was in pain. Of the forty students, sixteen stopped to help the young man, but twenty-four went right by him without stopping. One student even stepped over the victim. Do these data surprise you? Why didn't the seminarians stop to help?

Some of the students had been told that they would be ahead of time for recording their talks and so they could take their time in going from one building to another. Of these students, 63 percent stopped to help. Some of the students had been told that it was time to go and that they would have to hurry to get to the building where the recordings would be made. Of this group, 45 percent stopped to give help. Students in a third group were told that they were already late and that they would have to rush in order to have their talks recorded. Of this group, only 10 percent stopped to help the groaning young man. It is true that the number of students in each subgroup is small, but certainly there is a suggestion that whether or not a person stops to help someone depends at least to some extent on whether he thinks he has time to help.

In hurrying to get to a movie before it begins, would you stop to help a human being in distress?

Why do some individuals fail to give aid to persons in distress? At first thought, it would seem that the more individuals there were present in a situation of distress, the more likelihood there would be of help being given. Yet, in many social situations the opposite is true. Why?

One psychologist has suggested that three factors are involved. First of all, a person must notice that something unusual is happening. As we hurry along in crowds thinking about our individual problems, we may not even be aware that something unusual is happening. Second, a person must interpret the situation as an emergency. Maybe he sees a man lying at the side of the street but decides that probably the man is just drunk and in a short time will be able to get up and go home without assistance. In other words, he does not interpret the situation as an emergency. Third, a person must decide whether or not he has a personal responsibility to give help.

Whether or not a person feels he has a responsibility to help depends to a great extent on his background and previous experiences, but he will also be influenced by the crowd of bystanders at the scene. He looks around at others. If they seem to be unaroused and indifferent, the individual may not wish to stand out. He, too, will try to remain calm and look with indifference at the person who seems to be in distress. Perhaps each person in the crowd is thinking that someone else will do something about the distressful situation, and so nobody does anything. Actually, most, if not all, of the individuals in the crowd of bystanders may be quite emotionally upset, although they try to give an outward appearance of calmness. Experiments have indicated that often those who do not interfere to help a person in distress are more worried and upset about the situation than those who do interfere.

One reason why some individuals fail to give aid to persons in distressful situations is fear of being victimized themselves. In one case a man who had been shot succeeded in making his way to several houses, pleading for help. Because they were afraid of robbery or assault, the householders would not open their doors. A few did report the plea for help to the police, who responded immediately but could not find the man. When they eventually did locate him in a vacant lot, the man had died of his wounds.

Today if our automobile breaks down and we pull off to the side of the road, hundreds of cars may whiz by before anyone stops to give us assistance. We may have to wait until a police patrol car comes by to help us. If we leave our car to go for assistance, we may return to find that it has been vandalized or broken into and our personal possessions stolen.

We are more likely to receive help if our car breaks down on a nearly deserted road than if it stalls on a major highway. The next passing motorist is more likely to feel a personal responsibility to aid us. Again we see that the larger the number of individuals involved in an emergency situation, the less there is a feeling of personal responsibility to help.

Have you ever failed to give help because you were afraid you would be victimized?

Would you help a victim of exploitation? Many times individuals are the victims of unethical practices that are unfair to them—they are exploited.

In one experimental study of exploitation, forty high school girls served as subjects. Each subject observed two other "subjects" who, unknown to the subject, were actually confederates of the experimenter. One confederate, playing the role of exploiter, took unfair advantage of the other confederate, who played the role of victim. The assigned task for the three girls was the production of creative ideas. The true subject was told that the other two would work in separate rooms but that they would be permitted to communicate with each other by written notes that the true subject would carry from one to the other. Each girl's score on creative ideas was to be based entirely on her own production of ideas.

During the note-carrying sessions, the exploiter was unwilling to share any of her ideas with the other confederate. However, contrary to instructions, she wrote down ideas that she received from the other confederate with what obviously appeared to be the intention of presenting them to the experimenter as her own ideas. The confederate playing the role of victim gave the distinct impression of being more than ready to share her ideas with the exploiter and to help her in any way she could.

The experimenter developed a technique to determine if each true subject identified herself with—took sides with—the exploiter, with the victim, with both the exploiter and the victim, or with neither of them. The experiment was so planned that ten of the forty girls were classified under each of the four identification conditions.

Each true subject had two opportunities to intervene. One opportunity came when the experimenter simply asked her how things had gone during the experiment. The second opportunity came when, after supposedly counting the number of creative ideas produced by each of the confederates, the experimenter announced that the exploiter had produced more creative ideas than the victim (although he didn't use those terms).

Of the subjects who did intervene, most did so by telling the experimenter just what the exploiter had done. Some told the victim exactly what the exploiter was doing, or at least suggested that she be less helpful. A few subjects spoke to the exploiter, some expressing mild disapproval of her actions and others strongly criticizing her. More subjects might have indicated their disapproval to the exploiter if they had not been led to believe that they might have to work with the exploiter in a later part of the experiment. Intervention at the present time might lead to unpleasant relationships later.

The number of true subjects who intervened under each of the four identification conditions were as follows: identification with victim—10; identification with exploiter—5; identification with both—8; identification with neither—6. Although eleven subjects did not intervene, twenty-nine of them, or nearly three-fourths, did intervene in some way. You can see that all ten of the subjects intervened if they tended to identify with the victim, but only half of them intervened if they tended to identify with the exploiter.

Admittedly, the number of subjects in each group was small. However, we can say that the data suggest that identification with one or the other of two antagonists is a factor in determining whether or not a person is likely to intervene to render assistance.

Would you intervene if you knew that one student was exploiting another student by putting his own name on another student's written work and handing it in? What would you do if you knew that a student was copying answers on an examination?

Would you help a person who has had a minor mishap? We have discussed rendering assistance to persons suffering physical distress or being exploited, but what about giving help in cases of some minor mishap? Suppose you saw a woman drop a bag of groceries. Would you help her pick them up?

In one experiment two young women, college students, dropped their groceries just outside a supermarket. They were approximately the same age, height, and weight. They were dressed alike, had used little makeup, and wore no jewelry. Each woman was approximately twenty feet in front of the main exit from a supermarket, where most of the customers would pass her on their way to their

This woman has just had a minor mishap. She has tripped and fallen on the sidewalk. Her purse has opened and the contents are scattered. If you were walking by, would you help her?

cars. One woman was black and the other was white.

In addition to these two accomplices there was a "spotter" and an "observer." The spotter and the observer were also college students, both men. One was black and one was white. The spotter stood inconspicuously to one side of the exit where he could be seen by the grocery dropper. The observer took a position somewhere in the parking lot, where he could clearly see just what happened.

Twelve supermarkets were used in the experiment. Six of them were patronized primarily by black buyers and six primarily by white buyers. The markets were matched on prices, size of store, and volume of business. Judging from the customers, prices, and kind of commodities sold, all twelve supermarkets catered to people who were primarily of upper-lower to lower-middle socioeconomic status.

The subjects for the experiment were men and women shoppers who were selected as they left the store exit. They ranged in age from about twenty to about sixty years. Each subject had to be by himself or herself, and could not be so burdened down with groceries that he or she could not help. The 176 shopper subjects used in the experiment were divided into four groups—black women, white women, black men, and white men—each containing forty-four people.

When the spotter saw a suitable shopper leave the supermarket, he would turn quickly and walk away. This was the signal for the dropper to turn slowly away from the oncoming subject, tear open the bottom of her bag of groceries, and drop them when the subject was approximately ten feet away from her. The dropper gave appropriate gestures of surprise, displeasure, and dismay. She circled around the dropped groceries slowly for about five to ten seconds, thus giving the subject time to come to her assistance.

The behavior of the subjects fell into one of the following four categories: (1) ignores situation—subject ignores the dropper and walks by, (2) reacts without help—subject hesitates and shows surprise, (3) perfunctory help—subject helps dropper with a few of her groceries but then hurries on his or her

SOME SOCIAL RELATIONSHIPS **435**

way, and (4) positive help—subject helps the dropper with all of her groceries, offers to get her a new grocery bag, and so on. After each trial the observer, the dropper, and other students on the experimental team decided on the rating of the subject's behavior.

Data from the ratings revealed that nearly 20 percent of all the subjects gave complete positive help. On the other hand, 33 percent ignored the situation. Twenty-one percent offered perfunctory help, and 26 percent reacted without helping. Also, there was a sex difference in help given—men helped more than women. There is a suggestion that race made a difference, but among women only. The white women subjects helped the white dropper more often than they helped the black dropper. On the other hand, the white women subjects ignored the white dropper more often than the black dropper. The black women subjects tended not to help either dropper. Women in general tended to ignore the dropper of their own race. Can you offer any possible explanations for these differences? What do you think would have happened if the droppers had been men, one white and one black? Of course, this is only one experiment, based on a relatively small sampling. Do you think the same results would be obtained if this experiment were conducted at other supermarkets, perhaps patronized by customers of a different socioeconomic status?

Of the 104 subjects of both sexes and races who did not help the dropper, 46 percent did so in full view of another shopper. Would these other shoppers help the dropper, or would they follow the example of the first subject? Of these secondary subjects, 77 percent of the men and 46 percent of the women helped the dropper even though they had seen someone else fail to help.

If you saw another student drop his or her papers or books, would you offer assistance? Would it make any difference whether the dropper was white or black? male or female?

Victimizing those already in distress. In nearly every major disaster there are some individuals with such antisocial standards that they take advantage of those already in distress. Whenever there is a disaster such as a flood, hurricane, or earthquake, the police know that vandals and looters will promptly move into the stricken area to destroy or steal as much as they can from those who have suffered a great loss already. In one incident a young woman was involved in a very serious and almost fatal automobile accident. People in passing cars did stop to give whatever aid they could, and they did call the police. The young woman was unconscious and very near death. After she had regained consciousness in a hospital, she inquired about her purse, which contained several hundred dollars. It was then discovered that before the police arrived someone who had stopped to "help" had actually stolen the victim's purse. (The purse was not lost or misplaced, because it contained the name and address of the owner and therefore could have been returned.)

As our population rapidly expands and so many persons live in crowded cities, even in minor unfortunate situations we often seem to be losing our individual concern for the welfare of others. Are people becoming less compassionate?

Compassion. The word "compassion" means sorrow for the suffering or trouble of other persons, coupled with a desire to help them. Although incidents and experiments we have considered suggest that human behavior is far from perfect, in most cases at least some persons did offer help.

Compassionate individuals may form a

group to help others who are experiencing a similar kind of suffering or trouble. Each year about 27,000 families in Great Britain mourn the death of a child. A number of years ago, a group of bereaved parents formed an organization known as the "Society of the Compassionate Friends." Originally the purpose of the organization was to offer help and understanding to those who have lost a child through death, but the work has now been expanded to cover three areas: (1) the care of bereaved parents, (2) the care of parents, especially through group therapy, whose children are chronically ill, and (3) the support of research into medicine and road safety that will effectively reduce deaths among children.

Do you think our attitudes toward persons in distress would be altered if there were many different kinds of groups of compassionate friends?

There are numerous examples of compassionate individuals and groups. Once a year many communities raise large sums of money to be used by various agencies in helping individuals or families who, because of poverty, lack of education, poor health, or emotional disturbances, are in need of aid. Many individuals give their blood to be used in saving the lives of persons who are victims of accidents, whether or not they know the persons. In cases of natural disasters such as floods, tornadoes, and earthquakes, or in cases of fire or war-caused devastation, many, many individuals rush to give help by contributing food, clothing, or money. Many open their homes to victims of disaster, or even to the motorist stranded in a storm. Such help is given not only in times of local or national disaster, but also when disaster strikes in another part of the world. Undoubtedly you can think of other examples to add to the above suggestions. Is it easier to find examples of compassion or to find examples of unwillingness to help in time of trouble?

Social Facilitation

Sometimes businessmen complain that work production decreases as a result of their employees gathering in small groups to discuss and argue about social situations and problems. Maybe you have said to yourself, "If only I could get away from my family, or my classmates, I would really get some work done." Could the opposite be true?

Actually, the influence of the presence of other persons on an individual can cause the volume of his work output to increase. Whenever an individual in a group situation exceeds his characteristic level of performance when working alone, due to the presence of other persons, SOCIAL FACILITATION has occurred. The group situation increases motivation and the individual accomplishes more than he would otherwise because of the stimulation provided by other people. This does not mean that the individual is necessarily more efficient in a group situation. In fact, he may make more errors than when he is working alone. It also does not refer to individuals assisting one another in performing a specific task. Social facilitation refers only to the increase of an individual's work output due to the influence of other people's presence on him.

Social facilitation among animals. As is so often the case, we can learn much about human behavior by studying the behavior of organisms other than man. For many years psychologists and biologists have known that individual fish eat more when with other fish than when eating alone. Ants dig more dirt in a given length of time when working in the presence of other ants than when digging

Why do you think that fish eat more when they are with other fish than when they eat alone? If you have goldfish or tropical fish, you might try isolating one from the others and comparing how much the isolated fish eats to how much the fish who are together in a group eat.

alone. Also, rats eat and drink more when in group situations than when feeding alone, especially if there is a limited amount of food available or if they have to take turns at a water spout.

Social facilitation among human beings. Research with human beings, both children and adults, indicates that subjects doing the same tasks achieve more when working independently but near one another than when working alone.

In one classic experiment, for instance, adult subjects were given the tasks of crossing out certain letters of the alphabet from a page of scrambled letters, working multiplication problems, and writing arguments to disprove a given statement. First, the subjects worked on these tasks in separate rooms. At another time, they worked on similar tasks while seated around a common table. Although seated close to each other, they were asked not to compete or cooperate with one another. The data revealed that a majority speeded up their performance when working at the same table as others doing the same kind of work. However, the increase in quantity of work accomplished was accompanied by some loss in quality of work.

Another psychologist had subjects work in separate rooms, but all of their working times were controlled by the same starting and stopping signals. Even though the participants were in separate rooms, the common signals served to provide some social facilitation.

There is some evidence that greater production in group situations may be due to rivalry, although many times the individuals in the group do not realize that they are competing. One psychologist had individuals work near one another, but told them that their work records would not be compared to the work records of others. Social facilitation was not indicated by the data. The same psychologist had some individuals work in rooms by themselves, but told each one that his work record would be compared with the results of others working in other rooms. Their scores were very similar to the work scores of individuals working in group situations. The increase in their work output seemed to be due to rivalry.

Can you study more efficiently when others are around you? Some students find that they can study better in a library or study hall than when they study in a room by themselves. Just the fact that other students are around them, even though there is no communication by conversation or an exchange of notes, results in social facilitation.

One college freshman was close to dismissal from college because of very poor marks. She changed from studying alone to studying in the college library. In just a few weeks her marks improved and were above average. She had been raised in a large family, and all through elementary and high school she had studied with her brothers and sisters in the same room. Her room at college was in a private home where there were no other students. For her, it was "just too quiet to study there."

On the other hand, students with different home backgrounds may find it very difficult to study efficiently in group situations, or even with a roommate around. Unfortunately some college dormitories are not well designed for studying in isolation.

Social Competition

As we have seen, social facilitation is sometimes related to rivalry or competition. We find competition in many areas of American society. For instance, we thoroughly enjoy such athletic competitions as football, basketball, hockey, and baseball. Both players and spectators are anxious to have their teams win. Although such sports as track and swimming may be thought of as competition between individuals, there are many track and swimming meets that involve group competition. We enjoy both individual and group competition in such fields as music and debating.

Certainly we accept competition in business. For example, automobile manufacturers compete with one another for sales, as do electronics firms, book publishers, steel companies, and clothing manufacturers, to name but a few. In most schools students compete for high marks and scholastic honors, although in some schools attempts are made to encourage group effort and cooperation rather than competition.

What can experiments tell us about competition?

The pecking order in hens. In some species, when two or more animals desire the same objective, such as food or a mate, competition develops and a dominance hierarchy is established. The best example of such social competition has been observed in barnyard hens.

After several hens have been together for some time, a "pecking order" develops. The most dominant hen in the social competition pecks all other hens in the group and is pecked by none. The next most dominant hen pecks all other hens except the dominant one. This order continues down to one hen that is pecked by all the other hens but does not peck any hen. The order becomes relatively fixed and can be illustrated by the diagram below for five hens—*A, B, C, D,* and *E.*

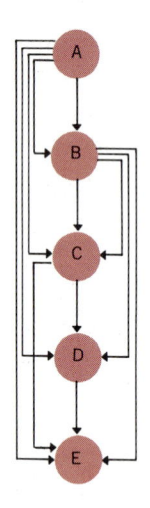

What happens if a new hen is put in the pen with a group of hens that has already established a pecking order? In that case, a new hierarchy develops. The new hen learns its relative position in the group.

There are several factors that determine the pecking order among hens. For instance, the most dominant hen, the *A* hen in our diagram, tends to be the largest and fastest hen in the group. Also, it tends to be the "smartest" one as shown by the fact that it learns quickly in experimental learning situations.

The pecking order in human beings. Can you think of examples of a pecking order in human social situations? What about the chain of command in military life? What about the seating of guests at formal dinners? If you attend a college commencement ceremony, you may find that faculty members enter marching in the order of their academic rank and tenure.

You may have an opportunity to observe a group of children at play. Does one child tend to boss and perhaps win fights over all the others? Is one child always picked on by the others? Does there seem to be a pecking order for the other children?

Studying competition between human beings in the laboratory. One psychologist studied social competition by having two subjects compete in a simulated business situation. Both players in this competitive game operate toy trucks. Each player tries to drive his truck over the shorter of two available roads in order to make as much profit as possible. To insure motivation, both drivers are actually paid money, although the amount of money for each trip is small—such as sixty cents, minus one cent for each second used in travel time. The road situation is shown in the figure on page 441. One firm is known as Acme, the other as Bolt. Trucks for both firms travel at the same speed, and can be made to go either forward or backward.

If a player takes his alternate route, the game is set up so that he will lose money on each trip. If both players try to use their shorter route, they will meet on a one-lane section of the road, where they cannot pass. If one of them backs up so that the other can go through on the one-lane section of the road, he will lose money and his competitor will make a profit, or at least suffer less of a loss. If neither driver gives in and permits the other to use the one-lane road, time costs will build up and both players will lose heavily. On the other hand, if the drivers learn to alternate in permitting each other to go through on the one-lane road, both will be better off financially.

The use of a threat by one person. The psychologist conducting the experiment introduced the possibility of a threat. One driver —for example, Acme—was given a gate that he could close. Sometimes after he had entered the one-lane road he would close the gate behind him. In that case, Bolt was forced to back up to a point past his end of the one-lane road, enabling Acme to proceed to his destination and make a profit, or at least reduce his loss. After Acme had left the one-lane road his gate would open and Bolt could proceed, but he would have wasted time and money. Of course, Bolt, knowing of Acme's threat of closing the gate, could take his alternate route from the start, but he would be certain to lose some money by doing so.

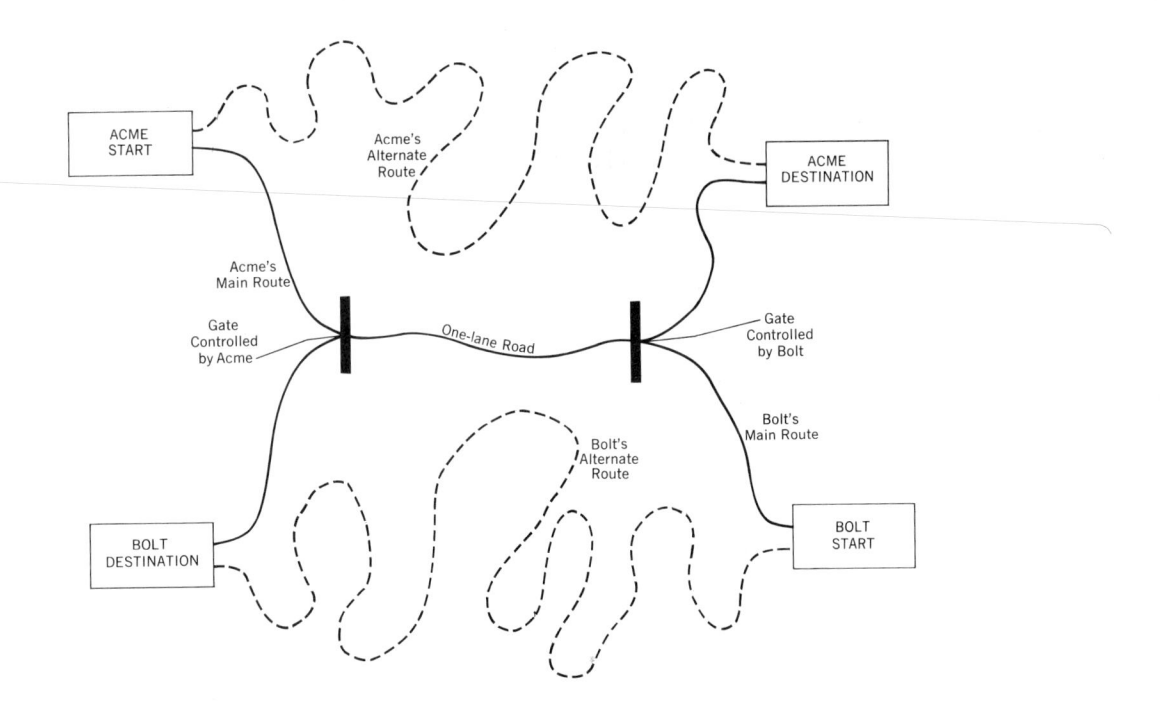

In this one-gate situation, data from the experiment indicated that the driver with a gate did better financially than his competitor, especially on the first few trips permitted by the experimenter. Interestingly enough, the driver with the gate gradually gave up his advantage of a threat and the two players began cooperating. The psychologist concluded this part of the experiment by saying, "If one member of a bargaining pair has a weapon, you are better off if you are the one who has it; but you may be even better off if neither of you has a weapon."

The use of threats by two persons. What happens if both drivers are given gates? It was found that both drivers lost more money than in the one-gate situation.

Then the two drivers were given intercoms so that they could talk to each other. Presumably this should have given them a great advantage, but such was not the case. Their conversations, which were held under the strain of competition and threats, were not constructive. They actually used words that worked against them rather than for them.

May there not be similar situations in social groups? One great world power threatens another great world power, which in turn produces a threat of its own. A minority group threatens a majority group, which in turn produces a threat of its own. Workers threaten management and management threatens workers. In such situations communication is attempted, as it must be, but will it

SOME SOCIAL RELATIONSHIPS **441**

be successful? When competition and threats are involved, doesn't communication often degenerate into conversations that are not constructive and for a time may even seem to be harmful to settling differences? At conferences between diplomats of opposing nations, communications often seem to break down and no constructive solutions are achieved, at least for a considerable period.

Playing "chicken." In another experiment using the same apparatus, high school boys were used as subjects. The game was altered to introduce the idea of "chicken."

The boys were told that if their two trucks met at any place along the one-lane road it would be considered a collision, which would cost each player at least ten cents. Instead of a gate as a threat, a player could use a "lock." This device enabled a player to lock his truck so that it could move in only one direction—forward. A signal informed the other driver that his competitor's truck was locked into a forward-only commitment. Data indicated that when one driver had the commitment device, he made significantly more money than the driver without a lock.

If both drivers could, and did, lock their trucks into a forward-only position, both would lose all of their profits. The psychologist found that the high school boys playing the game tended to be sufficiently prudent to resist the temptation of locking themselves into a position from which they could not compromise. This was especially true if they knew they were going to have repeated encounters with another player who could use the same threat. If they knew in advance that there was to be only a single encounter with another driver, they became less prudent, and also lost their money.

Minority groups and social competition. These experiments suggest some of the problems of competition between social groups in our society. Consider, for example, two ethnic or religious groups that are both striving to reach certain economic and social goals. Will they cooperate on the "one-lane road" that both must travel? Will one group try to use so much force that the other will have to give in? Will both groups try to threaten each other so that eventually one group will have to "chicken out"? Will they lock themselves into positions from which they cannot retreat?

National groups and social competition. What about two nations or two groups of nations that have separate goals but face some conflicts in achieving those goals? They can agree to alternate in negotiating the one-lane road of international relationships. Or one nation can build up such military and economic power that it can force the other nation to let it win all or most of the international disputes. Or both nations can build up military and economic might and so make any solution to their problems extremely difficult. One

Often when threats and counter-threats are used, as between these prisoners and New York State troopers at Attica State Prison, it is difficult to establish communication and settle differences amicably.

Sometimes people resort to cheating to win in a competitive situation. Two partners in this bridge game are cheating in an attempt to win the game—the girl who is fingering her necklace is indicating to her partner that she should bid hearts.

or both nations can lock themselves into a commitment situation so that they cannot back down or compromise. They can play the international game of "chicken," in which the stakes are millions of lives.

Social psychologists can present evidence from experimental studies on the values and disadvantages of competition and on some basic principles for the solution of international problems, but they cannot give final answers. You may wish to read about and discuss current international problems and the attempts being made to relieve the undesirable effects of competition among nations. In the light of your study of psychology and previously cited research findings, can you suggest possible solutions?

The Effects of Competition

It is easy to think of the advantages of competition. Instead, we will consider the possible disadvantages and how these disadvantages might be lessened. Some of the disadvantages of competition include undue agitation and confusion, the effects of winning at any price, the effects of losing on individuals, and the hostile aggression that may result.

Undue agitation and confusion. Some individuals do more and better work when they are not under the pressure of individual or group competition. One classic experiment used a horse race to study the effect of competition. Wooden horses were attached to a string and could be pulled along a track by winding the string onto a fishing reel. Working alone, without any element of competition, individuals could usually pull their horses along the track quite efficiently. When competing against others in a horse race, however, they would often tangle their lines and even reverse their reels. They became agitated and confused. They were less efficient than when "running" their horses alone.

Winning at any price. When competition is keen, some individuals may resort to dishonesty in order to win. Some children will cheat at party games to win a coveted prize. A student may resort to cheating to secure top marks and thereby attain public recognition, a college scholarship, or parental praise. Another student may not cheat, but he may go so far in competing to win high marks that he sacrifices needed social contacts and health-giving recreation. There are numerous examples throughout history of elections being

SOME SOCIAL RELATIONSHIPS **443**

rigged by political candidates who wanted to win at any price.

The effects of losing. Whether in beauty contests, musical competitions, athletic events, debates, or school marks, all too often we glorify the virtues and advantages of the winner without giving consideration to the effects of competition on those who do not win top prizes. It is true that some individuals who lose in a contest strive all the harder to win the next time in the same kind of competition, or to win in some other area of competition, but it seems that such individuals are often the exception rather than the rule.

What about the effects of rather consistently being a loser? Will the consistent loser become discouraged and cease to even try to win? Will he try to preserve his self-respect by lowering his level of aspiration?

These questions were considered in a research study involving school marks. Each member of a college class was asked to indicate what mark he expected to receive on an important examination to be given the next day. Half of the students did as well as or better than they expected. They had been successful. The other half of the students could be thought of as being unsuccessful, since they did not achieve their goals. Just before the next important examination, all students were again asked to indicate what mark they expected to achieve on that examination. Of the successful group, 62 percent indicated that they expected to achieve the same mark that they had expected on the first examination. Of the unsuccessful group, 66 percent gave the same response. There was not much difference. However, only 2 percent of the successful group lowered their expectations, whereas 34 percent of the unsuccessful group lowered their expectations. Of the successful group, 36 percent raised their expectations for the second examination, but no one in the unsuccessful group raised his expectation. Do you try harder in courses in which you have been successful than in courses in which you feel you have been unsuccessful?

Hostile aggression. If competition between individuals or groups becomes intense, hostile aggression may result. By hostile aggression we mean responding to a situation in ways that are deliberately harmful to another person or group and are not for purposes of self-defense.

Although athletic contests are generally conducted in a sportsmanlike way, athletes have been known to try to injure a particularly threatening rival. After a game some fans of the losing team may start a brawl, trying to injure fans of the opposing team, or they may destroy property associated with the rival team.

There are examples of hostile aggression among minority groups. Some members, believing that they cannot successfully compete with members of majority groups, become hostile and aggressive. They destroy the property of the majority group, injure, and perhaps murder members of that group. The same type of behavior is often used by the majority group against minority groups.

Leaders and their followers in some nations come to believe that they cannot compete successfully in world trade. They become hostile, possibly to the point of threatening to kill or actually killing people in rival nations. They destroy as much of the material wealth of the other nations as possible. We call such a situation "war."

Can the disadvantages of competition be reduced? Although we seem to be swinging somewhat away from the very competitive way of life that characterized the early days of

America, our society still emphasizes competition and tolerates its undesirable effects. Can anything be done to lessen the undesirable aspects without eliminating competition?

One possibility is to improve communication between competitors. We have seen that under conditions of competition, effective communication between competitors may break down. However, if two competing individuals or groups can talk or otherwise communicate without using threats or furthering the competition, they may be able to resolve their differences more often and work together in a constructive way.

Another possibility is to stress competition with the individual's own record rather than with the performance of others. In competing with others some individuals are bound to succeed and others are bound to lose. In the case of school marks, for example, a few students will receive high marks, a few will receive low marks, and most students will receive average marks. But if students compete against their own scores, every student has an opportunity to succeed.

Suppose at the beginning of a semester, students take a standardized test in some subject area. If a distribution of scores is made, some students would be at the bottom or close to the bottom. Suppose near the end of the semester the same test, or a statistically equivalent form of the test, is repeated. Even the students with the lowest scores on the earlier test may be able to enjoy the satisfaction of knowing that they have improved, that they have succeeded in this competition with themselves.

Another way to reduce the disadvantages of competition for those who do not win is by sharing the disappointment of failure. An athletic team may lose all, or nearly all, of its games in a given season. Each member of the team may be quite unhappy about the season. Nevertheless, there is some comfort in knowing that he is not alone but can share his disappointment over the results of the competition. "Misery loves company."

Some businesses have sales teams that compete with one another. One team is bound to lose, or at best tie for bottom place. The individual salesmen on this team may derive comfort from knowing that others in his group also tried and yet did not meet with the success they may have wished.

Competition seems to be a basic part of our social life. Nevertheless, it would be worthwhile for our society to place a greater emphasis on cooperation.

Social Cooperation

We have seen that both animals and human beings tend to do more work when in the presence of others of their kind than when working alone. In social facilitation, however, cooperation was not involved. Now we will examine some situations in which animals and humans are in the presence of others of their kind and cooperate to achieve various goals.

Social cooperation in animals. Certain insects, such as ants and bees, exhibit social cooperative behavior for survival of the species, but this behavior is biologically determined. Here we will devote our attention to learned social cooperation.

A number of experiments have demonstrated that rats can learn to cooperate with one another. The apparatus for one such experiment consisted of a box with an electrified floor through which a rat could be given a shock as it ate from a dish of food. However, the shock could be avoided if another rat would cooperate. At one end of the box and away from the food was a platform that turned off the current if a rat climbed on it. Alone in the apparatus, each rat initially learned two things: (1) to eat from the dish of food, and (2) to turn off the electrical current by stepping on the platform. Then two such trained rats were placed in the box together. At first the pair of rats displayed uncooperative behavior. Either they both endured the electrical shock in order to eat at the same time, or they both climbed on the platform to avoid being shocked.

In time, some pairs of rats did learn to cooperate. One rat ate without discomfort while the other remained on the platform. This was a pleasant situation for the rat that was eating, but not a pleasant situation for the hungry rat on the platform. The rat on the platform began pulling on the tail of the eating rat, apparently to get it to come to the platform. Eventually the rats learned to shuttle back and forth so that each could eat without discomfort from shock.

Social cooperation has also been demonstrated with the chimpanzee. Two chimpanzees can easily learn to cooperate with each other in a situation requiring that both pull on separate ropes to bring a box of food within reach of both. To study chimpanzee behavior in a more complex situation, two animals were placed in separate cages that were alike except that one cage contained a green and a blue panel and the other cage contained a red and a yellow panel. Food was given only if the chimpanzees pushed on their panels in a prescribed order. For example, one chimpanzee had to push its yellow panel and then wait for the other chimpanzee to push its green panel. Next, the first chimpanzee had to push its red panel, after which the second animal had to push its blue panel. If the pair cooperated and pushed their panels in the correct sequence, food became available to both. In some pairs, if one chimpanzee's partner was slow in pushing its panels, the first chimpanzee would reach through the bars of its cage and give the other chimpanzee a push, or even try to turn it in the direction of its panels. The chimpanzees' communication was limited to pushing or turning—they never pointed to the panels. Nevertheless, they did learn to cooperate.

There are even examples of social cooperation between two species that are ordinarily hostile to each other. A young rat and a young kitten were kept in the same cage, where they learned to live together. Then a screen was placed between the animals and their food. The experimental situation was such that if the rat pressed one lever at the same time that the kitten pressed another lever, the screen would open and they could both eat. Neither of the animals could open the screen by itself. They had to learn to cooperate. One time when the kitten was playing with the rat's tail, they both happened to press their respective levers and the screen opened, giving both access to food. The next time they were hungry the kitten began playing with the rat's tail, but the screen did not open because both levers were not pressed. In a later trial when the kitten had its paw on the lever, the rat pressed the other lever and both were able to eat. With repeated trials learning took place, and before too long the kitten and rat were cooperating whenever they desired food.

If animals, even those that are ordinarily hostile to each other, can learn to work together for a common good, what about the human species?

Social cooperation in man. In one experiment twenty children, ages seven to twelve years, were carefully matched into ten teams of two each. The two children on each team were seated on opposite sides of a table. Each child was given a stylus with an electrical connection, and had before him three holes. The apparatus was set up so that if the two children happened to place their styli in holes opposite each other, a red light would flash on and a single jelly bean was delivered. If the two children placed their styli in holes that were not opposite, no reinforcement was given. All ten teams learned the cooperative response within ten minutes after the experiment began, even though no team had been told that cooperation was necessary. Almost immediately, eight of the teams learned to divide the jelly beans in some manner. In the other two teams, one child took all of the jelly beans until his partner refused to cooperate. Then they began talking to each other and soon reached an agreement, such as "The first piece is mine, the next piece is yours." After establishing a verbal agreement, the two teams began cooperating.

In another experiment college students solved puzzles and worked out answers to human-relations problems under two conditions, cooperation and competition. Groups working under cooperative conditions were told that the members of their group were to work together, although each group would be in competition with other groups. All members of the highest ranking group would receive an honor mark in the course. Groups working under competitive conditions were told that only those individuals in each group who made the best contributions would receive the honor mark. Data revealed that in general, members of groups working under cooperative conditions solved their puzzles more rapidly and worked out more creative solutions to their human-relations problems than did members of groups working under competitive conditions.

In addition to such experiments, there is, of course, evidence of social cooperation in life outside the laboratory. Perhaps you have heard people say that competition, rather than cooperation, is "natural" for man. Most sociologists and anthropologists, as well as social psychologists, disagree.

Cooperation in the traditional Hopi Indian culture. Among Hopi Indians social cooperation is considered to be a virtue, whereas competition is discouraged. As farmers in the Southwest, the Hopi Indians had to rely on irrigation, and irrigation projects involve cooperation. The Hopi people learned that cooperation was socially much more desirable than competition.

Yet even in the Hopi culture children may display competitiveness, although such social behavior is frowned upon by adults. In one study Hopi children were asked about their preferences in certain social situations. For example, they were asked if they would prefer to make the best grades in their class or make the same grades as most of the other children. Sixty percent of the boys and 79 percent of the girls replied that they would prefer to make the best grades. Another question asked if they would prefer to run a race for a prize or just for fun. Seventy-two percent of the boys and 63 percent of the girls said they would rather run for a prize. It would be interesting to know how their parents would have answered these questions when they were children.

Social cooperation in a religious group. At various times and in various countries there have been attempts to establish communities in which social cooperation rather than social competition was the basic philosophy of life. Many of these communities consist of religious groups. One such community is the Amana Society.

Early in the eighteenth century a group known as the Amana Society was founded in Germany. Its members moved to a site near Buffalo, New York, in 1843, and then in 1855 migrated to their present seven-village

Above, the West German Chancellor Willy Brandt shakes hands with President Nixon at the end of a two-day summit meeting in Florida in December 1971. Whereas during World War II Germany and America were enemies, now the West Germans and Americans are allies who have learned to cooperate and work together for their mutual benefit.

site near Iowa City, Iowa. Simplicity marked their way of life. Land and industries were owned in common and were managed by the elders of the church. Members were assigned jobs on the basis of their abilities and the needs of the community. The strong helped the weak. Some men were assigned jobs on the farms; others worked in the various industries. Some women were assigned jobs of food preparation and serving, while others took care of the children of the community. Wages and salaries as we commonly know them were not paid. Members received only a small amount with which to satisfy their personal needs. Other than this, all profits went into a cooperative community fund for the good of all.

However, the Amanites lived as a minority group within the general economic structure of the United States, and their communal way of life was not in harmony with their neighbors. In 1932 the members voted to give up their economic communal way of life, but to maintain ther religious way of life. A cooperative stock company was formed and the stock was distributed to members of the community. General prosperity improved, based on the sale of farm products, furniture, textiles, and electrical appliances.

Social cooperation and communication among Americans. Although communication often fails to achieve its goal, it may make for greater cooperation both among Americans and with other nations. The United States seems smaller when brought together through communication and social contacts, thereby increasing the chances for social cooperation, just as the world seems smaller when brought together through international communication.

To study the likelihood of social contacts in the United States, one psychologist asked a group of American men and women to keep a record of all the individuals they happened to contact in a period of 100 days. On the average, each of these men and women reported that they had contacted and knew to some degree about 500 individuals. This meant that there was only about one chance in 200,000 that any two Americans chosen at random would know each other. However, there was a better than fifty-fifty chance that any two individuals might know mutual acquaintances.

Another psychologist chose at random 160 persons living in or near Omaha, Nebraska, and asked them to participate in a study of social contact in American life. Each of these individuals in Nebraska was known as a "starting person," because he initiated the chain of social contacts. He was asked to contact an individual living in Sharon, Massachusetts, who was known as a "target person."

Each starting person was sent a folder containing the name of a target person and a few facts about that person, such as place of employment, place of residence, and amount of schooling. Also in the folder was a set of rules for the experiment, the most important rule being, "If you do not know the target person on a personal basis, do not try to contact him directly. Instead, mail this folder ... to a personal acquaintance who is more likely than you to know the target person. It must be someone you know on a first-name basis."

The folder contained fifteen business reply cards. Each personal acquaintance receiving the folder was to send one card to the psychologist and the remaining cards to the next individual in the chain.

Of the 160 folders that started in Nebraska, 116 did not reach Massachusetts. Somewhere along the line participants did not cooperate. On the other hand, forty-four folders did reach the target person, although the distance from the starting position to the target position was 1305 miles. The chains varied from two to ten intermediate acquaintances, with a median of five. Some chains ended when they were only a few feet from the target person. The psychologist concluded, "Thus we see social communication is sometimes restricted less by physical distance than by social distance."

We know that people tend to limit their social contacts along socioeconomic and ethnic lines. We know that individuals of low income tend to know other poor individuals but do not know many individuals of high income. Wealthy persons tend to limit their social contacts to other persons of high income and tend not to know persons of low income. Individuals of one ethnic group tend to limit their social contacts to other individuals of the same general group.

The big social world might become a small world and many national and international problems might be solved, or conditions improved, if there could be a massive and friendly system of communication among individuals. If each of us could communicate in a friendly way with just a few individuals from different social, economic, ethnic, and national groups, we might become more sensitive to them as fellow human beings. We might be able to overcome some of our prejudices.

When you travel, near or far, do you try to communicate in a friendly way with people who do not have the same socioeconomic, ethnic, or religious background as your own, or do you limit your social contacts to persons much like yourself? Do you try to do your part in increasing social contacts and communication?

➔ Terms to Know

social competition   social cooperation   social facilitation

➔ Topics to Think About

1. In general, are people who live in rural areas and small towns more kind than those who live in large cities? Why do you think this is or is not so?

2. Would you say that people in other highly civilized countries are usually more helpful to individuals in distress than are people in the United States? If so, which countries? What is different in their society that makes them more helpful or less helpful?

3. Is there a "pecking order" in your school system—for example, among the different classes in your school? What is the pecking order among the members of your class?

4. Do you believe that school marks should be assigned on a competitive basis, as they usually are? If you were the teacher, on what basis would you assign marks?

5. Should we have a law to the effect that the first car to come upon the scene of any highway accident, or even a car breakdown, must stop and offer assistance or the driver will be subject to a fine?

➔ Suggestions for Activities

1. Set up an argument situation in which one student is shoved around by the other, without engaging in actual blows. Have an accomplice nearby where he will be inconspicuous but can count the number and record the various reactions of boys and girls who witness the argument. How many and to what extent do students of either sex attempt to aid the person being shoved around? Did some seem to enjoy the argument and try to promote it rather than attempting to stop it? For some possible interesting sex differences, try combinations of boy-boy; boy-girl, with the boy doing the shoving; boy-girl, with the girl doing the shoving; and girl-girl.

If the activity is to be carried out on school property, be sure to obtain the permission of the principal in advance. It would be well to have a teacher or someone else in authority near the scene of the argument and ready to explain the activity, should any difficulties arise.

2. Arrange a situation in which a student appears to be ill when in the halls between classes. He or she might give the impression of nausea or of abdominal pain. Have an accomplice nearby where he will be inconspicuous but can count the number of boys and girls, separately, who pass the student appearing to be in distress. How many look at the "ill" person, possibly stop for a few seconds, and then go on without offering help? How many boys offer to help another boy? How many boys offer to help a girl? How many girls offer to help another girl? How many girls offer to help a boy? If there are sex differences, how do you account for them?

You might vary the activity by having the student become "ill" in the hall during regular class time, when only an occasional student would be around. If only one student is in the hall at the time of the "illness," does he or she tend to offer assistance more readily than if the halls are full of students? Or you might have a student become "ill" at the beginning of the period between classes and also in the last few seconds of this time, when students are rushing to their next class. Does it seem to make a difference whether there is plenty of time to help or whether individuals are in a hurry?

Be sure to get the permission of the school authorities in advance for this activity.

3. Although sometimes people do fail to give help to those in need, we must not forget that there are many agencies as well as individuals who are always ready to help the unfortunate. Contact several organizations such as the Red Cross, Salvation Army, Volunteers of America, Alcoholics Anonymous, various church welfare organizations, and other groups that are devoted to helping in time of need, and learn of their work. Each student should report to the class what he or she finds out about such philanthropic organizations.

4. Have some student walk down a hall with a very awkward armful of books, notebooks, pencils, and other school supplies. At a prearranged place where you have stationed an accomplice, have the student drop all or most of the objects and try desperately to pick them up, only to drop them again and again. How many students walk by without paying any noticeable attention to the unfortunate student? How many laugh or smile but do not offer assistance? How many slow up or stop as they watch the student who is having difficulty, but do not offer assistance? How many assist the student by picking up some of the things he or she has dropped, but then hurry on? How many give complete assistance until the unfortunate student has all of the supplies under control and is able to go on his or her way? Does it make any difference whether the unfortunate student is female or male? Does it make any difference whether the dropping occurs early or late in the period between classes, when the student giving assistance might be late to his or her next class?

5. In times of disaster often new, and probably temporary, helping groups spring into existence. Perhaps your community has experienced some disaster such as a flood, earthquake, or tornado. From the mass media you can learn of disasters in various areas of our country and throughout the world. Note and report in class on how quickly and extensively many people respond to distress with various acts of kindness.

6. Secure the cooperation of some teacher who will give an objective examination covering a unit in his or her course. Have the teacher explain to the class in advance that marks on the examination will be based on the distribution of scores—that a certain percentage of the highest scores will receive A, a certain percentage of the next highest will receive B, and so on. Arrange for one student to "cheat" by making motions to two or three nearby students to hold their papers so that he or she can see the answers. The nearby students, who are really your accomplices, may even write answers on notes and quite openly pass them to the student who is cheating. The teacher will have to be very careless about watching the class, or else may leave the room for a short time while the cheating goes on.

After the papers are scored, have the teacher announce that the student who you know had been asked to cheat had by far the highest score in the class and comment that if he or she could do so well, the remainder of the class could have done much better than they did if they had studied harder.

Do any students report to the teacher that the person with the highest score had cheated? If so, were they the ones whose marks had been lowered a letter by the very high score of the cheater?

As always when subjects do not know the true nature of an activity, be sure to enlighten them after the activity is completed. It would not be fair to damage the reputation of the student who appeared to cheat or those who assisted him in the cheating.

7. If you have an opportunity to be with a group of children, try the following activity. Have the children line up to play a game for which there will be several prizes, but not enough for each child to receive a prize. Imply that the odds will be somewhat in favor of those nearest the front of the line. Have the children line up again to take their pick from a pile of presents in boxes of various sizes. Finally, have the children line up for refreshments. Note for yourself, or have someone note for you, the names of the children in rank order from first to last in line for each of the three situations. Is there any evidence of a pecking order? Does size or age seem to be related to the line-up order? Is there a sex difference?

Suggestions for Further Reading

Baron, Robert A., and Robert M. Liebert (eds.), *Human Social Behavior,* Dorsey Press. Included in this book are sections on social facilitation, social learning and imitative behavior, conformity, attitudes, aggression, violence, negotiation, bargaining, altruism, and prosocial behavior.

Bickman, Leonard, and Thomas Henchy, *Beyond the Laboratory: Field Research in Social Psychology,* McGraw-Hill. A collection of several dozen interesting and informative experiments, some of which can easily be adapted for high school students.

Holloway, Mark, *Heavens on Earth: Utopian Communities in America, 1680–1880,* Dover Publications. Various utopian experiments, such as the Shakers, New Harmony, and Amana, are described in this paperback.

Kagan, J., M. M. Haith, and Catherine Caldwell (eds.), *Psychology: Adapted Readings,* Harcourt Brace Jovanovich. See Selection 35 on bystander "apathy."

Latane, Bibb, and John M. Darley, *The Unresponsive Bystander: Why Doesn't He Help?* Appleton-Century-Crofts. An excellent collection of twelve experiments on bystander reactions to people in distress, written in nontechnical language in an interesting style.

Noyes, John H., *Strange Cults and Utopias of 19th-Century America,* Dover Publications. This book was originally published in 1870. The author was the founder of the Oneida Community in New York state.

chapter 18
Psychology and Problems of Society

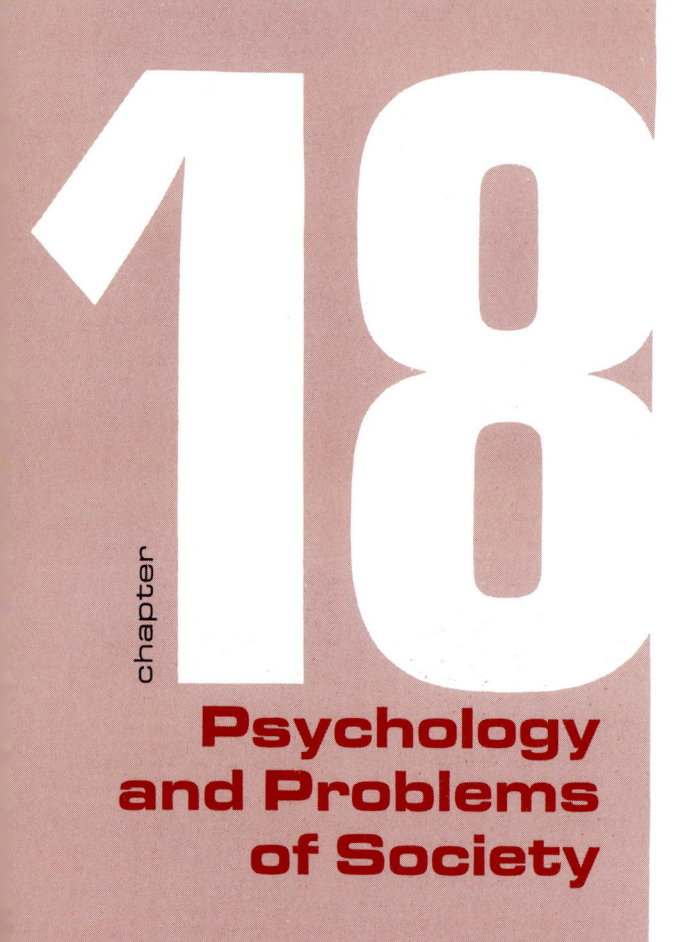

PSYCHOLOGY IS not the only field of science concerned with the problems of society, as you have probably discovered in other courses. Psychologists, especially social psychologists, are particularly interested in the psychological aspects of such problems. They search for the reasons behind man's behavior and try to find ways to change this behavior and thus diminish the problems. This chapter investigates some of the problems in our society, and discusses the role of psychology in working toward finding solutions to them.

Social Attitudes

An ATTITUDE may be defined as a readiness to respond favorably or unfavorably to a person, object, situation, or event. When a person expresses an opinion, he is revealing an attitude by verbalizing it. An attitude can be revealed in ways other than through an opinion. For example, the way a person treats the members of a minority group reveals his attitude toward them. People have attitudes toward everything from their pets to world problems. The attitudes that will be of primary concern to us in this chapter, however, are those which relate to social situations, problems, and questions. We call these attitudes SOCIAL ATTITUDES.

Of necessity, the social attitudes of all of us are based on very limited experiences. We often fail to realize this fact. Thus, we may find our friends and ourselves lightly expressing opinions, if not convictions, on social questions of all degrees of importance.

When does an attitude become a prejudice? Sometimes we hear it said that all politicians are corrupt, or that most of the Chinese smoke opium, or that all college professors are absent-minded and impractical. Such very general statements are often made quite emphatically and positively. How can it be held that all politicians are corrupt unless it has been proved definitely that every politician has been guilty of corruption? How can a whole people be characterized by those who have never visited or studied that nation?

At one time a questionnaire was given to 1725 native-born educated Americans. They were given a list of national and ethnic groups (English, Chinese, French, and so on) and asked to rank them from most preferred to least preferred in a variety of social situations. Some of the situations were "Would admit to close kinship by marriage," "Would admit to my club as personal friends," "Would admit to my street as neighbors." For all the situations given, the Hindu group was at or near the bottom of the list. That is, an overwhelming majority of these 1725 Americans were prejudiced against Hindus. How much do you think they knew about Hindus? How many of them do you suppose had ever met or even seen a Hindu?

Any attitude, either for or against a given social question, that prevents us from considering and evaluating new evidence objectively is spoken of as PREJUDICE. If we say that all politicians are corrupt because we know a few who are corrupt, we are merely expressing an attitude. Suppose we meet a politician who very evidently is not corrupt. If we refuse to recognize his honesty and do

This girl is expressing a prejudiced attitude. She has decided that she does not like oysters because they look strange, although she has never tasted one. She has become prejudiced against oysters without ever having tried them.

not change our statement concerning all politicians, our attitude is one of prejudice and is highly unjust.

One high school conducted an activity on prejudice during National Brotherhood Week. After careful planning, it was decided that for a period of four days all blonds in the school would be discriminated against. Blonds were chosen because they represented a minority group in the school and possessed an obvious common characteristic. During the four days blonds were denied certain privileges enjoyed by other students. They could not sit in specific areas in the cafeteria or use certain stairways, water fountains, rest rooms, and entrances. In addition, during the activity announcements were made over the public address system that blonds were undesirable and inferior persons. Other students intentionally ignored blonds, and an "underground" newspaper was distributed in the classrooms stating that blonds came from a different cultural background, lacked ambition, and had different interests. As a result, blonds began to develop some fairly typical behaviors—they learned to avoid restricted areas and groups of students who might criticize or make fun of them, and began to draw together as a group. At the conclusion of the four days, class discussions were held on such topics as "What is prejudice?" "Why does it exist?" and "How did you feel this week?" Although such an activity must be conducted with great care, it gave the participants—both the blonds and the other students—an opportunity to experience personally how prejudice grows and what effects it can have.

How are social attitudes measured? If we are to study social attitudes scientifically, we must have some means of measuring them.

One technique for measuring attitudes is to give an individual a sheet containing a number of specific statements on a given social problem. He is asked to indicate which statements he agrees with and which ones he disagrees with. For example, on one scale for measuring attitudes toward war we find such statements as "War is ennobling and stimulates our highest and best qualities"; "There is no progress without war"; "He who refuses to fight is a true hero"; "It is the moral duty of the individual to refuse to participate in any way in any war, no matter what the cause." A score value for each statement on the measuring scale is obtained. From these scores any individual can calculate just how his attitudes on specific social questions compare with the attitudes of a large number of other persons.

A somewhat similar technique consists of statements about a social problem. Instead of asking individuals whether or not they agree with each statement, this technique has persons indicate the degree to which they agree or disagree according to a definite rating scale.

Attitudes may also be measured by asking individuals to complete statements, such as "If a mentally retarded person were to come to my home, I would . . ." or, "If a mentally retarded person were to come to their homes, most people would . . ."

In measuring public attitudes, trained interviewers often call on randomly selected individuals and ask each person to express his opinion concerning certain issues or questions. The replies resulting from a large number of such interviews are carefully tabulated and analyzed. In this procedure, known as RANDOM SAMPLING, the sample group is selected in such a way that any individual in the given total population may be included in the sample group. For example, suppose you wished to measure the attitudes of students in your high school toward law enforcement. It

Any magazine, radio, or television advertisement, such as this televised ad, is a form of propaganda—it is an organized attempt to influence consumers' attitudes.

might be possible to get the opinion of every student in your school. However, if your school is very large or your time is limited, you might instead get a sample group by taking every other name, or perhaps every tenth name, from an alphabetically arranged list of all the students in your school.

Sometimes it is more desirable to use STRATIFIED SAMPLING, in which the individuals are selected by dividing the total population into a number of nonoverlapping groups, the number in each group being proportional to the total population. Suppose there are 500 students in your high school, which has four classes with the following distribution: freshmen, 200; sophomores, 150; juniors, 100; seniors 50. You might wish to select, in a random way, 20 freshmen, 15 sophomores, 10 juniors, and 5 seniors and then measure their attitudes.

Propaganda

The word "propaganda" appears frequently in any psychological discussion of attitudes. For many persons this term has come to have an undesirable connotation. Actually, PROPAGANDA refers to any organized attempt to influence social attitudes. The word has been somewhat humorously defined as "the art of making up the other man's mind." Propaganda may even be highly desirable.

Propaganda is not a twentieth-century invention. Excavators found walls of the old city of Pompeii (buried in 79 A.D.) covered with election appeals. There had been an organized attempt in this Roman provincial town to influence citizens to vote in a particular way. Politicians in our day can use newspapers, radio, and television for propaganda as well as the ancient means of signs and public gatherings.

What determines the effectiveness of propaganda? It is usually said that primacy is important in determining the effectiveness of propaganda. The advertiser who is first to call the attention of the public to his product is said to have a great advantage in sales. The nation that gets its propaganda into a neutral country before a rival nation can do so is said to have a great advantage in influencing the attitudes of the people in that country. In laboratory studies where propaganda on both sides of a question is presented systematically, however, primacy does not prove to be a very significant factor in influencing attitudes. Nevertheless, under the usual circumstances of social life, the side getting its propaganda before the public first has a great advantage because, having once been influenced by a given bit of propaganda, many individuals are no longer interested in and do not expose themselves to another point of view.

Some research studies have suggested that repeated exposure is an effective means of transmitting propaganda. An unfamiliar object or situation often elicits conflicting responses and uncertainty, which may produce negative feelings. Repeated exposure, on the other hand, produces familiarity, which is comfortable and makes the object or situation seem attractive. An individual at the supermarket trying to decide which brand of soap or breakfast cereal to buy will usually select the brand to which he or she has had repeated exposure and therefore is most familiar with. Much of commercial advertising is based on the effects of repeated exposure.

Propaganda seems to be a necessary part of our social life. Certainly it is a force in national and international affairs. Our problem is to recognize it, to get the propaganda from both sides, and then and only then to make our own decisions.

How can you avoid being manipulated by propaganda? Can you learn to recognize propaganda so that you will not be unduly influenced by it? In one study with subjects who earlier had been shown to be influenced by propaganda materials, it was found that a group who was given pamphlets to study explaining the methods and uses of propaganda was afterwards less influenced by propaganda than the control group, who was not given copies of the pamphlets.

There are a number of common techniques used in propaganda. If you become familiar with the following techniques, and use them to recognize and critically evaluate propaganda material when you see or hear it, you, too, will be less influenced by propaganda.

One technique consists of "name calling," or associating a person or object with some bad or disapproved of idea in the hope that he or it will be condemned and the accuracy of the label will not be questioned. For example, a person may be called a "warmonger," or a "radical," or a "racist." It is not unusual for a political candidate to resort to name calling, attaching tarnished labels to his opponents in the hope that the voters will reject these opposing candidates and vote for him.

Another technique, which is the opposite of name calling, is called "glittering generality." It is an attempt to identify a program or person with some known good, such as motherhood. There is evidence of a relation between the pleasantness of a proposition and the tendency to believe it. A person tends to accept as true those statements that are agreeable to him.

A third technique, "transfer," is the attempt to generalize from one portion of a statement or item to something else, in order to make the latter more acceptable or more unacceptable. For instance, the image of Uncle Sam is sometimes used in advertisements to make the product more acceptable and induce the public to buy it. It is hoped that we will associate the virtues of Uncle Sam with the advertised product.

Another technique is the "testimonial"—the endorsement of a product by some famous person, such as a well-known athlete or actor. The sponsor hopes that we will buy the product because it is used by a famous person.

Some propaganda is spread by persons seeking acceptance of themselves and their ideas because they are "just plain folks." During election years we often see politicians campaigning around our state or country, attending country picnics and visiting ghetto areas, trying to win votes by being just one of the folks.

Another propaganda technique is to "slant ideas," to mix truth with fiction. The individual includes enough truth or facts to make his case appear true, when actually he is intentionally overemphasizing certain issues, misrepresenting others, and not mentioning others.

One final technique, the "bandwagon technique," consists of giving the impression that large numbers of people are doing what the propagandist wants you to do. The fashion world attempts to have people believe that the new fashions are being admired and worn by just about everyone, on the theory that if everyone in your crowd is wearing them, you, too, will want to.

By recognizing these techniques, you can avoid being taken in by them. You can also avoid being manipulated by propaganda by developing resistance to it. One study has found that the ideal procedures for developing resistance to persuasion are to first subject the individual to a slight amount of threat to his presently held beliefs, which causes him to organize his defenses, and then to provide reassurance that his beliefs are correct.

Crime and Delinquency

By CRIME we mean any act that at the time it is performed is forbidden and punishable by the laws of the social group to which the culprit belongs. The word DELINQUENCY is used here to refer to crimes committed by those who are not legally of age.

Perhaps you are tired of hearing about delinquency. Newspapers, magazines, public speakers, clergymen, and teachers are constantly bringing up the subject of delinquency. As students of psychology, however, you cannot ignore the problem of delinquency. Since you are closer to the problem because of your age, we will emphasize delinquency rather than adult criminality. The juvenile delinquent of today may well be the adult criminal of tomorrow, unless preventive measures are taken.

How serious a problem is delinquency? There is no doubt that delinquency is an increasing social problem in the United States. Many social organizations and governmental agencies are concerned with the problem and are striving to solve it. Yet it is impossible to find data that give a true and complete picture of delinquency. Data from the various states are not always comparable because of differences in state laws and the organization of state courts. Furthermore, many communities have social agencies that adjust cases of delinquency without referring them to the juvenile courts.

We can say that at the present time well over one million juveniles each year find themselves in trouble with the law. Remember, however, that about 80 percent of the young people in the United States lead responsible social lives and do not become involved in delinquent activities. Unfortunately, some individuals tend to overgeneralize and condemn the majority of young people on the basis of the actions of the minority.

How may we account for the fact that so many young persons, as well as older ones, do not live within the general social rules? We will examine briefly a number of factors that people have associated with the development of delinquent behavior: heredity, low intellectual ability, the home, schools, neighborhood conditions, and personality patterns.

Heredity. Some people think that an individual inherits his criminal tendencies. But psychologists cannot accept the statement that criminality is inherited. There is some evidence that physical disabilities and deformities are found more frequently in criminals and other social-problem cases than in the general population. But only insofar as unfortunate physical appearance and bodily incapacities increase an individual's frustration can it be said that physical characteristics are even indirect causes of criminality.

Some research is being done to determine if individuals inherit certain structural defects of the brain and so tend, under unfortunate environmental conditions, to become antisocial in their behavior. In general, though, it is more profitable to look to sources other than heredity to understand the basic causes of delinquency and crime.

Low intellectual ability. There was a time when delinquency was thought to be very closely related to mental retardation. Today,

One problem of crime today is overcrowded court agendas. Here an individual protests against long waits in prison before court hearings.

with improved intelligence tests and techniques of research, psychologists are not inclined to think of mental retardation as a basic cause of delinquency. Actually, the overall intelligence test scores of delinquents are not greatly different from the overall intelligence test scores of nondelinquents, although scores on verbal factors of intellectual ability do tend to be lower for delinquents than for nondelinquents.

Sometimes persons of low intellectual ability do become involved in crimes because they are unable to understand our complicated social regulations, or because they are susceptible to suggestions made by persons of greater intellectual ability. On the other hand, considerable intellectual ability is required to carry out some crimes, such as fraud. One psychologist, studying the relationship between intellectual ability as measured by intelligence tests and the kinds of crimes committed by 3942 prisoners, found that 52.9 percent of the prisoners convicted of fraud were of above average intellectual ability and only 22.0 percent were below average.

The home. Social conditions in the home can be a factor in the development of delinquent behavior. Two investigators made a comparative study of a group of 500 delinquent boys and 500 nondelinquent boys. The two groups were matched for age, intellectual ability, national origin, and residence in underprivileged neighborhoods. As contrasted to the nondelinquent boys, the delinquent boys tended to come from homes of little affection and understanding; homes broken by divorce, desertion, separation, or death; and homes in which the parents were either too lax or too harsh in disciplinary measures.

The home is also the primary place where children's social attitudes are developed, and in some cases they develop attitudes favorable toward delinquency.

Schools. Schools as much as any social agency —and often more than any other—prevent delinquency. Modern schools with their varied curricula, clubs, social events, and recreational facilities give young people opportunities for self-expression, for developing feelings of adequacy, and for wholesome recreation.

Nevertheless, sometimes school situations are very frustrating to young people. In those communities in which the schools are crowded and the teachers are burdened with unduly heavy class and extracurricular duties, there is very little opportunity for the teachers to give attention to the problems and needs of individual students. The student who needs help so that he can compete scholastically and socially, but is unable to secure it, may turn to delinquent behavior for compensation, as a way to gain some feeling of achievement.

Sometimes, also, young people become involved in delinquent behavior while at school by associating with, and picking up the habits of, others of their peer group who engage in illegal activities, such as using drugs.

Neighborhood conditions. Neighborhood conditions can contribute to delinquency. Delinquency tends to be concentrated in the socially and economically poor sections of large cities. One way of studying crime and delinquency in a city is to get a detailed map of the city and then place a colored pin in the map to indicate the home address of each delinquent or adult criminal. The pins tend to concentrate in three kinds of areas: (1) business districts or areas near business districts, (2) manufacturing areas with their adjacent slum or rundown areas, and (3) districts in which the nature of the population is changing— that is, districts in which families of one race or nationality are moving out and being replaced by families of another race or nationality. The two groups probably differ in traditions, customs, and moral codes. Often neither the parents nor the children of the two groups get along well with each other.

Although most delinquents come from neighborhoods where there is overcrowding, poverty, adult friction, and lack of wholesome recreational facilities, some delinquents do come from the better and even the best socioeconomic districts. Crime is increasing at a faster rate in suburban areas than in either the large cities or rural areas.

Personality patterns. Unfavorable home, school, and neighborhood conditions are related to the production of delinquent behavior, but no single factor can be indicated as the basis of delinquency. Delinquency is the product of the interplay of many factors. Delinquent behavior can be understood only by examining the personalities of individuals who commit the antisocial acts.

A number of personality characteristics have been associated with delinquents. They tend to feel insecure and unacceptable, and try to compensate by defying society. They are often hostile, untrusting, resentful, stubborn, assertive, adventurous, unconventional, and defiant of authority.

Delinquents tend to be emotionally immature. The criminal is easily excited to anger and fear, and tends to worry. He may attempt to give the impression that he is big, tough, and superior, but actually he is afraid and feels inferior.

Some additional personality characteristics of delinquents include impulsiveness, thinking less highly of themselves than nondelinquents think of themselves, having difficulty in interpreting consequences of behavior, and, in many cases, experiencing less reaction to fear-provoking situations than do most persons. Many criminals show a paranoid trend. They say that they have never had a chance in life, that the teacher had it in for them when they were at school, that the police have it in for them. Accompanying this feeling of persecution is a desire to feel superior in some way, which may be satisfied for a time by committing some unusually bold crime.

Although there is no clear-cut general pattern of criminal personality, one psychologist experienced in prison work has characterized the prison inmate by saying, "On the average, he is a young man, emotionally unstable, vocationally untrained, a product of an environment economically, socially, morally impoverished. He is usually ... torn by conflicting values."

What can be done to prevent or cure delinquency and crime? No such simple answers as better neighborhoods and schools, valuable as they are, will magically change basic personality patterns that are responsible for delinquency and crime. Any steps that will lead to healthier personalities will lead toward the elimination of this social problem. Many delinquents and criminals have some desirable personality traits—loyalty and leadership, for example—that need redirection.

Punishment. If we believe that society should take revenge on a person who has disobeyed the laws, prisons are a simple answer to our problem of treatment. According to this view, the worse the prison, the better the punishment. We must be able to say that "justice" has been satisfied regardless of the damage the punishment may do.

The theory of deterrent treatment is a more enlightened one. According to this theory, imprisonment is not for revenge but so that the offender will not be able to continue his stealing or murder more victims, so that he will know better than to commit another crime. Furthermore, his imprisonment may serve as an example to deter others. Hangings were formerly carried out in public so that any potential criminals among the spectators might learn a lesson.

Instead of emphasizing punishment, a prison can focus on reforming inmates. It can offer useful information for reshaping their lives. Here inmates are studying English.

No doubt there is some justification for the theory of deterrent treatment. Mounting crime rates suggest, however, that it has not been a notable success. Often we hear or read about fitting the punishment to the crime. A more basic question would be how to fit the punishment to the criminal so that he would no longer be a criminal. Still more basic would be the question of how to guide personality development so that criminal behavior would not develop.

All too often punishment serves to increase criminality rather than to lessen it. Prisoners usually believe that they can expect only the worst from everyone they meet, especially law-enforcement officials. They tend to think that everyone is against them, and to feel worthless and inferior. The deeper such feelings become established in the personality structure, the greater is the tendency toward compensation through crime.

Also, imprisoning individuals allows contacts with other persons who have criminal records. Often such contacts provide a means for the younger offender, who has less experience in crime, to "learn the ropes" from the ones who are more experienced at violating the laws.

Furthermore, the extent to which punishment will be a deterrent is determined largely by the certainty and promptness with which it is administered. Unfortunately, in many American cases punishment for disobeying the law is neither certain nor prompt. Even a minor trial may be deferred for months.

Reform. The treatment of reform consists in literally "re-forming" the lives of those who have committed offenses rather than in punishing them for past offenses.

The report of one psychologist connected with the courts in a large city indicates that a psychologist can assist in reforming the lives of social offenders. After interviewing and testing offenders to learn something of their basic personality patterns, the psychologist recommended for or against granting probation. Over a period of one year, 193 persons recommended by the psychologist were placed on probation. These persons were helped and studied for six years while out on probation. In 69.9 percent of the cases the prediction of the psychologist was confirmed, the individuals were reformed—they had redirected their behavior.

One area currently under investigation is the use of chemical substances to help reform criminals. A research study on the effects of administering one chemical substance, lithium, produced some interesting results. The subjects were prisoners who volunteered to participate and who had a preprison history of violent assault, a prison history of continual verbal and aggressive behavior, and had no overt psychosis or brain damage. The volunteers were given daily doses of the chemical substance for four weeks, then doses of a placebo (a nonmedical substitute that appeared to be lithium) for the next four weeks. The doses continued to be alternated every four weeks for a total of three months. Results of the research showed a significant reduction in aggression during the periods when the subjects were taking the chemical substance.

Some reforming of an individual's life can take place while he is in prison. Modern prisons include training to prepare individuals to participate in socially approved activities when they are released. Modern prisons teach trades and provide classes in educational subjects. Prisoners have an opportunity to work and make small amounts of money. They are also trained to enjoy leisure time in a socially approved manner, such as playing baseball and football in the case of men, and playing cards and knitting in the case of women. As they readjust their lives, prisoners are given more and more responsibilities and an increasing number of privileges.

When the individual is released from prison, a psychologist or other social worker visits him frequently to help him become adjusted to nonprison life. The psychologist helps him in finding suitable work and wholesome recreational activities. The emphasis is on reform rather than revenge.

Social reforms take place slowly. Yet, with the elimination of poverty and economic insecurity, the day may come when adolescents and adults will not commit crimes to secure the necessities and common pleasures of life. Better housing and better general economic conditions will mean fewer feelings of frustration for children. When adult "big shots" find socially approved methods for meeting their needs and pleasures, children will not have undesirable examples to imitate. A permanent program of crime prevention will have been established. The old saying "An ounce of prevention is worth a pound of cure" is particularly true in the field of crime. The basic preventive measure is insuring better mental health for all citizens.

War

The crimes of individuals against their social group constitute a major problem. There is a far greater social problem, the crime called war. In terms of our definition of crime, war may not always be a "crime." Yet, when it is carried on in defiance of international laws, war is legally a crime as well as a socially tragic blunder.

Figures on the total financial cost of war soon become so astronomical in size that no one can appreciate them. Each adult realizes just a bit of the financial burden when he pays direct and indirect taxes for the support of recent and even long-past wars. The cost in human suffering is so great that people cannot comprehend it, although they have some understanding of it when injury or death affects their families or close friends.

What are the causes of war? Where can we place the blame for war? To eliminate one idea, psychologists do not believe that war can be attributed to instinct. No evidence of anything resembling warfare has been found in excavations of the remains of early man. Primitive man was, and in many cases still is, a hunter. Wars for conquest are not found among such primitive peoples. It is only after man begins to settle on the land, to acquire and hoard, that wars develop. Today social attitudes developing out of economic rivalry are usually, if not always, the basic factors in bringing about war.

Sometimes it is said that war is beastlike, but such a statement is not fair to the beasts. It does not agree with the facts. War is an organized attack of one social group on another social group. Such attacks are not made by animals. It is true that animals will prey upon other species to obtain food, but they do not "fight" in the way that man fights with his fellowmen. Sometimes, when very hungry, an animal will devour a member of its own species. An animal will also attack a member of its own species for possession of a mate. In warfare, however, the human individual is not generally fighting for personal gain or satisfaction. In many cases he does not even want to go to war.

It is said that wars are nature's method of improving the human species, in that only the most fit survive and later reproduce their kind. A moment's thought about this statement will indicate its falsity. The military services reject those who are physically weak, mentally retarded, or emotionally unstable. The best rather than the worst of the population is killed in time of war. Modern war acts as an agency of biological selection—but the selection is not in the best interests of the human species.

What can be done to prevent war? At one time some psychologists especially interested

The devastation of war, the amount of pain and suffering it inflicts, is overwhelming. In addition to those killed and wounded in battle, war also may harm the civilian population, as in the case of this Vietnamese family.

in social problems drew up a statement of psychological principles about war. This statement was submitted to members of the American Psychological Association, who were asked to sign and return the statement if, in their opinion as psychologists, the principles were psychologically sound. Of the 2038 psychologists who replied to the request, more than 99 percent subscribed to the statement. Because the statement is psychologically so basic, parts of it are given below.

1. *War can be avoided. War is not born in men; it is built into men.*
2. *In planning for permanent peace, the coming generation should be the primary focus of attention.*
3. *Racial, national, and group hatreds can, to a considerable degree, be controlled.*
4. *Condescension toward "inferior" groups destroys our chance for a lasting peace.*
• • • • •
8. *The root desires of the common people of all lands are the safest guide to framing a peace.*
9. *The trend of human relationships is toward ever wider units of collective security.*

How can the behavioral sciences help prevent war? Many groups are working frantically in the hope of finding a way to prevent war before it is too late.

Can scientists in the fields of psychology, sociology, and social anthropology, commonly called the behavioral sciences, make a significant contribution to world peace? There is reason to believe that they can. Already psychologists, and other behavioral scientists, have amassed a great deal of knowledge that can be helpful in bringing about peaceful international relationships, and they are constantly searching for more knowledge.

Psychologists do not limit themselves to the study of individual behavior; more and more they are studying the behavior of groups. Scientists have done much work in the area of cross-cultural research. They know a great deal about the causes and effects of frustration on individuals and on groups. They know something about the causes and aggressive expressions of hostility. They have learned that, under some conditions, hostility can be reduced by permitting people to express their feelings quite openly.

Scientists have learned the value of group discussion. They have learned that people are more likely to follow up on decisions that they make for themselves than they are to follow up on decisions that others impose on them. Psychologists and other behavioral scientists have made many studies of social attitudes and techniques of persuasion.

Through their studies on learning, psychologists know that reinforcing a given bit of behavior with expressed approval or some other form of reward is generally more effective in bringing about desired results than is punishment for undesired behavior. A nation might do well to express approval of what it considers to be desirable behavior on the part of another nation, instead of merely expressing disapproval of what it considers undesirable behavior.

All of these findings are available to the policymakers and the diplomats of the world who must make and carry out the decisions that determine the nature of international relationships. Hopefully, the continuing research of the behavioral scientists will provide still more information that can be used to further the cause of easing international tensions and of developing international cooperation and understanding.

Drugs

Psychologists and other scientists have also become involved in the social problem of drugs. Although the use of drugs has a long history, it is the present and future potential misuse of drugs that concerns behavioral scientists. Many statistics have been gathered on the number of individuals using drugs, and one fact emerges in all studies—there has been an increase in the use of drugs by Americans in recent years.

There is little doubt that drugs are a problem for many persons. During a recent year in one large American city, drug abuse was the leading cause of death among persons between fifteen and thirty-five years of age. The number of deaths caused by drugs is only part of the problem. There is the physical danger from the effects of some drugs and from mixing drugs so that the sum effect is much greater than the effects of any drug taken by itself at different times. Drugs are also partially responsible for the increase in the crime rate and for the human suffering of the drug user, those close to the user, and many innocent victims.

It is not the use but the overuse, or misuse, of some drugs that is dangerous. For example, taking an aspirin for a headache is an acceptable practice, but taking a dozen aspirins at one time would be dangerous.

Classifying drugs. There are many possible ways to define the word "drug." There are for instance, medical definitions and legal definitions. For purposes of this discussion, however, we will consider a DRUG to be any chemical substance that changes mood, perception, or awareness, and is misused to the extent that it is harmful to the individual or society.

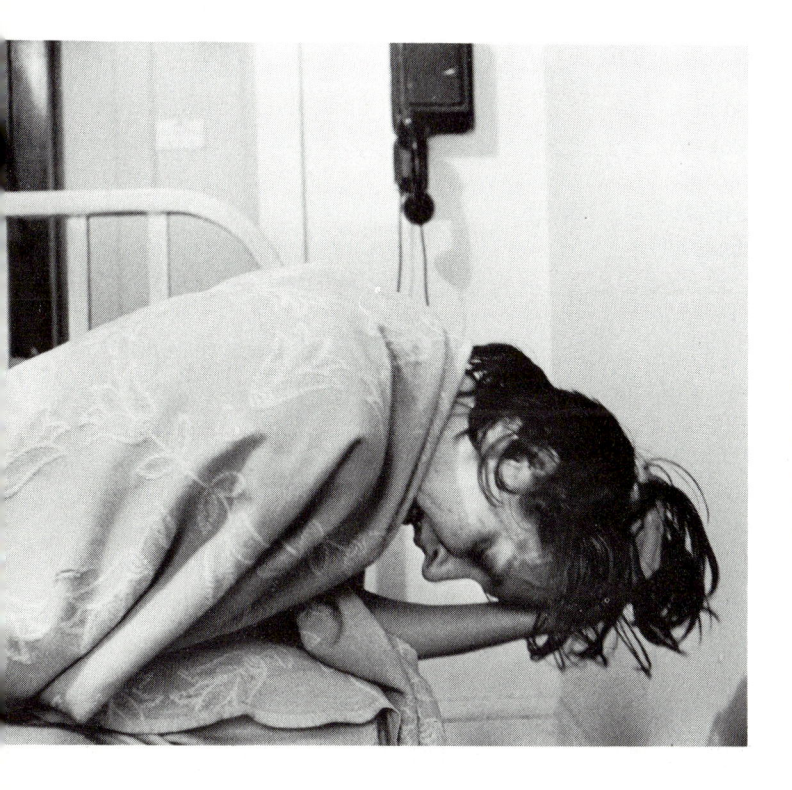

This drug addict is suffering withdrawal symptoms after having taken an overdose. One reason why drugs are a problem is that they can endanger your health. The misuse of some drugs—for instance, taking an overdose—can result in death.

The same drug may be called by many names. Heroin for example, is known as "H," "horse," "white stuff," and many other terms, some of which are coded so that only the seller and buyer of the drug will recognize the name.

Despite the lack of universal agreement on the definition, terminology, and classification of drugs at the present time, for convenience we can divide drugs into four categories: (1) hallucinogens, (2) stimulants, (3) depressants, and (4) narcotics. *Hallucinogens* are those drugs which produce pseudoperceptions, or sensory perceptions that have no true basis in reality, although the individual is sometimes able to distinguish between reality and his false perceptions. LSD, STP, DET, and marijuana are examples of hallucinogens. *Stimulants* are those drugs which result in increased functional behavior. The commonly misused stimulants are the amphetamines, especially benzedrine, dexedrine, and methedrine. *Depressants* ("downs") are drugs that decrease bodily functions, lessening the activity of the brain and other parts of the body. They include barbiturates, such as seconal and nembutal, and tranquilizers, such as librium and valium. *Narcotics* include drugs that are derived from opium, such as heroin, codeine, and morphine, and drugs that have the effects of opium, such as methadone. The effects of narcotics include an increased tolerance for the drug, a physical dependence, and certain withdrawal symptoms when the narcotic is stopped abruptly.

Computers are now being used to classify drugs and their effects. With an extremely large amount of data available on drugs, the computer offers a method of putting these data into a systematized and useful format. However, the most important aspect of drugs is not how they are classified, but rather the symptoms and the dangers involved in their use.

What are the physical symptoms of drug use? The effects of drugs are sometimes different not only for various persons but also for the same individual at different times. Nevertheless, there are certain physical reactions associated with each category of drug. The physical effects of hallucinogens include dilation of the pupils, chills and flushes, nausea, headache, increased heart rate and blood pressure, dry mouth, and extreme thirst. The use of marijuana produces some of these effects, as well as a reddening of the eyes, lowering of body temperature, and increased appetite. Stimulants such as amphetamines act on the sympathetic nervous system and cause physical reactions similar to those involved in fear and anger. The moderate use of depressants results in a slight decrease in respiration, blood pressure, and heart rate, but in large doses a coma may be induced, sometimes ultimately resulting in death. Probably you can name several famous individuals who have died from an overdose of barbiturates. Narcotics depress the central nervous system, reduce sensitivity to pain, and produce sleep, nausea, itching, and constriction of the pupils. An overdose can depress breathing and result in death.

What are the psychological and physical effects of some drugs? There is an even wider variation in psychological effects than in physical effects from one drug user to another. In addition, there is much less predictability of specific psychological symptoms, because they depend on such factors as the personality of the user, what the user expects from using the drug, the potency of the dosage, the social setting in which the drug is used, and the physical condition of the user.

The most conspicuous fact about the effects of hallucinogens is their unpredictability. Under the influence of hallucinogens an individual may have opposite feelings simultaneously, such as feelings of isolation and withdrawal at the same time as feelings of repressed anger leading to violence. Taking LSD sometimes makes the person believe that he is invincible and cannot die. Such persons have been known to attempt to fly from the roof of a tall building or stand in the path of an oncoming car.

An additional danger of LSD and another example of its unpredictability is a "bad trip," in which the person fears that he is becoming psychotic because he experiences a loss of contact with reality. No one can foresee who will take a bad trip or which of the times, if any, that a person takes LSD this state of panic will occur. Although relatively rare, some persons have a recurrence, or "flashback," of their LSD trip months after the last time they took the drug.

One of the possible physical effects of using LSD is brain damage and damage to chromosomes, although the evidence of either is inconclusive at the present time. Indications of brain damage are that persons taking LSD lose ambition, lack motivation, and generally become less sociable. Evidence of chromosome damage is based on experiments with animals and on babies born with birth defects whose mothers had taken LSD while they were pregnant.

There is some evidence that marijuana may cause injury to the brains of certain users. For example, lapses of memory not only become more frequent among marijuana users the longer they use the drug, but also the length of the memory lapses tends to increase. Although research on the possible hereditary effects of marijuana is just beginning, investigators are presently studying groups who have used "hashish," a potent relative of marijuana, for generations. Large groups of such people tend to "drop out" of their society and develop many of the psychological and physical symptoms found in chronic alcoholics on "skid row."

The effects of marijuana on drivers under the influence of the drug are similar to those exhibited by intoxicated drivers—reaction time is slow and judgment is poor in performing complicated or coordinated tasks, such as applying the brakes, flashing a turn indicator, and steering the car.

Scientists have isolated the specific compound in marijuana that makes the user feel "high," and can reproduce it in the laboratory. Recent experiments have shown that this compound, commonly called THC, has a tendency to accumulate in the tissues of human beings and animals when administered repeatedly.

The use of other drugs, such as heroin, produces specific and noticeable effects on the life style and mannerisms of its users. In one survey of some parents of heroin addicts, the following signs were noted by parents of the addicts before the use of the drug became known. (These are listed in order of frequency from highest to the lowest.)

1. Poor appetite
2. No interest in personal appearance
3. Unexpected absences from home
4. Spent long periods alone in room
5. Slept away from home
6. Slow and halting speech
7. Gave up organized activities
8. Received and made frequent phone calls

Does smoking marijuana lead to using heroin? At the present time there is no conclusive evidence that smoking marijuana definitely leads to the use of heroin. However, present evidence does indicate that marijuana smoking has become more common among opiate addicts in recent years. One study found the average age of opiate addicts who had not

Teen-agers often start smoking "pot" and taking other drugs because of pressure and encouragement to do so from drug-using friends. The peer group is a great influence in determining whether or not an individual tries drugs.

smoked marijuana was forty years, while the average of those who were addicts and had smoked marijuana was only twenty-nine years.

There are definite patterns of marijuana-opiate use in the United States. In the larger metropolitan areas there is a higher relationship between using marijuana and using opiates such as heroin, especially in the Southwestern states and the Eastern-Midwestern states. In these sections more than 50 percent of opiate users have smoked marijuana. Another pattern is found in the Southeastern states, where most of the opiate addicts have not smoked marijuana.

To what extent are drugs used in schools? There is little doubt that drugs are used by many students at both the high school and college levels, especially in the urban and suburban schools. The percentages of student users vary from about 5 percent to almost 50 percent of the total school populations, depending on what drug is being studied and when the study was made. In one early study of college students, 14 percent of the sample had used amphetamines without a doctor's prescription, 26 percent had used marijuana, and 5 percent had used LSD. A more recent survey of college students showed that the use of marijuana had increased to 42 percent; the use of LSD and other hallucinogens had risen to 14 percent; and barbituate use was at 14 percent. These data continue to change rapidly. Another study, performed only a year after the survey just mentioned, showed that although marijuana use was still growing, the use of LSD and heroin was declining.

Why do people take drugs? Contrary to the belief of many people, the "pusher," or seller of illegal drugs, is usually not the one who introduces an individual to his first drug experience. In the large majority of instances the individual is first introduced to a drug by a "friend" or member of his peer group.

One study found that students stated their main reason for using amphetamines was to help them study or get through their exams. Those who used marijuana reported that curiosity was the primary reason for trying it initially. Other students said that they took their first drug because of social pressures; still others because of the thrills or "kicks" associated with drugs.

Another reason why individuals turn to drugs is the social attitude toward drugs. We live in a drug-oriented society. We are constantly faced with advertisements showing how pills can be taken for gaining weight or losing it, for headaches and sore throats, for eliminating inconveniences and pain, for removing fears, for going to sleep or staying awake. How many people do you know who do not take drugs of some sort?

What can be done to help those who take drugs? Unfortunately the widespread availability of drugs has not been, and probably cannot be, adequately controlled. For example, the sniffing of glue, gasoline fumes, and aerosol propellants can produce effects similar to those of drugs, although the effects can sometimes be deadly. One study reported 110 cases of sudden death in youths who inhaled vapors from such substances.

Perhaps the best plan for dealing with the drug problem is a total educational program for students, parents, and school officials that is designed to *prevent* drug abuse. There are numerous sources that can be used to inform individuals about drugs, including local medical doctors, pharmacists, and public health officials.

For those who are addicted to drugs, the treatment should be both physical and social-psychological. One of the older methods of treating an individual who is physically addicted to drugs is to have him withdraw from drugs suddenly and completely, commonly called "cold turkey." Although fast, this method is generally not used in medical practice today because of the severe symptoms accompanying it. Another method is to decrease the amount of the drug given to the addict over a period of about ten days. During this time the addict may be given tranquilizers and sleeping pills at night, as well as vitamins to help restore any dietary deficiency.

A newer method for treating drug addicts involves administering a substitute drug to the addict. One such substitute is methadone. Although a narcotic itself, methadone does not produce the "high" associated with heroin. When obtained legally, it costs about the same as a cup of coffee. In one carefully supervised study in a hospital setting, it was reported that 82 percent of the individuals who had used heroin for five or more years were successfully treated in that they were no longer addicted to heroin, were not committing crimes, and were leading socially productive lives. However, a program using methadone has many disadvantages. Methadone does not work satisfactorily with all heroin addicts. Some addicts mix methadone with heroin to reduce their tolerance to heroin so that they can then use smaller does of heroin to become "high." Also, some people feel that methadone itself might produce additional addicts, because it is physically addicting.

Another substitute drug being studied at the present time is haloperidol. In experiments with rats haloperidol has relieved the anxiety and agitation associated with withdrawal from narcotics. The major promise of this drug is that it is not addicting. For effective treatment of drug addicts this type of drug should be supplemented with psychological treatment.

An individual who takes drugs, whether addicted or not, has usually developed the habit in a poor social environment. Any treatment of the physical aspects of drugs should also include social-psychological treatment, especially treatment involved in helping the person readjust to a productive social life. Unfortunately, many addicts do not respond to ordinary psychotherapy, because many of the factors necessary for successful psychotherapy operate at odds with traits found in addicts.

One of the most promising of present-day methods is self-help centers, many of which are established and run by ex-addicts. Addicts who come for help are required to live at the center, which has very strict rules set up by the center's members. Perhaps much of the success of such programs is due to the fact that those helping the addicts are personally familiar with their problems.

If you wish to become involved in the problem, become involved in the solutions—don't become part of the problem.

Pollution

In addition to drugs, another major problem facing our society today is the pollution of the environment. The activities of human beings are closely tied to the environment in which they live. The field that studies the relationship between organisms and their environment is called ECOLOGY.

People must learn to live in harmony with their environment. By damaging their environment, people are at the same time doing harm to themselves. Scientists today are trying to discover ways to diminish the damages that have taken place and to provide means by which future damage can be avoided. They are aware that problems of ecology are intricately woven together and that solving one problem may, in some instances, increase already existing ones.

We will now examine some of the problems connected with pollution. There are three major areas of the environment that are being polluted by man: air, water, and land.

Air pollution. The air is polluted primarily from the burning of fuels in automobiles (the largest single polluter of the air), airplanes, industrial plants, homes, and from the burning of refuse. There are about forty different substances that are regarded as pollutants of the air. Gases make up about 90 percent of the polluting substances, while particles (solids) and liquids make up the remaining 10 percent. The potentially dangerous gases in the air are carbon monoxide, sulfur oxides, nitrogen oxides, and hydrocarbons, which are all inhaled with each breath. We also breathe in particles, especially in metropolitan areas. In one large city there is an average of over forty billion particles per cubic foot of smog.

What are some effects of polluted air? Polluted air affects people indirectly by damaging the environment. For example, polluted air increases the corrosion of metals, harms animals, increases cleaning costs, and destroys crops and vegetation. Cleopatra's Needle, an ancient Egyptian obelisk, has corroded more in its ninety-three years in New York City than in the previous 3000 years it stood in Egypt. One study estimated that the economic loss from pollution in urban areas averages about sixty-five dollars a year per person.

Air pollution has a direct effect on the physical health of human beings. It has been related to bronchitis, lung and stomach cancer, heart disease, and infant mortality rates. However, in some of these studies certain important factors were not adequately controlled or taken into consideration. For example, in

In many cities polluting substances from industrial smoke stacks cloud the air.

one study socioeconomic status and income level were not taken into account, two factors known to be related to different kinds of physical illnesses.

One study conducted with pregnant rats indicated that the offspring of female rats subjected to low dosages of DDT (an insecticide) were less aggressive than normal rats. The offspring of females that had been subjected to sulfur were found to be significantly more aggressive than normal rats. It is thought that these behavioral changes came about because the pollutants caused an upset in normal brain chemistry. Another study exposed rats to carbon monoxide levels similar to those found on freeways. The young rats who were exposed exhibited slower physical growth and less spontaneous activity than normal rats.

Air pollution has probably caused thousands of deaths to human beings. London, England, had a fog that lasted for four days in the early 1950's and resulted in an estimated 4000 deaths. During those four days the average death rate tripled. (Since then, however, London has made giant strides in controlling its air-pollution problem.) In Tokyo, Japan, air pollution became so bad at one point that traffic policemen would pause at regular intervals to breathe oxygen from special containers, and vending machines supplied oxygen along the sidewalks for pedestrians.

There is probably no major American city that does not suffer from air pollution. Cities and towns located in valleys are very susceptible to accumulations of air pollutants over long periods of time, because the surrounding hills help prevent winds from scattering the pollutants.

What is being done to reduce air pollution? Many cities have begun campaigns to stop any further increase in air pollution and reduce the existing amount of air pollution. There is a nationwide surveillance system established in 1953 that is designed to identify airborne pollutants, establish areas of the largest concentrations of air pollution, study trends and patterns of air pollution, and provide data for creating laws related to air pollution. The system is primarily the responsibility of each state and local region.

Fortunately, within the past few years there has been an increase in the methods of controlling and eliminating air pollution, such as local laws regulating the use of incinerators, and federal laws requiring that cars meet certain standards. One consoling factor in connection with air pollution is that there has been no drop in the amount of oxygen in the atmosphere since it was first measured in 1910.

Are high school students concerned with the problems of air pollution? One study was conducted with high school students to assess their knowledge, awareness of, and concern with air pollution. The selected students were living, and had lived at least three years, in a large city with a severe air-pollution problem. In this city about twenty-two tons of solid particles settled on an average square mile each month within one mile of the school.

The first part of the study consisted of showing the students slides, in a random order, of various urban problems, such as rundown buildings, litter, air pollution, poor roads, and polluted streams. The subjects were asked to mark on a checklist what urban problems they saw on the slides.

The second part of the experiment measured the students' concern about air pollution. The subjects were given a two-part questionnaire. The first part dealt with how they would spend a large amount of money on different problems. The second part found out how much time each subject would spend in helping to solve an air pollution problem.

The third step in the experiment was to determine how much knowledge the subjects had about air pollution. This was done by administering a paper-and-pencil objective test on the economic, political, and scientific aspects of air pollution.

The fourth step in the experiment involved a simulated air-pollution problem, in which the subjects were presented with a hypothetical problem of a children's playground being threatened by smoke from a nearby junk yard. The subject was given ten plastic chips, representing ten friends. He could decide what activities these friends should undertake (on a gaming board) to convince the city council to solve the problem by passing an air-pollution control ordinance.

The following are some of the results of this experiment: (1) These high school students were concerned about social problems; (2) Some individuals who were concerned about air pollution were also very aware of this problem, while others who were aware of the problem cared very little about it; (3) Air pollution was ranked third highest in priority, after increasing job opportunities and improving police-community relations; (4) When the hypothetical city council did not pass the ordinance, all of the high school students recommended nonviolent ways of getting the council to reconsider; (5) Blacks with a high preference for exploratory behavior had a much greater interest in local community problems than did whites with a high preference for exploratory behavior; (6) Socioeconomic status and not race was the more important factor affecting awareness of the problem; (7) Low-socioeconomic-status subjects were less aware of air pollution than high-socioeconomic-status subjects.

The trend at the present is that individuals in the higher-socioeconomic-status groups are moving from the central parts of cities, where air pollution is heavier, to the suburbs. Will this result in an accumulation of individuals in urban areas who are less aware of the problem of air pollution? What can be done to increase awareness of the problem and concern for finding ways to solve it?

Water pollution. Another major problem facing our society today is the pollution of our waterways. The dumping of waste products into our waterways began when the number and size of towns located along water routes was small, and a simple solution to the disposal of waste products was to release them in the nearest waterway. Today the waste products dumped into our rivers, lakes, and streams has grown to enormous proportions, while the size of the waterways has remained relatively constant.

The increased volume and the types of

materials released upset the ecological balance in the waterways, affecting plant and animal life. Most cities today remove some sewage from the wastes before pouring them into waterways, but the purifying processes often upset the natural cycles in the rivers, lakes, and streams. In addition, fertilizers, containing nitrates and phosphates, wash into waterways and provide food for water plants, such as algae. The algae tend to grow so fast and become so thick that their underneath layer dies and sinks to the bottom. These decaying algae clog up the river and use up oxygen, making the water uninhabitable for fish.

Some additional problems of water pollution are due to oil spilling from tankers and offshore oil rigs, the release of industrial chemicals into waterways, the effects of petroleum products from marine engines, thermal (heat) pollution, the drainage of mines, and insecticides. An oil spillage in the ocean, for example, keeps oxygen from reaching into the depths, thereby killing untold numbers of fish. The results continue to affect sea life for years.

What direct effects does water pollution have on people? Water pollution can have direct economic effects on man. For instance, water pollution has resulted in the poisoning of fish in some rivers and lakes, which deprives commercial fishermen of income and prevents people from enjoying recreational fishing activities. The pollution of waterways also makes it more difficult and costly to provide homes with water for drinking and other household purposes.

Water pollution affects people in many other ways. Can you name a few? Can you think of things that you can do to help solve the problem?

Land pollution. The third type of pollution that has created a social problem in this country is pollution of the land. The average American generates more than six pounds of trash each day and the amount is growing steadily, as both the number of waste products and the population continue to increase. Also, there is a high demand for land so that land space for the disposal of solid waste becomes more and more scarce.

What is being done about solid-waste pollution? A few cities have partially solved the problem by filling over each layer of waste disposal with gravel and clay, eventually creating a large hill that is used for skiing and recreation during winter months. Other cities have compressed their garbage into small bundles, which they use for building foundations, and they have used crushed glass to help pave highways. Some companies are buying back their containers, such as aluminum cans, and reprocessing (recycling) them. The use

One of the effects of water pollution in many rivers is to kill off the fish, as shown above. Often the ecological balance is destroyed and the marine life cannot survive.

of bottles and cans that decompose when empty is also on the increase. Machines have been built that can compress an entire automobile into a few cubic feet. The metal is then recycled to build other cars. The burning of trash in some areas creates heat that generates electricity. Solid waste products have even been converted into food products. The possibility of burying some of our solid waste under the ocean floor has been considered. Perhaps you can suggest still other ways to handle the problem of land pollution.

Overpopulation

Overpopulation can be defined according to the number of persons living within a specific space—the amount of space per person. Many variables are involved in studying overpopulation. For instance, people living close together in a limited amount of space are affected by (1) temporal duration, or the length of time the individuals are together; (2) the richness of the environment available to the individual; (3) the ability or inability of the person to control his social role; and (4) prior experience with high- or low-density conditions.

Why is overpopulation a problem? As the population increases, each individual has more opportunities for social interaction. However, as the chances for social interaction increase, so does the possibility of more conflicts and frustrations arising from such interactions. Not only does overpopulation increase the problems of interpersonal relations, but it also adds to such problems as air and water pollution, crime, noise, and food and housing shortages.

Although at the present time the world's birth rate is declining, the death rates are also declining. Modern science is increasing man's life span and decreasing the mortality rates of infants. The end result is a rapidly increasing world population. In 1970 there were approximately 3.6 billion people, but it is estimated that by the year 2006 the world population will have doubled—to 7 billion people.

Ironically, those countries that can least afford an increase in their population have the largest increases. For example, in 1970 about 70 percent of the total world population lived in underdeveloped areas, but by the year 2006, if present trends continue, approximately 80 percent will live in these underdeveloped areas.

One expert recently calculated that the optimum number of persons who can live adequately in areas that are presently inhabitable is about 9 billion. However, predictions indicate that the world population will reach over 13 billion before it can be slowed down, stopped, and eventually returned to the optimum number of 9 billion.

Some possible effects of overpopulation on social behavior. In one series of fascinating experiments with rats, a scientist allowed rats to reproduce so that approximately twice the usual number occupied a space that ordinarily produces moderate stress from social interaction. The rats were given food, water, and nest-building materials in their confined space. Many signs of abnormality were observed under these overpopulated conditions. For example, the females did not take the usual care of their young. Male rats developed cannibalism, overactivity, and withdrawal from social contact. Also, the usual male-female ratios were upset.

In one pen a BEHAVIORAL SINK developed among the rats, that is, a situation that begins with organisms being distributed evenly over the space available to them, and then changes so that there are one or more heavily populated areas within the total space, the result-

As the world's population increases, people in high density areas must live under overcrowded conditions and deal with the physical, social, and psychological effects.

ing congregation far exceeding the optimum number of organisms that normally occupy such sections of the total space. The importance of the behavioral sink is that it creates a situation in which the density of the population far exceeds the desirable number of organisms that can adequately live in a normal social environment.

In another experiment rats were trained to drink water from a specially designed apparatus, which had two levers that could be depressed to deliver a drop of water. Two rats could stand side by side to lower the levers, but a wire partition kept them from having physical contact with each other. The floor and levers were wired so that three conditioning procedures could be used: (1) *no condition*—a rat could receive water whenever the lever was depressed; (2) *coop*—two rats had to be present, one on each side of the partition, and depress the levers at the same time before either one could receive water, and (3) *disop*—only one rat could be at a lever to receive water, the other lever being electrically locked if another rat was beside it.

Some of the results of this experiment were that when a group of more than sixteen *coop* rats were required to use the apparatus, their water consumption was reduced. The same was true when only eight *disop* rats were together. That is, when the number of rats increased, there was less time for any one rat to use the drinking apparatus. You are probably familiar with a similar situation when you try to obtain a drink of water from a fountain between classes and there is a long line of people ahead of you. In such overcrowded situations one's associates tend to interfere with the efforts of a single individual to, say, obtain water. Under these conditions, which are beyond the organism's ability to control, indications are that some organisms fail to adjust successfully. Other results were that the *disop* females produced smaller litters, and continued to do so months later. Also, the mortality rate of the rats increased rapidly.

One final result in this experiment may open new fields of study. Quite by accident one of the rats trained in the *disop* condition climbed over into the *coop* pen and went to the drinking apparatus. Before the *disop* rat had time to depress the lever to receive water, a *coop* rat entered the adjoining compartment and prepared to depress its lever to assist the *disop* rat in obtaining water. The *disop* rat immediately backed out of its compartment and attacked the *coop* rat, pulling it out of the apparatus. Remember that the *disop* rat had been trained to receive water when no other rat was present, while the *coop* rat had been trained to assist another rat in obtaining water. In other words, there was a direct conflict of learned behaviors between the two rats, which resulted in confusion. An organism introduced into a group with diametrically opposed learned behaviors completely disrupted the social situation. Compare this result to what happens when a person moves into a new environmental situation and immediately causes a conflict in learned values.

Other experiments have shown that the sudden introduction of a number of alien rats into a stable resident population of rats results in extreme disruption—death of half of the stable population and half of the alien rats. Even the sudden emergence of a large number of young rats into a population causes great disruption—the dominant male rats begin to viciously attack any associate, even female rats. Rats that are grouped together establish patterns of behavior, much like human beings establish particular patterns of behavior, and when a disruption occurs it affects the social relations within the group.

Possibly the results of these experiments will help us to better comprehend and reduce the difficulties encountered when individuals of different socioeconomic backgrounds and value systems are forced together. Psychology can provide immense help by aiding each of us to better understand not only ourselves but also those with whom we come into contact. As social contacts increase, due to increases in population and other factors, such awareness becomes even more important.

The Role of Psychology in Solving Social Problems

No one field of science can hope to solve the problems of society, because it will take the efforts of all fields and every individual. Each field of science must contribute its share of knowledge and skills to analyze the problems and offer solutions, just as each person must make his or her own contribution. The main contribution psychology can make is to determine the causes and effects of certain societal problems, helping individuals to better understand themselves, their relationships to their physical environment, and, perhaps most important, their relationships with other individuals.

Psychology can be of tremendous assistance in providing ways of promoting better communication among people. Some communities, for instance, are using psychologists and psychological procedures in the training and use of police to establish better communications, and thus improve relations between the police force and members of the community.

Finally, psychologists provide useful services as individual human beings—as authors, researchers, and teachers, and as members of local organizations concerned with the problems of society. Psychologists also join together to form professional groups dedicated to the promotion of public welfare. There is, for example, a division of the American Psychological Association devoted to the psychological study of social issues.

What can you do as an individual? Before anyone can help solve a problem, the person must first realize that a problem exists. You must be willing to take the time to recognize problems. The next step is then to search for solutions to recognized problems. You can learn more about the problems of society through reading sources of information beyond this text, through the mass media, and through discussions with friends, relatives, and experts in particular fields. You can also apply the knowledge you have acquired in this course to better understand yourself, others, and interpersonal relations. You can work toward developing better communications with all persons. If you remain flexible in your thinking, investigating specific social problems and actively seeking out solutions to them, you can make a significant contribution to the improvement of our society.

Terms to Know

attitude
behavioral sink
crime
delinquency
depressant drug

drug
ecology
hallucinogen
narcotic
prejudice

propaganda
random sampling
stimulant drug
social attitude
stratified sampling

Topics to Think About

1. How would big business and our economic life be affected if there were not such a thing as propaganda (advertising)? How would its absence affect your life personally?

2. If you knew beyond a doubt that some student in your school was using a dangerous drug, and without medical prescription, would you report the fact to the student's parents? to school authorities? to the police? If not, why not?

3. Should the advertising of nonprescription drugs, such as aspirin, as well as dangerous drugs be barred from radio, television, newspapers, magazines, and billboards? How much effect would the prohibition of such advertising have on the use of dangerous drugs?

4. Suppose a particular industry illegally causes pollution—but if you require the industry to add new equipment to stop the pollution, it will go bankrupt. What would you do? Ignore the situation? Prosecute the industry? Can you suggest some other solution?

5. Perhaps you know or have read about juveniles who have been arrested. Do you agree with the treatment they received? How would you change the laws regarding the treatment of juvenile delinquents?

6. Wars and highway accidents play some part in the prevention of overpopulation. Are either or both of them worth the price? Why or why not?

7. From past history it has been shown that the only requirement necessary for a society to justify killing another group within the society is to show that the deaths of the undesirables are necessary for the good of the society as a whole. Would you agree or disagree with this statement? Why?

8. Which is more important, the right of the individual or the right of the society in which that individual lives?

Suggestions for Activities

1. Bring to class for discussion editorials from newspapers differing radically in point of view on some social problem. Analyze the editorials in terms of techniques of propaganda.

2. Divide a bulletin board into two parts. On one side post newspaper and magazine articles that tell of juvenile delinquency. On the other side post clippings and articles that tell of desirable social activities of young people and organized youth groups. Which material is easier to find? Do most of the articles on delinquency refer to boys or to girls? Do most of them refer to young people who are in high school or to those who have dropped out of school? Consider the same questions for the articles on desirable social activities.

3. Have a police officer, judge, or social worker speak to your class on delinquency and crime. If this person can remain long enough, have a buzz session, breaking up the class into groups of five or six so that each group can come up with two or three important questions for the speaker. If the speaker cannot devote this much time to your class, have your buzz session before he or she comes and thus have some questions ready for the person in advance.

4. For a week, watch and report on television programs depicting crime. Are the programs realistic? Is the offender depicted as a hero? Are law-enforcement officers depicted as heroes? Are crime techniques demonstrated? Are the offenders young, middle-aged, or old persons? Are the offenders men or women? What suggestions are made for preventing crime, other than punishment? You may wish to make similar studies for films, magazine crime stories, and comic books or strips.

5. Have as a speaker someone trained and experienced in military life. Ask him to speak on war from his point of view. Have as another speaker someone who is frankly opposed to war. How do you account for the differences in attitudes of these two people? Do they have some attitudes in common? What is your attitude after hearing both speakers? Have you modified your attitude as a result of what the speakers have said?

6. With several other students, survey your community and surrounding areas for industries or other sources that pollute the air, water, or land. Determine the specific kind of pollution taking place and what each source is trying to do, or has done, to eliminate it. If possible, obtain a copy of any guidelines the industries must follow to prevent or end pollution. Also, try to find out what obstacles may hinder them in overcoming the pollution. Report your findings to the class.

7. One activity that can be very useful to you as well as to others consists of finding some area in your community that needs cleaning up, such as a vacant lot in which people have dumped trash. Obtain permission from the landowner, and then organize a group to meet and clean up the lot. You should not ask for or accept pay for this project.

Suggestions for Further Reading

Abelson, Herbert, *Persuasion—How Opinions and Attitudes Are Changed,* Springer. This book discusses over 100 published experiments on persuasion.

Allport, Gordon W., *The Nature of Prejudice,* Doubleday. A psychologist discusses how prejudice is learned, its effects, and ways in which it can be overcome.

Alpenfels, Ethel J., *Sense and Nonsense About Race,* Friendship Press. Written from an anthropological point of view, this book discusses common misconceptions about races.

Clark, Kenneth B., *Dark Ghetto: Dilemmas of Social Power,* Harper & Row. A discussion of social conditions and the segregation of blacks in New York City.

Clark, Kenneth B., *Prejudice and Your Child,* Beacon Press. A paperback on race awareness, child development, prejudices and antipathies, and segregation in education.

Grier, W. H., and P. M. Cobbs, *Black Rage,* Basic Books (paperback, Bantam). Written by two black psychiatrists, this book is a psychological study of the effects of racism on Black America.

Hilgard, E. R., R. C. Atkinson, and Rita Atkinson, *Introduction to Psychology,* 5th ed., Harcourt Brace Jovanovich. See pages 180–84, "Effects of Drugs"; pages 523–35, "Attitudes and Opinions"; and Chapter 23, "Psychology and Society."

Kagan, J., M. M. Haith, and Catherine Caldwell (eds.), *Psychology: Adapted Readings,* Harcourt Brace Jovanovich. See Selection 15, "LSD: A Novelist's Personal Experience," and Selection 33, "Like It Is in the Alley."

Kinkead, Eugene, *In Every Way But One,* Norton. A popular and well-written treatment of brainwashing—a form of persuasion.

Packard, Vance, *The Hidden Persuaders,* McKay. A study of how Americans are persuaded to buy and vote as they do.

Ruch, Floyd L., and Philip G. Zimbardo, *Psychology and Life,* 8th ed., Scott, Foresman. See Chapter 13, "Forces That Diminish Man."

Shepard, Paul, and Daniel McKinley (eds.), *Environ/Mental: Essays on the Planet as a Home,* Houghton Mifflin. A paperback collection of articles on overpopulation, the early environments of man, ecology, air pollution, and psychoecological aspects of population.

Shepard, Paul, and Daniel McKinley (eds.), *The Subversive Science: Essays Toward an Ecology of Man,* Houghton Mifflin. A collection of articles in paperback form that cover the problems of population growth, pesticides, A-bombs, ecosystems, and a number of other topics dealing with ecology.

Wertheimer, M., *Confrontation: Psychology and the Problems of Today,* Scott, Foresman. A book by an American psychologist on applying psychology to improve the interaction between man and his environment.

Wertheimer, M., et al., *Psychology: A Brief Introduction,* Scott, Foresman. See pages 146–61, 194–96, 220–22 on attitudes and their measurement, propaganda and advertising, group conflicts, racial differences, finding out what people think and believe, and psychology and law.

chapter 19

The World of Work

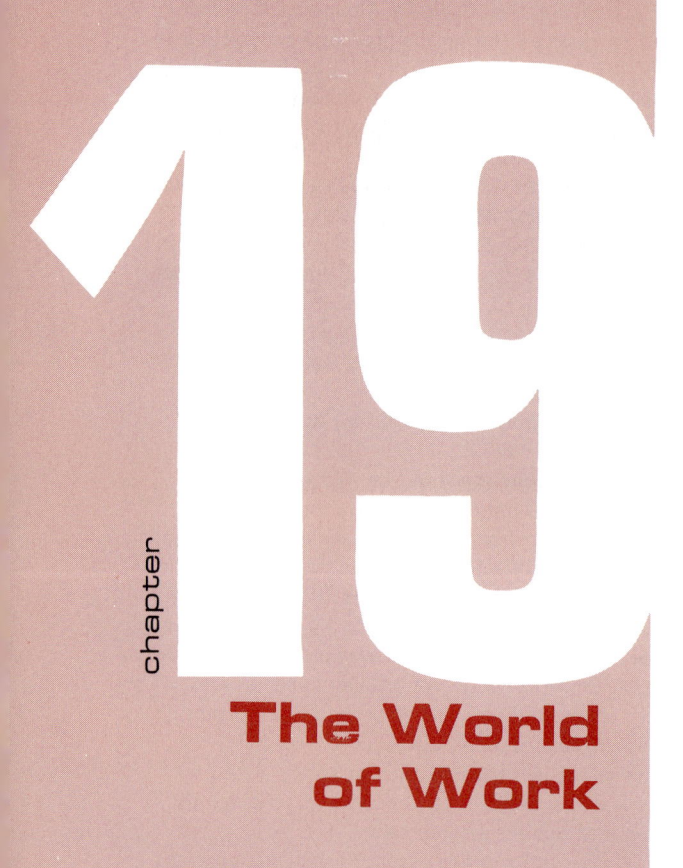

During your study of psychology you have learned many useful things, such as how to study more effectively, how you can help solve social problems, and how to make a more efficient adjustment to life. This last chapter will focus on problems of vocational adjustment. You will learn how psychology can help you in selecting a vocation, what psychologists have learned about the world of work, and, should you be interested in becoming a psychologist, more about psychology as a vocation.

Choosing Your Vocation

Young people may drift into jobs without seriously thinking about their abilities, suitability to the work, or their vocational interests. Therefore, many eventually become dissatisfied with their work and wind up shifting from one job to another.

Everyone should give serious thought to selecting a vocation. No one is born to fit only one particular job. Even so, individuals can spend a great deal of time before discovering what work best suits them. One study of college graduates found that 25 percent wished they had specialized in something else while in college. The smallest proportion of dissatisfaction was found among premedical students and the largest amount among pharmacy majors. About 50 percent of the clerical and manual workers reported that they were interested in their work, but only one-third stated that they would choose the same vocation if they were given another chance. It is inefficient either to spend many years hunting for a suitable vocation or to go through life without ever doing work for which you are particularly suited. Although there are no sure-fire schemes for helping people find suitable vocations, psychologists are able to assist young people in the very serious business of

The amount of job satisfaction is often related to the amount of self-involvement in your work. Here the noted artist Marc Chagall is absorbed in his vocation—painting.

selecting fields of work.

Your school guidance department can help you with your specific plans for the future, but here you can learn about how psychology contributes to vocational guidance.

What factors contribute to job satisfaction? Labor union agreements tend to emphasize that desirable wages, hours, and working conditions are important to an individual's satisfaction with his job. If asked what they want from a job, many people might say "money" on first thought. In one nationwide survey, however, employed men were asked, "If by some chance you inherited enough money to live comfortably without working, do you think you would work anyway?" Only 20 percent said that they would not work. In another study involving college students, the most important factor was a job that provided an opportunity to use their special abilities or aptitudes. Only 10 percent listed money as the most important factor. Although in our society some money is obviously a necessity, there are other factors that influence job satisfaction even more. A job contributes a great deal to an individual's self-respect, and a job serves as an indicator of an individual's social status.

Among the factors that influence job satisfaction is the extent to which the person is involved in his or her work. In general, the greater the involvement, the more satisfying the job. Another factor related to job satisfaction is education. Studies have indicated that college graduates are more likely to achieve vocational satisfaction than are individuals with less formal schooling. Still another factor that influences a person's satisfaction with his job is his self-concept. For instance, a student who has a favorable self-concept and a healthy degree of self-confidence in his abilities will be able to make vocational choices more satisfactorily than a student who has little self-confidence and an unfavorable self-concept.

What are some sources of dissatisfaction with jobs? In many cases individuals working for large organizations have very little independence or opportunity to display initiative. They are governed by numerous rules and regulations. If they aspire to the higher positions within the organization, they may become dissatisfied when they experience conflict between their vocational role and their family role. For example, a father may have promised to take his family on a picnic, an occasion that they are looking forward to. At the last minute he finds that he must attend an important meeting connected with his job. He must choose between fulfilling his job obligations and satisfying his family obligations.

In addition to possible conflicts between vocational and family roles, there may also be conflicts between roles within a vocation. Qualities that may lead to success in a vocation may also make the individual less successful with his or her fellow workers. For example, in one study, when insurance salesmen were asked what characteristics they thought a good salesman should possess, they listed "aggressiveness" and "hard-hitting" as primary qualities. "Sympathy" seemed to be of little importance as a desirable quality. Yet when they were asked to choose which salesmen they would like as house guests, they tended to choose salesmen who were sympathetic rather than those who were aggressive and hard-hitting. In other words, to be successful the insurance salesmen needed to be aggressive and hard-hitting, but if they had these qualities other salesmen were less likely to invite them to a social gathering.

In many large organizations a man can advance in position and salary only if he moves from one city to another at fairly frequent intervals. If he is married, such moving makes school adjustment difficult for his children and social adjustment difficult for his whole family.

Women may have special problems in finding job satisfaction. In our society a woman is expected to play the role of homemaker, yet she may also have a job outside the home. With two jobs making demands on her time and energies, she may have difficulty in doing both of them to her satisfaction.

She may also experience job dissatisfaction when she encounters job discrimination against women. In one study a survey was made to determine to what extent, if any, discrimination was practiced against women in the field of psychology. Two application forms, each describing the qualifications of a hypothetical psychologist looking for a job, were mailed to the heads of psychology departments at graduate schools. The only difference between the two forms was that one contained the name of a female and the other the name of a male. Of the 228 forms mailed out, a total of 147 useful answers were returned. Upon analyzing the data, it was found that males were offered higher positions than females, although both were identical in background and qualifications. This evidence supports the contention that discrimination practices do exist against females in the profession of psychology. Other studies have found that many females with the same background, qualifications, and experience as males have been making lower salaries.

How important is intelligence in choosing a vocation? There is some relationship between vocational success and intelligence as measured by tests. Remember, however, that all work is honorable if it is done well. Unfortunately some persons have the undemocratic idea that white-collar jobs are more honorable than blue-collar jobs. Anyone who is happy and efficient in his work is successful, no matter what the nature of that work may be.

If a person does not do well in his high school or early college work, even though he tries his best, and if scores on intelligence tests indicate that he is not above the average, he would probably not be happy in a professional career. On the other hand, if a student does well in high school or early college work, and his scores on intelligence tests indicate that he is above average, he may well consider preparation for some kind of professional work, such as that of a physician, lawyer, psychologist, high school teacher, or engineer. The professional field would offer a challenge to his abilities throughout life, and he would probably be happy in his work. If, however, everyone of above-average intellectual ability were to enter the professions, these fields would soon be overcrowded. There is a great need for individuals of high intellectual ability who can bring something of professional attitudes and skills to nonprofessional work.

Knowledge of the factors of intelligence can be valuable in choosing a vocation. If a person knows how he measures up in various mental abilities, he will have some clues as to what vocations he may be best suited for. For example, a person who scores high in verbal fluency might think about becoming a writer. If an individual has ability with numbers, he may choose to become an accountant.

A person's general intelligence and ability in various factors of intelligence, as measured by intelligence tests and as indicated by schoolwork, can help him determine both the level on which he can work and the kind of work he can do. He can also learn about his abilities from aptitude tests.

Aptitude tests. Psychologists have developed tests, known as APTITUDE TESTS, that help

This nurse performs essential duties in an emergency ward. Aptitude tests can help you find out if you are likely to be successful at a particular vocation, such as nursing.

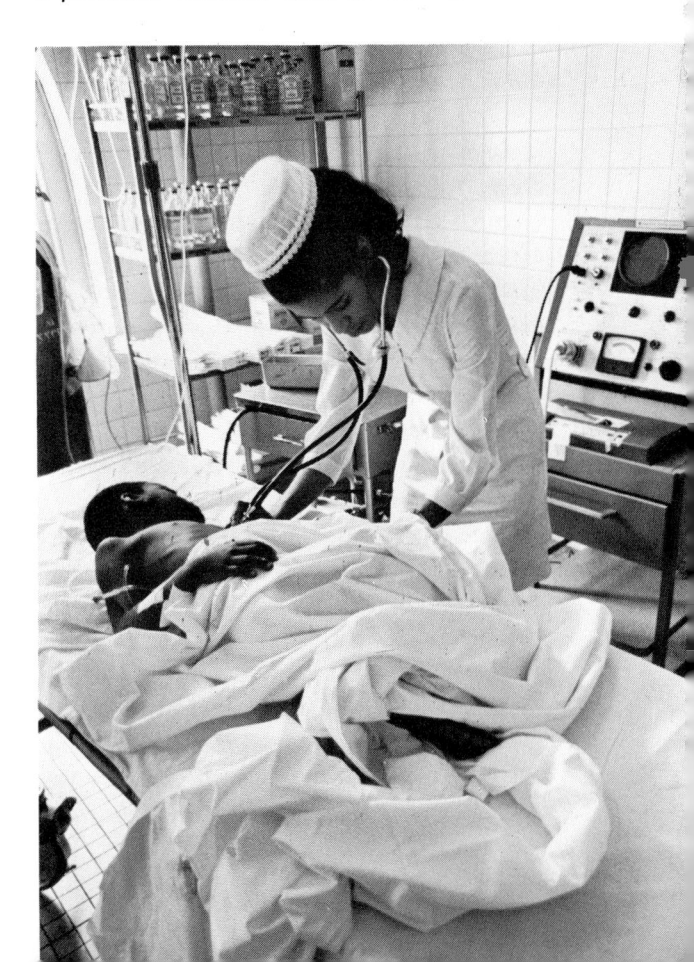

young persons, before they take specific training in a particular kind of work, to judge whether or not they are likely to succeed in that work. Aptitude tests do not provide a magic score that will tell a person just what kind of work he should train for, but they often give him information that may help him arrive at such a decision.

Sometimes business organizations use aptitude tests to assist them in selecting people who will be likely to profit from their training programs. For example, the president of a large company reported that the use of aptitude and other psychological tests had enabled his employment office to pinpoint 85 percent of the untrainable men who applied for work.

After an individual has taken an aptitude test, his score can be compared with the scores of others who have taken the same test and have gone on to training or work experience in the given field. For example, girls applying for admission to a hospital school of nursing can take a nursing aptitude test, and their scores can be compared with the scores of others who have successfully completed the required years of training. In one study of student nurses it was found that all the girls who had made a score of 130 or above on a nursing test graduated in the upper two-thirds of their class, whereas no girl with a score below 80 graduated in the upper two-thirds of the class. This particular aptitude test was a very good indicator of a girl's likelihood of succeeding in nurses' training.

One of the most widely used aptitude tests at the junior-senior high school level is the DAT (Differential Aptitude Tests). This test measures seven factors: verbal reasoning, numerical ability, abstract reasoning, spatial relations, mechanical reasoning, clerical speed and accuracy, and language usage (spelling and grammar). The results are useful in vocational guidance because they indicate the strong and weak areas of a student. The different subtest scores of the person can be compared to each other, as well as to the average for the person's grade level and sex. The verbal-reasoning and numerical-ability scores can be combined to estimate the person's scholastic ability, because there is a high relationship between these combined scores and school grades. Some of the factors are related to future vocational success. For example, it has been shown that the perception of spatial relationships is related to the profession of dentistry.

If possible, you should take some aptitude tests. Taking such tests will help you learn about your own aptitudes, although you must be careful not to jump to conclusions, not to place more faith in a few scores than is warranted. Aptitude tests are available in many fields—art, clerical work, mechanical work, music, sales, science, stenography, teaching, and so on. The procedure, conducted by such trained individuals as guidance counselors, of using the results of tests to aid an individual in determining which occupation he would probably be best suited for is known as VOCATIONAL GUIDANCE. In case you are unable to take such tests, the following examples will give you an idea of what they are like.

The person taking a mechanical aptitude test may be asked to do a bit of matching. In one column there may be pictures of a hammer, a wrench, and a saw; in a second column, pictures of a board, a nail, and a nut. We can at least imagine someone who knows so little about mechanical work that he would think a hammer should be used on a nut, a saw on a nail, and a wrench on a board. Instead of pictures, some mechanical aptitude tests use actual tools. One mechanical aptitude test contains a series of pictures of pulleys with belts connecting them. The pulleys are different sizes, and some of the belts are crossed while

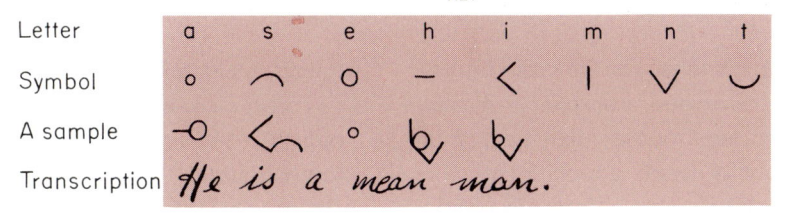

KEY								
Letter	a	s	e	h	i	m	n	t
Symbol	o	⌒	O	—	<	|	∨	∪
A sample	-o	<	o	b	b			
Transcription	*He is a mean man.*							

others are not. The person taking the test is asked to indicate whether the second pulley would turn in the same direction as the first of two pulleys or whether it would turn in the opposite direction, and whether the second pulley would turn faster, slower, or at the same speed as the first pulley.

Among other things, a stenographer must be able to write and transcribe symbols other than the letters of the alphabet. As part of one shorthand aptitude test the individual is asked to transcribe a page written in special symbols that look something like, but are not, regular shorthand. The symbols in the table on this page are a sample.

You will note that here, as in true shorthand, letters that are not pronounced are not written. "Mean" is written "m-e-n" because the "a" is not pronounced. How would you transcribe the following?

< α ʔ

Is personality a factor in choosing a vocation? Individuals differ greatly in their personality patterns. A very introverted person would probably not enjoy the work of a salesman or politician. Even though he might devote much time and energy to such work, he would probably never be as effective a salesman or politician as a very extroverted individual. On the other hand, the very extroverted individual would probably be unhappy and inefficient in research or clerical work, whereas the very introverted individual is likely to be successful in either of these fields.

Personality is also important for vocational success in machine-tending jobs and heavy manual work. Such jobs require dependability and good attendance. The person who is easily disturbed emotionally and who is unable to get along well with his fellow workers is likely to be absent from his work more frequently than the well-adjusted workman. There is evidence that personality factors affect the amount and quality of output of workmen.

The high school or college student considering the choice of a life occupation should give serious consideration to his predominant personality traits as measured by personality inventories and by the ratings of teachers and others who know him.

How important is interest? A person may have the general intelligence and the aptitude required to do a given kind of work, and his general personality pattern may indicate possible success in that work. Even so, he will probably be unhappy and not highly successful unless he is vitally interested in the work.

A case in point is that of a dentist who was neither very happy nor very successful in his profession. When he was in high school he was very interested in music and wished to become a professional musician. However, his parents wanted him to become a dentist. They refused to provide money for a musical education but offered to pay all expenses connected with dental training. The young man went to a university and succeeded in passing the necessary courses in the school of dentistry, but he spent as much time as possible in university musical activities. After graduation he opened an office, and his friends patronized him when they needed dental work. Nevertheless, his practice did not grow as it should have. He spent his evenings directing an orchestra. When the orchestra played for dances he would be up most of the night and often failed to meet his dental appointments the next morning. His interests were in music rather than in dentistry. If he had prepared for a musical career, he would probably have been successful in that field. As things actually turned out, he was neither an efficient dentist nor a really good musician.

Since interest is an important factor in selecting a vocation, it must be a genuine one. Young people often think that they would be interested in a specific kind of work. Yet after some training or experience in the field, they find that their original interest was based on a superficial knowledge of the vocation.

A girl may have a rather vague idea that she would be interested in teaching as a vocation. She has been in school and has seen something of what teachers do. But the essential point is whether or not her interests, her likes and dislikes, are similar to those of most teachers. Unless they are, she would probably not be happy and efficient in the career of a teacher. A boy may think that he would like to be an officer in one of the branches of military service. Perhaps he thinks the uniforms are attractive or that he would like to give orders. Such aspects of military life are very superficial. Unless a boy has the basic interests of most officers, he is not likely to succeed as an officer.

Many high schools today have files containing OCCUPATIONAL BRIEFS, which are usually short pamphlets or brochures containing pertinent information on specific occupations such as dentistry, engineering, psychology, and social work. From these briefs you can learn a good deal about different jobs. Often the better briefs will include such information as (1) academic work or experience generally required; (2) personality, interests, and aptitudes best suited for the job; (3) general salary ranges; (4) working conditions; (5) demand for applicants; and (6) future outlook. Many additional points may also be covered in occupational briefs. An individual interested in finding out more about a specific occupation can benefit from reading briefs on that vocation.

Measuring vocational interests. Psychologists have developed VOCATIONAL-INTEREST INVENTORIES that help the individual determine whether or not his interests are similar to those of persons engaged in a specific occupation. There is a definite relationship between success in a given kind of work and interests that are commonly associated with that type of work. Furthermore, there is evidence that as a rule, things liked best by an individual when he is young will be liked more and more with increasing age. Also, those things disliked by an individual when he is young tend to be disliked more and more as he grows older.

One widely used interest inventory of this kind is the *Kuder Preference Record—Vocational,* which requires about 45 minutes to administer. The individual indicates on each item which one of three activities he likes most and which one he likes least. For example, he might be asked which of the following three activities he likes most and which he likes least:

Collecting autographs
Collecting coins
Collecting butterflies

The results can be scored to indicate the strength of an individual's interests in each of ten vocational areas: outdoor work, mechanical work, computation, science, persuasion, art, literary work, music, social service, and clerical work. The individual can then determine how his interests compare with the

If you like to tinker with car engines, but vocational interest inventories show that you share few interests with auto mechanics, you may not be happy as a mechanic.

interests of others in a certain area or combination of areas.

Another interest-measuring device, the *Kuder Preference Record—Personal,* measures an individual's preferences for personal and social activities. It can be scored to indicate whether a person's interests are primarily those involving working with ideas, being active in groups, avoiding conflicts, directing others, or being in familiar and stable situations. Certainly these interests, as well as those mentioned in the previous paragraph, are important in planning one's school and job future.

There is also a *Kuder Preference Record —Occupational,* which relates an individual's interests to specific jobs, for example, the jobs of the accountant, architect, chemist, dentist, various types of engineers, farmer, lawyer, auto mechanic, minister, psychologist, and department store salesman.

One other widely used instrument to measure interests is the *Strong Vocational Interest Blank*. For this test the patterns of scores of individuals engaged in specific occupations were analyzed, and their interests were associated with their occupational group. The result is that individuals who answer items on the *Strong Vocational Interest Blank* are comparing their interests with the interests of persons who have been successful in particular occupational groups. For example, an individual giving answers similar to those given by psychologists would have interests that are similar to successfully engaged psychologists. If you are considering entering the field of psychology, where you would work with other psychologists, and you have interests vastly different from other psychologists, then you will probably be less happy in this field than in another field where your interests are more similar. Remember, however, that a lack of similar interests is not an absolute guarantee that you would be unhappy, nor does great interest absolutely guarantee that you will be successful in that field. Success and happiness in a specific occupation also depend on many other factors.

In one study of the interests of psychologists, using the *Strong Vocational Interest Blank,* it was found that psychologists in general have interests that are similar to those of artists, physicians, dentists, and architects. The implication is that psychologists are interested in an appreciation of beauty and in systematic investigation to promote the welfare of human beings. A large number of psychologists were also found to have interests similar to those of persons in the quantitative sciences, such as engineering, mathematics, and physics. On the other hand, in general, psychologists do not score very high in fields such as teaching, social science, school superintendent, and secretarial work.

Do your interests change? One point to remember is that interests may develop through experience. Young persons often think that they would not be at all interested in some occupations. Yet after they have learned something about these occupations, they may find that they are very much interested in them. Schools try to develop many interests in students that will put students in a better position to choose their life occupations. A person should not wait too long in deciding on an occupation; neither should he jump to a decision before he learns something about the field of his choice.

How accurate are vocational-interest inventories? Sometimes students take a vocational-interest inventory and are dissatisfied with the resulting scores. They say that the inventory is not valid, because it does not agree with their personal opinions of what they think they would like to do as a life vocation. Psychologists have found that interest-inventory scores may not relate closely to short-time interests and achievement. But inventory scores do tend to relate significantly when interests and achievement are measured over a considerable period of time. A point to remember is that scores on an interest inventory are arrived at by more scientific and standardized procedures than are opinions about interests and in the long run are usually more accurate.

The question is often raised as to whether or not the individual can bias the results of an interest inventory toward or away from specific areas. Actually, you can bias the results of some inventories but at the expense of working against your own future. If you wish, for example, to score high in social service to "prove" to others and perhaps yourself that you are interested in other human beings and that you should enter this occupation, you can intentionally give answers that do not truly indicate your interests. Later on, however, you may find that you have led yourself into an unsatisfactory job. The person administering the inventory is concerned with gaining as much valid and reliable information about you as possible to help you. Intentionally giving false information about yourself only hurts you.

What do industrial companies look for in college graduates? One university made a survey to learn what industry looked for in college graduates. Replies from executives in about seventy major companies indicated that, in general, industry looked for three things: (1) an effective personality, (2) participation in campus activities, and (3) high marks. They were anxious to have employees who would know how to work cooperatively with others, who had the knack of meeting and talking to people easily, and who were attractive in appearance and dress. Seventy percent of the executives said that they preferred graduates who had worked at part-time jobs while in college. One executive said, "We find that they have been willing to work harder. They realize the value of money, have taken their education more seriously, have developed greater qualities of initiative and responsibility." Yet students should be careful not to devote so much time to part-time jobs that they do poor, and even failing, college work.

Although the business executives pointed out that some students overdid extracurricular activities, they preferred graduates with extracurricular experience. They found that such persons cooperated and at the same time would not permit themselves to be left in routine positions. They tended to become the leaders and junior executives in industry. Only one-fifth of the executives indicated that high marks in college were essential for success in most of the positions in their businesses. In fact, one executive declared, "Frankly, we are scared of a person who has nothing but marks to offer." It should be added, however, that for technical and scientific jobs, the executives were interested in and required high marks in the records of those they employed.

Scientific Studies of Work

There are many areas within the total field of work that psychologists study. For many years they have been concerned with and worked in such areas as the training of personnel, personnel training programs, work motivation programs, the effects of fatigue and rest on work production, and the design of machines and displays. What, for instance, have psychologists found out about work patterns and the factors that increase and decrease efficiency?

A work curve. It would be very rare for anyone to work at the same level of efficiency over a long period of time. For example, after you have been studying for a long time, the degree of learning will eventually become less and less as time progresses. In other words, there will be a GENERAL DECREMENT, or decrease in amount of work done, with the passage of time. If you plot the efficiency of work on the vertical axis, or ordinate, and time on the horizontal axis, or abscissa, you may obtain a work curve like the one shown below for industrial production handwork. A WORK CURVE, therefore, shows the efficiency of work in a given task in relation to given units of time. Remember, though, that not all work curves are alike, because the efficiency depends on a number of factors, such as the number and length of rest periods, personal involvement in the task, and motivation. Work curves may also differ from one person to another when both are doing the same task.

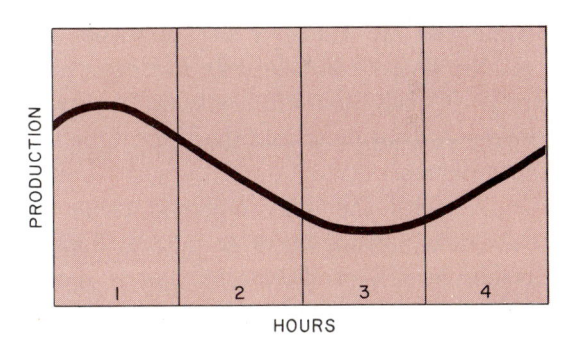

Some characteristics of work curves. Psychologists have found four general characteristics of work curves: a warming-up period, a beginning spurt, an end spurt, and fatigue.

The warming-up period, which may or may not appear in the curve, is probably familiar to you. You may have observed that prior to a sports event, such as football, the players spend some time in warming up. Or perhaps you have noticed that after you started studying for an exam, it takes a period of time before you are working at your best. By examining the typical work curve on page 491, you can see that efficiency is higher in the second hour than in the first hour. If the warming-up period is very slow, the work curve may rise slowly for the entire morning.

There may be a beginning, or initial spurt, in which the person begins work with enthusiasm. This burst of energy eventually wears off, perhaps because the person is bored or realizes that he cannot maintain this rate of work consistently, and a rather sudden drop to a more normal production occurs.

If activity increases toward the end of a task or workday, it is called an "end spurt." This is equivalent to a long-distance runner who puts forth maximum effort toward the end of the race because he realizes that he need not save his energy any longer. Perhaps while you are taking a test in school the teacher says, "You have only five more minutes." Usually you will work with renewed energy, displaying an end spurt, for those last five minutes.

A fourth and most important factor involved in a work curve is fatigue. Fatigue results in a work decrement, and is shown by the downward trend in a work curve. By fatigue we usually mean that the person feels tired or weary, but actually we have no consistent way of measuring fatigue. It can be measured by a decrease in work output, such as a decrease in the number of bricks a man will lay in a given period of time, or by an increase in errors, such as increase in the number of errors made in assembling small parts during a given period of time.

Also, factors other than fatigue can cause a work decrement. For example, a decrease in motivation can cause a decrease in work. Individuals may become bored with a specific task so that their willingness to work decreases. Work decrement can also be affected by the attitudes of the person toward the work. If the task requires high accuracy and not speed, such as assembling electronic parts, and the employer stresses that accuracy is important, when the worker becomes tired he may slow down to maintain a high degree of accuracy. Although his work curve would show a decrement, the decrement would be smaller if measured in terms of accuracy rather than in terms of the amount of work performed.

What have psychologists learned about production in industry? In the case of work that involves considerable muscular activity but is not overly monotonous, scientific studies usually show that there is a warming-up period in the morning while workmen get out their tools and settle down to work. Production decrement commonly begins about the middle of the morning. The noon rest eliminates some of this decrement, but it appears again toward the middle of the afternoon. The peak of production is usually lower in the afternoon than in the morning, and decrement is commonly more pronounced in the afternoon than in the morning. Remember, though, that individual records show considerable fluctuations in output, and general production records differ somewhat from one industry to another.

For work that is very monotonous and boring, individual work graphs tend to be very irregular, since individuals differ greatly in the way they react to monotonous work. Following a warming-up period there is a

What methods can you suggest for increasing the efficiency and performance of production workers on an assembly line, such as this assembly line for manufacturing cars?

very marked decrement, but as the relief from the work approaches, production may return to almost maximum for the work period.

Many weekly work production records show a warming-up period for Monday and Tuesday, with maximum production being achieved on Wednesday. This maximum production is followed by a decreasing daily production.

What can be done to increase industrial production? Scientific industrial studies show that the introduction of occasional short rest periods during the workday tends to improve total production by from 5 to 20 percent. For example, in one industry production was increased from 16 to 18 articles an hour by introducing a plan of having men work 25 minutes and then rest 5 minutes rather than working steadily. Even in clerical work, there is evidence that workers tend to pause and rest about 3 minutes out of an hour. The employer who not only permits but requires frequent rest periods, such as coffee breaks, actually gets more work done for his money.

Pay is often used to provide motivation in industrial work. Workmen may be paid a fixed amount per hour or per day, regardless of the amount of work done. This system of pay is known as a TIME-RATE SYSTEM. These workmen may then be offered a bonus for all

THE WORLD OF WORK

work done in excess of the usual amount. Or a PIECE-RATE SYSTEM of pay may be used, in which a fixed amount is paid for each piece produced.

Workmen sometimes report that they find it a strain to work under a piece-rate system and that they are not as happy in their work as under a time-rate system of pay. Factory superintendents often report that work done under a piece-rate system of pay is carelessly done and that there is greater waste of material than with a time-rate system.

There are a number of individuals, often called "time-study personnel," or "efficiency experts," who investigate industrial procedures to find easier and quicker ways of operation. To discover the best operating procedures, these individuals investigate the movements and procedures of each job separately. Sometimes they film the workers' actions and study them in detail, looking for a way to eliminate unnecessary movements. One of their basic aims is to discover the most efficient behavior patterns of performing various types of jobs.

Another way to increase production in industry is to discover the most efficient methods and conditions under which the individual learns various tasks. If the best learning conditions for various tasks can be found, and foremen of shops or other supervisory personnel can be taught to use them, production can be increased and the morale of employees kept higher. One example of industry adopting efficient learning methods that psychologists had developed is the case of programmed materials, which some industries use for teaching their employees basic facts about new jobs or new equipment. Efficient learning methods benefit both industry and the individual.

Another method of increasing productivity in industry utilizes behavior-modification techniques, in which certain behavior is improved by using conditioning procedures of positive and negative reinforcement. For example, in one warehouse productivity was down and the workmen were losing time and money because of back injuries resulting from lifting heavy loads incorrectly. Then foremen on the job were trained to use positive reinforcement—to compliment the workers when they used the correct procedures in lifting heavy loads. Productivity improved. In another company, when a group meets an established quota, they are rewarded by being allowed to set their next goal themselves.

Thinking Work

Many persons in industry and in the professions make their primary contribution to the world of work through thinking processes. Even those whose primary work is thinking do some muscular work in connection with their vocations. The accountant writes and operates calculating machines. The surgeon uses his arm and hand muscles in performing operations. The chemist handles test tubes and beakers. In vocations based primarily on thinking activity, though, the muscular activity is seldom great enough to produce such marked decrement as we noted in the preceding section.

How much work is involved in thinking? At one time a university student set herself the task of making a scientific study of the work involved in thinking. For example, she practiced doing such four-place multiplication problems as these:

$$\begin{array}{r} 2645 \\ \times 5784 \\ \hline \end{array} \qquad \begin{array}{r} 7954 \\ \times 3528 \\ \hline \end{array}$$

With practice she was able to do all of the multiplications without having the original problems in sight and without writing down any intermediate products. She did all the work in her head and wrote down the final product. (If you think such a task did not require much thinking, try it.)

After practice in this arduous thinking work, she began solving such problems on four successive days from about 11 A.M. to about 11 P.M., without any time out for meals. Each day she solved sixty-seven problems. The first day of the four-day experiment it took her, on the average, 9.47 minutes to solve each problem, the second day the average time was 9.13 minutes, the third day it was 7.55 minutes, and on the last day only 7.45 minutes. With the passing of the experimental days, she actually increased in speed efficiency.

It is true that she made slightly more errors in her work as the experiment progressed from day to day. The first day she made an average of 1.5 errors per problem, the second and third days an average of 1.9 errors per problem, and on the last day 2.3 errors per problem. A record was kept of the length of time required to solve each successive problem on each day. These data did indicate that, with the passing of the hours during a day, there was a tendency for more and more time to be required for each successive solution. For example, on the fourth day of the experiment the average time required for solving each problem was 4.45 minutes near the beginning of the day and 8.54 minutes near the close of the day. Also, there was a slight increase in number of errors, from 2.0 near the beginning of the fourth day to 3.1 near the close of the day. Yet at various times during the day she made fewer errors than she made at the beginning of the day.

In this well-known early experiment only one person was involved. A more recent repetition of the experiment, however, with more persons participating, confirmed these general findings. Another psychologist found that over a period of five hours of intense mental work (solving addition problems), there was a reduction of only 20 percent in output.

Do we become "too tired to think any more"? The above experiments did indicate some decrement in work efficiency with the passing of time. But the significant point is that individuals are able to do difficult mental work over considerable periods of time. After two or three hours of hard thinking work, most of us feel that we are just too fatigued to think any longer. It is true that a person doing very heavy muscular work would be so fatigued that he might be unable to do any work long before a twelve-hour work period was completed. In work that is primarily a matter of hard thinking, however, the point of complete exhaustion would probably not be reached for much more than twelve hours.

Experimental studies suggest that our complaints of being "too tired from thinking to think any more" are not justified in terms of actual fatigue. There must be some other explanation.

In one experiment subjects were asked to grade English compositions for a period of four hours. At intervals they were asked to estimate how much they were enjoying the work. Efficiency of the work was also measured. Results are indicated in the graph on page 496. The two top lines show that on the basis of initial efficiency, the percentage of drop in both speed and accuracy was slight. The lowest line plainly shows that there was a distinct and steady drop in the satisfaction or enjoyment that the work gave.

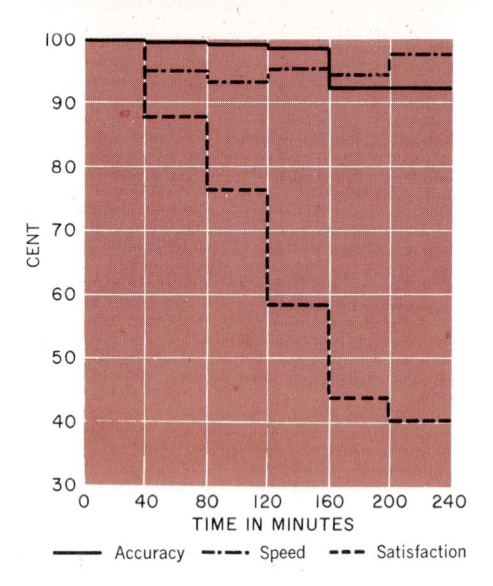

[Graph: Y-axis "PER CENT" 30–100; X-axis "TIME IN MINUTES" 0–240. Legend: Accuracy, Speed, Satisfaction]

In general, the evidence seems to indicate that what is usually considered to be fatigue in the work of thinking is really boredom. The work may be continuing at a high rate of efficiency, even though the worker no longer enjoys it and says that he is fatigued. In the work of thinking, feelings are a poor indication of efficiency. Often the efficient worker can continue with his work, even though he believes that he is too tired to do so.

Psychology As a Vocation

As you approach the end of this course in psychology, perhaps some of you are considering work in the field of psychology. Even if you do not plan to work in this area, you should have an understanding and appreciation of the work performed by psychologists, as well as of the requirements to become a psychologist. The fields in which psychologists specialize can be divided into six broad headings.

1. *Experimental and physiological psychologists.* The psychologists who work in a laboratory advance the scientific foundation on which all psychology is based. As you know, psychologists often do experimental work with animals. But many experimental psychologists work directly with human subjects, especially children.

In their laboratories experimental psychologists study not only overt behavior but also physiological processes—the functions of the glands and nervous systems, for example. Many experimental and physiological psychologists are employed in university and college departments of psychology. Some psychologists work as research scientists in laboratories maintained by private industries, governmental agencies, hospitals, and philanthropic foundations.

Sometimes psychological work is classified as either basic or applied, although there need be no sharp line drawn between the two. Experimental psychologists often engage in research aimed at discovering fundamental principles or laws—BASIC psychology. For example, such psychologists may strive to understand and explain basic principles and laws of color vision. Other psychologists take the basic principles and laws and apply them to current practical situations and problems—APPLIED psychology. On the basis of basic principles of color vision, an applied psychologist might develop a new test for color blindness. The psychologists in the remaining five classifications are concerned primarily with applied psychology.

2. *Industrial psychologists.* As the name implies, industrial psychologists work with industry. They develop programs for selecting, training, and promoting employees. They strive to improve morale. That is, they try to bring about good relations between groups of workers, and between workers and management, and to inspire job satisfaction. Some industrial psychologists form consulting firms used by business organizations.

Sometimes businesses call upon psychologists to assess consumer preferences and the relative appeal of various kinds of advertising. For example, a psychologist may survey a careful sampling of housewives to learn what kinds of articles they prefer in magazines written primarily for women readers. He is measuring consumer preference. A psychologist may be asked to investigate whether people prefer advertisements containing large illustrations and relatively little reading matter, or vice versa. In this case, he is measuring advertising appeal.

Human engineering psychologists work at designing machines that can be operated efficiently. They help design dials, gauges, and various instruments so that they can be read and operated with a minimum of error. They may also become involved in devising ways of training personnel to use these machines.

3. *Social psychologists.* These psychologists, often working with sociologists, study the behavior of individuals as members of groups. They conduct research concerned with such problems as leadership, segregation, prejudice, and the effects of disaster (floods, for example) on human behavior. They may specialize in public opinion surveys. In time of war, they may study the morale of defense workers, the influences of propaganda, the spread of rumors, and the attitude of the public toward the war effort.

Some social psychologists try to understand how individuals influence groups and how groups influence individuals. They study such social problems as the adaptation of immigrant groups to a new way of life.

4. *Educational and school psychologists.* Both educational and school psychologists are concerned with the problems of young people. No sharp line exists between the two fields of work.

Educational psychologists are most likely to be concerned with basic problems of teach-

A social psychologist might study the behavior of human beings reacting as a mob. How would you go about studying the behavior of this group of demonstrators?

ing, learning, and the personality development of children. Educational psychologists often work in university departments of psychology or education.

As the name implies, school psychologists work in school systems. They advise students about their educational and job plans. They help students with their personal, often highly emotional, problems. They strive to improve relationships between students, teachers, and parents. They are often called on to discover why certain students are having difficulty with their schoolwork and how such students can be helped. They work with crippled children and with children who have speech or reading difficulties. They often administer, or are responsible for the administration of, psychological tests—intelligence tests, aptitude tests, vocational-interest inventories, school achievement tests, and measures of personality. Some school psychologists devote part of their time to teaching psychology courses in the high schools of their school system.

5. *Clinical psychologists.* Clinical psychologists devote their time to counseling and otherwise helping persons who have disturbing personal problems. Their primary concern is with problems of mental health and individual adjustment. Their job is to help individuals to help themselves. Their work is not confined to clinics, for they may work in mental hospitals, in child guidance centers, in prisons, in connection with the work of juvenile and other courts, in social welfare agencies, in colleges, and even in some elementary and high school counseling centers. Some clinical psychologists establish offices to which anyone needing their help can come. In a hospital or clinic setting they are likely to work as members of a team along with psychiatrists (physicians who specialize in the prevention, diagnosis, and treatment of both mild and severe mental disorders), social workers, and other specialists. They may provide psychotherapy for individuals with emotional or personality disturbances. Many clinical psychologists carry on or direct research programs to learn more about basic problems and the treatment of disturbed individuals. Research is not limited to experimental psychology.

6. *Counseling and guidance psychologists.* The work of counseling and guidance psychologists is closely related to and at some points may overlap the work of both school psychologists and clinical psychologists. Whereas school psychologists work primarily with children, counseling psychologists are more likely to work with individuals in their late teens or with adults. They may specialize in assisting young persons to choose a lifework, although they also deal with other personal problems. They are often employed in vocational guidance centers, marriage clinics, and student counseling centers in schools, colleges, and universities.

Some areas in which psychologists specialize. Within the six general headings just mentioned, there are additional types of specialists. The following is a list of the different divisions of the American Psychological Association to give you an idea of the diversity present in the field of psychology. There are divisions on General Psychology, the Teaching of Psychology, Experimental Psychology, Evaluation and Measurement, Physiological and Comparative Psychology, Developmental Psychology, Personality and Social Psychology, the Psychological Study of Social Issues, Psychology and the Arts, Clinical Psychology, Consulting Psychology, Industrial and Organizational Psychology, Educational Psychology, School Psychologists, Counseling Psychology, Psychologists in Public Service, Military Psy-

A new area of psychological investigation is environmental psychology, which includes studying how astronauts such as these react to the environment of the moon.

chology, Adult Development and Aging, Engineering Psychology, Psychological Aspects of Disability, Consumer Psychology, Philosophical Psychology, the Experimental Analysis of Behavior, the History of Psychology, Community Psychology, Psychopharmacology, Psychotherapy, Psychological Hypnosis, and Humanistic Psychology.

A recent development in psychology is the area of environmental psychology, which studies man's relationships to his environment. This area deals with man's use of space, the physical environmental factors influencing choice of residence and migration, the results of prolonged exposure to environmental conditions such as overcrowding, and the effects of prolonged sensory deprivation on the psychological development of man. It is a relatively new and exciting area within psychology that promises to bring experimental and applied psychology more closely together. As man explores everything from the frontiers of outer space to the lower depths of the oceans, psychologists will play increasingly important roles to aid man to better understand man, the environments in which he lives, and his relationships to these different environments.

What training is necessary to become a psychologist? There is no short or easy road to becoming a psychologist. It is, however, an interesting road, and it leads to a rewarding, worthwhile destination.

Even in high school you can begin general preparation for becoming a psychologist. Basically, you must take your school's college preparatory course, including as many mathematics and science courses as possible, and courses in social studies, composition, and literature. You can broaden your background by participating in science fairs, junior academies of science, and other science activities. You may be able to visit a university department of psychology, tour its laboratories, observe some research in progress, and talk with members of the faculty and graduate students. A college or university near you may have special programs for high school students, such as a High School Science Day or a High School Career Day. You might even have an opportunity to participate in a high school science institute, spending part of a summer vacation visiting various university laboratories and then working as an assistant in some particular laboratory (possibly a psychology laboratory).

As we have just seen, psychologists do many different kinds of work. College preparation for such varied work must be broad. Later, specialization will be built on this broad foundation. You will need to take such college courses as history, philosophy, political science, and literature. You will also need thorough training in English composition. As a background for later specialization in the science of psychology, you will need to take basic college courses in physiology, biology, physics, mathematics, sociology, and anthropology.

Of course, in addition to a broad background in related fields, you will need to take undergraduate courses in psychology. This training should include courses in general psychology, something like the course that you are just completing but at the more difficult college level. You must take courses especially devoted to experimental theories and techniques. You will wish to get some training along such lines as physiological psychology, learning theories, abnormal psychology, social psychology, theories and practices of testing, statistical techniques, and developmental psychology. The college or university you choose will guide you in your selection of suitable courses.

The psychologist-in-training in a college or university, and even the high school student considering psychology as a vocation, can often gain valuable experience through summer or part-time nonprofessional work in mental hospitals, children's camps, or day-care centers.

The graduate training needed to become a psychologist. Following college graduation with a bachelor's degree, the future psychologist must go on to graduate training leading to the Doctor of Philosophy (Ph.D.), or a Doctor of Psychology (Psy.D.). For example, one large university offers a doctoral program in environmental psychology, which includes studying such topics as "how subways mold behavior." Training for the doctorate in psychology requires approximately four to five years of graduate work, depending on such factors as undergraduate and graduate majors, the specific school attended, marital status, and whether or not the person enters the doctoral program with a master's degree. Quite often the student may spend seven years or more in graduate training, although much of this time he is earning a living with part-time teaching, working under a research grant, or doing some other kind of work in his field. The mean age of a recipient of the doctorate in psychology is currently thirty-one years of age if the person enters the doctoral program with a master's degree, and thirty-two years of age if entering without a master's degree.

The doctorate is not granted simply on completion of a certain number of advanced courses. The candidate for the degree must be able to demonstrate that he has a broad as well as a specialized knowledge of psychology, that he can do and has already done research work, that he is ready to assume responsibility for carrying on and advancing psychology as a science and as a profession.

Even after such extensive training, he may need further specialized training, just as a physician may specialize after receiving his M.D. degree. The psychologist may gain experience working as an intern (under supervision) in his field of specialization, for example, in a mental hygiene clinic, a mental hospital, a factory or office, a child guidance center, a social welfare agency, or a school. Many psychologists take advantage of financial grants for doing postdoctoral research to gain further experience in scientific methodology and techniques.

Perhaps this seems like a long training program. It is, but it is no longer than that in many other professional fields. Perhaps you feel that you do not have sufficient money to spend eight or more years in a university. Such a program does require money, but colleges and universities have various programs for providing financial assistance to worthy undergraduate students. For the graduate student who has demonstrated his competence, there are governmental and private funds available.

In planning his training, the psychology student should prepare to meet the licensing or certification requirements of the state in which he plans to work in case the state has a law regulating the practice of psychology. If he plans to enter industrial, clinical or counseling psychology, he should prepare to take the examinations given by the American Board of Examiners in Professional Psychology.

Opportunities in psychological work for those without a doctorate degree. There are some opportunities for doing work of a limited psychological nature without the long and strenuous training just indicated. Strictly speaking, however, a person doing such work cannot be called a psychologist.

Two-year college programs are being designed to train subprofessional personnel for work of a psychological nature in mental hospitals, schools for the retarded, child-guidance clinics, and so on. Or possibly you are thinking of discontinuing your training after you have received a college bachelor's degree with a major in psychology. Will there be vocational opportunities for you with this amount of training? To answer this question, two psychologists sent a questionnaire to leaders in business and industry, schools and universities, governmental agencies, and social service organizations, asking about job opportunities for college majors in psychology. Almost all employers emphasized the importance of a broad liberal arts background rather than the particular field of study. They said they were seeking individuals who had not only excelled in schoolwork but who also had participated in extracurricular activities, had shown initiative, and had taken responsibility. The survey revealed that psychology majors would probably find their greatest opportunities in such areas as personnel administration, management training, and to some extent in sales, advertising, and production, although a college major in psychology was not a prerequisite for such jobs. In addition, there were opportunities for the college psychology major in educational, governmental, and social service areas. The employers stressed the importance of training in statistics and in English grammar, composition, and report writing. It was pointed out that most large organizations have their own in-training programs for providing the specialized preparation and experience needed for their jobs.

There are opportunities for psychological work for those who go on to a master's degree in psychology (usually awarded for one or two years' advanced study beyond the bachelor's degree). For example, such persons do work in connection with the problems presented by children having scholastic and behavior difficulties, including administration of various kinds of tests. They may do testing and other work in psychological clinics, although they do not have responsibility for final diagnosis and treatment. They may teach psychology in the increasing number of high schools that offer the course. In addition to their training in psychology, would-be teachers must take the courses necessary to get a teaching license and should prepare to teach in one or two other fields as well.

It is true that although work of a psychological nature can be done by those with less than doctoral training, the salaries are lower than for those individuals with the more complete training. It is also true that male psychologists have been receiving higher salaries than female psychologists with the same amount of training and experience, although some efforts are being made to end such salary discrimination.

This female psychologist is conducting a study of the relationships of some employees in the construction industry. Although still discriminated against, women psychologists are finding more openings than in the past, even in such areas as industrial psychology.

Opportunities for women in psychology. There are many opportunities for women in psychology, especially in child-guidance clinics and as school psychologists. There are a number of women doing research in psychology. Others are counseling psychologists. A few work in the personnel departments of large companies developing tests for job applicants and improving relations among existing employees.

One study compared gifted women psychologists with other gifted academic men and women. It was found that as a group, gifted women psychologists tended to be more intelligent, socially aloof, dominant, serious, sensitive, imaginative, unconventional (radical), secure, and self-sufficient than both adult women in the general population and college women. Although there was a great deal of similarity between gifted women psychologists and the profiles of successful academic men and women, women psychologists, as a group, scored higher than academic men in intelligence and unconventionality.

Looking Ahead

When most students begin their first course in psychology, they have many misconceptions about the field—about what psychology is, what it deals with, and what it can and cannot do. Hopefully any misconceptions you may have had have been cleared up, and many of your questions about psychology have been answered.

You have learned many things in this course. You now know that psychology is the science that studies the behavior of organisms. You know how to distinguish between psychologists and pseudo-scentists who may work in this field. You have learned something about the development of personality and behavior, what intelligence is, the social problems involved in caring for the mentally retarded and the mentally ill, the influences of heredity and environment on behavior, and how to keep in better mental health. You have studied about behavior in groups, such as the peer group, about social problems and how psychology helps to solve them, about the problems involved in dating, marriage, and family life, and about many other areas that can benefit you and also enable you to better understand and help other people.

You have now come to the end of your course in psychology. Some of you will take other courses in psychology, others will major in psychology in college, and a few of you will take the remaining training necessary to reach the top levels of psychology. For many of you this course will be your only formal study of psychology, although in the years to come you will be reminded of it constantly through material that you read, hear discussed, or see presented on the screen.

Regardless of the future you may seek, whether within the area of psychology or in some other field, it is sincerely hoped that you will make use of what you have learned to improve not only yourself but everyone with whom you come into contact, thereby making our world a better place in which to live.

➡ Terms to Know

applied psychology	general decrement	vocational guidance
aptitude test	occupational brief	vocational-interest inventory
basic psychology	piece-rate system	work curve
	time-rate system	

➡ Topics to Think About

1. Suppose that incomes for all vocations were the same. Would such a condition change your present vocational plans?

2. *If* a governmental agency of some kind were able to predict with accuracy how many doctors, electrical workers, truck drivers, teachers, clergymen, nurses, and workers in many other fields were going to be needed during your lifetime, would you be willing to have psychologists and guidance personnel give you a battery of tests and then tell you what vocation you must prepare for and enter?

3. Suppose a psychologist gave you some vocational aptitude tests, and also some vocational interest tests. Which set of scores would you place the greater confidence in? Why?

4. If you had your choice between two jobs, one of which would be quite monotonous but with very high pay and the other quite interesting but with relatively low pay, which one would you choose? Why?

5. Sometimes the term "workingman" is used to refer to an individual who does rather heavy muscular work or at least uses his hands a great deal in his work, in contrast to a person who sits at a desk and whose primary job is one of thinking —the implication being that the person with a desk job is not really working. In the light of your study of behavior, is this distinction justified? Should these two general vocational groups be paid at the same rate? If not, which should receive the higher pay?

6. Why do you think that males discriminate against females in many areas of work? Are you in favor of maintaining present conditions or of striving for equality? If the latter, what changes would you suggest to help bring this about?

Suggestions for Activities

1. If you have a school counselor or guidance person, make arrangements to take an aptitude test, such as the *Differential Aptitude Test* (DAT), (published by The Psychological Corporation). Since the entire series is quite time-consuming, you may wish to take only those parts of the DAT that are most highly related to your chosen occupation. If you have not selected an occupation, you might take several sections of the DAT to help you decide on one. However, remember that scores on a test are only additional data to consider in selecting an occupation and should be used in conjunction with many other factors, such as your interests, possible futures in that field, and the demand for persons in that field.

2. A number of measuring devices are available that measure interests rather than aptitudes. In connection with the work of the guidance department or in connection with your class in psychology, you may wish to take the *Kuder Preference Record* (published by Science Research Associates). The Kuder record has three forms: Vocational, Personal, and Occupational.

3. Ask a psychologist to speak to the class about his or her work. Your school system may have a full- or part-time psychologist. Local industries may employ psychologists. There will be one or more psychologists on the staff of any child-guidance clinic. Institutions for the care of the mentally retarded, the mentally ill, and people who have broken the law will have psychologists who might be willing to discuss their work.

4. Write a report on "How my ideas of psychology and psychologists have changed during my study of psychology" or "Why I think I might wish to become a psychologist."

5. Assume that you are the person in charge of promoting employee-employer relationships. One section of your plant has serious disagreements with management about working conditions. These employees claim that the plant area is too hot (or cold), there is not enough light (or too much light), and there is a lack of adequate safety measures. You may add other "complaints" as you see fit.

Write a short paper on the general procedures you would use to improve employee-employer relations, using as many principles as possible that you have learned in this psychology course. You may wish to review your notes and the text.

6. If you have selected your future career, find someone who is successfully engaged in that particular occupation and talk with him or her about the occupation and its duties.

Suggestions for Further Reading

American Psychological Association, *A Career in Psychology,* Washington, D.C.: American Psychological Association. Information on what is involved in becoming a psychologist and what psychologists do.

The Encyclopedia of Careers and Vocational Guidance, vols. 1 and 2, Doubleday. Provides material on determining your goals, vocational planning, how to find a job, and what specific occupations are like.

Hilgard, E. R., R. C. Atkinson, and Rita Atkinson, *Introduction to Psychology,* 5th ed., Harcourt Brace Jovanovich. See pages 356–60 on testing aptitudes and achievements.

Jobs in Psychology, Job Family Series, Science Research Associates. Although this booklet is an elementary discussion of various jobs available in the area of psychology, there is much useful information on the different kinds of work that psychologists perform and the general qualifications for these jobs.

Occupational Outlook Handbook, Washington, D.C.: U.S. Department of Labor, Bureau of Labor Statistics. An excellent guide to practically all occupations. Includes information on the nature of the job; training, requirements, and advancement opportunities; and salaries and working conditions.

Seidman, Jerome M. (ed.), *The Adolescent: A Book of Readings,* rev. ed., Holt Rinehart & Winston. See pages 456–68, "Looking at Occupations."

Wertheimer, M., et al., *Psychology: A Brief Introduction,* Scott, Foresman. See pages 182–84, 208–16 on aptitude, industrial psychology, clinical psychology, and school psychology.

STUDYING AND PREDICTING BEHAVIOR

Do you sometimes try to predict what your future life will be like? You know what your behavior has been and what it is like now in your home, your school, and your community. Can you predict your future behavior with some degree of confidence?

All sciences study the past as well as the present, and all make some kinds of tentative predictions. Psychology is no exception. But human, and even animal, behavior is extremely complex. The problem of isolating all the variables makes prediction of behavior—of what people will say or do—more difficult than predictions in the physical sciences—in chemistry, for example.

Various schools or systems of psychological thinking have developed as psychologists have tried to understand and predict behavior. Below are very brief descriptions of some of these systems. They indicate the wide range of research and theoretical discussion over human behavior and its predictability that has taken place in the past and continues at the present.

An early system of psychological thought was *structuralism*, which grew out of the work of a German psychologist, Wilhelm Wundt (1832–1920), who founded the first purely psychological laboratory. Structuralist psychologists were trying to break down complex behavior forms into basic elements. They used a method of introspection in which a subject was presented with, say, a colored light and then was asked to report on his sensation, without giving any interpretation. This approach to psychology was scientific in its attempt, but it proved to be too narrow.

Another early system of psychological thinking was *functionalism*. Leaders in this field, such as American psychologists William James (1842–1910) and John Dewey (1859–1952), said that all behavior served some adaptive function—all behavior enabled the individual to adjust to his environment.

A system of psychological thought that developed out of medical practice was *psychoanalysis*, founded by Sigmund Freud (1856–1939). Psychoanalysis stresses the importance of the unconscious in motivating and determining human behavior. It has had a considerable effect on the development of clinical psychology.

About 1912 a system known as *gestalt* psychology had its beginnings in Germany. The German word "gestalt" is usually translated as form, pattern, or configuration. The gestaltists were concerned with the overall pattern of behavior, with wholes rather than parts, with insight rather than trial-and-error learning. Their views have influenced modern cognitive psychology.

Gestaltists used a method of psychological study called *phenomenology*, which studies human experiences and behavior —phenomena—without elaboration or analysis into elements. Phenomenologists are more interested in the inner world than the external environment of the individual. To them, each individual is unique. They give as much weight to the reported perceptions of a child as to the more sophisticated report of an adult. The phenomenologists say that man can be described meaningfully in terms of his consciousness, and that he is unpredictable.

Beginning about 1913 a famous American psychologist, John B. Watson (1878–1958), suggested that psychologists concern themselves solely with the study of overt behavior. This school of thinking became known as *behaviorism*. Psychologists following the lead of Watson focused on the relationship between stimulus and response. They wanted to be very objective in their methods, and insisted that any experiment should be so reported that another psychologist could repeat it and thus check on the data and conclusions. Today most experimental psychologists favor some form of behaviorism. They claim that man can be described meaningfully in terms of his behavior, and that man is predictable.

We have spoken very briefly of several schools or systems of psychological thinking. Each has contributed to the science of psychology, although emphasizing different aspects. None can be taken as completely right or completely wrong. Today psychologists do not stress these different systems, but accept the best of each.

Do you lean more toward one system of psychological thinking than another? Do you think the authors of this book lean a bit more toward one system of thought than toward others?

GLOSSARY

absolute threshold The minimum amount of stimulus that a subject can detect.

acceleration On a graph of a learning situation, **positive acceleration** is a curve showing increasing returns; **uniform acceleration** is a curve indicating the same amount of improvement for equal units of practice; and **negative acceleration** is a curve showing decreasing returns.

acute hallucinosis A condition, often of alcoholic origin, characterized by hallucinations, especially auditory hallucinations.

adjustment mechanism Any form of behavior that aids the organism to adapt to its environment, reduce anxiety from frustration, and help satisfy needs.

adolescence The period between childhood and adulthood; roughly from ages twelve to twenty-one for girls and from thirteen to twenty-two for boys.

adrenal glands A pair of endocrine glands located over the kidneys.

affective experience An emotional experience that is measured in terms of both pleasantness or unpleasantness and intensity.

aggression Hostile or angry activity in which there is attack on other persons—physical injury, destruction or taking of their property, or ridicule.

all-or-nothing thinking A form of uncritical thinking.

alpha wave (or **rhythm**) An electrical brain wave that maintains a steady rhythm of fluctuations during normal waking periods.

amnesia Loss of memory as a result of physical or psychological factors.

anthropomorphism The attribution of human characteristics to beings other than man, as in fairy tales when animals talk to one another or to human beings.

anxiety A state of generalized fear and dread, which usually seems unattached to a specific object or event, and is often related to the future.

anxiety reaction A neurotic behavior disorder characterized by chronic, acute, diffuse anxiety and uneasiness.

approach gradient The increase in the strength of the tendency of an organism to move toward a desired goal the closer it gets to the goal.

aptitude The ability to acquire or the likelihood of acquiring, with training, some knowledge or skill. An **aptitude test** measures what an individual is likely to be able to accomplish with training rather than what he has accomplished already.

artificial punishment Punishment that is not the logical outcome of the behavior with which it is associated.

atmospheric perspective The difference in clarity between objects close by and objects far away. Objects that appear to be hazy are perceived as being distant; well-defined objects are perceived as being near.

attitude A persisting readiness to respond to a situation in a given evaluative way. **Social attitude** is the readiness to respond in a definite way to either general or specific social stimuli.

aura A sensationlike experience preceding or marking the onset of an epileptic seizure.

autistic thinking Wishful thinking in which the individual imagines his world as being more like the world in which he would like to live than is justified by the facts of reality.

autokinetic illusion The apparent motion of a small, fixed dot of light located in a dark room.

autonomic nervous system A functional classification for those parts of the central and peripheral nervous systems that govern involuntary behavior.

aversive therapy A method of treatment in which the organism is conditioned to avoid a previously desired object or goal.

avoidance gradient The increase in the

strength of the tendency of an organism to avoid an undesirable goal the closer it gets to the goal.

behavior The activity of an organism, including muscular, glandular, and thinking activity.

behavior disorder Activities of an individual that are considered as deviant from some norm, and that impair the person from meeting everyday responsibilities and functioning adequately in society.

behavior modification The changing of some undesirable behavior through the use of conditioning procedures.

behavior sampling A method of measuring certain specific traits of personality by means of an actual sampling of behavior.

behavioral sink An extreme increase in the density of a population in a given area so that the optimum number of individuals who can live in that area is exceeded.

brain lesion The destruction of a specific area of the brain through surgery, accident, or disease.

brainstorming A method of creative thinking in which all ideas that seem to have any bearing on a problem are noted but are not critically evaluated until some later time.

branching program A form of instruction that progresses step by step but also provides alternative, or branching, supplementary information if the subject makes incorrect responses.

brightness The quality of light as determined by the amplitude or intensity of the stimulating light waves. A dimension of a color in terms of its nearness in brilliance to white as contrasted with black.

case-study method A means of studying human behavior by constructing an impartial record of the individual's development, using documents and verbal reports of remembered events.

central nervous system A structural classification for the part of the nervous system composed of the brain and spinal cord.

chromosomes Small rodlike bodies in the cell nucleus. A human cell normally has 46 chromosomes, arranged in 23 pairs. (See **genes**.)

chronological age (CA) The number of years and months a person has lived from birth to the present.

clairvoyance The perception of an external object without the use of known sense organs.

classical (or **Pavlovian**) **conditioning** The repeated pairing of an unconditioned stimulus, which originally elicited a given response, with another stimulus until this conditioned stimulus elicits the given response.

clinical psychologist A psychologist who specializes in the diagnosis and treatment of personal and social maladjustment.

coding The process of transforming energy from one form to another. In relation to memory, the process whereby information temporarily stored in the short-term memory is translated into smaller "chunks" that can be more readily stored in the long-term memory.

cognitive dissonance Inconsistency or disagreement between the feelings and beliefs, or between the thoughts and overt behavior of an individual.

color blindness (color weakness) Inability to discriminate certain hues. In the most common form, red and green are seen as alike and are confused with a faded yellow.

communication The process of transmitting or exchanging symbols, such as words or gestures, which are understood by the two or more organisms engaged in the interaction.

compensation An attempt by an individual to make up for a deficiency in one area by expending extra time, effort, and energy in order to excel in some other area.

complementary colors Colors whose light waves when mixed in proper proportions are seen as gray.

concept The meaning, expressed in words or other symbols, which an individual attaches to the common property of a variety of objects or situations.

conditioned response (CR) The new or acquired response elicited by a stimulus not originally capable of arousing it.

conditioned stimulus (CS) The new stimulus, in a conditioning process, that was originally ineffective in eliciting a given response but has become capable of doing so.

conditioning The learning of some particular response to a stimulus.

conflict The state of tension or stress involved when an individual is faced simultaneously with either opposing or mutually exclusive impulses, tendencies, or desires. The most common kinds of conflict situations are *approach-approach, avoidance-avoidance,* and *approach-avoidance.*

conscience An individual's awareness of what is considered right or wrong by the culture or society in which he lives.

consciousness Awareness at the present moment, with resulting ability to react to the environment.

continuous reinforcement Rewarding an organism every time it gives a correct response.

control group A comparison group of subjects in an experiment usually matched to an experimental group but with whom the independent variable (condition being studied) is not present or is controlled.

convergence The movement of eye muscles that causes our pupils to come closer together as an object is brought closer than about twenty feet to our eyes, providing a cue to distance.

conversion reaction A neurotic reaction in which an individual's psychological disturbances are changed or converted into bodily disturbances, such as paralysis of an arm or inability to recall past experiences. This term is replacing the older terms *hysteria* and *conversion hysteria.*

convulsive disorders Diseases often characterized by varying degrees of convulsive behavior and unconsciousness, such as *grand mal, petit mal, Jacksonian,* and *psychomotor.*

correlation The tendency of certain paired measures to vary in relationship to each other.

cortex (cerebral) The surface or outer layer of the brain in man and higher animals.

counter-conditioning Replacing one conditioned response to a stimulus with another (usually incompatible) response. The process is often used to eliminate undesirable behavior.

creative thinking Nonroutine directed thinking in which the individual seeks new solutions to problems or new forms of artistic expression; the thinking is along new lines for the individual, although others may have done similar thinking.

crime An act or the performance of an act which, at the time of its commission, is forbidden and punishable by the laws of the place where it is committed and the society of that place, and which is subject to social condemnation.

cross-sectional method A means of studying human behavior by observing individuals of different age levels simultaneously.

cybernetics The study of mechanisms for the automatic control of information, such as automatic control systems.

data The mass of measured, factual materials collected and recorded for large groups. (*Data* is plural; the singular is *datum.*)

daydream Imaginative thinking engaged in by an individual while awake and usually involving fulfillment of wishes in some form. In the **conquering-hero daydream** the individual imagines himself performing great and heroic deeds while an appreciative audience applauds. The **suffering-hero daydream** is based on self-pity. Although the dreamer's imaginary suffering is painless or pleasantly painful, it elicits sympathy from others.

deductive reasoning The process of reasoning from general principles or rules to particular cases or consequences.

delinquency Socially nonconforming behavior, or crimes, committed by those who are not legally of age.

delirium tremens A behavior disorder of a chronic alcoholic characterized by apprehension, trembling, confusion, and hallucinations.

delusion A false belief that persists in spite of evidence or proof to the contrary.

dependent variable The factor the changed condition of which is considered to be a consequence of, to correspond to, or to depend on the independent variable in an experiment; it is often a response to a definite, measured stimulus.

desensitization A therapeutic technique based on classical conditioning principles used to reduce severe anxiety. The anxious situation is associated with pleasant stimuli to make it less threatening.

deviation IQ A method for computing an intelligence quotient by comparing the test score of an individual to the average score of a large number of persons of the same chronological age.

difference threshold The amount of change necessary for a subject to detect a difference in stimulation 50 percent of the time. **Just-noticeable difference** (JND) is the minimum amount of change necessary for a subject to be able to detect it.

discrimination The tendency to respond to certain stimuli of a given kind in one way and to respond to somewhat different stimuli in another way, as when an animal or person makes one response to a reinforced stimulus and another response to a stimulus that is not reinforced.

displaced aggression An adjustment mechanism in which an individual transfers his hostility from the original source of frustration to an object or person not directly associated with it.

dissociative reaction A behavior disorder in which certain parts of an individual's activities are in disagreement with, and separate from, the remaining parts of his personality—as in amnesia.

DNA (deoxyribonucleic acid) A chemical substance in the cell nucleus that is largely responsible for genetic inheritance.

dominant characteristic A characteristic that appears in all individuals of the first generation of descendants. A characteristic that prevents the appearance of the corresponding recessive characteristic.

drive A physiological condition that impels an organism to activity. The activity is usually directed toward some appropriate goal; for example, the hunger drive impels a person to food-seeking activity.

drug Here, any chemical substance that changes mood, perception, or awareness and can harm the individual or society if misused. **Hallucinogens** are drugs that produce sensory perceptions that have no basis in reality. **Stimulants** are drugs that cause increased functional behaviors. **Depressants** are drugs that decrease bodily activity. **Narcotics** are addictive drugs that relieve pain and induce sleep and coma.

duct gland A gland that discharges its secretion through an outlet onto an external or internal surface of the body.

ductless gland A gland having no duct (outlet). Its secretions are absorbed by the lymph or the blood.

ecology The study of the relationship between organisms and their environment.

ego An individual's conception of himself. Also, a psychoanalytic term referring to the rational aspect of the personality.

eidetic image An exceedingly vivid image (usually visual) which may be as clear as a perception but is generally recognized as subjective. Much more common in children than in adults. Popularly spoken of as a "photographic mind."

electroconvulsive therapy (ECT) A form of shock therapy in which an electric current is passed through the head for a very brief period of time, producing temporary loss of awareness. It is used in the treatment of behavior disorders.

electroencephalograph (EEG) An instrument that records the minute electrical oscillations, or brain waves, that accompany the activity of the brain. The record of the electrochemical changes is called an **electroencephalogram.**

emotion A stirred-up state of an individual. An acute disturbance of the individual involving widespread physiological changes, which are either pleasant or unpleasant.

empathy The ability to understand another person's attitudes, especially those that are emotionally toned. Sometimes spoken of as "inner mimicry."

environment The external forces, conditions, and influences that surround an organism's life and affect its activities.

epilepsy (See **convulsive disorders.**)

equilibrium sense The sense used to help a person maintain position of the body in space. It is governed by the inner ear.

ergograph An instrument for recording the amount of continuous work done with a certain set of muscles.

eugenics The science of heredity, especially as it is concerned with measures for improving the human species by attention to breeding.

exclusive group A group whose members place restrictions and limitations on the opportunity for others to participate.

experimental group A group of subjects in an experimental situation on whom the independent variable, or condition being studied, is varied.

explicit behavior Behavior that is easily observed and measured. Sometimes referred to as *overt* behavior.

extinction The dying out of an established conditioned response as a consequence of presenting the conditioned stimulus without the usual reinforcement.

extrasensory perception (ESP) Becoming aware of objects or events without the use of sense organs.

extrinsic reward An artificial reward, not inherently associated with the behavior being reinforced.

extroversion A general term indicating the tendency for an individual to center his interests in his external environment and in social life. Also spelled *extraversion*.

fantasy Imaginative thinking or daydreaming that is usually pleasant and provides the individual with some temporary relief from his frustrations.

feedback In problem-solving, the process of having a given bit of information or activity modify subsequent activity. (See **psychological feedback.**)

feelings Experiences of pleasantness or unpleasantness, including passions, desires, interests, likings, and dislikings. Also, *feeling* may refer to the sense of touch.

figure-ground relationship A situation perceived as divided into two parts—the part that is focused on is the figure, and the remaining part is the background.

filial love The love of children for their parents.

frame The single unit displayed at each step in programmed learning.

fraternal twins Twins developing from two ova (eggs) fertilized by two sperms. They may be of the same sex or different sexes.

friendship A social relationship between two persons in which there is mutual attraction, cooperation, trust, and reinforcement. The term is usually applied to relationships in which attraction for a person of the other sex is not present or is not emphasized. Friendship implies more than a casual acquaintanceship.

frustration The thwarting or blocking of motivated behavior so that a prompt and effective adjustment cannot be made. **Frustration tolerance** is the ability of an individual to withstand frustration without developing undesirable modes of response, such as becoming emotionally upset or neurotic.

fugue Amnesia with flight, in which a person with amnesia runs away from the area in which he usually resides.

functional disorder A mental illness with no demonstrable organic basis (although there may be such a basis). A behavior disorder depending on previous experiences in the person's life rather than on bodily defects.

galvanic skin response (GSR) The change in electrical resistance of the skin, especially as such change accompanies an emotional state.

galvanometer An instrument that measures the amount of resistance offered to an electric current passed through some area of an organism's body.

general decrement A decrease in the efficiency with which work is done over a period of time, due to such factors as fatigue.

generalization In conditioning—after a conditioned response has been established to a certain stimulus, other similar stimuli will also result in that response. Also, the reaching of a general conclusion or judgment based on specific facts or observations.

generation gap The belief that there are distinct differences in the attitudes and values of younger and older generations.

generosity error A tendency, when rating some situation or person, to overrate.

genes Factors in a cell that determine the transmission and development of hereditary characteristics. Tiny parts within chromosomes.

genius An individual of very superior intellectual ability. Used by some psychologists to refer to individuals with IQ's of 180 or higher.

genotype The sum of all the biological characteristics that an individual is capable of transmitting to his offspring, or a single such characteristic.

gifted Used to describe persons with exceptional or special abilities or persons of high intellectual ability (IQ's of about 140 to about 180.)

goal gradient The theory that the shorter the delay in time between performance of the correct response and reinforcement of that response, the more likely it is that an organism will learn that response.

gonads Sex glands that provide the sperm and egg cells for reproduction, and produce hormones which determine secondary sex characteristics and influence sexual behavior.

group atmosphere The general emotional state of a group at a particular time.

group climate The kind of atmosphere that prevails in a group over a considerable period of time.

group cohesiveness The mutual, general attraction that all members feel toward the others in the group.

group dynamics The study of the foundation and functioning of groups, and the interpersonal relationships that develop between the members.

group morale The prevailing attitude of members of the group to work willingly and loyally toward group goals.

group therapy A psychotherapeutic treatment in which a small group of people meet to discuss their problems and to interact.

hallucination A misinterpretation of ideas as perceptions. A senselike perception for which there is no appropriate external stimulus, as in the case of a psychotic person who hears voices speaking to him although there are no voices or other sounds that might be interpreted as voices.

halo effect A tendency, when one person is rating another, to be influenced by an estimate of some other trait or by a general impression of the individual being rated. The general impression may be either favorable or unfavorable.

heredity The sum of the characteristics transmitted from parent to child by the germ plasm.

heuristic concept A formulation that originates in order to explain something. It is an approximation, unprovable, having no existence on its own.

hormones Chemical substances produced by endocrine glands.

hue A technical term for "color" (red, green, blue, yellow, etc.). The characteristic of a visual impression as determined by the wavelength of the light stimulus.

hypnosis An artificially induced state characterized chiefly by extreme suggestibility. Usually, though not always, resembling sleep but physiologically different from it.

hypochondriac A person who is preoccupied with his health and bodily ailments, and tends to exaggerate or imagine numerous symptoms.

hypothesis An assumption adopted as a tentative explanation of observed facts and as the basis for further reasoning or investigation.

id A psychoanalytic term referring to the unconscious primitive urges, mainly sexual and aggressive in nature, that underlie behavior.

identical twins Twins developing from a single fertilized ovum (egg), thus having the same heredity. Always of the same sex.

identification An adjustment mechanism in which an individual imitates, or closely affiliates with, the behavior of some other person or group.

illusion A false perception.

imagination The reproduction and reorganization of past experiences into a present ideational experience.

implicit behavior Behavior not easily observable by another person without the aid of special, sensitive measuring instruments. For example, implicit speech consists of inaudible, tiny muscular movements of the speech apparatus during thinking, which can be detected only by use of very delicate instruments. Sometimes referred to as *covert* behavior.

imprinting A special kind of very rapid learning that occurs in some animals, notably birds, at a certain early stage in their development. It is relatively insusceptible to forgetting or extinction.

inclusive group A group whose members strive to expand their activities and include more people.

incubation A stage in creative thinking characterized by absence of active thinking about a given problem. A period in which no obvious progress in problem-solving occurs.

independent variable The factor the effects of which are being examined in an experiment. It is selected and then manipulated by the experimenter in some systematic and predetermined manner while all, or as many as possible, other variables are held constant. The independent variable is often a stimulus, the response to which is the dependent variable.

inductive reasoning The process of reasoning from particular facts or cases to general conclusions.

insanity A legal term for any behavior disorder in which an individual is judged to be incapable of assuming normal responsibility for his acts. (See **psychosis.**)

insight An apparently rather sudden grasp of the relationships involved in problem solving.

inspiration A step in creative thinking which follows preparation and incubation and in which there is a rather sudden solution of the problem under consideration.

instinct (See **species-specific behavior.**)

intelligence The ability of a complex organism to adapt itself adequately to its environment. Now thought to include a number of specific factors.

intelligence quotient (IQ) The ratio of mental age to chronological age times 100. IQ = (MA/CA) × 100. (See **deviation IQ**.)

interaction Face-to-face communication among persons in a group.

interaction-oriented group A group whose primary purpose is to establish social contacts and to interact with others.

interest A set or preparation that motivates a person in a certain direction.

intermittent reinforcement The rewarding of some, but not all, correct responses.

interposition A cue to depth perception which indicates that when one object partially blocks the view of another, the object blocking the view is closer than the object behind it.

interviewing A method of judging a person in a relatively short time by means of standardized (or an informal) conversational situation.

intrinsic reward A reward that is logically associated with, and an integral part of, the behavior being reinforced.

introversion A general term indicating the tendency for an individual to center his interests in himself and his own experiences.

inventory, personality A standardized questionnaire or self-rating scale in which an individual gives information about his attitudes and overt behavior, which can then be evaluated in terms of norms.

just-noticeable difference (See **difference threshold**.)

kinesthetic sense The muscle, tendon, and joint sense, which is important in determining body movement and position.

Korsakoff's psychosis A behavior disorder of some older chronic alcoholics that is characterized by an inability to remember previous experiences, especially events that have just taken place. Often there is also an unsystematic falsification of memory.

laissez-faire A French term meaning "allow to do." A laissez-faire leader exercises little, if any, control, guidance, or assistance to his group.

latent learning Learning that takes place in the absence of reinforcement but is utilized when reinforcement is given. Learning that becomes evident only when it is being used.

leader The individual in a group who exerts the greatest influence on the members of the group. He or she guides the thinking of the group and initiates, directs, or organizes the activity of the group.

learning Acquiring the ability to respond adequately to a situation. The modification of behavior through experience.

linear perspective The perception of objects as smaller and closer together the more distant they are from the observer.

linear program A form of instruction that contains a series of statements arranged in a step-by-step progression to which the subject responds and then learns immediately whether or not his answer is correct.

long-term memory The storage and retention of information that has been situated briefly in the short-term memory.

longitudinal method A means of studying human behavior by observing the development of the same individual or group over a considerable period of time.

loudness The intensity of a sound, determined primarily by the amplitude of the sound waves.

manic-depressive A psychosis that usually includes periods of excitement with overactivity and periods of melancholy with underactivity.

maturation Bodily growth or development and the accompanying behavioral changes.

maze A learning device consisting of a correct pathway and blind alleys. It can be used in both animal and human learning experiments.

memory trace The assumed changes that occur in the nervous system between the time learning takes place and the time it is recalled. It is hypothesized that these changes explain the process of retention.

mental age (MA) A measure of mental development in terms of the ability of average individuals of various ages, especially children.

mental deficiency A term used to refer to the condition of individuals of subnormal intellectual ability. Some psychologists reserve this term for those whose lack of ability is a result of brain damage or other organic defect. (See **mental retardation.**)

mental maturity The condition of complete general mental development. In terms of intelligence testing, mental maturity is attained at the time when a person ceases to improve his score on a general intelligence test as he grows older. Also, may be called *intellectual maturity*.

mental retardation A term used to refer to the condition of individuals of subnormal intellectual ability. Some psychologists reserve this term for those who have undue difficulty in learning but with no evident organic basis for the difficulty.

mind The organization of behavior. (The word is seldom used in psychological writings.)

mnemonic device An artificial aid to learning; a catchword or formula employed to facilitate recall. Usually of very limited and temporary value.

mood A mild emotional state that lingers for some time, but not permanently, after the emotion-producing situation has passed.

motivation A general term referring to regulation of behavior in such a way as to satisfy the individual's needs and enable him to work toward his goals. Aspirations, attitudes, and interests are involved.

multiple personality A dissociative reaction involving the development of two or more usually separate personalities within the same individual.

nerve impulse The current or disturbance that travels along a nerve fiber following stimulation.

neurosis (plural, *neuroses*) A milder form of behavior disorder than a true psychosis. A neurotic person needs medical and psychological care, although usually he does not have to enter a mental hospital for treatment.

nonsense syllable. A meaningless syllable that can be pronounced but does not represent a meaningful word. For example, *lar, bic, ral*.

norm A standard or representative value for a group.

observation A method used in psychology to gather data; may be **natural** (uncontrolled) or **directed** (controlled in the laboratory). Usually done by someone trained in the procedure.

obsessive-compulsive Describes psychoneurotic behavior characterized by preoccupation with unwanted ideas and persistent impulses to repeat certain acts over and over.

operant conditioning The strengthening of a given response by immediately presenting a reinforcing stimulus if (and only if) the response occurs.

ordinal position The place of an individual in the family as determined by birth order: first child, second child, and so on.

organic disorder A behavior disorder that can be attributed to damage to or disease in the body, especially the nervous system.

organism Any living thing capable of maintaining its existence by itself. Organisms may be divided into two classes, plants and animals. In psychology, the term almost always refers to animals.

organismic approach A theory of personality that emphasizes the total combination of forces, both external and internal, that interact to form personality.

overcompensation An extreme effort by an individual to overcome feelings of weakness, guilt, or inferiority in some area; excessive compensation.

overlearning Learning in which practice goes beyond the point of bare, required mastery.

panic A rather sudden, highly emotional reaction of fear.

paradoxical sleep The first stage of sleep, in which an individual is only slightly asleep according to EEG records and yet is difficult to arouse when having rapid eye movements (REMs).

paranoid personality A personality disorder characterized by emotional detachment, fear, and feelings of being persecuted.

paranoid reactions Reactions characterized by persistent, systematized delusions of grandeur, persecution, and reference (the individual believes, without justification, that people are talking about him or doing things to him).

parapsychology A branch of study concerned with phenomena that are generally considered very unusual, fantastic, and even allegedly supranormal: trances, telepathy, clairvoyance, apparitions, and so on.

parathyroid glands A pair of ductless glands, located beside the thyroid gland, that regulate the balance of calcium and phosphorus in the body.

parental love The love of parents for their children.

paresis, general An organic psychosis resulting from syphilitic infection of the brain. A person suffering from paresis is spoken of as a *paretic*.

partial reinforcement (See **intermittent reinforcement**.)

pathological intoxication A behavior disorder of an alcoholic who reacts in a violent and extreme way (he may kill), often after having consumed only a small amount of alcohol.

peer A person considered to be one's equal, or a companion or associate of about the same age or ability.

perception Sensation plus meaning. The process of getting to know the environment by means of the senses.

performance test A specialized test in which verbal directions play a minimum role.

peripheral nervous system A structural classification for the nerves that branch out from the spinal cord and brain.

personality The unique or individual pattern of a person's life; the fundamental organization of an individual's characteristic adjustment to his environment; that which sets a person apart from other individuals and determines how they respond to him.

phenomenon (plural, *phenomena*) Any observable fact or event.

phenotype The actual, observable characteristic that makes its appearance or is manifested in an individual.

phi phenomenon Successive presentations of two separated stimuli, which are perceived as a single stimulus in motion—the simplest form of stroboscopic motion.

phobia A strong, unreasonable, persistent fear.

pitch The highness or lowness of a sound as determined chiefly by the vibration frequency.

pituitary gland A ductless gland, located on the underside of the brain, secreting several hormones that influence growth, sex development, and metabolism.

placebo Any preparation that contains no medicine but is given to an individual who believes that he is receiving a medicine.

plateau In a learning graph, an intermediate period of little or no apparent progress preceded and followed by periods of measurable progress.

popularity The state of being pleasing to, admired by, or esteemed by many persons.

posthypnotic suggestion The procedure of suggesting to a subject during hypnosis that he or she perform a particular activity some time after being awakened from the hypnotic state.

precognition The seeming "perception" of a future event through extrasensory means and without rational inference.

prejudice An attitude, either for or against a given social question, which prevents one from evaluating new evidence dispassionately.

proactive inhibition The tendency for present learning to interfere with the recall of later learned material. (See **retroactive inhibition**.)

procrastination An escape or withdrawal mechanism that gives an individual temporary relief from a distressful situation by postponing his attack on a task.

programmed book A teaching device, combining modern principles of learning with traditional teaching methods, in which material to be learned is broken up into a series of prearranged simple steps. Such a book is so arranged that correct responses are reinforced immediately.

programmed learning Learning from material arranged in a series of sequential steps that enable the learner to proceed with a minimum of error and receive a maximum of reinforcement.

projection An adjustment mechanism in which an individual attributes to others his own unacceptable motives or thoughts, or places the blame for his difficulties on others.

projective technique A method of evaluating personality in which an individual externalizes his ideas, emotional states, and motives by attributing them in a free and unrestricted manner to other individuals or objects in the environment, for instance, telling what he "sees" in ink blots or in a given picture.

propaganda Any organized attempt to influence attitudes—that is, to spread particular ideas or beliefs.

pseudogroup effect Falsely attributing certain results to group influence when no group communication has occurred.

psychiatry A division of the body of medical knowledge pertaining to the diagnosis, care, and treatment of persons suffering from both mild and severe mental disorders. A **psychiatrist** is a physician specializing in the study and treatment of mental disorders.

psychoanalysis A system of psychological theory and treatment first devised by Sigmund Freud.

psychodrama A spontaneous play in which individuals act out situations relevant to their personal problems.

psychokinesis The subdivision of parapsychology in which it is said that the thoughts of an individual influence the activity of some physical object or the outcome of some event.

psychological feedback Knowledge of results. The process of providing the individual with information as to the correctness of previous responses so that he can make adjustments in his behavior.

psychology The science that studies the behavior of organisms.

psychosis A serious prolonged behavior disorder. The individual having a psychosis is said to be *psychotic*.

psychosomatic disorder An illness in which physical disturbances, such as ulcers and allergies, are attributable to or aggravated by prolonged emotional disturbances.

psychotherapy The treatment of behavior disorders through the use of psychological techniques by psychologists, psychiatrists, and psychoanalysts.

punishment Any form of unpleasant or painful stimulation applied to an experimental subject for nonperformance of a response which the experimenter has chosen as the correct response. Popularly, it is any penalty inflicted on a person or animal for wrongdoing.

pupillometrics A method of studying emotional reactions to pleasant and unpleasant stimuli by measuring the size of the pupil of the subject's eye when stimuli are presented. A pleasant stimulus causes the pupil to enlarge; an unpleasant stimulus results in contraction.

questionnaire method A means of studying behavior by giving a list of questions on some subject to a selected group of individuals, and treating the answers statistically.

rapid eye movements (REMs) The movements of an individual's eyes that occur when he is asleep and usually indicate that he is dreaming.

rating The assigning of a rank or score to an individual. Also, an individual's position in a scale of values. A **rating scale** provides a uniform method of securing judgments of an individual's personality traits.

rationalization The process of justifying conduct or opinions by inventing socially acceptable reasons. The rationalizer may not realize that he is explaining his behavior in terms of socially approved and high-sounding reasons instead of real reasons.

reaction time The interval of time between the beginning of a stimulus and the beginning of a voluntary response to it.

reasoning A form of thinking in which one attempts to solve a present problem on the basis of general principles derived from elements in two or more previous experiences. A form of thinking in which experiences are organized in such a way that conclusions can be reached that are consistent with all known relevant facts.

recessive characteristic A characteristic that is latent and does not appear in the first generation of descendants, although it may appear in subsequent generations. A characteristic that does not appear in the presence of the corresponding dominant characteristic.

reflex A relatively simple, unlearned, involuntary response to a stimulus.

regression An adjustment mechanism by which a frustrated individual retreats to an earlier known, less mature, and usually less adequate, way of meeting his problems.

reinforcement In classical or Pavlovian conditioning, presentation of the unconditioned stimulus immediately following the conditioned stimulus, such as giving an animal an electric shock immediately following the sounding of a bell. In operant or instrumental conditioning, the strengthening of a response when it leads to satisfaction, typically a reward of some kind. If the reinforcement does not directly satisfy a need but had previously been associated with such satisfaction, the term **secondary reinforcement** is used. Reinforcement is said to be **positive** if its presentation strengthens a response and **negative** if its removal strengthens a response.

repression An unconscious process by which an individual selectively "forgets" unpleasant or undesirable situations that, remembered, would result in feelings of shame, pain, or guilt.

research Any systematic, careful, firsthand observation of phenomena in order to better understand the constitution or operation of the environment.

response Any organic process involving activity of a muscle or gland and resulting from stimulation. A reaction.

retarded individuals Persons of limited intellectual ability, usually classified under three headings: (1) **Mildly retarded.** Individuals who can take care of their personal needs and can often make a fairly satisfactory adjustment in the community, especially if given some social guidance. They have IQ's that range from about 53 to 69, and they are educable. (2) **Moderately retarded.** Individuals who can learn to take care of themselves to a limited extent and can do some useful work but need constant supervision. Their IQ ranges from about 36 to 52, and most are educable. (3) **Severely retarded.** Individuals who are of such low intellectual ability that they are unable to care for their needs or make any kind of adequate social adjustment. Their IQ's range from about 35 down to as low as can be measured. Those in the upper reaches of this classification can be trained to take care of their bodily needs. The most extreme cases (IQ's 20 and below) are known as **profoundly retarded.**

retention Persistent aftereffect of an experience, which may result in modified subsequent experience; a holding onto what has been learned.

retinal disparity The difference in the two images projected onto the retinas of the right and left eyes. This slight difference in the viewing angle of the two eyes contributes to depth perception.

retroactive inhibition The tendency of later learned material to interfere with the recall of previously learned material. (See **proactive inhibition.**)

reward (See **reinforcement.**)

RNA (ribonucleic acid) A chemical substance, manufactured by DNA, which helps to implement cellular development and is thought to be important in memory.

role The kind of behavior expected of an individual in a specific situation. **Role model** is a person whom another individual selects to pattern his behavior after. **Role playing** is a technique for teaching principles of interpersonal relationships by having individuals act out parts in a spontaneous play.

Rorschach test A projective technique for evaluating personality. Ten ink blots as standardized by Hermann Rorschach are presented to the individual under study.

sampling The selection for study of a set of individuals or measurements from the total population or group. In **random sampling** the selection is made solely by chance and in such a way that every individual or measurement has an equal and independent chance of being included in the sample. In **stratified sampling** the total number of individuals or measurements in the population is first divided into a number of nonoverlapping groups and then a random sampling is taken within each group. The number of cases in each group is proportional to that group's representation in the total population.

saturation The degree to which any "color" differs from a gray of the same brightness. Pure colors are highly saturated; such colors as maroon and pink are low in saturation.

scapegoat An individual (or group) that bears the blame for the misdeeds or mistakes of others.

schizoid personality A personality disorder characterized by emotional coldness and detachment, and avoidance of competition.

schizophrenia A psychosis characterized by seclusiveness and extreme withdrawal from the realities of life, peculiar mannerisms, emotional blunting, delusions, and disorientation as to time and place. Includes such forms as *simple, hebephrenic, catatonic,* and *paranoid schizophrenia.*

secondary reinforcement When, as a result of being associated with a primary reinforcement, some object or event becomes itself a reinforcer.

self-actualization The belief that man innately strives to make his potential abilities develop into actual or real abilities.

self-concept The view that an individual has of himself. In Freudian terms, his ego.

semantic differential The different qualities and values given to the same words by different individuals.

senility Mental and physiological damage or injury incident to old age.

sensation The physiological arousal of a sense organ by a stimulus. Sensation does not involve organization, meaning, or association.

sensory deprivation Making it physiologically impossible for an organism to use one or more of its senses or placing it in an environment where there is practically no sensory stimulation.

serial learning Learning responses in a prescribed sequence; verbatim learning of poetry, prose, a list of words, or syllables; learning motor activities in a prescribed order.

short-term memory The process of initial and brief storage of sensory information, which is accessible to immediate recall.

sibling rivalry A child's inability to share parental affection and recognition with a brother or sister, regardless of respective ages.

siblings Offspring of the same parents, irrespective of age or sex of such offspring.

size constancy The tendency of a known object to appear to be the same size, regardless of how close or far away it is.

social facilitation The increase in motivation and effort that arises from the stimulus provided by the presence of other people.

sociodrama A spontaneously acted short play in which the members of a group act out the roles of the characters in the play, thus helping the group to study some problem of interpersonal behavior.

sociometry The study of the interpersonal relations of a group by having each member express an opinion about every other member. A diagram of the interaction among group members is called a **sociogram**.

sociopathic personality A personality disorder characterized by violations of the customs, rules, mores, and laws of the society in which the person lives.

sour-grapes rationalization A form of rationalization in which a person says that he does not want that which he cannot have or achieve.

species-specific behavior Behavior characteristics of the members of a given species acting under the same or highly similar circumstances. This term is replacing the term *instinctive behavior*.

spontaneous recovery The reappearance of a conditioned response after a rest period following extinction but without further reinforcement.

status An individual's position and degree of acceptance in a group.

stereotype A preconceived idea of the appearance or behavior of individuals of a given group—racial, political, occupational, etc.

stereotyped behavior An adjustment mechanism in which an individual displays inflexible behavior—behavior that is not altered by circumstances.

stimulus An energy or energy change acting on a receptor (sense organ) and exciting it. A situation or event inside or outside an organism that results in activity of some kind.

stimulus generalization A situation in which an organism associates one stimulus with a similar stimulus and because of the similarity responds to the second stimulus in the same way that it responds to the original.

stroboscopic motion Apparent motion produced by the presentation of stationary stimuli in rapid succession.

subject The person or animal exposed to any kind of experimental treatment and whose behavior is then observed and measured.

sublimation The transfer or redirection of emotionally aroused energy, especially sexual energy, into more socially approved forms of creative or social expression.

subliminal perception The perception of stimuli so weak that the individual is not aware of their influence on his behavior.

successive approximations The reinforcement of overt responses on successive trials that more and more closely resemble the ultimate desired response.

superego A psychoanalytic term for that which is commonly called "conscience" and which criticizes the ego. The ethical or moral aspects of personality.

surrogate An organism (or object) that serves as a substitute for some other organism in the life of an animal or human being.

sweet-lemons rationalization A form of rationalization in which a person has something he does not want, but says that what he has is just what he wants.

symbol An object, act, or sound that becomes a representative substitute for something else.

task-oriented group A group whose primary purpose is to perform a specific job or task.

teaching machine A somewhat mechanical auto-instructional device in which the learner indicates his answers to a question or his solution of a problem and then is reinforced immediately. The material presented for learning may be determined by the learner's performance.

telepathy The alleged communication of thought from one person to another by other than the usual means of sensory stimulation.

theory A logically organized principle, based on considerable data, proposed as an explanation for what is observed. A theory is based on more evidence than is a hypothesis.

therapy Treatment of behavior disorders to bring about psychological and social adjustment. Includes such forms as drug, environmental, supportive, client-centered, and group therapy. (See **psychotherapy**.)

thinking Implicit activity by means of which a person or animal manipulates past experiences (not physically present to the senses) through the use of symbols. Much human thinking is subvocal or covert speech behavior.

thyroid gland A ductless gland, located in the front of the neck close to the larynx (in the upper part of the windpipe), which influences metabolism and growth. The hormone secreted by this gland is thyroxin, largely iodine in content.

tic A twitch of a muscle or muscle group, especially in the face. It is not subject to voluntary control.

timbre The quality of a sound as determined by the complexity of the sound waves—that is, by the pattern of overtones.

tone A sound whose stimulus consists of a regular wave.

trait A relatively constant pattern or dimension of behavior. The characteristics that indicate similarities between people. Those traits which are characteristic of most persons are spoken of as *primary traits*.

transfer In psychology, the effect of prior learning on later learning. If the prior learning facilitates later learning, there is said to be **positive transfer**. If the prior learning interferes with later learning, there is said to be **negative transfer**.

unconditioned response (UCR) The response elicited by the original (unconditioned) stimulus at the beginning of a conditioning process.

unconditioned stimulus (UCS) The original stimulus that elicits the desired response before the conditioning process begins.

unconscious The absence of an awareness of some desires, experiences, concepts, and information which, under ordinary circumstances, are not generally available on the conscious level.

unit character A characteristic of an individual that is inherited on an all-or-none basis and is dependent on the presence or absence of a single gene.

variable A condition in a research study that can change in amount or quality.

visible spectrum Hues that are visible to the eye arranged according to wavelengths, with violet being a short wavelength and red a long wavelength.

work curve A graphical representation of the relationship between work efficiency and time in carrying out a particular task.

Zeigarnik effect The theory that uncompleted tasks are remembered longer than completed tasks.

INDEX

Page numbers in *italics* that have *c, f* or *p* written before them refer to charts or tables (*c*), features (*f*) or pictures (*p*). Page numbers in **boldface** show that the word's meaning is given on that page. (In addition, many words are defined in the Glossary.)

Abilities, 159, 164. *See also* Intelligence
Absolute threshold, 242
Acceleration curves in learning, 73
Achievement: inferiority feelings and, 296; intelligence and, 172, 174–75, 182–83
Addicts. *See* Drugs
Adjustment mechanisms, 278; aggression, displaced, 282–**83**, *p283;* cognitive dissonance, **286**–88, *p287;* compensation, **278**–79; decision avoidance, 283; identification, **280,** *p280;* overcompensation, **279**–80; procrastination, **282;** projection, **281;** rationalization, **283**–86; regression, **281**–82; repression, **281;** stereotyped behavior, **281**
Adler, Alfred, 121
Adolescents: boy-girl relationships, 154–55, *c306,* 306–07; cultural differences in behavior, 142; dating, 154–55, 305–06; daydreaming, 297–99; drug use (*see also* Drugs), 470, *p470;* emotional problems, 292–312; family conflicts, 155, 302–04, *c303;* friendships, 379–80, *p381;* independence, striving for, 155; inferiority feelings, 292–97; love, romantic, 155, 305, *p307,* 307–09; motor development, 148; older persons and, 304, *p304,* 371–74; puppy love, 155; role learning, **309**–12; sibling rivalry, **302–03;** social development, 155; thrills and thrill-seeking, 299–302, *p300*
Adrenals, 151, 224–25
Advertising: personality, popular concept of, and, 116; as propaganda (*see also* Propaganda), *p457,* 458
Affection: deprivation experiments, 376–79, *p377;* family and, 118, 349, *p350,* 352–54, *p353;* need for, 378. *See also* Love
Affective experience, 292
Age: chronological, **169**
Aggression: displaced, 282–**83**, *p283;* hostile, and competition, 444; love and, *f424–25;* world, *f342–43*
Aid in distress, *p430;* assault reactions, 429–30; compassion, 436–37; exploitation victims, aid to, 433–34; failures to offer, 428–29; failure to offer, reasons for, 430–33, *p432;* mishaps, minor, and, 434–36, *p435;* victimizing distressed, 436
Air pollution, 472, *p473;* effects, 472–73; reduction, 473; student concern, 474
Alcoholism: acute hallucinosis, 332–33; alcoholic psychosis, **332**–33; counter-conditioning, 34–35; delirium tremens, 332; drunkenness, 332, *p332;* help for alcoholics, 333–34; pathological intoxication, 333; Korsakoff's psychosis, 333
"All-or-nothing" thinking, 94–95
Alpha waves, 220
Amanites, 447–49
American Psychiatric Association, 318, 329
American Psychoanalytic Association, 318
American Psychological Association (APA), 13, 15, 21, 206, 318, 466
Amnesia, 322
Anastasi, Anne, *f264–65*
Animals: affection deprivation and, 376–78; aggression and affection, *f424–25;* anthropomorphism, **20;** behavior, 20, 144; brains, 218, 219, 225; classical conditioning, 32–33, *p33,* 34, *p34;* concepts and, 89–90, 92–93; emotions and digestion, 229–30; experiments, 20–21; fear of, 152, 363, *p363, p365;* heredity experiments, 196–97; imprinting, 201–02, *p202;* insight learning, 49–50, *p50,* 51; instincts, 230–33, **231,** *p233;* latent learning, 71; malnutrition effects, 203–04; maturation and learning, 199, 201–02, *p202;* memory trace transmission, RNA and, 80–81; operant conditioning, 38–41, *p39, p40,* 43–46, *p45;* overpopulation and behavior, 476–78; pecking order, 440, *c440;* pollution effects, 473; psychosomatic disorders, *p323,* 323–24; social cooperation, 445–46; social facilitation, 437–38; speech and concepts, 92–93; trial-and-error learning, 31–32; visual cliff, 252
Anthropology, 6–7
Anthropomorphism, 20
Anxiety, 320; bound, 322–23; free-floating, 322; reactions, neurotic, **322**–23
Appearance: inferiority feelings and, 294–95
Applied psychology, 496
Approach gradient, 271–72, *c272, c273*
Approximations, successive: in operant conditioning, 40
Aptitude tests, *p485,* **485**–87
Assault: failures to offer aid, 428–29; reactions to, 429–30
Astrology, 8–9
Athletic ability: popularity and, *c382,* 382–83
Atmosphere, group, 404, *p404*
Attention: divided, 241; inattention, and forgetting, 79; individual and, 240–41; maintenance, 241; stimulus, **239**–40, *p240*
Attitudes, 254. *See also* Social attitudes
Aura, 221
Autistic thinking, 101
Autokinetic illusion, 420–21
Autonomic nervous system, 215–16; operant conditioning, 39
Aversive therapy, 337

Basic psychology, 496
Beers, Clifford, 318
Behavior, 5; animal, 20; biological influences, 214–35; conditioning, *see* Classical conditioning, Operant conditioning; cross-sectional studies, **143**–44; cultural differences, 142; development and, 140–44, *c141;* emotional, *p4,* **150**–53, *c151, p226,* 226–30, *p230;* environment and, *f112–13,* 192, *f342–43;* explicit, **88;** handicaps and, 146; heredity and, 192; hypnotized, 11–12; implicit, **88;** imprinting, 201–02, *p202;* instinctual, 230–33,

231, *p233;* language development and, *p149,* 149–50, *c150;* learning and, 30–31; longitudinal studies, **143,** 144; mental development and, **158**–60, *c159;* motor development and, *p147,* 147–49; overpopulation effects, 476–78; personality and, 116–36, 156–58; physical development and, **144**–46; punishment and, 46; reflex, **31,** 231; sleep and, 233–36; social development and, **153**–56, *p154;* species-specific, 230–33, **231,** *p233;* stereotyped, **281;** study methods, *p143,* 143–44; theories, *f506*–08; unlearned, 31, 231. *See also* specific subjects

Behavior disorders, 316–17; aggression and social survival, *f342*–43; biochemistry, 317; curability, 325; functional, **317;** functional psychoses, 326–30; job opportunities in fields of, 319; institutional care, 318–19, *p319,* 334, 335, 338; misconceptions concerning, 324–25; neurosis (psychoneurosis), 319–24; organic, **317;** organic psychoses, 330–34; personality, 334; prevalence, 317; prevention, 318–19, 338; psychosis, **324**–34; treatment, 7, 318–19, *p319,* 334–38, *c335, p336*

Behaviorism, *f507–08*

Behavior modification, 52, 337; aversive therapy, 337; counter-conditioning, 337; desensitization, 337; employee productivity and, 494; token economies, 338

Behavior sampling, *p132,* 131–32; cautions in using, 133; of cheating, 132; graphology, 133; and prediction of behavior, 132–33

Binet, Alfred, 165–66

Biochemistry: emotions and, 151; functional disorders and, 317; memory and, 80–81; mental retardation, 180; schizophrenia and, 329

Biology: brain, 217–23, *p219, p220, p222;* drives and, 206–07; glands, *p223,* 223–26; nervous systems, 214–16, *p215;* psychology and, 6, 214; reaction time, 216–17, *p217;* roles, social, and, 310. *See also* specific subjects

Birth injuries, 180

Birth order (ordinal position): and personality, 118

Blacks: dehumanizing influence of ghettos on, *f342*–43; intelligence of, *f189,* 206, 209

Body type: personality and, 123,

124–25; ectomorph, 123; endomorph, 123; mesomorph, 123

Brain, 215, 217, *p220;* cortex, **217,** 218–20, *p219, p220,* 227; disorders, acute and chronic, **331;** disorders, convulsive, 220–23, *p222,* 225; drugs and, 469; electrical stimulation, 217; electroencephalograph (EEG), **217,** 220–21, *p222;* hydrocephalus, 181; hypnosis and, 11; hypothalamus, 227; lesion, **217;** localization of functions, 218–19, *p219,* 227; malnutrition and, 180, 203, 204; personality and, 219–20; pollutant damage, 473; size and intelligence, 218, 225; syphilitic infection, 331; waves, 217, 220, *p222*

Brainstorming, 98–99

Brainwashing, 260

Buzz sessions, *c415,* 415–16

Case-study method, 17

Catatonic schizophrenia, 329

Central nervous system, 214–15, *p215*

Character, 117

Cheating, 132, 358, *p359;* attitudes toward, 358; competition and, 358–59, *f443,* 443–44; learning to cheat, 357–58; and programmed learning, 48–49, 358, *p359;* thrill-seeking, 357

Chemistry, 6

Chromosomes, 193–96

Clairvoyance, 13

Clark, Kenneth B., *f342*–43

Classical conditioning, 32–34, *c33;* animal training, 32–33, *p33,* 34, *p34;* applications, *p34,* 34–35; conditioned response, **33**–34, 35–36; conditioned stimulus, **33**–34; counter-conditioning, **34–35;** counter-conditioning therapies, 337; discrimination in, **38,** extinction, **35**–36, *c36,* 38; generalization in, *p37,* **37**–38; operant conditioning compared with, 38–42; Pavlov's experiments, 32–33, *p33;* recovery, spontaneous, **36,** *c36,* 38; reinforcement, **36,** 38; terms related to, 35–38; unconditioned response, **33**–34, 35–36; unconditioned stimulus, **33**–34, 35–36

Classroom techniques, 413; buzz sessions, *c415,* 415–16; discussion, group-centered, 413–17, *c414, c415;* lectures, 413; question-answer, 413

Client-centered therapy, 336

Clinical psychologists, 8, 498

Clothing, and inferiority feelings, 295

Coding: memory and, 81

Cognitive dissonance, 286–87, *p287;* reducing or justifying, 287–88

Cognitive psychology, *f507*

Cognitive theory of learning, 52

Coincidence: confusion of with cause, 95

Color(s): blindness or weakness, 245–46; brightness, **243**–44, *p244;* complementary, **244**–45; effects, 245; hue, **243;** saturation, **244,** *p244,* 245; spectrum, visible, 243

Communication, 405–06; benefits, 407; competition and, 441–42, *p442,* 445; cooperation and, 449–50; empathy, **406;** feedback, group, **407**–08; gap, 372; gestures and signs, *p406,* 407; group size and, 407; jargon, **407;** language development and, 149–50; patterns in groups, 408–13; *c409–10, c412;* in small groups, 405–13, *c409–10, c412;* status and, **408**

Compassion, 436–37

Compensation, 278–79; overcompensation, **279**–80

Competition, 439; cheating and, 358–59, *p443,* 443–44; communication and, 441–42, *p442,* 445; disadvantages, 443–45; hostile aggression, 444; international, 442–43, 444; learning and, 63, *p64;* losing, effects of, 444; minorities and, 442, 444; pecking order, 439–40, *c440;* reducing disadvantages of, 444–45; studies of, 440–42; threats and, 440–42, *p442;* winning at any price, 443–44

Computers: analogue, 104; dating and, 305–06; digital, 103–04; psychotherapy and, 337; "thinking," 103, *p104,* 104–05

Concepts, 89; animals and, 89–90, 92–93; children and, *p90,* 90–91; formation, 91–92, *p93;* heuristic, **6;** thinking and, 89–93

Conditioning, 32; classical, **32–38;** friendships and, 380–81; insight compared with, 51; operant, **38**–49, therapies, 337–38. *See also* Classical conditioning; Operant conditioning

Conflict: approach-approach, *c271,* **271**–72, 275, *c275;* approach-avoidance, *c273,* **273**–74, 275, *c275;* avoidance-avoidance, **272,** *c272,* 275, *c275;* as cause of frustration, 270–71. *See also* Frustration and conflict

Conformity: generation gap and,

371–74, *p372;* to small-group norms, *p420,* 420–21; ordinal position (birth order) and, 118; to peer group standards, 373–74
Conscience, 354, development, 354–55; "hurting," and behavior standards, 355–56
Control group, 19
Convergence: in spatial perception, **246**
Conversion reaction (conversion hysteria), **322**
Convulsive disorders, 220–21, *p222,* 225; aura, **221;** causes, 222; grand mal, 221; helping victims of, 222–23; Jacksonian, 221; petit mal, 221; psychomotor, 221
Cooperation: social, 446–47; animals, 445–46; communication and, 449–50; Hopi Indians, 447; international, *p448,* 449–50; religious groups, 447–49
Counseling: family therapy, 352; marriage, 352; as vocation, 498; vocational guidance, **486**
Counter-conditioning, 34–35, 337
Creativity, 95–96; artistic, 96; brainstorming, **98**–99; characteristics, personal, and, 99; environment and, *f265;* incubation period, 96–97; individual vs. group performance, 98–99; inspiration, 97, *p97;* preparation and, 96; steps in, 96–98; verification and revision and, 97–98
Cretinism, 181, 224
Crime and delinquency, 459; courts and, *p460;* heredity and, 460; intelligence and, 460–61; neighborhoods and, *f342–43,* 461–62; personality and, 462; prevalence of delinquency, 459–60; prevention, 461, 462–63; punishment, 462, 463; reform treatment, *p463,* 463–64; schools and, 461; war as crime, 464–66
Cross-sectional method, 143–44
Culture. *See* Society; specific subjects

Dating, 154–55, 305; computer-arranged, 305–06
Daydreaming, 297; "conquering hero," 297–98, 299; "suffering hero," 298–99; usefulness, 299
Deafness, 150, 256–57
Death: fear of, 363–64
Decrement: general, and work curves, **491**
Deductive reasoning, 103
Definition of psychology, 5–6
Delinquency, 459–62

Delirium tremens, 332
Delusion, 95, 326; of grandeur, 329–30
Dementia praecox, 328
Dependent variable, 19
Depressants, 468. *See also* Drugs
Desensitization, 337
Development, 140–41, *c141;* continuity, 142; culture and characteristics of, 142; emotional, 150–53, *c152;* environment and, 202–10, *p204, p207, c208, c210;* genetics and, 194–95; importance of periods of, 142–43; language, *p149,* 149–50, *c150;* maturation and, **141**–42; mental, **158**–60, *c159;* motor, *p147,* 147–49; of responses, 142; pattern predictability, 142; personality, *p117,* 117–19, **156**–58; physical, 144–46, *p145,* 224; principles of, 142–43; prenatal, 192, 202–03; rate, 142; social, 153–56, *p154,* 375; study methods, *p143;* 143–44
Dewey, John, *f507*
Dickens, Charles, 182
Difference threshold, 242
Differential Aptitude Tests (DAT), 486
Discipline, 359; artificial punishment, **362;** consistency, 360; corporal punishment, 362–63; extrinsic rewards, **361;** fear and, 366; intrinsic rewards, **361**–62; purpose, 359–60; reward vs. punishment, 360–63, *c361*
Discrimination: in classical conditioning, **38;** in operant conditioning, 45–46
Discussion technique: group-centered, 413–15, *c414;* buzz sessions, *c415,* 415–16
Dissociative reactions, 322
Distributed practice, 66–68, *c67*
Dix, Dorothea, 318
DNA (deoxyribonucleic acid), 194
Dominant characteristics, 193
Dreaming: duration of, 235; need for, 235–36; REMs (rapid eye movements) and, 235, *p235*
Drives, biological, 206–07
Drugs, 467; classification, **467**–68; effects, psychological and physical, 468–69; marijuana and opiates, 469–70, *p470;* methadone, 471; prevention of abuse, 471; reasons for taking, 470–71; self-help centers for addicts, 472; student use, 470; substitute, 471; symptoms, physical, 468; treatment of addicts, 471–72; withdrawal symptoms, *p467*

Drug therapy, 6, 334, *p335,* 464
Dwarfism, 224

Ebbinghaus, Hermann, 75, *c75*
Ecology, 472–76. *See also* Pollution; subjects
Ectomorphs, 123
Education: classroom techniques, 413–18, *c414;* of mentally retarded, *p178,* 179–80, 181; programmed learning, 46–49, *p47;* psychologists, educational and school, 498. *See also* specific subjects such as Intelligence tests; Learning; etc.
Edwards Personal Preference Schedule, 129
EEG (electroencephalograph), **217,** 220–21, *p222*
Ego. *See* Self-concept
Eidetic imagery, 99–101, *p100*
Einstein, Albert, 96, *p97*
Electroconvulsive shock (ECS): and retention, 81
Electroconvulsive therapy (ECT), 334–35
Emotions: adolescence and problems of (*see also* Adolescents), 292–312; affective experience, **292;** common, and age, 153; development, 150–53, *c151;* digestion and, 229–30, *p230;* emotional state, **227;** feelings, **292,** galvanic skin response (GSR), **228,** *p228;* inferiority feelings, 292–97; learned, 152–53; lie detectors and, 228–29; love, romantic, 305, *p307,* 307–09; measuring, 227–29, *p228;* personality and, *p156,* 156–57; physical response, *p4, p226;* physiology and, 151, 224–25, 226–30, *p230;* pupillometrics, **229;** studies of, 227–30, *c228*
Empathy, 406
Employment. *See* Vocations; Work
Endocrine glands, *p223,* 223–25
Endomorphs, 123
Environment: adjustment to, intelligence and, **163**–64, *f188–89;* behavior and, 192; control of, *f112–13;* creativity and, *f265;* delinquency and crime, *f342–43,* 461–62; enriched sensory stimulation, effects of, 260; ghetto, *f342–43,* 461–62; glands and, 225–26; heredity interaction, 206–11, *p207, c208;* home, 117–18, 205, 461; intelligence and, 172, *f188–89,* 198, *p204,* 204–11, *c208, f264–65;* learning about senses and, 239–60; personality and, 117–18;

pollution, 472–76; postnatal, 203–06; prenatal, 202–03; psychosis, functional, and, 327; sensory deprivation, effects of, 259–60, *p260;* social, and personality, 118–19, 121, 124
Environmental therapy, 335
Equilibrium sense, 259
Eugenics, 198–99
Examinations. *See* Tests
Experimental method, 19; animal experiments, 20–21; control group, **19;** experimental group, **19;** hypothesis, **19;** mazes, 31–32, *p32;* procedures, 19–20; puzzle boxes, 31; reports, 21; stimulus, **19;** subject, **20;** variables, **19**
Epilepsy. *See* Convulsive disorders
Explicit behavior, 88
Exploitation: aid and, 433–34
Extinction: in classical conditioning, **35**–36, *c36,* 38; in operant conditioning, 42
Extrasensory perception, 13, *f26–27;* clairvoyance, **13;** precognition, **13;** psychologists and, 13, 15, *f26–27;* research, 15, *p15,* 26–27; telepathy, **13,** 14–**15,** *p15*
Extroversion, 120–**21,** 124

Family, 346–47; adolescent conflicts, 302–04, *c303;* affectionate, 118, 349, *p350,* 352–54, *p353;* conscience development and, 354–56; delinquency and, 461; discipline, **359**–63; extended, 346; father role, 350; foster parents, affection and, 352–53; generation gap, **371**–74; identification of child with parents, 355; kibbutz, 346–47; love between children and parents, 352–54; lying by children, *p356,* 356–57; marital relationships and, 348–52; ordinal positions in, **118;** personality influenced by, 117–18; role and job role conflicts, 484; structure, *p347,* 347–48; television watching, 366–68, *p368;* therapy, 352
Fantasy, 101
Fear: age patterns, 153; causes in children, 364; of death, 363–64; discipline and, 366; of fear, 364; of injury, and aid in distress, 430; learned, 152, *p363,* 363–64, 366; needed fears, 364; overcoming, 364–65, *p365;* prevalence among children, 363; stimulus generalization and, 37–38
Feedback: group, **407**–08; psychological, and learning, *c65,* **65**–66; of results, and motivation, 63

Feelings, 392
Figure-ground relationship, 396, *p396*
Fixed-interval schedule, 44
Fixed-ratio schedule, 44
Ford family, *p198*
Forgetting: biochemical distortion of memory trace, 80–81; inattention, 79; inhibition, proactive, **80;** inhibition, retroactive, 79–**80;** long-term and short-term memory, 81–82, *c82;* motivated, 80; time elapse, 79; Zeigarnik effect, **80**
Freud, Sigmund, 7–8, 121, 122, 336, *f507*
Friendships, 374, **377;** conditioning, 380–81; development in childhood and adolescence, 379–80, *p381;* isolation experiment with animals, 376–78; popularity and, 381
Fromm, Erich, 121
Frustration and conflict: adjustment mechanisms, **278**–288, *p280, p283, p287;* aggression, displaced, 282–**83,** *p283;* approach-approach conflict, *c271,* **271**–72, 275, *c275;* approach-avoidance conflict, *c273,* 273–74, *c274,* 275, *c275;* approach gradient, 271–72, *c272, c273;* avoidance-avoidance conflict, **272,** *c272,* 275, *c275;* compensation, 278–79; conflicts as causes of frustration, 270–74, *c271–74;* cooperation and, 276; daydreaming, 297; decision avoidance, 283; determination as response, 276; flexibility and, 277–78; frustrating situations, 268–70, *p269;* frustration tolerance, **270;** identification, *p280,* **280;** motor development and, 148; overcompensation, 279–80; planning to avoid, *p277;* procrastination, 282; projection, 281; rationalization, **283**–86; regression, 281–82; repression, 281; responses to, 275–88; seeking alternative solutions, 277, 278; seeking help and, 276; solving conflicts, 274–75, *c275;* stereotyped behavior, **281**
Fugue, 322
Functional psychoses, 326–30. *See also* Psychoses, functional; Psychosis
Functionalism, *f507*

Galvanic skin response (GSR), 228, *p228*
Galvanometer, 228
Gambling, 301–02
Generality: glittering, 458–59
Generalization: in classical condi-

tioning, *p37,* **37**–38; in operant conditioning, 45
Generation gap, 371–72, *p372;* causes of current, 372–74; communications gap, 372
Generosity error, 126
Genetics, 193–96, *p194, p195;* DNA (deoxyribonucleic acid) and RNA (ribonucleic acid), 194–95; dominant characteristics, **193;** genotype, **193**–94, *p195;* LSD and, 469; phenotype, **194,** p195; recessive characteristics, **193;** unit characters, **193.** *See also* Heredity
Genius, 181
Genotype, 193–94, *p195*
Gesell, Arnold, 143, *p143*
Gestalt, *f507*
Ghettos: and behavior, *f342–43;* delinquency and crime, *f342–43,* 461–62
Giantism, 224
Gifted persons, 181–83
Glands, 214; adrenal, 224–25; duct (exocrine), 223; ductless (endocrine), *p223,* 223–25; environmental effects on, 225–26; gonads or sex glands, 225; malnutrition, prenatal, and, 203; mental retardation and, 180, 181; pancreas, 224; parathyroids, 224; physical development and, 142, 224; pituitary, 142, 224; thyroid, 224, 225, 321
Goals: motivation and, 62
Gonads, 225
Graphic rating scale, 126
Graphology, 133
Groups: control, **19;** experimental, **19;** personality influenced by, 118–19; rationalization by, 285–86; social, and personality, 119; social facilitation, **437**–39. *See also* Family; Groups, small; Peer groups
Groups, small, 393–94; alliances within, 419–20; atmosphere, **404,** *p404;* behavior studies of, 418–21, *p420;* classroom, 413–18; *c414;* cohesiveness, **402**–03, *p403;* communication in, 405–13, *c409–10, c412;* conformity to norms of, *p420,* 420–21; creative performance of individuals vs., 98–99; disadvantages, 400–01, *p401;* efficiency improvement, 398–99; exclusive, **395**–96; family, 346–68; figure-ground relationship, **396,** *p396;* feedback, **407**–08; inclusive, **395;** interaction-oriented, **395;** judgment influenced by, 419–21; membership characteristics, 402;

membership motives, 399–400; morale, **403**; peer, 371–89; pseudogroup effects, **418**–19; roles, individual, in, **404**–05; size and efficiency, 396–97; status, **408**; task-oriented, *p394*, **394**–**95**
Group therapy, 336, *p336*
Growth. *See* Development
Guilford, J. P., 164, 165

Habits: changes in, 129–30; intermittent reinforcement and, 44
Hallucinations, 252, 325–26
Hallucinogens, 468–69. *See also* Drugs
Halo effect, 126–27
Handicaps, 146, 150; and inferiority feelings, *p293,* 293–94; programmed learning and, 49
Harlow, Harry F., *f424*–25, 377
Hearing, 239, 253; deafness, 150, 256–57; noise, 255–56, *p256;* sound characteristics, 254, *p255*
Hebephrenic schizophrenia, 329
Height and weight, 144–46, *p145*. *See also* Physical development
Help, offering. *See* Aid in distress
Heredity: animal experiments, 196–97; ancestors vs. parents as sources of inherited characteristics, 195–96; behavior and, 192; characteristics, inherited, 193–96, *p195;* criminality, 460; environment interaction, 206–11, *p207, c208;* eugenics, **198**–99; genetics, 193–96, *p194, p195,* 469; intelligence and, 172, 180, 196–99; maturation and, **141**–42, **199**–202; mental retardation, 180; pregnancy and, 192
Heroin, 469–70. *See also* Drugs
Heuristic concept, 6
Holtzman Inkblot Test, 135
Home: delinquency and, 461; personality and, 117–18. *See also* Family
Hopi Indians, 447
Hormones, 223–25. *See also* Glands
Horney, Karen, 121
Hospitals: mental health, 318–19, *p319,* 334, 335
Hydrocephalus, 181
Hypnosis, 9; behavior in, 11–12; laws restricting, 13; medical uses, *p12,* 12–13; methods of inducing, 10, *p11;* posthypnotic suggestion, **12;** psychology and, 9, 13; psychotherapy and, 13; sleep compared with, 9, 12; states or degrees of, 12; susceptibility to, 10; uses of, *p12,* 12–13
Hypochondria, 320

Hypothesis, 19

Identification, *p280,* **280;** with parents, 355
Illusions, 252–53, *p253;* autokinetic, **420**–21; stroboscopic motion, **253**
Imagery, eidetic, **99**–101, *p100*
Imagination, 101; autistic thinking, **101;** fantasy, **101**
Implicit behavior, 88
Imprinting, 201–02, *p202*
Inattention: forgetting and, 79
Independent variable, 19
Inductive reasoning, 103
Industry: hiring criteria for college graduates, 490–91; industrial psychologists, 496–97; piece-rate system of pay, 494; production, daily and weekly patterns of, 492–93; production, ways of increasing, 493–94; programmed learning used in, 49; progress of learning job, 74, *p74;* time-rate system of pay, 493–94; time-study personnel or efficiency experts, 494; turnover and employee intelligence, 175–76, *c176*. *See also* Vocations
Inferiority feelings, 292–93; achievement, academic, and, 296; appearance and, 294–95; dress and, 295; physical abnormalities and, *p293,* 293–94; prejudice, *p295,* 295–96; symptoms of excessive, 296–97
Inhibition: proactive, **80;** retroactive, **79**
Inkblot tests, *p134,* 134–35, 136
Insecticides, 473. *See also* Pollution
Insight learning, 49; animals, 49–50, *p50,* 51; conditioning compared with, 51; experience, preparatory, 51
Inspiration: creativity and, 97, *p97*
Instinct, 230–33, **231,** *p233*
Institutionalization of children: effects of, 379
Intelligence, 163–64, *f188*–89; abilities, 159, 164; age and changes in, *c159;* brain size and, 218, 225; delinquency and criminality, 460–61; environment and, 172, *f188*–89, 198, *p204,* 204–11, *c208, f264*–65; factors, 159, 164–65; gifted children, 181–83; heredity and, 172, 189, 196–99; innate potential vs. observable aspects of, 172; malnutrition and, 180, *f189, p204,* 204–05; mental development, **158**–60, *f188*–89; mental maturity, **172;** mental retardation, *p177,* 177–181, *p178;* physical development and, 182; quotient (IQ) (*see also* IQ), **169**–73, *f188*–89; superior, 181–84, *p181;* of twins, **208**–09; vocations and, 176, 485. *See also* Intelligence tests; IQ
IQ (intelligence quotient), **169**–71; brain wave measurement, 171; calculation of, 169–71; classification, 173, *c173;* deviation, **171;** environment and, 172, *f188*–89, 205–06; mental retardation, 177–79; prediction, 171; race and, *f189,* 206, 209; stability, 171–72; television watching and, 367, *c367*. *See also* Intelligence; Intelligence tests
Intelligence tests: achievement and, 172, 174–75, 182–83; criticisms of, 184–85; employment and, 175–76, *c175;* group, 168–69; individual, 165–68, *p166, f188*–89; interpretation, 169; IQ and, **169**–72; multi-media, *c170,* 171; performance or nonverbal, *p167,* 167–68; reaction time, *f189;* school use, 168–69, 173–75, *p174;* score changes, *c159,* 171–72; sleep and scores, 234. *See also* Intelligence; IQ (intelligence quotient)
Interests, vocational, 487–88, *p489;* inventories, **488**–90
International relations: aggression and, *f342*–43; competition, 442–43, 444; cooperation, *p448,* 449–50; war, 464–66
Interval schedule: of reinforcement, **44;** fixed-interval (FI), 44; variable-interval (VI), 44
Interviews, 17, 130; improved, 131; validity, *p130,* 130–31
Introversion, 120–**21,** 124
Inventories, interest, 488–90
Inventories, personality, 128–29; cautions in using, 129–30; *Edwards Personal Preference Schedule,* 129

James, William, *f507*
Jargon, 407
Jensen, Arthur Robert, *f189*
Job: dissatisfaction, 484–85; satisfaction, *p483,* 483–84. *See also* Vocations; Work
Judgment: group influence and, 419–21, *p420*
Jung, Carl, 120–21
Just-noticeable-difference, 242
Juvenile delinquency, 459–62. *See also* Crime and delinquency; Delinquency

Kinesthetic sense, 258–59
Korsakoff's psychosis, 333

Kuder Preference Record: Occupational, 489; **Personal,** 489; **Vocational,** 488–89

Land pollution, 475–76. See also Pollution
Language: abilities, 159, 164; deafness, and development of, 150; development, *p149,* 149–50; jargon, 407; progress of learning, 73; relearning, 76; semantic differential, **150,** *c150;* thinking and, 89; transfer in learning, 57–58, 60; verbal abilities, 159, 165; vocabulary, and retention, 77–78
Latent learning, 71
Law enforcement, *p460,* 463. See also Crime and delinquency; Delinquency
Leadership: autocratic, 387–88; democratic, 387, 388, *p389;* followers and leaders, comparison of attitudes toward, 389–90; functions, 385; in school and in later life, 387; kinds of, 385, 387–88; laissez-faire, 388; learned, 388–89; motivation, 385; peer groups, 384–90, *p389;* personality and, 385–86; physiology and, *p386,* 386–87; role playing as training for, 388–89; world, aggressiveness of, *f342–43*
Learning, 30–31; acceleration curves, **73;** behavior modification and, 52; classical conditioning and (*see also* Classical conditioning), 32–38; cognitive theory, 52; competition and, 63, *p64;* conditioning, 32; controversies, 51–52; efficiency in, 57–82; emotions, 152–53; feedback, psychological and, *c65,* **65**–66; forgetting, 79–82; imprinting, 201–02, *p202;* industrial productivity and, 494; inhibition of, 79–80; by insight, 49–51, *p50;* intelligence factors and, 165; latent, **71;** maturation and, **141**–42, **199**–202, *p200, p202;* mazes, 31–32, *p32;* meaningfulness and, 64–65; method of savings, 75; mnemonic devices and, **69**–70; motivation and, 62–63; needs and, 52; nonserial, 67; operant conditioning and (*see also* Operant conditioning), 38–49; overlearning, **70**–71, *c71;* plateaus, **74**–75, *c74;* practice, massed vs. distributed, and, 66–68, *c67;* principles of applied to examinations, 105–06, *p107;* programmed, 46–48, *p47;* progress, 72–75, *c74;* puzzle boxes, 31; readiness, 141–42, *p174,* 201; recall, 76; reinforcement, need for, 52; relearning, *c75,* 75–76; retention and forgetting, *c75,* 75–82, *c78, c79, c82;* sensory deprivation and, 260; serial, **71**–72, *p72;* skills, *p58,* 58–59, *p61,* 67, *c74,* 74–75; sleep-learning, 78; speed of, 52; stimulus-response and cognitive theories compared, 52; transfer of, 57–62, *p58, p61;* trial-and-error, 31–32, *p32;* verbatim, 68, 77–78, *c78;* whole vs. part, 68–69, *p69.* See also Thinking
Lectures as technique, 413
Lie detectors, 228–29
Life expectancy, 156
Longitudinal method, 143, 144
Long-term memory, 81–82, *p82*
Love, aggression and, *f424–25*
Love, filial, 352–53
Love, parental, *p353,* 353–54
Love, romantic, 155, 305, *p307;* at first sight, 309; characteristics of, 307; physiology and, 308–09
LSD, 468, 479. See also Drugs
Lying: by children, *p356,* 356–57

Malnutrition: animal experiments, 203–04; development and, 203–05, *p204;* intelligence and, 180, 181, *f189, p204,* 204–05; prenatal, 203, 204
Manic-depressive, 327–28, *p328;* drug therapy, 334
Marijuana, 469–70, *p470.* See also Drugs
Marriage: counseling, 352; factors conducive to, 350, *p350;* happy, characteristics of, 348–50; problems, 351, *c351.* See also Family
Maslow, Abraham, 122–23
Massed practice, 66–68, *c67*
Maturation, 141–42; heredity and, **141**–42, **199**–202; learning and, 141–42, 199–202, *p200, p202*
Maturity, mental, **172**
Mazes, 31–32, *p32*
McConnell, R. A., *f27*
Meaningfulness: learning and, 64–65
Measurement techniques, 18, *p18;* behavior sampling, 131–33, *p132;* galvanic skin response (GSR), **228,** *p228;* graphology, 133; intelligence, *see* Intelligence tests; interviews, *p130,* 130–31; inventories, interest, **488**–90; inventories, personality, 128–30; lie detectors, 228–29; personality, 125–36; projective techniques, **133**–36; pupil-lometrics, **229;** ratings, personality, **125**–28; sampling, random, **456**–57; sampling, stratified, **457;** sociogram, **402**–03, *c403;* voice printing, 133. See also Methodology; Tests; subjects
Medical professions: and hypnosis, *p12,* 12–13
Memory, 75, 164; amnesia, **322;** biochemistry and, 80–81; coding and, 81; long-term and short-term, 81–82, *c82;* recall, 76; recognition, 76–77; relearning and, *c75,* 75–76; repression, **80;** RNA (ribonucleic acid) and trace transmission, 80–81; trace, 79, 80–81; Zeigarnik effect, **80.** See also Forgetting; Retention
Mendel, Gregor, 193
Mental development, 158–60, *c159;* problems of studying, 158. See also Intelligence
Mental health: motor development and, 147; programs, 318–19
Mental illness. See Behavior disorders; subjects
Mental retardation, 177; causes, 180–81; cretinism, 181, 224; delinquency and criminality, 460–61; education and, *p178,* 179–80, 181; eugenics and, **198**–99; mild, *p178,* 179; moderate, 178–79, 180–81; profound, 177–78, 180–81; severe, *p177,* 177–78; therapy for, 181; vocabulary development and, 89
Mesomorphs, 123
Methadone, 471. See also Drugs
Methodology: case study, 17; cross-sectional method, **143**–44; development study, 143–44; electroencephalograph (EEG), **217,** *p222;* experiments, 19–21, *p20;* interviews, 17; language study, 150; longitudinal method, **143,** 144; mazes, 31–32, *p32;* measurement techniques (*see also* Measurement; Tests, psychological), 18, *p18;* observation, 16, *p16,* 143, *p143;* personality measurement, 125–36; puzzle boxes, 31; questionnaires, 17–18; reports, 21
Mind: in psychology, 6–7; "photographic," 100; reading, 13, 14–15, *p15*
Minorities: inferiority feelings and, 295–96; prejudice and, 454–56; social competition and, 442, 444
Mnemonic devices, 69–70
Morale: group, **403**
Motion: autokinetic illusion, **420**–21; spatial perception of, 246, 253; stroboscopic, **253**

Motivation, 62; achievement, academic, and, 183; competition as (*see also* Competition), 63, *p64;* feedback of results and, 63; in forgetting, 80; goals as, 62; heredity-environment interaction, 206–07, *p207;* leadership, 385; learning efficiency and, 62–63; production, industrial, and, *p493,* 493–94; for psychology study, 2–4; punishment fear as, 63; social facilitation, 437; tests as, 62–63; transfer and, 61

Motor development, *p147,* **147**–48; from childhood to old age, 148–49; frustration and, 148; of infant, 148; self-concept and, 147; sex differences, 149; socialization and, 147

Multiple-personality reaction, 322

Name calling, 458
Narcotics, 468. *See also* Drugs
National Association for Mental Health, 318
National Committee for Mental Hygiene, 318
National Mental Health Act, 318
Needs: learning and, 52; personality and, *c122,* 122–23
Negative acceleration in learning, 73
Negative transfer, 58
Neo-Freudian theories of personality, 121, 124
Neosensory perception, 13
Nervous systems, 214; autonomic, 39, **215**–16; central and peripheral, 214–**15,** *p215. See also* Brain
Neurosis, 319–**20;** amnesia, **322;** causes, 321; conversion reaction (conversion hysteria), **322;** dissociative reactions, **322;** fugue, **322;** hypochondria, **320;** multiple personality, **322;** obsessive-compulsive, **320,** *p321;* phobia, **320;** psychosomatic disorders, *p323,* **323**–24; symptoms, 320–21; therapy, 334–38; tics, **320**
Noise, 255–56, *p256*
Numerical ability, 159, 164
Numerology, 8–9

Observation, as technique: directed, 16, *p16;* experimental or laboratory, 16, *p16;* natural, 16; one-way-vision, 143, *p143*
Obsessive-compulsive neuroses, 320, *p321*
Occupational briefs, 488
Operant conditioning: animal training, 38–41, *p39, p40,* 43–46, *p45;* approximations, successive in, 40;

autonomic nervous system functions and, 39; behavior, human, and, 41–42; classical conditioning compared with, 38–42; counter-conditioning therapies, 337–38; discrimination in, 45–46; environment control and, *f112–13;* extinction in, 42; generalization in, 45; programmed learning and, 46–49, *p47;* punishment and, 46; recovery, spontaneous, in, 42; reinforcement in, 40, 42–45; schedules of reinforcement, **44;** secondary reinforcement, **45,** *p45;* terms, 42–46; token-economy therapy, 338

Optical illusions, 252–53, *p253,* **420**–21
Order-of-merit rating, 125
Ordinal position, 118
Organic psychoses, 330–34. *See also* Psychoses, organic; Psychosis
Organism, 5
Overachievers, 183–84
Overcompensation, 279–80
Overlearning, 70–**71,** *c71*
Overpopulation, 476, *p477;* optimum population, 476; social behavior effects, 476–78

Pancreas, 224
Paranoid personality, 334
Paranoid schizophrenia, 329
Parapsychology, 13; extrasensory perception, **13**–15, *p15,* 26–27; psychokinesis, 13, 14
Parathyroids, 224
Paresis, 331
Part learning vs. whole learning, 68–69, *p69*
Pavlov, Ivan, 32–33, *p33*
Pecking order, 439–40, *c440*
Peer group, 371, attitudes toward school, 375–76; drug use, *p470,* 471; friendships, 374, **377**–81; generation gap and, 373–74; influences, 373–76, *p375;* leadership, 384–90, *p389;* physical development and acceptance by, 144; popularity and, **381**–84, *p384;* rebellion feelings, 375; role models, 375; self-concepts and, 376; self-evaluation and, 374
Perception, 242; color, 243–46, *p244;* insight and, **49;** sensation and, 241–43; spatial, 159, 164, 246–53, *p251, p252;* subliminal, **242**–43
Performance, group vs. individual: creative thinking and, 98–99; social facilitation and, **437**–39

Performance tests (intelligence tests), *p167,* 167–68
Peripheral nervous system, 214–**15,** *p215*
Personality, 116–**17, 156;** assessment, 125–36; behavior sampling as measurement of, 131–33, *p132;* body type and, 123, 124–25; brain and, 219–20; change, 157–58; character and, 117; of creative persons, 99; of delinquents and criminals, 462; development, *p117,* 117–19, **156**–58; disorders, 334; ectomorph, 123; emotions and, *p156,* 156–57; endomorph, 123; experimental theories, 121–22, 124; extrovert, 120–**21;** family influence on, 117–18; Freudian theory, 121–22; glands and, *p223,* 224–25; graphology and, 133; home influence on, 117–18; hypnosis, susceptibility to, and, 10; independent, 118; informal theories, 119–20, *p120;* intelligence factors, 165; interviews in measurement of, *p130,* 130–31; introvert, 120–**21;** inventories, 128–30; leadership, 385–86; learning concept theories, 121–22; measurements, 125–36; mesomorph, 123; multiple, **322;** needs and, *c122,* 122–23; neo-Freudian theories, 121, 124; ordinal position and, **118;** organismic theories, 122–23, 124; paranoid, 334; pleasing, 383–84; popularity and, *c382,* 382–84, *p384;* primary traits, **120;** projection, **133**–36; ratings, **125**–28; schizoid, 334; self-actualization, *c122,* 122–23, 124; self-concept, 146, 147–48, 157; social influences on, 118–19; sociopathic, 334; theories, 119–25; traits, **120,** 123–24; vocations and, 487; voice-printing and, 133
Perspective: linear and atmospheric, **246**
Phenomenology, *f507*
Phenotype, 194, *c195*
Phenylketonuria, 181
Phi phenomenon, 253
Phobia, 320
Phrenology, 8–9
Physical development, 144; abnormalities, 146, *p293,* 293–94; effect on individual of, 144; height and weight, 144–46, *p145;* intelligence and, 182; maturation, **141;** motor development, *p147,* **147**–49; overconcern with, 294; pituitary gland and, 142, 224
Physique: personality and, 123, 124–25

INDEX **531**

Piaget, Jean, 90, *f188–89,* 182
Piece-rate system of pay, 494
Pigeonhole error: in rating, **127**
Pituitary: development and, 142, 224
Polls: public opinion, 17; random sampling, **456**–57; stratified sampling, **457**
Pollution: air, 472–74, *p473;* ecology, **472**; insecticides, 473; land, 475–76; recycling and, 475–76; student concern with, 474; water, 474–75, *p475*
Popularity, 381–82; friendship and, 381; price of, 382; traits and, *c382,* 382–84, *p384*
Positive acceleration in learning, 73
Positive transfer, *p58,* 58–59
Practice: massed vs. distributed, 66–68, *c67*
Precognition, 13
Pregnancy: development and, 192, 202–03, 204–05; LSD use in, 469; mental retardation and, 180
Prejudice, 454–56, **455,** *p455;* inferiority feelings, *p295,* 295–96
Proactive inhibition, 80
Problems, personal: emotional, adolescent, 292–312; and psychology, 203, *p8. See also* subjects
Procrastination, 282
Productivity: industrial, 492–94, *p493;* social facilitation and, 437–39
Programmed learning: advantages, 49; books, 48–49; branching programs, *p47,* 48; cheating and, 48–49, 358, *p359;* frames, 47; handicapped and, 49; industrial use of, 49; linear programs, 47–48; operant conditioning and, 46; teaching machines, 48, 49
Projection, 281
Projective technique, 133–34; circles, representative, placement of, 135; cloud picture interpretation, 135; ink blot tests, *p134,* 134–35, 136; play with toys, 135; problems of using, 136; scoring responses, 136; sentence completion, 136; using pictures, 135–36
Propaganda, *p457,* 457–58; bandwagon technique, 459; effectiveness, 458; glittering generality, 458–59; name calling, 458; resistance to, 458–59; slanting ideas, 459; testimonial as, 459; transfer in, 459
Pseudogroup effects, 418–19
Pseudo-scientists, 8–9
Psychiatry: compared with psychology, 7

Psychoanalysis, 7, 336, *f507;* compared with psychology, 7–8
Psychodrama, 336
Psychokinesis, 13, 14
Psychological Bulletin, 21,
Psychology as vocation, 503; applied psychology, **496**; basic psychology, **496**; clinical psychology, 8, 498; counseling and guidance, 498; educational and school psychology, 497–98; experimental and physiological psychology, 496; industrial psychology, 496–97; nondoctoral opportunities, 501–02; social psychology, 497, *p497;* specialties, 496–99, *p499;* training for, 499–501; women and, 502, *p502*
Psychology, studying: curiosity, intellectual, and, 4; definition of psychology, 5–6; hypnosis used in psychology, 9, 13; methods of study, *p16,* 16–21, *p18, p20, p21;* mind in psychology, 5–6; motivations for, 204; parapsychology and, 13–15, *p15;* problems, personal, and, 2–3; pseudo-sciences vs. psychology, 8–9; sciences, other, in relationship to psychology, 6–8; social problems and, 3–4, 478–79
Psychoneurosis. *See* Neurosis
Psychopharmacology, 6, 334, *p335,* 464
Psychoses, functional, 326–27; acute and chronic brain disorders, **331**; causes, 327; manic-depressive, **327**–28, *p328,* 334; paranoid reactions, 329–30; schizophrenia, **328**–29, *p330,* 334
Psychoses, organic, 330–31; alcoholic, **331**–32; paresis, **331**; senile, **331**–32
Psychosis, 324; brain disorders, acute and chronic, **331**; diagnosis criteria, 325–26; functional, 326–30; misconceptions concerning, 324–25; organic, 330–34; therapy, 334–38
Psychosomatic disorders, *p323,* 323–24
Psychotherapy, 7, 336; client-centered, 336; computer-assisted, 337; as drug-addiction treatment, 471–72; family, 352; hypnosis, 13; interview use, 131; psychoanalysis, (*see also* Psychoanalysis), 336; psychodrama, 336; supportive, 336
Punishment: artificial, **362**; corporal, 362–63; of criminals, 462, 463; discipline and, 359, 360–63, *c361;*

as learning motivation, 63; operant conditioning and, 46
Pupillometrics, 229
Public-opinion polls, 17; random sampling, **456**–57; stratified sampling, **457**
Puzzle boxes, 31

Question-answer method, 413
Questionnaire method, 17–18

Race: intelligence quotient and, *f189,* 206, 209
Racism: inferiority feelings and, 295–96; and prejudice, *f342–43,* 454–56
Ratings, personality, 125; dangers in, 126–28, *p127;* generosity error, **126**; graphic rating scale, **126**; halo effect, **126**–27; order-of-merit, **126**; pigeonhole error, **127**; stereotypes, **127**, *p127;* type error, **127**
Rationalization, 283–84; "chance" as, 299–300; constructive, 285; group and national, 285–86; scapegoat, **285**–86; sour-grapes, 284; sweet-lemon, 284–85
Ratio schedule of reinforcement, 44; fixed ratio (FR), 44; variable ratio (VR), 44
Reaction time, 216–17, *p217;* intelligence test, *f189*
Reasoning, 101, 159, 164; of children, 101–02, *p102;* of college students, 102–03, *p103;* deductive, **103**; inductive, **103**
Recall, 76; mnemonic devices and, 69–70; under hypnosis, 11–12, 13
Recessive characteristics, 193
Recognition: retention and, 76–77
Recovery, spontaneous: in classical conditioning, 36, *c36,* 38; in operant conditioning, 42
Reflex, 31
Regression, 281–82
Reinforcement, 52; in classical conditioning, **36,** 38; group, 407–08; habits and, 44; interval schedules, **44**; in operant conditioning, 40, 42–45; partial or intermittent, **36,** 43–44; ratio schedules, **44**; secondary, **45,** *p45*
Repression, 281; forgetting and, **80**
Response, 19; conditioned (CR), **33**–34, 35–36; development and, 142; in transfer, 59–60; unconditioned (UCR), **33**–34, 35–36
Retardation. *See* Mental retardation
Retention, 75; following rest or other learning, *c79;* recall and, 76; recognition and, 76–77; relearning

and, *c75,* 75–76; sleep and, 81; sleep-learning, 78; verbatim, 77–78, *c78;* vocabulary and, 77; Zeigarnik effect, 80. *See also* Forgetting; Memory
Retroactive inhibition, 79–80
Revised Stanford-Binet, 166, *p166,* 167
Rewards: extrinsic, **361;** intrinsic, **361**–62; vs. punishment, 46; vs. punishment in discipline, 360–63, *c361*
Rhine, Joseph B., *f26*–27
RNA (ribonucleic acid), 194; memory trace transmission and, 80–81
Rogers, Carl, 122
Role: in small groups, 404–05
Role playing: classroom, 416–18, *p417;* as leadership training, 388–89; psychodrama, 336; sociodrama, **416**–18, *p417*
Roles, social, 309; biology and, 310; changing, 310–12, *p311;* culture and, 310–12; family and job conflicts, and, 484; peer group as models, **375**
Rorschach, Hermann, 134
Rorschach test, 134–35, 136

Sampling: of behavior, 131–33, *p132;* graphology, 133; random, **456**–57; stratified, **457**
Savings: method of, 75
Scapegoat, 285–86
Schizoid personality, 334
Schizophrenia, 328–29, *p330;* drug therapy, 334; forms of, 329; prevalence, 329; recovery chances, 329
Science(s), 5; methodology (*see also* Measurement techniques; Methodology; specific subjects); pseudosciences, 8–9; psychology in relation to other, 6–8; theory, **5**
Secondary reinforcement, 45, *p45*
Self-actualization, *c122,* **122**–23, 124
Self-concept (ego), 157; handicaps and, 146; motor development and, 147–48; peer groups and, 376; physical development and, 144
Semantic differential, 150, *c150*
Senile psychosis, 331–32
Sensation, **242;** perception and, 241–43; thresholds, **242**
Sense(s), 239; attention and, 239–41, *p239;* deprivation, effects of, 259–60, *p260;* of equilibrium, 259; of hearing, 239, 253–57, *p255, p256;* kinesthetic, 258–59; number of, 239; sensation and perception and, *p241,* 241–43; skin, 258, *p258;* of smell, 239, 257; stimulation, enriched, and, 260; of taste, 239, 257–58; of vision, 239, *p244,* 243–53, *p252, p253*
Sensitivity-training group, 335
Sensory deprivation, 259–60, *p260;* brainwashing, 260; learning and, 260; in space travel, 259
Serial learning, 71–72, *p72*
Sex glands, 225
Sheldon, W. H., 123
Short-term memory, 81–82, *p82*
Sibling rivalry, 302–03
Simon, Theodore, 166
Sinclair, Upton and Mrs., *f26*
Skills, learning: plateaus in, *c74,* **74**–75; practice and, 67; transfer of, *p58,* **58**–59, *p61*
Skinner, B. F., 38–40, *p39, f112*–13, *f189*
Skin senses, 258, *p258*
Sleep: hypnosis compared with, 9, 12; learning during, 78; need, 234; paradoxical, 235; REM (rapid eye movement), and dreams, *p235,* 235–36; retention and, 82; stages, 234–35
Smell sense, 239, 257
Social attitudes, 454; measuring, 456–57; prejudice, 454–56; **455,** *p455;* propaganda and, *p457,* **457**–59
Social competition, 439–45. *See also* Competition
Social cooperation, 445–50; aid in distress, 428–37. *See also* Cooperation
Social development, 153–54, *p154;* in adolescence, 155; in adulthood and old age, 155–56; in early childhood and preschool years, 153–54; during early school years, 154–55; motor development and, 147; peer groups and, 475
Social facilitation, **437;** animals and, 437–38; studying and, 439
Socialization: motor development and, 147
Social problems: attitudes, 454–59, *p457;* crime and delinquency, 459–67, *p460, p463, p465;* drugs, *p467,* 467–72, *p470;* overpopulation, 476–78, *p477;* pollution, 472–76, *p473, p475;* psychology and, 3–4, 478–79
Social psychologists, 497
Society: development characteristics and, 142; personality influenced by, 118–19; roles and, 309–12; *p311. See also* specific subjects
Society for the Psychological Study of Social Issues, 206, 209
Sociodrama, 416–18, *p417*
Sociology, 6, 7
Sociometry, 402; sociogram, **402**–03, *c403*
Sociopathic personality, 334
Sound: audible range, 254; loudness, **254,** *p255;* noise, 255–56, *p256;* pitch, **254,** *p255;* timbre, **254,** *p255;* tone, **254,** *p255. See also* Hearing
Spatial perception, 159, 164, *p251;* convergence, 246; hearing and, 254–55; interposition, 246; learned vs. innate, 251–52, *p252;* of movement, 246, 253; optical illusions, **252**–53, *p253,* 420–21; perspective, linear and atmospheric, 246; phi phenomenon, 253; retinal disparity, 246; standards of size and distance and, 246–51; stroboscopic motion, 253; visual cliff, 251–52, *p252*
Species-specific behavior, 230–33, **231,** *p233*
Stanford Revision of the Binet-Simon Test, 166, 170
Status: communication and, 408
Stereotyped behavior, 281
Stereotypes, 127, *p127*
Stimulants, 468. *See also* Drugs
Stimulus, 19, 239; absolute threshold, **242;** attention and, 239–41, *p240;* conditioned (CS), **33**–34, 35–36; counter-conditioning, **34**–35; deprivation, 259–60; difference threshold, **242;** discrimination, **38,** 45; enriched environment, effects of, 260; figure-ground relationship, **396,** *p396;* generalization, *p37,* **37**–38, 45; just-noticeable-difference, **242;** response, 19; subliminal, 242–43; thresholds, **242;** unconditioned (UCS), **33**–34, 35–36. *See also* Classical conditioning; Operant conditioning
Stimulus-response: and cognition theories of learning compared, 52
Stroboscopic motion, 253
Strong Vocational Interest Blank, 489–90
Structuralism, *f506*–07
Stuttering, 146
Subliminal perception, 242–43
Suggestion, posthypnotic, 12
Sullivan, Harry Stack, 121
Superstitions, 43
Supportive therapy, 336
Surrogate mothers, *p377,* 377–78
Symbols, *p88,* **88**–89

Task-oriented groups, *p394,* **394**–95; size and efficiency, 396–98; size, optimum, 397–98
Taste sense, 239, 257–58

Teaching machines, 48, 49
Teaching techniques: *See* Classroom techniques; subjects
Telepathy, 13, 14–15, *p15;* psychologist's judgment of, 15
Television: "all-or-nothing" thinking and, 94, *p94;* effects of, 367–68, *p368;* time devoted to, 366, 367, *c367;* watching, 366
Tension, 320
Terman, Lewis M., 166, 182–83
Testimonial: as propaganda, 459
Tests (examinations): checking answers, 65-66; essay-type, 77, 105–06; feedback, psychological, and, **65–66;** learning principles applied to taking, 105–08, *p107;* motivation and, 62–63; objective, 66, 76–77, 106–08, *p107*
Tests, psychological, 18, *p18. See also* Intelligence tests; Measurement techniques
T-groups, 335
Theory: scientific, **5**
Therapy: drug, 6, 334, *p335;* family, 352; group, **336,** *p336;* occupational, 352. *See also* Psychotherapy
Thinking, 87, **88;** "all-or-nothing," *p94,* 94–95; artistic creativity, 96; autistic, **101;** brain localization, 218–19, *p219;* brainstorming, **98–99;** computer vs. human, 103–05, *p104;* concepts and, **89**–93, *p90, p91, p93;* confusion of coincidence with cause, 95; creative, 95–99, *f265;* delusion, **95;** elements, basic, of, 87–89, *p88;* fantasy, **101;** imagery, eidetic, and, **99**–101, *p100;* imagination and, **101;** individual vs. group performance, 98–99; inspired, 97, *p97;* language and, 89; reasoning and, 101–03, *p102, p103;* steps in, 96–99, *p97;* symbols and, *p88,* **88**–89; "too tired to think," 495–96, *c496;* uncritical, *p94,* 94–95; verification and revision, 97–98;

as work, 494–96, *c496. See also* Learning
Threats: and competition, 440–42, *p442,* 445
Threshold, stimulus: absolute, **242;** difference, **242;** just-noticeable-difference, **242**
Thrills and thrill-seeking, 299–301, *p300;* "chance" as rationalization, 299–300; cheating, 357; gambling, 301–02
Thurstone, L. L., 164
Thyroid, 224, 225, 321
Tics, 320
Time-rate system of pay, 493–94
Time studies of industrial productivity, 494
Token economies, 338
Touch (pressure): sense of, 239, 258
Traits, 120, 123–24; primary, **120**
Transfer, in learning, 57–**58;** attitude and efficiency of, 61; experiments, 59; increasing, 61–62; negative, 58; positive, *p58,* 58–59
Transfer, in propaganda, 459
Trial-and-error learning, 31–32, *p32*
Twins: fraternal, **208;** identical, **208**–09
Type errors, in rating, **127**

Underachievers, 183–84
Uniform acceleration in learning, 73
Unit characters, 193
U.S. Public Health Service, 318

Variable-interval schedule, 44
Variable-ratio schedule, 44
Variables, 19; dependent, **19;** independent, **19**
Vision, 239; binocular, 246; color, 243–46, *p244;* monocular, 246; retinal disparity, **246.** *See also* Spatial perception
Visual cliff, 251–52, *p252*
Vocabulary: development of, 73, 89, 149–50, *p149;* retention and, 77–78; thinking and, 89; verbal

abilities, 159, 164. *See also* Language
Vocational-interest inventories, 488–90
Vocations: aptitude tests, *p485,* **485**–87; choosing, 482–83; discrimination against women, 484–85; guidance in choosing, **486;** industry criteria, 490–91; intelligence and, 176, 485; intelligence tests and, 175–76; *c175;* interest inventories, **488**–90; interests, 487–90, *p489;* job dissatisfaction, 484–85; job satisfaction, *p483,* 483–84; in mental health field, 319; occupational briefs, **488;** personality and, 487; in psychology, 496–503; work studies, scientific, 491–96
Voice printing, 133

War, 464–65, *p465;* causes, 465; leadership aggression, *f342–43;* prevention, 465–66
Water pollution, 474–75, *p475*
Watson, John B., 152, *f507*–08
Wechsler Adult Intelligence Scale (WAIS), 166–67
Wechsler, David, 188
Wechsler Intelligence Scale for Children (WISC), 166–67
Wechsler Preschool and Primary Scale of Intelligence (WPPSI), 166–67
Weight and height, 144–46, *p145. See also* Physical development
Whole learning vs. part learning, 68–69, *p69*
Work: curves, *c491,* 491–92; general decrement, **491;** industrial, 492–94, *p493;* piece-rate system, **494;** production, increasing, *p493,* 493–94; thinking, 494–96, *c496;* time-rate system, 493–94; time studies and productivity, 494. *See also* Vocations
Wundt, Wilhelm, *f506–07*

Zeigarnik effect, 80

ILLUSTRATION CREDITS

Cover: Harbrace

UNIT I
1, © 1958 United Features Syndicate Inc.; 3, Kenneth Murray—Nancy Palmer; 4, Harbrace; 8, David Margolin; 11, Harbrace; 12, Wide World; 15, Harbrace; 16, David Linton; 20, Joe Short & Tim Weaver—PHI DELTA KAPPAN; 21, © 1972 by Scientific American, Inc. All rights reserved.

UNIT II
29, Ellen Kirouac—Monkmeyer; 32, Authenticated News International; 34, David Margolin; 37, Harbrace; 40, Central Press—Pictorial Parade; 43, APA Monitor, May 1971 (p. 4); 45, Yerkes Laboratory of Primate Biology; 50, Three Lions; 58, American Airlines; 61, Christa Armstrong—Rapho-Guillumette; 64, 69, James Carroll, Laurence Fink—Nancy Palmer; 72, Harbrace; 90, Dr. Jerome Kagan; 94, 97, Brown Brothers; 100, Harbrace; 104, Sybil Shackman—Monkmeyer; 107, Harbrace; 112, Ken Heyman; 113, Photo: Stuart.

UNIT III
115, Hugh Rogers—Monkmeyer; 117, David Margolin; 120, Harbrace; 123, Michael Ramus, *Introduction to Psychology* by Clifford T. Morgan, McGraw-Hill Co., 1956 (p. 235); 127, Wide World; 130, 132, Harbrace; 134, from *The Rorschach Technique: An Introductory Manual* by Bruno Klopfer and Helen H. Davidson, © 1962 by Harcourt Brace Jovanovich and reproduced with their permission; 143, Edmund B. Gerard, LIFE Magazine, © Time, Inc.; 145, Harbrace; 147, 149, Hans Truol, Charles Sanders—D.P.I.; 151, Redrawn from Fig. 1, "Emotional Development in Early Infancy" by Katherine M. B. Bridges from *Child Development* (p. 340), © 1932 by the Society for Research in Child Development, Inc. Reproduced with the permission of the author and publisher; Redrawn from fig. 1 (p. 31) of *The Measurement and Appraisal of Adult Intelligence,* 4th ed., by David Wechsler, © 1958, Williams & Wilkins Co., Baltimore; 154, David Strickler—Monkmeyer; 156, Stratford Shakespeare Festival, Ontario; 164, David Margolin; 166, Courtesy of Houghton Mifflin Co.; 167–174, Harbrace; 177, David Margolin; 178, Wide World; 181, The Bettmann Archive; 188, Harbrace.

UNIT IV
191, "Blaze I 1962" by Bridget Riley; 194, Dr. Lorne MacHattie; 198, Culver Pictures; 200, Harold Lambert—Frederic Lewis; 202, Reprinted by permission from the SATURDAY EVENING POST, © 1961, Curtis Publishing Co.; 204, Florita Botts—Nancy Palmer; 207, Harbrace; 217, Charles Gatewood; 222, The Epilepsy Foundation of America; 226, Mickey Palmer—D.P.I.; 230, Harbrace; 233, William A. Garnett; 235, © Walt Disney Studios, Dr. William C. Dement (insert); 240, Harbrace; 244, Francis Laping—D.P.I.; 247 (top) After I. Dvorine, Dvorine Pseudo-Isometric Plates, 1953, reproduced by permission of the author; (bottom) Redrawn from Pl. IV, bot., of *Psychology: A Scientific Study of Man* by Fillmore H. Sanford, © 1965, Wadsworth Publishing Co.; 249, (top) Harbrace, (bottom) Harbrace; 250, (top) Harbrace, (bottom) After Evans, 1948; 251, Jan Lukas—Rapho-Guillumette; 252, William Vandivert; 258, Jesse Alexander—Nancy Palmer; 260, Charles Gatewood; 264, Tommy Weber—Fordham University.

UNIT V
267, Harbrace; 269, 277, David Margolin; 280, David Stickler—Monkmeyer; 283, 287, Harbrace; 293, U.P.I.; 295, Amando del Rivero; 297, © 1967, United Features Syndicate; 300, Wide World; 304, David Margolin; 307, Harbrace; 311, U.P.I.; 319, Courtesy of Community Psychiatric Centers, San Francisco; 321, Ewing Galloway; 323, Walter Reed Army Institute of Research, U.S. Army; 326, APA MONITOR, June 1971 (p. 3); 330, The Guttman-Maclay Collection, Institute of Psychiatry; 332, 336, Harbrace; 342, Wide World.

UNIT VI
345, Harbrace; 347, Marion Faller—Monkmeyer; 350, Tana Hoban—D.P.I.; 353, Bill Anderson—Monkmeyer; 356–372, Harbrace; 375, David Margolin; 377, Primate Laboratory, University of Wisconsin; 381, Harbrace; 384, Marion Faller—Monkmeyer; 386, Courtesy of Dr. Jose M. R. Delgado; 389, Martin Schneider Associates; 394, U.P.I.; 398–420, Harbrace.

UNIT VII
427, Hugh Rogers—Monkmeyer; 430, David Margolin; 432, Shelly Rusten; 435, 438, Harbrace; 442, Wide World; 443, Harbrace; 448, Wide World; 455, Harbrace; 457, David Margolin; 460, *The New York Times;* 463, C. Wolinsky—Stock Boston; 465, *The New York Times;* 467, Archie Lieberman—Black Star; 470, Shelly Rusten; 473, Syd Greenberg—D.P.I.; 475, Ewing Galloway; 477, Curt Kaufman—Editorial Photocolor Archives; 483, Photo IZIS—Rapho-Guillumette; 485, Bob West—Photo Trends; 489, David Margolin; 493, General Motors Co.; 497, Lida Moser—D.P.I.; 499, NASA; 502, 506, Harbrace.

A	3
B	4
C	5
D	6
E	7
F	8
G	9
H	0
I	1
J	2

535